THE ROUTLEDGE COMPANION TO METAPHYSICS

The Routledge Companion to Metaphysics is an outstanding, comprehensive and accessible guide to the major themes, thinkers and issues in metaphysics. The Companion features over fifty specially commissioned chapters from international scholars which are organized into three clear parts:

- History of Metaphysics
- Ontology
- Metaphysics and Science

Each section features an introduction which places the range of essays in context, while an extensive glossary allows easy reference to key terms and definitions. *The Routledge Companion to Metaphysics* is essential reading for students of philosophy and anyone interested in surveying the central topics and problems in metaphysics, from causation to vagueness and from Plato and Aristotle to the present day.

Robin Le Poidevin is Professor of Metaphysics at the University of Leeds; Peter Simons is Professor of Moral Philosophy at Trinity College, Dublin; Andrew McGonigal and Ross P. Cameron are Lecturers in Philosophy at the University of Leeds.

THE ROUTLEDGE COMPANION TO METAPHYSICS

Edited by
Robin Le Poidevin
Peter Simons
Andrew McGonigal
Ross P. Cameron

London and New York

This edition published 2009 by Routledge
2 Park Square, Milton Park, Abingdon, Oxon, OX14 4RN

Simultaneously published in the USA and Canada
by Routledge
270 Madison Ave, New York, NY 10016

Routledge is an imprint of the Taylor & Francis Group, an informa business

© 2009 Robin Le Poidevin, Peter Simons, Andrew McGonigal and Ross P. Cameron for selection and editorial
matter; individual contributors for their contributions
Typeset in Goudy Old Style Std by Saxon Graphics Ltd, Derby
Printed and bound in Great Britain by MPG Books Ltd, Bodmin

British Library Cataloguing in Publication Data
A catalogue record for this book is available from the British Library

Library of Congress Cataloging in Publication Data
A catalog record for this book has been requested

Hbk ISBN 13: 978-0-415-39631-8
Ebk ISBN 13: 978-0-203-87930-6

CONTENTS

CONTENTS

CONTENTS

CONTENTS

NOTES ON THE CONTRIBUTORS

Lucy Allais is Senior Lecturer in Philosophy at the University of the Witwatersrand and Lecturer in Philosophy at the University of Sussex. She is the author of a number of articles on Kant's transcendental idealism, and is currently completing a book on the topic. She is also working on forgiveness, punishment and retributive emotions.

Louise Antony is Professor of Philosophy at the University of Massachusetts, Amherst. She is the author of numerous articles on the philosophy of mind, the philosophy of language, epistemology and feminist theory and the editor of *Philosophers without Gods: Meditations on Atheism and the Secular Life*. She is currently working on issues concerning the place of normativity in a computationalist theory of mind.

Elizabeth Barnes is Lecturer in Philosophy at the University of Leeds. She works mostly in metaphysics, and has published or forthcoming papers in *Noûs*, *Philosophical Studies*, *Mind* and *Analysis*, among others.

John Bigelow is Professor of Philosophy at Monash University. He was an early contributor to "truthmaker" theories, the emergence (or re-emergence) of "presentist" theories of time, "modal realism," "Australian Realism" and platonism in the philosophy of mathematics.

Alexander Bird is Professor of Philosophy at the University of Bristol. He is author of *Nature's Metaphysics: Laws and Properties* (2008) and articles in the metaphysics and philosophy of science. He is also Principal Investigator on the Arts and Humanities Research Council project Metaphysics of Science: Causes, Laws, Kinds, and Dispositions.

Ross P. Cameron is Lecturer in Philosophy at the University of Leeds. He has published a number of papers on truthmakers, modality, the metaphysics of time, mereology, the nature of properties, etc. His most recent work has been on understanding the open future, defending presentism from the truthmaker objection, and arguing that we can have mathematical truth without mathematical ontology.

John Campbell is Willis S. and Marion Slusser Professor at the University of California, Berkeley. He is the author of *Past, Space and Self* (1994) and *Reference and Consciousness* (2002) and is currently working on causation in psychology.

Roberto Casati is Research Director of CNRS at Ecole Normale Supérieure, Paris, France. He is the author of *The Shadow Club* (2002, translated in nine languages) and, with A. C. Varzi, of *Holes and Other Superficialities* (1994) and *Parts and Places* (1999). He has worked on object cognition and on the philosophy of the cognitive sciences, and is currently writing a text on *Creative solutions*.

Maudemarie Clark is Professor of Philosophy at the University of California, Riverside. She is the author of *Nietzsche on Truth and Philosophy* (1990) and numerous articles on Nietzsche. She is currently finishing *Nietzsche's Manificient Tension of the Spirit: An Introduction to* Beyond Good and Evil, with David Dudrick.

Peter Clark is Professor of Philosophy and Head of the School of Philosophical, Anthropological and Film Studies in the University of St Andrews. He works primarily in the philosophy of the physical sciences and mathematics, and was editor of the *British Journal for the Philosophy of Science* (1999–2005). He is co-editor (with Katherine Hawley) of *Philosophy of Science Today* (2003) and is currently Secretary General of the International Union of the History and Philosophy of Science, Division of Logic, Methodology and Philosophy of Science.

Ursula Coope is Professor of Ancient Philosophy at Oxford University and a Tutorial Fellow at Corpus Christi College. She is the author of a book, *Time for Aristotle*, and of articles on Aristotle's metaphysics and philosophy of action, and was the winner of a Philip Leverhulme Prize (2005).

Chris Daly is Senior Lecturer in Philosophy at Manchester University. He is the author of two forthcoming books, *Introduction to Philosophical Methods* and *Philosophy of Language*.

John Divers is Professor of Philosophy at the University of Leeds. He is the author of over twenty articles on modality in addition to his *Possible Worlds* (2002).

Julian Dodd is Professor of Philosophy at the University of Manchester. He is the author of *An Identity Theory of Truth* (2000) and *Works of Music: An Essay in Ontology* (2007), and the co-editor (with Helen Beebee) of *Truthmakers: The Contemporary Debate* (2005). He is currently working on topics in metaphysics and in the philosophy of music.

Lisa Downing is Professor of Philosophy at the Ohio State University. She is the author of numerous articles on early-modern philosophy, most focusing on connections between natural philosophy and metaphysics in the period. She is working on a book on empiricism and Newtonianism, among other projects.

Nikk Effingham is Lecturer in Philosophy at the University of Birmingham. His interests in metaphysics include metaontology, persistence, composition and supersubstantivalism.

Peter Forrest has the Chair of Philosophy at the University of New England. He is the author of *The Dynamics of Belief* (1986), *Quantum Metaphysics* (1988), *God without the*

Supernatural (1996), and *Developmental Theism* (2007). He is currently working on a book to be called *The Necessary Structure of Space–Time*.

Richard Glauser is Professor of Philosophy at the University of Neuchâtel in Switzerland. He is the author of *Berkeley et les philosophes du 17e siècle* (1999) and of a number of articles on various early-modern philosophers. He is currently writing a book on Locke's theory of freedom.

Richard Hanley is Associate Professor of Philosophy, University of Delaware. He has written on metaphysics, philosophy of language and the philosophy of science fiction. With Michael Devitt he co-edited the *Blackwell Guide to the Philosophy of Language* (2002), and he is the author of *Is Data Human? The Metaphysics of Star Trek* (1998).

Katherine Hawley is Professor of Philosophy at the University of St Andrews. She is the author of *How Things Persist* (2001), and of various articles in metaphysics and epistemology.

John Heil is Professor of Philosophy at Washington University in St Louis. He is author of articles in metaphysics and philosophy of mind and *From an Ontological Point of View* (2003).

Herbert Hochberg is Professor of Philosophy at the University of Texas, Austin. His books include *Thought, Fact and Reference* (1978), *Logic, Language and Ontology* (1984), and *Russell, Moore and Wittgenstein: the Return to Realism* (2001). He has taught at Northwestern, Minnesota, Ohio State, Indiana and Göteborg universities and has held Guggenheim and Fulbright fellowships.

Rolf-Peter Horstmann is Professor Emeritus of Philosophy at the Humboldt University, Berlin, Germany. He has published, edited and contributed to numerous books on Kant and German idealistic philosophy, especially Hegel. He has also written on topics in Schopenhauer and Nietzsche, as well as epistemology and metaphysics. Currently he is a regular visiting professor of philosophy at the University of Pennsylvania.

Robin Le Poidevin is Professor of Metaphysics at the University of Leeds. He is the author of *Travels in Four Dimensions* (2003) and *The Images of Time* (2007) and editor of *Questions of Time and Tense* (1998) and *Being: Developments in Contemporary Metaphysics* (2008). In 2007 he was the Stanton Lecturer in the Philosophy of Religion at Cambridge, and is currently writing a book on the subject of those lectures: the metaphysics of the Incarnation.

Peter J. Lewis is Associate Professor of Philosophy at the University of Miami. He is the author of articles on the foundations of quantum mechanics and on scientific realism.

Fraser MacBride is Reader in Philosophy, Birkbeck College, London. He has written on metaphysics, the philosophy of mathematics, and the history of analytic philosophy. He is currently completing a monograph entitled *Overcoming Division: F.P. Ramsey and the Theory of Universals*.

George MacDonald Ross is Senior Lecturer in Philosophy at the University of Leeds, and he has published widely on the history of philosophy. As Director of the Subject Centre for Philosophical and Religious Studies of the Higher Education Academy, he has a special interest in making the outcomes of historical research accessible to students. He is currently writing an introductory book on Hobbes, which is due to be published in 2009.

Stephen Makin is Reader in Ancient Philosophy at the University of Sheffield. He has published on the Presocratics, Aristotle and Aquinas and is the author of the Clarendon Aristotle volume on *Metaphysics* Θ, comprising a translation and substantial commentary.

W. J. Mander is Fellow in Philosophy at Harris Manchester College, Oxford. He is the author of numerous articles on British idealism, a history of which he is in the process of completing.

John Marenbon is a Senior Research Fellow at Trinity College, Cambridge. His recent books include *The Philosophy of Peter Abelard* (1997), *Boethius* (2003) and *Medieval Philosophy: An Historical and Philosophical Introduction* (2007), and he is editor of the forthcoming *Cambridge Companion to Boethius*.

Tim Maudlin is Professor of Philosophy at Rutgers University. He is the author of *Quantum Non-Locality and Relativity* (1994, 2002), *Truth and Paradox* (2004), and *The Metaphysics within Physics* (2007). He is currently writing a book on the foundations of topology and its application to physics, entitled *New Foundations for Physical Geometry*. This project is supported by a Guggenheim Fellowship.

Andrew McGonigal is Lecturer in Philosophy at the University of Leeds. He has written on aesthetics, philosophy of language, and meta-ethics. He was a visiting professor at Cornell University in 2007.

D. H. Mellor is Emeritus Professor of Philosophy at the University of Cambridge. He is the author of numerous articles and several books on metaphysics, including *Matters of Metaphysics* (1991), *The Facts of Causation* (1995), *Real Time II* (1998) and *Probability: A Philosophical Introduction* (2005).

Alexander Miller is Professor of Philosophy at the University of Birmingham. He is the author of *An Introduction to Contemporary Metaethics* (2003), *Philosophy of Language* (2nd edn, 2007), and co-editor with Crispin Wright of *Rule Following and Meaning* (2002).

Cheryl Misak is Professor of Philosophy at the University of Toronto. She is the author of *Truth and the End of Inquiry: A Peircean Account of Truth* (1991), *Verificationism: Its History and Prospects* (1995), and *Truth, Politics, Morality: Pragmatism and Deliberation* (2000) and the editor of the *Cambridge Companion to Peirce* (forthcoming), *New Pragmatists* (2007), and the *Oxford Handbook of American Philosophy* (2008). She is currently working on a book titled *American Pragmatism*. In her spare time, she is Interim Vice-President and Provost of the University of Toronto.

Kevin Mulligan, Ordinary Professor of Analytic Philosophy at the University of Geneva since 1986, has published on analytic metaphysics, the philosophy of mind, and the history of Austrian philosophy from Bolzano to Wittgenstein. He has recently edited, with Armin Westerhoff, *Robert Musil – Ironie, Satire, falsche Gefühle* (forthcoming, 2009).

Stephen Mumford is Professor of Metaphysics at the Department of Philosophy, University of Nottingham. He completed a Ph.D. at Leeds (1994) and since then has written *Dispositions* (1998), *Laws in Nature* (2004) and *David Armstrong* (2007). He has edited the books *Powers*, by George Molnar (2003), and *Russell on Metaphysics* (2003). He has published a wide variety of papers in journals such as *The Monist*, *Philosophical Quarterly*, *Synthese* and *Ratio* and is a regular contributor to handbooks and encyclopaedias. He is a co-investigator on the Arts and Humanities Research Council-funded Metaphysics of Science project with Alexander Bird and Helen Beebee.

Dugald Murdoch is a Professor of Theoretical Philosophy at the University of Stockholm. He is one of the translators of *The Philosophical Writings of Descartes* (3 vols., 1985–91), and the author of *Niels Bohr's Philosophy of Physics* (1985).

Daniel Nolan is Professor of Philosophy at the University of Nottingham. He is the author of *Topics in the Philosophy of Possible Worlds* (2002) and *David Lewis* (2005), as well as numerous articles in metaphysics, methodology and other areas of philosophy.

Eric T. Olson is Professor of Philosophy at the University of Sheffield. He is the author of *The Human Animal* (1997) and *What Are We?* (2007), as well as many articles on metaphysics.

Claude Panaccio holds the Canada Research Chair in the Theory of Knowledge at the University of Quebec at Montreal. He has published extensively on medieval nominalism, and is the author of *Le Discours intérieur: De Platon à Guillaume d'Ockham* (1999), which won the 2000 Grammatikakis-Neumann Prize from the Institute of France, and of *Ockham on Concepts* (2004), which won the 2007 book prize of the Canadian Philosophical Association.

Richard Patterson is Professor of Philosophy at Emory University. He is the author of *Image and Reality in Plato's Metaphysics* (1985) and *Aristotle's Modal Logic* (1995), and a variety of articles on Plato, Aristotle, and more recently, topics in cognitive psychology.

Philip Percival is Professor of Philosophy at the University of Nottingham. He has published several articles in the areas of metaphysics, philosophy of science, epistemology and philosophical logic.

Herman Philipse is Research Professor at the University of Utrecht, The Netherlands. He has written numerous articles in Dutch and in English on metaphysics, epistemology, philosophy of religion, and continental philosophers such as Edmund Husserl and Martin Heidegger. His best-known publication on the latter is *Heidegger's Philosophy of Being: A Critical Interpretation* (1998).

Graham Priest is Boyce Gibson Professor of Philosophy at the University of Melbourne, and Arché Professorial Fellow at the University of St Andrews. He is well known for his controversial views on logic and metaphysics. His books include: *In Contradiction*, *Beyond the Limits of Thought* (2002), *Towards Non-Being* (2005), *Doubt Truth to be a Liar* (2006), and *Introduction to Non-Classical Logic* (2001).

David Robb is Associate Professor of Philosophy at Davidson College. He is the author of articles in metaphysics and the philosophy of mind, and the co-editor of *Philosophy of Mind: Contemporary Readings* (2003). He is currently working on the metaphysics of properties and its application to problems in the philosophy of mind.

Howard Robinson is University Professor in Philosophy, Provost and Academic Pro-Rector at Central European University in Budapest. He is the author of *Matter and Sense* (1982), *Perception* (1994, 2001) and the World's Classics' edition of Berkeley's *Principles* and his *Three Dialogues* (1996). He is also author of a variety of articles on the philosophy of mind, the philosophy of perception, idealism and the history of philosophy.

Gonzalo Rodriguez-Pereyra is tutorial fellow at Oriel College and a lecturer at the University of Oxford, where he holds the title of Professor of Metaphysics. He is the author of *Resemblance Nominalism* (2002) and of articles on diverse themes on Metaphysics (on topics like truthmaking, identity of indiscernibles, the slingshot argument, metaphysical nihilism, resemblance nominalism and others), Leibniz and Descartes.

David Sedley is Laurence Professor of Ancient Philosophy at the University of Cambridge, where he is also a Fellow of Christ's College. His books include *The Hellenistic Philosophers* (1987, with A. A. Long) and *Creationism and Its Critics in Antiquity* (2007).

Peter Simons is Professor of Moral Philosophy at Trinity College Dublin. Prior to that he held posts at the University of Salzburg (1980–95) and the University of Leeds

(1995–2009). His areas of research cover metaphysics (pure and applied), philosophical logic, and the history of philosophy in the last two centuries, with emphasis on Central Europe and on early analytic philosophy. He is the author of *Parts* (1987), *Philosophy and Logic in Central Europe from Bolzano to Tarski* (1992) and some two hundred articles. He is currently working on the metaphysics of quantities.

Barry Smith is Julian Park Distinguished Professor in the University at Buffalo. His primary research focus is in applications of ontology to biomedical research. He is Coordinating Editor of the Open Biomedical Ontologies Foundry initiative and a Scientific Advisor to the Gene Ontology Consortium.

Tom Stoneham is Professor of Philosophy at the University of York (United Kingdom). He is the author of *Berkeley's World* (2002) and several articles on Berkeley and his contemporaries. He has also published articles on self-knowledge, perception and modal metaphysics, and is currently thinking about mirrors, their use in early-modern arguments about perception, and the metaphysics of reflections.

Avrum Stroll is Research Professor of Philosophy at the University of California, San Diego. He is the author of about twenty books and many papers. His newest manuscript, *Informal Philosophy*, will be published in 2009.

Amie L. Thomasson is Professor of Philosophy and Parodi Senior Scholar in Aesthetics at the University of Miami. She is the author of *Fiction and Metaphysics* (1999) and *Ordinary Objects* (2007), and co-editor (with David W. Smith) of *Phenomenology and Philosophy of Mind* (2005). She has also published numerous articles and book chapters on topics in metaphysics, philosophy of mind, the ontology of the social and cultural world, and philosophy of art.

Michael Tooley is Distinguished College Professor in the Philosophy Department at the University of Colorado at Boulder, and a Fellow of the Australian Academy of the Humanities. He is the author of *Abortion and Infanticide* (1983), *Causation* (1987), and *Time, Tense, and Causation* (1997), a co-editor of *Causation* (1993), and the editor of the five-volume anthology *Analytical Metaphysics* (1999). He is also a co-author, with Alvin Plantinga, of *Knowledge of God* (2008), and a co-author of the debate volume, *Abortion: Three Perspectives* (2008).

ACKNOWLEDGEMENTS

The editors would like to express their grateful thanks to the editorial team at Routledge for all their work and support, and especially to Tony Bruce, for the original invitation to edit the volume, and whose idea this was, to Adam Johnson, who helped us see the project to completion, and to Jim Thomas, for doing a wonderful job with the copy-editing and whose suggestions improved the text in countless instances. We are also very grateful to Steven Appleby for permission to reproduce one of his characteristically erudite cartoons in the entry on Berkeley.

GENERAL INTRODUCTION
What is metaphysics?
Robin Le Poidevin

In 1869 the British architect and writer James Knowles, together with the poet Alfred Lord Tennyson, founded a new society whose purpose was to bring together clergy, scientists, and other intellectuals, to explore the relationship between science and religion (relations between which being then somewhat fraught), in their attempt to explain the cosmos and our role in it. Meetings were held in London, and the society's members during the ten or so years of its existence included the biologist Thomas Henry Huxley, the philosophers Henry Sidgwick and James Martineau, the head of the English Roman Catholic Church, Cardinal Manning, the art critic John Ruskin, and the Prime Minister W. E. Gladstone. It was called the Metaphysical Society. It came to an end in 1880 because, in Tennyson's view, "after ten years of strenuous effort no one had succeeded in even defining the term 'Metaphysics'" (quoted in Tennyson 1899: 559).

To attempt a task that apparently defeated some of the greatest minds of the Victorian age might seem foolhardy, even arrogant, but in an introduction to a volume calling itself a Companion to Metaphysics, the attempt cannot be avoided. What follows does not pretend to be comprehensive, or detailed: it does no more than to sketch, in very general terms, some of the features that characterise the Western analytical tradition in metaphysics, the tradition in which most of the contributions to this volume are situated.

Many disciplines can be captured by their distinctive subject matter: geology, for instance, is the study of the earth, its physical structure and composition and the processes that shape these. But, as A. J. Ayer once observed, philosophy seems to have no special subject matter (Ayer 1973: 1). And the same is true of metaphysics. Metaphysics is sometimes described as the study of reality, but the sciences also study (parts of) reality, so what is distinctive about metaphysics? One way of distinguishing metaphysics from science is by pointing to the level of generality in metaphysical discussion. Physics, for instance, concerns itself with particular processes, laws and entities: the conversion of one energy form into another, the laws of motion or thermo-dynamics, protons, neutrons and quarks. Metaphysics operates at a higher level of abstraction, and looks at those features the particular processes or entities might have in common: causal connection, taking place or existing in space and time, or being composed of matter. This distinction is not as sharp as one might suppose, however, since physics too has to deal in abstractions, and cosmology, for instance, is concerned with the nature of space and time themselves, and not just what takes place in them.

Metaphysics is also interested, as physics is not, by *what it is* to be real. Is there anything informative we can say about the distinction between what is real, or existent, and what is not? Are there general principles that govern the whole of reality (for instance, that everything that exists must have a cause of its existence)? Having reached a view on what it is to be real – perhaps that the character of reality is (unlike fiction) independent of our beliefs – we may be in a better position to say what is real: that is, to catalogue, in the most abstract terms, those things that are real. Our list may include such familiar entities as persons and material objects, but it may also include items very different from these, such as numbers. The part of metaphysics that is concerned with what exists is known as *ontology* (see Introduction to Part II). We might wonder whether there could be anything to metaphysics other than ontology, and indeed ontology does seem to be a large part of the metaphysical enterprise. But metaphysics is concerned not just with *what is*, but also with the *way* that it is. Objects do not merely exist: they have certain features. A building may be octagonal, a leaf brown, a bird in motion, and so on. Simply to list the things that are (even where "things" is used in its widest sense) does not capture the way things are. Of course, recognising that things have features may itself lead us to expand our ontology to include *properties* as well as the things that have those properties. And we may have to allow not only the individual property instances but also what is common to those instances, the property types. Does this show that saying how things are just amounts, after all, to saying what there is? No, because listing all the objects and properties that exist is consistent with any number of different allocations of those properties to those objects. So something has to be said about what relates a property to an object, by virtue of which the object can truly be said to have that property.

Two other cases appear to indicate that saying how things are does not reduce to saying what things there are (even though it may involve it). The first case concerns identity through time. One of the more interesting facts about persons, our common sense tells us, is that they have the capacity to go on existing, to *persist* through various kinds of change. It is one thing to understand that, and how, something exists; it is another to understand what it is for that same something to continue to exist, and to have existed in the past. To characterise persistence is not just to say what does, did and will exist: it is to say what relates those three.

The second case concerns contingency and necessity. You need not have been reading this page just now. You could, instead, have been going for a walk, or doing some shopping. Indeed, allowing our imaginations a little more freedom, your whole life might have been different: instead of studying philosophy (let us suppose, not unrealistically, that that is the actual state of affairs), you could have trained as an astronaut, and been about to set off on a journey to Mars. Why not? There is nothing absurd in such an idea. So the fact you are doing what you are doing right now is a purely contingent matter: it could have been otherwise. But there are other properties you have that we might be more reluctant to suppose you possess only contingently. Is it merely contingent, for instance, that you belong to the species *Homo sapiens*? Or (if you have no difficulty imagining yourself as a giant beetle) is it merely contingent that you occupy space? Could you have been a number? There does seem to be a limit to the possibilities. If so, then there are certain properties that you have not merely contingently but of necessity. If this distinction is legitimate, then we can recognise what we might call a second-order way of being. There is a way things are, and there is a way *that that way* is. Some ways things are appear to be contingent; other ways things are appear to be necessary.

None of this is beyond dispute. It may be disputed, for instance, that contingency and necessity apply to reality itself, rather than to our descriptions of reality. One could imagine someone arguing as follows: "If I say 'all white swans are white', I have said something necessarily true, but I do not appear to have identified some necessity in the world. What I have said is true even if there are no white swans, or if white swans turn from time to time into black swans. Any actual state of affairs is consistent with my statement. This is a rather obvious case in which the necessity attaches just to the statement, but in fact *all* apparent cases of necessity have their source in language rather than the world." This is certainly a plausible line of reasoning, but it faces two kinds of objection. First, it is not clear that all apparent cases of *de re* necessity (that is, necessity attaching to things themselves) can be construed as *de dicto* necessity (necessity attaching to sentences). Second, if we say that "all white swans are white" by virtue of the fact that "some white swans are not white" is self-contradictory, we assume that there are no true contradictions. But that there are no true contradictions could be a substantial fact about this world, not a trivial one. That is, it may be a *de re* necessity that ultimately explains the *de dicto* ones.

So far, then, we have characterised metaphysics as concerned with what it is to be or be real, with what things there are, with the way that they are, and with the connection between the way things are and what things there are. And all this is pursued at a higher level of abstraction than typifies any of the special sciences like physics, geology or chemistry. But this is to characterise metaphysics in terms of its subject matter, and that only provides half the story, for it still leaves room for very different conceptions of the ambitions and methods of metaphysics. What, in doing metaphysics, are we aiming to achieve, and how should we set about doing so?

In 1959, during the heyday of "ordinary language philosophy," P. F. Strawson published a book entitled *Individuals: An Essay in Descriptive Metaphysics*. He begins by contrasting two approaches to metaphysics: the descriptive and the revisionary (Strawson 1959: 9). Descriptive metaphysics aims to describe how we actually conceptualise the world, often making explicit what is often implicit in our thinking. Revisionary metaphysics, by contrast, aims to discover how we should conceptualise the world: how the world truly is. Revisionary metaphysics, as the name implies, will often show the world to be quite different from the way we ordinarily think it to be. We may wonder whether descriptive metaphysics really counts as metaphysics at all, as opposed to a prelude to metaphysics, given that it concerns our mental mirror of reality rather than reality itself. It may, of course, be all that is available to us, if all that is presented to our minds is reality's image. But one reason to think that we can in principle move beyond description is that we may discover hitherto hidden contradictions in our ordinary thought, forcing us to revise our beliefs to some extent. This is often precisely how the revisionary metaphysician will proceed. If a given model of reality is found to be self-contradictory, then it must be replaced by some other model, which of course will be subject to the very same test. Ultimately, we may hope to arrive at a model that is a more accurate description of reality than the one with which we started. (Again, however, this presupposes, what for some philosophers is a matter of controversy, that there can be no true contradictions: see Priest [1987].)

This brings us to methodological issues. Is the "ordeal by consistency test" the only weapon in the metaphysician's armoury? If so, we are left with no means of choosing between equally consistent models. What else might guide our choice at this point? Very often a viewpoint is described as "intuitive," the implication being that this is a merit. And equally, a "counterintuitive" result is supposed to indicate that something has gone wrong somewhere. But what is it that is informing this intuition? It is presumably guided by the conceptual scheme that descriptive metaphysics seeks to uncover. If, then, intuition is accorded any authority, revisionary metaphysics will still to some extent be answerable to descriptive metaphysics: even if revealed contradictions force us to revise our ordinary conceptions of the world, we are still urged to choose the consistent scheme that diverges least from whatever scheme descriptive metaphysics throws up. But the very drive towards revisionary metaphysics should make us suspicious of "intuition" as a source of metaphysical knowledge.

Another constraint on our choice of model might be an epistemological one. Some metaphysical theories make it mysterious how we could acquire knowledge of the kinds of entity, property or relation that those theories say exist. And this might reasonably be held to be a point against such theories. The theory that underlying an object's properties is some bare "substratum," or that mathematical statements are made true by abstract entities that have no location in space and time, has been subjected to just this kind of epistemological objection.

The methods I have mentioned so far – attending to internal consistency, compatibility with our original conceptual scheme, and epistemological consequences – are wholly or largely a priori, making no direct appeal to experience or experiment. And this is often how metaphysics is popularly conceived, as a wholly a priori enterprise, this being precisely what differentiates it from science. But in sharp contrast to this is a naturalistic metaphysics, which is informed by physical science. The naturalistic metaphysician may be less concerned with a priori structures than with the metaphysical picture of the world suggested by, for example, the special and general theories of relativity, quantum mechanics, or string theory. As we might put it, metaphysics tells us what is possible; science what is actual (see Lowe 1998: 22–7, for a more careful statement of this idea). This does not make metaphysics redundant, because the philosophical implications of scientific theories, concerning a principle like the identity of indiscernibles, for instance, may need to be made explicit, since the scientist's concern in putting forward these theories is not likely to be primarily philosophical. But a note of caution is in order. In drawing out the supposed consequences of these theories, how much are we revealing what is already there, deep within the scientist's picture of reality, and how much are we bringing independent metaphysical models or principles to the interpretation of that picture? And how much are scientists themselves making metaphysical assumptions that need to be scrutinised before being incorporated into scientific theory?

References

Ayer, A. J. (1973) *The Central Questions of Philosophy*, Harmondsworth: Penguin.

Lowe, E. J. (1998) *The Possibility of Metaphysics*, Oxford: Clarendon Press.

Priest, Graham (1987) *In Contradiction: A Study of the Transconsistent*, Dordrecht: Nijhoff.

Strawson, P. F. (1959) *Individuals: An Essay in Descriptive Metaphysics*, London: Methuen.

Tennyson, Hallam (1899) *Alfred Lord Tennyson: A Memoir by His Son*, London: Macmillan & Co.

Part I
HISTORY OF METAPHYSICS

INTRODUCTION TO PART I
Millennia of metaphysics
Peter Simons

Metaphysics traces its ancestry to ancient Greek civilisation. Centuries before the idea of metaphysics was outlined by Aristotle, longer still before it got the name "metaphysics," Presocratic philosophers speculated about the nature of the world, what it was made of, and according to what principles it developed. Metaphysics is thus one of the oldest branches of thought, and despite several attempts to remove it, retains a place in philosophy.

Whereas the Presocratics from Ionia concerned themselves with the nature of the observable natural world, attempting natural rather than supernatural explanations, the Eleatic philosophers Parmenides and Zeno offered logical arguments to demonstrate that reality is one and unchanging, so the physical world we observe must be mere appearance, while the Pythagoreans contended that the principles of the world are not material things but numbers.

This opposition between the physical or natural world (*physis* means "nature" in Greek) and the world of the eternal or unchanging has been a dominant theme in Western metaphysics ever since. Plato compromised by admitting change and plurality to the perceptible world, but ascribing to it a lower reality, derivative from a realm of unchanging ideas or forms, which possess greater reality and provide the patterns to which the perceived world imperfectly conforms. But Plato's student Aristotle rejected separate eternal forms and took an object's form to be in it, so located in space and time and part of physical reality.

Another major division that early caught, and thereafter held, the attention of metaphysicians was whether the human mind, spirit or soul was itself part of the natural world, or whether it could somehow stand apart. Again Plato stoked the controversy by holding that the soul is strictly eternal and immortal, communing with the forms, but is temporarily shackled to the material body during life. Aristotle characteristically held the soul to be in the human body as its form. The issue whether there is one, two or even three fundamental subdivisions of things (material, mental, ideal) has still to receive a consensual resolution.

It was Aristotle who first explicitly separated the branch of knowledge now known as metaphysics. He called it "first philosophy," to distinguish it from second philosophy or the theory of nature (physics). Metaphysics is variously characterized by him as the science of being *qua* being, of first principles and causes, and of the divine. Unlike other branches of knowledge, which concern themselves with part of what there is, metaphysics is universal: it is about absolutely everything, not with every detail, but only those matters which all things share. It was only some centuries later (first century CE) that Aristotle's highly compressed texts, probably lecture notes, were put together by his editors and dubbed "the works coming after the works on nature" (*ta meta ta physika*), from which cataloguing tag the subject received its name. Surprisingly, the more appropriate "ontology," meaning "science of being," was only coined in the seventeenth century by German scholastics.

Most of Western philosophy before the rise of modern natural science stood in the shadow of Plato or Aristotle. The man regarded as the first medieval philosopher, the Irishman Johannes Scotus Eriugena (ninth century), took many of his ideas from Plato. Aristotle's works were initially better known in the Islamic world, and the great medieval commentators al-Farabi, Avicenna and Averroes wrote in Arabic. When their works and the Greek originals were eventually translated into Latin, Europe caught up, and the apogee of Aristotelian influence coincided with the rise and spread of universities in Europe. The great scholastic philosophers Thomas Aquinas, John Duns Scotus and William of Ockham were at once Aristotle scholars and metaphysicians in their own right, pursuing their metaphysical differences under the guise of disagreements about what Aristotle meant. At the same time medieval Christian metaphysics benefited from the urgent need to provide sound intellectual underpinnings to difficult points of Christian dogma, including the Holy Trinity, Christ's Incarnation, the transubstantiation of bread and wine at communion, the freedom of individuals despite divine foreknowledge, the status of the soul after death and before resurrection, and whether God could be rationally proved to exist.

Metaphysics began its long slide from intellectual pre-eminence with the coming of modern natural science. Galileo expressly set his new world-system against that of the Aristotelians. René Descartes promised to found knowledge not on authority or tradition but on self-evidence. It was Descartes who both returned to Plato's emphasis on *a priori* rational justification and gave the opposition between mind and matter its modern urgency, though Descartes' dualism was strenuously opposed by the materialist Thomas Hobbes. The stress on the *a priori* was carried further by Spinoza, who contended one could infer the nature of reality by logical deduction from self-evident axioms. By contrast, the role of experience in our knowledge was stressed by John Locke, who, while he shared many assumptions with Descartes, emphasized the importance of reflecting on our intellectual capacities and the way we attain knowledge, initiating the critical and introspective attitude to metaphysical claims that peaked with Kant but has never thereafter lost its importance to metaphysics. Locke's inconsistencies were exposed by George Berkeley, whose anti-materialist metaphysics was carried further by the greatest of all critics of metaphysics (as of other intellectual pretensions) David Hume. Hume's ironical injunction to burn all books of "divinity or school [i.e., scholastic] metaphysics" for being neither mathematics nor natural science, and so containing "nothing but sophistry and illusion," haunts all subsequent metaphysics.

Until the rise of modern natural science there were two major sources of knowledge carrying the stamp of official and academic approval: divine revelation (as interpreted by the church) and, second to this, the authority of ancient philosophers. Experimental and mathematically formulated natural science threatened and in many cases supplanted these sources. Aristotle's physics was shown to be fundamentally flawed, and the authority of the church was challenged by the Reformation. While Newton and Leibniz, like nearly all their contemporaries, believed in God, their God increasingly had to conform to the discerned patterns of nature rather than the other way around. Enlightenment thinkers across Europe stressed the autonomy of human knowledge, and God began to be pushed into the metaphysical corner.

Hume's challenge to the claims of metaphysics could not remain unanswered. One native Scottish answer was to stress the literal truth and reliability of most of our everyday beliefs, by contrast with Hume's sparse and flawed Berkeleyan metaphysics of ideas. A more radical answer was provided by the erstwhile rationalist Immanuel Kant, who safeguarded *a priori* metaphysics by withdrawing its claims to be about an independently existing real world in itself (*an sich*), instead confining it to the critical examination of knowledge dealing with the world as we experience it. On Kant's account, this is principally formed by us, rendering space and time "forms of intuition" and the basic kinds or categories not divisions of the *an sich* but concepts we employ to turn our experience into knowledge.

Kant's position was unstable, retaining as it did a last *an sich* remnant of unknowable reality. His German successors replaced this by an all-encompassing creative mind, culminating in Hegel's systematic vision of a unified rational and spiritual universe, understandable from within by *a priori* insight. Hegel's grandiose pretensions echoed through nineteenth-century philosophy, but were quickly dismissed in his native Germany, where the sceptical stance of Hume and other British empiricists inspired philosophers to turn to the natural sciences for their knowledge, and a generation of philosophers–scientists from Weber and Kirchhoff to Helmholtz and Mach followed the Frenchman Auguste Comte in confining their claims to those which could be experientially justified. Comte envisaged thought advancing from theology via metaphysics to "positive" science, augmented by the rising sciences of psychology and sociology. Darwin's theory of evolution at last provided a naturalistic explanation for those aspects of reality which had seemed to call for a supernatural designer–creator. Darwin's ideas were taken up enthusiastically by German philosophy's great debunker Friedrich Nietzsche, whose disdain for metaphysics (his own metaphysics of centres of power notwithstanding) was surpassed only by his disdain for religion.

The sceptical attitude to metaphysics did not prevail among the philosophy professors, however. In Germany, a "back-to-Kant" movement gathered momentum, while British metaphysicians such as Francis Herbert Bradley belatedly discovered the German idealists. Absolute idealism and Spencer's Darwinian "synthetic philosophy" provided an eclectic but metaphysically vibrant background to the new realism of Moore and Russell at the turn of the twentieth century. While Moore sought to escape idealism, whether Berkeleyan or Hegelian, Russell was concerned to refute Bradleyan monism, using the new mathematical logic. The philosophy of mathematics, despite steady progress in rigorization through the nineteenth century, had, following Georg Cantor's invention of set theory, been plagued by a series of paradoxes, culminating in Russell's paradox of the set of sets which are not elements of themselves. Russell discovered that the German mathematician Gottlob Frege had refined his logic to the point where the paradox could be rigorously derived as a theorem, undermining Frege's attempt to show arithmetic to be extended logic.

While Moore and Russell were preoccupied with providing solid foundations for ethics and mathematics, respectively, students of the German neo-Aristotelian Franz Brentano ventured anew into metaphysics, under the titles "theory of objects" (Alexius Meinong) or "formal ontology" (Edmund Husserl). Russell's underpinning to the new logic, developed partly in opposition to Meinong, was logical atomism, a realist metaphysics of facts and their parts. This was refined by Russell's student Wittgenstein, who coupled an austere world of independent atomic facts with a severe critique of attempts to "say anything metaphysical" as nonsense. Wittgenstein's strictures were taken up in interwar Vienna by the Vienna Circle, an interdisciplinary group around Moritz Schlick, and the Circle put flesh on Wittgenstein's bare bones by classifying all statements as "meaningless" if they could not be verified. This enhancement of empiricistic positivism with the tools of modern logic, especially by Rudolf Carnap, put the brakes on metaphysics, which had enjoyed a brief heyday in the 1920s with systematic treatises by Samuel Alexander, John McTaggart and Alfred North Whitehead. The European political situation soon scattered the logical positivists, and they, together with foreign visitors to Vienna such as W. V. Quine and A. J. Ayer, spread their anti-metaphysical brand of linguistic analysis abroad.

Throughout the mid-twentieth century, positivism and the metaphysically deflationary ordinary language philosophy of Wittgenstein, Ryle and Austin kept metaphysics subdued. From mid-century onwards, however, things began to change. Quine combined pragmatist naturalism with a denial of any separation of philosophy from science. His logical criterion of ontological commitment re-awoke interest in ontology, although his own attitude to metaphysics was distinctly light touch, favouring a schematic structural ontology supported only by an interlocking network of beliefs, lightly secured by experiential evidence. A more traditional idea re-emerged with Peter Strawson's descriptive metaphysics, a Kantian project to determine *a priori* the perennial conceptual scheme we need to make sense of the world we find. The positivists' verifiability criterion of meaningfulness was found to be self-defeating, and Karl Popper's similar falsifiability criterion separated, not sense from nonsense, but science from meaningful non-science, including metaphysics. In time Popper came to embrace an ebullient "three-world" metaphysics of physical, mental and abstract things, echoing similar ideas of Frege, and even earlier, Bernard Bolzano.

Although one strand of analytic philosophy gave home to the most stringent anti-metaphysics, other forms of philosophy from phenomenology to post-structuralism have been equally anti-metaphysical. Indeed it is within analytic philosophy that metaphysics has experienced its strongest comeback. Issues of mind and modality have driven much of this. Australian materialism rescued metaphysical discussion of the mind–body problem, while the mental characteristics of intentionality and consciousness have resisted attempts at naturalization. The semantics of modal logic and the widespread adoption of the concept of possible worlds have fuelled intense discussion as to how realistically such talk should be interpreted. The frank modal realism of David Lewis constitutes the late twentieth century's most systematic metaphysical project. Meanwhile, classical metaphysical problems such as universals, free will, mathematical Platonism, and the metaphysical implications of causation, laws of nature, and truth have spawned a wide range of debates about metaphysical issues, no longer carried on in the shadow of anxiety about meaninglessness. At the beginning of the twentieth-first century, metaphysics appears to be enjoying an astonishing golden age.

1

PRESOCRATIC THEMES
Being, not-being and mind

David Sedley

Introduction

European philosophy started life as speculative science. The remarkable pantheon of Greek thinkers classed as "Presocratic" on the ground that they are philosophically antecedent to Socrates (BC 469–399) treated the world itself as their primary *explanandum*. But deep questions concerning the world's physical structure turned out to be inseparable from still deeper ones about what it is to be a discrete thing, what being entails, and whether there is any parallel role for its negative counterpart, not-being. In what follows, it should be borne in mind that, although all the thinkers we will be considering wrote one or more books, none of those books survives intact. Their thought must be reconstructed from fragments (purportedly verbatim quotations) and other testimonies. This makes an already risky historical exercise even more hazardous. But the ultimate sources of our own thinking are a topic we cannot lightly set aside.

Heraclitus

> Teacher of most is Hesiod: him they recognize as knowing most. And he did not understand day and night. For that is one thing. (Heraclitus, in Diels and Kranz 1952: B57)

If we can succeed in deciphering this characteristically cryptic utterance of Heraclitus (c. BC 500), and work out what mistake he was trying to expose, we will be well on our way to the heart of Presocratic metaphysics. That will require starting even earlier, with Hesiod, the target of Heraclitus' complaint.

The poet Hesiod (c. BC 700) was, even more than his approximate contemporary Homer, a canonical author for the Greek philosophers, who repeatedly felt obliged to come to terms with him when formulating their own ideas. His poem the *Theogony* had become the classic Greek creation myth. It takes the form of a genealogical cosmogony, charting the emergence of the world in the guise of a growing family of divinities: first Chaos, who was superseded by Earth, followed by a series of further cosmic entities, including Night, herself in turn the mother of Day. Day shares the house of her mother Night, because, conveniently, both are never in at the same time: they meet only on the doorstep, as the one arrives home and the other sets out on her round (*Theogony*, 746–57).

What in Heraclitus' eyes was Hesiod's error? It seems to have lain in the latter's naïve assumption that the two names, "day" and "night," in virtue of the very fact that they are two, must pick out two discrete items. His casting the two of them as co-resident goddesses is no more than a traditionally mythological showcasing of that naïve assumption. The same metaphysics of personification runs right through Hesiod's worldview, which includes literally hundreds of minor deities, as diverse as Love, Lightning, Hunger and Victory. That the Hesiodic way of carving reality up into discrete components is a fundamental misunderstanding is in a way Heraclitus' pivotal insight (see Mourelatos [1973], who calls it "the Naïve Metaphysics of Things"), and the driving force behind his radical reanalysis of reality. Even Heraclitus' most significant philosophical forerunner Anaximander (early to mid sixth century BC) had maintained the same primitive assumption of discrete thinghood, apparently speaking of such opposites as hot and cold, and wet and dry, as pairs of antithetical forces whose members, during the cycle of seasons, advance or retreat in the face of each other. Heraclitus is implicitly setting Anaximander right when he puts it this way: "Cold things warm, hot cools, moist parches, dry dampens" (Diels and Kranz 1952: B126).

Both in the case of Day and Night, and in that of pairs like hot and cold, it is easy enough to see why Heraclitus objects to his predecessors' simplistic assumption: they have been misled by the structure of language into assuming a one-to-one correlation of distinct words and distinct things. Yet on closer inspection language itself challenges the distinction between these items. For in the opening quotation Heraclitus' names for Day and Night are, respectively, *Hēmera* and *Euphronē*, both of which can mean "the kindly one"; and it is entirely characteristic of Heraclitus to regard such linguistic patterns as metaphysically revealing. (This particular example, curiously unremarked in the literature on Heraclitus, is owed to Hayden Pelliccia [pers. commun.].) In a comparable passage (Diels and Kranz 1952: B48), challenging the familiar duality of life and death, Heraclitus leans on the double meaning of *bios*, which differently accented can mean "life" and "bow": "The name of the bow is life, but its work is death." Heraclitean metaphysics flows from a desire to make us not so much abandon the way we familiarly talk as understand its meaning all the way down. The very discourse (*logos*) that Heraclitus constructs for us is, in addition to being his own, one that he insists has all along been publicly available for anyone with the wit to fathom its meaning (Diels and Kranz 1952: B1).

The denial of Day and Night's duality makes sense as a reaction to Hesiod's primitive ontology, itself no doubt emblematic of pre-philosophical ontology more generally. The harder question to answer is how Heraclitus would defend his own contention that, in the case of Day and Night, precisely *one* thing is in the frame. We will do best to return to this after broader consideration of the principle at stake.

Some of Heraclitus' other illustrations of the unity of opposites, as his most celebrated motif has come to be known, are helpfully transparent. In particular, "The road up and down: one and the same" (Diels and Kranz 1952: B60) is a saying which not only exemplifies the unity principle but also offers a possible model for interpreting the more puzzling cases. If I call "the road up" what you call "the road down," both of us are missing its essential unity because we arbitrarily privilege our own perspectives on it. Unity, in Heraclitus' view, transcends the duality as soon as one eliminates perspective and adopts a neutral god's-eye vantage point.

In the case of Day and Night, however, the misleadingness of their separation from each other seems to be established by partly different considerations. The sun is a curiously minor player in Heraclitus' cosmology – a bowl filled with fire, restricted by a higher power to possessing a diameter of one foot, and replaced every day by a new sun. And yet "if there were no sun," Heraclitus remarks, "it would be night" (Diels and Kranz 1952: B99). That is, the sky is sometimes illuminated by this transient bowl of fire, sometimes not. To make that fact the basis for postulating two discrete cosmic entities is to privilege a superficial variation over the underlying unity.

The ways in which human discourse generates polarities are then many and various. Although the underlying unity of the continuum is the deep truth that Heraclitus is most at pains to uncover, and this leads him to deplore the polarizing tendencies of common human perspectives, humans are not the victims of simple error. The unity, or "harmony," is precisely a harmony of opposites, which in turn makes the existence of opposites a necessary precondition of true unity. "They do not understand how it is by being at variance with itself that it is in agreement with itself: a back-turning harmony, as of a bow and a lyre" (Diels and Kranz 1952: B51).

Parmenides

> From this point on, learn the opinions of mortals, listening to the deceitful ordering of my words. For they have decided to name two forms, one of which they should not, and that is where their error lies. (Parmenides, in Diels and Kranz 1952: B8, lines 51–4)

We have now moved on a generation, to Parmenides, the most revolutionary thinker of the entire Presocratic era, and inaugurator of the "Eleatic" school, so named after his city Elea in southern Italy. His poetic discourse, placed in the mouth of a goddess, contrasts the duality implicit in ordinary human beliefs with the strong unity thesis that Parmenides himself advocates. The way in which "mortals" are described in the above-quoted lines as polarizing reality into paired opposites has a strikingly Heraclitean ring. As for Parmenides' monism, his thesis that what-is is a unity, this was not in itself new. Heraclitus had not just defended the essential unity of opposed pairs of opposites, but had himself progressed from there to a global unity thesis: "*All* things are one" (Diels and Kranz 1952: B50), that underlying unity being identifiable with god: "The god: day and night, winter and summer, war and peace, satiety and hunger. But he varies, just as fire, when mixed with different spices, is named after the savour of each" (Diels and Kranz 1952: B67). Even before him Thales, Anaximander and Anaximenes, the celebrated trio of Milesian philosophers, had espoused what is widely interpreted as material monism, seeking to trace the world and all its phenomena back to some single primary stuff. In short, the ultimate unity of being was not in itself news. But Parmenides' monism goes far beyond that of his predecessors. It is *eliminative* monism: the single entity which it postulates does not for him, as it had done for Heraclitus, underlie, and thus in a way account for, the more superficial plurality of ordinary experience, but at a stroke eliminates that plurality. As traditionally understood (although there has been a wide spectrum of interpretations) Parmenides really does insist that what-is is a literal unity, entirely undifferentiated across time and space alike.

How could a worldview so contrary to experience and common sense be defended? His methodology is to set aside empirical data such as had been used to favour one physical analysis of the world over another, and instead to examine the concept of being itself. If the logic of being turns out already to place constraints on what could possibly serve as the subject of the verb "be," we had better ensure that those constraints are in place before we proceed to ask what, as a matter of fact, there "is."

The key constraint that emerges is that the verb "be" is un-negatable. The expression "… is not," that is, could never have a subject, because to supply a sentence with a subject one must either *name* or *think of* the item in question, and both options are ruled out when it comes to naming or thinking something which *is not*. What-is-not is unavailable for referring to, so cannot be successfully named; nor can you succeed in thinking of it, given that you could not do so without knowing what it is, and that you could not know what something is when it is not anything at all. This last expression, "anything *at all*," conveys a key assumption at work in Parmenides' argument. Some, he foresees, will try to evade his trap by saying that not-being is normally not absolute, but relative to some chosen complement: thus what *is not*, e.g. is not wooden or is not in Cambridge, also *is*, e.g. is plastic or is in Oxford. Parmenides' refusal to allow qualified or partial non-being, the most contentious of all his argumentative moves, is summed up in his words "The choice on this matter lies in the following: it is, or it is not" (Diels and Kranz 1952: B8, lines 15–16), which we may choose to think of as an early predecessor of the law of the excluded middle.

Parmenides has been suspected here of confusing different senses of "be," in particular its complete use, equivalent to "exist," and its incomplete use as the copula. More recent work on the Greek verb "be" (see especially Brown 1994), however, has cast doubt on the accusation. In Greek, to be is regularly to *be something*. Most of the time the something is specified: the bottle is a plastic object, is in my bag, etc. Occasionally it is not: the bottle simply "is." But the latter use, which to Anglophone readers may look like a switch to the existential sense, is in ancient Greek usage still a way of saying that the bottle *is something*, albeit without this time specifying what. Parmenides is not equivocating between two senses of "be," the one incomplete and the other complete, but is advising that the only correct way to use this univocal verb is without restricting the complement, since to do so would be implicitly to import some not-being (if the bottle is plastic, for example, it is not glass).

If we accept that not-being is an incoherent notion, we will endorse Parmenides' conclusion that whatever turns out to be the proper subject of "… is" must in no context or relation admit of any predicate that would entail its also at any time *not being* something. But *any* variation in being across time or space would imply some phase or component of the illicit not-being. If something comes-to-be, it previously *was not*; if something has distinct parts, each part *is not* what the others are; if something moves, there must be a place for it to move into, where it *is not* already. Therefore being must be altogether invariable, and all apparent change and qualitative difference an illusion. Most surprisingly of all (many scholars doubt it, but the text is particularly clear on the point), being must be spherical, since any asymmetric shape would import a component of not-being to explain its projecting less in this direction than in that. Since the world itself was already understood by the Greeks as mathematically spherical (because bounded by a spherical heaven), we can if we wish read Parmenides' project as a re-description of that very same sphere, in such a way as to eliminate all the apparent variations from it.

Parmenides' poem describes his journey in a chariot to the House of Night, at whose gates the paths of Day and Night meet. It is from this vantage point, where regular temporal distinctions collapse, that the unnamed goddess proceeds to divulge to him the true unvarying nature of reality. The artificial separation of Day from Night had been the focus of Heraclitus' complaint against Hesiod's multiplication of entities. Parmenides' symbolic withdrawal to the place where their paths merge can be seen as his continuation of that same resistance to Hesiodic ontology, with his radical monism being its ultimate culmination.

After Parmenides

The interpretation of Parmenides is, even by the standards of Presocratic philosophy, fraught with controversy. But there are plentiful signs that in subsequent generations he was understood as an eliminative monist, and that the various attempts to rehabilitate plurality were framed as replies to his challenge. Some of the evidence is found in thinkers who will otherwise not feature in this chapter, notably Empedocles, who interpreted the world as a cyclical alternation between an ideal Parmenidean One and a cosmic Many, and Parmenides' follower Zeno of Elea, who argued in reply to the likes of Empedocles that the pluralist premise "There are many things" embodies a whole series of self-contradictions.

There is, however, one oddity which casts some doubt on the nature and degree of Parmenides' influence. On the one hand, everyone in the next generation agreed with Parmenides that strictly speaking nothing comes into being or perishes, and their unanimous emphasis on this tenet reads like their concession of a partial victory to him. On the other hand, there is no evidence that any of them took seriously his specific ground for the tenet, namely that prior to its putative coming-to-be and after its putative ceasing-to-be the entity in question would *not be*, and that not-being is an illicit notion. Instead, they seem to have relied on a much older and more intuitive premise, that nothing can come to be *out of nothing* or perish *into nothing*, in the light of which change as such may prove unobjectionable, so long as it is reanalysed as the endless redistribution of permanent stuffs. That principle had been tacitly at work even in much earlier physical theorists. What Parmenides seems to have prompted is a more explicit recognition of its importance, resulting in its frequent introduction as an explicit premise. Anaxagoras (on whom more below) even went so far as to outlaw from his philosophical writing the verbs "come-to-be" (or "become") and "perish," rejected as representing a popular misunderstanding of the nature of change, and to replace them with verbs signifying mixture and separation (Diels and Kranz 1952: B17).

Melissus

One reason for this switch from Parmenides' idiosyncratic argument against change to the intuitive premise outlawing absolute generation and annihilation may lie in the work of Melissus, although it remains a matter of dispute whether he wrote his book, *On Nature or on What-Is*, early enough to have influenced our other protagonists (the only recorded date in his life is BC 440, when he memorably led his island, Samos, to victory in a naval engagement with the Athenians). Melissus presented a revised version of Parmenides' monism as, in effect, a revolutionary physics, defending the solitary existence of a single infinite entity which he calls "the One," and using the kind of premises and arguments that were typical of cosmological writing. Because his work is primarily physics and not metaphysics, he does not earn more than a walk-on part in this chapter. But we should note that his relatively clear arguments came to be more widely echoed, and therefore probably more directly influential, than those of Parmenides. The intuitive and widely accepted "Nothing could ever come to be out of nothing" (Diels and Kranz 1952: B1) was the very first premise in his chain of arguments, from which all his conclusions ultimately stemmed.

Anaxagoras

The great physicist Anaxagoras, who wrote in the first half of the fifth century BC, can be placed in the direct aftermath of Parmenides. It is not Anaxagoras' physics as such that will concern us here, but his singular way of escaping Parmenides' trap. Parmenides' monism is founded on the constraints imposed by rational thought, yet so strictly monistic is it that it can allow no distinct role for thought itself, or for the thinking subject. His line "For it is the same thing to think and to be" (Diels and Kranz 1952: B3) has been interpreted in various ways, but the likeliest meaning remains that what is thinks and what thinks is. That is, there can be no distinction between the thinking subject and the object thought. To permit any such distinction would be to abandon monism for dualism. And that vital move to dualism is to be credited not to Parmenides but to Anaxagoras, who has the historical distinction of being the very first dualist of mind and matter. It is a natural guess that this dualism originated as his chosen way of cutting himself free from Parmenidean monism.

The default assumption had always been top–down: that matter has certain attributes all the way down, and that these include vital properties like life and intelligence. Whatever the basic stuff of the universe may be, it is inherently and irreducibly alive, and in fact probably divine. Since Hesiod had treated the world itself as a collection of divinities (Heaven, Earth, etc.), it is no surprise that his successors should, in the course of scientific rationalization, have left in place the explanatorily helpful implication that the major stuffs constituting the world are inherently alive. This hylozoism leaves it unproblematic to explain nature's inclusion of living and even intelligent beings. It raises only the relatively minor problem of explaining why, given that matter is irreducibly alive, some things appear *not* to be alive. Thales (Diels and Kranz 1952: A22) had explicitly maintained that in reality everything is animate ("All things are full of gods") – even stones, regarding which he pointed to the motive powers of the lodestone or natural magnet. Presumably in some things, e.g. other stones, the vital powers were still present but too muted to show. This same hylozoist assumption accounts for Parmenides' lack of concern to separate reality from the mind that conceives it, and for remarks made by Melissus in which he betrays his un-argued assumption that the One is a living being (Diels and Kranz 1952: B7, lines 4–6).

Against this background, Anaxagoras' radical dualism is a remarkable break with tradition. The universe, according to his treatise, has two major constituents. First there is a single material blend of all ingredients, in which "there is a portion of everything in everything." Second, and entirely unmixed with the first item, there is *nous*, translatable as "mind" or "intelligence." Why mind is unmixed is explained as follows (Diels and Kranz 1952: B12):

> The other things share a portion of each, but mind is something infinite and autonomous, and is mixed with no thing, but it alone is by itself. For if it were not by itself, but were mixed with something else, it would share in all things, if it were mixed with any of them – for in each thing a portion of each is present, as I have said earlier – and the things mixed with it would prevent it from controlling any thing in such a way as it does in being alone by itself.

The impression may be given here of mind's having the transcendent status of a detached divinity. But although for Anaxagoras a great extra-cosmic mind does sometimes take on the role of a creator divinity, he also speaks of portions of mind as being present *in* living things, and there should be no doubt that he is talking about mind as we know and ourselves possess it.

Rather, what Anaxagoras means by making mind unmixed seems to be as follows. The mixed ingredients either are, or (on a more widely accepted interpretation) include, a full set of pairs of opposite properties: hot and cold, wet and dry, bright and dark, heavy and light, etc. The omnipresence of these opposites in the mixture, albeit in varying proportions, is what guarantees that every physical object has some temperature, some weight, etc. Now if mind were "mixed" with the other things, it too would have some temperature, some weight, and so on. And if that were the case, it would be subject to control by physical forces, for example being heated or cooled, dried or dampened, by the prevailing weather conditions. By remaining unmixed, mind is invulnerable to physical control, and is instead left free to exercise its natural control *over* matter.

Thus what mind's being "unmixed" amounts to is its being *free of physical properties*. Its power over matter depends on it itself being non-physical. If that is what Anaxagoras is getting at, it is a breakthrough of sorts. No other philosopher before Plato fully succeeded in distinguishing the incorporeal from the corporeal (see Renehan 1980). Anaxagoras does not go all the way either, since (elsewhere, in Diels and Kranz 1952: B12) he speaks of mind as if it were a very special *stuff*: it is the "finest and purest of all things," and occurs in larger and smaller quantities. Nevertheless, his declaring it unmixed is as close as anyone came in the Presocratic era to making mind something non-physical, and that move lies right at the heart of the dualism of mind and matter with which he counters Parmenidean monism. If mind can be shown to be sufficiently distinct from the rest of being, and powerful enough to exert control over it, it can rescue us from a static and undifferentiated Eleatic monism and account for the world as we experience it.

The atomists

The suggestion above has been that Anaxagoras, seeking an escape route from Parmenides' One, found it in the separateness of mind, thus becoming the first mind–body dualist. A competing ontological duality, consisting of "limiters" and "unlimiteds," is credited to the Pythagorean Philolaus in the late fifth century BC, but there is no space to discuss it here. A better-understood dualism contemporary with Philolaus is that of the atomists – Leucippus, about whom we know little, and his successor Democritus, a voluminous writer of great power and originality. Once again a Parmenidean inspiration can be discerned behind their dualism.

Parmenides' argument, as we have seen, turned on the incoherence of not-being. By outlawing not-being from his ontology, he rendered coming-to-be and perishing inexplicable. The atomists, adopting a premise that we have seen to be typical of the entire era, accept that absolute coming-to-be and perishing are impossible and must be replaced by mere redistribution of eternal elements. But not only are their reasons for respecting this principle of conservation not the ones urged by Parmenides, their theory of elements goes so far as to administer a direct rebuff to Parmenides' veto on not-being.

In Parmenides, one of the guises of the rejected not-being had been as empty space, without which movement becomes impossible. This equivalence between not-being and void is anything but clear in Parmenides' verses, but is brought to the fore by an argument of Melissus' (Diels and Kranz 1952: B7, lines 7–10), according to which (a) there is no motion without void; and (b) void, being nothing, does not exist. What our evidence puts beyond doubt is that the atomists stood that Eleatic argument on its head by asserting a symmetrical dualism of being and not-being. Being is equated with body (or "the full"), and is argued to come in indivisible chunks called "atoms" ("indivisibles"); not-being is equated with void or vacuum (or "the empty"), which provides the intervals separating atoms. Both atoms and void equally exist, because "being no more is than not-being is." In saying this they vindicate the taboo term "not-being," insisting, *contra* Parmenides, that it designates something real. They also, for good measure, allow it the deflationary label "nothing": as Democritus put it with a touch of linguistic inventiveness, "Thing [den] no more is than nothing [mēden] is" (Diels and Kranz 1952: B156).

How they defended their great metaphysical paradox, that "not-being is," is nowhere recorded. Indeed, if void is assumed to be empty space, and empty space in turn equated with nothing and with not-being, there is an obvious danger that its being will thereby be being negated rather than asserted. For this reason there is some attraction (see Sedley 1982) in identifying the atomists' "void," not with empty space itself, but with the portion of emptiness that occupies this or that space. For if the *occupant* of a space is called nothing and not-being, that seems a safer way of asserting that the space *is* empty, and hence that void exists. Moreover, if void is a space-occupier in this way, that seems as good a ground as any for asserting its existence.

To end, it is important to note certain further metaphysical consequences of atomism. For in this system we meet the very first reductionist ontology. Atoms and void, which are the sole constituents of the universe and its occupants, have only ineliminable physical properties like volume and shape. Colour, temperature, flavour, etc., are not part of the core reality but observer-dependent epiphenomena, generated when atomic complexes interact with the sense organs. In Democritus' famous slogan, "By convention [*nomōi*] sweet, by convention bitter, by convention hot, by convention cold, by convention colour; in reality [*eteēi*] atoms and void" (Diels and Kranz 1952: B9).

This bottom–up treatment of sensible properties applies, *mutatis mutandis*, to mental properties too. We saw earlier how an originally monistic psychology, in which mind was assumed to be as inseparable an aspect of matter as density and temperature are, was radically refashioned by Anaxagoras into a dualism of mind and matter. Atomism reverts to monism, but this time of a strictly physicalistic stamp. For Democritus the soul (*psychē*) is an atomic structure, whose distinctively mental properties are not part of the underlying atomic reality but epiphenomenal accretions.

Of all the metaphysical ideas generated in the Presocratic era, this brand of bottom-up materialism is not only chronologically the last, but also, appropriately, the one that can most directly engage twenty-first-century metaphysical concerns.

One or two?

Recall once more Parmenides' criticism of popular ontology: "For they have decided to name two forms, one of which they should not, and that is where their error lies." If this means that popular ontology rests on a counting error – two instead of one – it captures a surprisingly large part of the metaphysical agenda of the Presocratic era. For the ancient Greeks (and for none more than for Aristotle, the founder of metaphysics as a distinct discipline) ontology was indeed a counting game. Metaphysical speculation began life in Heraclitus' critical reflection on a naïve, pre-philosophical ontology which had tended to bifurcate unities into dualities. Parmenides' continuation of his reunification project culminated in a monism so extreme that it made the world itself threaten to collapse into illusion. And the subsequent rehabilitation of a pluralist ontology in several cases took the form of a search for the explanatory duality – matter and mind? being and not-being? – best equipped to rise from the ashes of Parmenidean monism.

References

Brown, Lesley (1994) "The Verb 'To Be' in Greek Philosophy: Some Remarks," in S. Everson (ed.), *Language*, Cambridge: Cambridge University Press, pp. 212–36.

Diels, H., revised by Kranz, W. (1952) *Die Fragmente der Vorsokratiker*, revised by W. Kranz (and later edns), Berlin.

Mourelatos, A. P. D. (1973) "Heraclitus, Parmenides, and the Naïve Metaphysics of Things," in E. N. Lee, A. P. D. Mourelatos, and R. Rorty (eds), *Exegesis and Argument*, Assen: Van Gorcum, pp. 16–48.

Renehan, Robert (1980) "On the Greek Origins of the Concepts Incorporeality and Immateriality," *Greek, Roman and Byzantine Studies* 21: 105–38.

Sedley, David (1982) "Two Conceptions of Vacuum," *Phronesis* 27: 175–93.

Further reading

Two user-friendly introductions to Presocratic philosophy as a whole are Catherine Osborne, *Presocratic Philosophy: A Very Short Introduction* (Oxford: Oxford University Press, 2004); and James Warren, *Presocratics* (Trowbridge, UK: Acumen, 2007). Three navigable sourcebooks are G. S. Kirk, J. E. Raven, and M. Schofield, *The Presocratic Philosophers*, 2nd edn (Cambridge: Cambridge University Press, 1983), with Greek texts, translations and commentary; Richard D. McKirahan, *Philosophy before Socrates* (Indianapolis; Cambridge: Hackett, 1994), with translations and commentary; and Robin Waterfield, *The First Philosophers: The Presocratics and the Sophists* (Oxford: Oxford University Press, 2000), with translations and commentary. Fuller discussion of individual philosophers will be found in Jonathan Barnes, *The Presocratic Philosophers* (London: Routledge, 1979), with philosophically the best available comprehensive discussion of the Presocratics; Daniel Graham, *Explaining the Cosmos: The Ionian Tradition in Scientific Philosophy* (Princeton, NJ: Princeton University Press, 2006), including important reservations about "monism"; and A. A. Long (ed.), *The Cambridge Companion to Early Greek Philosophy* (Cambridge: Cambridge University Press, 1999). For the significance of individual philosophers, see further C. H. Kahn, *The Art and Thought of Heraclitus* (Cambridge: Cambridge University Press, 1979); and Patricia Curd, *The Legacy of Parmenides: Eleatic Monism and Later Presocratic Thought* (Princeton, NJ: Princeton University Press, 1997), an innovative study, frequently differing from the above account.

2
PLATO
Arguments for forms

Richard Patterson

Plato's "middle dialogues," especially the *Phaedo, Republic, Symposium* and *Phaedrus*, along with the late *Timaeus*, bring the reader's attention to a previously unnoticed sort of thing that he calls "forms" (*eide*). Forms are entirely imperceptible but grasped in thought; non-spatial and non-temporal yet fully real; independent of and separate from worldly things yet "participated in" by them and somehow responsible for their being what they are; useless in the way one would use a hammer or a doctor's expertise yet the source of all objective value, including that of hammers and doctors, in the world. Although Plato seldom explicitly argues for these curious entities he indicates that they serve numerous purposes, and these in turn point to corresponding implicit arguments. Later philosophical tradition has drawn extensively on this generous store of reasons for postulating one or another sort of Platonistic entity, tending to classify such arguments as metaphysical, epistemological or logical. But as a rule Plato's forms are distinct from the abstract objects of other Platonists, and his fundamental argument for forms was in fact normative. That is, forms are not such things as value-neutral, shared attributes of things or meanings of general terms. They are rather the types of thing and relationship entailed directly or indirectly by the nature of some objective good – e.g., a good cosmos, human community, or soul. This is the focus of the fourth and tenth sections, which link the epistemological and metaphysical arguments introduced in other sections to Plato's value-based conception of forms.

The One-over-many argument and uniqueness

Near the beginning of Plato's celebrated and, some would say, devastating examination of young Socrates' theory of forms, the title character of the *Parmenides* proposes a motive for forms:

> I suppose you think each Form is one for some such reason as this: whenever some group of things seems to you to be large, there seems to be some one character which appears the same as you look at all of them; and thus you think the large is one. (*Parmenides*, in Cooper and Hutchinson 1997: 132a)

Similarly the mature Socrates of the *Republic* remarks that "our usual procedure is to postulate a single form for each multiplicity of objects to which we apply the same term" (596a). Thus sensibles' shared relation to a single form accounts for their being similar in some respect. The *Republic* also extends the principle from pluralities of sensibles to pluralities of forms themselves, arguing that if God had created two forms of Bed rather than one, these would have something in common by virtue of which they were both called "what-is-Bed." If so, that common factor would be the form of bed, and would be unique (597b–c). In this way, the One-over-many principle implies not just the reality of forms, but also the uniqueness of each form.

But the *Parmenides* passage quoted above cleverly turns the One–many principle against the claim of uniqueness by extending the principle to a plurality including both intelligible and sensible items – large sensibles and the Large itself. This mixed group of larges (*megala*) entails a further form of Large "over" it, whereupon this new Large along with all the previous larges constitutes yet another plurality calling for yet another form of Large; and so on (132a–b). The regress applies to other forms as well (Human, Equal) and has become known as the "Third Man argument."

But what force does the regress in fact have against Platonism based on a One–many argument? "Parmenides" evidently assumes that the form of Large is itself large, so that its size can be imaginatively visualized "in the same way" as that of sensibles. Many later readers have also interpreted forms in one way or another as instances of themselves – either as (a) the sole "perfect particular" of a given kind; (b) the paradigm case of a given type; or (c) the only token of any given type F that is F without qualification as to time, relation or context. Sensible participants are then, respectively, imperfect approximations to the form, non-paradigm instances of the form, or things that are F only in some respect or relation, or at some time, etc. These "self-exemplifying" forms all stand in contrast to forms read as (d) natures or properties having themselves no visualizable shape or size, and exemplifying themselves only in special cases. Thus the form of Large is not, *pace* "Parmenides," a large thing, but the property possessed by large things, and Human is not the perfect or paradigm human being, but the nature of Humanness, etc. Difference, however, is both a characteristic possessed by sensibles and itself an instance of Difference (hence "self-exemplifying") in that it is, as Plato's *Sophist* argues, different from Sameness.

So are the self-exemplificational readings (a)–(c) inescapably liable to the regress? And is even (d) vulnerable in cases like Difference? It turns out that on any of these readings the dread Third Man can be disarmed by formulating the notion of a *many* in a manner suggested by more than one ancient commentator:

A plurality of things similar to one another in a certain respect F is a *many* if and only if there is no one member of the group by virtue of which all the rest are F.

This makes the world safe for a One-over-many principle, since it now generates a form only where one was intended in the first place. But since it will save all known interpretations of forms from the regress, it does not in itself establish any one reading.

The One-over-one principle

Plato also formulates the closely related principle that each particular F is F because of its participation in the form of F (e.g., *Phaedo*, 100c–101e). He also sometimes argues that the existence of an instance entails the reality of a type to which it belongs (what Michael Frede calls the "converse use" of "is"; Frede 1967). This "One–one" principle expresses directly, without appeal to any actual or potential plurality of instantiations, Plato's fundamental distinction between a thing and the intelligible nature(s) it instantiates. He does not examine the relation of the One–many and One–one principles, and they might seem in the end equivalent. But the One–one principle applies even if a form necessarily has only one instance – e.g., the *Timaeus*' unique created world. For this reason forms, unlike Aristotelian universals, are not definable as that which "potentially applies to more than one subject."

Interestingly, the One–many and One–one principles correspond to two later-emerging versions of "abstraction": one focusing attention on what is common to a plurality of things and ignoring their other properties to get at a universal, the other "subtracting" away all but one property of a single given object. Plato acknowledges neither version of abstraction, for (separate) forms are not "in things," and thus not literally accessible via abstraction. But why, then, should anyone believe in *separate* forms? And how are they to be apprehended?

Separateness

Plato affirms separateness directly or symbolically in numerous passages (e.g., *Symposium*, 211a–b; *Timaeus*, 52a–b), and "Parmenides" emphasizes it repeatedly in his critique of Young Socrates' theory. But in fact Parmenides' objection to participation in forms as "having a share of" them (*metechein*) amounts to an argument for separateness:

(1) Forms are either separate from or in their participants.
(2) If forms are in their participants, they are either (a) divided into parts, with one part in each participant as its "share," or (b) present as a whole in each participant.
(3) Forms are neither present as a whole in each participant, since then they would be separated from themselves (131a–b), nor as divided into parts, since this leads to numerous absurdities (131c–e).
(4) Therefore forms are separate from their participants.   .

Some readers think premise (2) treats forms as corporeal objects, and certainly the argument works on such a conception. But if, as is historically plausible, Aristotle was present in Plato's Academy at the time of the *Parmenides* and urging his theory of immanent universals (as found in the *Categories*), it may be that Plato is here responding to the challenge of immanent universals, and doing so in a manner familiar from medieval and modern debates; i.e., it is incoherent to say of anything that the whole of it is in one place and simultaneously in another. Similarly Socrates asserts in the late

Philebus that if a form is "one and the same," then its being in many things at the same time and being thus "dispersed, multiplied, and entirely separated from itself," would seem "most impossible of all" (15b). This is not to say that separate forms occupy a location other than that of their instances; rather, forms are not in any place at all (*Timaeus*, 52a–b).

Separateness, independence and the Good

Separateness and independence do not strictly entail one another, and in fact Plato argues for both via a single, normative, argument. *Republic* VII describes Goodness (the Good itself, the form of the Good) as the "source of the being and essence of all the other Forms" (in Cooper and Hutchinson 1997: 509b). Interpreted along lines strongly suggested by the *Timaeus* and *Republic*, this oracular utterance makes sense and yields an argument for independence of forms from their worldly participants:

(1) Goodness is real and exists independently of this world.
(2) Goodness determines the kinds of things and relationships necessary for a good cosmos, city, soul, et al.
(3) Goodness and the kinds it determines are forms.
(4) Therefore there are forms independent of worldly things.

The natural kinds directly specified in the description of the best cosmos or soul (e.g., types of citizens, parts of the soul, and their proper relationships) are not created by politicians or philosophers, but discovered through critical investigation. These basic kinds of things and their proper interrelations are eternally determined and real, even if no good worlds, cities or souls ever come into being. (Of course these forms entail many others that are not directly specified in the structure of, say, a good city; for details see Patterson [1985].)

This normative vision greatly influenced Christian and Jewish thinkers who made forms into archetypes in the mind of God so that, unlike Plato's Demiurge in the *Timaeus*, the creator contained within himself the foundations and standards of all created goodness. But whether forms are outside of and apprehended by God, or exist in the mind of God, they are independent of the created world. As Socrates reflects in *Republic* IX, the good city there created in logos perhaps exists nowhere on earth, but "only in heaven." Thus the *Timaeus*' Demiurge creates the well-ordered cosmos looking to eternal forms as a guide, as the philosopher describes the best city guided by apprehension of Justice.

Although the Good entails a diverse population of forms, it still supports only a limited domain of forms, for not every plurality or general term corresponds to a kind entailed directly or indirectly by the Good. Plato's late "method of division" confirms this selectivity, since it "carves reality at the natural joints," rather than hacking off arbitrary parts like a clumsy butcher (*Phaedrus*, 265d–e). It discovers genuine *gene* or natural kinds (forms) rather than mere parts (*mere*, *Statesman*, 262a–263b); and some groups of particulars do not even deserve a name of their own (e.g., *hagglers about contracts*, *Sophist*, 225b–c). Natural kinds, sub-kinds and differentia correspond to forms, but merely arbitrary ones do not.

Does the normative argument show the One–many and One–one arguments to be superfluous or even seriously misleading, in that the latter do not yield a select population of forms, or separate and independent forms, or any particular connection to value? Not entirely, for Socrates often finds the One–many principle useful for prodding discussants into thinking about what is common to many objects, and about definitions rather than examples; and either principle can serve as a customary first step in discussion, where the genuine formhood of an assumed One is not (yet) in question. This would be a reasonable interpretation of the *Republic* passage (596a) quoted earlier as evidence for the One–many argument.

Notice, however, that Platonists could consistently accept both the One–many and normative arguments, with the former establishing (immanent) universals for every plurality and the latter establishing selective, value-based, separate and independent forms – with some groupings of things corresponding to both a universal and a form. Universals could explain similarity in general, while forms would be essential for explaining the rationality and goodness of the world. But Plato seems uninterested in this possibility. At least, he has Timaeus pose the dilemma that either there are forms of Fire, etc., or these sensibles are "just what we see" (*Timaeus*, 51b). And again, the *Parmenides* and *Philebus* formulate what would be a powerful objection to immanent universals.

On Plato's view it holds nonetheless that all things must participate in forms to be whatever they are, and thus that all similarities among things are due ultimately to their participation in forms. This is so because his selective realm of forms provides the sorts of materials necessary for constructing any and all sorts of thing, good, bad or indifferent. These "materials" include microscopic constituents of all sorts of corporeal things whether natural or arbitrary, an array of qualitative opposites and their intermediates, numbers, shapes, relations of greater, less and equal, civic and psychic types and their hybrids, et al. So every property of things, and every point of similarity, is accounted for ultimately in terms of basic form-properties, even though arbitrary categories do not as such correspond to forms.

Forms as objects of thought

"Parmenides" concludes his critique of forms, not by rejecting them outright, but by affirming that *eide* are needed as something on which to "fix one's thought." This and similar passages (e.g., *Phaedrus*, 249b–c) suggest one of several closely related but distinguishable epistemological arguments for forms:

(1) General human logos (thought or language involving general concepts or terms) is in some way about or signifies forms.
(2) If thought and language are about or signify forms, then forms are real.

The argument identifies a recognized capacity of humans, but accounts for it in a way most philosophers would reject. Moderate Platonists would respond (as to the One–many argument) that all it shows is the need for immanent universals; conceptualists, that universal concepts existing only in minds will suffice to explain general human logos; nominalists, that all we need is general terms referring indifferently to members of some plurality. Even Plato should object, since this argument, like the One–many argument, generates Ones over merely arbitrary kinds, and provides no grounds for separateness or independence. But as before, Plato can do without immanent universals so long as his (select) forms provide conceptual materials – quantitative, qualitative, relational, etc. – adequate for the formation of concepts and classifications in general. Thus the *Timaeus* provides for human perception and thought in general by constructing the moving circles of the soul from being, sameness and difference of "both sorts" (corporeal and intelligible), and inscribing in these circles arithmetic, geometric and harmonic proportions. The detailed operation of this cognitive apparatus is left obscure, but the Demiurge evidently means to equip the soul for all-purpose cognition of similarities and differences on the basis of a small number of built-in fundamental discriminative capacities, and to provide for apprehension of good and bad states of things in particular via cognition of harmony, proper measure or proportion, or fitting "means." So the argument for forms as intelligible unities presupposed by the human capacity for general thought is consistent with Plato's fundamentally normative vision of reality and thought.

(Innate) cognition of forms and sense perception

One of Socrates' arguments in the *Phaedo* for immortality maintains that there are forms if and only if we have prenatal knowledge, and also that we have such knowledge. We must have such knowledge because (i) when, for example, we make perceptual judgments about sensible sticks and stones being equal we are aware that they also appear to be or actually are unequal – to another person, in another respect, in relation to a different object, or at a different time; (ii) we are aware of this deficiency because sensible equals put us in mind of the Equal itself, which never seems or is unequal. And since (iii) we make perceptual judgments from the moment of birth, we must be born with latent knowledge of relevant forms, and "recollect" this knowledge upon perceiving sensibles. This, along with other "recollection" passages (e.g., in the *Meno*), is recognizably the godfather of the Western "innate ideas" tradition.

Although Socrates indicates how the deficiency of sensible equals could amount to their being equal in some way and unequal in others (see Owen 1965 [1953]) his talk of sensibles "trying to be like" the Equal but "falling short" (74d–e) may suggest that sensibles are never exactly, but only approximately, equal (see Vlastos 1965 [1954]). The former sort of deficiency motivates a limited range of forms corresponding to "incomplete predicates" – i.e., those implying some relevant completion or qualification (e.g., "equal *to* ___," "beautiful *in respect of*___," or "father *of* __"). By contrast the "approximation" reading would apply to all forms, including those for living things and artifacts as well as for equality and beauty. Thus putting aside the *Phaedo's* connection to immortality we have either a narrow or broad epistemological argument for forms, depending on the deficiency one alleges of sensibles:

(1) Our comprehension of general predicates presupposes experience of complete exemplars of those predicates.
(2) In the sensible world there are no complete exemplars of incomplete predicates (e.g., equals that are not equal to something, or in some respect).
(3) Therefore we must experience *non*-sensible complete exemplars of the incomplete predicates we comprehend.

This narrower argument concludes that these complete, non-sensible exemplars are forms. The broader argument would be structurally similar, maintaining that to grasp a general concept we need experience of perfect instances of that concept; sensibles are never perfect exemplars of their type; therefore we must experience *non*-sensible perfect instances of concepts.

Both arguments make Plato's theory glaringly incoherent, the former by postulating non-sensible things that are equal without being equal to anything, the latter by postulating purely intelligible perfect instances of types whose instances cannot possibly be invisible and purely intelligible (e.g., Horse, Shuttle). But defenders of these readings will say that these are Plato's problems.

A more plausible reading is again that forms are not in general instances of themselves, but are rather the intelligible natures or properties instantiated by sensibles – and by themselves in certain cases. The form's superiority to its deficient worldly participants consists in its being, in its own essential nature, intelligibly, eternally, purely what it is (e.g., Equality itself, Beauty itself). But on all three readings the core of the argument is that we exercise some comprehension of relevant natures or properties whenever we make perceptual judgments; that these natures or properties cannot be anything we perceive by the senses, since sensible instances necessarily "fall short" of such natures in their manner of being *F*; that perceptual judgments of the form "*x* is *F*" therefore presuppose cognition of relevant non-sensible, intelligible entities – i.e., forms.

Knowledge, opinion and "Being and not being"

Republic V, 476–80, argues that there is a difference between knowledge (expertise, understanding; *techne, episteme*) and opinion (*doxa*), such that knowledge necessarily concerns "what always is" while opinion concerns "what is and is not." The argument is complicated by Socrates' efforts to engage rather than simply to refute certain "lovers of beautiful spectacles" who would reject outright the very idea of a single nature of Beauty itself:

(1) Knowledge and opinion are different capacities (*dunameis*), since knowledge is unerring, but opinion is not.
(2) Capacities are individuated by what they relate to and what they accomplish.
(3) Therefore knowledge and opinion are related to different things.

(4) Knowledge relates to what simply is, opinion to what both is and is not.

(5) Beauty (*kalon*) itself always is what it is (*kalon*), whereas the sensible beauties admired by the "sight-lovers" are and are not (beautiful, *kalon*), depending on the context.

(6) Therefore knowledge pertains to Beauty itself, and opinion to sensible beauties.

The passage raises many thorny problems of interpretation. Is the inference to (3) fallacious, in that it should say only that knowledge and opinion relate to different objects *or* accomplish different things? Is "is" objectionably used in different ways, for "exists," or predicatively for "is___," or veridically for "is the case that___"? Does the argument assume that the objects of opinion and knowledge are strictly and mutually exclusive, or only that knowledge must always somehow involve forms but opinion need not? Does it assume that every particular beauty is also not-beautiful, or only that every sort of sensible property that is beautiful in one instance will have other instances that are not beautiful? Let it suffice here simply to sketch a plausible reading that links forms to the manner in which Socrates distinguishes knowledge from opinion, then look for further help to a similar argument in the *Timaeus*.

Socrates has in mind knowledge consisting in or based on answers to definitional questions of the form, "What is ___?" The *Republic* focuses on defining justice, then on the derivative question, "Is justice good for its possessor?" One cannot know, for example, that paying one's debts is essentially or by definition just, if paying one's debts is in some situations just and in others not (e.g., giving back a borrowed dagger to a homicidal neighbor). The same holds for instances of beauty (e.g., a shade of purple that is beautiful in the king's robe but not in his iris). Accordingly any "ABC is *F*" proposition one *knows* must simply and without qualification be true, not true or false depending on the situation or on which particular instance of ABC one chooses. This allows, but does not require, that every instance of ABC be both *F* and not-*F* (see Fine 1978; Irwin 1999). But in fact the beautiful sights and sounds pursued by the lovers of appearances, whether particular or general (e.g., an actor's *particular* gesture or given *sort* of gesture), would in some possible contexts be beautiful and in others not, and so in that specific sense "are and are not" beautiful. Thus sensibles can be opined, but not known, to be beautiful. Knowledge evidently implies a *non*-sensible object that is *kalon*, and never in any context not *kalon*, and what Socrates calls Beauty itself would qualify. (In fact, to show that Beauty is *kalon* the argument would need to show, given there is knowledge that some ABC is *kalon*, either that no other non-sensibles qualify, or that if anything else is *kalon*, Beauty itself is *kalon*. Socrates implies the latter, even regarding aspects we are perceiving, at *Phaedo*, 100c.)

Aside from its application to the anti-Platonistic lovers of appearances, Socrates' reasoning is of interest because it sometimes is tempting (even for Platonists) to suppose that certain sensible qualities of, say, a painting or a musical performance are in themselves beautiful and account for the beauty of the painting or performance we perceive. According to Socrates this is always a mistake. Also, the argument generalizes to some important cases of moral qualities – for example, when relevant observable qualities of a person's behavior (such as its "slowness") are thought to make it moderate or temperate, as discussed in the *Charmides*.

Knowledge vs. true opinion

Still, *Republic*, 476–80, does not say much about the nature of knowledge. Furthermore if knowledge differs from opinion simply in never being mistaken, how does it differ from *true* opinion, which is by definition not mistaken? The *Timaeus* addresses such points, arguing for forms on the basis of a detailed distinction between knowledge and true opinion: (a) understanding comes through teaching, true belief through persuasion; (b) understanding involves a true account, whereas true belief lacks an account; (c) understanding is unmoved by persuasion, but true belief gives in to persuasion; (d) all humans have a share of true belief, but only the gods and a few humans have understanding. Therefore that is real which (i) keeps its own form unchangingly, (ii) has not come into being and is not destroyed, (iii) does not receive into itself anything else from anywhere else or enter into anything else anywhere. Further, (iv) it cannot be perceived by the senses at all, and (v) is the proper object of understanding (51d–52a).

Since knowledge differs from true belief in the respects here marked (a)–(d), knowledge requires the sort of object described by (i)–(v). Timaeus is almost entirely concerned to establish the knowledge/true opinion distinction (a)–(d), and evidently takes it for granted that knowledge entails objects as described in (i)–(v). Many readers will find (a), (c) and (d) question-begging; but these points may derive from the more promising mention of an "account" (*logos*) in (b). *Logos* would cover definitions, descriptions, arguments and explanatory accounts of why things are as they are. Thus on the important "method of hypothesis" promoted in the *Republic*, *Meno* and *Phaedo* one justifies and/or explains certain propositions on the basis of further "hypotheses"; or, one obtains knowledge rather than true opinion by "figuring out the cause or reason why" (*aitias logismos*, *Meno*, 97d–98b). The *Republic* speaks of the philosopher tracing matters all the way up to an "unhypothetical starting point" (511), probably the Good itself, on which all being and knowledge depend. So (b) may reflect a foundationalist picture of knowledge, with insight into Goodness (not "mystical" or ineffable, but expressed in *logos* and defended against refutation, 534b–c) as the foundation of understanding, and more local principles involved in distinct branches of knowledge. Having such an explanation is quite different from merely opining correctly that some proposition is true. Moreover (a), (c) and (d) have some force after all, for conveying a foundationalist explanation/justification is not merely a matter of persuading someone to believe something; explanations firmly rooted in first principles withstand dissuasion; and only a few humans – along with the gods – ever achieve such understanding.

Absolutely stable knowledge and objects manifest to reason

Earlier in his creation story Timaeus had emphasized that

> the accounts we give of things have the same character as the subjects they set forth. Accounts of what is stable and fixed [*tou monimou kai bebaiou*; see (i), (ii), above] and manifest to reason [*meta nou kataphanous*] are themselves stable

and unshifting [*monimous kai ametaptotous*] … [but] accounts we give of [the world of change], which has been formed to be like that reality, are themselves likely [*eikotas*]. (29b; Zeyl trans., adapted)

The notion of completely stable and fixed objects of knowledge suggests an interesting further argument: knowledge is of objects that are in principle fully manifest to reason, and this holds of forms but not sensibles. We can never know sensibles because (a) we can perceive them only perspectivally and therefore partially, since there are infinitely many perspectives from which they may be perceived (*Republic*, 598a), and (b) sensibles are always in principle subject to change and destruction. Utterly stable accounts require at a minimum objects (a) whose natures we can apprehend in all their essential aspects and (b) whose essential aspects we can know to be utterly immutable. Forms meet both conditions, sensibles neither. So if there is utterly stable knowledge, there are forms.

Knowledge and the Good: separate, independent forms

From at least the *Gorgias* on, expertise, knowledge or understanding (*techne, episteme*) is not just a knack or a matter of experience, but is essentially normative and explanatory (*Gorgias*, 464b–465a). All *technai* – e.g., arithmetic, medicine, legislation – (a) aim at some genuine good and (b) can give a principled explanation of how this is achieved. In general, it appears that *technai/epistemai* just are the ways in which rational (roughly, principled and beneficial) activity enters our world. True, humans can misapply *technai* (building too many houses, making hay in the rain), and can practice pseudo-*technai* that pleasurably flatter rather than genuinely benefit the palate or eye (confectionery, cosmetics). But every genuine *techne* is by definition a rational means of realizing some genuine rather than merely apparent good.

A *techne* itself corresponds to a form (Medicine, Statecraft, Mathematics, Grammar); indeed the extensive "divisions" into natural kinds found in the late dialogues are largely concerned with distinguishing various sorts of *technai*. In addition, each type of expertise or branch of learning corresponds to a group of interrelated forms constituting its domain, such as the different types and subtypes of letter, or the functional parts of a good city. This implies a normative epistemological argument for forms:

(1) There are *technai/epistemai*.
(2) Each *techne/episteme* itself corresponds to an intelligible type and involves mastery of a domain of intelligible types.
(3) Therefore there are intelligible types – i.e., forms.

If *technai* are essentially normative in aiming at some genuine good, then the forms they imply exist separately from and independently of worldly agents and their activities. The types of goods at which *technai* aim are the eternally determined objective goods, for example, of human beings – food, shelter, education, defense, etc. – where humans are themselves one kind of living creature essential to the best sort of cosmos.

These types of goods, and the naturally best means to their attainment (*technai*), do not depend upon the opinions or activities of humans or gods: they are eternally "fixed in the nature of things," as Socrates says of forms at *Parmenides*, 132d.

It is more speculative, but likely, that every knowable object (form) is essentially part of the domain of one or more type of knowledge/expertise. So if all *technai/epistemai* are normative in the sense that they and their intelligible domains are the sorts of thing entailed directly or indirectly by the necessary conditions for some genuine good, then the argument from *techne/episteme* is the epistemological twin of the normative argument discussed earlier ("Separateness, independence and the Good," above), and converges on the same selective, value-based, separate and independent realm of intelligible forms.

In sum, all of Plato's many arguments and motivations for postulating forms are of great interest, and have stimulated variants and adaptations for 2,500 years (and counting). Plato's view appears to be, however, that the ultimate grounds for believing in eternal, immutable, intelligible entities that are what they are separately and independently of spatial and temporal things, and that are the source of all that exists and all that is of value in the universe, are normative.

References

Cooper, John and Hutchinson, D. S. (1997) Plato, *Complete Works*, Indianapolis, IN: Hackett.

Fine, Gail (1978) "Knowledge and Belief in *Republic* V," *Archiv für Geschichte der Philosophie* 60: 121–39; reprinted in *Plato 1: Metaphysics and Epistemology*, Oxford: Oxford University Press, 1999.

Frede, Michael (1967) *Prädikation und Existenzaussage*, Göttingen: Vandenhoeck & Ruprecht.

Irwin, Terrence (1999) "The Theory of Forms," in Gail Fine (ed.) *Plato 1: Metaphysics and Epistemology*, Oxford: Oxford University Press, pp. 145–72.

Owen, G. E. L. (1965 [1953]) "The Place of the *Timaeus* in Plato's Dialogues," in R. E. Allen, *Studies in Plato's Metaphysics*, London: Routledge & Kegan Paul, 313–38; originally published in *Classical Quarterly*, n.s., 3: 79–95.

Patterson, Richard (1985) *Image and Reality in Plato's Metaphysics*, Indianapolis, IN: Hackett.

Vlastos, Gregory (1965 [1954]) "The Third Man Argument in the *Parmenides*," in R. E. Allen, *Studies in Plato's Metaphysics*, London: Routledge & Kegan Paul, 231–64; originally published in *Philosophical Review* 63: 319–49.

Further reading

For further reading, see Plato, *Complete Works*, edited by John Cooper, associate editor D. S. Hutchinson (Indianapolis, IN: Hackett, 1997); Harold Cherniss, *Aristotle's Criticism of Plato and the Academy* (Baltimore, MD: Johns Hopkins University Press, 1944) (a detailed discussion of Plato's metaphysics organized around Aristotle's criticisms; not for the casual or "Greekless" reader, but amply repays careful study); and G. M. A. Grube, *Plato's Thought* (London: Athlone Press, 1980 [1938]) (an accessible, compact, thematically organized presentation with a minimum of ax-grinding). Several collections contain important discussions of Plato's thought concerning forms: R. E. Allen, *Studies in Plato's Metaphysics* (London: Routledge & Kegan Paul, 1965); Gail Fine, *Plato 1: Metaphysics and Epistemology* (Oxford: Oxford University Press, 1999); Richard Kraut, *The Cambridge Companion to Plato* (Cambridge: Cambridge University Press, 1992); Nicholas D. Smith, *Plato: Critical Assessments* (London: Routledge & Kegan Paul, 1998); and Gregory Vlastos, *Plato I: Metaphysics and Epistemology – A Collection of Critical Essays* (New York: Doubleday Anchor, 1971).

3

ARISTOTLE
Form, matter and substance

Stephen Makin

Basic things: the notion of substance

Some philosophers are interested in the extremely general issue of just what there is in the world. But their curiosity would not be much satisfied by a bare list of things-which-exist, however exhaustive it was. First, metaphysically inclined philosophers are interested in the *types* of thing the world contains. And second, it seems that some among the world's items are more basic than others, and that what would be really interesting would be to find out which types of thing – if any – are the *most basic*. Aristotle uses the term *substance* for the most basic type of item. Of course, being given that term tells us nothing about what there is in the world. But it provides a crisp way in which to pose the two questions which face us when we think about what there is in the world. First, just what is meant when we say that substances are basic, or fundamental, or primary? And second, which types of things are the substances?

A good place to gain entry to Aristotle's account of substance is his short work *Categories*, especially chapters 1–5. The *Categories* identifies individual persisting things as substances, and Aristotle says this about them:

> It seems most distinctive of substance that what is numerically one and the same is able to receive contraries. In no other case could one bring forward anything, numerically one, which is able to receive contraries. For example, a colour which is numerically one and the same will not be black and white, nor will numerically one and the same action be bad and good; and similarly with everything else that is not a substance. A substance, however, numerically one and the same, is able to receive contraries. For example, an individual man – one and the same – becomes pale at one time and dark at another, and hot and cold, and bad and good. (*Categories*, in Barnes 1984: Ch. 5, 4a10–21)

The driving thought is that substances are those things which persist through change. Other things depend in one way or another on substances. Some are temporary properties of substances, for example something's colour. Some are kinds into which these temporary properties are grouped (scarlet and crimson are both types of red). Yet others are kinds into which substances are grouped (being human). But none of these could exist without the individual persisting things which Aristotle identifies as substances – the individual man, the individual horse, and the individual ox are the examples he gives. Without these individual substances there would be no temporary properties because there would be nothing for them to be properties *of*; and there would be no kinds, neither of the absent individual substances nor of the temporary properties which at different times attach to the substances. (Aristotle offers an argument for this conclusion at *Categories* [in Barnes 1984: Ch. 5, 2a35–2b6]: "if the primary substances did not exist it would be impossible for any of the other things to exist.")

The view Aristotle expresses here – that what is "most distinctive" of substances is the fact that a single substance can have opposed properties at different times – helps fill out the way in which substances are basic.

First of all, it suggests that a substance is more robust than the properties it can lose or acquire. Suppose Sandie grows over the next year. Sandie will still be around that year (in that year it will be *Sandie* who is six foot tall), but Sandie's previous height will have gone (the height five feet and six inches can't itself increase to six feet).

Second, the view that substances are singular things which can persist from one time to another ties in with the appealing intuition that individuals have a more secure ontological status than general kinds. It is the individual man walking his individual dog with which I come into contact most immediately, and the status of those individuals looks more secure than that of the kinds – human and canine – under which they fall.

Third, we are introduced to the idea that substances are basic insofar as they *underlie* the other things, and that the other things depend on them because they are (in various ways) features *of* them. The fact that what is most distinctive of substances is that they can underlie one property today, and an incompatible property tomorrow reinforces the idea that substances are basic in that they are persisting subjects for properties.

Fourth, Aristotle's examples of substances are noteworthy: things which are not merely persisting but natural, and not merely natural but living (an individual man, horse or ox rather than an individual mountain or an individual house). Aristotle's preference for living things should be unsurprising, for they are indeed prime examples of individuals which persist through change. What is characteristic of living things is precisely that they keep themselves going through changes; in fact the life of a living thing is a series of changes – of size, shape, position, etc. – through and by which it develops. We probably have a more thorough understanding of how it is that a living thing changes and develops than we do about the alterations to which a mountain or a house can be subject.

Finally the idea that what is distinctive of substances is their persistence through change points to another Aristotelian contrast. When we characterise an individual as a substance of a certain kind (the individual Sandie as *human*) we are saying what Sandie *is* (a human being); whereas when we characterise an individual as having a quality (she is pale) we are saying what Sandie *is like*. If it is to be possible that Sandie first have one property (she's pale) and then an incompatible property (she's tanned), then what she *is* must remain stable (after all it is one and the same Sandie) while what she is *like* can change (pale yesterday, tanned today).

The main point to take from the *Categories* is that the basic things – the substances – are individual living things. And while much else about the *Categories* is controversial, this view of substance is sufficient for now (for further reading on the *Categories* see Ackrill 1963; and "Categories in Aristotle," in Frede 1987: 29–48).

Nature

We can come to the *Categories* view of substance from another direction. At the start of *Physics*, Book 2, Aristotle reflects on this general feature of the world around us: that there is a difference between what is natural and what is artificial. By thinking through what precisely the difference is between the natural and the artificial, Aristotle comes to an account of what it is for something to have a nature of its own. His statement is nuanced and difficult, but the general idea is appealing. We live in a world in which a great deal happens, and we are bound to wonder where all these happenings come from. Which things in the world are producing all the activity we observe around us? To say that something has a nature of its own is to characterise *it* as one of the origins of change in the world, is to identify it as one of the things from which the changes in the world emerge, one of the things it would be sensible to appeal to in explaining why things change and remain the same in the various ways they do. The things which have natures are those which "drive" the world, things which activate change rather than merely responding to the activities of other things.

Further, it is tempting to suppose that the types of things which "drive" the various happenings in the world are in some sense the "basic" things in the world. They are those things the activities of which we would want to discover in order to understand what goes on in the world. Aristotle recognises and emphasises the connection between these different issues: which things are the natural things, which sorts of things have natures, what their natures are on the one hand, and which things are substances on the other. Towards the middle of chapter one of *Physics*, Book 2, he says,

> Nature, then, is what has been stated. [i.e. a principle or cause of being moved and of being at rest in that to which it belongs primarily, in virtue of itself and not accidentally.] Things have a nature which have a principle of this kind. Each of them is a substance; for it is a subject, and nature is always in a subject. (*Physics*, in Barnes 1984: Bk 2, ch. 1, 192b33–4, with back reference to 192b21–3)

And the same connection is apparent in this remark from *Metaphysics*, Book 8:

> Perhaps neither of these things themselves [house or utensil], nor any of the other things which are not formed by nature, are substances at all; for one might say that the nature in natural objects is the only substance to be found in destructible things. (*Metaphysics*, in Barnes 1984: Bk 8, ch. 3, 1043b21–3)

So, understanding what it is for something to be a substance, and identifying the sorts of things which are substances, is part and parcel of doing science, of investigating and understanding the workings of the world around us. And once we start to think of substances in the context of the natural world and its workings, further reflection on the view of substance stated in the *Categories* is inevitable. Identifying substances as individual living things retains much of its appeal. Living things look to be star examples of agents, origins of change rather than simply reagents to the doings of other things. But the view is also likely to require refinement and development. (For further reading on Aristotle's account of nature see Lear [1988: Ch. 2] and Waterlow [1982: Chs 1–2].)

Form and matter

We have seen that what is most distinctive of substances is that they can have incompatible properties at different times, and thereby persist through change. But the idea of a persisting thing changing is really very puzzling, since it involves two aspects which appear *prima facie* to be in tension. Suppose Sandie changes from Monday to Tuesday. Then, on the one hand, she is different on the two days: she has *changed*, and so she is not on Tuesday as she was on Monday. But, on the other hand, she is the same on the two days: it is *Sandie* who has changed, *Sandie* who is not on Tuesday as *she* was on Monday. Indeed so puzzling is the notion of change that various of the Presocratic philosophers had abandoned one or the other of the seemingly conflicting requirements it embodies, some denying that there is any difference from one time to another, others denying that there is any sameness from one time to another.

Now it might seem easy to resolve this tension. It is obvious, is it not, that when something changes between Monday and Tuesday, it is *in one respect* different on the two days, while *in another respect* the same. However a bare statement like that is little more than a slogan, indicating roughly how to proceed with the problem. Aristotle's rich distinction between *form* and *matter* is intended to expand on the slogan and take us further (see Aristotle's treatment at *Physics*, in Barnes 1984: Bk 1, Chs 7–9).

"Matter" translates a Greek term, *hulê*, which is an everyday word meaning "wood"; and among the various terms which "form" translates is an everyday word, *morphê*, meaning "shape." These ordinary usages give us the basic idea. We can think of a table as some stuff (wood) arranged in a certain shape (flat surface with supporting legs). We can similarly think of a cardigan as wool knitted and stitched into the shape of a human torso, of a lake as water contained and arranged in a fairly extensive inland area, and so on. And we can go beyond these fairly simple examples, thinking of a word as some letters (matter) put in a certain order (form), of an archway as some stone (matter) in a certain shape and position (form), of a plant as some variety of chemicals (matter) in a certain dynamic structure (form). Further, the form/matter distinction can be applied and reapplied at different levels of composition. A house is bricks (matter) linked together in a certain structure (form). But equally a brick is, for example, clay (matter) in a rectangular shape (form). And a village will be houses (matter) related geographically in a particular way (form).

While some of the cases are (much) more difficult than others, the general scheme running through them should be clear enough. The matter of something is what composes it. The form is that in virtue of which the composing matter actually does compose it. This might be something as simple as shape in the case of a table, or something as complex as a set of abilities in the case of a horse (for what makes something a horse is the ability to live an equine life, to gallop, canter and trot, to eat certain foods, to hear sounds within a certain range, etc. – a pickled and preserved equine corpse, regardless of its shape, *isn't* a horse, but at best a laboratory specimen or a work of art).

Aristotle develops a variety of views around his form–matter distinction, and those views are often referred to by scholars as hylomorphism (recall that "matter" translates the Greek *hulê*, and "form" the Greek *morphê*). Hylomorphism provides Aristotle with the resources to give a more carefully worked out account of change. Speaking quite generally, when something changes we can think of the matter (the material aspect) as what remains the same over the change, and the form (the formal aspect) as what is gained or lost as a result of the change. Now this hylomorphic analysis can be applied to the individual living things which Aristotle identifies as substances in the *Categories*. There are two types of application to consider. The first is fairly straightforward, while the second leads to further reflection on the substantial status of individual living things.

First, consider the type of case which was to the fore in the *Categories* in which an individual living thing persists through a change. First of all Sandie is one height, then she is another: we can think of Sandie as what persists and underlies the change, as the subject first for one height and then for another. (Aristotle's prime example in *Physics*, Bk 1, ch. 7, of someone learning music, is a little more nuanced. The starting point is a privation [ignorance of music] understood as a subject's lack of the form [knowledge of music], the acquisition of which form constitutes the change in the persisting subject.)

Second, the hylomorphic analysis can be applied to the individual living thing itself, that thing which was taken as persisting through the change in height. Aristotle said nothing in the *Categories* about the structure of an individual living thing such as Sandie. But it should seem clear that the individual living thing is itself a form–matter complex. For the crucial fact is that Aristotle's favoured substances come into and go out of existence. In fact, as living things, they come into and go out of existence in regular and predictable ways. They have natural and fairly determinate life spans.

Now the idea that substances could be temporally limited things is striking. Many would feel tempted to think that the basic things in the world are eternally persisting things, and that their being basic is grounded in their indestructibility. According to Aristotle a number of his predecessors thought along these lines, looking for some permanent underlying stuff for the universe, and viewing other things as rearrangements of that stuff (for example, Democritus' idea that everything is atoms and void). We also find the same downgrading of the temporally limited in Plato's very different outlook, according to which the true beings are immaterial, eternal and unchanging forms, while other transient things are mere reflections or imperfect instantiations of the eternal forms. However, anyone who takes substances to be eternal pays a high price for doing so, for while Democritean atoms or Platonic forms would be eternal, they are not directly empirically accessible to us, and so the world views of Democritus or Plato are far more distant from commonsense than that of Aristotle. So the task for

Aristotle is to see how far he can hold to the view that empirically accessible individual living things are substances.

Existential and non-existential change

The fact that individual living things are subject to existential change (they come into and go out of existence) – as well as non-existential change (they increase in height and weight) – requires us to think of an individual living thing itself as a form–matter complex. But is this as straightforward a requirement as it seems?

Of the two types of change – existential and non-existential – the former is if anything more puzzling than the latter. If something new comes into existence at noon, then it might seem that at noon we have *something* where before noon there was *nothing*. If it were not so, how else could we get at the idea that there is something new (existential change) rather than something which was there all along undergoing non-existential change? But in that case existential change looks particularly paradoxical, for it would appear to involve something new coming from nothing.

Aristotle accepts that existential change cannot involve something coming out of nothing, and he acknowledges that in the case of existential change too we require some precursor from which the new substance arises.

> But that substances too, and anything that can be said to be without qualification, come to be from some underlying thing, will appear on examination. For we find in every case something that underlies from which proceeds that which comes to be; for instance animals and plants from seed. (*Physics*, in Barnes 1984: Bk 1, ch. 7, 190b1–4)

Now a seed cannot be merely a precursor. There will have to be some degree of material continuity between the seed and the living thing which develops from it. For if there were no material continuity between seed and organism there would be no reason to think of what occurs as a seed giving rise to an organism rather than a seed vanishing and an organism appearing in the same place out of nowhere. But in that case a problem looms. For if there is some material continuity involved in both existential and non-existential change, then the temptation resurfaces to think of putative coming-into-existence as, in fact, *non*-existential change in some underlying material. So if Aristotle is to stand any chance of preserving his preference for individual living things as substances, he has to resist this slide back towards the idea that true basic substances are eternal, ungenerated and indestructible.

Aristotle considers the difference between existential and non-existential change in some detail at *De Generatione et Corruptione*, Book 1, chapters 3–4 (in Barnes 1984). Consider those transitions (to put it neutrally) in which there is something from which the transition starts, which is lost and replaced by something with which the transition ends, and where there is also something which persists through the transition. Aristotle offers a principled way of distinguishing among these transitions between those which count as non-existential change and those which count as existential change. The crux is the relation between the new item at the terminus of the transition and the persisting item. If the new terminal item is a feature of what persists then we have a non-existential change in what persists. For example, take a transition in which green is replaced by red, while an apple persists. Since what is new at the end of the transition (red) is a feature of what persists through the transition (the apple) – i.e. since it is the apple which is red – we have a non-existential change in the apple. By contrast, if the new terminal item is not a feature of the persisting item, we have an existential change. Aristotle's example is some elemental air (hot–wet stuff, according to him) being destroyed by cooling, and some elemental water (cold–wet stuff) coming into existence in its place. There is something at the start of the transition (hotness) which is lost, and which is replaced at the end of the transition by something new (coldness); and there is also something which persists (wetness). In this case, however, the coldness, which is new, is *not* a feature of the wetness, which persists. Rather, both are features of something else – water. That is to say, it is not the persisting wetness which is cold, but the resultant water which is both wet and cold. And so this counts as an existential change: some air ceases to exist, and some water comes into existence.

How does any of this help with the idea of substances which are subject to existential change? It fills out the way in which we view an individual living thing as a hylomorphic complex. Living things come into existence out of precursors (seeds); and there is some material continuity between the seed and the organism. But the stuff of the seed does not persist as a subject of which the properties of the new organism are features. It is, rather, transformed in various ways – for example, in the course of embryonic development – into new stuff appropriate to compose the body and organs required for the life of the organism in question. The form of a horse – what it is in virtue of which some stuff composes a horse – is a set of abilities (for example, to eat, move, and perceive in various ways). The fairly simple and unstructured types of stuff found in seeds are not sufficient for those abilities. The equine form requires bone, muscle, hair, nerve tissue etc., which in turn make up the type of skeleton and musculature which enables galloping, the type of teeth and stomach which enable the eating and digestion of vegetable matter, and so on. There is no bone or muscle or hair in the precursors from which a horse develops. The flesh and bone which are the matter of a horse – unlike the bricks which are the matter of a house – are not pre-existent components from which the horse is made; and while a horse comes into existence from a seed, neither that seed nor its stuff persist as subjects for the horse's features.

Substance and substantial form

Now once we see that an individual living thing is itself a hylomorphic complex, the question of what should most properly be identified as substance re-arises. Aristotle considers a number of the issues surrounding this question in Books 7–9 of his *Metaphysics* (these "central books" of the *Metaphysics* are standardly referred to by Greek letters: Books Z, H and Θ). These books stand out in the Aristotelian corpus as particularly complex and obscure. Still, while practically everything about the interpretation of these books is controversial, it does seem – particularly in *Metaphysics*, Book 7 – that

Aristotle comes to prefer another candidate for the title of substance: not the hylomorphic complex which is a individual living thing (for example, the individual dog) but the substantial form (that in virtue of which something is a dog). It is not necessary for us to decide here quite what to make of this shift in focus. It may be that Aristotle has changed his mind about which items are substances (not living things, but their substantial forms); or it may be that he has retained his view that individual living things are substances while arguing that they owe this privileged status to their substantial forms. In either case a common question strikes us: why should it be plausible to move from the claim that there is something metaphysically special about living things to the thought that there is something special about their substantial forms? Here are two lines of argument

The first starts from the idea, familiar from the *Categories*, that what is most distinctive of substances is that they can have incompatible properties at different times while remaining one and the same thing. Living things seemed *par excellence* to satisfy that requirement. But we now see that living things themselves involve both change and persistence, that one and the same living thing is born, grows and develops, and eventually dies. Living things start from material precursors. They constantly take stuff from, and return stuff to, their environment in the course of producing new complex types of material in new organic structures. They eventually die, and the complex matter of which they are composed rots down and returns to the environment as the sort of lower level stuffs which can be taken up by other living organisms. What is it that persists through, guides, and controls that constant material change? The appealing answer is: the substantial form, the form which makes that individual living thing the type of thing it is. Consider the human Sandie. The matter of which she is most immediately composed – her flesh, bone, muscle, nerve tissue, etc. – are manufactured from other environmental stuffs through the processes of nutrition and growth which are in part, what her human form consists in (only in part, since there is far more to being human than eating and growing). The way in which that material change proceeds is fixed by the human form. How much material variation Sandie can survive is likewise fixed by the human form: given what is required by the abilities and dispositions which render something human, Sandie can grow and shrink within limits, but not to something over ten miles long or weighing less than an ounce. Changes which are not consistent with the continuation of the human form – for example, being diced into small chunks – are changes which destroy Sandie. In that case it will seem natural to think that the special status Sandie has as a living organism is due to, and should be inherited by, her substantial form.

The second argument starts from the observation that living things are highly organised, and their organisation goes a long way down into their hylomorphic structure. Not only the organism as a whole, but also the organs and the organic tissue, exhibit a great deal of structure. It is in virtue of this complex organisation that living things are such strongly unified items, and it is the fact that they are strongly unified which allows us to view individual living things as deserving of substantial status. For the more that some whole is a mere agglomeration of parts, the more drawn we are to take the parts as more basic than the whole – each individual sheep, for example, as more basic than the flock. So, if we want to understand what it is about living things in virtue of which they can be complex and yet also strong candidates for substantial status, we should consider what it is which accounts for the high degree of unity which they exhibit. Now, as Aristotle argues in *Metaphysics* Book 7, chapter 17, what explains this degree of unity cannot itself be just another component of the unified whole, since then we would need to know what unifies *it* with all the other components. Rather it must be something to which we can appeal in explaining why all this stuff and all these parts taken together make up, for example, a single living human being. And that will be the substantial form – a structure rather than a component, a "principle" rather than an "element," as Aristotle puts it:

> It would seem that this is something, and not an element, and that it is the cause which makes *this* thing flesh and *that* a syllable. And similarly in all other cases. And this is the substance of each thing; for this is the primary cause of its being; and since, while some things are not substances, as many as are substances are formed naturally by nature, their substance would seem to be this nature, which is not an element but a principle. An *element* is that into which a thing is divided and which is present in it as matter, e.g. *a* and *b* are the elements of the syllable. (*Metaphysics*, in Barnes 1984: Bk 7, ch. 17 1041b25–33; substituting "explanation" for "cause" makes Aristotle's point clearer)

So we can see why individual living things should have a strong claim to be substances; why individual living things themselves have to be hylomorphic complexes; how they might be both substantial and yet undergo existential change; and why ascribing a privileged status to individual living things would lead Aristotle to turn his attention to substantial forms.

References

Ackrill, J. L. (1963) *Aristotle's* Categories *and* De Interpretatione, Oxford: Clarendon Press.

Barnes, Jonathan (ed.) (1984) *The Complete Works of Aristotle: The Revised Oxford Translation*, 2 vols, Princeton, NJ: Princeton University Press.

Frede, M. (1987) *Essays in Ancient Philosophy*, Oxford: Clarendon Press.

Lear, J. (1988) *Aristotle: The Desire to Understand*, Cambridge: Cambridge University Press.

Waterlow, S. (1982) *Nature, Change and Agency*, Oxford: Clarendon Press.

Further reading

I have referred to four Aristotelian texts: *Categories*, *Physics*, *Generation and Corruption* and *Metaphysics*. Where I have quoted I have used the translations in *The Complete Works of Aristotle: The Revised Oxford Translation*, 2 vols, edited by Jonathan Barnes (Princeton, NJ: Princeton University Press, 1984). For detailed commentary on the texts and passages on which I have concentrated (along with a translation generally alternative to the Revised Oxford Translation) there are the following volumes in the Clarendon Aristotle Series: J. L. Ackrill, *Aristotle's* Categories *and* De Interpretatione (Oxford: Clarendon Press, 1963); D. Bostock, *Aristotle* Metaphysics Books Z *and* H (Oxford: Clarendon Press, 1994); W. Charlton, *Aristotle's* Physics Books I *and* II, revised edn (Oxford: Clarendon Press, 1992); and C. J. F. Williams, *Aristotle's* De

Generatione et Corruptione (Oxford: Clarendon Press, 1982). J. Barnes (ed.), *The Cambridge Companion to Aristotle* (Cambridge: Cambridge University Press, 1995) contributes a particularly helpful section on Aristotle's metaphysics. M. F. Burnyeat *A Map of* Metaphysics *Zeta* (Pittsburgh, PA: Mathesis, 2001) is a major study of *Metaphysics* 7 (an advanced book). M. Frede, *Essays in Ancient Philosophy* (Clarendon Press, Oxford, 1987) is a collection of Frede's papers, including both "Categories in Aristotle" (1981) and "Substance in Aristotle's Metaphysics" (1985). J. Lear, *Aristotle: The Desire to Understand* (Cambridge: Cambridge University Press, 1988) is a general introduction to Aristotle, with chapter 2 particularly helpful on nature, form and matter. V. Politis, *Aristotle and the Metaphysics* (Abingdon, UK: Routledge, 2004) is a guide book designed to make Aristotle's *Metaphysics* more easily accessible. C. Shields, *Aristotle* (Abingdon, UK: Routledge, 2007) is a recent general introduction to Aristotle's philosophy (chapters 4 and 6 concentrate on the *Categories* and *Metaphysics*). S. Waterlow, *Nature, Change and Agency* (Oxford: Clarendon Press, 1982) (chapters 1 and 2, in particular, concentrate on Aristotle's concept of nature). M. V. Wedin, *Aristotle's Theory of Substance* (Oxford: Oxford University Press, 2000) is an advanced discussion of Aristotle's treatment of substance in the *Categories* and *Metaphysics* Z.

4
ARISTOTLE
Time and change

Ursula Coope

Aristotle's account of time in *Physics*, Book 4, chapters 10–14 (translated in Hussey 1993), is at once fascinating and frustratingly obscure. In it, he discusses time's relation to the present, to change, and to the mind. The view that emerges is one on which temporal order depends on a more basic order: an order of the stages within changes. On this view, for there to be time, there must be changes. Moreover, Aristotle holds that if there is to be time, changes must be marked out, or "counted" in a certain way. Because of this, time also depends on the mind: for there to be time, there must be beings capable of counting. These are intriguing claims, but what exactly do they mean? This essay suggests one way in which we might make sense of them.

Time and the now

Is time something that "is"?

Aristotle starts out with a puzzle about whether there can be such a thing as time. Time seems to be divided into two parts, neither of which exists. The past is something that was, but is no longer; the future is something that will be, but is not yet. How can time be something that exists, if none of its parts exists? (*Physics*, Bk 4, ch. 10, 217b29–218a3).

You might think that there is a third part of time – the present – and that the present is something that exists. But Aristotle argues that the present (or "now" as he calls it) is not really a part of time (218a6). The now (he claims) is a mere boundary between the past and the future; it itself has no duration. If the now is a mere boundary, its existence cannot be what grounds the existence of time. For how can there be a boundary between two things, neither of which exist? No one would think it possible for the coast to exist in a world in which there was neither sea nor land: the coast just is the boundary between the sea and the land. How, then, can the now be all there is to time, if the now is simply a boundary between two parts of time (the past and the future)?

Aristotle himself never explains how to answer this puzzle. After presenting it, he goes on to give his own positive account of time. As we shall see, he says that time is something that depends for its existence on change. Perhaps he thinks that he can establish that there are such things as changes and can use this fact to solve the puzzle about time. However, it is not immediately clear how such a solution would work. At least on the face of it, the puzzles about time's existence would seem to apply also to the existence of change. Any change that is going on will have a part that is past and a part that is future. So we can ask: is the present part of the change anything more than an instantaneous boundary between the past and the future?

A moving now?

Aristotle also raises another puzzle about the now. Is the now always the same or is it always different? The best way to understand his question is to perform the following thought experiment. Consider the present *now* … wait a bit … consider the present *now*. What is the relation between the two times you have identified? On the one hand, they seem to be two different times: one of them is earlier than the other. On the other hand, each of them was present (or now) when you identified it. What is this feature *presentness* that the two times have in common?

Aristotle explains the relation between earlier and later "nows," using an analogy. He compares the now to a moving thing. Imagine a man, Coriscos, moving from the marketplace to the Lyceum. In some respects Coriscos remains the same throughout this movement, but in other respects he is always different: he is first at one place and then at another. Similarly, earlier and later nows are in some respect the same, but in another respect different (*Physics*, Bk 4, ch. 11, 219b9ff.).

What exactly is Aristotle trying to establish when he makes this comparison? Many philosophers have thought that he is endorsing a "moving-now" view of time (see, for instance, Hussey 1993: xliii–xliv). On such a view, one and the same thing, the now, moves through time, being first earlier and then later. So if, on two different occasions, you refer to *the present*, you are each time picking out one and the same thing, the present, but you are picking it out at different stages of its movement. On this view, time itself is the movement of the present (or now), as it progresses further and further into the future.

But there is reason to doubt whether this is really Aristotle's view. For he argues that time itself is not a kind of movement. His argument is that movement is the sort of thing that can be quicker or slower, but time cannot be quicker or slower (*Physics*, Bk 4, ch. 10, 218b13–18). A very similar argument would show that the now does not move. The now is not the sort of thing that can move more or less quickly. This suggests that on Aristotle's own view the now is not the kind of thing that can move.

What, then are we to make of his comparison between the now and a moving thing? One clue is that Aristotle here invokes *what the sophists say* about Coriscos in the Lyceum and Coriscos in the marketplace: the moving thing is different in definition "*in the way in which the sophists assume* that being Coriscos-in-the-Lyceum is different from being Coricos-in-the-marketplace" (my italics; *Physics*, Bk 4, ch. 11, 219b20–21; here, and in what follows, translations are from Hussey [1993]). The sophists were notorious for raising puzzles about how a thing could retain its identity though changing in some respect. For instance, at *Metaphysics* Book 4, chapter 2, 1026b15–18, Aristotle presents a sophistical worry about whether musical-Coriscos and Coriscos are one and the same. Perhaps, then, Aristotle's point is that the now is analogous to a moving thing, *as a moving thing would be conceived by the sophists*.

What would this sophistic view be? A sophist might hold that, as Coriscos moves from the Lyceum to the market, there are a series of different entities: Coriscos-in-the-Lyceum, Coriscos-at-a-point-partway-to-the-market, Coriscos-at-another-point-partway-to-the-market, and so on, to Coriscos-at-the-market. These different entities all have something in common (they are all part of the series that makes up Coriscos-in-motion-from-the-Lyceum-to-the-market), but they are nevertheless distinct things.

If Aristotle is comparing the now to the moving thing *as conceived of by the sophists*, then we do not have to saddle him with the view that the now is a thing that moves. His view is that just as (on the sophistic view) what we call Coriscos is, in fact, a series of different entities, so also what we call *now* is on each occasion something different. Similarly, just as the series Coriscos-in-the-Lyceum, and so on, to Coriscos-in-the-market all have something in common (they are members of the series that makes up Coriscos-in-movement-from-the Lyceum-to-the-market), so also different nows all share membership in a series: they are all members of a single temporal before-and-after ordering.

Change as more basic than time

Aristotle defines time as a "number of change in respect of the before and after" (*Physics*, Bk 4, ch. 11, 219b1–2). There are at least two things that are puzzling about this definition: the claim that time is a kind of number, and addition of the qualification "in respect of the before and after."

Time as a kind of number

It is odd to describe time as a kind of number. After all, time is something continuous: it is not a *collection* of things that can be counted. For this reason, some interpreters have suggested that Aristotle really means to say that time is that by which we *measure* change (see, for instance, Annas 1975). In support of this, they point out that Aristotle himself says (later in his account) that time is that by which we measure change (though he adds that we also measure time by change) (*Physics*, Bk 4, ch. 12, 220b14–16). However, it is unlikely that this is the point he is making when he defines time as a kind of number. Aristotle presents this definition as if it follows uncontroversially from claims he makes about how we are aware of time by being aware of the occurrence of change, but nowhere in these claims does he mention the need to be aware of any regularly repeated change, of the sort that could be used as a kind of measure.

We shall get closer to understanding Aristotle's definition if we look at his immediately preceding remarks about our awareness of change. He says that we are aware that time has passed when we mark off earlier and later stages in a change, recognising that these stages are different from one another. When we do this, we identify two different nows. Time is what is between these two nows: "what is marked off by the now is thought to be time" (*Physics*, Bk 4, ch. 12, 219a29–30).

This emphasis on marking off different nows suggests a solution to our problem about the sense in which time is "counted." We count nows, but by so doing, we also (in a derivative sense) count the time that is between them. Suppose that I identify a now at an early stage of Coriscos' movement to the market and a now at a later stage of Coriscos' movement to the market. Since the nows are each at different stages of one and the same change, they must be two different nows. I can, then, count them as two and recognise that there is a period of time between them.

If this is Aristotle's view, then the counting that goes on here is of a very special type. Normally, when we count things, the point of doing so is to find out how many of them there are. Aristotle thinks that whenever we mark out two nows, we could always have marked out another now between them. So the point of counting nows cannot be to find out how many there are. Counting must, then, have a different purpose. We can find a hint as to what this purpose might be if we look back at the definition: time is a number of change *in respect of the before and after*. In counting nows, we are putting them in a certain *order*. If this is right, then to say that time is a number of change is to say that it is a kind of order within which changes occur. Time is what is marked out by the nows that we count, and to count these nows is to arrange them in a single order within which every change has a position.

To understand this claim more fully, we need to look at the other puzzling aspect of Aristotle's definition. What exactly does it mean to say that time is a number of change *in respect of the before and after*?

The before and after

To define time as a number of change "in respect of the before and after" might seem self-defeating. *Before* and *after* are themselves naturally understood as temporal notions. How, then, can a definition of time that uses them in this way be explanatory?

The answer to this question lies in Aristotle's earlier remarks about the relations between time and change. (For the sake of simplicity, I pass over his difficult remarks about the relation between change and *magnitude*. For discussion of these, see Coope [2005].) Aristotle says that time follows change (*Physics*, Bk 4, ch. 11, 219a16–18). By this he seems to mean that certain features of time depend upon corresponding features of change. One such feature is *the before and after*. There is a before-and-after relation in change and because of this there is a before-and-after relation in time. What does this mean?

Aristotle's view seems to be that within any one change there is a pre-temporal before-and-after series. Consider, for instance, the growth of a particular acorn into an oak tree. There is a series of stages in this change: acorn, shoot, small sapling, oak. Aristotle's claim is that these stages have a pre-temporal before-and-after order. That is, they have an order that is not itself derived from their order in time. It is an order that is defined only on the stages of one and the same change: the acorn-stage is *before* the shoot-stage *in this change*. There is no one change that has as stages, say, the acorn-stage and the *Coriscos-in-the-market* stage, so there is no relation of before-in-change or after-in-change that holds between the acorn-stage and the Coriscos-in-the-market stage.

When Aristotle says that the before and after in time follows the before and after in change, his point is that temporal order (the order of nows) depends on the pre-temporal orders of before-and-after series within changes. For example, suppose that the acorn-stage is before the shoot-stage in the change that is the acorn's growth into an oak. Aristotle thinks that because of this, the time of the acorn-stage will be temporally before the time of the shoot-stage. If we mark out a now when the acorn appears and another now when the shoot appears, the now of the acorn-stage will be temporally before the now of the shoot-stage.

But this just raises the question: what is the basis for thinking that the order of the stages in a change is pre-temporal? Isn't it more natural to think that this order itself depends upon time: that the acorn-stage is before the shoot-stage in the change just because it is *temporally* before the shoot stage? To see how Aristotle might answer this, we need to look at his account of change.

Aristotle's view of change

Modern philosophers have sometimes defined changing as being in incompatible states at different times. Bertrand Russell, for instance, says that motion "consists merely in the fact that bodies are sometimes in one place and sometimes in another, and that they are at intermediate places at intermediate times" (Russell 1953 [1918]: 83). Aristotle must reject any account that appeals to time in this way. Since he thinks that temporal order depends upon a prior order that holds between stages of a change, he needs some independent account of what it is for something to change.

In *Physics*, Book 3, chapters 1–2, he seems to be providing just such an account. He gives a definition of change in terms of two other notions: potentiality and actuality. Change, he says, is "the actuality of that which potentially is, *qua* such" (*Physics*, Bk 3, ch.1, 201a10–11). What does he mean by this?

The notions of potentiality and actuality that Aristotle employs in this definition figure centrally in much of his thinking about metaphysics. Unfortunately, they are notoriously difficult to understand. His thought here seems to be this. For there to be a change, there must be something that exists before the change and that has the potential to be in the end state of the change. Consider, for example, the change that is the coming-to-be of a statue. For this change to occur, there must be some stuff (some bronze, perhaps) that is not (yet) a statue but has the potential to be a statue. When Aristotle writes of "that which potentially is," he is referring to that which is potentially in the end state of the change. For instance, in our example, "that which potentially is" is the bronze and the potential that the bronze has is the potential to be a statue.

The change into a statue is the actuality (or fulfilment) of the bronze, insofar as the bronze is potentially a statue. In other words, *becoming a statue* is the fulfilment of the bronze's potential to be a statue. This leaves one obvious difficulty. It might seem that the bronze's potential to be a statue is most fulfilled when the statue exists in its finished state. But at that point the change we are trying to define is already over: the bronze is no longer becoming a statue. Given that he wants to define change as the actuality of a potential to be in some end state, how can Aristotle distinguish between *changing into* that state and *statically being in* that state? How, in our example, can he distinguish between becoming a statue and simply being a statue?

To answer this, it is necessary to think about the significance of the *"qua"* clause in the definition. The change in question is the actuality of the bronze *qua potentially (but not actually)* a statue. Aristotle explains that, as he is using the notion of "potential" here, something only counts as potentially F, when it is not in fact F. When the statue has been made, the bronze is no longer something that is (in this sense) "potentially a statue." Or, as he puts it (using a different example), "when the house is, the buildable [i.e. what is potentially but not actually a house] no longer is" (*Physics*, Bk 3, ch.1, 201b11). Change is the actuality of something that is, in this way, merely potential. When something is becoming F, its potential to be F is *as actual in a way compatible with merely being a potential.* Though *being a statue* is a kind of actuality of the bronze, it is not the actuality of the bronze's potential to be a statue, considered as a *mere* potential. *Becoming a statue* is the actuality of the bronze insofar as it is potentially, but only potentially, a statue. That is to say, it is "the actuality of that which potentially is, *qua* such" (201a10–11). Another way to put this (suggested by Aristotle's remarks at *Physics*, Bk 3, ch. 2, 201b31–3) is to say that the changing thing is fulfilling a certain potential, but fulfilling it incompletely. When the bronze is becoming a statue, it is fulfilling its potential to be a statue, but it is fulfilling this potential incompletely.

There are, of course, several objections one might make to this account of change. What about the kind of change that is not a progression towards some definite end state? What account can Aristotle give of infinitely long changes, which have no end at all? Can we really make sense of the notions of potentiality and actuality without covertly smuggling in the notion of time? It is interesting to speculate how Aristotle might answer such questions. For our purposes, though, there are two important points to note. First, this is, at least *prima facie*, an account of change that does not appeal to time. Second, there is an obvious way in which one might try to use this account to generate a pre-temporal order for the stages of any change.

On Aristotle's view, while the bronze is changing it is incompletely fulfilling a certain potential (the potential to be a statue); when the change finishes, this potential is completely fulfilled. This suggests the following account of the order of the stages within this change: for any two stages, x and y, x is earlier than y in the change just in case the potential that governs the change is less fulfilled at x than it is at y. For example, the molten bronze (when it is about to be poured into its mould) is earlier in the statue-becoming change than the setting bronze (that is in the mould). This is because the potential to be a statue is less fulfilled at the molten-bronze stage than it is at the set-bronze stage. Similarly, the acorn is before the shoot in the oak-becoming change, because the potential to be an oak is more fulfilled (more fully "actual") in the shoot than in the acorn.

Aristotle's definition and some residual problems

If the interpretation I outlined above is correct, then Aristotle has the following view. Any particular change, such as the acorn's growth into the oak tree, can be divided into a series of stages: stages that stand in a pre-temporal before-and-after order. When we identify a now, we identify a dividing point in any change that is then occurring: a point at which that change could be divided. So in marking out nows, we also mark out stages within changes. The before and after in time is the series we mark out when we count nows in such a way as to reflect the pre-temporal before-and-after orderings within all changes. Time is, thus, a single universal order within which all changes are related to each other. It is an order that depends on the various pre-temporal orders within changes, but which (unlike them) is common to all change.

This interpretation allows us to take seriously Aristotle's claim that time is a kind of number. It also makes sense of his view that the before and after in time depends upon the before and after in change. However, it does leave Aristotle with an account that faces certain problems. For instance, he never explains what justifies the assumption that there *is* a single temporal order that reflects all the different orders within changes. If the before-and-after within a change is pre-temporal, couldn't it turn out that two changes have before-and-after orderings that run in different directions? Couldn't it turn out, for instance, that a is before b in change C_1; p is before q in change C_2, but a and q are simultaneous and b and p are simultaneous? Since he is committed to the view that there is a *single* temporal order, Aristotle must assume that this cannot happen. Again, what account should be given of the relation of simultaneity? For Aristotle, the stages of different changes are simultaneous just in case they are at one and the same now. But we want to ask: *in virtue of what* are these change-stages at one and the same now? This is another question that Aristotle never raises.

(3) Time and the soul

Towards the end of his account of time, Aristotle asks about the relation between time and the mind. Could there be time in a world in which there were no ensouled beings? His answer is that there could not. Time can only exist in a world in which there are beings capable of counting it: "if there is nothing that has it in its nature to count except soul, and of soul [the part which is] intellect, then it is impossible that there should be time if there is no soul" (*Physics*, Bk 4, ch. 14, 223a21–6). He goes on to say, though, that in such a world there might still be change, "if it is possible for there to be change without soul" (223a26–8). His earlier definition of time as a kind of number has, in a way, prepared us for these claims. As we saw, he introduced this definition with remarks about how we perceive that time has passed. Time, he said, is what we mark out when we count nows in a certain way.

Nevertheless, these claims raise further questions. One puzzle arises from Aristotle's remark about change. He seems to say that a world without ensouled beings would be a world in which there could be change, though there could not be time. Does this show that change is possible without time? If so, it conflicts with Aristotle's earlier claim that every change is in time (*Physics*, Bk 4, ch. 14, 223a15–16). The answer to this is that when Aristotle asks what would be true if there were no ensouled beings, he is not asking about (what a modern philosopher might call) a possible world. He does not think that it is possible to have a world without ensouled beings. Hence, he is not committed to the view that a world without ensouled beings is a possible world in which there is change but no time.

But if this is so, what does it mean to say that there would be change but no time in a world without ensouled beings? Aristotle's point is that it follows simply from the nature of time that if there is time, there must be things capable of counting. However, it does not follow simply from the nature of change that if there is change there must be things capable of counting. On Aristotle's view, it is a necessary truth that there are beings capable of counting, so a world in which there is change will in fact be a world in which there are such beings. But this is just because any possible world is a world in which there are such beings, it is not something that follows specifically from the nature of change.

A further question is this. Why does Aristotle think that there must actually be things capable of counting if there is to be time? According to the view sketched earlier, time is a single order that depends on the various before-and-after orders within changes. Why does the existence of this single temporal order depend upon there being someone to count it? What exactly is the contribution of our counting?

The claim that time depends upon counting might be thought to signal a radically subjectivist view. On such a view, our counting would determine which of two events was temporally before the other. It would be *because of the way we count* that the Trojan War was before the Battle of Hastings and not vice versa. One might wonder, then, whether different people could count differently: might the Trojan War be before the Battle of Hastings for me, but not for you?

In fact, though, there is nothing in Aristotle to suggest he would endorse these radically subjectivist conclusions. On his view, our counting must reflect independent facts about the ordering of stages within a change and about the relations of simultaneity that hold between different changes. But why, then, is this counting necessary at all? Why aren't these independent facts about order themselves enough for the existence of time?

Aristotle's answer seems to be that it is by marking out nows that we create certain divisions in changes. When we count a now, we make a division in all the changes that are then going on. When we count another now, we make a second such division. On Aristotle's view, when we do this we *create* a series of divisions, each of which is a single point cutting through *all* the changes that are then going on. Without counting, there could be changes, and there could be certain before and after relations within them; but without counting there would be no single series of nows. Because of this, Aristotle holds that without counting, there would be no time.

References

Annas, J. (1975) "Aristotle, Number and Time," *The Philosophical Quarterly* 25: 97–113.

Coope, U. (2005) *Time for Aristotle*, Oxford: Oxford University Press.

Hussey, E. (trans.) (1993) *Aristotle's* Physics *Books III and IV*, with an introduction and notes by E. Hussey, Oxford: Clarendon Press.

Russell, B. (1953 [1918]) "Mathematics and the Metaphysicians," in *Mysticism and Logic*, London: Penguin, pp. 74–94.

Further reading

J. Annas, "Aristotle, Number and Time," *The Philosophical Quarterly* 25 (1975): 97–113, is a defence of the view that Aristotle defines time as a kind of measure. S. Broadie, "A Contemporary Look at Aristotle's Changing Now," in R. Salles (ed.), *Metaphysics, Soul, and Ethics in Ancient Thought* (Oxford: Oxford University Press, 2005), pp. 81–93, is an interesting investigation of the relation between Aristotle's account and modern discussions of time. A detailed discussion of the whole of Aristotle's account of time is found in U. Coope, *Time for Aristotle* (Oxford: Oxford University Press, 2005). Coope's forthcoming "Change and Its Relation to Actuality and Potentiality" in G. Anagnostopoulos (ed.), *Blackwell Companion to Aristotle*, explains Aristotle's account of change and discusses alternative interpretations. R. Heinaman, "Is Aristotle's Definition of Change Circular?" *Apeiron* 27 (1994): 25–37, defends an alternative interpretation of Aristotle's account of change. E. Hussey (trans.), *Aristotle's* Physics *Books III and IV*, trans., with an introduction and notes (Oxford: Clarendon Press, 1993) is a translation with a helpful, thought-provoking (though sometimes difficult) commentary. M. Inwood, "Aristotle on the Reality of Time," in L. Judson (ed.), *Aristotle's* Physics: *A Collection of Essays* (Oxford: Clarendon, 1991), pp. 151–78, is a clear and lively discussion of the puzzles with which Aristotle begins his account. L. A. Kosman, "Aristotle's Definition of Motion," *Phronesis* 14 (1969): 40–62, is a classic, though controversial, attempt to explain Aristotle's account of change. Chapter 3 of J. Lear, *Aristotle: The Desire to Understand* (Cambridge: Cambridge University Press, 1988) is a good introduction to Aristotle's account of change and the infinite. G. E. L. Owen discusses the relation between time, change and magnitude and objects that Aristotle's account of time is circular in "Aristotle on Time," in P. Machamer and R. Turnbull (eds), *Motion and Time, Space and Matter* (Columbus: Ohio State University Press, 1976), pp. 3–27; reprinted in Martha Nussbaum, ed., *Logic, Science and Dialectic* (Ithaca, NY: Cornell University Press, 1986, pp. 295–314). R. Sorabji, *Time, Creation and the Continuum* (Ithaca, NY: Cornell University Press, 1983), offers a good introduction to some of the questions raised by Aristotle's account of time.

5

MEDIEVAL METAPHYSICS I
The problem of universals

Claude Panaccio

The medieval controversy over universals was rooted in a crucial disagreement between Plato and Aristotle. While Plato wanted to explain the natural order and the cognizability of the material world by postulating immaterial and mind-independent ideal Forms, Aristotle argued that it was entirely mysterious how a separate Form such as Horseness, say, could account for the substantial identity of each concrete material horse. Much of the late Greek and Arabic philosophical traditions had striven to reconcile the two great thinkers on this central issue, but by the time the discussion was taken over by the European Latin scholars, the common wisdom came to be that Plato was basically wrong after all and that the truth of the matter lay within Aristotle's doctrine, from which it had to be retrieved somehow. This, however, turned out to be a difficult task to carry through. Aristotle is notoriously ambiguous as to his positive account of how it is that two different individuals can be of the same species, or of the same genus, as one another, and the medievals in the end had to figure out by themselves what the right answer was. This gave rise, from the twelfth to the fifteenth century, to one of the richest and most sharply argued discussions in the history of Western metaphysics.

Sources

Apart from Aristotle himself, three main sources deeply influenced this medieval debate. First, the very formulation of the problem was standardly borrowed from Porphyry's introduction to Aristotelian logic, his famous *Isagoge* (the Greek word for "Introduction"), written towards the end of the third century AD and translated from Greek to Latin in the early sixth century by Boethius. Porphyry, at the beginning of the treatise, raised three questions about genera (such as *animal* or *flower*) and species (such as *man* or *tulip*):

(a) whether genera and species are real or are situated in bare thoughts alone;
(b) whether as real they are bodies or incorporeals; and

(c) whether they are separated or in sensibles and have their reality in connection with them (Spade 1994: 1).

Porphyry himself declined to answer such "profound" questions – as he qualified them – in the context of a mere introduction to logic and was content to forward them to some "deeper" field of investigation, metaphysics presumably. In the wording he gave them, nevertheless, these three questions came to jointly constitute the problem of universals for the Latin medieval intelligentsia.

Plato's position, for example, was commonly understood to have been that universals – genera and species, that is – were (a) real, (b) incorporeal, and (c) separated from the sensible things. Since this was supposed by most to have been refuted by Aristotle, the medieval problem was to work out some more acceptable combination of answers to Porphyry's questionnaire.

Another influential guide for the medieval thinking on these issues was Porphyry's translator, Boethius, who provided in his *Second Commentary on Porphyry's Isagoge* the first thorough discussion of the three questions available in Latin. His final answers were not as crystal clear as one might have wished, but he did bring to the debate at least one major contribution by arguing that universals can be successfully isolated in thought by abstraction, even if they do not exist as separate entities in the world. No falsehood, Boethius insisted, need ensue from such a discrepancy between the way universals are present to the mind and how they exist in reality (if indeed they do so exist). For many late-medieval thinkers, this opened the way to what can be called "immanent realism," of which Boethius is often seen as the first Latin proponent: the doctrine, namely, that universals only exist out there within the singular things that exemplify them, rather than (as Platonists held) as separate entities of their own, but can be extracted somehow from these singular things by the intellect. Yet Boethius's main point about an acceptable, and cognitively harmless, structural disparity between mental universals and external reality, was most welcome to the medieval nominalists as well: although there is no generality at all in the external world itself, these nominalists wanted to say, general concepts can legitimately be used by the human mind to correctly categorize the external individuals that do exist. Boethius's main legacy, in the end, was to bring into focus, with respect to universals, the question of *intellectual abstraction*: How is it that general concepts arise from our encounters with singular things and how can they manage, as a result, to adequately represent these singular things in our thoughts? Does the process require, in particular, the acceptance of real extra-mental universals within the singular things, as immanent realists insisted, or can it be accounted for without such an assumption, as nominalists held? Thanks to Boethius, the ontological Porphyrian problems appeared to depend for their solution upon how conceptual cognition was understood to proceed.

In addition to Porphyry and Boethius, the third major influence on the Latin medieval quest for a good Aristotelian theory of universals was the great Islamic eleventh-century thinker, Ibn Sînâ, known in the West as Avicenna. Many of his works were translated into Latin during the twelfth and early thirteenth century, even anteceding in some cases the translation of the corresponding treatises of Aristotle himself on which they were based.

As to the problem of universals, Avicenna's most distinctive single contribution was his so-called theory of the *indifference of essence* as he expounded it in the *Metaphysics* of his great philosophical encyclopaedia, the *Shifa*. Considered in itself, Avicenna taught, the essence of certain things – the humanity of men, for instance – is neither universal nor singular, but can indifferently become one or the other, according to whether it is intellectually entertained by the mind (in which case it is realized as a universal in the mind) or concretely exemplified within a singular thing (in connection to which, then, it can be said to be singular itself). The suggestion was that the very *same* essence can exist in two different ways: either as a universal in the mind or as a singular in some determinate external thing. Yet Avicenna did not want to posit these essences "considered in themselves" as additional beings in the world. His doctrine of the indifference of essence could thus appear as a way of avoiding Platonism while still countenancing universals in reality, and as a key theoretical component, consequently, for immanent realism.

Peter Abelard's quasi-nominalism

The first round of discussion that we are aware of among European Latin scholars over the problem of universals took place in Paris towards the late eleventh and early twelfth century. This was before Avicenna's writings became available in the West. Even such important works by Aristotle as the *Metaphysics*, the *Physics* and the *De Anima* were still untranslated and, consequently, unread. Aristotle's *Categories* and his treatise *On Inter-pretation*, along with Porphyry's introduction and Boethius's commentaries, were the main bases for the theoretical attempts of the time to tackle Porphyry's questionnaire. The debate for all that lacked neither profundity nor subtlety. Thanks to the high degree of logical sophistication attained by the Parisian schools at the end of the eleventh century, the very thinness of the authoritative corpus might even have favoured creativity in this circumstance. One towering figure, at any rate, stands out from the rest, that of Peter Abelard (1079–1142), who came to be posthumously considered in the late twelfth century as the chief of the nominalists.

Commenting upon Porphyry's text, Abelard proposed on the problem of universals both an incisive criticism of various realistic doctrines and an exciting positive theory of his own. The main target of his devastating attacks was his former master William of Champeaux, who had successively tried, with respect to Porphyry's first question, different ways of upholding the reality of universals without returning to Platonism. None of them, Abelard wanted to say, was successful. His detailed arguments constitute, even in today's eyes, a marvellously instructive piece of rigorous philosophizing. Against all forms of realism, for example, Abelard argued from the commonly accepted definition of a universal as "what can be predicated of many," that no external thing can ever be *predicated* of anything: realists, he suggested, often tend to conflate talk about words with talk about things.

Against the specific suggestion that universals should be identified with the common substances of individual things (as Champeaux had first held), Abelard objected – among other things – that the very same substance, then, would end up having contradictory essential properties. Since some animals are essentially rational (human beings) while some are essentially irrational (beasts), the universal animal substance which is supposed to be common to all of them would be both essentially rational and essentially irrational, a consequence which is surely unacceptable!

Against another realist theory, according to which the universal man was to be identified with each individual man, but insofar only as he is a man, Abelard interestingly argued on the basis of what we call today the principle of the indiscernibility of identicals: if *x* is identical with *y*, then whatever is true of *x* is also true of *y*; "for no thing," Abelard says, "is diverse from itself at one and the same time" (Spade 1994: 36). The fine point here is that Socrates insofar as he is a man and Socrates insofar as he is Socrates are the same reality; if the latter is an individual, then, and not a universal, so is the former.

Abelard's negative conclusion was that universals are not real things out there. His positive theory, however, was that universality, in the strict sense, can be ascribed "only to words" (Spade 1994: 37). Only words indeed can be "predicated of many." A universal is nothing but a general linguistic predicate, and its universality depends not on its mode of being, but on its mode of signifying. Just like proper names, general predicative terms such as "man," "flower" or "animal" refer only to singular individuals (since nothing else exists); but contrary to proper names, they simultaneously – and "confusedly", as Abelard puts it – refer to several such individual things. The English word "tulip" is a universal term insofar as it "confusedly" designates several individual things, all the singular tulips namely. Abelard lucidly acknowledged, along Boethius's line, that there is a disparity between the *mode of signification* of a general term (universality) and the *mode of existence* of what it designates (singularity), and that this is no hindrance – quite to the contrary – for our capacity of talking or thinking about reality: that no universal thing exists does not make general terms semantically empty. The key to ensuring the required connection between generality in language and the absolute singularity of whatever exists is, in Abelard's view, to countenance "confused" (or plural) signification as a perfectly appropriate device.

Despite these brilliant insights, Abelard did not quite succeed, however, in keeping clear of all realist commitments with respect to universals. When he undertakes, in his *Logic for Beginners*, to account for the general signification of common terms, he does it, saliently, by positing that each one of them is semantically associated somehow with a concept or "common conception" which determines which individual things exactly it will confusedly represent. But since human mental representations are hardly adequate for the right understanding and categorization of things, Abelard's supposition is that each general term receives its full signification by being associated ultimately with a common conception *in God's mind* (Spade 1994: 45, 53). This guarantees that the correct signification of general words does not crucially depend upon human variable representations and opinions: spotting a certain kind of things, the inventor of the corresponding general term meant to associate it with God's conception of such things, "even if he did not know himself," Abelard says, "how to think out the nature or characteristics" of those things (Spade 1994: 46). But Divine Ideas in this context obviously are but theological surrogates for Plato's separate Forms, and they ultimately play the same metaphysical and epistemological roles in accounting both for the essential natures of singular things (since God is supposed to have created reality in accordance with his Ideas) and for their rightfully falling under general predicates. Abelard, therefore, does not really dodge Platonism.

Moreover, he doesn't quite avoid immanent realism either. His account of abstraction, indeed, explicitly rests on the notion that the mind isolates somehow certain "forms" such as rationality or animality which are really present within the perceived things, although not in a separate way. Several commentators have suggested that such internal forms might not be universal at all for Abelard: Socrates's rationality, after all, might be seen as a singular form of its own. The problem, however, is that it is not clear how these forms could do the job they are supposed to do – to account for abstraction, namely – if they were purely singular aspects. Abelard actually expresses himself at times just as a typical immanent realist would, writing for example, in connection with the theory of abstraction, that "by the phrase 'this man' I attend only to the nature *man*, but as regards a certain subject thing, [while] by the word 'man' I attend to the same nature simply in itself, not as regards any one man" (Spade 1994: 50). Such formulations strongly suggest that there is in each human being something like a human nature, common to them all, just as immanent realism wants. The basic difficulty, then, was still unresolved: How can anything like a common nature be present within singular things?

John Duns Scotus and immanent realism

After Peter Abelard's death, the debate over universals continued to be lively for a while in Parisian schools. Besides the *nominales*, who followed Abelard, there were several varieties of realists around, each one named after its original leader: the *Porretani* (after Gilbert of Poitiers), the *Albricani* (after Alberic of Paris), the *Robertini* (after Robert of Melun) and the *Parvipontani* (after Adam Parvipontanus), with quite a number of doctrinal differences among them. By the mid-thirteenth century, however, as a new brand of teaching institutions, the universities, was flourishing across France, England and northern Italy, a consensus was reached among scholars that immanent realism, under one guise or another, had to be the right answer; and nominalism was all but forgotten.

Thomas Aquinas (c. 1225–74), for example, rejected Platonism for having wrongly supposed that universals have to exist in a separate manner in the extra-mental world to be correctly isolated by the mind. Yet he can hardly be labelled as a nominalist either. Even though universals *in the strict sense* exist only in the mind for him, they nevertheless have an external foundation within the singular things: human nature really is somehow in each singular human being. Aquinas's point is that only mental – or linguistic – units can literally be "predicated of many" (as Abelard had insisted). This being the technical definition of what a universal is, it follows that only mental – or linguistic – units can be said to be universals in this technical sense. But it does not follow that several external things, such as singular horses, cannot correctly be said to have anything in common: they do share a certain nature. As Aquinas wrote in his famous *Sum of Theology*: "the very nature, therefore, which happens to be understood or abstracted under the guise of universality is nowhere but within the singulars; but its being understood or abstracted under the guise of universality is within the intellect only" (Pt 1, Question 85, art. 2, *ad* 2; my translation).

How such a nature could simultaneously exist within several singular beings was left utterly unexplained, however, by Aquinas as well as by the other immanent realists of the time until the English Franciscan John Duns Scotus (1266–1308) addressed the point head on in the late thirteenth and early fourteenth century. Scotus agreed with Aquinas that, technically speaking, there are no universals out there in the world, since only what is in the mind can be "predicated of many." But he was very explicit that this did not rule out, in his view, the external existence of *common natures*: "Community," he wrote in his *Ordinatio*, "belongs to the nature outside the intellect" (in Spade 1994: 67). Scotus, consequently, is rightly labelled as a realist with respect to common natures, and this is what matters, after all, in the context of the metaphysical debate over universals.

Against the nominalist notion that everything is singular by itself from the very start and that no objective common feature is ever to be postulated in the ontology, Scotus argued in two main ways. First, science would be impossible. Science, indeed, always proceeds with general concepts and, since generality not only differs from, but is the very opposite of, singularity, such general concepts would be inescapably inadequate for the understanding of reality if reality was composed only of purely singular entities. Second, there must be some non-singular aspects of things, since there are some "less than numerical" differences among them. A horse and a tulip differ numerically from each other, just as two horses do, each one of them counting for exactly one thing. But there is some respect under which a horse and a tulip differ more from each other than two horses. This shows that in addition to their numerical distinctness, the horse and the tulip do have with respect to each other another sort of difference, which Scotus calls a "less than numerical difference": a difference in species, namely, or in genus. But no such difference would be possible, he claims, if there was not in each of the two things a "less than numerical" unity at work, such as that of their respective nature. If only purely singular things existed, there could be only numerical differences among them; but this, obviously, is not the case (see Spade 1994: 59–62).

According to Scotus, in short, there is in each singular thing a less-than-numerical unity which is the unity of its *nature*. A common nature, however, such as horseness or humanity, never exists in reality without being either thought out by the intellect (in which case it is a universal) or singularized in a certain particular thing (in which case it ends up being ontologically singular insofar as it is now the nature of *this* particular thing). Scotus explicitly resorts there to Avicenna's notion that a common nature, although it never exists by itself, is in itself indifferent as to being a universal in the intellect or a singularized nature within a given particular thing (Spade 1994: 64–5). His originality on the matter is to provide a distinctive account of how a common nature gets singularized within each particular being. The nature, he says, is "contracted" in each of these individuals by an "individuating difference." Given that all individuals of the same species share a common nature, there must be something in each one of them, Scotus argues, that differentiates it from any other: this is the "individuating difference." It is neither a nature, in his view, nor a form, nor an accident, nor a particular parcel of matter, nor a composite of any of these, but a special *sui generis* component of any individual thing, which is unique to that thing and which combines with the nature of the thing – its horseness, for example – to constitute one singular being, thus singularizing, or "contracting," the nature which it combines with, into becoming the nature of *this* particular individual (see Spade 1994: 101–7).

This account requires that a distinction be drawn within the individual being between the nature and the individuating difference, between, in other words, what makes it belong to a certain natural kind and what differentiates it from the other members of the same kind. Yet Scotus did not want to acknowledge a *real* distinction here, since that would amount to countenancing common natures as real entities of their own, and bringing us back to Platonism. And he did not want to say either, that it was a distinction of reason, a mere mind-dependent distinction. Scotus attempted to escape the dilemma by introducing one of his most famous – and controversial – theoretical innovations: the idea of a third sort of distinction, *formal distinction*, namely. A formal distinction in Scotus's sense holds between two entities *a* and *b* when:

(1) *a* and *b* can in no possible circumstances occur separately from each other in reality;

(2) *a* and *b* are, however, ontologically irreducible to each other.

Condition (1) dissociates the formal from the real distinction (since any two really distinct things *could* exist separately if God so wanted), while Condition (2) provides an objective foundation for *a* and *b* being isolated from each other by the mind. This, Scotus proposed, is precisely the sort of distinction that holds between the internal nature of a given singular thing and its individuating difference. Scotus thus managed to avoid the position of common natures as really distinct entities, while guaranteeing an ontological foundation for scientific abstractions.

William of Ockham and fourteenth-century nominalism

The next major intervention in the debate came from Scotus's younger Franciscan confrere William of Ockham (c. 1287–1347), who energetically revitalized the nominalist position. His main target, as can be expected, was immanent realism. Against Scotus, in particular, Ockham argued in his *Ordinatio* on the basis of what is now known as the principle of the indiscernibility of identicals, just as Abelard had in his time against his own realist opponents. If the common nature of a certain thing, for Scotus, is not *really* distinct from the individuating difference within that thing, Ockham remarked, then it must be really identical with it, and it must, therefore, be utterly singular by itself, since this is what the individuating difference is supposed to be. Scotus cannot have it both that the common nature is really identical with the individuating difference and that it is not singular by itself although the individuating difference is singular by itself, for "among creatures the same thing cannot be truly affirmed and truly denied of the same thing" (Spade 1994: 156). Moreover, if each common nature was identical in reality with some individual, as Scotus held, there would be just as many common natures as there are individuals, which is tantamount to saying that there would be no common nature at all (Spade 1994: 161). Scotus's formal difference, in short, was entirely rejected by Ockham as an artificial device, ultimately incompatible with the most fundamental principles of sound reasoning.

Ockham's conclusion was radical: whatever exists is irreducibly singular and no component of it is anything but singular. To accommodate observable accidental changes, he distinguished two basic sorts of such individuals: substances such as Socrates or a particular horse; and their qualities, such as a feeling within Socrates's mind or the color of a particular horse. All the other Aristotelian categories – especially quantity and relation – were accounted for as semantical phenomena, without special corresponding entities being postulated in addition to substances and qualities. Universals, *a fortiori*, were dismissed out of the ontology and confined exclusively to mind and language. Not that there is for Ockham a special mode of mental or linguistic existence that would circumvent somehow the metaphysical law that everything is singular: from an ontological point of view, mental and linguistic units are just as singular as anything else, being ultimately nothing but particular qualities of the mind or of some material medium (such as paper in the case of written words). Ockham's point, like Abelard's before him, was that generality is a semantical feature, not an ontological one: "every universal," he wrote in his *Sum of Logic*, "is one particular thing and it is not a universal except in its signification, in its signifying many things" (Loux 1974: 78).

Ockham's originality is that he was much more systematic than Abelard in his ontological rejection of universals and that he skilfully used, in the process, all the technical resources of the recently developed "terminist" logic, including the so-called "supposition theory" (a theory of reference, basically), which was still unknown to Abelard. His main move in this respect was to transpose the theoretical apparatus of this new semantics to the fine-grained analysis of intellectual thought and concepts. Thought, then, comes out as a kind of mental discourse endowed with a syntax pretty much like that of external languages. Its basic units are *concepts*, seen as natural signs in the mind, from which spoken and written words inherit their own semantical properties as the result of linguistic conventions. A general concept such as *horse* is naturally acquired on the basis of the subject's encounters with real singular horses, and it operates within the mind of that subject, from then on, as a sign for all singular horses: when it is combined with other such signs into mental propositions, it can stand for – or "supposit for" (this is where supposition theory comes in) – some or all of them in various ways, according to the context, and contribute in each case in a precise manner to the truth-conditions of those mental thoughts. Across different propositions – such as "all horses are mammals" or "Socrates owned horses" or "Bucephalus is a horse" – the concept *horse* maintains its natural signification (it signifies all horses), but it stands in various ways for various individuals in each case, as made explicit by the details of supposition theory. Even a proposition such as "man is a species" could be accepted as true by Ockham insofar as the term "man" in it was understood to stand for the corresponding mental concept rather than for its external significates (a case of "simple supposition" in Ockham's vocabulary), just as "man is a noun" is true if "man" in it stands for the corresponding word rather than for individual men (a case of "material supposition").

The semantical properties of concepts and words, and the truth-conditions of all kinds of propositions were thus accounted for by Ockham with the help of technical semantical notions such as *signification* and *supposition* (plus *connotation* in some cases), without countenancing in reality anything but individuals. The truth of a universal proposition such as "all horses are mammals," for example, never requires that the terms "horses" and "mammals" should stand in it for anything but singular beings. For this to work, it had to be admitted, of course, that all horses (or all mammals, for that matter) were truly and mind-independently akin to each other. How, otherwise, could a mental concept acquired on the basis of just a few individual encounters end up signifying all horses or all mammals rather than any other random combination of individual things? For general natural signs to be possible, things in the world must be correctly categorizable into natural kinds. But this is something Ockham had no qualms about. That two horses should be *essentially* similar to each other to some degree is just a plain fact of nature for him, in no way depending upon human intellectual or linguistic activity. His ontological point was merely that this fact does not require the admission of extra universal entities or common natures either within or outside the individual horses themselves.

This nominalist doctrine was enthusiastically adopted by many of the most influential thinkers of the fourteenth century, such as John Buridan (c. 1295–1361), Adam Wodeham (d. 1358), Nicole Oresme (c. 1320–82), Albert of Saxony (c. 1316–90), and Marsilius of Inghen (c. 1340–96). Those were original philosophers of their own – especially Buridan, who is still vastly underrated in the standard histories of philosophy – but they all evicted universals and common natures out of the basic furniture of the world as Ockham had, and they all did it on the basis of a semantical theory of concepts quite similar to Ockham's. They did not occupy alone, of course, the whole philosophical spectrum: Thomists and Scotists were still very active in the European universities. Yet they jointly provided, with respect to the problem of universals, the most distinctive and most sophisticated contribution of the late Middle Ages and they deeply influenced in so doing later major authors, such as Hobbes, Locke or Leibniz.

References

Loux, Michael J. (trans.) (1974) *Ockham's Theory of Terms: Part I of the* Summa Logicae, Notre Dame, IN: University of Notre Dame Press.

Spade, Paul V. (trans.) (1994) *Five Texts on the Medieval Problem of Universals*, Indianapolis, IN: Hackett; English translations of major texts by Porphyry, Boethius, Abelard, Scotus and Ockham.

Further reading

The best overall monography on Ockham's thought is Marilyn M. Adams, *William Ockham* (Notre Dame, IN: University of Notre Dame Press, 1987). Alain De Libera, *La querelle des universaux: De Platon à la fin du Moyen Âge* (Paris: Seuil, 1996) is an excellent historical survey. John Marenbon, *Peter Abelard* (Cambridge: Cambridge University Press, 1997) is the best introduction to Abelard in English. Claude Panaccio, *Ockham on Concepts* (Aldershot: Ashgate, 2004) is a revisionist account, on the basis of the latest discussions on the subject. Paul V. Spade, *The Cambridge Companion to Ockham* (Cambridge: Cambridge University Press, 1999) is a very useful collection. Martin Tweedale, *Scotus vs Ockham: A Medieval Dispute over Universals*, 2 vols (Lewiston, NY: Edwin Mellen Press, 1999) is an in-depth study, with several important texts translated. Thomas Williams (ed.), *The Cambridge Companion to Duns Scotus* (Cambridge: Cambridge University Press, 2003) is a good collection of introductory studies.

6

MEDIEVAL METAPHYSICS II
Things, non-things, God and time

John Marenbon

On a narrow conception, metaphysics in the Middle Ages was the subject called by that name and directly linked to Aristotle's *Metaphysics*. On a wider conception, it includes both that subject and medieval treatments of whatever topics are now considered metaphysical. I shall follow the wider conception here, but very selectively. My aim is to give an impression of the range and complexity of medieval metaphysics, not by setting out themes or positions in the manner of an encyclopaedia, but by looking a little more closely at a few texts or passages. In the first section I shall discuss accounts of the basic constituents of things, before and then after Aristotle's *Metaphysics* became current. It will also give the chance to look at the debate over the subject of metaphysics and the relationship between metaphysics and theology. In the second section, I discuss some accounts of non-things – items that seem to figure in an ontology, without being considered properly speaking as entities. In the third section, I look at a central issue in the medieval philosophy of time: how is the notion of eternity to be understood?

Two thinkers, Peter Abelard and Thomas Aquinas, act as anchors for these discussions. Abelard worked in the period from c. 1100 to 1140, mainly in the Paris schools, at a time when Aristotle's *Metaphysics* was still unknown and philosophers were led into metaphysical questions mainly through texts of Aristotelian logic. By contrast, Aquinas, who was working in the 1250s to 1270s, knew the *Metaphysics* thoroughly, along with the discussions of it in the Arabic tradition.

I have had to exclude far more of medieval metaphysics than I can include. Among the many other areas that particularly deserve treatment are mereology, especially with regard to artefacts (see Henry 1995; Arlig 2005); modality (see Knuuttila 1993); and the "transcendentals" (attributes such as unity, truth and goodness that it was believed every existing thing has; see Gracia 1992; Aertsen 1996).

The basic constituents of things

In the Latin West, Aristotle's *Categories* was known (first indirectly, then directly in Boethius's translation) about four centuries before the *Metaphysics* started to become available. It was from this text, along with the *Isagoge* ("Introduction") to it written by the third-century Neoplatonist Porphyry, that philosophers in the early medieval Latin West derived their basic ontology. The *Categories* makes a distinction between what is "in a subject" (accidents, nowadays usually called "tropes") – for example, my whiteness or baldness – and what is "said of a subject" (universals) – for instance, "human being" is said of me. Particular substances, such as John, are what is *neither* in a subject *nor* said of a subject. These divisions correlate with another: of what is signified by all things "said without combination" into ten categories, the first of which is substance, and the others each sorts of accidents – translating literally from Boethius's version: quantity, quality, to something (relation), when, where, posture, having, doing and suffering. Porphyry's *Isagoge* regroups these distinctions, by considering the five main types of term that can be used as a predicate: two of them – "genera" and "species" – name classes of universal substances; two – "accident" and "distinguishing accident" (*proprium*: an accident that attaches to all and only the members of a certain species, such as ability to laugh for humans) – name classes of accidents. The fifth, "*differentia*," is the essential property that distinguishes species within a genus: in a scheme often represented by medieval logicians as a tree-diagram ("Porphyry's Tree"), substance was divided by the *differentiae* corporeality and incorporeality; corporeal substances, i.e. bodies, were divided into living and nonliving; and so on, until human being – that is to say, corporeal, living, sensibly perceiving, rational and mortal substance – was reached. Human being is a most specific species, beneath which there are no other species. A *differentia* is not a substance; nor is it an accident of any sort, because Porphyry defines an accident as that which can come to and go from its subject without the subject's being destroyed, but it is not even conceivable that something should continue to exist as a substance of a certain sort without any one of its *differentiae*.

From these two texts, then, by the eleventh century, if not before, philosophers had drawn up a basic metaphysical picture. Every natural thing, apart from God, is either a particular or universal substance or form (that is to say, *differentia* or accident); artefacts are assemblages of natural things. It was, however, a matter of debate whether there really existed items of all these sorts. Realists held that there also exist particular universal substances forms; nominalists like Abelard held that only particulars – both substances and forms – exist; extreme nominalists, like Abelard's teacher, Roscelin, seem to have held that only particular substances exist (Marenbon 2004: 27–34, corrected by Marenbon 2008a).

For Abelard, Porphyry's tree becomes, not a hierarchy of more and less universal classes, but a model for the constitution of particular things. A given human, Socrates for instance, has his or her own particular *differentiae* of corporeality, being alive, ability to perceive with the senses, rationality and mortality; and there also attach to him or her at any given time a cluster of accidents of various categories, such as whiteness (a quality), being-six-foot-tall (a quantity), wearing-sandals (a having) and writing (a doing). Each of these forms is a real particular thing, though not a substance. Though forms can exist only in a substance, and when an accident leaves one substance, it cannot go on to be in another; they have an individual identity that does not depend on the substances they inform. Socrates might have been made white by the particular whiteness that, in fact, makes Plato white. Socrates could not exist without having a form of rationality attached to him, but it might not have been the same form numerically as in fact informs him (Abelard 1919–31: 129, lines 34–6, and 84, lines 19–21; see Marenbon 2008b).

It might seem to follow that there are bare substances, to which *differentiae* are added to make them into stones, for instance, or roses or humans. But this is not Abelard's view. Rather, he puts forward two different positions about bodily substances, which are not obviously reconcilable. According to the first, the *differentiae* attach, not to substance, but to body. After having created primordial bodily matter – an amorphous mixture of the four elements – God then adds to it the *differentiae* which make it into a particular of some natural kind or another. According to the second, even apart from forms of any kind, substances have an identity as particular members of a species and genus: "even if the forms were removed, things could none the less subsist discrete in their essences, because their individual discreteness [*personalis discretio*] is not through forms but through the very diversity of essence" (Abelard 1919–31: 13, lines 22–5) (but see Marenbon 2008c King [2004] offers the best account yet of Abelard's metaphysics).

From roughly the turn of the thirteenth century, Latin translations of Aristotle's non-logical books, including the *Metaphysics*, came into use. From the 1250s onwards, all university students (including those who would go on to study theology) followed a curriculum based around Aristotle's texts. The *Metaphysics* develops a view of the constitution of things different from that in the *Categories*, in the context of an investigation into being and into God. The relationship between these two topics was already a matter of dispute in the Arabic tradition, where the *Metaphysics* had been known since the ninth century. Al-Kindî (c. 801–66) had taken metaphysics, the branch of knowledge as presented by Aristotle, as a way of doing theology to be pitted against the more home-grown Islamic thinkers. Avicenna (Ibn Sînâ, before 980–1037) reacted against this interpretation. He argued that it was in metaphysics that the existence of God was demonstrated. God cannot, therefore, be the subject of metaphysics, because a branch of knowledge must have as its subject matter something the existence of which is already certain. The subject of metaphysics is therefore, he contends, being as being. Averroes (Ibn Rushd, c. 1126–98) disagreed. He contended that Aristotle proved the existence of God in the *Physics*, and so God could be the subject of the *Metaphysics*. Thirteenth and fourteenth-century Latin thinkers debated the two views, tending to prefer Avicenna's. But, whichever was chosen, a tight connection – absent in twelfth-century accounts based on the *Categories* – was made between thinking about the constitution of things and considering the nature of God. A closer look at some of Aquinas's ideas and their background illustrates this point.

Although substance and accident continued to play a central part in thirteenth-century treatments of how things are constituted, thinkers were led by Aristotle's *Physics*, *On Generation and Corruption*, as well as his *Metaphysics*, to lay more emphasis on an Aristotelian idea already known earlier: that each particular natural thing is a composite of matter and form, and that matter is potentiality which form actualizes. The prevalence of this scheme is strikingly illustrated by the model adopted widely to explain human thought about universals. Socrates is matter made actual by an individualized form of being-a-human; when I grasp the universal, human being, the aspect of my intellect that is in potency acts as the matter to the form of being-a-human, which actualizes it.

Forms were considered to be either accidental or substantial. Although there were many variations in teaching, accidental forms usually were given less ontological independence than in Abelard's account. For instance, while Aquinas clearly accepts that accidents are real things, distinct from the substances in which they inhere, in some of his discussions, at least, he is ready to admit that they exist only because their subjects exist (Wippel 2000: 253–65). A substantial form was not, as it had been for Abelard, any *differentia*, but rather that form according to which a particular is the kind of thing it is, and its parts are unified into a whole. It was also envisaged in a more concrete way, as a sort of internal efficient cause for all the features of a thing that do not come to it from outside – Socrates's blue eyes, for example, and the fact that he is by birth light-skinned, but not the redness of his eyes the morning after or his designer suntan (Pasnau 2004). Both in its explanatory and causal aspects, and in its variation between individuals of the same species, this conception of substantial form fitted well with the theory taken from Aristotle's *On the Soul* that the soul (or life principle) in living things is the form, to which the body is the matter.

In the *Metaphysics*, substance is discussed in the wider context of its investigation into what it is to be. This perspective is evident in Aquinas's *On Being and Existence* (*De ente et essentia*, 1252–6). One of the positions he argues against is the universal hylomorphism that had been advocated by the Jewish philosopher, Solomon ibn Gabirol (d. 1057/8). All things except for God, argued Solomon, even incorporeal ones, are composites of matter and form. By introducing a more fundamental distinction, Aquinas is able to allow some created beings, angels, to be pure forms, without thereby imperilling the uniqueness of God. In everything, Aquinas, argues – taking a position that many of his fellow theologians would reject – essence and existence are distinct, not merely "by reason" (conceptually), but really. What does he mean by this distinction? Not the view, sometimes wrongly attributed to Avicenna, that existing is an accident of essence, as if there were many essences and just some happened to exist. Rather (Chapter 4), that not only any form–matter composite, such as a stone or a human, but also an angel, considered by Aquinas to be a pure form, can be grasped mentally without its also being known that any such thing exists. Even, therefore, things in which there is no composition of form and matter are composed of the sort of thing they are, their essence, and existence (*esse*). The one exception will be that of which the essence is just to exist – and this, Aquinas, argues, is God. Although the relation between form and matter is one of act to potentiality, this does not mean that pure forms, apart from matter, are pure actuality. Even pure forms are themselves in potency to *esse* itself – that is, to God, who is pure act. They would fail actually to exist were existence not given to them by God. By requiring that the existence of any thing be explained through this activity of pure existing, Aquinas has succeeded in placing God at the basis of his metaphysical analysis of all things. An unorthodox but insightful way of presenting this doctrine (Pasnau 2002: 131–40) is to see Aquinas's account of things based fundamentally *not* on form and matter, but on degrees of actuality, ranging from the pure potency which is matter to the complete actuality which is God.

The claim that what God is is just to be can seem puzzling, but it can be read in terms of negative theology: any attempt to specify God as a certain sort of thing is misguided. The whole basis of Aquinas's theory of being has been attacked, from a Fregean standpoint, as a confusion (Kenny 2002). But the simple response is that Aquinas's standpoint is not Frege's (Klima 2004). It remains true, however, that, despite its greater sophistication, the theological leanings of much later medieval treatment of being and substance make it harder for most philosophers to grasp today than some of the twelfth-century discussions.

Non-things

The Mu'tazilites, the speculative theologians of early Islam, had a non-Aristotelian conception of accidents, according to which each lasted only for an instant and had to be freshly recreated the next. Tenuous though these accidents' hold on existence may be, it is far stronger than that of the non-things which appear in different forms in medieval philosophy. The ninth-century thinker, John Scottus Eriugena, begins his masterpiece, the *Periphyseon*, by dividing nature into what is and what is not. Among the things that are not are those which "through the excellence of their nature escape not only the sense but all intellect." According to Eriugena, these are not only God, but also the essences or reasons of all things made by him (Scottus 1996–2003: Bk 1, 443AB). It is hardly surprising, then, that Eriugena considers that there are more things in nature than contained in Aristotle's ten categories, since "none of those who philosophize rightly" will deny that possible things and impossible things are counted among things – the impossibles being precisely those which it is impossible should appear to the sense or the intellect (Scottus 1996–2003: Bk 2, 596D–7C).

Eriugena's negative theology led him to postulate things that lack being. In Abelard's thinking, and then again, in the fourteenth century, a more rigorously worked out notion of an item that fails to be a proper entity is found. Unlike Eriugena, these philosophers described them explicitly as *not* being things at all. The metaphysical question was raised by an issue in semantics. Consider a simple sentence such as "It is a rose." "Rose" signifies a substance. Does the whole sentence also signify something, and, if so, what sort of entity is it (on the medieval semantics of sentences in general, see Nuchelmans 1973)? Abelard gives a very good reason to think that the sentence must have something it signifies as a whole, by considering the complex sentence "If it is a rose, it is a flower." This conditional, he argues, would always be true, even if there existed no roses and no flowers, and so there were no entities which the words "rose" and "flower" could signify (Abelard 1919–31: 366, lines 6–12). It cannot be that the "if … then …" connection is being asserted simply of the two sentences "It is a rose" and "It is a flower," because the truth of the antecedent of a true conditional *requires* the truth of the consequent, whereas the first sentence can perfectly well exist without the second one (Abelard 1970: 156, lines 1–21). Similarly, it cannot be maintained that what the antecedent and the consequent signify are thoughts, since I can perfectly well think "It is a rose" without *thinking* "It is a flower" (Abelard 1970: 154, line 30, to 155, line 11). There must, then, be some special sort of quasi-entities, distinct from substances or forms of any kind, to which whole sentences refer. Abelard calls them *dicta*, a Latin word which means "the things said." It is a moot point whether Abelard has in mind truth-bearers – something like propositions in the contemporary sense – or truth-makers, that is to say states of affairs. But he leaves no doubt about the ontological status of these *dicta*. They are, Abelard insists, *not* things: they are "entirely nothing" (Abelard 1919–31: 369, line 1–2).

In denying that *dicta* are things of any sort, is Abelard incoherently allowing himself to speak as if an item of a certain sort exists while at the same time denying that any such item exists? There seems to be a plausible defence he could make. Since the system of substances, *differentiae* and accidents accounts for everything about the world (where any substance is at a given time and in exactly what state and relations), a *dictum* is not some new item: it can be explained completely by these other, genuine things. But there is a problem, because Abelard believes that a *dictum* such as "It is a rose" requires the *dictum* "It is a flower," even when none of the objects they concern exists (Marenbon 1997: 207–8; but for a defence of Abelard, see King [2004: 105–8]).

In the fourteenth century, two thinkers Adam of Wodeham (d. 1358) and Gregory of Rimini (d. 1358, too), were led by arguments quite similar to Abelard's – though they would not have known his work – to posit, as signified by sentences, what they characterized as non-things. Their name for them was not *dicta*, but the more precise *complexe significabilia* – what are signifiable by a complex (i.e. not a single word but words combined). These signifiables seem more clearly than Abelard's *dicta* to be states of affairs – for instance, that a human being is an animal.

Adam of Wodeham is forced to clarify the ontological status of *complexe significabilia* by the following objection (Adam of Wodeham 1990: 193, lines 5–8): a signifiable is either something or nothing, but if it is nothing it cannot play the semantic role it was introduced to serve. If it is something, it is either a substance or an accident. But every substance and accident can be signified by a non-complex utterance. So it is purposeless to posit *complexe significabilia*. Adam answers (Adam of Wodeham 1990: 195) by saying that a *complexe significabile* such as "that a human being is an animal" is "not a something or a substance," but it is that a human being is something and that a human being is a substance or an accident. Against the argument that such a signifiable must be something or nothing, Adam suggests that the reasoning is parallel to saying that a people is either a human being or not a human being. So, if it is not not a human being, it is a human being. This obviously sophistical argument is based on insisting on the pair of alternatives, is or is not a human being, when really a people is human beings. Similarly, a *complexe significabile* is not something, nor does it follow that it is nothing: it is not a what (*quid*), but a being-a-what (*esse quid*).

Faced by a similar objection ("either the significate of the whole sentence is something or nothing"), Gregory of Rimini (1981: 8, line 25, to 10, line 3) distinguishes three ways in which "being" (*ens*) or "thing" (*res*) can be understood. In the broadest sense a thing or being is whatever can be signified by a single word or a combination of words; or, secondly, it is whatever can be *truly* signified by a single word or a combination of words; or, thirdly, a being or thing is "some essence or existing entity." Gregory is willing to allow his objector to use "thing" in the third of these senses, and so he accepts that *that a human is an animal* is nothing, and that therefore nothing is an object of scientific knowledge, both in the sense that a non-being (*non ens*) is the object of scientific knowledge and in the sense that there is no being which is the object of scientific knowledge. He rejects, however, the further conclusion that, therefore, scientific knowledge has no object. It *does* have an object, he replies, which is not a being.

The two fourteenth-century thinkers force themselves to try to explain more clearly than Abelard had done what precisely they mean by denying that states-of-affairs are things. It has been argued (Perler 1994) that, for Adam, states of affairs supervene on a set of entities, in the way that fragility supervenes on certain molecular structures. He avoids any tendency to treat states of affairs as if they were things, even while denying that they are. Gregory's treatment veers rather in the direction of seeing "non-thing" as a label for what is unlike substances, accidents, or artefacts, but is still a special type of item, part of a broad, inclusive ontology though excluded by a narrower one.

Time and eternity

Perhaps the most interesting area of the medieval philosophy of time is the discussions about eternity. Their intensity was the result of theological needs. God, all accepted, is eternal, but what does this mean? The theological background also provided an extra complication not faced by most contemporary philosophers who think about eternity.

To us now, it may seem as if there are just two, very obviously distinct, meanings of eternity. Something is eternal either by existing for an infinite duration of time (its existence has no beginning and/or no end) – call this "sempiternity"; or something is eternal because it is timeless: it lacks extension and position in time. According to most historians, the generally accepted view in the Middle Ages about divine eternity was that it is timeless. The classic statement of this position is supposed to be the definition given in the early sixth century by Boethius (*Consolation of Philosophy*, Bk 5, prose 6, 4) eternity is "the whole, perfect and simultaneous possession of unending life." Clearly, Boethius is not thinking of sempiternity, and he indeed makes an explicit contrast between eternity, which is God's way of being, and the unending duration of the world (according to some philosopher's views). But is his definition of being eternal really reducible to a lack of temporal extension and position? Boethius is describing a perfect way of living, in which everything happens all at once; our way of living in time he considers an unsuccessful attempt to imitate it.

Many of the discussions of eternity in the period up to the later thirteenth century resemble Boethius's in suggesting that God is in some sense outside time and yet *not* seeing his eternity simply as timelessness (Marenbon 2005). They had good reason to resist eternity as simple timelessness. The objects that some contemporary philosophers consider timeless, such as numbers and universals, do not interact with things in time as cognizers or makers, whereas God, the medieval thinkers held, knows and, ultimately, brings about all things. It is hard, then, to sacrifice the idea that God exists at every time, though there are also strong theological pressures towards divine timelessness. Anselm (*Monologion*, Chs 18–22; see Leftow 1991: 183–216) tries to combine the two, apparently antithetical views. He considers that because God lacks not merely an end but a beginning, and so he exists at every time, he is also outside time, because he cannot be measured by it. Early thirteenth-century treatments draw on Anselm's view, but they extend it by considering time and eternity as different types of duration, in a way rather similar to how some philosophers today discuss multiple time-streams (Marenbon 2003: 55–6).

I would like to look in a little more detail at what happens when, for the first time, some medieval thinkers do analyse divine eternity as timelessness in a sense near to ours: how then are they to explain God's relation to temporal things? The setting of this discussion is the analysis of God's omniscience. God knows all things, Christian doctrine holds, even those which are in the future. In order to explain *how* God could know future contingent events – events the nature of which is not certain, because they might happen one way or another – Boethius invokes God's way of existing not in time but eternity. Future events, it is contended, are not future so far as God's knowledge of them is concerned. A careful reading of the text suggests that Boethius is not, however, basing this idea on the metaphysical claim that God is himself timeless, but on an epistemic claim – that, in some scarcely explicable way, God is able to know events which really are in the future, just as if they were happening in the present: "the divine gaze runs ahead of what is future and twists it and recalls it back to the present of its own understanding" (*Consolation*, Bk 5, prose 6, 40). Over seven centuries later, Aquinas – contrary to what most of his modern interpreters contend – adopted, at least in most of his discussions, the same approach, epistemic rather than metaphysical. "God's knowledge", says Aquinas (*Quaestiones de quolibet*, Quodlibet 11, question 3), "is above time and is measured only by eternity, and so it does not know things, both necessary and contingent, as they are in time, but as they are in eternity, that is as present to him; and so he knows all things as present in his own presentness." As he explains (*Compendium Theologiae*, Bk 1, ch. 133): "Although particular temporal things are not simultaneous, God however has a simultaneous cognition of them: for he knows them according to the mode of his being, which is eternal and without succession." (On Aquinas and other thirteenth-century writers on eternity, see Fox 2006.)

Shortly after Aquinas died, a fierce controversy about his teachings began. They were attacked by the Franciscans, and defended by his own Dominican Order. It was, it seems, as a way of *attacking* Aquinas that there was first formulated and attributed to him the idea that "because eternity is present to every difference of time and every difference of time is present to eternity, therefore contingent things, which do not yet exist really and actually in time, already exist really and actually in eternity through their natures and so are subject to the divine vision" (as Aquinas's critic, William de la Mare, put it; quoted in *Correctorium* 1954: 17). Some of Aquinas's Dominican supporters kept to his epistemic approach, but others were happy to accept the metaphysical view, though their attempts to bolster were little more than rhetoric. Take, for instance, Jean Quidort (Quidort 1941: 26, lines 37–44; in Pt 1, art. 3):

> eternity is a measure or duration which goes beyond bounds and is simple. Because it goes beyond bounds and is without limits, it includes in itself all the course of time with its limits ... But because it is simple, it is as a whole simultaneous with time and as a whole outside time and as a whole with all time and as a whole is present to every difference of time.

It was left to a Franciscan, Richard of Middleton, to work out (c. 1281–4) a principled way of *defending* a position which his confreres had invented, it seems, just so as to attack it. Richard (Richard of Middleton 1559: Quodlibet 3, question 1) forcefully asserts the coexistence of divine eternity with all of time: "The whole present of eternity is before our present and the whole of it coexists with our present and it is infinitely beyond our present." But he goes on to explain the nature of this coexistence in a special way. Since divine eternity is immense, it does not merely coexist with our present but stretches before and after it infinitely. And because divine eternity is entirely simple, the *whole* of it both coexists with our present and is infinitely before and after it. These two different aspects of eternity in its relationship with time allow Richard to offer an explanation of why future things are *not* actually present, although eternity coexists with time. There is one aspect of eternity, call it Eternity A, which coexists with our present. There is another aspect of eternity, call it Eternity B, which does not coexist with our present, but stretches infinitely before and after it. Future things coexist with Eternity B, but not Eternity A. Therefore it does not follow that they exist in our present. The problem with this view, of course, is to explain how divine eternity, which is entirely simple, can have these different aspects, and to answer the objection which, a little later, would be put by Durandus of St Pourçain: if all events really stand in the relation of presentness to God, then they must all be simultaneous (Durandus of St Pourçain 1964: 104v; *In Sententias*, Bk 1, distinction 38, question 3, note 14; nearly 700 years later, Anthony Kenny [1969: 264] formulated, independently, the same objection).

References

Abelard, Peter (1919–33) *Peter Abaelards philosophische Schriften* (Beiträge zur Geschichte der Philosophie und Theologie des Mittelalters 21), edited by B. Geyer, Münster: Aschendorff.

—— (1970) *Dialectica*, 2nd edn, edited by L. M. De Rijk, Assen; Van Gorcum.

Adam of Wodeham (1990) *Lectura secunda in librum primum sententiarum: Prologus et distinctio prima*, edited by R. Wood, St Bonaventure, NY: Franciscan Institute.

Aertsen, J. (1996) *Medieval Philosophy and the Transcendentals: The Case of Thomas Aquinas* (Studien und Texte zur Geistesgeschichte des Mittelalters 52), Leiden: Brill.

Arlig, A. (2005) "A Study in Early Medieval Mereology: Boethius, Abelard, and Pseudo-Joscelin," Ph.D. dissertation, Ohio State University; available: http://www.ohiolink.edu/etd/view.cgi?osu1110209537

Brower, J. E. and Guilfoy, K. (eds) (2004) *The Cambridge Companion to Abelard*, Cambridge: Cambridge University Press.

Correctorium (1954) *Le Correctorium Corruptorii "Quaestione"* (Studia Anselmiana 35), edited by J.-P. Muller, Rome: Herder.

Durandus of St Pourçain (1964) *In quattuor libros* Sententiarum, Venice 1571; facsimile Ridgewood, NY: Gregg.

Fox, R. (2006) *Time and Eternity in Mid-Thirteenth-Century Thought*, Oxford: Oxford University Press.

Gracia, J. J. E. (ed.) (1992) "The Transcendentals in the Middle Ages," *Topoi* 11, no. 2: 113–21.

Gregory of Rimini (1981) *Lectura super primum et secundum sententiarum*, edited by A. D. Trapp and V. Marcolino, I, Berlin; New York: De Gruyter.

Henry, D. P. (1995) *Medieval Mereology* (Bochumer Studien zur Philosophie 16), Amsterdam; Philadelphia: Grüner.

Kenny, A. (1969) "Divine Foreknowledge and Human Freedom," in A. Kenny (ed.), *Aquinas: A Collection of Essays*, Notre Dame: University of Notre Dame Press, 255–70.

—— (2002) *Aquinas on Being*, Oxford: Oxford University Press.

King, P. (2004) "Metaphysics," in Brower and Guilfoy (2004), pp. 65–125.

Klima, G. (2004) "On Kenny on Aquinas on Being: A Critical Review of *Aquinas on Being* by Anthony Kenny," *International Philosophical Quarterly* 44: 567–80.

Knuuttila, S. (1993) *Modalities in Medieval Philosophy*, London; New York: Routledge.

Leftow, B. (1991) *Time and Eternity*, Ithaca, NY: Cornell University Press.

Marenbon, J. (1997) *The Philosophy of Peter Abelard*, Cambridge: Cambridge University Press,

—— (2003) "Eternity," in A. S. McGrade (ed.), *The Cambridge Companion to Medieval Philosophy*, Cambridge: Cambridge University Press, pp. 51–60.

—— (2004) "Life, Milieu and Intellectual Contexts," in Brower and Guilfoy (2004), pp. 13–44.

—— (2005) *Le temps, la prescience et les futurs contingents de Boèce à Thomas d'Aquin*, Paris: Vrin.

—— (2008a) "The Turn of the Twelfth Century," in D. Gabbay and J. Woods (eds), *A Handbook of the History of Logic*, vol. 2: *Medieval and Renaissance Logic*, Amsterdam: Elsevier, pp. 65–81.

—— (2008b) "Abelard on Differentiae: How Consistent Is His Nominalism?" *Documenti e Studi Sulla Tradizione Filosofica Medievale* 19: 1–12.

—— (2008c) "Was Abelard a Trope Theorist?" in *Compléments de Substance. Études sur les propriétés acciden-telles offertes a Alain de Libera*, ed. C. Erisman and A. Schiewind, Paris: Vrin, 85–101.

Nuchelmans, G. (1973) *Theories of the Proposition. Ancient and Medieval Conceptions of the Bearers of Truth and Falsity*, Amsterdam; London: North Holland.

Pasnau, R. (2002) *Thomas Aquinas on Human Nature: A Philosophical Study of* Summa Theologiae 1a, 75–89, Cambridge: Cambridge University Press.

—— (2004) "Form, Substance, and Mechanism," *The Philosophical Review* 113: 31–88.

Perler, D. (1994) "Late Medieval Ontologies of Facts," *Monist* 77: 149–69.

Quidort, John (1941) *Le correctorium corruptorii "Circa"* (Studia Anselmiana 12–13), edited by J.-P. Muller, Rome: Herder.

Richard of Middleton (1559) *Quodlibeta*, Brescia.

Scottus, John (1996–2003) *Periphyseon* (Corpus Christianorum Continuatio Mediaeualis 161–5), edited by E. Jeauneau, Turnhout, Belgium: Brepols.

William de la Mare (1956) *Declarationes magistri Guilelmi de la Mare de variis sententiis S. Thomae Aquinatis* (Opuscula et Textus Historiam Ecclesiae Eiusque Vitam atque Doctrinam Illustrantia, Series Scholastica 21), edited by F. Pelster, Münster: Aschendorff.

Wippel, J. (2000) *The Metaphysical Thought of Thomas Aquinas: From Finite Being to Uncreated Being* (Monographs of the Society for Medieval and Renaissance Philosophy 1), Washington, DC: Catholic University of America Press.

7

DESCARTES
The real distinction

Dugald Murdoch

Descartes' *Meditations on First Philosophy* (1641) is probably the most widely read book of metaphysics ever written, and one of its most widely discussed theses is that the mind is really distinct from the body, and can exist without it. His argument for this thesis has puzzled his readers ever since it was put forward. My aim in this chapter is to elucidate the argument, and to comment on some objections to it.

The translations below are those of the standard edition of Descartes' philosophical writings in English, referred to as CSM (the translators, Cottingham, Stoothoff and Murdoch), I (vol. 1) and II (vol. 2), and CSMK (the translators, Cottingham, Stoothoff, Murdoch and Kenny) (see Descartes 1984–5, 1991).

The real distinction

Descartes' argument for the real distinction first appears in rudimentary form in the *Discourse on the Method* (1637). After arguing that he cannot doubt that he exists, Descartes goes on to say that if it were not for his thinking, he would have no reason to believe that he exists. From this he concludes that his essence consists only in thinking, and that his mind is entirely distinct from his body and would be what it is even if his body did not exist (CSM I 127).

Descartes had invited readers of the *Discourse* to point out to him anything they found worthy of objection. One of his readers pointed out that from the fact that Descartes does not perceive himself to be anything other than a thinking thing it does not follow that his essence consists only in his being a thinking thing. Descartes replies that in the passage in question he was not intending the exclusion indicated by the word "only" to apply to how things are in reality, but only to how they are in his perception of them. In the *Meditations*, however, he undertakes to show how, from the fact that he is not aware of anything else belonging to his essence, it follows that nothing else does in fact belong to it (CSM II 7).

The place in the *Meditations* where Descartes purports to show how, from the fact that he is not aware of anything else belonging to his essence, it follows that nothing else does in fact belong to it, is the following passage in Meditation Six (CSM II 9, 11, 95) (I have added the numbers in the following [passage A] for the sake of reference).

[1] First, I know that everything which I clearly and distinctly understand is capable of being created by God so as to correspond exactly with my understanding of it. [2] Hence the fact that I can clearly and distinctly understand one thing apart from another is enough to make me certain that the two things are distinct, since they are capable of being separated, at least by God. [3] The question of what kind of power is required to bring about such a separation does not affect the judgement that the two things are distinct. [4] Thus, simply by knowing that I exist and seeing at the same time that absolutely nothing belongs to my nature or essence except that I am a thinking thing, I can infer correctly that my essence consists solely in the fact that I am a thinking thing. [5] It is true that I may have (or, to anticipate, that I certainly have) a body that is very closely joined to me. [6] But nevertheless, on the one hand I have a clear and distinct idea of myself, in so far as I am simply a thinking, non-extended thing; and on the other hand I have a distinct idea of the body, in so far as this is simply an extended, non-thinking thing. [7] And accordingly, it is certain that I am really distinct from my body, and can exist without it. (CSM II 54)

This passage is puzzling in many ways. The key to understanding it, I believe, lies in the distinction which Descartes makes between the mental acts of abstraction and exclusion (see Murdoch 1993). He does not introduce this distinction explicitly in any of his published writings, but he explicates it in a letter to Gibieuf of 19 January 1642, which he wrote not long after the publication of the *Meditations* (CSMK 201). In the case of abstraction, Descartes explains, we turn our attention away from a part of the content of a richer idea and focus it on another part. For example, we focus our attention on some shape without thinking of the extended substance whose shape it is. We can tell that this act is an abstraction from the fact that while we can think of the shape without paying any attention to the extended substance, we cannot deny the one of the other when we think of them both together, that is, we cannot think of the shape and at the same time deny that it has an extension, and we cannot think of the extension and at the same time deny that it has a shape. In the case of exclusion, by contrast, we focus our attention on the contents of both ideas while denying the one of the other. For example, we focus our attention on a thinking substance and on extension while denying that the thinking substance is extended or that extension is a thinking substance. We can tell that this is an act of exclusion by the fact that we can deny the one of the other. We can deny the one of the other because we recognise that no contradiction is involved in the denial.

Passage A should be understood in terms of exclusion, not abstraction. When Descartes says in sentence (2), "I can clearly and distinctly understand one thing apart from another," what he intends is an act of exclusion. It is not that Descartes can clearly and distinctly understand the one thing while not attending to the other thing, but that he can clearly and distinctly understand the one thing while denying the other thing of it. When he says in sentence (6), "I have a clear and distinct idea of myself, in so far as I am simply a thinking, non-extended thing," what he intends is an act of exclusion, for he is conceiving of himself as a thinking thing while denying of himself that he is extended.

The importance of exclusion for Descartes' reasoning in passage A is emphasised in a letter which he wrote to Mesland on 2 May 1644:

> There is a great difference between *abstraction* and *exclusion*. If I said simply that the idea which I have of my soul does not represent it to me as being dependent on the body and identified with it, this would be merely an abstraction, from which I could form only a negative argument, which would be a poor result. But I say that this idea represents it to me as a substance which can exist even though everything belonging to the body be excluded from it; from which I form a positive argument, and conclude that it can exist without the body. (CSMK 236; I have altered the CSMK translation at "which would be a poor result")

By "a negative argument" Descartes means that the conclusion would be "I do not know that the mind is dependent on the body," and by "a positive argument" he means that the conclusion would be "I know that the mind is not dependent on the body."

Exclusion is crucial for Descartes' reasoning in passage A, for it is thanks to exclusion that Descartes' understanding of himself simply as a thinking thing is clear and distinct. A perception, in the generic sense which covers conception, understanding, recognition, and perception in the specific sense, is clear when it is "present and accessible to the attentive mind," and distinct when, as well as clear, "it is so sharply separated from all other perceptions that it contains within itself only what is clear" (CSM I 207–8). His perception of himself simply as a thinking thing is clear, because it is present and accessible to his attentive mind, and it is also distinct, because it is sharply separated from his perception of every other thing. What makes it thus sharply separated is Descartes' act of exclusion. While understanding himself as a thinking thing, he can, without self-contradiction, deny of himself every attribute other than that of thinking and the modes of this attribute, such as perception and willing. It is his ability to make this denial which makes his understanding of himself simply as a thinking thing distinct as well as clear, and which entails that his understanding of himself simply as a thinking thing is not a mere abstraction; if it were a mere abstraction, then for all he would know, he might be essentially extended.

It may seem from passage A that Descartes' knowledge that he, a thinking thing, is really distinct from his body, and can exist without it, depends entirely upon the power of God to separate him from his body. But this is not the case, as is shown by sentence (3), where he says, "The question of what kind of power is required to bring about such a separation does not affect the judgement that the two things are distinct." Descartes makes the same point again at the end of the First Replies, where he says, "Our knowledge that two things are really distinct is not affected by the nature of the power that separates them" (CSM II 120). What he means by this is, I believe, as follows.

The fact that Descartes has a clear and distinct understanding of himself simply as a thinking, non-extended thing is sufficient for him to know that he is a thinking, non-extended thing, and hence distinct from his body; this is sufficient, because whatever we clearly and distinctly understand is true in a way which corresponds exactly to our understanding of it (Synopsis, CSM II 9). Descartes had introduced the latter thesis (call it "the truth thesis") at the beginning of Meditation Three (CSM II 24), and proved it to his satisfaction in Meditation Four (CSM II 41–3). However, the fact that Descartes is distinct from his body does not entail that he is *really* distinct from his body, that is, that he can exist without it (as Wilson notes [1978: 190]). It may be that although Descartes is distinct from his body, his existence depends upon his body, owing to some close connection between himself and his body. There seems to be just such a close connection, as he observes in sentence (5) of passage A, and consequently some power may be required to break the connection if he is to exist without his body. There is a power capable of breaking this connection, namely, God's power. Hence Descartes is really distinct from his body, and can exist without it. This is not to say that God's power is necessary to break the connection, for as Descartes says at the end of the Second Replies, he introduced the power of God not because some extraordinary power was needed, but because in the preceding arguments he had dealt only with God, and hence there was no other power he was aware of (CSM II 120).

The present interpretation is supported by what Descartes says in the letter to Gibieuf cited above. He states there that there can be no such thing as an atom, an extended thing which is indivisible, because it is impossible to have an idea of some extended thing without having the idea of half of it, or a third of it, and so on, and hence the thing in question is in reality divisible, since God has given Descartes the faculty of conceiving it as divisible. Someone might object that from the fact that Descartes can conceive of the parts it does not follow that they are separable, since God may have joined them so tightly together that they are completely inseparable. To this, Descartes replies that in that case, God can separate them. He adds, "so that absolutely speaking I have reason to call them divisible, since he has given me the faculty of conceiving them as such." The same holds, he says, where the mind and the body are concerned (CSMK 202–3). In light of this, it is clear that Descartes' knowledge that he is really distinct from his body depends primarily on the truth thesis, and only secondarily on the power of God to separate him from his body.

The argument for the real distinction can be set out as follows:

(1) Whatever I clearly and distinctly understand is true.
(2) I clearly and distinctly understand myself as a thinking, non-extended thing.
(3) Therefore I am a thinking, non-extended thing.
(4) Therefore I am distinct from my body.
(5) Yet some power may be needed to separate me from my body.
(6) There is such a power, namely, God's power.
(7) Therefore I can exist without my body.
(8) Therefore I am really distinct from my body.

Descartes gives a second argument for the distinction between the mind and the body in Meditation Six, which is that the mind is indivisible, whereas the body is not (CSM II 59). When Descartes considers the mind, he cannot distinguish any parts, whereas when he considers the body, he can. Modes of thinking, such as perceiving and willing, understanding and denying, and so on, are not parts of the mind, for it is one and the same mind which perceives and wills, understands and denies, and so on. This one argument, Descartes says, would be enough to show that the mind is completely different from the body if he did not know this from other considerations (what he is alluding to here is the argument of passage A). Exclusion plays a tacit role in this second argument, for Descartes must be assuming here that when he considers the mind, his conception of it is formed by exclusion, and not by abstraction from the richer idea of a single substance which is both thinking and extended, for if it were so formed, he could not be certain that the mind has no parts.

The role of exclusion in Descartes' "Replies"

The notion of exclusion plays a crucial role in Descartes' replies to his critics in the Objections and Replies, though he does not employ the term "exclusion" there. For example, the author of the First Objections, Caterus, objects that to understand one thing apart from another there need not be a *real* distinction between them; it is enough that there should be a *formal* distinction (CSM II 72). Descartes replies that a formal distinction is what he calls a *modal* distinction. A modal distinction is a distinction either between an attribute and a mode of that attribute or between two different modes of an attribute. In the case of a modal distinction we can understand the one item apart from the other by abstraction, but not by exclusion. We can understand the shape of a body apart from its motion, and vice versa, but we cannot deny that the body which has that shape has some motion or other, and we cannot deny that the body which has that motion has some shape or other. This shows that the distinction between the shape and the motion is not real, that the one cannot exist without the other. In the case of the mind and the body, by contrast, we can understand the mind as a thinking thing while denying that it is extended, and we can understand the body as an extended thing while denying that it is thinking. These denials would not be possible if there wasn't a real distinction between the mind and the body (CSM II 85–6; see also CSM II 213–14).

The author of the Fourth Objections, Arnauld, had read Descartes' Replies to Caterus, and in light of his reading he puts forward the objection that although Descartes can deny that the mind is extended, he may be mistaken in doing so, for by the same token someone could clearly and distinctly understand that a triangle inscribed in a semicircle was right-angled yet mistakenly deny that the square on the hypotenuse was equal to the sum of the squares on the other two sides (CSM II 141–3). Descartes replies that the said person does not *distinctly* understand that the triangle is right angled, for there is no way in which this person could distinctly understand that the triangle is right-angled and at the same time deny that the square on its hypotenuse is equal to the sum of the squares on the other two sides. This person's understanding of the triangle is not distinct, but confused (and, we should add, could be shown to be confused) (CSM

II 158–9). Descartes makes essentially the same point in the First Replies, where he says that even if he can understand what a triangle is if he abstracts from the fact that its three angles are equal to two right angles, he cannot deny this property of the triangle by a clear and distinct act of the intellect, that is, while understanding what he means by his denial (CSM II 84).

The role of exclusion in other key arguments in the *Meditations*

Exclusion plays a crucial part in other key arguments in the *Meditations*, such as the argument for Descartes' existence in Meditation Two. Descartes is supposing there that his former beliefs are all false, but while supposing this, he recognises that he cannot suppose the thought "I exist" to be false. In other words, he cannot *deny* "I exist." His reasoning can be formulated as a classical *reductio ad absurdum* argument:

(1) I do not exist.   (supposition)
(2) I am trying to suppose premiss (1).   (beyond doubt)
(3) I do not exist and I am trying to suppose premiss (1).   (from [1] and [2] by
                                                                 "and" introduction)
(4) Conclusion (3) is absurd.   (beyond doubt)
(5) I exist.   (from [1] to [4] by
                                                                 classical *reductio*)

This formulation captures the part which exclusion plays in Descartes' reasoning, for what Descartes is trying to do in line (3) is to perform an exclusion, and what he recognises in line (4) is that he cannot perform the exclusion and at the same time understand what it is he is doing.

Exclusion plays a crucial part also in Descartes' argument in Meditation Two that he is a thinking thing. Now that Descartes is certain *that* he exists, he goes on to ask *what* he is. He considers the attributes which he formerly ascribed to himself, and rejects those which presuppose the existence of the body, for at this stage he is still supposing that no body exists. At last he hits upon an attribute which he is unable to suppose he does not possess: "Thinking? At last I have discovered it – thought; this alone is inseparable from me" (CSM II 18). Thinking is inseparable from Descartes in the sense that he cannot *deny* "I am thinking." His reasoning, again, can be formulated as a classical *reductio* argument.

(1) I am not thinking.   (supposition)
(2) I am trying to suppose premiss (1).   (beyond doubt)
(3) I am not thinking and I am trying to suppose premiss (1).   (from [1] and [2] by
                                                                 "and" introduction)
(4) Conclusion (3) is absurd.   (beyond doubt)
(5) I am thinking.   (from [1] to [4] by
                                                                 classical *reductio*)

In concluding here that he is thinking, Descartes is not concluding that thinking is essential for his existence, but only that thinking is the only attribute which he knows for certain he possesses. This is shown by his statement that "it could perhaps be that were I totally to cease from thinking, I should totally cease to exist." He is saying, in other words, that if he were to cease from thinking, he *might* cease to exist, not that he *would* cease to exist.

Exclusion is at work also in Descartes' argument for the existence of God in Meditation Five. He argues there that he cannot suppose the thought "God exists" to be false, cannot *deny* "God exists." He takes himself to perceive clearly and distinctly that existence is part of the essence of God, and that what is part of the essence of a thing can be truly affirmed of the thing. Again, his reasoning can be formulated as a classical *reductio*:

(1) God does not exist.   (supposition)
(2) Existence is part of God's essence.   (beyond doubt)
(3) God does not exist and existence is part of God's essence.   (from [1] and [2] by "and" introduction)
(4) Conclusion (3) is absurd.   (beyond doubt)
(5) God exists.   (from [1] to [6] by classical *reductio*)

Comments on some objections to the argument for the real distinction

At the heart of Descartes' argument for the real distinction lies the truth thesis, that whatever Descartes clearly and distinctly understands is true. He introduced the thesis (with the generic term "perception" rather than the specific term "understanding") in Meditation Three (CSM II 24–5), and took himself to have proved it in Meditation Four, as a corollary of his proof in Meditation Three that God exists and is not a deceiver. If anything which Descartes clearly and distinctly perceived was false, then God would be a deceiver, by giving Descartes a faculty which caused him to err, and without providing him with any other faculty which would enable him to correct the error (CSM II 41–3). The trouble is that in proving that God exists and is not a deceiver, Descartes has relied on his clear and distinct perception, and hence his proof that whatever he clearly and distinctly perceives is true appears to be circular.

As I have argued elsewhere, however, in Meditation Three Descartes convinces himself, *before* he draws the conclusion that God exists, that he can rely on what he calls "the natural light" (CSM II 26–7; see Murdoch 1999). By "the natural light" Descartes means, I believe, the faculty of clear and distinct perception. He argues that whatever is revealed to him by the natural light cannot be open to doubt in any way, because there can be no other faculty which he trusts as much as the natural light and which could show him that what the natural light revealed was not true (the CSM translation "trustworthy" here is not quite right). Descartes' point is that if he could not trust the natural light, then he could not trust any other faculty, for if he could be deceived by the natural light, he could be deceived by that other faculty. What he perceives by the natural light, then, is absolutely incorrigible. Thus, before he proves that God exists, Descartes recognises that whatever he perceives by the natural light is absolutely incorrigible and beyond all doubt. It does not follow from this that whatever he thus perceives is true. But this follows, he believes, once he clearly and distinctly perceives that God exists and cannot be a deceiver.

Many philosophers today, though not all, reject the view that we have a faculty of non-sensory cognition which enables us to know that certain things are true, for, they point out, we have no idea how this faculty is supposed to work. Nevertheless, it is a fact which needs explaining that when we consider certain sentences, such as one of the form "If *a* is taller than *b*, and *b* is taller than *c*, then *a* is taller than *c*," they immediately strike us as evidently true, without the aid of the senses. The hypothesis that we recognise such truths by means of a faculty of non-sensory cognition is a hint at a possible explanation of this fact. The fact that a sentence is immediately evident to us is good evidence that it is true, and as Saul Kripke says, "I really don't know, in a way, what more conclusive evidence one can have about anything, ultimately speaking" (Kripke 1980: 42). The rival hypothesis, the Quinean view that whatever we know, we know only because it belongs to a system of beliefs which agrees with experience as a whole, is itself not much more than a hint at a possible explanation of the said fact.

What counts as a clear and distinct perception, for Descartes, is not simply whatever strikes us as evident, for, as he repeatedly stresses, much of what strikes us as evident is mere prejudice and dogma, and some of it is simply false, as we sometimes discover. What counts as a clear and distinct perception is only what strikes us as evident after the meticulously critical kind of analysis which Descartes describes in detail in his *Rules for the Direction of Our Native Intelligence* (written c. 1628), and which he puts into practice in the *Meditations*. Unless we practise this methodical kind of analysis, we may believe that our perception is clear and distinct when it is not. A classic example of this, one might think, is Frege's learning, when it was pointed out to him by Russell, that the fifth axiom of his system in the *Grundgesetze* led to a contradiction. Frege had not taken his usual scrupulous preliminary analysis of his concepts far enough. The example, however, is not quite accurate, for Frege had been troubled by the lack of self-evidence of this axiom long before Russell discovered the contradiction. Still, how can we ever know that we have taken our preliminary analysis far enough? How, in other words, can we ever know that we have reached a belief which is incorrigible? Perhaps we cannot, but nevertheless there comes a point at which further analysis would be absurd.

As for the distinctness of the mind from the body, Descartes got this wrong, one might argue, on the grounds that he failed to recognise that some identity sentences, such as "Hesperus is Phosphorus," are contingently true, and what is more, empirical. The sentence "The mind is identical to the body" is of this kind. To this, Descartes might have replied, anticipating Kripke, that all identity sentences, be they positive or negative, are necessarily true, if true, though some which are true are indeed empirical. Nevertheless, Descartes might have added, in cases where an identity sentence is an empirical truth, as in the Hesperus case, the thing in question can be known to exist only with the aid of sensory experience, whereas in the case of the mind, the thing can be known to exist without the aid of sensory experience, by the mind's awareness of its own awareness. In cases like this, the identity sentence cannot be known to be true with the aid of sensory experience; all that can be known with the aid of sensory experience is that the one thing, a mind, is present only when another thing, a body, is present. But is this not good evidence that the mind and the body are one and the same thing? No, Descartes would have said, for the defining attributes of the mind and the body, thinking and extension, have nothing whatever in common, apart from being attributes. No mode of extension is a mode of thinking, and no mode of thinking is a mode of extension; thinking has no shape, size or motion and is not divisible, let alone infinitely divisible. The fact that the attributes are completely different suggests that the mind is distinct from the body.

Besides, Kripke's view of identity sentences works in Descartes' favour. For, as Kripke points out, many identity sentences appear to be contingently true, even though they must be necessarily true, if true at all. This fact calls for explanation. In the case of the sentence "Heat is identical to the rapid motion of molecules," the explanation is, Kripke suggests, that we pick out the referent of the word "heat," namely, heat, by means of a contingent attribute of heat, namely, the sensation of heat. Since this attribute is contingent, it is possible that, had things been different, heat would have been corre-lated with a different sensation. A similar explanation, however, will not work in the case of the sentence "Pain is identical to C-fibres firing," for we pick out the referent of the word "pain," namely, pain, not by a contingent attribute of pain, but by an essential attribute, namely, the specific phenomenological quality of pain, and it is not possible that, had things been different, pain would not have had this specific quality, for it is of the essence of pain that it has this quality (Kripke 1980: 146–55).

Kripke's argument applies to type–type identities, but a similar argument can be given for token–token identities. A similar argument, moreover, can be given for any mode of thinking whatever, or as we say today, for any mental state.

References

Descartes, René (1984–5) *The Philosophical Writings of Descartes*, vols 1 and 2, trans. John Cottingham, Robert Stoothoff, and Dugald Murdoch, Cambridge: Cambridge University Press.
—— (1991) *The Philosophical Writings of Descartes*, vol. 3: *The Correspondence*, trans. John Cottingham, Robert Stoothoff, Dugald Murdoch, and Anthony Kenny, Cambridge: Cambridge University Press.
Murdoch, Dugald (1993) "Exclusion and Abstraction in Descartes' Metaphysics," *Philosophical Quarterly* 43, no. 170: 38–57.
—— (1999) "The Cartesian Circle," *Philosophical Review* 108, no. 2: 221–44.
Kripke, Saul (1980) *Naming and Necessity*, Cambridge, MA: Harvard University Press.
Wilson, Margaret Dauler (1978) *Descartes*, London: Routledge & Kegan Paul.

Further reading

The present chapter is based on Dugald Murdoch, "Exclusion and Abstraction in Descartes' Metaphysics," *Philosophical Quarterly* 43, no. 170 (1993): 38–57. A thorough and careful introduction to Descartes' metaphysics is Margaret Dauler Wilson, *Descartes* (London: Routledge & Kegan Paul, 1978). For further reading on this topic, see also S. Schiffer, "Descartes on His Essence," *The Philosophical Review* 85, no. 1 (1976): 21–43. Saul Kripke, *Naming and Necessity* (Cambridge, MA: Harvard University Press, 1980) is a modern classic on issues essential to metaphysics.

8
HOBBES
Matter, motion and cause

George MacDonald Ross

Introduction

Thomas Hobbes (1588–1679) is now known mainly as a political philosopher; but in his lifetime, he was equally famous as a metaphysician and natural philosopher. Along with others such as Descartes, Mersenne and Gassendi, he was in the vanguard of the modern movement which swept away the scholastic world view in the middle of the seventeenth century.

Hobbes was a late developer, and his first philosophical writing to appear in print was the third set of objections to the *Meditations* of his younger contemporary, Descartes, which was published in 1641, when Hobbes was 53. However, his major project was to write a three-volume work in Latin called the *Elements of Philosophy*, of which part 1, *On Body*, would be about metaphysics and natural philosophy; part 2, *On the Human Being*, would be about individual psychology; and part 3, *On the Citizen*, would be about political philosophy. For various reasons these parts were written and published out of order: *On the Citizen* was published in 1642; *On Body*, in 1655; and *On the Human Being*, in 1658.

Hobbes was a royalist, and he fled to France in 1640, in advance of the civil war. He did not return to England until 1652. While in exile he made it his priority to write a separate work on political philosophy, *Leviathan*, justifying the absolute authority of the sovereign. He wrote it in English for an English audience, and some of the contents were specific to the English political situation. It was published in 1651. Just as the structure of the *Elements of Philosophy* was determined by Hobbes's belief that the science of politics depends on human nature, and that the science of human nature depends on certain metaphysical principles, the first part of *Leviathan* covers some of the same ground as *On Body* and *On the Human Being*. Towards the end of his life, Hobbes wanted to secure his international legacy by publishing an edition of his Latin writings, and for this he rewrote *Leviathan* in Latin, adding three appendices vindicating his theological views. This edition appeared in two volumes in 1668.

Although the main sources for Hobbes's metaphysics are *On Body* and *Leviathan*, there are metaphysical discussions in other writings, such as the early *Elements of Law* (which was circulated in manuscript in 1640), his debates with John Bramhall about the freedom of the will, and *Ten Dialogues of Natural Philosophy* (1678).

Denial of the immaterial

The scholastic world was full of different kinds of entity. As well as material objects, there were immaterial souls, God, angels, spirits, ghosts, underlying substances, essences, forms, quiddities, space, time, visible species, occult virtues, powers, universals, numbers and so on. Hobbes took the radical step of reducing everything to matter in motion, and the main question for his philosophy is whether the phenomena of human experience can be accounted for on the basis of these two concepts alone. Hobbes spent little time arguing that matter exists: he thought it was proved by reason, since there must be some external cause of our "phantasms," or sensory images. He spent much more time arguing that nothing other than matter exists.

The most controversial aspect of Hobbes's materialism is his denial of immaterial substance. One of his reasons for denying immaterial substance is that he holds that the only things before our minds when we think are images derived from sense experience. Since we do not have sense experiences of immaterial substances, we can have no conception of them, let alone any grounds for supposing that they exist. Thus in the Fifth Objection, he says:

> But when people think of angels, they sometimes have in their minds an image of a flame, and sometimes an image of a pretty little boy with wings. This makes me feel certain that the image does not resemble an angel, and therefore that it is not an idea of an angel. But since I believe that there do exist various created beings which serve God, and that they are invisible and immaterial, I apply the name "angel" to the thing I believe in or suppose to exist, even though the idea through which I imagine an angel is a compound of ideas of visible things. In the same way, we have no image or idea corresponding to the holy name of God. This is why we are forbidden to worship God through images, in case we come to think we can form a conception of Him who cannot be conceived.[1]

At this stage in his development he accepted that there were immaterial beings, even though we could have no conception of them. Presumably he considered it to be an article of Christian faith that such beings existed. However, detailed study of the Bible soon convinced him that there was absolutely no scriptural authority for the concept of immaterial substance. And without this authority, there were no grounds for conceiving of any kind of substance other than material substance, or body. Consequently, there was no distinction between substance and body, and the very concept of an immaterial substance was a contradiction in terms. In *Leviathan* chapter 34, he writes:

> According to this interpretation of the word "body," "body" and "substance" have the same meaning; and consequently the compound expression "incor-

poreal substance" is as meaningless as if you were to say "non-bodily body." And neither that expression, nor the word "immaterial" is to be found anywhere in Holy Scripture.

God as body

It follows from the above that allegedly immaterial substances are either non-existent, or material. So, in the case of God, Hobbes says in the Third Appendix to *Leviathan* (written in dialogue form, with B representing Hobbes's position), "A. [Hobbes] denies that there are any incorporeal substances. What else is this than to deny the existence of God, or to assert that God is body? / B. He does indeed assert that God is body." This raises the question of whether God is one body among many, or all-pervasive. The Latin is ambiguous, since it can be translated either as "God is body" or as "God is *a* body." The former is the only plausible interpretation, because Hobbes did not conceive of God as a remote entity beyond the stars. But what sort of body is he? Hobbes wavers between two positions. In the Third Appendix he tends towards the view that God is the totality of the material universe (a view subsequently taken up by Spinoza). He cites St Paul's statement that "We all have our being and move in God," which could be interpreted as meaning that God is the whole universe; and he denies that God is no more than a rarefied spirit, since rarefaction dilutes the existence of matter: "Those who attribute purity to God are right to do so, since it is an honorific title. But it is dangerous to describe him as a rarefied being, since rarefaction is on a scale leading to nothingness." However, in *An Answer to Dr Bramhall*, he says: "I maintain that God exists, and that he is a most pure, and most simple corporeal spirit." And in the *Ten Dialogues*, he argues that there can be no vacuum, because God is an omnipresent material substance (similar to the ether, which Hobbes also believed in):

> A. Given the rapid vibration of all natural bodies, why should not some small parts of them be thrown off, and leave empty the places they were thrown out of?
> B. Because He who created them is not a phantasm, but the most real substance that exists. Since he is infinite, no place where He is can be empty, and no place where He is not can be full.

Angels imaginary

As for angels, Hobbes dithers as to whether they actually exist as rarefied material spirits, or whether they are no more than mental images conjured up by God as a means of communicating with people. The latter seems to be his preferred view. As he says in *Leviathan*, chapter 34:

> If we consider the passages in the Old Testament where angels are mentioned, we will find that (usually if not always) the word "angel" denotes some sort of an idea which God conjures up in the phantasy, in order to signify the divine presence in some supernatural action of his.

No immaterial soul

Hobbes's assertion that the expression "immaterial substance" is a contradiction in terms commits him to denying the existence of an immaterial soul as well. Human beings are bodies, and everything they do is the product of the motions of their bodily parts. As long as these bodily parts are in motion, humans are alive, and death is when the motions cease.

In fact Hobbes's account of the human body is not so very different from Descartes's. Descartes believed that sensory images were carried by the material "animal spirits" which filled the cavities of the brain, and that most human behaviour was purely automatic. The soul was needed only for intellectual functions, such as talking or writing about philosophy, and for altering the behaviour of the body by an act of will. One might be tempted to add consciousness, in the philosophical sense of being aware of oneself while being aware of other things, but neither Descartes nor Hobbes seem to have had any such concept, and they certainly had no word for it (terms like "consciousness" and "apperception" came into use only towards the end of the seventeenth century).

Descartes's argument for the existence of the soul as an immaterial, naturally immortal, thinking thing was the *cogito* argument, by which he claimed to have a direct awareness of himself as a thinking thing. Hobbes makes two main criticisms of the argument in the Second Objection. The first criticism is that Descartes's argument depends on the principle that there cannot be a thought without a thinker. That is true, but it does not follow that the thinker must be immaterial. Rather, it shows that the thinker must be material, because only material objects can be the subject of actions: "it could be that a thinking thing is that which underlies mind, reason, or understanding as its subject, and hence that it is something corporeal. Mr. Descartes assumes without proof that it is not corporeal." The second criticism is, in effect, the criticism later made by Hume and Kant, that the subject of thought cannot simultaneously be its own object, otherwise there is an infinite regress:

> Even though you can think about your having thought (this form of thinking is nothing other than remembering), it is absolutely impossible for you to think about your present thinking, any more than you can know that you know. That would lead to an infinite regress: how do you know that you know that you know that you know?

In short, we humans know that we can think, because it is something we do all the time. But neither Descartes nor anyone else has shown that it is impossible for a suitably developed material object, such as the human body, to be capable of thinking; and the alternative supposition of an immaterial substance is simply unintelligible.

Immortality

From a theological perspective, a major difficulty with Hobbes's materialism might seem to be that it is incompatible with Christian belief in immortality. Clearly it is inconsistent with the Platonic and Cartesian belief that there is an immaterial realm which is more real than the world of matter, and that the soul naturally returns to it on being released from the body. But, as Hobbes makes clear in the Third Appendix to *Leviathan*, this is not the Christianity of the Bible. According to the Bible, at the Second Coming, Christ will return to earth, and the dead will be raised. The Last Judgment will condemn sinners to a second death (not to eternal punishment), and reward the virtuous with eternal paradise on earth under the rule of Christ. Between the death of the individual and the Second Coming, there is nothing more than a dead body; and making the dead live again is no more miraculous than giving them life in the first place.

Humans and animals

From a philosophical perspective, the problem with Hobbes's materialism is that of how he can articulate the distinction between humans and animals without recourse to an immaterial, rational soul. Hobbes fully accepted the traditional definition of man as a rational animal. Where he diverged from tradition was in holding that human rationality consisted not in possession of a rational soul, but in a capacity which less developed animals lacked. This capacity was a language rich enough to contain general terms. There is nothing magical about language. Words are arbitrarily chosen names of things, and we can communicate with each other successfully when we agree on how names are to be defined. Names can refer to individual things, to properties of things, to classes of things which resemble each other in respect of some property, and to names themselves.

For language to be meaningful, words must directly or indirectly refer back to material objects we experience. Thus we use arithmetical terms for counting things, but there are no numbers; we use geometrical terms for describing the shapes and sizes of things, but there are no abstract geometrical entities; we use general terms for referring indifferently to any number of things which share the same property, but there are no universals or essences or forms. And the abstract terms beloved of metaphysicians and theologians are simply meaningless because they have no application to experience at all.

To return to the question of the distinction between humans and animals, Hobbes makes it clear in the Sixth Objection that animals might have the same thoughts as humans, where by "thoughts" he means a sequence of mental images, but only humans can accompany the thoughts with a linguistic judgment about truth or falsehood, as a sort of running commentary on their experiences:

> Besides, assertion and negation cannot exist without language and names, which is why animals cannot assert or deny anything; nor can they exist without thought, which is why dumb animals cannot make judgments either. All the same, thought can be similar in humans and animals. When we assert that a person is running, we do not have a thought which is any different from that had by a dog watching its owner running. So the only thing that assertion or negation adds to simple thoughts is perhaps the thought that the names which the assertion consists of are the names of the same things in the

mind of the person doing the asserting. This is not to involve in a thought anything more than its resemblance to its object, but to involve that resemblance twice over.

Reasoning

Just as language is a purely natural phenomenon, reasoning is an equally natural process depending on it, and not requiring an immaterial soul. According to Hobbes, reasoning is nothing other than "computation," or adding or subtracting names or sentences. For example, adding "rational" to "animal" gives you a human being; and subtracting "rational" from "human being," gives you an animal. As he says in *Leviathan*, chapter 5:

> These operations are not peculiar to numbers, but apply to any kind of thing of which one can be added to or taken away from another. Just as arithmeticians add and subtract with numbers, so geometricians teach us to do the same with lines, shapes, angles, ratios, times, degrees of speed, forces, powers, and the such like. Logicians too do the same with sequences of words, adding two names together to make a proposition, and two propositions together to make a syllogism, and a number of syllogisms to make a proof; and from the sum or conclusion of a syllogism they subtract one proposition to find another … Wherever there is scope for addition and subtraction, there is also scope for reasoning; and where there is no scope for them, there is no scope for reasoning either.

Hobbes distinguished between empirical (or "historical") knowledge derived from experience, and scientific knowledge (or "science") which depends on reason. He valued the latter more highly than the former, as being distinctive of human intelligence. However, he never managed to explain how it is possible for scientific knowledge to have any *content*, if it consists merely in analytic deductions from definitions; nor how it can apply to reality, if it depends ultimately on arbitrarily defined names. As Hobbes himself admits in the Fourth Objection:

> reasoning can tell us nothing at all about things in the real world, but only about their names. This is so whether or not we combine the names of things in accordance with arbitrary agreements we have made about their meanings. And if this is true (as is possible), then reasoning will depend on names; the names will depend on images; and the images will perhaps (as I believe) depend on the motion of the bodily organs. It follows from this that mind will be nothing other than motions in various parts of an organic body.

His solution was to say that scientific knowledge is essentially hypothetical. Reason alone can supply us with a range of possibilities, but only experience can tell us which is actual.

Matter

Let us now consider what Hobbes has to say about matter itself. In *On Body*, chapter 7, Hobbes discusses the nature of space and time before discussing body. He is absolutely explicit that both space and time are imaginary, and mere phantasms. To put it another way, we have an internal space and time in which we represent things spatiotemporally, but space and time do not exist independently of human perceivers (though in earlier writings he did allow that space and time also existed objectively). Hobbes's implicit argument for saying that there is no objective space and time corresponding to our subjective space and time is that only material objects exist, and if space, for example, were a material object, there would be no room for material things to exist *in* it, since two bodies cannot occupy the same space. However, this creates difficulties for his definition of body in chapter 8. He says:

> We now understand the nature of imaginary space, in which we suppose nothing external to exist, but only the pure absence of the things which, when they existed, left their images in the mind. Let us next suppose that one of these things is put back again, or re-created. It is therefore necessary for that re-created or replaced thing not only to occupy some part of the said space (i.e. to coincide and be coextensive with it), but also to be something which does not depend on our imagination. But this is the very thing which is customarily called *body* on account of its extension; *self-subsistent* on account of its independence from our thought; *existent* because it subsists outside us; and finally *substance* or *subject* because it seems to support and underlie imaginary space, so that it is not by the senses, but only by reason that we understand that something is there. So the definition of body is something like this: *Body is whatever coincides or is coextensive with a part of space, and does not depend on our thought.*

The problem is that the very thing which occupies imaginary space is supposed to exist outside us. This is just about intelligible if we take Hobbes as meaning that we reason that there is an external object corresponding to our image of it in subjective space, and that it has the spatial dimensions we perceive it as having. But there is still the difficulty that it has spatial dimensions, even though there is no objective space for it to occupy. Nevertheless, it is clear that Hobbes believed that bodies are spatially extended, and exist independently of us.

Then there is the question of how body is different from an equivalent volume of empty space. Hobbes seems vulnerable to the same objection as Descartes, that by defining body in terms of its extension, there is no difference between a body and the same amount of empty space. Ancient philosophers had defined matter as extension plus resistance to penetration, and modern philosophers would define it as extension plus mass.

Motion

Although Hobbes does not include this in his explicit definition of body, he makes it axiomatic that all bodies are in motion, and this distinguishes bodies from empty space, because empty space cannot be in motion. In the *Ten Dialogues*, chapter 2, Hobbes comes close to saying that matter would cease to exist if it were not in motion:

> you must enquire thoroughly into the nature of motion, since the differences between one phantasm and another, or (which is the same thing) between one phenomenon of nature and another, all have one universal efficient cause, namely the differences between one motion and another. If all the things in the world were absolutely at rest, there could be no difference between one phantasm and another, and living creatures would be without any sensation of objects; which is hardly less than to be dead.

The motion he is referring to is the motion of the microscopic *parts* of objects, rather than the objects themselves. One of Hobbes's most original concepts was that of conation or endeavour, which he defined as an infinitesimal motion. In *On Body*, chapter 15, article 2, he writes: "I shall define *conation* as *a motion through space and time which is less than any given quantity ... in other words, it is a motion through a point.*" Conation is the ultimate source of all motion in the universe, and hence of all change, since the only change is motion. Hobbes had to define it as an infinitesimal *motion*, because he held that a motion could be caused only by a motion; but the function of the concept is more like that of the modern force or energy. It had a powerful influence on Leibniz, both for the infinitesimal calculus, and for his theory that force or energy is the essence of matter. So in short, for Hobbes, a body is in effect a collection of conations occupying a particular volume of space; and it is by virtue of these conations that bodies resist penetration and acceleration, exert gravitational forces, and do everything that distinguishes them from empty space.

Causation

Conation is also the means by which events are *caused*. Like the other modern philosophers, Hobbes rejected the Aristotelian four causes, and insisted that the only causes are "efficient," or mechanical ones. Further, he restricted mechanical causes to the pushing of one body by another in immediate contact with it (*On Body*, Ch. 9, article 7). Given that there do seem to be many instances in nature of objects attracting or pulling each other, he had hard work explaining how "pulling is really pushing", as he attempts to do in *On Body*, chapter 22, article 12.

Determinism

Hobbes believed that there was no such thing as empty space or a vacuum, but that the whole universe was filled with a subtle ether. This ether was responsible for transmitting light and other forces. For example, the light of the sun is generated by a rapid pulsation of the sun's matter. The surface of the sun pushes against the ether particles closest to it, and they push against the next, and so on to infinity (although in some places he says that the motion will eventually cease). The consequence is that every part of the universe is affected by many other parts, and to know the complete cause of an event would involve knowing almost everything. As he says in *Of Liberty and Necessity*:

> Nor does the co-operation of all causes consist in one simple chain or concatenation, but in an innumerable number of chains. They are not joined together at every point, but they are in the first link, which is God Almighty. Consequently, the whole cause of an event does not always depend on one single chain, but on many together ... (See "Hobbes: Supplementary Extracts on Cause," page 246)

If the complete cause is present, then the effect happens necessarily. As he defines it in *On Body*, chapter 9, article 3:

> *a complete cause is the totality of all the accidents, both of the agents (however many there may be) and of the patient, such that assuming all to be present, it is inconceivable that the effect should not be produced together with it; and assuming one of them to be absent, it is inconceivable that the effect should be produced.*

And again in chapter 9, article 10, he says that the word "contingent" can be used only in a relative sense, and: "In relation to their causes, all things happen with equal necessity; for if they did not happen necessarily, they would not have causes – something which is unintelligible in the case of things which have come into being."

Causation and scientific knowledge

Hobbes made a sharp distinction between empirical (or "historical") knowledge, which consists in reports of particular experiences, and scientific knowledge, which is universal, hypothetical and necessary, and which is due to reason. As we have seen, Hobbes holds that reasoning consists in deducing consequences from arbitrary definitions, and there is a problem over how this can hook on to reality and give us genuine knowledge.

At least a partial solution to this conundrum lies in geometry. In Hobbes's day, it was universally accepted that geometry was necessarily true, and that it was true of the world. Euclid's method was to start with definitions of key concepts, indubitable axioms and less certain postulates, and then deduce theorems from them by logic. Because of the power of Euclidean geometry to yield necessary truths about the world, his method was meticulously followed by Newton, Spinoza and others. Hobbes's emphasis on definitions led him to believe that axioms and postulates were unnecessary, and that everything could be derived from definitions alone. So there was a strong precedent for believing that definitions could yield necessary knowledge of the world.

Next, for Hobbes (as also for Descartes), geometry was not separate from physics. Physics was the science of matter; matter was principally extension, and geometry was the science of extension. A complete description of the world of matter would consist of its geometrical properties (the sizes and shapes of bodies) together with their transformations in time (their motions). So it was not unreasonable to suppose that mechanics might be also an *a priori* science, like geometry.

Then there is Hobbes's belief that geometry is not about abstract entities, but about material objects. When we do geometry, we generate geometrical figures using a straight edge, a scribe and a pair of compasses. The definitions of geometrical figures are in effect rules for generating them. For example, a circle is generated by rotating a pair of compasses round a fixed point; and a sphere is generated by rotating a circle round its diameter. As geometers, our physical constructions coincide exactly with our rational proofs, and the necessities of reason are instantiated in the world of experience.

Finally, we have necessary knowledge of what we ourselves know how to create (in particular, geometrical figures), but not of what depends on the divine will. Using our reason we can make hypothetical judgments about possible causes, but we cannot be certain as to which actual causes God used to generate the observed phenomena. As he says in *On the Human Being*, chapter 10, article 5:

> By contrast, we cannot deduce the properties of real things from their causes, because we do not see these causes – they are not in our power, but lie in the divine will; and the most significant of them, namely the ether, is invisible. However, by drawing consequences from the properties we do see, it is granted to us to advance as far as to be able to prove that such and such *could* have been their causes.

So in the case of geometry we have God-like power, in that we know the only possible ways of generating geometrical figures. However, in the case of physics, we have power enough to imagine different ways in which God might have brought the world into being, but not to know which one he chose.

Conclusion

Hobbes was remarkably bold in rubbishing most of the previous history of philosophy, and attempting to create a complete science of nature, man and society on the assumption that nothing exists apart from matter in motion. No-one, except perhaps for Hobbes himself, would accept that he succeeded in his task. Nevertheless, he earned himself a well-deserved place in the history of metaphysics through his arguments against immaterial beings, his naturalistic account of human language and reason, and his concept of matter as essentially active.

Note

1   All references are to my own translations (http://www.philosophy.leeds.ac.uk/GMR/hmp/texts/modern/ hobbes/hobbesindex.html). The translations are from William Molesworth (ed.), *The English Works of Thomas Hobbes*, 11 vols (London: John Bohn, 1843); and *Opera Latina*, 5 vols (London: John Bohn, 1839–45). I have translated his English writings into modern English, because his English, though beautiful, is sometimes difficult for a modern reader to understand.

Further reading

Most writings about Hobbes focus on his politics, rather than on his metaphysics, or are highly specialised – for example, Steven Shapin and Simon Schaffer, *Leviathan and the Air-Pump* (Princeton: Princeton University Press, 1985) is primarily about Hobbes's argument with Robert Boyle about the existence of a vacuum.

A. P. Martinich, *Hobbes: A Biography* (Cambridge: Cambridge University Press, 1999) is the fullest biography in existence, and it includes extensive coverage of the development of Hobbes's philosophical ideas in their historical context. R. S. Peters, *Hobbes* (Harmondsworth: Penguin, 1956), J. W. N. Watkins, *Hobbes's System of Ideas*, 2nd edn (London: Hutchinson University Library, 1973), and T. Sorell, *Hobbes* (London: Routledge & Kegan Paul, 1986) are classic expositions of Hobbes's philosophy. A simple and brief introduction is R. Tuck's *Hobbes* (Oxford: Oxford University Press, 1989).

9

SPINOZA
Substance, attribute and mode

Richard Glauser

Baruch Spinoza (1632–77), born in Amsterdam of Jewish parents of Portuguese origin, expounded his definitive metaphysical views in his monumental *Ethics: Demonstrated in Geometric Order*. He began writing this work around 1662 and prepared it for publication in 1675, although he may have revised it somewhat before its posthumous publication in 1677. Other relevant sources are his early *Short Treatise on God, Man and His Well-Being* (probably written between 1660 and 1662), his correspondence, and the *Tractatus Theologico-Politicus* (published 1670). Because Spinoza's main concern is ethical in nature, he explains only enough of his metaphysics in *Ethics* as to enable him to reach his goal, which is to show what human freedom is and how it can be attained. Along with Spinoza's fondness of concision, this explains in part why his metaphysics raises important unanswered questions, and why, too, there is little consensus among scholars even on the most basic issues.

In his day, one of the most accomplished exponents – but by no means an advocate – of Descartes' philosophy, Spinoza was fully acquainted with Descartes' criticism of Aristotelian scholasticism. He knew that there nevertheless remained quite a bit of metaphysical ground common to Descartes and the scholastics, namely the claim that, God apart, nature contains an indefinitely large quantity of created substances. Spinoza's metaphysics is revolutionary for many reasons, one of which is his attempt to explode this common ground by showing that there is only one substance, God. All minds and bodies, their states and qualities, that make up nature as produced by God are merely modes of this substance.

Substance and mode

One of the guiding lines throughout Spinoza's metaphysics is his correlation of – and constant distinction between – ontological and conceptual independence and dependence. This is clear, for example, in Spinoza's sharp division of reality between two sorts of particulars, substance and modes. Nothing can be both a substance and a mode; and if something is thought of as being neither (e.g. number), it is not a real being but an *ens rationis*, a figment due to our way of thinking. A substance is defined as what is both in itself and conceived through itself. To say that a substance is in itself is to say that it does not inhere in, or belong to, anything else. It is an ultimate subject of predication; hence it is ontologically independent in comparison with modes, which can exist only by inhering in a substance. To say that a substance is conceived through itself is to say that it is conceptually independent, i.e. the concept of a substance depends on the concept of no other particular being. This is consistent with the fact that the concept of a substance depends on the concepts of its essential properties, for these are not particulars.

Substance is contrasted with mode, which comes from the Latin "modus," meaning "manner." Modes are determinate manners of being or "affections" – qualities or states – of a substance. At the same time many modes are also particular beings inasmuch as they, too, have "affections," states or qualities. The relation of mode to substance is that of unilateral ontological and conceptual dependence. A mode is in a substance, or inheres in a substance, because it is a determinate manner of being of a substance, and so it is ontologically dependent on it. It is also conceptually dependent because the concept of a mode involves the concept of the substance in which it inheres. To say that the concept of A *involves* the concept of B is to say that A cannot be adequately conceived without the concept of B (E IIP49D; see Spinoza 1972 [1925], 1985, 1994).[1] For instance, a mind, its ideas, emotions and other mental states are modes that involve the concept of a thinking substance; a body and its physical states are modes involving the concept of an extended substance.

Attribute

As to thought and extension (three-dimensional space), they are attributes of a substance. These two are the only attributes that can be known by finite minds, although we learn that there is an infinite quantity of other attributes which we do not know, but which God knows. Attributes are essential properties of a substance, and so they are not part of nature as produced by God. All attributes are really distinct, which is to say that no attribute can be conceived by means of the concept of another attribute; all attributes are specifically, or essentially, different.

Spinoza's apparently less than straightforward definition of an attribute has caused much speculation: "By attribute I understand what the intellect perceives of a substance, as constituting its essence" (E ID4). "Perceives" is used here in the very broad sense of the seventeenth century, which includes "conceives," or "intellectually cognises." Further, in speaking of "the intellect" Spinoza surely wishes to include God's infinite (and presumably infallible) intellect. Thus, if God conceives attributes as constituting his essence, then they do, and there can be nothing illusory about the matter. Even so, why does Spinoza not say outright that an attribute is constitutive of a substance's essence? Bennett suggests that attributes are not the most basic properties of a substance, so they are not really, but only apparently, constitutive of a substance's essence (Bennett 1994). One should resist this interpretation because attributes fit Spinoza's definition of an essence: "to the essence of any thing belongs that which, being given, the thing is necessarily posited and which, being taken away, the thing is necessarily taken away; or that without which the thing can neither be nor be conceived, and which can neither be nor be conceived without the thing" (E IID2). In other words, the relation between a substance and whatever constitutes its essence is that of bilateral ontological and conceptual dependence. (As the relation does not obtain between a mode and God, God is not part of a mode's essence.) Because this is presumably the relation that obtains between a substance and any of its attributes, the latter can safely be taken to be a substance's essential properties. Why, then, Spinoza's roundabout definition of an attribute? Because, when using the expression "the intellect" in the definition Spinoza wants to include not only God's infinite intellect, that knows all of his attributes, but also our finite intellects which can know only thought and extension. Far from implying an appearance–reality distinction between a substance's attributes and its essence, Spinoza's definition of an attribute is meant to suggest that, although a substance's essence is really constituted by its attributes, it may be constituted by far more attributes than those conceivable by our finite minds.

When Spinoza occasionally says that an attribute is conceived through itself, he does not mean that the concept of an attribute does not involve the concept of the substance of which it constitutes the essence, for this would contradict his definition of an essence. He means that the concept of an attribute involves the concept of no other attribute. In sum, a substance is ontologically and conceptually independent in comparison with modes. An attribute is conceptually independent with regard to other attributes. But there is bilateral ontological and conceptual dependence between a substance and any one of its attributes. Furthermore, because the essence of a substance is constituted by its attributes, a mode's ontological and conceptual dependence on a substance implies its ontological and conceptual dependence on an attribute of the substance of which it is a manner of being. However, as Descartes, Spinoza believes that a mode depends on only one attribute of only one substance. For instance, the concepts of a certain mind, of all of its ideas, emotions and other mental states involve the concept of thought, but not of extension, nor of any other attribute; the concepts of a certain body and of all of its physical states involve the concept of extension, but not of thought, nor of another attribute. This is why our knowledge of minds and bodies affords us no knowledge of any attributes apart from thought and extension.

Contrary to Descartes, who held that the attribute of thought is instantiated in an indefinitely large number of substances, in Spinoza no attribute can belong to more than one substance. (For if, *per impossibile*, there were two substances, say S_1 and S_2, and if attribute A were instantiated in both of them, the two numerically distinct attributes, A_1 in S_1 and A_2 in S_2, would be conceptually indiscernible, so that it would be possible to conceive S_1 by means of A_2, and S_2 by means of A_1. In the first place, this would contradict Spinoza's definition of what constitutes an essence. Second, it would not be the case that a substance can be conceived only through itself. For, if S_1 could be conceived by means of A_2, and given that A_2 is conceived by means of S_2, then S_1 could be conceived by means of S_2.) Spinoza also holds it true by definition that the more perfection or reality a substance has, the more attributes it has. This is why, contrary to Descartes, a substance can have any quantity of attributes according to its degree of perfection; thus, it is possible for the thinking substance to be extended, too.

Causality and the principle of sufficient reason

Contrary to Hume, in Spinoza the ontological dependence of an effect on its cause is correlated with, yet distinct from, conceptual dependence. The concept of an effect involves, and so depends on, the concept of its cause. If something exists, either a substance or a mode, there is a cause of its existence. Because the knowledge of a cause explains the existence of its effect, Spinoza assimilates causes and reasons, and so – before Leibniz – he holds a certain form of the principle of sufficient reason: nothing exists without a cause or reason. Thus, there is always an answer to the question: Why does something – a substance or mode – exist rather than not? Spinoza also believes that there is always an answer to the converse question: Why does something not exist rather than exist? If something does not exist, there is a reason for its not existing, a cause that prevents it from existing. In a similar vein, if something is finite, there must be a reason for its being finite rather than infinite. For, there must be a cause that prevents the thing from existing beyond the precise limits in virtue of which it is finite.

If something exists, then either (1) the cause or reason of its existence lies within the very nature of the thing, or (2) it is external to it. In the first case the thing is a substance, a necessary being; it is *causa sui*, cause of itself. (Spinoza found the expression *causa sui* in Descartes, but whereas Descartes strove to give it a causal meaning, Spinoza takes it in a more logical sense: a *causa sui* is a being whose essence involves existence.) In the second case the thing is a mode, and it may be called contingent. Conversely, if something does not exist, then either (3) the reason for its not existing lies in the very definition of the thing, or (4) it is external to the thing's nature. In the former case the thing is logically impossible (e.g. the reason for the impossibility of a square circle is its definition); in the latter case the thing is a mode and it may be called contingent. Thus, modes are contingent inasmuch as their mere essence neither involves nor excludes existence. This notion of contingency is based on a mode's *essence*. However, due to its external causes, the *existence* or *non-existence* of a mode is always necessary.

No mode of a certain attribute can be caused, or causally affected, by a mode in another attribute. Otherwise, a mode-effect, say mode X in attribute A, would have to be conceived by the concept of its mode-cause, say mode Y in attribute B, thus making it necessary to conceive X by the concept of Y which involves the concept of B; this is impossible, since a mode conceptually depends on no other attribute than the one it modifies. All the modes that cause, or that are caused by, a certain mode in one attribute are modes of the same attribute. Thus, Spinoza's system rules out any possibility of mind–body or body–mind causation. Minds and their mental states do not cause any actions as realised in bodily movements; bodies and affections of bodies do not cause any of a mind's perceptions.

God's existence

In a system designed not only to incorporate a version of the principle of sufficient reason, but also to account for the possibility of a finite mind's coming to know, to at least some extent, the real causal order of things by adequate knowledge of their causes or reasons, there must be an ultimate reason of all things, and the ultimate reason must be accessible, to some extent, to human knowledge. The ultimate reason of all things is God's essence, the essence of an infinitely infinite substance. It is a complex essence constituted by an infinite quantity of attributes, all of which are specifically different, and each of which is infinite in its own kind. To prove that God exists Spinoza relies on a version of the ontological argument, which, as with Descartes' attempt, is logically flawed. (The flaw consists in taking existence to be a first-order, rather than a second-order, property.) That being said, one can see how Spinoza could easily be drawn into his position on God's necessary existence as *causa sui*, given his conception of causality mentioned above. Furthermore, Spinoza takes it to follow from God's existence that no other substance is possible. Why? Because an attribute can be instantiated in only one substance, and because Spinoza infers – perhaps mistakenly – that since God's essence is constituted by an infinite quantity of attributes, then no attribute can be denied it, and it therefore contains *all possible* attributes. (The move from "infinite" to "all possible" is disputable.) Thus, no attribute can be left to constitute the essence of any other substance.

The question whether God is immanent to the universe or whether he transcends it is controversial. It seems, however, that he is both immanent and transcendent. On the one hand, God is immanent because two of his attributes are thought and, especially, extension. On the other hand, it seems that in at least two respects God transcends the natural world we live in and know. First, God has an infinite quantity of attributes that we cannot even conceive. Second, God's existence is defined as eternity. By "eternity" Spinoza means a form of being that "cannot be explained by duration or time, even if the duration is conceived to be without beginning or end" (E ID8Exp). In other words, God's existence is not infinite duration, but a durationless and timeless being.

God's power

Spinoza was often considered an atheist in his century and the next. Given what we have seen the accusation might seem absurd. What was meant is that Spinoza's conception of God is utterly incompatible with standard theological views in which God is considered an infinite person, and there is much truth in the accusation so construed. God's essence was customarily viewed as principally comprising three infinite attributes: (1) an intellect, by which God is omniscient; (2) a will infallibly directed to the good, thus (Descartes apart) ensuring that the universe is created and causally ordered for a certain purpose or end; and (3) infinite power or omnipotence. From Spinoza's perspective such a representation of God as an infinite person is sheer anthropomorphism.

According to Spinoza God does have an infinite intellect, and an infinite will, but he believes – scandalously at the time – that they are not part of his essence. Instead, they are infinite modes *produced* by God's essence. This means that it is not the case that God thought of the world and willed it before producing it. Instead, God produces together the world and his knowledge of it. He does so by producing, all together, modes of thought, i.e. his true ideas of bodies, and modes of extension, i.e. bodies, so that each and every body is adequately known by God by means of a corresponding true idea. As for God's power, Spinoza follows Descartes in holding that God's essence and power are one and the same thing. But he gives the claim a meaning far removed from anything Descartes imagined. For Spinoza, God's power is nothing more nor less than God's essence considered as productive. On the one hand, God's essence explains his existence, since he is *causa sui*; on the other hand, God's essence is an *essentia actuosa* (E IIP3S), an active essence, inasmuch as it is considered in relation to its effects (so conceived, God is *natura naturans*). The effects are all modes, both infinite and finite; they make up *natura naturata*. God's causality is not creation. He cannot properly be said to create anything at all, for his causality is entirely immanent: all the effects he causes are modes of his attributes.

Spinoza compares the relation of God's essence to his effects with the relation between the essence of a triangle and the property of having the sum of its three angles equal to two right ones (E IP17S). With the comparison kept in mind some of the most daring features of Spinoza's metaphysics readily follow. For example, given God's essence, (1) God produces not only the existence of modes, but also their essences (E IP25); (2) although modes may be called contingent inasmuch as their essences neither involve nor exclude their existence, their existence (whenever they exist) and causal action necessarily follow from God's attributes (E IP29D); (3) there is nothing that God has the power to produce that he does not produce (E IP17S) (are there any geometrical properties that might – but do not – follow from a triangle's essence?); (4) "things could have been produced by God in no other way, and in no other order than they have been produced" (E IP33); therefore (i) it is not the case that God (freely) chooses to produce a world rather than not, and (ii) it is not the case that God (freely) chooses to produce this world rather than another (does a triangle's essence choose its geometrical properties?); (5) God's producing effects, indeed his producing the entire *natura naturata*, aims at no end or goal (is there any end for which a geometrical property follows from the essence of a triangle ?); (6) in a nutshell, "God must be called the cause of all things in the same sense in which he is called the cause of himself" (E IP25S), because "the reason ... or cause, why God, or Nature, acts, and the reason why he exists, are one and the same" (E IVPref).

The causal order of modes

What difference would it make if, instead of there being one substance with an infinite quantity of attributes, there were an infinite quantity of one-attribute substances, or any quantity of substances with attributes distributed between them in various quantities? The answer is that in both of the latter hypotheses, either it would not be the case that the order and connection of ideas is (one and) the same as the order and connection of things, or, if it were the case, no reason could be given for it. This calls for some explanation.

Let us make two preliminary remarks about the claim that "the order and connection of ideas is the same as the order and connection of things" (E IIP7). First, Spinoza says "things," not "bodies," thereby including not only the modes of extension, but also the modes of the other attributes. Second, the Latin wording seems to indicate that "the same," here, means "one and the same." So the claim is that there is only one series, or causal chain, of effects produced by God throughout the infinity of his attributes. This presupposes that, in some sense, God's (true) idea of a certain body, for instance, and the body itself are one and the same item considered, on the one hand, as a mode of thought, and, on the other, as a mode of extension (E IIP7S). Thus, all the ideas that cause, or are caused by, any idea in the attribute of thought are in some sense identical with the bodies and bodily affections that cause, and are caused by, the corresponding body in the attribute of extension. Because Spinoza identifies a finite mind with God's (true) idea of that mind's body, the idea–body identity claim is the basis for Spinoza's mind–body identity claim (E IIIP2S). The idea–body (or mind–body) identity claim, however, is notoriously mysterious for the following reason. A certain body is transitively caused by, and causes, other modes of extension; thus, if an idea of that body is identical with the body, it seems to follow that the idea is caused by, and causes, other modes of extension. This would contradict Spinoza's claim that there can be no cross-attribute causation (Delahunty 1985: 197). Della Rocca (1996) offers an elegant interpretation, based on intensionality, that makes good sense of the identity claim while avoiding Delahunty's difficulty. An alternative reading, however, might be built upon Spinoza's definition of a true idea. A true idea "must agree with its object … i.e. (as is known through itself), what is contained objectively in the intellect must necessarily be in nature" (E IP30D). The definition presupposes an ontological thesis inherited from Descartes. That is, one and the same entity (say a certain body) can have two manners of being: it can exist both formally, i.e. actually, in extension, and also objectively, i.e. as (the content of) a true idea of that body, in thought. According to this comparatively deflationist reading, a finite mind and its body are one and the same thing expressed in two different attributes, inasmuch as the body exists both formally in extension and objectively in thought, as the content of one of God's true ideas, a finite mind.

To return to our main point, the claim that "the order and connection of ideas is the same as the order and connection of things" depends on the cross-attribute identity Spinoza posits between items conceived as modes of extension and the same items conceived as modes of thought (E IIIP2S), and so on throughout the other attributes. The cross-attribute identity of modes depends, in turn, on the fact that all attributes are instantiated in only one substance. Spinoza suggests, therefore, that the reason for there being only one order and connection of the caused items throughout the infinity of attributes is that the series of effects is produced by (the complex essence of) one and the same substance (E IIP7S). Such would not be the case if the attributes belonged to different substances, or, if it were the case, it would lack a reason, thus violating Spinoza's version of the principle of sufficient reason.

Modes again

Curley holds that "the relation of mode to substance is one of causal dependence, not of inherence in a subject" (1991: 37). This reading faces the obvious difficulty of explaining why a mode is called, precisely, a mode, i.e. a manner of being of something else. If Curley were to reply that *immanent* causation suffices to account for the dependence of mode on substance, the rejoinder would be that the very notion of immanent causation depends on the notion of inherence: what makes immanent causation immanent is the fact that the effect inheres in the substance that causes it. So, it is preferable to maintain that inherence and the effect-to-cause relation are distinct. In any case, it is interesting to note that there are other unilateral ontological-dependence relations in Spinoza apart from these two. For instance, Spinoza says that "There are no modes of thinking, such as love, desire, or whatever is designated by the word affects of the mind, unless there is in the same Individual the idea of the thing loved, desired, etc. But there can be an idea, even though there is no other mode of thinking" (E IIA3). In other words, because love, desire and other affects are intentional states, they depend on a mind's having the idea of the thing loved, desired, etc. However, a mind can have an idea of something without loving it or desiring it, etc. This is a unilateral ontological dependence relation that is distinct from both causation and inherence, for the mere idea of X does not suffice to cause love or desire of X, and such affects do not inhere in the idea.

What are the implications of the fact that finite minds and bodies are modes of God?

God's eternity is durationless being. Yet, a finite mode – a mind or a body – finitely echoes God's eternity inasmuch as the duration of the mode's existence is determined neither by its essence nor by the modes that cause it to exist (E IID5Exp). In other words, once finite mode M_1 has caused finite mode M_2 to exist, and if, *per impossibile*, there were no other modes preventing M_2 from existing after a certain time, M_2 would exist indefinitely. Second, God's infinity is the "absolute affirmation of the existence of some nature" (E IP8S1). This can be said, too, of God's power as *causa sui*. Yet, God's infinite power is finitely echoed in a finite mode's *conatus* (its striving to persevere in existence). Although minds and bodies are not *causa sui*, they nevertheless have something in common with God, namely the fact that "the definition of any thing affirms, and does not deny, the thing's essence, *or* it posits the thing's essence, and does not take it away" (E IIIP4D). This is why a finite mode will strive to persevere in its existence for as long as possible, and this striving to persevere is nothing but the mode's actual essence. Thus, just as God's essence, or power, involves his eternal (durationless) existence, a finite mode's actual essence involves a power of indefinite duration of existence (E IIIP7D and P8D). In this way minds and bodies finitely express both God's eternity and his infinite power. One might object that so much could equally be said in a system other than Spinoza's, in which minds and bodies are finite substances created by God and really distinct from his own substance. After all, is it not an accepted theological commonplace that God created man as an image of himself? True, but the fundamental difference between such a system and Spinoza's is that, in Spinoza, because finite minds and bodies are modes of God, the power by which they strive to persevere in existence – and by which they would succeed in existing indefinitely were it not for the action of other finite modes – is part of God's own power as finitely expressed. This is what Spinoza means when he says that minds and bodies are "modes ... that express, in a certain and determinate way, God's power, by which God is and acts" (E IIIP6D). Such would not be the case if minds and bodies were not modes, that is, if – per impossibile – they were finite substances rather than inherent manners of being of God's substance and attributes.

Each attribute has two infinite modes, about which Spinoza says precious little: an infinite mode immediately produced by a certain attribute, and an infinite mode mediately produced by the attribute, that is, produced by the attribute as modified by its immediate infinite mode. The infinite modes of extension are, respectively, motion and rest, and "the face of the whole universe, which face, although it varies in infinite ways, nevertheless always remains the same" (Spinoza 1994: 271–2). The immediate infinite mode of thought is God's intellect, the infinite idea by which God knows his attributes and everything that follows from them. Spinoza does not name the mediate infinite mode of thought. What seems clear enough, though, is that the infinite modes of a certain attribute contain all the finite modes of that attribute. Whereas the immediate infinite mode contains the eternal essences of the finite modes, the mediate infinite mode contains the existing finite modes as they appear and disappear in duration according to their causal sequence and interactions. But, surely more must be involved, and presumably this has to do with causal laws. For instance, Curley plausibly suggests that an attribute contains fundamental principles and causal laws, whereas the infinite modes contain particular laws derived in some way from the former (1988: 42ff.). For all that, though, one of the basic implications of Spinoza's theory of modes is that an existing finite mind is a part of the mediate infinite mode of thought, and a finite mind's essence is a part of God's intellect, the immediate infinite mode of thought. Whereas a finite mind is the very idea by which God knows the finite mind's body, whatever adequate ideas a finite mind has are the very ideas by which God knows the things those ideas are of. A finite mind's adequate knowledge is a part of God's own.

A finite mind's activity depends on acquiring adequate ideas. The effort to acquire such ideas is the effort to free oneself from the bondage imposed by passions. Thus, a finite mind can heighten its conatus and master its passions to some extent by acquiring adequate knowledge of the causal order of things as following from God's attributes. In this life a finite mind can never be entirely free of passions, but it can considerably reduce their bondaging influence. According to Spinoza, "That thing is called free which exists from the necessity of its nature alone, and is determined to act by itself alone" (E ID7). Only God is fully free in this sense. A finite mind, not being causa sui, cannot exist "from the necessity of its nature alone." Yet, the more a finite mind acquires adequate knowledge and develops its conatus, its activity and its mastery over its passions, the more it comes to be "determined to act by itself alone" in comparison with other modes, and the more it comes to love God as the only truly free being. Furthermore, by its adequate knowledge a finite mind can come to know (1) that it is a part of God's intellect; (2) that whatever adequate knowledge it acquires is part of God's infinite knowledge; and (3) that its love of God is a part of God's love of himself. This would be impossible if a finite mind were not a mode of the divine substance.

Note

1   References to Spinoza's *Ethics* are abbreviated as follows: E, *Ethics*; I–V, parts 1–5; A, axiom; D, demonstration, if it follows a proposition (definition, otherwise); Exp, explication; P, proposition; Pref, preface; S, scholium.

References

Bennett, J. (1994) "Eight Questions about Spinoza," in Y. Yovel (ed.), *Spinoza on Knowledge and the Human Mind*, Leiden: Brill, pp. 11–26.

Curley, E. (1988) *Behind the Geometrical Method*, Princeton: Princeton University Press.

—— (1991) "On Bennett's Interpretation of Spinoza's Monism," in Y. Yovel (ed.), *God and Nature – Spinoza's Metaphysics*, Leiden: Brill, pp. 11–25.

Delahunty, R. J. (1985) *Spinoza*, London: Routledge & Kegan Paul.

Della Rocca, M. (1996) *Representation and the Mind–Body Problem in Spinoza*, Oxford: Oxford University Press.

Spinoza, B. (1985) *The Collected Works of Spinoza*, vol. 1, trans. E. Curley, Princeton: Princeton University Press.

—— (1994) *A Spinoza Reader: The Ethics and Other Works*, trans. E. Curley, Princeton: Princeton University Press.

—— (1972 [1925]) *Opera*, 5 vols, edited by C. Gebhardt, Heidelberg: Carl Winter.

Further reading

J. Bennett, *A Study of Spinoza's Ethics* (Cambridge: Cambridge University Press, 1984) is an original and thought-provoking work. R. Brandom, *Tales of the Mighty Dead* (Cambridge, MA: Harvard University Press, 2002), chapter 4, contains a fine discussion of intentionality in Spinoza's theory of ideas. A. Donagan, *Spinoza* (Chicago: Chicago University Press, 1988) is the work of a great scholar. M. Gueroult, *Spinoza*, 2 vols. (vol. 1: *Dieu*, vol. 2: *L'Âme*) (Paris: Aubier-Montaigne, 1968) is a detailed commentary of the first two parts of the *Ethics*. Charles Jarrett, "The Logical Structure of Spinoza's *Ethics*, Part I," *Synthese* 37 (1978): 15–65, is just what it says. Very useful. O. Koistinen and J. Biro (eds), *Spinoza: Metaphysical Themes* (Oxford: Oxford University Press, 2002) is a fine selection of papers on Spinoza's metaphysics. Two collections of papers by leading scholars are Y. Yovel (ed.), *God and Nature – Spinoza's Metaphysics* (Leiden: Brill, 1991) and his *Spinoza on Knowledge and the Human Mind* (Leiden: Brill, 1994).

10
LOCKE
The primary and secondary quality distinction

Lisa Downing

The three distinctions

In Book 2, chapter 8, of John Locke's *magnum opus*, the *Essay Concerning Human Understanding*, he formulates perhaps the most famous and influential version of the distinction between primary and secondary qualities. (It is also the first version to use the terminology of primary and secondary qualities. Important early-modern precedents include Galileo, Descartes and Boyle.) Before one can begin an attempt to analyze Locke's distinction between primary and secondary qualities, one must confront the question: which distinction? The difficulty is that there seem to be at least three primary/secondary-quality distinctions in play in the *Essay*, including a metaphysical distinction, an epistemological distinction, and a physical/scientific distinction. Our first task, then, is to characterize these three distinctions and, then, to consider their relations.

The metaphysical distinction

An unrefined and misleading first pass at Locke's metaphysical distinction might be this: primary qualities are really in bodies, and secondary qualities are not, being merely appearances in our minds. The first amendment we need is that Locke does not deny that secondary qualities are in bodies; however, they are not in bodies in the way that we naïvely take them to be, and they are in bodies in some way inferior to the way in which primary qualities are there. Thus, the metaphysical distinction is, most broadly, a distinction between qualities which are really in bodies and qualities which are, at best, in bodies only in some lesser or dependent fashion. Such a distinction is suggested by the beginning of 2.8.9,[1] where Locke describes the primary qualities as "utterly inseparable from the Body, in what estate soever it be," and is clearly indicated by Locke's repeated insistence that he is identifying the qualities which "*are really in them, whether any one's Senses perceive them or no*" (2.8.17), as opposed to those which are "*imputed*" (2.8.22), and "nothing in the Objects themselves, but Powers" (2.8.10) or "*are no more really in them, than Sickness or Pain is in Manna*" (2.8.17). Let us attempt some further refinements. Perhaps the clearest thing in these matters is that secondary qualities, for Locke, are powers, mere powers, and nothing in the object but powers. They are *dependent* because these powers are causally derived from more basic primary qualities. Primary qualities, then, are really in bodies in that they are intrinsic and irreducible; unlike secondary qualities, they cannot be removed by a reconfiguration of more basic qualities. Such primary qualities ground all of the other powers and behaviors of bodies. Thus, the core of this metaphysical distinction can be captured by the distinction between the intrinsic and irreducible qualities of bodies (the qualities that are always in them and inseparable from them) and other qualities which are dependent on and reducible to those primary qualities.

Now, not *all* powers derived from the intrinsic and irreducible qualities count as secondary for Locke. We have yet to take account of the special role of the senses in the notion of secondary quality. Roughly, it is the powers to produce sensory ideas in us directly that Locke singles out as secondary qualities. Below (in the third section), we will refine this further by considering macroscopic qualities generally and Locke's notion of resemblance. For present purposes, however, of outlining and relating Locke's three distinctions, we should keep our focus on the primary qualities. Locke's metaphysical notion of primary quality can be captured fairly simply by the formula, "the intrinsic and irreducible qualities of bodies."

The epistemological distinction

To locate what I will call the epistemological version of Locke's primary/secondary quality distinction, we need to examine a notorious passage from 2.8:

> Qualities thus considered in Bodies are, First such as are utterly inseparable from the Body, in what estate soever it be; such as in all the alterations and changes it suffers, all the force can be used upon it, it constantly keeps; and such as Sense constantly finds in every particle of Matter, which has bulk enough to be perceived, and the Mind finds inseparable from every particle of Matter, though less than to make it self singly be perceived by our Senses. *v.g.* Take a grain of Wheat, divide it into two parts, each part has still *Solidity, Extension, Figure,* and *Mobility*; divide it again, and it retains still the same qualities; and so divide it on, till the parts become insensible, they must retain still each of them all those qualities. For division (which is all that a Mill, or Pestel, or any other Body, does upon another, in reducing it to insensible parts) can never take away either Solidity, Extension, Figure, or Mobility from any Body, but only makes two, or more distinct separate masses of Matter, of that which was but one before, all which distinct masses, reckon'd as so many distinct Bodies, after division make a certain Number. These I call *original* or *primary Qualities* of Body, which I think we may observe to produce simple *Ideas* in us, *viz.* Solidity, Extension, Figure, Motion, or Rest, and Number. (2.8.9)

The initial thought, that primary qualities are "utterly inseparable from the Body" sounds consistent with the metaphysical version of the distinction canvassed above. However, Locke immediately goes on to provide what seems to be a method of identifying a particular list of qualities by means of sensory and conceptual criteria (Davidson and Hornstein 1984). The primary qualities, here, are those that (1) we always find in every observable particle of matter, no matter how small; and (2) we cannot conceive of bodies being deprived of. The grain of wheat example goes on to illustrate the application of the second, conceptual, criterion. This passage raises many questions about how the sensory and conceptual criteria are supposed to pick out just solidity, extension, figure, motion, rest and number as primary. (Can we conceive of bodies as lacking color? Descartes thought we could, and also thought that we sense bodies that lack color, but this won't work if Berkeley was right that "pellucid is a colour" [Descartes 1984–5: Vol. 1, 227; section 11 of part 2 of the *Principles*, Berkeley 1993: 357; entry 453 of the notebooks]. What about temperature?) But the most serious question raised by this passage is, What are these criteria for? So as not to presuppose an answer to this question without further consideration, I will use "the epistemological distinction" as a name for a version of the distinction according to which the primary qualities are those that the senses constantly find in body and the mind finds inseparable from bodies.

The scientific distinction

To diagnose yet a third distinction, we need only observe the remarkable coincidence between Locke's typical lists of primary qualities, and the lists of basic physical qualities proffered by the corpuscularian natural philosophy of Locke's time. Locke's friend and sometime collaborator, the natural philosopher, chemist and natural theologian Robert Boyle, coined the word "corpuscularian" as an adjective to identify a mechanist physics that attempts to be neutral between Cartesianism and atomism (Boyle 1991: 7). The most central feature of corpuscularian physics was the view that body can be exhaustively characterized by a short list of qualities, including size, shape, impenetrability, number, motion or rest. (Interestingly, Boyle doesn't put impenetrability on his list of "primary affections," presumably because it is a universal characteristic of all matter on his view, and thus not a characteristic that diversifies bodies [Boyle 1991: 50–1].) Locke's discussion of primary and secondary qualities, especially his lists, often seem like they could be taken straight from Boyle. Notably, Locke frequently uses the corpuscularian term of art "texture," meaning a particular spatial arrangement of particles, each with their own set of primary qualities (e.g. 2.8.18). He also uses the corpuscularian term of art, "corpuscle" (2.8.21). It thus appears that Locke has taken his distinction between primary and secondary qualities directly from what he regarded as the best physics of his day. This impression is reinforced by Locke's explicit apology for "this little Excursion into Natural Philosophy" (2.8.22). I will use the label "scientific" for this version of the distinction, despite the anachronism of it, to avoid the long-winded "natural philosophical." On this version of the distinction, "primary quality" denotes whatever qualities the best extant scientific theory takes to be intrinsic and irreducible in bodies. Since, on Locke's view, this turns out to be Boylean corpuscularian, we get corpuscularian lists of primary qualities.

In what follows, I will refer to Locke's core *list* of primary qualities – size (or bulk), shape (or figure), solidity and motion/rest – as the corpuscularian primary qualities or corpuscularian primaries. Locke's lists of qualities vary quite a bit; often he includes number and also texture (spatial arrangement). Not much of philosophical interest hangs on the variation, except for the issue of microscopic vs. macroscopic primary qualities, which is addressed below (in the third section, under "Macroscopic primary qualities").

How are the three distinctions bound into one position?

How are these three distinctions related, for Locke? Of course, one possibility is that Locke simply conflated them, moving from one to another without clear distinction. This would be an exceedingly uncharitable interpretation. It is also unnecessarily uncharitable. Our next step is to explore three different accounts of how the three distinctions are supposed to be related. I will argue that the third interpretation is the best interpretation of Locke's mature position.

The naïve interpretation (the first interpretation)

I call this interpretation naïve because it is the most obvious reading of the text, which, of course, should count as a point in its favor. As we will see, however, it has significant philosophical problems. This interpretation asserts that Locke held that the epistemological distinction tells us that the scientific and metaphysical distinctions coincide. That is, the sensory and conceptual criteria establish that Boyle was right – corpuscularian physical theory correctly characterizes the intrinsic and irreducible qualities of body. So, the metaphysically primary (intrinsic and irreducible) qualities of body are size, shape, solidity, motion/rest, and we know this by reflection on the (purported) fact that these are all and only the qualities that both (1) are always sensed in bodies and (2) cannot be conceived of as absent from bodies. This interpretation is a natural one for two reasons. First, Locke often writes as if we knew that the corpuscularian list of qualities (size, shape, solidity, motion/rest) are metaphysically primary, intrinsic and irreducible. Second, the way in which the sensory and conceptual criteria are presented in the very paragraph that introduces the notion of primary quality suggests that they are supposed to allow us to identify the metaphysically primary qualities.

Against the obviousness of this interpretation, however, stands Locke's epistemic modesty, a commitment at the core of his philosophical identity. Why would Locke rashly assume that sense perception and reflection on sense perception reveal to us the intrinsic and irreducible qualities of bodies? This seems unjustifiably optimistic and goes against the grain of Locke's consistent interest in reminding us of our epistemic limitations. Furthermore, he lectures Descartes harshly for what would seem to be a very similar infraction:

I shall not now argue with those Men, who take the measure and possibility of all Being, only from their narrow and gross Imaginations: but having here to do only with those, who conclude the essence of Body to be *Extension*, because, they say, they cannot imagine any sensible Quality of any Body without Extension, I shall desire them to consider, That had they reflected on their *Ideas* of Tastes and Smells, as much as on those of Sight and Touch; nay, had they examined their *Ideas* of Hunger and Thirst, and several other Pains, they would have found, that they included in them no *Idea* of Extension at all, which is but an affection of Body, as well as the rest discoverable by our Senses, which are scarce acute enough to look into the pure Essences of Things.

If those *Ideas*, which are constantly joined to all others, must therefore be concluded to be the Essence of those Things, which have constantly those *Ideas* joined to them, and are inseparable from them; then Unity is without doubt the essence of every thing. For there is not any Object of Sensation or Reflection, which does not carry with it the *Idea* of one: But the weakness of this kind of Argument, we have already shewn sufficiently. (2.13.24–5)

Our senses are "scarce acute enough to look into the pure Essences of Things" and we ought not to expect our "narrow and gross Imaginations" to fare better. This is quintessential Locke and moreover it seems correct: It is optimistic to expect that the intrinsic and irreducible qualities of bodies are so readily identified.

In defending the naïve interpretation against this critique, one might defend optimism: Why not suppose, defeasibly, that Locke's sensory and conceptual criteria successfully identify the metaphysically primary qualities of bodies and thus show that Boyle was right? After all, Locke thought that Descartes' views about the essence of body were in fact defeated and he did not eschew all conceptual argument (see Jacovides 2002). Arguably, it would have been reasonable for Locke to trust the sensory and conceptual criteria if the results – a corpuscularian account of the primaries – were unproblematic. As a matter of fact, however, Locke became over time increasingly dissatisfied with mechanist physics: It could not explain cohesion, impulse, or how ideas are caused (4.3.29). And the success of Newton's *Principia Mathematica* and his attractionist theory of gravity convinced Locke, by the time of the correspondence with Stillingfleet and the fourth edition of the *Essay*, that the corpuscularian account of body's nature that fits with our conception of matter could not be fully adequate (see also Locke 1989: 246):

The gravitation of matter towards matter, by ways inconceivable to me, is not only a demonstration that God can, if he pleases, put into bodies powers and ways of operation above what can be derived from our idea of body, or can be explained by what we know of matter, but also an unquestionable and every where visible instance, that he has done so. (Locke 1823: Vol. 4, 467–8)

... gravitation of matter towards matter, and in the several proportions observable, inevitably shows, that there is something in matter that we do not understand. (Locke 1823: Vol. 4, 464–5)

Surely these difficulties suffice to motivate the search for other interpretations of the relations among Locke's three distinctions.

The naturalist interpretation (the second interpretation)

An interpretation made prominent by Peter Alexander (1985) is that the *Essay* simply begins from the assumption that the best scientific theory of the time is broadly correct; the *Essay* is premised on the truth of corpuscularianism. So, Locke assumes that the scientific distinction and the metaphysical distinction coincide. The sensory and conceptual criteria, on this sort of interpretation, can function merely as reminders of the appeal of corpuscularian theory: it coheres with the conception of body we derive from reflection on sensory experience.[2]

This interpretation undeniably has its attractions. Since naturalism is attractive to many contemporary philosophers, this seems a charitable interpretation of Locke. More significantly, it neatly explains the above-noted remarkable coincidence between Locke's lists of primary qualities and corpuscularian physical theory. Against it, however, there are at least three points. First, as briefly argued in the second section, under "The naïve interpretation," above, by the time of the fourth edition of the *Essay*, Locke holds that Newton has shown that corpuscularianism isn't an adequate physical theory. If the *Essay* were premised on the truth of corpuscularianism, this surely would have called for more revision. Second, in every edition, Locke thinks of the work of the *Essay* as being prior to physical theorizing.

Third, and most importantly, there is good reason to take the metaphysical distinction to be the central version of the distinction. If we look at the beginning of 2.8, we see that it is introduced as a sort of appearance/reality distinction, as an important qualification to the earlier thought that because we are passive in sense perception, the mind is a sort of mirror (2.1.25). This is the point of Locke's introductory discussion in 2.8 of positive ideas (e.g. the idea of cold) from privative causes (e.g. the absence of motion). But if the distinction is first and foremost a metaphysical one, why foreclose the possibility that our science hasn't yet hit on the correct account of it? That Locke's notion of primary quality is metaphysical, and that he regards the correct account of it as an open question, is further established by the fact that he sees it as logically connected to the notion of real essence, which is manifestly an abstract, metaphysical notion in his theorizing. It is this last point that motivates the third interpretation, so I will turn to expounding it.

The third interpretation – corpuscularianism as uniquely good exemplar of the metaphysical distinction

Locke officially introduces his notions of real and nominal essence as follows:

> *First, Essence* may be taken for the very being of any thing, whereby it is, what it is. And thus the real internal, but generally in Substances, unknown Constitution of Things, whereon their discoverable Qualities depend, may be called

their *Essence*. This is the proper original signification of the Word, as is evident from the formation of it; *Essentia*, in its primary notation signifying properly *Being*. And in this sense it is still used, when we speak of the *Essence* of particular things, without giving them any Name.

Secondly, The Learning and Disputes of the Schools, having been much busied about Genus and Species, the Word Essence has almost lost its primary signification; and instead of the real Constitution of things, has been almost wholly applied to the artificial Constitution of *Genus* and *Species*. 'Tis true, there is ordinarily supposed a real Constitution of the sorts of Things; and 'tis past doubt, there must be some real Constitution, on which any Collection of simple *Ideas* co-existing, must depend. (3.3.15)

The notion of real essence outlined here is an abstract, metaphysical one; the real essence of something is its fundamental principle or constitution, the source of its further qualities. Locke goes on in 3.3.17 to note two different hypotheses about what the real essences of material substances are like: the first, an Aristotelian hypothesis, and the second, broadly corpuscularian. While in much of the *Essay*, Locke describes real essences in thoroughly corpuscularian terms, I suggest that this passage tells us exactly how to understand such talk. Locke considers that corpuscularian theory *illustrates* the abstract metaphysical notion of real essence and provides a concrete *hypothesis* about what real essences might be like. But real essence and primary quality are closely connected notions. A real essence is the ultimate source of a thing's observable qualities. Primary qualities are the intrinsic and irreducible qualities of bodies that ground their other powers. A body's real essence is thus some particular instantiation of a set of primary qualities, i.e. a configuration of primary qualities. Textual evidence that Locke sees the logical connection between these two abstract, metaphysical notions is provided by passages such as 4.6.7: "we know not the real Constitutions of Substances, on which each *secondary Quality* particularly depends." "Real constitution" is systematically used by Locke as synonymous with "real essence." He says here, then, that secondary qualities depend on real essences. But, of course, Locke usually describes secondary qualities as depending on *primary qualities*. This highlights the logical relationship between these two notions.

What falls out of this observation is the following interpretation of Locke's threefold primary/secondary quality distinction: The notion of primary quality is first and foremost an abstract, metaphysical one, the notion of an intrinsic and irreducible quality of bodies. The scientific version of the distinction, the corpuscularian account, *illustrates* this metaphysical notion and provides a concrete *hypothesis* about what the intrinsic and irreducible qualities of bodies in fact are. Officially, however, it is just an hypothesis; Locke remains open to the possibility that the metaphysically primary qualities of bodies are in fact different from the corpuscularian list. (They might, for example, include qualities unfamiliar from sense perception, say, spin or charm.)

Of course, this raises as a puzzle the question of what the sensory and conceptual criteria are doing in 2.8.9. The answer is that they point out the way in which corpuscularianism is more than a *mere* hypothesis: It represents a uniquely intelligible hypothesis for us, because it corresponds to the way in which we conceive of bodies based on reflection on sense perception. Corpuscularianism thus provides a uniquely good illustration of the abstract notions of primary quality and real essence, and a uniquely natural proposal as to what the primary qualities might be and what real essences might be like (see Downing 1998; also compare McCann 1994). Another way to put this point is that what's unique about corpuscularian physical theory is that it proposes that the real essence of body corresponds to the nominal essence that we assign to body (Ayers 1981: 229; Atherton 1984: 418).

But if the corpuscularian list is just an hypothesis about what the primary qualities of bodies might be, why does Locke not present these lists in some more qualified fashion? The reply is twofold. First, it is simply the case that Locke often writes in terms of the most intelligible hypothesis about what might fill this metaphysical role. Additionally, at an early stage of the writing of the *Essay*, he was inclined to assume that Boyle's theory was true, and while revisions to the fourth edition of the *Essay* amend this, they don't remove all traces of the earlier view (see Downing 2008).

The central advantages of this interpretation are that it respects the fundamentally metaphysical character of the distinction, it recognizes the parallel status that ought to attach to real essence and primary quality, it represents the sensory and conceptual criteria as meant to accomplish something they can accomplish, and it gives Locke a consistent attitude towards corpuscularian physical theory throughout the *Essay* – it is an hypothesis upon whose truth it is not his business to pronounce (4.3.16).

Remaining issue: Is the distinction founded on relativity arguments?

In passages such as 2.8.21, some have read Locke as arguing in something like this fashion: The water feels cold to one hand and warm to the other. But the water cannot be both cold and warm. Therefore, temperature is not a quality of the water itself. This sort of relativity argument might seem a convenient way of stripping the secondary qualities from bodies, leaving the primary. It would be possible to defend an analog of the "naïve interpretation" above, suggesting that Locke is trying to use relativity arguments to ground, philosophically, the claim that size, shape, solidity, motion/rest, number are metaphysically primary. This seems to be how Berkeley read Locke. However, such arguments are so bad and Berkeley's criticisms so good that this is nowadays a very unpopular reading. The central problem with such arguments is that, as Berkeley observed in section 14 of his *Treatise Concerning the Principles of Human Knowledge*, they don't establish that the quality in question isn't in bodies, just that we do not know by sense which quality (heat or cold) is in the body. And, as Berkeley also pointed out, there is plenty of perceptual variability when it comes to qualities such as size, shape, and motion; so if this argument is taken to show that color is in the mind, it should be taken to show that shape is there as well (Berkeley 1993: 94). Most contemporary commentators agree that in one way or another we should see these arguments as illustrating the explanatory power of corpuscularian mechanism. On interpretation one above, this offers further confirmation that Boyle was right. On interpretation two, this further illustrates the attractiveness of Boyle's mechanism, though it isn't supposed to establish its truth. On interpretation three, it further exhibits the naturalness of Boyle's theory and further illustrates how metaphysically secondary qualities may be grounded in and explained by metaphysically primary ones.

Refining the metaphysical distinction

I have argued that the primary/secondary quality distinction for Locke was primarily a metaphysical distinction, that a primary quality is an intrinsic and irreducible quality, and that a secondary quality is a power to produce an idea in a perceiver, grounded in primary qualities. We can refine this distinction further by asking two difficult questions: (1) What about macroscopic primary qualities? (2) What are powers and to what extent are secondary qualities dependent on our senses?

Macroscopic primary qualities

On the interpretation of the primary/secondary quality distinction laid out thus far, the core distinction is between fundamental (primary) properties and other qualities which causally result from these fundamental properties. This suggests that primary qualities are properties of the inner constitutions of things, which, if the corpuscularians were right, would be corpuscular constitutions. This fits with many of Locke's descriptions of primary qualities (e.g. 2.8.10, which attributes primary qualities to the "insensible parts" of objects); however, he also speaks of macroscopic qualities, e.g. the size, shape, motion of observable material objects, as primary qualities. But the situation is complicated, for Locke also specifically acknowledges that all macroscopic, observable qualities are *powers*, powers to produce ideas in perceivers (2.8.8). The key here is Locke's (much-debated) notion of resemblance. Some of our ideas may resemble the ultimate qualities of bodies, that is, may give us an accurate conception of the types of qualities that are intrinsic and irreducible in bodies. Any qualities corresponding to such ideas count as primary for Locke. Thus, the notion of primary quality turns out to be disjunctive: both the intrinsic, irreducible properties of bodies (which might belong only to submicroscopic parts, and so be unobservable) *and* those macroscopic qualities or powers (which might themselves be reducible) which provide us with an accurate conception of the intrinsic, irreducible properties count as primary qualities (see Downing 1998). Thus, again, if the corpuscularians were right, the shapes of corpuscles would be primary qualities, and so would be the shapes of apples. (It is theoretically possible, however, that all observable qualities are primary, or that none are. Locke is inclined to suppose that the truth lies in-between.)

What sorts of powers are secondary qualities?

Secondary qualities, then, are powers to produce ideas in us directly, ideas which do not resemble the ultimate qualities of bodies, that is, do not give us an accurate conception of the sorts of qualities that are intrinsic and irreducible in bodies. Such qualities are "mere" powers because of the non-resemblance. The point of adding "directly" is so as to distinguish secondary qualities from what scholars usually call "tertiary qualities" (and Locke calls at 2.8.26 "secondary Qualities, mediately perceivable"), which are powers to affect other objects such that they produce different ideas in us, e.g. the sun's power to melt wax. Color, taste, temperature, odor would all be such secondary qualities, if the corpuscularians were right. (And, although I've argued above that Locke isn't committed to the truth of corpuscularianism, I do think he thinks it overwhelmingly likely that colors, etc., are merely secondary and not intrinsic and irreducible.)

At least one tricky issue remains: How should we understand the powers that secondary qualities are? A fairly standard reading here is that secondary qualities are dispositions to produce ideas in perceivers. So the greenness of an apple is (something like) the disposition it has to produce a certain sort of idea in normal perceivers under standard circumstances. The object retains the disposition and remains green even if all perceivers leave the room or all perceivers are annihilated. Against this, it has been observed that Locke asserts emphatically that "Porphyre has no colour in the dark" (2.8.19). Matthew Stuart (2003) has argued powerfully from such passages that secondary qualities for Locke are "degenerate powers," that is, powers that objects have just in case an actual n-place relation obtains between an object, a perceiver and whatever other $(n-2)$ items are required for the production of an actual idea. Although there is a real tension in Locke on this issue, I think we are better off with the standard reading. Degenerate powers would be actualities, not potentialities. This does not fit with Locke's account of power in 2.21, which surely should be taken as his considered account. Furthermore (as Stuart himself observes), if things lose and gain secondary qualities at the drop of a hat, they will also lose and gain membership in kinds at the drop of a hat, something Locke shows no signs of countenancing. (E.g. the ring on my hand will cease to be gold whenever I avert my gaze, since yellowness is part of the nominal essence of gold.) The best explanation for the porphyry-type passages is that Locke is inclined to think that what are primarily (or, at least, in one important sense) green, red, colored, hot, etc., are our ideas, and that he is shifting to color-as-idea in these passages (see 2.8.17; for different versions of this sort of interpretation see Alexander [1985, 118] and Jacovides [1999, 2007]). Color-as-quality, however, is a disposition. Such dispositions depend for their existence on the primary qualities of bodies, and for their individuation on the faculties of perceivers.

Notes

1   All references to Locke's *Essay* are to Locke (1975), given by book, chapter and section numbers.
2   Note that this is not exactly how Alexander treats 2.8.9; see Alexander (1985: 119).

References

Alexander, Peter (1985) *Ideas, Qualities, and Corpuscles: Locke and Boyle on the External World*, Cambridge: Cambridge University Press.
Atherton, Margaret (1984) "Knowledge of Substance and Knowledge of Science in Locke's *Essay*," *History of Philosophy Quarterly* 1: 413–27.

Ayers, Michael (1981) "Mechanism, Superaddition, and the Proof of God's Existence in Locke's *Essay*," *Philosophical Review* 90: 210–51.

Berkeley, George (1993) *Philosophical Works: Including the Works on Vision*, edited by Michael Ayers, London: J.M. Dent & Sons; Rutland, VT: Charles E. Tuttle.

Boyle, Robert (1991) *Selected Philosophical Papers of Robert Boyle*, edited by M. A. Stewart, Indianapolis, IN: Hackett.

Davidson, A. I. and Hornstein, N. (1984) "The Primary/Secondary Quality Distinction: Berkeley, Locke, and the Foundations of Corpuscularian Science," *Dialogue* 23: 281–303.

Descartes, René (1984–91) *The Philosophical Writings of Descartes*, 3 vols, edited, trans. by John Cottingham, Robert Stoothoff, Dugald Murdoch, and Anthony Kenny, Cambridge: Cambridge University Press.

Downing, Lisa (1998) "The Status of Mechanism in Locke's *Essay*," *Philosophical Review* 107: 381–414.

—— (2008) "The 'Sensible Object' and the 'Uncertain Philosophical Cause'," in D. Garber and B. Longuenesse (eds), *Kant and the Early Moderns*, Princeton, NJ: Princeton University Press, pp. 100–16.

Jacovides, Michael (1999) "Locke's Resemblance Thesis," *Philosophical Review* 108: 461–96.

—— (2002) "The Epistemology under Locke's Corpuscularianism," *Archiv für Geschichte der Philosophie* 84: 161–89.

—— (2007) "Locke on the Semantics of Secondary-Quality Words: A Reply to Matthew Stuart," *Philosophical Review* 116: 633–45.

Locke, John (1823) *The Works of John Locke*, 10 vols, London: for Thomas Tegg.

—— (1975) *An Essay Concerning Human Understanding*, edited by Peter H. Nidditch, Oxford: Clarendon Press.

—— (1989) *Some Thoughts Concerning Education*, edited by J. W. Yolton and J. S. Yolton, Oxford: Clarendon Press.

McCann, Edwin (1994) "Locke's Philosophy of Body," in V. Chappell (ed.), *The Cambridge Companion to Locke*, Cambridge: Cambridge University Press, pp. 56–88.

Stuart, Matthew (2003) "Locke's Colours," *Philosophical Review* 112: 57–96.

Further reading

The best analysis of Boyle on qualities is Peter Anstey, *The Philosophy of Robert Boyle* (London: Routledge, 2000). Michael Ayers, *Locke*, 2 vols (London: Routledge, 1991) is of interest on every aspect of Locke. E. M. Curley, "Locke, Boyle, and the Distinction between Primary and Secondary Qualities," *Philosophical Review* 81 (1972): 438–64, is an influential article. E. J. Lowe, *Locke on Human Understanding* (London: Routledge, 1995) is an introduction to the *Essay*, with a dispositionalist interpretation of Locke on secondary qualities. An influential treatment which helped to revive interest in Locke's connection with Boyle is Maurice Mandelbaum, "Locke's Realism," in *Philosophy, Science, and Sense Perception: Historical and Critical Studies* (Baltimore, MD: Johns Hopkins University Press, 1964), pp. 1–60. Michael Jacovides, "Locke's Distinctions between Primary and Secondary Qualities," in Lex Newman (ed.), *The Cambridge Companion to Locke's Essay* (Cambridge: Cambridge University Press, 2007), pp.101–29, diagnoses multiple (six) versions of the distinction in Locke (an excellent source for further references). Samuel Rickless, "Locke on Primary and Secondary Qualities," *Pacific Philosophical Quarterly* 78 (1997): 297–319. Robert Wilson, "Locke's Primary Qualities," *Journal of the History of Philosophy* 40 (2002): 201–28. Kenneth Winkler, "Ideas, Sentiments, and Qualities," in Phillip D. Cummins and Guenter Zoeller (eds), *Minds, Ideas, and Concepts: Essays on the Theory of Representation in Modern Philosophy* (Atascadero, CA: Ridgeview, 1992), pp. 151–65, includes a short but judicious treatment of the distinction in Locke. A very good introduction to Locke, with a chapter on the distinction that provides useful historical context emphasizing Locke's anti-scholasticism, is R. S. Woolhouse, *Locke* (Minneapolis: University of Minnesota Press, 1983).

11
LEIBNIZ
Mind–body causation and pre-established harmony

Gonzalo Rodriguez-Pereyra

Causation was an important topic of philosophical reflection during the seventeenth century. This reflection centred around certain particular problems about causation, one of which was the problem of causation between mind and body. The doctrine of the pre-established harmony is Leibniz's response to the problem of causation between mind and body.

In this chapter I shall (a) explain the problem of mind–body causation; (b) explain Leibniz's pre-established harmony; and (c) assess his case for it.

The problem of mind–body causation and the pre-established harmony

There is a regular correlation between what happens in the mind and what happens in the body. This correlation is manifested in two groups of cases, one concerning perception and sensation, and the other concerning action. For instance, if my body were to be cut then, normally, I would feel a sensation of pain. Or if something with certain characteristics, say brown and round, were placed within my visual field in certain circumstances, say under optimal conditions of illumination etc., then I would have a visual perception of something brown and round. Similarly, if in certain circumstances, for instance that my arm were untied, I had the desire of moving my arm, then my arm would move.

The correlation between mind and body, or between states thereof, constitutes the data of the problem. And the problem consists in explaining these data. Initially this looks like an easy problem: what explains the correlation between mind and body is causation between mind and body. When I perceive or feel a sensation, the state of a part of my body, my brain, causes my mind to be in a certain state, a perceptual state or the state of having a certain sensation. And when I act, a state of my mind, the state of desiring to move my arm, causes the state of being in movement in my arm, a part of my body.

This solution was deeply problematic in the context of seventeenth-century metaphysics. Descartes was inclined towards such a solution, but it caused him and his followers quite a problem. For Descartes maintained the following two propositions:

(1) Cause and effect must be similar.
(2) Mind and body are dissimilar.

The sense in which mind and body are dissimilar is that they have different natures or essences. That is the sense in which, at least when both cause and effect are finite beings, they must be similar. Now, those two propositions are clearly inconsistent with this one, to which anyone adopting the causal explanation of the correlation between the states of mind and body is committed:

(3) Mind and body causally interact.

Some have argued that it was precisely this inconsistency that led to the downfall of Cartesianism as a school of thought in the late seventeenth century (Watson 1966). (That Descartes was committed to (1), or to a version of (1) that creates philosophical trouble, is controversial (see Loeb [1981] and Schmaltz [2006] for discussion and criticism of this view)).

To solve this problem it is sufficient to reject one of those three propositions – for any two of those three propositions are mutually consistent. Let us ignore propositions (1) and (2) and concentrate on proposition (3). Leibniz rejected (3): for him, the mind does not act upon the body and the body does not act upon the mind. This is not a doctrine that Leibniz restricts to the case of mind and body. For him only God can act upon a created or finite substance. But for Leibniz no finite, created substance acts upon another. So Leibniz denies any sort of causation among finite or created substances. As he says,

> There is also no way of explaining how a monad can be altered or changed internally by some other creature ... The monads have no windows through which something can enter or leave. Accidents cannot be detached, nor can they go about outside of substances, as the sensible species of the Scholastics once did. Thus, neither substance nor accident can enter a monad from without. (*Monadology*, in Leibniz 1989: §7)

"Monad" is Leibniz's technical term for individual substances. Leibniz is, in the passage just quoted, putting forward an important metaphysical thesis: the denial of inter-substantial causation between created or finite substances. For Leibniz the world is composed of infinitely many finite substances which are completely causally isolated from one another, since they cannot act upon each other. This is what led Leibniz to say that every substance is like a world-apart, independent of any other thing save God (*Discourse on Metaphysics*, in Leibniz 1989: §14).

But if Leibniz denies inter-substantial causation, what is his solution to the problem of mind–body causation? How does he explain the correlations between the states of the mind and the states of the body? This is the function of his doctrine of the pre-established harmony. Leibniz states it in the following passage:

> ... the soul does not disturb the laws of the body, nor the body those of the soul; and ... the soul and the body ... only agree together; the one acting freely, according to the rules of final causes; and the other acting mechanically, according to the laws of efficient causes ... God, foreseeing what the free cause would do, did from the beginning regulate the machine in such manner, that it cannot fail to agree with that free cause. (Fifth letter to Clarke, in Leibniz and Clarke 1956: Para. 92)

According to this doctrine although the mind and the body do not causally interact, God has made them coordinate perfectly, so that both act as they would act *if* they causally interacted. Thus the harmony that obtains between mind and body has been previously established by God.

But in what sense do the states of the mind and the body harmonise or correspond? They correspond in the way in which they would correspond if they causally interacted with each other. For instance, God made the mind and the body such that when the mind is in a state of willing to move a certain arm in a certain way at time t_1, the arm in question moves in that way at t_1; and when the body is cut with a knife, the mind has, at that very same time or shortly thereafter, a sensation of pain. So although there is no inter-substantial causation, substances act as if there were: "... bodies act as if there were no souls (though this is impossible); and souls act as if there were no bodies; and both act as if each influenced the other" (*Monadology*, §81). Although for Leibniz no created substance acts upon another, there are passages where Leibniz speaks of a substance acting upon another. This does not mean that Leibniz contradicts himself: in such passages he is speaking with the vulgar while thinking with the learned. In *Discourse on Metaphysics*, §15, Leibniz explicitly says that we must reconcile the language of metaphysics with practice. Basically he says that we say that a substance A acts upon a substance B when A expresses what happens in B more clearly than B expresses what happens in A. Here expression is a non-causal relation of correspondence or correlation.

Thus Leibniz can solve the problem of mind–body causation. He does not deny the data to be explained, but instead of explaining the correspondence in terms of causation between the mind and the body, he explains it in terms of a divinely pre-established harmony between them.

But this doesn't mean that the Leibnizian world is wholly devoid of causation. There are two kinds of causation for Leibniz:

(1) Causation by God: God creates and sustains finite substances in existence.
(2) Intra-substantial causation: the states of a finite substance are caused by the active force inherent to the substance.

The doctrine of the pre-established harmony can be taken to consist of the following elements:

(a) No finite substance acts upon any other finite substance.
(b) Every non-miraculous state of a finite substance is a causal effect of its inherent active force.
(c) God has set up the mind and the body so that there is a correspondence between their states.

Component (b) is Leibniz's doctrine of the spontaneity of substances, according to which substances have their principle of action within themselves, and so each non-miraculous state of a substance is caused by something internal to the substance. (As stated, [b] is the view attributed to Leibniz by Bobro and Clatterbaugh [1996: 409]. Other authors, like Sleigh [1990] and Kulstad [1993] attribute to Leibniz a position, for which there is also textual basis, according to which every non-miraculous non-initial state of a substance is a causal effect of the preceding state. Bobro and Clatterbaugh [1996] discuss this other view.)

Note that the thesis of spontaneity is not equivalent to the thesis that no finite substance acts upon any other finite substance. Indeed the French philosopher Nicolas Malebranche (1638–1715) denied inter-substantial causation without maintaining intra-substantial causation and therefore without maintaining the thesis of spontaneity for finite substances. For Malebranche no finite substance is causally efficacious and so no finite substance acts upon any other finite substance, but he thought that every state of every substance is an effect not of its own active force but of the action of God.

It is important to note that the three components of the pre-established harmony are logically independent. For instance God could have set up the mind and body so that there is a correspondence between their states, by making it the case that each state of one is an effect of the other, and never of its own inherent active force. Thus (c) is logically independent of (a) and (b). Similarly (b) could be true even if God did not exist and some states of finite substances (or indeed all of them) were also an effect of other finite substances – so some states of substances would be causally overdetermined in this situation. Thus (b) is logically independent from (a) and (c). Finally, (a) could be true even if there were no correspondence between the states of the mind and body and each state of every substance were uncaused. Thus (a) is logically independent from (b) and (c). If so, that Leibniz has arguments for some of the components of the pre-established harmony is no guarantee that he has arguments for the others.

Note that the doctrine of the pre-established harmony is contingent, since it is not true in every possible world. It might be that Leibniz thought that components (a) and (b) of the pre-established harmony are necessary. But even if that is the case, the whole doctrine is contingent because component (c) is contingent, since there are possible worlds where minds and bodies don't harmonise with each other.

The arguments for the pre-established harmony

How does Leibniz argue for the pre-established harmony? One of Leibniz's characteristic theses on substance was that each substance has an individual concept so complete that it contains all the predicates of the substance, in the sense that it is possible to deduce from its concept everything that happens to the substance in question. Thus if one had perfect knowledge of the concept of Caesar one would be able to deduce that he crossed the Rubicon and that he wrote *De bello Gallico*. Some texts suggest that Leibniz attempted to derive component (a) of the pre-established harmony from this doctrine about the individual concepts or notions of substances. The following passage provides textual basis for this interpretation:

> The complete or perfect notion of an individual substance contains all its predicates, past, present and future. For certainly it is now true that a future predicate will be, and so it is contained in the notion of a thing [...] Strictly speaking, one can say that no created substance exerts a metaphysical action or influx on any other thing. For ... we have already shown that from the notion of each and every thing follow all of its future states. (*Primary Truths*, in Leibniz 1989: 32–3)

The idea seems to be that since all the predicates of a substance are contained in its concept, the having of any states corresponding to such predicates does not result from the action of another finite or created substance. As pointed out by C. D. Broad (1975: 46–7), this idea is fallacious. From the fact that all predicates are contained in the concept of a substance it does not follow that nothing external acts upon a substance. After all, the concept of a substance could contain a predicate like "is caused to be F by substance *x*."

It might be replied that the concepts of substances do not contain such causal predicates. But for Leibniz *every* predicate of a substance is contained in its concept. Thus one needs another argument to deny that such causal predicates are true of substances.

Since Leibniz's argument doesn't establish even (a), it doesn't establish the whole doctrine of the pre-established harmony. Another argument against inter-substantial causation appears in the *Monadology* (§7), where Leibniz says this:

> There is also no way of explaining how a monad can be altered or changed internally by some other creature, since one cannot transpose anything in it, nor can one conceive of any internal motion that can be excited, directed, augmented, or diminished within it, as can be done in composites, where there can be change among the parts.

A problem with this argument is that it assumes that the only way in which a monad could be affected would be by affecting its parts. But this assumption is unwarranted since Leibniz admits intra-monadic causation, and such causation cannot be effected by affecting the monad's parts, since monads have no parts. And Leibniz does not say why while intra-substantial causation does not work by affecting parts, inter-substantial causation would (see Broad 1975: 48; Loeb 1981: 271–2).

In other texts, Leibniz attempts to establish the pre-establish harmony as a whole, rather than parts of it. From 1695 onwards he usually uses an argument from elimination to support the pre-established harmony. Typically, he thinks that there are three theories that can explain the correspondence between mind and body, and that pre-established harmony is the best. These are the following:

(a) Interactionism, or "the way of influence"
(b) Occasionalism, or "the way of occasional causes"
(c) Pre-established harmony.

This argument succeeds only if the list of solutions is exhaustive. But it is not, since Spinoza's solution has been left out. But in many writings Leibniz makes clear why he rejects Spinozism. Nevertheless it is not clear that Spinozism is the only omission. But let us ignore the inexhaustiveness of the list and proceed to examine Leibniz's reasons to discard interactionism and occasionalism.

What Leibniz calls "the way of influence" is the theory that there is causal inter-action between the mind and the body. But Leibniz finds this inexplicable, because he thinks that if there were causal interaction between mind and body there would be transmission of properties from one to the other and that properties cannot be detached from one substance and pass into another (*Third Explanation of the New System*, in Leibniz 1998: §5; *Monadology*, §7). But these reasons are weak. It is not a very plausible model of causation that pictures it as a literal transmission of properties from one thing to another. Furthermore, this seems to undermine even cases of intra-substantial causation. For sometimes a mental state can cause another which is completely different from it and which has virtually no properties in common with it. For instance, sometimes a state of guilt can be caused by considering doing something wrong, but it is difficult to see how this causal fact could consist in the transmission of any properties.

The case against the way of influence is thus weak. Nevertheless it may have carried more weight in Leibniz's time than today, since in the seventeenth century it didn't seem so implausible as it seems today to demand some sort of similarity between causes and effects, a similarity that could be accounted for if one requires that causes transmit properties to their effects.

But discarding the way of influence is not enough to ensure the victory of pre-estab-lished harmony, for Leibniz still has to defeat occasionalism. What is occasionalism, and what are Leibniz's objections to it?

Occasionalism, developed in the seventeenth century by Malebranche and others, says that the only efficient cause is God. Like Leibniz, Malebranche denied that the pain I feel when my body is damaged is produced by the wound in the body. But for Malebranche, God intervenes and produces my pain when my body is damaged. Here the wound in the body is simply an occasion for God to produce the pain in the mind. Similarly, Malebranche denied that my desire to move my arm may cause my arm to move. According to him, when I have a desire to move my arm, God intervenes and makes my arm move. The desire to move the arm is simply an occasion for God to move my arm.

Since events in the mind and the body function as occasions for God to intervene one may call those events *occasional causes*. But here the word "cause" is deflated. The events in the mind and the body are not causes in the sense of efficient and productive causes. The events in the mind and body have, of themselves, no power to produce anything anywhere. They just give God an opportunity to intervene and change the mind according to what happens in the body and vice versa. The only thing that has causal powers is God.

Leibniz liked to explain the differences between his theory and occasionalism by means of an analogy. Suppose there are two clocks that are perfectly coordinated and give exactly the same time. There are different ways of obtaining this perfect coordination. One way would be to have a man who constantly looks after them and who adjusts them from moment to moment so as to maintain the clocks giving the same time. This corresponds to occasionalism. Another way would be to construct the clocks, from the beginning, with such a skill and accuracy that we could be sure they would always keep the time together without needing to readjust them. This corresponds to pre-established harmony (*Third Explanation of the New System*, §§2–4).

So occasionalism is like pre-established harmony in that it denies real causation between created substances. But the difference between occasionalism and pre-established harmony is that in occasionalism God is acting whenever a change occurs in the world. When I move my arm on occasion of my desire of doing so, God is acting then – he is making my arm move; when I feel pain on occasion of my body's being damaged, God is acting then – he is making me feel pain. In the doctrine of the pre-established harmony God is not acting permanently in the world. He acts only once, at the very beginning when he creates the world and then, if he acts later, this is only to perform a miracle. But normally he does not intervene in world affairs. When my body is damaged I do not feel pain because God intervenes and produces it. I feel pain because the active force inherent in me produces pain in those circumstances.

What are Leibniz's arguments against occasionalism? Leibniz did not think occasionalism was unintelligible, but he thought it had many problems:

(1) Occasionalism explains phenomena in terms of miracles.
(2) Even if occasionalism does not posit miracles, a pre-established harmony is more worthy of God.
(3) Occasionalism rules out intra-substantial causation.
(4) Occasionalism leads to monism.

The objection on which Leibniz put most weight was (1). Why did he think occasionalism explains phenomena in terms of miracles? Because occasionalism explains them in terms of God intervening in the world and acting directly upon the mind and the body at any time the mind and the body change. The defender of occasionalism will reply that when God acts upon the mind on occasion of the body and vice versa, he is not performing miracles. For God acts according to general laws. That is, it is not that at time t_1 and under circumstances C God makes a body have property F on occasion of mental state G, and at time t_2 and under the same circumstances God makes a body have property H on occasion of mental state G. Unless performing a miracle, God always makes, under circumstances C, a body have property F on occasion of mental state G. So, according to occasionalists, occasionalism does not make the world full of miracles, because although God is permanently intervening in the world, he intervenes in a regular way.

Leibniz's response to this is to distinguish two senses of the word "miracle": the popular sense and the strict and philosophical sense. According to the popular sense a miracle is something rare and infrequent. But according to Leibniz this understanding of miracles is wrong. It makes, for instance, every unique or merely rare event a miracle. Leibniz points out that, on this understanding of the word, the existence of a monster should count as a miracle (Fourth letter to Clarke, in Leibniz and Clarke 1956: Para. 43). For Leibniz, a miracle, in the strict sense, is something that exceeds the powers and forces of any finite or created being, and so it is something that cannot be explained in terms of the powers and forces of created entities. And so occasionalism leads to a perpetual miracle. For on occasionalism created substances have no efficient or productive powers; they are incapable of causing anything. Which is why occasionalists postulate permanent divine intervention to account for changes. So, on Leibniz's understanding of miracles, occasionalism requires a perpetual miracle.

But why is this an objection? Why is it bad to explain phenomena in terms of God and miracles? After all, Leibniz also believed that God exists, and Leibniz did not deny God's *power* to intervene in the world and do what Malebranche thought God actually did. The answer is that Leibniz had a clear view about what sound philosophical methodology was. He thought that we must try to explain things by reference to the notion of the subject we are dealing with: "In philosophy we must try to show the way in which things are carried out by the divine wisdom by explaining them in accordance with the notion of the subject we are dealing with" (*New System of the Nature of Substances and Their Communication, and of the Union Which Exists between the Soul and the Body*, in Leibniz 1998: §13). Of course, if we cannot explain things by reference to the notion of the subject we are dealing with, then we should find a different explanation, for instance one in terms of God's performing a miracle. But Leibniz's point is that *other things being equal* one should prefer an explanation that proceeds in terms of the powers and forces included in the notion of the subject. Occasionalism explains the states of a substance by appealing to God's intervention. Pre-established harmony, on the contrary, explains them by reference to the powers and forces included in the notion of the substance in question.

Both occasionalism and the pre-established harmony rule out inter-substantial causation. But pre-established harmony admits intra-substantial causation and so it can do without God and miracles. But when Leibniz presses objection (3) he is not normally thinking along these lines. What he has in mind, in general, is that by denying intra-substantial causation, occasionalism makes God responsible for our actions and so takes away our responsibility and makes God responsible for the evil in the world (*On Nature Itself*, in Leibniz 1989: §10). But this is not a good objection, for if accepted then Leibniz should accept that on his theory one is not responsible for what happens to other things as a result of one's actions. Perhaps God is not responsible for the suffering that an evil person inflicts, but if Leibniz's third objection to occasionalism goes through, then on Leibniz's view the evil person is not responsible either; instead the person responsible would be the recipient of evil.

Another problem Leibniz points out is that occasionalism contradicts our consciousness of intra-substantial causation (*On Nature Itself*, §10), but this is not a good point either, for the pre-established harmony also contradicts our consciousness of our influence on the body.

Objection (2) is a minor point. Leibniz says that even if occasionalism does not lead to miracles, a pre-established harmony is more worthy of God. For it is better to make a machine that keeps working by itself than having to intervene again and again to fix it. But this is more rhetorical than philosophical.

Objection (4) is better, but it assumes Leibniz's own ideas about substances. For Leibniz thought that everything that is a substance acts, and so on occasionalism there is only one substance, namely God. This makes occasionalism close to Spinoza's system (*On Nature Itself*, §15). Why is a monism in which the only substance is God, bad? One reason why such a position is bad might be that since there are modifications, those will be God's and so this position makes God modified, i.e. limited (I owe this point to Paul Lodge. I know of no passages where Leibniz says explicitly that this is the problem).

So perhaps the best objection here is (1), if we understand it as based on methodological considerations. But the case against the way of influence was rather weak, although we saw as well that it might have been considered stronger in the context of seventeenth-century assumptions about causation. And we saw his case for component (a) of the pre-established harmony on the basis of the doctrine of the complete concept of a substance is also weak. Thus, it seems that, overall, Leibniz's case for his doctrine of the pre-established harmony is weak.

Acknowledgements

I am grateful to Paul Lodge for discussion of the topics of this chapter and for allowing me to use his invaluable (unpublished) review of the literature on the pre-established harmony.

References

Works by Leibniz

Leibniz, G. (1989) *Philosophical Essays*, edited, trans. by R. Ariew and D. Garber, Indianapolis, IN; Cambridge, MA: Hackett.
—— (1998) *Philosophical Texts*, edited, trans. by R. S. Woolhouse and Richard Francks, Oxford: Oxford University Press.
Leibniz, G. and Clarke, S. (1956) *The Leibniz–Clarke Correspondence*, edited by H. G. Alexander, Manchester, UK; New York: Manchester University Press.

Works by others

Bobro, M. and Clatterbaugh, K. (1996) "Unpacking the Monad: Leibniz's Theory of Causality," *Monist* 79, no. 3: 408–25.
Broad, C. D. (1975) *Leibniz: An Introduction*, London: Cambridge University Press.

Kulstad, M. (1993) "Causation and Pre-established Harmony in the Early Development of Leibniz's Philosophy," in S. Nadler (ed.), *Causation in Early Modern Philosophy*, University Park, PA: Pennsylvania State University Press, pp. 93–117.

Loeb, L. (1981) *From Descartes to Hume: Continental Metaphysics and the Development of Modern Philosophy*, Ithaca, NY: Cornell University Press.

Schmaltz, T. (2006) "Deflating Descartes's Causal Axiom," *Oxford Studies in Early Modern Philosophy* 3: 1–31.

Sleigh, R. C., Jr (1990) "Leibniz on Malebranche on Causality," in J. Cover and M. Kulstad (eds), *Central Themes in Early Modern Philosophy*, Indianapolis, IN: Hackett.

Watson, R. (1966) *The Downfall of Cartesianism*, Hague: Martinus Nijhoff.

Further reading

K. Clatterbaugh, *The Causation Debate in Modern Philosophy 1637–1739* (New York; London: Routledge, 1999) is an accessible history of the debate on causation during the early modern period; it contains chapters on Descartes, Malebranche, Leibniz and any other major philosopher of the period. Mark A. Kulstad, "Causation and Pre-established Harmony in the Early Development of Leibniz's Philosophy," in S. Nadler (ed.), *Causation in Early Modern Philosophy* (University Park, PA: Pennsylvania State University Press, 1993), pp. 93–117, discusses the influence of Malebranche, Geulincx and Spinoza on Leibniz's thought on causation and pre-established harmony. The first full statement of Leibniz's mature philosophy was the *Discourse on Metaphysics*, and Leibniz presented a comprehensive statement and defence of the pre-established harmony in the *New System of the Nature of Substances and Their Communication, and of the Union Which Exists between the Soul and the Body* in *Philosophical Texts*, edited, trans. by R. S. Woolhouse and Richard Francks (Oxford: Oxford University Press, 1998); the final presentation of his philosophical system is the *Monadology*, in *Philosophical Essays*, edited, trans. by R. Ariew and D. Garber (Indianapolis, IN; Cambridge, MA: Hackett, 1989). Paul Lodge, "Leibniz's Commitment to the Pre-Established Harmony in the Late 1670s and Early 1680s," *Archiv für Geschichte der Philosophie* 80, no. 3 (1998): 292–320, argues that developments in Leibniz's thinking during his earliest years in Hanover suggest that he was committed to the pre-established harmony in all but name by June 1682 and possibly as early as the Summer of 1679. R. Woolhouse, "Leibniz and Occasionalism," in R. Woolhouse (ed.), *Metaphysics and Philosophy of Science in the Seventeenth and Eighteenth Centuries: Essays in honour of Gerd Buchdal* (Dordrecht: Kluwer Academic Publishers, 1988), discusses Leibniz's objections to occasionalism and their relations to Leibniz's objections to Cartesian interactionism and Spinozism.

12
BERKELEY
Arguments for idealism

Tom Stoneham

Berkeley's idealism, which he called immaterialism, has two fundamental theses, which we can call the ontological and the metaphysical.

(ONT) Everything which exists is either a mind or an object of perception.
(MET) Objects of perception exist when, only when, and in virtue of, being perceived by some mind.

(ONT) has some anti-realist consequences all on its own, ruling out unobserved particulars (e.g. a small rock on a distant planet with no sentient life) and unobservable kinds (e.g. quarks). (MET) is common to Berkeley and indirect realists (see below), so does not immediately have anti-realist consequences. But the combination of the two theses is a distinctive and radical view of the world, characterized, or perhaps caricatured, by the consequence that things pop in and out of existence, depending on whether they are perceived or not (Figure 12.1).

(ONT) and (MET) are indeterminate in a few ways. (ONT) does not specify what kind of thing a mind is and what kind or kinds of thing might be objects of perception, while (MET) says nothing about how something could exist "in virtue of being perceived." Berkeley says very little in his published works about what kind of things minds are, and we will follow him in that. He calls the objects of perception "ideas," and this leads many to think there is an easy answer to the question of how they could exist in virtue of being perceived: they are mental items, feelings or sensations like pains and tickles. If that is right, immaterialism is even more radical, for it says that everything that exists is mental, that there is no physical world, just minds and what happens to them.

But notice that someone who held (ONT) + (MET) and yet thought that the objects of perception were not mental, would be saying something much more amenable to common sense – so long as they could persuade us that (MET) might be true of those non-mental objects of perception. And this is exactly what Berkeley intended, despite his misleading use of "idea" for the objects of perception: the objects of perception are

Figure 12.1 A popular view of Berkeley's metaphysics (Appleby 17 November 2002; courtesy of Steven Appleby)

not states of our own minds but things in the world. It is just that they only exist when perceived. As he put it (PHK 38; see also DHP3 251):[1]

> If you agree with me that we eat and drink, and are clad with the immediate objects of sense which cannot exist unperceived or without the mind: I shall readily grant it is more proper or conformable to custom, that they should be called things rather than ideas.

And more bluntly (DHP3 244):

> I am not for changing things into ideas, but rather ideas into things.

Furthermore, Berkeley was confident that ordinary, non-philosophical folk cared little or none about unperceived objects, and thus that consequences of holding (MET) for the ordinary physical objects we take ourselves to perceive would not be too much in conflict with common sense (PHK 45, DHP3 249).

The dialectic

The opponents of Berkeley's immaterialism can be divided into three camps. Two have a common assumption, namely that ordinary objects like apples and houses are material:

(MAT) Ordinary physical objects (OPOs from now on) can exist unperceived.

The indirect or representative realists accept (MET), which combined with (MAT) entails that OPOs are not among the objects of perception. So if such physical objects exist, (ONT) is false. The direct realists accept that OPOs are amongst the objects of perception and thus, given (MAT), deny (MET). When considering Berkeley's arguments, it seems that the *Principles* is primarily addressed to indirect realists and more attention is paid to direct realists in the *Three Dialogues*. But dialectically speaking it looks as if he needs first to argue against the direct realist to establish (MET) and then against the indirect realist to establish (ONT). Though Berkeley has some things to say about the merits of (ONT) itself, he prefers to argue indirectly: the indirect realists' conjunction of (MET) and (MAT) forces them to deny that OPOs are amongst the objects of perception, which Berkeley takes to be unreasonable. (The conjunction of (MET), (MAT) and (ONT) is worse, for it forces one to deny that there are any ordinary physical objects. That view is sometimes erroneously attributed to Berkeley.) So if (MET) has been established then (MAT) must go, and once we deny (MAT) we are a long way towards establishing (ONT).

The third opponent of immaterialism appears at this point in the dialectic. This philosopher accepts the arguments for (MET) and against (MAT) but still denies (ONT), for he or she thinks that even if ordinary physical objects are not material, they do have material counterparts which cause or occasion our experiences. A version of this view can be found in Berkeley's contemporaries Malebranche and Norris, but it may be more familiar to contemporary readers as a form of scientific realism: (MET) is true, and thus the table exists only when perceived, but the swarm of particles which physics finds in its place (quite literally: in the location where we take the table to be) exists unperceived.

As Figure 12.2 makes clear, to argue for idealism Berkeley needs at least three distinct arguments: one for (MET), one against (MAT), and one against there being other, unperceivable, matter. In fact, Berkeley offers dozens of arguments, and it is not always clear exactly which version of materialism is the intended target of each. Furthermore, there are about as many different interpretations of his arguments as there are interpreters. To avoid scholarly bickering, the arguments I am going to discuss are Berkeleian in spirit and based in the texts, though they go beyond what can be indisputably found there.

For (MET)

Berkeley does not have a single argument for (MET), but a great variety of arguments which work in many different ways. Some are variants of traditional arguments from illusions and perceptual variations across individuals and species, others seem original to Berkeley, such as his argument that a great heat is indistinguishable from a pain, for which (MET) is obviously true (DHP1 175–8).

A so-called "Master Argument" is often attributed to Berkeley (Gallois 1974), namely that it is impossible to imagine or conceive an unperceived tree (PHK 22–3, DHP1 200). Whatever the merits of that claim about what we can and cannot conceive, it would only support an argument for (MET) with the further premise that what is inconceivable is impossible, and there is no evidence that Berkeley accepted that. What he did accept was the reverse thesis – what is conceivable is possible (e.g. PHK Intro 10, PHK 5) – and thus needed to show that unperceived trees are not conceivable to avoid an obvious and decisive objection to (MET) (see Stoneham 2005: 159–62).

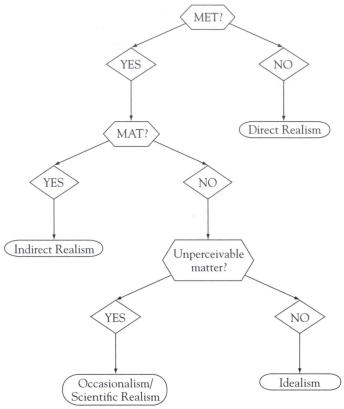

Figure 12.2 The dialectic of Berkeleian idealism

His most original and challenging argument is his denial that there is any substantive difference between primary qualities such as shape, size and motion, and secondary qualities such as colour, taste and texture. One way he makes this point is to follow the example of the seventeenth-century sceptic Pierre Bayle and apply the arguments from perceptual variation to the primary as well as the secondary qualities (PHK 15–5, DHP1 188–91). But he has a much more powerful and general argument to the effect that *whatever reason you have for thinking (MET) is true of the secondary qualities*, you must also think it is true of the primary qualities. Berkeley summarizes his argument thus (PHK 10; see also DHP1 194): "Now if it be certain, that those [primary] qualities are insepa-rably united with the other [secondary] sensible qualities, and not, even in thought, capable of being abstracted from them, it plainly follows that they exist only in the mind."[2] All Berkeley's arguments for (MET) rely on the claim that the only true objects of perception are the objects of *immediate* perception, though ordinary language is careless on this point. The distinction between immediate and mediate perception is not quite the same as the distinction between direct and indirect perception. Berkeley's thought is that what is immediately perceived can always be experienced in a single perception, that our perceiving it now does not depend upon our perceiving anything else, either now or at some other time. His examples, such as our immediately perceiving a painting or words in a book but not what the painting is of or the words describe, tend to emphasize that what is immediately perceived is present. But it is important to see it is not just being present but being *wholly present* that matters for immediate perception. Specific instances of colours, textures, shapes, etc., clearly fall into this category for the presence of such qualities does not depend upon anything which is not given in a single perceptual experience. However, the properties which correspond to sortal concepts, such as *being an apple*, do not seem to be immediately perceivable, since to be an apple something must have a complex combination of qualities, thus one can only perceive that something is an apple by perceiving it in a variety of sense modalities and over a period of time: no particular look or smell or taste or feel is sufficient for appleness.

Of course, we will sometimes judge there to be an apple in the fruit-bowl on the basis of a single glance, but that is only because of past connections between what we see and the other experiences which go to make up perception of appleness. As Berkeley says, if we have previously had these other experiences, the look of an apple will "suggest" the taste and smell, but we do not thereby immediately perceive that taste and smell and thus we do not immediately perceive appleness. Furthermore, while we do not immediately perceive properties such as *being an apple*, we also do not immediately perceive the object, the apple itself, which has the sensible qualities which we do immediately perceive: we do not have distinct perceptual experiences of physical objects over and above our experiences of their properties (PHK 1, DHP1 174–5). So Berkeley concludes that only a very limited range of things are immediately perceived, and thus properly considered objects of perception, namely "light, and colours, and figures, … sounds, … tastes, … odours" and textures. But this list can include all primary and secondary qualities: what it excludes are objects, if those are taken to be something more than collections or bundles of properties, and sortal properties.

Berkeley's inseparability argument is meant to work against anyone who accepts the mind-dependence of secondary qualities. There has been almost universal agreement among philosophers and scientists since the beginning of the seventeenth century that there is something subjective about the secondary qualities; unfortunately for Berkeley, this recognition of a subjective aspect to the secondary qualities does not have to take the form of accepting (MET). In particular, some philosophers, including Locke (*Essay*, Pt 2, ch. 8, §15), have thought that the connection between possessing a given secondary quality and appearing a particular way can be captured by saying that the secondary qualities are dispositions to cause appearances in suitable observers: to be red, for example, just is to have a certain visual appearance, but red things need not actually have been perceived to be red – it is enough that they would look red. Consequently, (MET) is false of secondary qualities, since the dispositions to cause experiences may exist even if they are and remain unperceived.

Berkeley does not have much sympathy for this dispositional account of secondary qualities for a very simple reason (DHP1 187). Dispositions, as opposed to their manifestations, are not immediate objects of perception. We do not see the disposition of the leaf to look green, rather we see a manifestation of that disposition: the leaf actually appears green to us. And if the disposition in question is a disposition to appear a certain way, all manifestations of that disposition exist when, only when, and in virtue of being perceived. If we want to identify the greenness of the leaf with the disposition to look a certain way, then we have in effect denied that the secondary quality is a sensible quality, i.e. it is not an object of immediate perception. However, when we go back to the data of experience and consider a case of looking at a leaf, it is undeniable that among the things we see, that is, among the objects of perception, are both the shape of the leaf and its colour. Since (MET) is concerned with objects of perception, it is those actual sensible qualities, rather than any dispositions the object might have, which Berkeley's argument addresses.[3]

Some commentators claim that Berkeley only accepted the inseparability claim because he had an imagistic theory of conception, namely that to conceive of something is to form a mental image of it. True, one cannot form a mental image of, say, the shape of a coin, without also imagining the coin to have some colour, so if one thought that all conceiving was imagining, Berkeley's argument would be effective. Whether or not Berkeley held this rather implausible view of conception, there is another Berkeleian reason to accept inseparability. This reason begins with the point that we cannot *perceive* primary qualities without perceiving secondary qualities – e.g. you only see the shape of the coin because you see its edges and you only see its edges because of a colour contrast between the coin and the background – and once we understand why this is the case, then we can see that no conception of an object lacking secondary qualities will be a conception of it possessing the very primary qualities which we immediately perceive. I will first present the argument in the abstract and then give a concrete example.

When we perceive a property, the property we perceive, be it a shape or a colour, has a qualitative character: there is something it is like for the subject to perceive that property, which is why we call it a sensible *quality*. A property with no qualitative character cannot be immediately perceived, and thus cannot be a sensible quality. Nothing can have a qualitative character without having some secondary qualities. So if, *per impossibile*, someone conceives of an object possessing some property but lacking secondary qualities, they conceive of it lacking qualitative character and thus lacking all sensible qualities. Hence no such conception can show the object possessing *those very primary qualities we perceive* in the absence of secondary qualities.

Take, for example, a round coin I can see and feel. Suppose, for the sake of argument, I can conceive (as opposed to imagine) the coin lacking colour but still being round: perhaps I conceive of it rolling down a gentle gradient without conceiving of anyone perceiving it doing so. The question Berkeley will then ask about that conception is whether the property called "roundness," which in my conception it has in virtue of how it rolls when unobserved, is *the very same property as* the one I see it to have. If it is not, then the conception shows nothing about the separability of the primary from the secondary sensible qualities. In response, I might insist that it is the same property, because I conceive of its unperceived roundness as its having all the points on its edge equidistant from a single point, and that is also true of its perceived roundness. However, this only proves my point if I have conceived of it as having an edge without conceiving of its secondary qualities and to do that we would have to conceive of the boundary between coin and non-coin in terms of a difference in some primary property. But a *perceived* edge is always and necessarily marked by a difference in secondary qualities and hence no difference in primary properties alone is sufficient for the existence of a perceiv*able* edge. Of course, some differences in primary properties are sufficient for there to be a boundary between the coin and the non-coin, but such boundaries are only perceivable in virtue of some difference in secondary qualities. So if I have success-fully conceived of the coin as being round without conceiving of it as having any secondary qualities, I have conceived of it as having a property distinct from any property I can perceive. Hence I have not shown that I can separate the primary sensible qualities from the secondary.

Berkeley's point is that when we try to conceive of an object possessing primary qualities and no secondary qualities, the most we could achieve is a conception of it as possessing some properties and no secondary properties, but those properties are not "the *very* figure and extension which you perceive by sense" (DHP1 188; my emphasis). And because of this inseparability of primary and secondary sensible qualities, whatever persuades you that (MET) is true of the secondary qualities will thereby require you to think (MET) is true of the sensible primary qualities as well. All we perceive are sensible qualities and it is in the nature or essence of those sensible qualities to be perceived, hence "their *esse* is *percipi*" (PHK 3).

There are two ways one might object to this argument. First, one might argue that we can separate the cognitive from the sensuous elements of perception and the former does not depend upon the latter. Thus, even though whenever we do perceive something as, say, square, we also perceive it as having a certain qualitative character, that quali-tative character is not constitutive of our perceiving it as square. Berkeley would say that to argue thus confuses perception, which is passive and involuntary, with thought or judgement, which is active (e.g. PC 286). Second, one might argue that some secondary qualities are not in fact mind-dependent. Perhaps such a view can be defended, but it will not be easy.

Against (MAT)

Berkeley gives a very blunt and direct argument against (MAT) at the beginning of the *Principles*:

> But with how great an assurance and acquiescence soever this principle [MAT] may be entertained in the world; yet whoever shall find in his heart to call it in question, may, if I mistake not, perceive it to involve a manifest contradiction. For what are the forementioned [ordinary physical] objects but the things we perceive by sense, and what do we perceive besides our own ideas or sensations; and is it not plainly repugnant that any one of these or any combination of them should exist unperceived? (PHK 4)

Unfortunately, this argument looks like a classic equivocation (Stoneham 2003). The premises are:

1. Ordinary physical objects are amongst *the things we perceive by sense*.
2. All *the things we perceive by sense* exist only when perceived.

The problem is that, as we have seen, the reasons Berkeley gives for accepting 2. require us to restrict "the things we perceive by sense" to the immediately perceived sensible qualities, but the reasons we have for 1. do not hold with this restriction in place: ordinary physical objects do not appear to be amongst the immediately perceived sensible qualities, for those are only colours, shapes, textures, sounds, odours, etc.

Berkeley's solution is to say that the ordinary physical objects consist in collections of sensible qualities, thus the argument does not equivocate. But the indirect realist has a different approach, which Berkeley needs to rule out first. According to the indirect realist, "the things we perceive by sense" picks out two classes of object: the sensible qualities (which exist only when perceived) and the physical objects. She then claims that we perceive the physical objects *by* perceiving the sensible qualities, so objects of each kind are perceived, but the relation is different in each case.

If sensible qualities are a different class of objects from physical objects and we perceive the latter by perceiving the former, there must be some relation between the two types of object which makes this possible. Berkeley considers two: the sensible qualities represent the physical objects; and the sensible qualities inhere in the physical objects. Either would explain how we perceive one indirectly by perceiving the other directly.

Against the first, Berkeley makes the important point that nothing can resemble an idea but an idea. Of course, there are other sorts of representation than resemblance, but the position Berkeley is objecting to here accepts that sensible qualities are mind-dependent objects of perception and that by perceiving them we perceive something else, something material and not otherwise perceivable. So this is a case of perceiving something indirectly by perceiving something else. The relation which makes this possible cannot be a matter of convention, nor can it be one which requires us to experience both *relata* to know that it holds, such as a causal relation. So it does seem that resemblance is the best candidate. But it will not do because only things which are themselves perceivable can resemble each other, and according to the indirect realist, the material objects are not themselves perceivable. As Berkeley puts it (DHP1 206),

> But how can that which is sensible be like that which is insensible? Can a real thing in itself *invisible* be like a *colour*; or a real thing which is not *audible*, be like a sound? In a word, can any thing be like a sensation or idea but another sensation or idea?

Against the second proposed relation, Berkeley offers three arguments. One is that he simply does not understand inherence (DHP1 190, DHP2 234). The second is that, whatever the inherence relation is, it implies an existential dependence, but if we accept (MET), sensible qualities existentially depend upon being perceived, so they cannot inhere in unperceiving matter (PHK 7 and 76, DHP1 197). The third is most general: if we perceive material things by perceiving sensible qualities, we must thereby gain some sort of idea of those material things. But what sort of idea could that be? It could not be the sort of idea found in direct perceptions, so it must be a "relative idea," i.e. our idea of material objects is as the thing related in such a way to the sensible qualities (PHK 16). Relative ideas are not uncommon: most readers of this chapter will only have a relative idea of me, namely as the author of this chapter. But there is a plausible necessary condition upon having a relative idea: one must have a grasp of the relation holding between things of which one has non-relative ideas. This creates two problems for the indirect realist. One is that we are supposed to have a relative idea of matter even though we cannot have a non-relative idea. The other is that it is self-defeating to explain the relation of inherence in terms of relations we have experienced because (MET) applies to them (DHP1 198).

So the indirect realist's claim that "things we perceive by sense" equivocates between direct and indirect objects of perception cannot be sustained (see also Hume, *Treatise*, Bk 1, pt 4, §2, para. 4, for a phenomenological objection). However, if OPOs are just bundles or collections of sensible qualities, then it can be true both that we only immediately perceive sensible qualities and we immediately perceive OPOs.

Against other material things

We now need to consider how Berkeley argues against someone who accepts his arguments for (MET) and against (MAT), but who thinks that this does not prove that there is no matter, merely that material objects are unperceivable. One form of this view is the occasionalism of Malebranche and Norris, against which Berkeley has a panoply of arguments turning on the fact that the matter they postulate is unknowable, does nothing, and would have been pointless for God to create (DHP2 *passim*). But a more plausible form of the view is that through science we come to know of the unperceived material world: science shows (ONT) is false. We can call this scientific realism.

One way of reaching this conclusion is from our experience with scientific instruments like microscopes and telescopes. These show us that as we improve our perceptual acuity, we discover previously unperceivable features of the world. Since there are no non-contingent upper bounds to acuity, this implies that there could always be more to the world than we can perceive, so (ONT) is implausible. Furthermore, microscopes do not just show us new things, as looking over a mountain might, but show us what appear to be the otherwise imperceptible inner workings of things we can perceive (PHK 60).

Berkeley's response is that microscopes do just show us new things and there is no prior reason to think they will have any connection with the ordinary objects of experience. Where we do find such a connection, it is entirely contingent. Thus when we look at some object through a microscope, it is not necessary that we will see anything, let alone something which will help us understand the behaviour of that object. Of course, that we do see such things makes the working of nature more law-like and easier to predict which, if we believe in such a thing, we might count as another instance of Divine Providence (PHK 62, DHP3 245).

Another way of denying (ONT) on the basis of science is via the positing of theoretical objects. According to this view, ordinary physical objects like tables and trees consist of sensible qualities which do not exist unperceived. However, there are other objects, the objects of scientific theory, which lack sensible qualities but do exist unperceived. We know about these purely theoretical objects because the theories in which they figure are successful in predicting what happens to perceptible objects.

The first problem for this view comes when we ask where these imperceptible material things are located. It is tempting to answer that they are in the same place as the ordinary physical objects whose behaviour they explain. Thus I see a table in front of me, what I see is just a collection of sensible qualities, but in the very place I see that table, there is a collection of unperceivable, material things, perhaps a swarm of atoms. But this will not do, for the spatial properties of the table are among the sensible qualities of the table, and thus cannot be possessed by the unperceivable matter which the scientific realist introduces. So if there is this matter, it is not merely unperceivable, it is also not spatially related to anything we can perceive (PHK 67):

> But secondly, though we should grant this unknown substance may possibly exist, yet where can it be supposed to be? That it exists not in the mind is agreed, and that it exists not in place is no less certain; since all extension exists only in the mind, as hath been already proved. It remains therefore that it exists no where at all.

This point is in fact devastating for the scientific realist, for science postulates unperceivable objects to explain perceivable phenomena and the explanations require those theoretical objects to be spatially related to the phenomena. If nothing unperceivable can be spatially related to something perceivable, then science cannot be giving us reason to believe in unperceivable material objects. In fact, if we accept (MET) and include spatial relations in the objects of perception, the only consistent interpretation of these scientific theories which postulate unperceivable objects is instrumentalist: the theory and its postulates are just a tool we use to predict and explain phenomena and thus we are not committed to the existence of those postulates, only of the phenomena they predict. Here Berkeley's position relies very heavily on the objection to the primary–secondary quality distinction, for if the spatial properties we perceive are such as might exist unperceived, then they could be possessed by theoretical entities.

Conclusion

A complete defence of Berkeleian idealism would have two parts. First, one would have to argue against the existence of matter. Then one would have to show that the denial of matter does not bring with it any insuperable philosophical problems. In this chapter I have tried to make some of Berkeley's arguments against matter as plausible as possible. Of course those arguments are not watertight, but objecting to them incurs costs elsewhere in one's metaphysics. Only in the light of a consideration of whether Berkeley's denial of matter is itself a cogent metaphysics can we properly assess the true merits of immaterialism.

Acknowledgements

I would like to thank Steven Appleby for his kind permission to reproduce part of his cartoon, "The Science of Philosophy" (see Figure 12.1), which first appeared in the *Sunday Telegraph* on 17 November 2002.

Notes

1   There are many different editions of Berkeley's main philosophical works and they differ only in the finest details. I have used the following conventions to refer to Berkeley's writings:

PC 154 = *Philosophical Commentaries* (Jessop and Luce 1948 [1707–8]), entry 154.
PHK 89 = A *Treatise Concerning the Principles of Human Knowledge* (Jessop and Luce 1949 [1710]), sec. 89.
DHP2 216 = *Three Dialogues between Hylas and Philonous* (Jessop and Luce 1949 [1713]), Second Dialogue, p. 216, of the Jessop and Luce edition (1949) (these page references are included in many recent editions).

2   There is another reading of Berkeley's argument here which goes as follows:

(1) Secondary qualities exist only in virtue of being perceived.
(2) So an unperceived object would have only primary qualities.
(3) We cannot conceive of an object having primary qualities without secondary qualities.
(4) So it is impossible for an object to have only primary qualities.
(5) So it is impossible for there to be unperceived objects.

While this is an interesting argument, I doubt it is Berkeley's for the same reason I doubted he used the Master Argument, namely that he does not accept the principle that what is inconceivable is impossible.

3   It is worth noting here that Berkeley's argument at this point does not need the strong thesis that we can never perceive dispositions, though I think he would have accepted that, but merely that at least sometimes when we immediately perceive secondary qualities, we are not perceiving dispositions but their manifestations.

References

Appleby, Steven (17 November 2002) "The Science of Philosophy" (cartoon), *Sunday Telegraph*.
Gallois, A. (1974) "Berkeley's Master Argument," *Philosophical Review* 83: 55–69.
Jessop, T. and Luce, A. (1948) *The Works of George Berkeley*, vol. 1, London: Thomas Nelson.
—— (1949) *The Works of George Berkeley*, vol. 2, London: Thomas Nelson.
Stoneham, T. (2003) "On Equivocation," *Philosophy* 78: 515–9.
—— (2005) "Berkeley's Principles of Human Knowledge," in J. Shand (ed.), *Central Works of Philosophy*, vol. 2, Chesham, UK: Acumen, pp. 137–65.

Further reading

(1) Selected interpretations of Berkeley: R. Cummins, "Berkeley's Ideas of Sense," *Noûs* 9 (1975): 55–72, defends Thomas Reid's interpretation of Berkeley's ideas as sensations. J. Dancy, *Berkeley: An Introduction* (Oxford: Blackwell, 1987) interprets Berkeley as making heavy use of the principle that what is inconceivable is impossible. R. Fogelin, *Berkeley and* The Principles of Human Knowledge (London: Routledge, 2001) interprets Berkeley as taking (MET) to be intuitively obvious. G. Pitcher, *Berkeley* (London: Routledge

& Kegan Paul, 1977) is a thorough and systematic, if slightly unsympathetic, account of all aspects of Berkeley's thought. J. Roberts, *A Metaphysics for the Mob* (Oxford: Oxford University Press, 2007) is an original interpretation of Berkeley as a "spiritual realist." Part 3 of T. Stoneham, *Berkeley's World* (Oxford: Oxford University Press, 2002) tries to show that idealism can be developed into a cogent metaphysics. A sympathetic account, with detailed discussions of other scholars, is found in K. Winkler, *Berkeley: An Interpretation* (Oxford: Oxford University Press, 1994). (2) Other works relevant to the arguments discussed here: K. Allen, "The Mind-Independence of Colour," *European Journal of Philosophy* 15 (2007): 137–58, defends the view that colours are mind-independent, which would undermine the inseparability argument. J. Austin, *Sense and Sensibilia* (Oxford: Oxford University Press, 1963) argues against (MET) and the restriction of the immediate objects of perception to qualities. Chapter 3 of A. Ayer, *The Central Questions of Philosophy* (London: Weidenfeld & Nicholson, 1973) responds to Austin, and chapter 4 attempts to give a non-idealist "construction" of the world. Many of Berkeley's views about the immediate objects of perception, and vision in particular, are developed in his *An Essay Towards a New Theory of Vision* (1709), in T. Jessop and A. Luce (eds), *The Works of George Berkeley*, vol. 1 (London: Thomas Nelson, 1948). J. Campbell, "A Simple View of Colour," in J. Haldane and C. Wright (eds), *Reality, Representation and Projection* (Oxford: Oxford University Press, 1993) distinguishes between objectivity and mind-independence and applies the distinction to colours; and "Berkeley's Puzzle," in T. Gendler and J. Hawthorne (eds), *Conceivability and Possibility* (Oxford: Oxford University Press, 2002) presents Berkeley as offering a very serious challenge to realism. M. Dummett, "Common Sense and Physics," in G. Macdonald (ed.), *Perception and Identity* (London: Macmillan, 1979) contains a sophisticated discussion of scientific realism (§3, on what it is to be immediately perceived). C. McGinn, *The Subjective View* (Oxford: Oxford University Press, 1983) discusses the relation between the inseparability thesis and the imagistic account of conception (see pp. 80ff.). J. McDowell, *Mind and World* (Cambridge, MA: Harvard University Press, 1994), tries to reconcile the passivity of perception with its being cognitive. P. Strawson, "Perception and Its Objects," in G. Macdonald (ed.), *Perception and Identity* (London: Macmillan, 1979) offers a form of empirical realism strongly influenced by Kant.

13
HUME
Necessary connections and distinct existences

Alexander Miller

Introduction: causal realism

A white billiard ball collides with a stationary black billiard ball at time t and a fraction of a second later, at time $t+$, the black ball moves off towards one of the pockets on the billiard table. At $t+$, a spectator sneezes. Call the collision of the white ball with the black ball at t event e_1, the black ball moving off at $t+$ event e_2 and the spectator sneezing at $t+$ event e_3. Intuitively, we would judge that e_1 caused e_2 but that e_1 did not cause e_3. What are we doing when we make *causal judgements* such as these? One answer is that we are expressing *beliefs*: when we judge that e_1 caused e_2 but not e_3 we are expressing the belief that e_1 stands in a relation to e_2 that it does not stand in to e_3. What relation? One answer is the relation of *necessary connection*: the occurrence of e_1 *made necessary* the occurrence of e_2. On the other hand, although e_1 was *followed* by e_3, the occurrence of e_1 did not make necessary the occurrence of e_3. Given e_1, in some sense e_2 (unlike e_3) *had to happen*. *Causal realism*, as understood here, holds that causal judgements express beliefs about necessary connections between events, that at least some of these beliefs are true (and justified), and that they are true in virtue of the obtaining of mind-independent states of affairs. (We can also think of the causal relation as obtaining between objects or facts, but throughout this entry we will think of it as obtaining between events). So causal realism holds that the judgement that e_1 caused e_2 expresses a belief that there is a relation of necessary connection between them, that this belief is true (and justified), and that the obtaining of this relation in no way depends upon the thoughts, feelings or mental activity of humans.

Causal realism seems like a piece of common sense. Historically, however, it is challenged by the writings of the Scottish philosopher David Hume (1711–76), especially part 3 of book 1 of his *A Treatise of Human Nature* (1739) and §4–7 of his *An Enquiry Concerning Human Understanding* (1748). In the second and third sections, we outline the ingredients of Hume's case against causal realism, and in the fourth section we outline some possible alternatives to causal realism that might be attributed to

Hume. (Note that it is *logically possible* for e_1 to occur without e_2 following: in Humean terminology e_1 and e_2 are "distinct existences." The central issue about causal realism raised by Hume is thus whether there are mind-independent "necessary connections" between "distinct existences").

Hume's naturalism and empiricism

Hume's project, announced in the *Treatise*, is to provide a "solid foundation" for the "science of man" by explaining the "principles of human nature" (1978 [1739]: xvi): in effect, a naturalistic account of the workings of the human mind that views it as susceptible to a broadly scientific treatment. Hume writes: "the only solid foundation we can give to this science itself must be laid on experience and observation" (1978 [1739]: xvi). The challenge to causal realism emerges from Hume's attempt to apply this naturalistic–empiricist approach to causal judgement.

Hume uses a generic term – "perceptions" – to refer to states of mind, and distinguishes between *impressions* and *ideas*. Impressions are, roughly, experiences: sense-experiences, "outward sentiments" or "impressions of sensation," such as visual or tactual experiences, and introspectable experiences, "inward sentiments" or "impressions of reflection," such as joy, sadness, anger and desire. The cornerstone of Hume's empiricism is his claim that all concepts – or ideas – are copies of resembling impressions: "By ideas I mean the faint images of [impressions] in thinking and reasoning" (1978 [1739]: 1). However, since we have the concept of a golden mountain, yet no corresponding impression (we've never experienced one), Hume refines his empiricist claim by distinguishing between simple and complex ideas and impressions: "Simple perceptions or impressions and ideas are such as admit of no distinction or separation. The complex are the contrary to these, and may be distinguished into parts" (1978 [1739]: 2). The empiricist claim is then enshrined in Hume's Copy Principle: all our ideas are either (a) simple ideas copied from some resembling impression or (b) complex ideas ultimately composed of simple ideas. Since the idea of a golden mountain is a complex idea, the fact that we have it despite never having experienced one is consistent with Hume's empiricism, since it is composed of ideas (such as that of gold) that do correspond to resembling impressions.

The Copy Principle can be viewed as a semantic principle, according to which the *content* of our ideas ultimately derives from experience, or as a genetic claim, according to which experience is the ultimate causal *source* of our ideas, or both. Either way, it imposes constraints upon accounts of causal judgement. If the judgement that e_1 caused e_2 expresses the belief that e_1 and e_2 stand in a relation of necessary connection, then we either have to show that the idea of necessary connection implicated in this belief is a complex idea composed ultimately of simple ideas copied from resembling impressions, or, if the idea of necessary connection is held to be simple, find an impression from which the idea of necessary connection itself is copied. If neither of these is possible, then the notion that we are so much as capable of making causal judgements is threatened, either because there is no idea of necessary connection (semantic) or there are no grounds for attributing such an idea to us (genetic). Either way, causal realism would be threatened.

Hume's search for the impression of necessary connection

Hume can thus be viewed as attempting to clarify the idea of necessary connection (or "power") by looking for the impression or impressions from which it is ultimately derived:

> To be fully acquainted ... with the idea of power or necessary connection, let us examine its impression; and in order to find the impression with greater certainty, let us search for it in all the sources, from which it may possibly be derived. (1975 [1748]: 63)

Consider again our example involving the billiard balls. When we look outward at the goings-on on the table, we see a sequence of events – including e_2 following e_1 – but, Hume argues, we receive no impression of a relation of necessary connection between them:

> When we look about us towards external objects, and consider the operation of causes, we are never able, in a single instance, to discover any power or necessary connection; any quality, which binds the effect to the cause, and renders the one an infallible consequence of the other. We only find, that the one does actually, in fact, follow the other. The impulse of one billiard-ball is attended with motion in the second. This is the whole that appears to the *outward* senses. The mind feels no sentiment or *inward* impression from this succession of objects: Consequently, there is not, in any single, particular instance of cause and effect, any thing which can suggest the idea of power or necessary connection. (1975 [1748]: 63)

In favour of this claim, Hume argues that given all of the information that our senses yield about the white billiard ball up to and including the point at which it strikes the black billiard ball, we could not predict what will happen to the latter the instant immediately after it is struck. If we did receive an impression of necessary connection from observing the billiard table up to and including the point at which the collision takes place, we would be in a position to make such a prediction. So Hume concludes that we do not get an impression of necessary connection from observing a single causal transaction between external events.

Hume next considers whether we might get an impression of necessary connection from introspecting on a single causal transaction involving our own minds, e.g. the event of my willing my arm to move causing my arm to move upwards. He rejects this suggestion. First, if we had an impression of necessary connection between the mental act of volition and the bodily event of my arm's moving upwards, we would understand the mind–body relationship. But far from understanding "the secret union of soul and body," there is no relationship "in all nature more mysterious" (1975 [1748]: 65) than this. Second, if we had such an impression we would understand why it is that I can move my arm but not my liver. Since we don't understand this, it again follows that we have no such impression. (To the rejoinder that we do in fact understand – courtesy of modern physiology – why I can move my arm but not my liver, Hume would reply that this understanding is not based on the experience of a single causal transaction). Third, there is a complex sequence of events between the mental act of willing and the movement of my arm, events involving "certain muscles, and nerves, and animal parts" (1975 [1748]: 66). Since all of these events are part of a sequential causal process, one event in the sequence causes the next, which causes the next, and so on. So all of these events are necessarily connected to their neighbours. If we had impressions of necessary connection between the events and their neighbours we would understand, independently of further experience, how one link in the causal chain causes the next. We don't, so again Hume's conclusion is that we have no such impressions.

Could we get an impression of necessary connection from reflecting on a single instance of a causal transaction involving an act of will and another *mental* event, e.g. the event of my willing myself to think of a glass of Laphroaig leading to an idea of such a glass appearing in my mind? Hume argues against this suggestion. First, if we had such an impression we would understand the mind's ability to produce ideas at will. But according to Hume we don't, since "This is a real creation; a production of something out of nothing" and this is "entirely beyond our comprehension" (1975 [1748]: 68). Second, if we had such an impression, we'd be able to understand, on the basis of a single experience, why we can conjure up at will an idea of Tony Blair but not a sentiment of approbation towards him. Since we're not able to understand this on the basis of a single experience, we have no such impression. Likewise, we'd be able to explain on the basis of a single experience why "we are more master of our thoughts … fasting, than after a full meal" (1975 [1748]: 65). We can't, again showing that we have no such impression.

Indeed, the fact that the impression of necessary connection is so hard to track down, that "even in the most familiar events, the energy of the cause is as unintelligible as in the most unusual," leads philosophers such as Malebranche (1638–1715) to the doctrine of occasionalism, according to which, when one billiard ball collides with another "it is the Deity himself … who by a particular volition, moves the second ball" (1975 [1748]: 70). Hume rejects this theory as taking us "into fairy land": it does not help us trace the impression of necessary connection, since we are equally ignorant "of the manner or force by which a mind, even the supreme mind, operates either on itself or on body" (1975 [1748]: 72).

Does it follow from the arguments above that we have no idea of necessary connection and that our "causal judgements" are in fact meaningless? No: according to Hume we can locate the impression from which the idea of necessary connection is copied, but only by looking *beyond* single instances of causal transactions.

On all previous occasions on which a billiard ball has struck another stationary ball, the collision has been followed by the stationary ball's moving off. Also, when we saw the white billiard ball approaching the stationary black ball, we inferred that the black ball would likewise move off. When this happens, we say that the white ball's colliding with the black ball is the cause of the black ball's movement:

> [W]hen one particular species of event has always, in all instances, been conjoined with another, we make no longer any scruple of foretelling one upon

the appearance of the other, and of employing that reasoning, which can alone assure us of any matter of fact or existence. We then call the one object, *Cause*; the other, *Effect*. (1975 [1748]: 74)

How can exposure to many more instances of billiard ball collisions help us in the search for the impression of necessary connection? Is it that such exposure reveals something in the sequence of events (or "in the objects") that yields the impression of a necessary connection between them?

Hume suggests not. When we view the 1,000th instance of a billiard ball being struck by another and then moving off, as far as the external events are concerned there is nothing experienced in that transaction that wasn't also experienced in the first:

> 'Tis evident … that the repetition of like objects in like relations of succession and contiguity *discovers* nothing new in any one of them; since we can draw no inference from it, nor make it a subject either of our demonstrative or probable reasonings. (1978 [1739]: 163)

Causal claims cannot be established by demonstrative (*a priori*) reasoning: "I shall venture to affirm, as a general proposition, which admits of no exception, that the knowledge [of the relation between cause and effect] is not, in any instance attained by reasonings *a priori*" (1975 [1748]: 27). For any given pair of causally related events we can always conceive of the cause happening without the effect:

> When I see, for instance, a Billiard-ball moving in a straight line towards another; even suppose motion in the second ball should by accident be suggested to me, as the result of their contact or impulse; may I not conceive, that a hundred different events might as well follow from that cause? (1975 [1748]: 29).

We can conceive of e_1 being followed, not by e_2, but by e_4, in which both balls instantaneously become stationary. So no *a priori* reasoning can allow us to infer the occurrence of e_2 from the occurrence of e_1.

Moreover, even after exposure to the prior constant conjunction of e_1-type events with e_2-type events we are unable to rely on *a posteriori* or "probable" reasoning to infer the occurrence of e_2 from the occurrence of e_1. To infer the occurrence of e_2 from the occurrence of e_1, and the fact that all previous e_1-type events have been followed by e_2-type events, we would need to rely on the supposition "that instances, of which we have had no experience, must resemble those, of which we have had experience, and that the course of nature continues uniformly the same" (1978 [1739]: 89). But this proposition cannot be established either by *a priori* or *a posteriori* reasoning. It cannot be established by *a priori* or "demonstrative" reasoning, since we can conceive of a situation in which the black ball doesn't move off after being struck by the white ball, despite the fact that in the past, events of the latter type have always been followed by the stationary ball's moving off. Nor can it be established by *a posteriori* or "probable" reasoning.

Arguing that since *in the past*, instances of which we have had no experience have resembled those of which we have had experience, *in the future* instances of which we have had no experience will resemble those of which we have had experience, would be to argue in a circle. (This argument – in Book 1, pt 3, §6 of Hume's *Treatise* and §4 of his *Enquiry* – is clearly related to the traditional "problem of induction," but various commentators have questioned whether it is in fact a genuine concern of Hume's [see e.g. Beebee 2006: 7]).

Hence, experience of the constant conjunction of e_1-type events with e_2-type events reveals no impression of necessary connection obtaining between them. So how does the experience of the constant conjunction yield the sought-after impression of necessary connection? Hume answers:

> [T]here is nothing in a number of instances, different from every single instance, which is supposed to be exactly similar; except only, that after a repetition of similar instances, the mind is carried by habit, upon the appearance of one event, to expect its usual attendant, and to believe that it will exist. This connection, therefore, which we *feel* in the mind, this customary transition of the imagination from one object to its usual attendant, is the sentiment or impression from which we form the idea of power or necessary connection. (1975 [1748]: 75)

Thus, the impression of necessary connection is an impression of reflection that arises in the following way. When we experience a constant conjunction of two types of events, say e_1-type events and e_2-type events, they "acquire a union in the imagination" (1978 [1739]: 93): we become disposed, in virtue of "Custom" or "Habit" (1975 [1748]: 43), to infer an e_2-type idea from an e_1-type impression. This "customary transition of the mind" is accompanied by a *feeling* of *irresistibility* or *compulsion*. Given an impression of a white ball striking a black ball we feel compelled to form the idea of the black ball's moving off. This feeling of compulsion is the impression from which the idea of necessary connection is copied.

Causal anti-realism

What are the implications for causal realism of Hume's search for the impression of necessary connection? What, according to Hume, are we doing when we judge that e_1 caused e_2?

Hume claims that in making causal judgements we exhibit a tendency to *project* aspects of our psychology on to the world:

> [T]he mind has a great propensity to spread itself on external objects, and to conjoin with them any internal impressions, which they occasion, and which always make their appearance at the same time that these objects discover themselves to the senses. Thus as certain sounds and smells are always found to attend certain visible objects, we naturally imagine a conjunction, even in

place, betwixt the objects and qualities, tho' the qualities be of such a nature as to admit of no such conjunction, and really exist nowhere ... [T]he same propensity is the reason, why we suppose necessity and power to lie in the objects we consider, not in our mind, that considers them; notwithstanding it is not possible for us to form the most distant idea of that quality, when it is not taken for the determination of the mind, to pass from the idea of an object to that of its usual attendant. (1978 [1739]: 167; see also 1975 [1748]: 78)

How can we best make sense of Hume's talk of "the mind spreading itself on external objects" and "transferring the feeling of customary connection to objects"?

Projectivism

Causal realism holds that the judgement that e_1 caused e_2 expresses a *belief*, a psychological state that can be assessed in terms of *truth* and *falsity*. In general, an account of a type of judgement that views them as expressing beliefs is called a *cognitivist* account of judgements of that type. The projectivist interpretation of Hume sees him as rejecting causal realism by giving a *non-cognitivist* account of causal judgement, according to which causal judgements do not express beliefs or states with truth-evaluable propositional contents.

In the case of moral judgement, non-cognitivism holds that e.g. the judgement that murder is wrong does not express the *belief* that actions of a certain sort instantiate the *property* of moral wrongness, but rather expresses a *feeling* or *sentiment* of revulsion or disapproval towards acts of that kind, where these feelings or sentiments are non-cognitive in the sense that they are incapable of truth and falsity. According to the ethical non-cognitivist, what appears to be an ascription of a moral property is in fact a projection of a feeling on to a world that contains no such properties. Could something like this be what Hume has in mind in the case of causal judgement where he speaks of the mind spreading itself on the world? Simon Blackburn suggests that it is:

[According to Hume], the causal connection between events is something of which we have no impression, hence no idea, so a Humean theory of causation instead sees us as projecting on to events our own tendency to infer one from another [...] [For Hume] the causal order is a projection of our own confidences in the way they follow from one another. (Blackburn 1994: 180, 306)

According to the projectivist, then, when we judge that e_1 caused e_2, we are expressing our *feeling of confidence* that e_1-type events are always followed by e_2-type events, or our *habit* of inferring that an e_2-type event will occur from the occurrence of an e_1-type event, or perhaps the *feeling of being compelled* to form an e_2-type idea that we get when given an impression of an e_1-type event.

How plausible is this? Arguably, for Hume, where a judgement expresses the belief that *a* is G the constituents of the belief are ideas, where these ideas – according to the Copy Principle – are ultimately copied from impressions. If the judgement that *a* is G expresses a belief, it is true if and only if the object represented by the idea of *a* instantiates the property represented by the idea of G. However, a non-cognitivist account of the judgement *denies* that there is a property of G-*ness*, so it denies that there is such a thing as an idea of G (see Blackburn's remarks above). In the moral case, e.g., the non-cognitivist denies that we have an idea of moral goodness, since ideas are constituents of beliefs or propositions, and the non-cognitivist's claim is that moral judgements do not express beliefs or propositions.

Thus, according to the projectivist interpretation, Hume says we have no impression of necessary connection, hence – by the Copy Principle – no idea of necessary connection: we are not expressing beliefs whose constituents are ideas that are ultimately copied from impressions.

But this is clearly not what Hume is claiming: far from *denying* that we have an idea of necessary connection, the entire thrust of Hume's discussion is to *locate* the impression from which our idea of necessary connection is copied. Recall: "This connection, therefore, which we *feel* in the mind, this customary transition of the imagination from one object to its usual attendant, is the sentiment or impression from which we form the idea of power or necessary connection" (1975 [1748]: 75). How can Hume be a projectivist – as opposed to a cognitivist – when he claims to have *found* the impression from which the idea of necessary connection is copied?

Perhaps the projectivist view expressed by Blackburn above is over-simple, and some more complex projectivist account is available that does not deny the existence of an impression of necessary connection. Beebee, for example, writes: "It is the *transition of the mind* that is projected, and not the impression of necessary connection: the impression of necessary connection just *is* the modification of visual experience that we undergo when the transition takes place" (Beebee 2006: 146). Beebee's sophisticated projectivism deserves an extended discussion not possible here, but one problem at least should be plain: although her projectivist view talks of an impression of necessary connection, the suggestion that the *idea* of necessary connection is *copied* from it seems to have dropped out entirely. Indeed, the Copy Principle – the very thing motivating Hume's search for an impression of necessary connection – is not even mentioned in the course of her discussion of projectivism. At the very least, then, further explanation is required of how the projectivist interpretation coheres with what Hume says about the impression and idea of necessary connection and the Copy Principle that motivates his search for the former.

Error theory

The error theory holds that causal judgements do indeed express beliefs, but that they are systematically and uniformly false: the mind's projection of its feelings on to external objects is an error of presupposition. The judgement that e_1 caused e_2 expresses the belief that there is an objective relation of necessary connection between them. However, there are no objective relations of necessary connection obtaining between events, only a determination of the mind to move from an impression of one kind of event to an idea of another: "Hume's thesis is that a necessary connection is never observable between distinct events, whether mental or physical, since no two distinct events are necessarily connected" (Noonan 2007: 83). So the judgement that e_1 caused e_2 is *false*, as are all other (positive, atomic) causal statements (Stroud 1977).

On some views (Mackie 1974), Hume proposes a (revisionary) *regularity theory* of causation as a way of avoiding the error theory implied by our ordinary concept of causation. According to the regularity theory, to say that e_1 caused e_2 is to say that e_1 preceded e_2 and that all e_1-type events are followed by e_2-type events. The event of one billiard ball's striking another is invariably followed by motion in the second, but not by sneezing in nearby spectators.

This is the "traditional" interpretation of Hume, but it faces serious problems. First, it doesn't sit well with the Copy Principle. How can our concept of the causal relation be a concept of an objective relation between events if our idea of necessary connection is copied from a subjective feeling that accompanies a transition from one idea to another? Second, as Beebee argues (2006: 136–41), if Hume had held a regularity theory, he would surely have confronted the problem of distinguishing between genuine causal claims (e_1-type events cause e_2-type events) and accidental regularities (e_2-type events always follow e_1-type events). Since he didn't, it is strained to view him as proposing a regularity theory, even as a philosophically hygienic revision of our actual practice.

Subjectivism

Hume writes the following:

> [N]ecessity is something that exists in the mind, not in objects; nor is it possible for us ever to form the most distant idea of it, considered as a quality in bodies. Either we have no idea of necessity, or necessity is nothing but that determination of the thought to pass from causes to effects and from effects to causes, according to their experienced union. (1978 [1739]: 165–6)

Could Hume be rejecting causal realism by claiming that our concept of necessary connection is a concept of a determination of the mind to pass from an idea of one type of event to another? According to this *subjectivist* interpretation, when we judge that e_1 caused e_2 we express the belief that e_1-type events are always followed by e_2-type events *and that the idea of an e_1-type event leads irresistibly to an idea of an e_2-type event*: causal judgements express beliefs, at least some of which are true, but in virtue of facts about our mental propensities rather than objective, worldly relations.

Subjectivism faces various problems. First, it sits ill with facts about the *phenomenology* of causal judgement: if our concept of necessary connection is a concept of a determination of the mind, why is the first place that we look for the relation *outward*, between the events themselves? (This is the first place Hume looks: see the third section, "Hume's search for the impression of necessary connection," above.) Second, if Hume holds that subjectivism gives a descriptively adequate account of our concept of necessary connection, why does he expect us to be shocked by his view, as when he imagines us reacting as follows:

What! The efficacy of causes lie in the determination of the mind! As if causes did not operate entirely independent of the mind, and wou'd not continue their operation, even tho' there was no mind existent to contemplate them … Thought may well depend on causes for its operation, but not causes on thought. This is to reverse the order of nature, and make that secondary, what is really primary. (1978 [1739]: 167)

Without further explanation, the subjectivist interpretation is implausible.

Sceptical Realism

A claim common to the projectivist, error-theoretic and subjectivist interpretations is that according to Hume there are no such things as objective relations of necessary connection between events. According to proponents of "the New Hume," however, Hume does not deny that there are objective relations of necessary connection, only that we ever possess knowledge of them. In defence of this claim they point to passages such as the following:

[E]xperience only teaches us, how one event constantly follows another; without instructing us in the secret connexion, which binds them together, and renders them inseparable. (1975 [1748]: 66)

[N]ature has kept us at a great distance from all her secrets, and has afforded us only the knowledge of a few superficial qualities of objects; while she conceals from us those powers and principles on which the influence of those objects entirely depends. (1975 [1748]: 32–3)

The scenes of the universe are continually shifting, and one object follows another in an uninterrupted succession; but the power or force which actuates the whole machine, is entirely concealed from us, and never discovers itself in the sensible qualities of body. (1975 [1748]: 63–4)

In general, realist views combine *modesty* and *presumption*. As Crispin Wright puts it, they "modestly allow that humankind confronts an objective world" (1993: 1), but nevertheless presume "that we are … capable of acquiring knowledge of the world and of understanding it" (*ibid.*). The sceptical realist interpretation thus views Hume as departing from causal realism by rejecting its presumptuous but not its modest component. Whether or not this combination of a realist metaphysic with a sceptical epistemology can plausibly be attributed to Hume is a matter of current controversy (see e.g. Beebee [2006: Ch. 7] for a balanced overview). However, although there is no consensus as to whether Hume should be viewed as a projectivist, error-theoretic, subjectivist or sceptical-realist opponent of causal realism, his writings do indisputably form the starting point for all current discussions of the metaphysics of causation.

References

Beebee, H. (2006) *Hume on Causation*, London: Routledge.

Blackburn, S. (1994) *The Oxford Dictionary of Philosophy*, Oxford: Oxford University Press.

Hume, D. (1975 [1748]) *An Enquiry Concerning Human Understanding*, edited by L. A. Selby-Bigge and P. H. Nidditch, Oxford: Clarendon Press.

——— (1978 [1739]) *A Treatise of Human Nature*, 2nd edn, edited by L. A. Selby-Bigge and P. H. Nidditch, Oxford: Clarendon Press.

Mackie, J. (1974) *The Cement of the Universe*, Oxford: Oxford University Press.

Noonan, H. (2007) *Hume*, Oxford: Oneworld.

Stroud, B. (1977) *Hume*, London: Routledge.

Wright, C. (1993) *Realism, Meaning and Truth*, 2nd edn, Oxford: Blackwell.

Further reading

A superbly clear introduction to the first *Enquiry* is A. Bailey and D. O'Brien, *Hume's* Enquiry Concerning Human Understanding: *A Reader's Guide* (London: Continuum, 2006). H. Beebee, *Hume on Causation* (London: Routledge, 2006) contains a defence of a projectivist interpretation that incorporates a critical survey of competing interpretations. See also S. Blackburn, *Spreading the Word* (Oxford: Oxford University Press, 1984) (chapter 6 contains a brief exposition of a projectivist account); and "Hume and Thick Connexions" (originally published in 1990), in his *Essays on Quasi-Realism* (Oxford: Oxford University Press 1993) (more on projectivism, plus a critique of sceptical realism). An excellent introduction to book 1 of the *Treatise* is H. Noonan, *Hume on Knowledge* (London: Routledge, 1999); and Noonan's *Hume* (Oxford: Oneworld Publications, 2007) is a high-level introduction to Hume's overall philosophy. J. Mackie, *The Cement of the Universe* (Oxford: Oxford University Press, 1974), views Hume as an error theorist and regularity theorist. S. Psillos, *Causation and Explanation* (Chesham, UK: Acumen, 2002) contains a survey of views of causation, beginning with Hume. An influential study viewing Hume as an error theorist is B. Stroud, *Hume* (London: Routledge, 1977).

14

KANT
The possibility of metaphysics

Lucy Allais

In metaphysics we have to retrace our path countless times, because we find
that it does not lead where we want to go, and it is so far from reaching
unanimity in the assertions of its adherents that it is rather a battlefield, and
indeed one that appears to be especially determined for testing one's powers in
mock combat; on this battlefield no combatant has ever gained the least bit of
ground, nor has any been able to base any lasting possession on his victory.
(Kant 1998: Bxv)

Kant opens his *Critique of Pure Reason* with a damning assessment of the state of
metaphysics, especially when compared with the progress made in mathematics and
science. He thinks that philosophers have attempted to have knowledge of reality
through reason alone, but they have not succeeded: the problems they discuss, such as
whether we have freedom of the will, are as controversial as they were in ancient
Greece. Part of the problem, he thinks, is that a lot of the questions with which philosophers are concerned are in fact impossible for humans to answer, and part of the
problem is that there is no established method for making progress in metaphysics. The
point of his *Critique* is to solve these problems, by taking a step back and asking how it
is possible for us to have substantial (nontrivial) knowledge of the world through reason
alone, i.e., *a priori*. Kant thinks that an explanation of the possibility of metaphysical
knowledge will give us a method for establishing metaphysical claims, at the same time
as clearly delimiting which kinds of metaphysical questions it is possible for us to answer,
thereby ending pointless dispute about those of which we cannot have knowledge.

Kant presents the *Critique* as addressed to the question, "How are synthetic *a priori*
judgements possible?", which he takes to be the same as the question, "How is
metaphysics possible?" His two-part answer to the question of synthetic *a priori*
knowledge is his account of how metaphysics is possible, as well as of the possible
extent of metaphysical knowledge. Kant says that the question of how synthetic *a priori*
judgements are possible is not a problem in logic, and he thinks that the only way of
answering it is by invoking a complex and subtle metaphysical and epistemological

position, which he calls "transcendental idealism." This solution will explain what metaphysical knowledge Kant thinks is possible for us, as well as the principled limits he places on it. Further, Kant thinks that it provides the basis of empirical knowledge and science, at the same time as creating essential space for the quite different knowledge involved in thinking about morality.

Synthetic *a priori* knowledge

Kant says that all propositions are either analytic or synthetic, and are known either *a priori* or *a posteriori*. A priori knowledge is justified independently of experience, and Kant thinks that all claims which contain necessity and universality can be known only *a priori* (Kant: A1). For example, the claim "every event has a cause" could never be established empirically, since we cannot, in principle, experience every event. For Kant, analytic propositions can be seen to be true through analysis (i.e., decomposition) of the concepts they contain (breaking them down into their sub-concepts [A151/B190]). He also says that they can be seen to be true in accordance with the principle of non-contradiction (A6–7/B10–11); this brings his definition close to a common contemporary definition, which says that a proposition is analytic if it is a basic proposition of logic, or if it is translatable into a basic proposition of logic by substituting synonyms for synonyms. It is thus relatively easy to see how analytic propositions can be known *a priori*: through our grasping relations between the concepts in them. For example, the claim "bachelors are unmarried" can be analysed or decomposed into the claim "unmarried men are unmarried"; no investigation of particular bachelors is required to see that this is true. In contrast, synthetic propositions go beyond what is contained in the concept of the subject, and can be denied without contradiction; an example is the claim "bachelors are lazy." This claim is synthetic and *a posteriori*: we need to investigate bachelors to see whether it is true. Synthetic *a priori* propositions will be more than mere logical claims, yet they *cannot* be seen to be true through investigation of the way the world is, since they are *a priori*. For example, take the claim that "every event has a necessitating cause." Kant agrees with Hume both that this claim is not a truth of logic (it can be denied without contradiction) and that it cannot be established empirically. However, he does not agree with Hume that we should therefore dismiss it: Hume overlooks the possibility of synthetic *a priori* knowledge.

At the start of the *Critique*, Kant treats the possibility of our knowing *metaphysical* claims as an open question, but he thinks it is obvious that there is at least *some* synthetic *a priori* knowledge, since he thinks that mathematics is synthetic and *a priori*, and that physics is based on synthetic *a priori* claims. This view of mathematics is a reasonable one for Kant to hold, since it is not possible to reduce mathematics to logic given the logical tools available to him; indeed, whether this is completely possible with the logic we have today remains an open question. In the first half of the twentieth century Kant's claim that there is synthetic *a priori* knowledge was widely rejected, by those philosophers who went back to the empiricist idea that our *a priori* knowledge is restricted to analytic propositions. In the second half of the twentieth century, Kant's account was rejected even more radically, by those who questioned the analytic–

synthetic distinction, and the notion of *a priority*. There has not, however, been consensus around these rejections, and we will not concern ourselves with them here.

Why does Kant align the possibility of metaphysics with the question of synthetic *a priori* knowledge? Kant presents his position as a synthesis of rationalism and empiricism. On the one hand, philosophers like Leibniz and Descartes think we can have substantial knowledge of the world through reason alone, independent of experience. Kant agrees that this is what we aspire to in metaphysics, and he thinks that the drive to this kind of knowledge is a natural and unavoidable part of the way we think. But he thinks that all that these philosophers achieve is completely different accounts, neither supported nor contradicted by experience, and therefore with respect to which we have no clear way of adjudicating between them and of making progress. On the other hand, empiricists like Hume think that, in Kant's terms, all our *a priori* knowledge is trivial, analytic knowledge, and that all our substantial knowledge is empirical. Hume ends his *Enquiry Concerning Human Understanding* by saying the following:

> When we run over libraries, persuaded of these principles, what havoc must we make? If we take in our hand any volume; of divinity or school metaphysics, for instance; let us ask, *Does it contain any abstract reasoning concerning quantity or number?* No. *Does it contain any experimental reasoning concerning matter of fact and existence?* No. Commit it then to the flames: for it can contain nothing but sophistry and illusion. (*Enquiry*, in Hume 1988: §12, pt 3)

If we accept this, then it seems that all we have are the empirical sciences on the one hand, and logic on the other, with nothing left for philosophy in between (the two main conceptions of philosophy in the twentieth century – as conceptual analysis, and as part of the natural sciences – seem to be a result of accepting this view). Against this view, Kant wants to find a substantive role for philosophy, a metaphysics that is more than just clarifying relations between concepts used by the sciences. If metaphysics, as an investigation into reality, is to be different from the empirical sciences, and in particular, if we strive for knowledge of necessary truths, then metaphysics is *a priori*; for it to be substantive, it must be synthetic. Not only does Kant think that our minds strive after such knowledge, he thinks that empirical knowledge cannot be explained without it. While he is extremely impressed by the explanatory power and progress of the empirical sciences, there are two respects in which he thinks that they are limited. First, he thinks we cannot explain empirical knowledge without appealing to some substantive *a priori* propositions which provide a framework within which empirical knowledge can proceed: we cannot gain knowledge from experience without principles with which to interpret the sensory input. Second, he thinks that there are limits to empirical knowledge, and there is reason to think that it cannot explain everything there is. Kant thinks that it is the failure to recognise the possibility of synthetic *a priori* knowledge that led Hume to dismiss metaphysics; at the same time, Kant respects the objections empiricists have to the idea that we could have substantial knowledge of mind-independent reality. Synthetic *a priori* judgments are the only way we could have non-trivial knowledge of reality through reason alone, yet synthetic *a priori* judgments seem to be a mystery (Kant: A10/B13).

Transcendental idealism

Kant's answer is that our synthetic *a priori* knowledge is not knowledge of an entirely mind-independent world. In other words, he invokes a kind of idealism, his famous transcendental idealism. Kant's transcendental idealism makes three basic claims. (1) There is a distinction between the world as it is in itself and the world as it appears to us. (2) The world as it appears to us depends on our minds, in some sense and to some extent. (3) We cannot have any knowledge of the world as it is in itself. Kant argues that our synthetic *a priori* knowledge is knowledge of the world as it appears to us, and that the fact that synthetic *a priori* truths hold of the world of experience is explained by the fact that our minds impose them on the world. As opposed to the *tabula rasa* of the empiricists, Kant thinks that the mind actively contributes to the way we experience the world as being, and that the world we experience is a combination of what is contributed by mind-independent reality and the structuring principles our minds use to process and arrange this input. Principles we use to interpret and structure our experience could not all have been derived from experience; some must be independent of it, and are therefore due to the mind and not the way the mind-independent world is. Thus, we can have nontrivial knowledge of necessary features of the world that we experience because the necessary structure of the world of experience is imposed on it by our minds. Kant famously says that "We can cognize of things *a priori* only what we ourselves have put into them" (Kant: Bxviii). What the mind contributes is *a priori* structure, which includes space and time, as well as *a priori* concepts and principles.

Ever since the publication of the first edition of the *Critique*, and continuing to the present day, there has been no agreement amongst commentators as to how to interpret Kant's transcendental idealism. Commentators disagree as to how Kant's distinction between things in themselves and things as they appear to us should be understood, about the sense in which things as they appear to us depend on our minds, and about whether Kant's idea of things as they are in themselves involves a metaphysical commitment to an actually existing but essentially unknowable aspect of reality, or whether he merely thinks that we cannot avoid using the concept of things as they are in themselves. Some commentators have read Kant as a strong metaphysical idealist in the way that Bishop Berkeley is – as thinking that empirical objects exist only *in* our minds. At the other extreme, Kant's transcendental distinction between things as they are in themselves and things as they appear to us has been read as a merely epistemological or methodological distinction between two ways of thinking about the objects of knowledge, two aspects of the world, or two perspectives on the world. In between this deflationary view and the extreme idealist view are any number of different accounts; what follows is one interpretation.

Repeatedly, and throughout the *Critique*, Kant makes strongly idealist-sounding claims, such as that if we remove our own subject or even only the subjective constitution of the senses in general, then all constitution, all relations of objects in space and time, indeed space and time themselves would disappear … as appearances they cannot exist in themselves, but only in us. (A42/B60)

It is hard to reconcile these statements with any interpretation of transcendental idealism that does not see Kant as committed to the world as we experience it being mind-dependent in a substantial sense. On the other hand, there are clear objections to seeing Kant as a Berkeleyan idealist with respect to appearances, not least that Kant himself explicitly and repeatedly rejects this interpretation of his position (B70, B274; *Prolegomena*, in Kant 2004: 293, 374). Further, Kant explicitly rejects an important assumption that empiricists like Hume and rationalists like Descartes share, which is that what the mind is immediately and directly in contact with is something mental; on the contrary, he argues that we have immediate experience of objects distinct from us and in space (which he explicitly says are the very objects whose existence Berkeley denies and Descartes doubts, and these are clearly not mental entities), and that our knowledge of our mental life depends on this. As well as saying that the world as it appears to us depends on our minds, Kant also stresses what he calls its "empirical reality." He says that appearances are *transcendentally ideal but empirically real*, and part of his concern in stressing their empirical reality is to distinguish appearances from mere mental states. Kant thinks that he can prove that empirically real objects are public, external objects, which exist in space and time, are made up of indestructible stuff (matter which is conserved), exist unperceived, and are in necessary causal relations with each other. One of the challenges of interpreting transcendental idealism is to do justice to both the empirical reality and the transcendental ideality of appearances.

Here is one way of thinking about the mind-dependence of appearances. Think of viewing a scene through a pane of glass. You do not see objects in virtue of seeing images on the pane of glass, rather, you see straight through the glass to the objects themselves. Now imagine that the glass has a distorting effect, such that, for example, the shapes of things are seen as being somewhat different to the way they actually are – perhaps as being more curved. Just as in the first case, you do not see the objects in virtue of seeing images on the pane of glass; you still see through the glass to the objects beyond it. However, you now see the objects as being different, to some extent, from the way they are in themselves – the way they are independent of your perceiving them. It would not be incoherent to say that what you see is in some sense a representation of the objects: what you see is the world as it is represented in your perceptual experience, which is partly dependent on its being seen through glass. At the same time you still see things which exist outside of your mind, although you do not see them as they are in themselves. Now imagine that the glass is more radically distorting, such that it actually affects how you see objects arranged in the scene – and even what you perceive as an object – and imagine that you have no way of finding out how objects are independently of the way you perceive them. Put the cognitive-processing apparatus of the mind in the place of the glass, and you might think of Kant's view as something like this. We are directly consciously presented with the world, as opposed to representing the world by constructing mental images, but the way we perceive things as being is partly a function of the way the mind is. Kant thinks that the way we perceive things is radically determined by our minds in such a way that the way they appear to us is nothing at all like the way they are independently of our perceiving them.

It is sometimes objected that Kant is not entitled to say both that there are things in themselves and that we cannot have any knowledge of them. However, what he says is that we cannot have any substantial knowledge of their nature, not that we cannot know any truths about them at all – for example, we can know that analytic propositions are true of things in themselves. Kant thinks that we cannot have any nontrivial knowledge of the world as it is in itself: our empirical knowledge is limited to the world as it appears to us (which is partly dependent on our minds), and our *a priori* knowledge is limited to knowledge of the conditions of the possibility of experience (necessary truths about the world as it appears to us) and logic.

Kant's distinction between things in themselves and things as they appear to us is almost, but not quite, the same as his distinction between noumena and phenomena; the reason it is not quite the same is that Kant distinguishes between a positive and a negative notion of noumena. He says that a noumenon in the positive sense would be an object of a kind which, in principle, could not be experienced through our sense organs (think of Platonic numbers, God or Cartesian souls). Kant says that we do not even really understand what such objects would be (Kant 1998: B307), but that we have the concept of such objects as a limiting concept: it stops us from arrogantly asserting that there could not be more to reality than the kinds of things of which we have experience. But he says that a noumenon in the negative sense is a thing which we experience, thought of in abstraction from the ways we experience it (B307), and that this is not a merely limiting concept, but something to whose existence we are actually committed. This suggests that his notion of things in themselves is neither the notion of distinct supersensible objects, nor merely a limiting concept: rather, Kant thinks that there is an actually existing aspect of the world which is partly responsible for how the world appears to us, but of which we cannot have knowledge.

The negative and positive projects: transcendent and immanent metaphysics

Kant thinks that his transcendental idealism both explains how it is possible for us to have knowledge of (synthetic *a priori*) metaphysical claims, and at the same time clearly delimits the scope of our metaphysical knowledge. He argues that most of the traditional questions of metaphysics transcend our capacity to answer them, because they attempt to have knowledge, through reason alone, of things which we could not, in principle, experience, such as the beginning of the universe, God or a Cartesian soul. Kant refers to such attempts as "transcendent metaphysics." A large part of the *Critique* is devoted to debunking transcendent metaphysics, and trying to show that it is not possible for us to know, for example, whether we have souls which are essentially different from matter and are immortal, whether the world is finite or infinite in space and time, whether matter is infinitely divisible or made up of simple parts, whether we have free will, and whether there is a God. He aims to explain why it is that we cannot help *trying* to answer these questions, but to show that reason necessarily falls into contradiction when it tries to answer them. While this part of Kant's project is primarily negative, he thinks it serves a positive purpose in two ways. First, showing which questions we cannot answer and why, enables us to end pointless disputes. Second, he thinks that the impossibility of knowledge with respect to God and whether we have free will is crucial for the way we think of ourselves as moral beings, and that moral thought and experience can partly complete what theoretical reason on its own cannot achieve.

While Kant rules out most of the traditional metaphysical concerns of philosophers as unknowable, he does not take this to mean that we cannot have any *a priori* knowledge of nontrivial necessity; as we have seen, he thinks that we can have knowledge of necessary features of the world of experience. Necessity and contingency are often explained in terms of possible worlds: the idea is that necessary truths are true in all possible worlds, and contingent truths are not. Since synthetic propositions are not logical truths, they can be denied without contradiction, or, in other words, there are possible worlds in which they are not true. But if they are not true in all possible worlds, how can they be necessary? Kant's idea that there is both analytic and synthetic necessity can be explained by thinking of a division in the set of all possible worlds. First we have all the barely possible worlds – the worlds which are described by sets of propositions which do not logically contradict each other. A smaller subgroup of the possible worlds consists of those worlds of which it is possible for us to have empirical knowledge, and to experience as objective: synthetically necessary truths are true in all and only these worlds. Thus, they can be denied without contradiction, but they are still necessary, in the sense that they are not true merely of the actual world, but rather of all the possible worlds of which we can have experience. Kant thus distinguishes between merely logical possibility and what he calls "real possibility" (A244/B302), where real possibility is given by necessary truths about worlds of which we could have experience, or, as Kant puts it, the formal conditions of experience (A218–21/B265–8). This gives him an account of metaphysical necessity, as well as a sense in which the laws of nature are necessary that is irreducibly different from logical necessity. A metaphysics of synthetic *a priori* propositions will be a description of the necessary features of the actual world of which we have experience: an "immanent metaphysics." What makes it metaphysics is that it is *a priori* knowledge of necessary features of the world. What distinguishes it from previous metaphysics is that it is a description of necessary features of the world that we experience, not an attempt to describe that which goes beyond what we can experience.

Transcendental arguments

In addition to his proposed general solution (transcendental idealism), Kant has a method for establishing particular (synthetic *a priori*) metaphysical claims: he thinks that we can show that a claim is true of the actual world by showing that it is a condition of the possibility (or presupposition) of experience and empirical knowledge. If it is a presupposition of experience, then it will be true of any world of which we could have experience. Commentators label this strategy "transcendental argument"; these arguments are supposed to demonstrate the truth of some controversial claim (in Kant's case, a synthetic *a priori* judgment) by showing it to be a presupposition of a less controversial claim. Kant takes his way of establishing (synthetic *a priori*) metaphysical claims to be inseparable from his transcendental idealism, but it is arguable that one could accept his notion of metaphysics as synthetic *a priori* knowledge, and make use of transcendental arguments, without accepting the idealism, or *vice versa*.

A famous example of Kant's use of the strategy is his response to Hume's scepticism about causal necessity. Hume denies that events involve – or could be known to involve – necessary connections, but he does not doubt that we experience *events*, in the sense of one thing following another in the world. Kant argues that we could not know ourselves to have experienced an event (an objective succession in the world, as opposed to a succession of subjective mental states) if we did not know that every event has a necessitating cause. He points out that all of my mental life consists of one experience following another, whether or not what I am experiencing is objectively successive: when a ball drops, my experience of it in one place follows my experience of it in another place, but similarly, when I experience parts of a house, my experience of one part (perhaps the roof), follows my experience of another part (perhaps the walls), although these parts do not *exist* successively in the way that the ball's being at different places is objectively successive. This means that the mere experience of my successive mental life is not enough for me to know that I am experiencing something objectively successive. Kant puts forward a complex argument designed to show that having knowledge of an objective temporal order requires there being necessitating causal relations. If successful, the argument shows that Hume is not entitled to his starting point, using the materials at his disposal.

Kant thinks that he can show that our empirical knowledge depends on the truth of the claim that every event has a necessitating cause: this means that we can know the claim to be true of any world of which we can have knowledge and experience, and therefore that we can know of all the events that we experience that they have a law-governed necessitating cause. Because this principle is a condition of empirical knowledge, and as such serves us so well, we are naturally led to think we can apply the concept to the beginning of the world as a whole, as ask whether *it* has a cause. But here we try to apply the principle to something which is, in principle, impossible for us to experience, and this leads us into contradiction: we find that we have equally good arguments for thinking that there must be, and that there cannot be, a necessary first cause of the world. Kant points out that we are not entitled to take our natural and irresistible inclination to ask for a sufficient explanation for everything for insight into the way reality actually must be: while we can know that every event that we could experience has a necessitating cause, we cannot know that this is true of everything that could exist. It is thus not possible for us to have the ultimate explanation which we cannot help seeking.

Freedom of the will

Kant's account of freedom of the will is an example of how he thinks his negative project of debunking transcendent metaphysics has a positive role. Kant thinks that the way we think about morality commits us to thinking that we have freedom of the will in a strong sense which is incompatible with deterministic laws of nature: he thinks it requires believing in a kind of causality which is different to empirical causality in that it involves the ability to initiate events which are not a deterministic function of previous states of the universe. He thinks that if we knew that deterministic laws of nature were true of the world we would have to give up on both the ideas of freedom and morality, and he thinks that deterministic laws of nature are an *a priori* presupposition of scientific knowledge. But he thinks that when we try to think about everything that exists, in itself, in terms of deterministic causal explanation, we find ourselves with equally compelling arguments for thinking that there can be only deterministic causation and for thinking that there must be another kind of causation (which involves the ability to initiate an event in a way which is not a function of previous states of the universe), and we are thus driven to contradiction (A444–52/B472–80). His transcendental idealism is supposed to enable us to avoid this contradiction, by limiting deterministic causation to the world as it appears to us. This allows for the possibility of a different kind of causation in the world as it is in itself, which opens a space in which it is rationally permissible for us to believe that we have free will, although we cannot know that we have it, or even really understand what it would involve.

Clearly, how we understand Kant's attempt to reconcile freedom of the will and deterministic laws of nature will directly depend on how we interpret his transcendental idealism, and there are more strongly metaphysical, and relatively deflationary, accounts of his solution to the free will problem, corresponding to interpretations of his transcendental idealism. In one respect, Kant's is an unambitious response to the problem of free will: he is not trying to demonstrate that we have strong (incompatibilist) free will, nor to explain what it is or how it is possible. He is merely trying to show that it is not ruled out by what we know about the world, and therefore that we are entitled to believe in it. However, merely attempting to show that a conception of freedom of the will which is inconsistent with deterministic laws of nature is *coherent* is a large project, and one many philosophers have rejected. Kant remained concerned with the problem of reconciling the presuppositions of morality and science throughout his further writings; along with his concerns with the nature of space and time, the explanation of how mathematics applies to reality, and the nature of causation, amongst others, this remains a live question. While large parts of Kant's project and his method were rejected by twentieth century philosophers, they were not refuted, and there is still much to be learnt from him on these subjects.

References

Kant, I. (1998) *The Critique of Pure Reason*, edited, trans. by Paul Guyer and Allen Wood, Cambridge: Cambridge University Press.
—— (2004) *Prolegomena to Any Future Metaphysics*, edited by Gary Hatfield, Cambridge: Cambridge University Press.
Hume, D. (1988) *Enquiry Concerning Human Understanding*, edited by A. Flew, Chicago, IL: Open Court.

Further reading

There are a number of excellent commentaries on the *Critique of Pure Reason*, of which a sample is listed here: H. Allison, *Kant's Transcendental Idealism: An Interpretation and Defence* (New Haven, CT; London: Yale University Press, 2004); J. Bennett, *Kant's Analytic* (Cambridge: Cambridge University Press, 1966); *Kant's Dialectic* (Cambridge: Cambridge University Press, 1974); G. Bird, *The Revolutionary Kant* (Chicago: Open Court, 2006); A. C. Ewing, *A Short Commentary on Kant's Critique of Pure Reason* (Chicago: University of Chicago Press, 1996); S. Gardner, *Kant and the Critique of Pure Reason* (London: Routledge, 1999); P. Guyer, *Kant and the Claims of Knowledge* (Cambridge: Cambridge University Press, 1987); H. J. Paton, *Kant's Metaphysics of Experience* (London: George Allen & Unwin, 1936); P. F. Strawson, *The Bounds of Sense* (London: Methuen & Co., 1966); R. C. S. Walker, *Kant* (London: Routledge & Kegan Paul, 1978); and A. Ward, *Kant: The Three Critiques* (Cambridge: Polity, 2006). There are many different interpretations of Kant's transcendental idealism; below is a sample, roughly grouped into different approaches. Phenomenalist: J. Van Cleve, *Problems from Kant* (New York and Oxford: Oxford University Press 1999). Metaphysical but nonidealist: A. Collins, *Possible Experience* (Berkeley; Los Angeles: University of California Press 1999); R. Langton, *Kantian Humility: Our Ignorance of Things in Themselves* (Oxford: Clarendon Press, 1998). Epistemological/methodological: H. Allison, *Kant's Transcendental Idealism* (above). Metaphysical, idealist but not phenomentalist: L. Allais, "Kant's One World," *The British Journal for the History of Philosophy* 12, no. 4 (2004): 655–84.

15

HEGEL AND SCHOPENHAUER
Reason and will

Rolf-Peter Horstmann

Metaphysics, according to a caustic remark by the British philosopher F. H. Bradley, is "the finding of bad reasons for what we believe upon instinct" (1897 [1893]: x). If one does not take offence at the word "bad" one can use this characterization as a telling starting point to come to an understanding what metaphysics is all about and why it has been and still is a topic of considerable concern not only to professional philosophers. Even a normal person will experience situations that lead to questions concerning the basis of his beliefs. Thus an average taxpayer who happens to believe in the funda- mental reasonableness of the world might wonder, on getting an unexpected and unwarranted huge tax bill, how to think about the rationality of a world in which such a thing can happen. This arguably is or at least implies a metaphysical question, in this case a question concerning the general organization of the world. Another person who under the most unlikely circumstances meets the man of her dreams and learns at the very same time that she has won the first prize in the lottery might be tempted to think she is dreaming, and that what she is experiencing is just a representation, something not "really real," something she makes up, though until now she had no reason whatsoever to have doubts about the reality of the world she inhabits. She too is drawn into a metaphysical question as to the ontological status of the world of experience.

Though neither the unlucky taxpayer nor the lucky lady is likely to develop a metaphysical theory about the world as a whole, the philosopher does. This characteri- zation of the objective of a metaphysical theory restricts metaphysics to what was called "metaphysica generalis" or "ontologia" in the rationalistic tradition of continental philosophy in the eighteenth century. Though the term "metaphysics" has since been used with a number of different connotations it is in the traditional meaning of "general metaphysics" that we use the term here. Coming to metaphysical questions in much the same way as the common person the philosopher is not content with just asking them: he wants to answer them. The resulting theory is intended to uphold a specific view of the world. The two philosophers discussed here, Georg Wilhelm Friedrich Hegel

(1770–1831) and Arthur Schopenhauer (1788–1860), both argue for very distinctive worldviews, which are alike in being difficult to understand in their own right and even more difficult to reconcile with deeply rooted convictions of everyday life. Thus Hegel maintains what is called a "monism of reason," according to which one has to think of reality as a process which consists in the self-cognition of reason (*Selbsterkenntnis der Vernunft*), whereas Schopenhauer insists on what one could call a "monism of the will" which asserts that reality is ultimately nothing but a purposeless force, called "will," which for a cognizing subject like a human being appears in the mode of presentation in different objectivations (hence the title, *Die Welt als Wille und Vorstellung*).[1] Even though both of these claims seem to be highly counterintuitive they are not just the outcome of some personal preconception. Both Hegel and Schopenhauer are convinced that there are quite compelling reasons in favour of their respective views. In what follows I will first discuss the basis and the meaning of Hegel's metaphysical monism before giving an outline of Schopenhauer's position in metaphysics.

Hegel: metaphysical monism

To understand Hegel's position in metaphysics as an answer to problems whose solution, according to Hegel, depends on endorsing a monistic worldview, one has to go back both to everyday life and to philosophy, in particular to Immanuel Kant (1724–1804). For Hegel the origin of all philosophical reflection is the experience of alienation and bifurcation characteristic of modern times. Already in his early works, he critically notes the loss of unity in human life which leads modern human beings to inconsistent and even contradictory conceptions of the world and their situation in it. Under these circumstances the task of philosophy in general and metaphysics in particular consists in establishing a view of reality that overcomes alienation and the sense of an insurmountable opposition between the modern individual and the world he is living in and allows the modern individual to think of himself as an integral part of a rationally organized totality. For Hegel – and for all the other post-Kantian idealistic philosophers like Johann Gottlieb Fichte (1762–1814) and Friedrich Wilhelm Joseph Schelling (1775–1854), who then became known as German idealists – this task is formulated and pursued most impressively by Immanuel Kant, which made his philosophy the natural starting point for a modern metaphysical theory. However, this assessment was not unequivocally positive and led to a very ambivalent attitude towards Kant's achievements. On the one hand, Hegel – like all the German idealists – considers Kant's philosophical theory to be the most advanced attempt of modern times of bringing together in a systematically ordered way all the different branches of philosophy into a unified system thus allowing people to think of themselves and the world surrounding them as a somehow coherent unity. This assessment of Kant's achievements turned not only Hegel into an unreserved Kantian. On the other hand, he is equally convinced that Kant did a very bad job in realizing his own programme (at least within the "official" statement known as the three Critiques) in that he chose to rely heavily on conceptions which flatly contradicted his guiding intentions and which led him, according to Hegel and the other German idealists, to what they called irreconcilable dualisms and to a totally unjustified subjectivist interpretation of the world. It was these alleged shortcomings which made Hegel and his idealist contemporaries into critics of Kant. Connected with that ambivalent relation is the belief that in order to achieve a more satisfying philosophical realization of the Kantian programme one has to explore highly unconventional methodological and conceptual means, because according to Hegel, Kant made the best use possible of traditional conceptions and methods and he nevertheless failed badly.

In Hegel's eyes the most obvious problem with Kant's approach is that he has to distinguish between a world of appearances and a world of things in themselves, and he restricts cognition to the world of appearances. According to Hegel, the distinction and the restriction together amount to the admission that we cannot gain knowledge of the essence of reality, but have epistemic access only to its subjective complement, i.e. to the way reality appears to us. For Hegel this admission, though unavoidable from a Kantian perspective, not only violates our sense of reality, but also prevents us from conceiving reality as an objective unity. Hegel claims that the reason for this unwelcome result lies in Kant's distorted subjectivist conception of the role and the status of what he calls "transcendental unity of apperception" or transcendental self-consciousness. Since metaphysics is supposed to give an account of the objective constitution of reality that can integrate the idea of the world as an organized whole and at the same time can accommodate the fact of self-consciousness, one has to abandon the Kantian version of metaphysics and start all over again. And this is precisely what Hegel wants to do. The guiding intention in his endeavour can be stated roughly as the attempt to overcome the Kantian divide between the world as it appears to us (subjectively) and the world as it is in itself (objectively), by changing the status of self-consciousness from a merely subjective principle as in Kant to one that is also objective. The hope is thereby to reconcile the opposition between the subjective and the objective and thus to allow for reality to be conceived as a "monistic whole," i.e. a totality constituted by subjective as well as objective elements.

Presented in this rather sketchy way the strategy attributed to Hegel seems to be both ad hoc and trivial. But neither charge really sticks. The ad hoc charge does not count because Hegel and his idealistic contemporaries all took great pains to demonstrate that unless it was an objective principle the transcendental unity of apperception could not be a fundamental principle constitutive of both cognition and of reality. That they all had different and somewhat idiosyncratic conceptions of cognition as well as reality, which are not easy to bring into line with what Kant meant by these notions, is another story. The allegation of triviality does not stick either. It turned out to be an enormously complicated endeavour to integrate transcendental self-consciousness into a coherent monistic conception of reality. It was necessary both to avoid objective reality becoming a mere function and product of subjectivity and thus dependent on it, and to avoid subjectivity becoming merely the passive mirror of an independent reality with no role in its organization.

That it is complicated to formulate a monistic metaphysics can be shown very clearly in the case of Hegel. To show this we mention the most crucial of the basic convictions he relied on: his particular conception of what reality understood as a monistic whole consists in. This conception embodies the following three constitutive claims: (1) We have to think of the sum total (*Gesamtheit*) of reality as a rational unity or, as Hegel quite often says, as reason. This claim implies that for Hegel the term "reason" has primarily (though not exclusively) an ontological meaning: it refers to the totality of what there is. (2) This rational unity or reason has to be thought of as the product of the process of the realization of its concept. This claim amounts to a dynamic conception of reality as a process of self-realization of reason. (3) This dynamic process is determined by those conceptual elements that are contained in the (Hegelian) concept of reason, i.e. in the concept of reality understood as a rational unity. This claim makes Hegel something like a conceptual realist.

These assertions shape the structural design of Hegel's system in that they commit him to a theory of what he calls the concept of reason and a theory of the so-called process of the realization of this concept. The former he calls "Science of Logic," the latter he calls *Realphilosophie*. The central role in terms of metaphysics is assigned to the "Science of Logic" because it is here that Hegel analyses the internal conceptual structure or organization of reason taken in the ontological sense of the totality of what is real. This structure then determines the specific ways in which reason realizes itself in all the different forms of physical and non-physical reality, i.e. as nature and "spirit" (*Geist*). Here, "spirit" refers to the realm of psychological (subjective spirit), social–political (objective spirit) and aesthetic, religious as well as more secular cultural (absolute spirit) phenomena. The leading idea behind this conception is perhaps not that mysterious if one imagines it by analogy with the way in which one can conceive of the development of an organism: a fully grown individual organism can be described as the product of the successful realization of all its constituent characters and traits. One can think of the totality of these characters and traits as that which forms the concept of that organism. Here "concept" just means the set of all qualities and dispositions which in the course of the development of a specific organism account for its being the particular organism it has become. Thus the term "concept" functions here as shorthand for the characterization of the underlying structure which determines the developmental process of an organism.

We noted above that a major problem for a monistic metaphysics was how to integrate self-consciousness as an objective principle. Hegel contends that, in order to account for self-consciousness within the framework of such a monistic conception of reality one has to make sure that one can identify structural or conceptual elements within the concept of what is taken to be an internally differentiated totality, i.e. reason or reality, which can be the basis for self-consciousness as a feature in the world (where "world" is to be understood as the objective manifestation of this concept). This could be done in a number of different ways. Hegel chooses to give a description of the structure of self-consciousness and then trace this structure back to its conceptual foundation. For reasons of method this procedure – if it is not to become circular – commits Hegel to the claim that in his notion of the concept of reason (as distinguished from its process of realization) this structure is contained albeit in an unrealized form. This commitment has some interesting consequences (e.g. that for Hegel the concept of reason has to be maximally complex), but they are not really relevant here.

The structural description of self-consciousness, the self or "I" that Hegel prefers is given in different contexts in different ways. Because of the rather intricate if not idiosyncratic nature of his suggestion, none of these formulations can claim to be immediately transparent or intuitively plausible. They all are deeply embedded in his general perspective on a monistic ontology of reason. They address the conceptual elements which play a role in Hegel's notion of self-consciousness or of the self from different points of view. Each of these is in need of a thorough explanation which cannot be given here. We need only mention that there is a phenomenological, an epistemological and a metaphysical aspect connected with this conception of the self. The metaphysical aspect will be considered more closely below. The other two aspects may be outlined briefly. The phenomenological aspect consists in the claim that his conception fits our "normal," commonsense understanding of what we mean if we ascribe to an entity the attribute of self-consciousness: what we mean in attributing self-consciousness to someone is that he is in the position to distance himself from something which at the same time he knows to be identical with himself. The epistemological aspect is based on the assumption that knowledge or cognition has to be explained in accordance with and in terms of a relational model of self-consciousness: for someone to know or to cognize something means to relate to something else in such a way that it loses its quality of sheer otherness or externality (*Äußerlichkeit*) and becomes the other of oneself (*Andere seiner selbst*).

In regard to the metaphysical aspect it is mainly one line of thought in Hegel's account of self-consciousness which indicates paradigmatically his strategy in integrating the self into the framework of his monistic metaphysics. Within the phenomenological description just mentioned Hegel emphasizes as the main structural feature of self-consciousness a specific kind of relation. This relation occurs only in the case of the self if one accepts that the self must be taken to be an internally differentiated unity, where what is distinguished is the self-functioning as the subject and the very same self-posited as the object to which this subject refers. This peculiar relation that holds between the subject- and the object-element of such a unitary self Hegel describes as consisting in being with or by itself in its other (*in seinem Anderen bei sich selbst sein*). Whatever is meant exactly by this expression and whatever one may think of the adequacy of this description of the characteristic structure of the self, and even forgetting the question whether there are good or only bad historical and systematic reasons for such a view of the self, to integrate such an assessment into a monistic metaphysical scheme one has to claim that it would be impossible without it to get a coherent conception of reality as a whole. This is so because otherwise the structure claimed to be characteristic of self-consciousness would have to be viewed as a contingent feature of reality, one which could be omitted without affecting the way in which reality is organized in any other way.

That there is no other way to think of reality properly than by including the relational structure characteristic of self-consciousness into the set of elements constitutive of reality must be shown by demonstrating that we could not account for even the most basic forms of internal differentiation within any part of reality if we were not prepared to attribute to reality as a whole the complex relational structure characteristic of self-consciousness. Because, according to Hegel's idea of reality as a self-realizing concept, whatever can be found in the real world has to be an integral part of the concept of reality, he is required to establish this complex relational structure already in his theory of the concept. It is precisely the fulfilment of this obligation that Hegel pursues in his theory of the concept, i.e. in his *Science of Logic,* by pointing out that already the conceptual possibility of thinking of reality as an ensemble of qualitatively different objects presupposes our possession of a concept of self-relation founded in that self-relation characteristic of self-consciousness. His claim is a conditional one: if we agree that the most basic elements of reality are individual objects with qualities then we have to accept reality as a rather complex self-conscious totality, because otherwise we cannot account for the very concept of an individual object. Stated in this short, maybe even crude, form this claim is a good example of one of Hegel's most cherished metaphysical convictions: To make sense of what is taken to be simple you have to look at it as the partial or one-sided exemplification of something more complex.

Ultimately one can say that Hegel's metaphysics is motivated by his conviction that philosophy is about constructing a unified worldview which allows us to think of reality as an intrinsically rational affair structured by consistent laws and uniform processes. What had to be avoided is the impression of contingency and irrationality as essential characteristics of reality. This supreme interest in taking the world to be rational finds its most famous (and most controversial) expression in Hegel's pointed statement in the Preface to his *Philosophy of Right,* according to which one has to start in philosophy with the premise that what is real is rational and what is rational is real. Rationality for Hegel (as for Fichte and Schelling, who both followed Kant here) had to be conceived in terms of (systematic) unity. Thus the establishment of unity understood as organized or organic connectedness of everything with everything else became the foremost and exclusive task of philosophy.

Schopenhauer: will and presentation

Hegel's confidence in the rationality of reality was not shared by Arthur Schopenhauer. On the contrary: the view Schopenhauer wanted to establish is deeply rooted in his belief that the world, viewed from a metaphysical perspective, is a thoroughly irrational and senseless affair. Though this outlook puts him in severe opposition to Hegel, whose philosophy he often and notoriously scorns, he nevertheless shares at least two convictions with Hegel. The first concerns Kant. Like Hegel, Schopenhauer insists on taking Kant's philosophy as the starting point in metaphysics because every metaphysical theory has to integrate Kant's profound results in both theoretical and practical philosophy. This does not prevent Schopenhauer from being an outspoken and erudite critic of almost all parts of Kant's philosophy. The extensive appendix to his *The World as Will and Presentation,* which has the title "Critique of the Kantian Philosophy," contains what is even by contemporary standards one of the most informative and acute critical discussions of central Kantian topics. The second common conviction concerns monism. Schopenhauer like Hegel wants us to think of the world as a monistic totality, one that is not the result of putting together independent facts or objects, but as a whole that generates a manifold of facts and objects through internal differentiation. What distinguishes them is their answer to the question of the essential quality of this totality, i.e. to the question: is the world fundamentally rational or is it ultimately irrational?

Schopenhauer puts forward his metaphysical doctrine in a work first published in 1818, when he was just thirty years old. It appeared the year after Hegel's *Encyclopedia of the Philosophical Sciences in Outline* (1830) and in the year in which Hegel became a professor at the University of Berlin. There was, however, a huge discrepancy between the public success of Hegel and of Schopenhauer. Whereas Hegel became the leading figure in philosophy of his time Schopenhauer's work was virtually unacknowledged, either academically or publicly. This undeniably was a reason for Schopenhauer's lifelong animosity against Hegel and his philosophy. The very title of Schopenhauer's work sets down his main thesis in a nutshell. It is named *The World as Will and Presentation*. On the very first page of the book, Schopenhauer declares that the work contains but one thought, that expressed by the title. According to this, one must distinguish between the world as will and as presentation. This distinction, according to Schopenhauer, is forced on us by reflecting on the two modes in which we experience the world. In the one mode we encounter the world as an object of cognition, in the other we come into contact with it as the environment of our acting. The world understood as an object of cognition is the world as presentation, the world grasped as the setting for actions is the world as will. Concerning the way we experience the world as an object of cognition the leading idea seems to be that what is going on in cognition is that a subject represents an object or, what is the same for Schopenhauer, that a subject is related to the presentation of an object. Thus, from an epistemological point of view the world is nothing but a collection of presentations. Schopenhauer makes a distinction between two kinds of presentation. There are intuitive presentations which represent an object directly, and there are abstract presentations or concepts which represent an object indirectly. Now, in order to be qualified as a direct presentation of an object a presentation has to obey a number of rules without which the representing subject could not have presentations of objects at all. According to Schopenhauer there are ultimately three constitutive subjective rules which he calls principles of individuation (*principia individuationis*): space, time and causality. These rules demarcate the domain of what is cognitively accessible to us and determine the way objects appear to us. Regarding his theory of presentation and the epistemology based on it Schopenhauer is very eager to point out (correctly) that he relies heavily on elements of Kant's theory of cognition.

The theory of presentation is intended to prepare the way for his genuine metaphysical doctrine according to which the world is ultimately will. Schopenhauer arrives at this conclusion by pointing out that we experience the world not just as an object of cognition but that we also are aware of ourselves as acting individuals in the world who feel immediately that their acts are an expression of their will. Because this experience is intimately connected with our bodies and because the body (*Leib*) is the mode of being of an individual as a presentation, the individual has to acknowledge that it is distinct from all the other objects to which it has epistemic, i.e. presentational access, in that it is both presentation (as body) and will (as acting). Though this reasoning might give some credibility to the thought that the individual person, if not considered as a presentation, has to be taken to be will, it does not immediately follow that all objects that are given to us as presentations are will too. The decisive move in Schopenhauer's argument to the effect that all objects of presentation are ultimately will, takes place at the end of the famous §19 (2008), which reads as follows:

> The double cognizance that we have, given to us in two utterly heterogeneous manners, of the essence and effectuality of our own bodies ... will accordingly be further employed as a key to the essence of every phenomenon in nature, and we will assess all objects that are not our own body, thus are not given in a double manner but only as presentations to our consciousness, precisely by analogy with that body, and therefore assumes that, just as they are on the one hand, entirely like the body, presentations, and in this respect of a kind with it, so on the other hand, setting aside their existence as the subject's presentations, what remains with respect to their inner essence must be the same as what we call in our own case will.

Whatever one may think of this argument from analogy, it is the basis of Schopenhauer's metaphysical claim that the world considered in itself and in its totality is nothing but will, whose appearance or manifestation is the presentational world of objects to which we have epistemic access. It is easy to see that this double aspect view of the world is not only meant to bring together our epistemic and our more practical attitudes towards the world into a coherent picture but is also put forward with the intention of remaining faithful to the Kantian distinction between unknowable things in themselves and knowable appearances.

From his metaphysics of the will Schopenhauer derives his two most influential doctrines, namely his aesthetic theory and his pessimism. In his theory of art his main contention is that it is in aesthetic experience that we can become acquainted with the real nature of the world, i.e. the will. This is so, according to Schopenhauer, because in aesthetic experience we overcome the divide between subject and object characteristic of and basic to the presentational world of cognizable objects and fall into a contemplative mode of awareness which sets us free from the principles of individuation that govern the world of presentation, and leads us beyond this world to an insight into what lies behind it as its real essence. Schopenhauer takes the different forms of art (sculpture, painting, literature, music) to reveal to the contemplating mind different states of the will, where the most adequate contemplative experience of the will takes place in the experience of music. On pessimism Schopenhauer is of the opinion that the will, because it transcends all rational order, is ultimately just a senseless and directionless striving. This striving we experience in our lives as the fundamental absence of lasting satisfaction. Because for Schopenhauer restricted satisfaction is suffering, he feels justified in claiming that his analysis of the human condition shows that living necessarily means suffering.

Though the metaphysical doctrines of Hegel and Schopenhauer have found very few followers who would endorse their teachings without reservation, both have been quite influential. The better known of those who relied in their own philosophical work on elements of Hegel's metaphysical system are Marx, Kierkegaard and, in the English speaking world, Bradley, McTaggart and Collingwood. Schopenhauer's metaphysics has had a strong impact not so much on academic philosophers but on the work of eminent figures in art and literature such as Wagner, Nietzsche, Thomas Mann and Beckett. It is also said that Schopenhauer was of significance for Freud and Wittgenstein.

Note

1 In English editions, this title has been translated in three different ways. The oldest translation (by Haldane and Kemp) has *The World as Will and Idea*, in the translation by Payne it became *The World as Will and Representation*. The newest translation is the one quoted here and used throughout the text (2008).

References

Bradley, F. H. (1897) *Appearance and Reality*, 2nd edn, Oxford: Clarendon Press.
Hegel, G. W. F. (1830) *Enzyklopadie der philosophischen Wissenschaften im Grundrisse*, 3rd edn, Heidelberg: Verlag Osswald.
Schopenhauer, A. (2008) *The World as Will and Presentation*, vol. 1, trans. Richard E. Aquila, in collaboration with David Carus (Longman Library of Primary Sources in Philosophy), New York: Pearson Education.

Further reading

For further reading, see T. Pinkard, *German Philosophy 1760–1860: The Legacy of Idealism* (Cambridge; New York: Cambridge University Press, 2002); J. Young, *Schopenhauer* (London; New York: Routledge, 2005); and Hegel's *Phenomenology of Spirit* (1807).

16
ANTI-METAPHYSICS I
Nietzsche

Maudemarie Clark

Metaphysics aims to establish what there is to know about the world that goes beyond what can be discovered by science. In this sense, Nietzsche himself put forward metaphysical views in his final works. But he is better known for the criticism of metaphysics he began developing in the works of his middle or "positivistic" period. This criticism is specifically directed against "two-world" metaphysics, the kind of metaphysic put forward by Parmenides, Plato, Leibniz, Kant and Schopenhauer, among others, according to which there is a second world in addition to the empirical world studied by science, and it is the "true" or real world whereas the empirical world is mere "appearance." Although he turns against metaphysics in this sense in the works of his middle period, Nietzsche began his philosophical career as a devotee of Schopenhauer's two-world metaphysics.

Nietzsche's early work

Nietzsche's main concern in his early work was the condition of contemporary European culture, which he judged to be inferior to that of the pre-Socratic Greeks. He used Schopenhauer's metaphysics to interpret the achievements of the latter and the falloff of modern culture from its standard. He criticizes modern culture in effect for having become anti-metaphysical, for having accepted that the empirical world is the only one. By following Socrates' preference for the rational and clear over the artistic and mythical, it has come to assume that only science gives us truth. Nietzsche's early work sets out to combat this assumption.

One argument he gives against it in his first book, *The Birth of Tragedy* (1999 [1872]; *BT*), is that Kant and Schopenhauer have demonstrated that the empirical world of individuals, the only reality recognized by science, is mere appearance. A second argument is based on Schopenhauer's claim that the deeper truth about existence is that it is will and therefore suffering without end or point. Nietzsche argues that modern culture's blindness to this truth has led it to a shallow optimism. According to *BT*, the Greeks were not shallow optimists. They recognized that the empirical world is mere appearance and that the character of the underlying reality is horrifying, and were therefore in effect Schopenhauerian pessimists. Their great art was produced in the attempt to deal with their pessimism, to find a way to affirm life in spite of it. Apollonian art induced affirmation by presenting an idealized version of life, thus by means of a beautifying illusion, but the Dionysian affirmation of tragedy was undertaken in full appreciation of the horrifying character of the underlying reality, i.e., of the Schopenhauerian truth.

Nietzsche probably did not think that "will" captured the literal truth about the thing in itself (or that the Greeks would have thought it did). In unpublished notes written before BT, he rejects Schopenhauer's proofs that the thing in itself is will and says that only a "poetic intuition" allowed him to substitute will for the "Kantian X." Nietzsche seems to agree with Kant, claiming that the thing in itself is "wholly outside the sphere of cognition," but thinks that Schopenhauer helps us see that we can nevertheless have a kind of intuitive or pre-linguistic grasp of it, which we can only put into language by describing the thing in itself in terms borrowed from the world of appearance. He thinks that this is what Schopenhauer did when he called the thing in itself "will," and that something similar happened in the case of ancient tragedy: the members of the (originally) dancing, chanting chorus produced in themselves an ecstatic state in which they identified with and thus gained an intuitive grasp of the inner nature of the world, which they expressed in words and images as the "Apollonian dream image" of the play itself. It seems probable that he understands his use of Schopenhauer's metaphysics in the same way, as a translation of his inchoate sense of the thing in itself into the language of appearance.

Nietzsche did not remain satisfied with this "artist's metaphysics" for long. After BT, he no longer held that art provides access to a truth that is beyond the grasp of science, although he did try out other ways of defending "the metaphysical significance of culture" (1995 [1874]: Third Essay, §6), the idea that by means of culture human activity becomes "explicable only by the laws of another, higher life" (Third Essay, §4). The main suggestion seems to be that we should act as if it's true even though we know it's not. In his 1874 essay on history, he urges that history be practiced as art rather than as science, on the grounds that certain scientific doctrines, clearly meaning Darwin's theory of evolution and its implications, are "true, but deadly," apparently fearing that the loss of the myth that humans are more than animals – that they belong to "another, higher life" – will foster a disintegration of culture into "systems of individual egoism, brotherhoods whose purpose will be the rapacious exploitation of non-brothers" (1995 [1874]: Second Essay, §9).

Nietzsche middle ("positivistic") period

In the works of his middle period, Nietzsche turns his back on the attempt to imbue culture with "metaphysical significance." In Human, All Too Human (1986 [1878]; HA), he abandons his polemic against the high value placed on science in modern culture, now taking it as "the mark of a higher culture to value the little unpretentious truths discovered by means of rigorous method more highly than the errors handed down by metaphysical and artistic ages and men, which blind us and make us happy" (1986 [1878]: §3). Hereafter he never doubts that science gives us truth. In fact, in the works of his middle period (at least in *HA* and *Daybreak* [1997 (1881)]), *only* science gives us truth, which leaves no room for metaphysics as Nietzsche understands it. He regards philosophy as he now practices it as part of natural science (1986 [1878]: §1).

HA aims to induce skepticism about any metaphysical world, thus contributing to the anti-metaphysical modern culture against which Nietzsche directed his first book, by showing that it is cognitively superfluous. He concedes that "there might be a metaphysical world," meaning that the true nature of reality (the thing in itself) might in fact differ from the empirical world studied by science. For "we behold all things through the human head and cannot cut this head off; while the question nonetheless remains what of the world would still be there if one had cut it off" (1986 [1878]: §9). We can only know things as they can appear to us, and therefore cannot rule out the "absolute possibility" that they differ from how they appear (and would appear even to idealized human observers). Nietzsche's metaphorical formulation of this point above might also seem to imply that we could know nothing about the metaphysical world even if it does exist. But he does not rely on such an argument in *HA*, presumably because he knows that metaphysicians have always thought that special methods – usually *a priori* ones, which do not belong merely to the "human head" – provide access to a reality that is inaccessible empirically. So his strategy is to induce skepticism about metaphysical assumptions by arguing that

> passion, error, and self-deception … the worst of all methods of acquiring knowledge, not the best of them, have taught belief in them. When one has disclosed these methods as the foundations of all extant religions and metaphysical systems, one has refuted them! Then that possibility still remains over; but one can do absolutely nothing with it, not to speak of letting happiness, salvation and life depend on the gossamer of such a possibility. (1986 [1878]: §9)

To make good on this claim, Nietzsche offers a genealogy of philosophers' belief in a metaphysical or non-empirical world. The first idea of a "second world" came from dreams, he claims: primitive human beings thought that in dreaming they were "getting to know a *second real world*" (1986 [1878]: §5). Philosophers later exploited this idea to explain how they could have knowledge of things they recognized they could not know empirically. These things include what "all metaphysics has principally to do with," namely, "substance and freedom of the will" (1986 [1878]: §18). Instead of concluding that these things did not exist, metaphysicians claimed that empirical methods were faulty, and that the real world was accessible only to non-empirical methods. The empirical world was thus taken to be a mere appearance or distortion of a second world, which was thereby constituted as the "true" one.

Nietzsche assumes that it is already clear to his readers that the beliefs in substance and free will that led philosophers to posit a metaphysical world are contradicted by the "disclosed nature of the world," the world as disclosed by modern science (1986 [1878]:

§§10, 29). This is because he assumes that substance is unchanging and that free will requires uncaused events whereas science shows that everything changes and that all events have causes. *HA* aims merely to counteract any remaining tendency to think there must be some truth in these beliefs by showing that we can explain how they arose without assuming that they contain any truth. His explanation seems highly implausible, however. The basic idea is that both beliefs are shared by "everything organic" and that we have inherited them from lower organisms who did not notice change, in the case of substance, or have a grasp of causality, in the case of free will (1986 [1878]: §18).

Nietzsche's more interesting concern in *HA* is a second reason philosophers had for positing a metaphysical world, namely, to explain the existence of things they held to possess a higher value than typical occupants of the empirical world – for instance, knowledge, objectivity, art, the virtues. Because metaphysicians assumed that things cannot "originate in their opposite, for instance, rationality in irrationality ..., disinterested contemplation in covetous desire, living for others in egoism," they could explain the origin of such things only by assuming "for the more highly valued thing a miraculous source in the very kernel and being of the 'thing in itself'" (1986 [1878]: §1). Nietzsche's strategy here gives his book its name: to show that these more highly valued things are "human, all too human," mere sublimations and transformations of things of lower value. By showing that we can explain disinterested contemplation as a sublimation of lust, altruistic acts as disguised egoistic ones, etc., he shows that the things of higher value provide no basis for positing a metaphysical world.

If these two lines of argument succeed, Nietzsche expects interest in the purely theoretical problem of the thing in itself and appearance to die out (1986 [1878]: §10). Indeed, it may be considered worthy of a "Homeric laugh": for "it appeared to be so much, indeed everything, and is actually empty, that is to say, empty of significance" (1986 [1878]: §16). That is, no one is driven to metaphysics by the question of what things are like apart from our knowledge of them (in the terms of his earlier passage: what the world would be like if we could cut the human head off). That is a purely theoretical problem and is "not very well calculated to bother people overmuch; but all that has hitherto made metaphysical assumptions *valuable, terrible, delightful* to them, all that has begotten these assumptions, is passion, error, and self-deception."

Error is involved when a metaphysical world is postulated to explain the existence and knowledge of things that do not in fact exist (substance and free will) or that can be explained by empirical methods (things taken to be of a higher value). Nietzsche evidently takes passion and self-deception to play a role in generating and sustaining the belief in things of a higher value.

> It is probable the objects of the religious, moral and aesthetic sentiments belong only to the surface of things, while man likes to believe that here at least he is in touch with the world's heart; the reason he deludes himself is that these things produce in him such profound happiness and unhappiness, and thus he here exhibits the same pride as in the case of astrology. For astrology believes that the starry firmament revolves around the fate of man; the moral man,

however, supposes that what he has essentially at heart must also constitute the essence and heart of things. (1986 [1878]: §4)

Although the actual objects of religious, moral and aesthetic feelings probably belong only to the empirical world, metaphysicians posit other objects for them, ones they situate in the metaphysical world – as when the object of awe is taken to be God instead of the features of the natural world, or when morality is taken to be the perception of Platonic Forms rather than the expression of a "human, all too human" attitude – thereby taking the empirical world to be only the "surface of things." They do so in an attempt to convince themselves that their concerns are not theirs alone, that support for them is somehow woven into the fabric of the universe. This is why they concern themselves with questions about "appearance" and the thing in itself: because the latter provides a space that can be furnished with the objects of the moral, religious and aesthetic feelings, thus seeming to provide external support for them. Note that this explains Nietzsche's own concern with such questions in *BT*: he was seeking external support for the importance of art and of his own aesthetic experience. But this is all illusion and self-deception as far as he is now concerned. *HA* sets out to show that aesthetic, moral and religious feelings are to be explained as merely human reactions to natural features of the world, hence that "the origin of religion, art and morality" can be "perfectly understood" without invoking a metaphysical world (1986 [1878]: §10). Only self-deception remains to motivate metaphysics.

Nietzsche's final works

The works of Nietzsche's third and final period show significant changes in his analysis of two-world metaphysics. To begin with, he no longer claims that "there might be a metaphysical world," evidently recognizing the problem with the metaphor that led him to this conclusion in *HA*. In *The Gay Science* (2001 [1882, 1887]), he denies that appearance is to be contrasted with an essence or "unknown X," claiming that we have no conception of the latter except in terms of "the predicates of its appearance" (2001 [1882]: §54). He makes the consequence of this explicit in *Beyond Good and Evil* (1973 [1886]), calling the thing in itself (the "unknown X") a "contradiction in terms" (1973 [1886]: §16). Finally, in *Twilight of the Idols* (1954 [1889]), he offers a history of "How the 'True World' Finally Became a Fable." This is a six-stage history of metaphysics, including Plato, Christianity, Kant, and the various stages of Nietzsche's criticisms of metaphysics, which ends with the denial that there is any "true" world and a recognition (which was missing, for instance, in *Gay Science*) that the remaining world, the empirical world, can no longer be considered the merely "apparent" world. It is the only demonstrable world, but also the only world of which we have any conception. Why, then, have philosophers thought otherwise? Nietzsche revises and refines his earlier answer and in doing so seems to develop some sympathy with the aims of metaphysics, perhaps recognizing the possibility of a kind of metaphysic that does not conflict with science or reduce the empirical world to mere "appearance."

One change is that he no longer locates the origins of metaphysics' errors in beliefs inherited from lower organisms, but instead, anticipating Wittgenstein, gives language the major role in generating them. He sometimes seems to claim that language itself falsifies reality, as when he holds the subject–predicate structure of Indo-European languages responsible for philosophers' propensity to think that reality itself must consist of ultimate subjects that could never be part of the experienced world: God, the ego or soul, and indivisible atoms of matter. But he is better interpreted as saying of language what he ultimately says of the senses: only what we make of its testimony introduces error ("'Reason' in Philosophy," in 1954 [1888]: §2). Language misleads us into traditional philosophy only if we in effect assume that the grammar of some natural languages offers us a blueprint of reality that is a substitute for and can be used to challenge the adequacy of empirical theories.

In *Twilight of the Idols* (1954 [1888]), Nietzsche tells us that grammar seduced human beings into a "realm of crude fetishism," a primitive "metaphysics of grammar," as soon as they started thinking about what the world was like. This metaphysics sees "a doer and a deed" everywhere: "it believes in will as *the* cause," that is, as the cause of all events we would now explain mechanistically. It also believes in the ego "as being," "as substance, and it projects this faith in the ego-substance upon all things – only thereby does it first *create* the concept of 'thing'." When philosophers "very much later" recognized "the sureness, the subjective certainty, in our handling of the categories of reason" and realized that these could not be derived from experience, indeed did not apply to the empirical world, they concluded that it applied instead to a "higher world" in which they had once been at home and to which they now had access "since we have reason" (1954 [1888]: "'Reason' in Philosophy," §5). They believed that they possessed "pure reason," that their ability to reason brought with it the ability to reach truth without reliance on empirical data. Nietzsche often refers to the "errors" or "prejudices of reason," but what he thus refers to are the prejudices derived from the "belief in grammar," the implicit assumption that grammar reveals the truth about reality. It is from this assumption that the "categories of reason" were actually derived. Only the primitive "metaphysics of grammar" so derived provided philosophers with a basis for thinking that they grasped the structure of a world (the "true world") that differed from the empirical one.

But metaphysics isn't a matter of innocent confusion or error that philosophers simply fall into (contrary to what *HA* sometimes seems to suggest). Philosophers are willingly seduced by grammar; they exploit it for their own purposes, in particular, to express and defend their own values. This is the more important change in Nietzsche's understanding of metaphysics, the greater emphasis he now gives to the role of values in it. One well-known example of how the "metaphysics of grammar" is exploited to underwrite value conclusions is his account of the "belief in a neutral 'subject' with free choice" in *On the Genealogy of Morality*.

> A quantum of power is just such a quantum of drive, will, effect – more precisely,
> it is nothing other than this very driving, willing, effecting, and only through the
> seduction of language (and the basic errors of reason petrified therein), which

understands and misunderstands all effecting as conditioned by an effecting something, by a "subject," can it appear otherwise. For just as common people separate the lightning from its flash and take the latter as a doing, as an effect of a subject called lightning, so popular morality also separates strength from the expression of strength as if there were behind the strong an indifferent substratum that is free to express strength. But there is no such substratum; there is no "being" behind the doing, effecting, becoming; the "doer" is simply fabricated into the doing – the doing is everything (1998 [1887]: First Treatise, §13).

Nietzsche is not denying that there are doers in the sense of persons or agents; he denies only that the doer is a "neutral 'subject'" or "indifferent substratum," something that is the bearer or cause of all its properties, but which is itself distinct for any and all of them, and so is completely free to choose what kind of person to be. Nietzsche's claim is that people are seduced into this belief in a real subject behind "doing" by the necessity of a grammatical subject for every predicate, just as scientists were seduced into positing indivisible atoms. But in the case of the materialistic atom, the empirical evidence eventually overcame the metaphysics of grammar (1973 [1886]: §12). In the case of the "neutral 'subject'," things are more difficult because the error was exploited "by the suppressed, hiddenly glowing affects of revenge and hate" to "hold the bird of prey *accountable* for being a bird of prey" and to interpret certain effects of powerlessness – e.g., patience and humbleness – as a "voluntary achievement, something willed, something chosen, a *deed*, a *merit*" (1998 [1887]: First Treatise, §13).

According to later Nietzsche, two-world metaphysics involves the same kind of exploitation of the errors of reason that one finds in the pre-philosophical notion of free will. Holding "the moral (or immoral) intentions in every philosophy" to be "the real germ of life out of which the entire plain has grown," he suggests that such intentions explain how its "most abstruse metaphysical assertions have actually been arrived at" (1973 [1886]: §6). His most important example is that of the Stoics, who claimed to derive an ethical imperative from nature, when they actually arrived at their view of nature (as following rational laws) by reading their own ethical ideal of self-governance into it (1973 [1886]: §9). Because he claims that all philosophy does what the Stoics did, Nietzsche can't criticize metaphysicians for reading their values into the world (unless he is willing to dispense with all philosophy, which he is not). His objection is twofold: that self-deception keeps metaphysicians from recognizing that their "truths" are actually a matter of reading their values into reality, and that the values their metaphysics reads into reality are those of the ascetic ideal.

The ascetic ideal is the ideal of self-denial shared by most of the major religions. The assumption or value behind the idealizing of self-denial, according to Nietzsche's diagnosis, is that merely natural (earthly) existence has no intrinsic value, that it has value only as a means to something else that is actually its negation (e.g., heaven or nirvana.). This life-devaluing ideal infects all the values supported by most religions. Although these values originally came into existence in support of some form of life, the ascetic priest gives them a life-devaluing interpretation. For instance, acts are interpreted as wrong on the grounds that they are selfish or animal, that they affirm natural instincts, and thus become not merely wrong but "sinful." Nietzsche sees traditional ("metaphysical") philosophers as successors to the ascetic priest because they interpret what they value – truth, knowledge, philosophy, virtue – in non-natural terms. He thinks that the assumption of the ascetic ideal lies behind this: that whatever is truly valuable must have a source outside the world of nature, the world accessible to empirical investigation. What ultimately explains the traditional assumption that philosophy must be *a priori*, and therefore concerned with a metaphysical world, is philosophers' assumption that nothing as valuable as philosophy or truth could be intimately connected to the senses or to the merely natural existence of human beings. Nietzsche therefore understands two-world metaphysics as an act of disguised revenge against life, and his later philosophy aims to provide a life-affirming alternative to it.

The question remains as to whether his later philosophy has room for some other kind of metaphysics, one that would not run afoul of his criticism of the two-world variety. Much is unsettled on this issue, and it must be admitted that what is said here about it will inevitably be more controversial than the claims about Nietzsche's rejection of two-world metaphysics. The notorious doctrine that life and the world are will to power is one reason to take later Nietzsche to leave room for metaphysics, for the doctrine seems clearly metaphysical, a mere variation on Schopenhauer's claim that the world is will. Richardson (1996) is the most successful attempt to work out the details of this doctrine and argue that it does not conflict with Nietzsche's criticism of metaphysics. But this interpretation is based to a large extent on Nietzsche's unpublished notebooks, a notoriously unreliable basis for interpretations, and, as Richardson (2004) admits, there is no empirical or scientific basis for the doctrine in this unrestricted form. In this form, the doctrine evidently needs an *a priori* basis, and Nietzsche's criticism of metaphysics makes it difficult to see where he would find a basis for that. Indeed, in *Beyond Good and Evil*, §15, he seems to embrace "sensualism" (that is, empiricism) as a "regulative hypothesis," which seems in line with the recent interpretation of Nietzsche as a methodological naturalist, who insists not only that philosophy aim for consistency with what the best science tells us, but also that it follow the methods of the sciences (Leiter 2002). Embracing a doctrine of the will to power on *a priori* grounds would therefore seem to be inconsistent with his overall philosophical orientation.

However, one problem for interpreting later Nietzsche as a methodological naturalist is his suggestion in the second edition of *The Gay Science* (1887), addressed to "Mr. Mechanic," that a "'scientific' interpretation of the world, as you understand it, might still be the *stupidest* of all possible interpretations of the world," precisely because it would allow no room for its own reality (2001 [1882, 1887]: §373). Nietzsche's wider point in this passage is that there are certain things that cannot be recognized or understood using only the methods of the natural sciences, e.g., the intellect and its products, agents and their actions, ethical and aesthetic properties. These show up only from a perspective that is constituted by value commitments. Just as one cannot recognize the value of a piece of music from a purely scientific perspective, but only if one is equipped with aesthetic standards from which to judge it, one cannot recognize behavior as constituting an action or as exhibiting thought unless one is equipped with standards for differentiating good from bad, rational from irrational, action and thought. And Mr

Mechanic cannot respond that the "real" world knows nothing of such value properties without admitting that his interpretation of the world has no place in reality, but is just a collection of marks or sounds.

Later Nietzsche thus seems to recognize that there is more to reality than what science can tells us, and this opens the possibility of recognizing metaphysics as a legitimate discipline. One example of the kind of metaphysics this might involve will have to suffice. Consider that if thought and actions can't be recognized from the viewpoint of science, the one who thinks and performs actions – the person – cannot be recognized from that perspective either. But what is a person? Nietzsche's answer is given in *Beyond Good and Evil* in terms of the traditional metaphysical notions of the soul and the will. Of course he rejects the soul as it was conceived by two-world metaphysics – as "indestructible, eternal, indivisible" – but makes explicit that this does not require us to "get rid of 'the soul' itself and thus forgo one of the most venerable of hypotheses," unlike "clumsy naturalists who cannot touch 'the soul' without losing it" (1973 [1886]: §12). Clark and Dudrick (forthcoming) argue that the "venerable" hypothesis referred to is Plato's tripartite soul. Nietzsche wants to revise and refine that hypothesis because he doesn't believe that conceiving reason as a separate part of the soul, as an independent source of motivation and therefore of values, can be squared with what we know of human beings from science, which is that our cognitive faculties always operate in the service of some interest. But he aims to explain the possibility of values, as distinguished from desire or appetite, and thereby to make conceivable weakness of the will. He attempts to do this with the hypothesis that the soul is the "political order of the drives and affects." Briefly put, drives are dispositions to behavior, and their relative strength at any time determines how one behaves at that time. But what gives a human being values, hence a soul, and makes her a person is that her drives also have a political order. Some drives are recognized as having authority to command and be obeyed, and therefore to speak for the whole; as such, they constitute the viewpoint of the person. How such a political order of the drives came about is precisely what Nietzsche attempts to explain in his account of the origin of "bad conscience" in his *Genealogy of Morality*. The upshot is that Nietzsche aims to rehabilitate traditional metaphysical notions on a normative basis. What science can't tell us is precisely what is revealed only from the viewpoint of values. Nietzsche's own notions of the soul and the will are presumably grounded in the value he places on rational and self-governed behavior. If so, this leaves questions about the metaphysics of value that scholars have only begun to raise.

References

Primary sources

Nietzsche, F. (1954 [1888]) *Twilight of the Idols*, in *The Portable Nietzsche*, trans. Walter Kaufmann, New York: Viking.
—— (1973 [1886]) *Beyond Good and Evil*, trans R. J. Hollingdale, New York: Viking Penguin.
—— (1986 [1878]) *Human, All-Too-Human*, trans. R. J. Hollingdale, Cambridge: Cambridge University Press.
—— (1995 [1874]) *Unfashionable Observations*, trans. Richard T. Grey, Stanford: Stanford University Press.

—— (1997 [1881]) *Daybreak*, trans. R. J. Hollingdale; edited by Maudemarie Clark and Brian Leiter, Cambridge: Cambridge University Press.

—— (1998 [1887]) *On the Genealogy of Morality*, edited, trans. by Maudemarie Clark and Alan Swensen, Indianapolis, IN: Hackett.

—— (1999 [1872]) *The Birth of Tragedy*, trans. Ronald Speirs; edited by Raymond Geuss and Ronald Speirs, Cambridge: Cambridge University Press).

—— (2001 [1882, 1887]) *The Gay Science*, trans. Josefine Nauckhoff; edited by Bernard Williams, Cambridge: Cambridge University Press.

Secondary sources

Clark, Maudemarie and Dudrick, David (forthcoming) *Nietzsche's Magnificent Tension of the Spirit: An Introduction to* Beyond Good and Evil, Cambridge: Cambridge University Press.

Leiter, Brian (2002) *Nietzsche on Morality*, London: Routledge.

Richardson, John (1996) *Nietzsche's System*, Oxford: Oxford University Press.

—— (2004) *Nietzsche's New Darwinism*, Oxford: Oxford University Press.

Further reading

The basis for much of the material in this essay was Maudemarie Clark, *Nietzsche on Truth and Philosophy* (Cambridge: Cambridge University Press, 1990). Maudemarie Clark and David Dudrick's *Nietzsche's Magnificent Tension of the Spirit: An Introduction to* Beyond Good and Evil (forthcoming) contains the argument that Nietzsche aims to rehabilitate traditional metaphysical notions of the soul and the will on normative grounds. Brian Leiter, *Nietzsche on Morality* (London: Routledge, 2002) gives an important interpretation of Nietzsche as a methodological naturalist. Peter Poellner, *Nietzsche and Metaphysics* (Oxford: Oxford University Press, 1995) offers a detailed examination of various aspects of Nietzsche's later metaphysics. Richard Schacht, *Nietzsche* (London: Routledge, 1983) gives very complete coverage of all the various aspects of Nietzsche's philosophy and metaphysics.

17
BRADLEY
The supra-relational Absolute

W. J. Mander

British philosophy has usually been too anchored in common sense to permit much scope for speculative metaphysics, but during the last quarter of the nineteenth century and the first quarter of the twentieth there occurred a great flowering of constructive philosophy. This period saw the creation of several original philosophical systems, but chief of these in terms of its renown and influence was that put forward by the Oxford philosopher F. H. Bradley. Widely revered as the greatest philosopher of the age, and paid as much attention by his opponents as by his followers, Bradley was a monist and an idealist, that is, he believed in the existence of but a single unified substance – which he called the Absolute – conceived as broadly mental or experiential in nature. The bulk of this essay looks at his argument for the first of these claims, but in the final section I discuss also the second.

A useful way to understand his system is to observe that for Bradley there are three distinct levels or orders of experience: immediate experience (which he also terms "feeling"), relational experience, and absolute experience. It is his position that these three together form a developmental sequence in which immediate experience gives birth to relational experience which in turn gives birth to absolute experience, although whether this sequence is just notional or manifested in an actual chronological development, either in the life of the individual or of the species, is something he never took a clear position upon. From the point of view of philosophical understanding the best place to begin to understand this sequence is not in fact the beginning but in the middle, with relational experience, which as a state points beyond itself in two directions, both to its origin and its goal.

Relational experience

Bradley's philosophy begins with a critique of what he calls "relational experience." What is this? At its simplest, it is any experience or thought about the world that employs relations in any way at all; which, of course, takes in *all* experience or thought in any everyday sense.

To appreciate this we need simply to recognise the sheer pervasiveness of relations. Wherever we go, whatever we encounter, we meet with a myriad of relations, for they are what give structure to the world in which we live. Everything is related to the world around it, often in many different ways. Moreover we should note that relations hold, not just between things, but between their parts, between their temporal segments, between them and their properties, as well as between properties themselves.

We tend to think of a relation as something that *unifies* two or more distinct elements, as something that brings otherwise disparate items together into a single relational fact. However, for Bradley, relations are more than just unifiers, they also *divide*. Thus what he is considering here is as much the notion of division or separation, as that of union or togetherness. His topic is, not just relations, but (as he puts it) the whole machinery of *terms and relations*. They are a pair. It is obvious that there could be no relations without distinct terms for them to relate, but Bradley finds it equally obvious that terms could not be distinct were it not for the relations which hold between them. And in this way distinction presupposes relation just as much as relation presupposes distinction – they must be considered as a pair.

What then was his view of relations? A statement is easy enough to find. He says "The conclusion to which I am brought is that a relational way of thought – any one that moves by the machinery of terms and relations – must give appearance and not truth. It is a makeshift, a device, a mere practical compromise, most necessary but in the end, most indefensible" (Bradley 1897: 28). "The very essence of these ideas is infected and contradicts itself" (Bradley 1897: 21) he says, and the contradictions that he claims to find are famous. But before we look at them more closely, a word of warning is due – we should not expect to derive from relational statements some neat little *reductio* of the form "*P* and not *P*." The contradictions are less a matter of what is being *said*, than of the *practical implications* of what is being said, almost, we might say, of what is being *done* – like using a pair of scissors to glue two things together, or trying to support both sides at a football match. The problem Bradley identifies is that the relational apparatus (the mechanism, that is, of terms and relations) is trying to describe a situation for which there is, as it were, no "room" conceptually – like the concept of "divorce" for certain strict Christians, or the difference between "compromise" and "defeat" to ultra hard-line political activists. Bradley's argument against relations proceeds by considering a variety of ways in which we might try to understand them, each of which fails. The arguments have achieved a certain fame, even notoriety, so let us follow Bradley in his own presentation of this sorry tale.

What then, we must ask ourselves, is a relation? The options, as Bradley sees it, are limited. Taking any two-term relation (and these are the only kind he recognises) we can think of the relation either as some third sort of component placed somehow "between" the other two, or else as some kind of property or quality "attaching to" the terms themselves. (Bradley does not distinguish between "relation" and "relational property.")

The first is easily ruled out. We cannot take the relation to be any kind of extra element, for the question would then have to be asked how that element itself stood to the terms, introducing two new relations and so launching us on an infinite regress. It would, says Bradley, be like supposing that to attach two chains together, we need a further link, and then two more, and then another four, and so on, indefinitely (Bradley 1897: 28).

But if we turn to the second option, we fare no better; in the end, indeed, we seem to face the very same problem. For to take the relation as but a feature of either of the objects related requires us to make a division within its nature between those of its features that enter into the relation and those that don't. To illustrate, being wiser than the Vice-Chancellor is, we may take it, a matter of one's intelligence or insight but not one's height or shoe size. But faced with such a division, if we then ask how the former set of features stands to the latter we would seem to have found a new relation to worry about – one which, were we to treat it in the same fashion, could only lead us into another endless regress (Bradley 1897: 26). And it is hardly surprising that this should be so, for it would take a subtle logician to find other than a verbal distinction between the question of how a thing stands to its own relations and the question of how stands its non-relational to its relational nature.

The only remaining option we have for understanding relations is to say that they are indeed aspects or qualities of the terms that they relate, but that they are so fused with them as to render impossible any separation between the term's relational and non-relational nature. But either we have lost our relation altogether here and are left with simply a term (something we have already dismissed as absurd), or else what is being offered is nothing but a relation – there being no aspect of it that is not relational. But nothing can consist solely in its relation to others; the notion of a world of relations without any terms is, argues Bradley, even more absurd than that of a world of qualities without relations (Bradley 1897: 27). And with that we must certainly agree. The options for making sense of them exhausted, Bradley concludes that relations are impossible.

Assessment of Bradley's case

It is only to be expected that so radical a line of argument was to be challenged, and one of its greatest critics was Bertrand Russell. Indeed the story of Russell's rise as a philosopher and of the emergence of analytic philosophy with which he is so closely associated was in large part the story of his break with Bradley's Absolute. One consequence of that triumph is that it is still widely believed that Russell refuted Bradley's view of relations, but if we look at the details the matter is less clear; for many of Russell's objections were based on fundamental confusions about or misrepresentations of Bradley's position.

In his 1903 book *The Principles of Mathematics* Russell distinguishes between two theories of relations, the monadistic which he attributes to Leibniz and Lotze and the monistic which he attributes to Spinoza and Bradley (Russell 1937: §§212–16). In the first a relational proposition, *aRb*, is understood by analysing it down into two separate propositions, ar_1 and br_2, each attributing a different property to the two terms involved. In the second by contrast the relational proposition is understood by taking the two terms together and attributing a property to the pair, giving the schema (*ab*)R. Russell rejects both analyses on grounds of their inability to deal with asymmetrical relations; on the monistic theory, for example, the distinct propositions "*a is greater than b*" and "*b is greater than a*" would both receive the same analysis, (*ab*)*Greater than.*

To a large extent this objection fails to touch its target for the monistic theory which Russell identifies as Bradley's is really a long way from his actual position. The analysis Bradley proposes is not merely a redistribution of the roles of subject and predicate within the proposition, but rather the translation of the entire propositional content into a predicate then referred to reality as a whole. Thus, in the judgment "S is P," instead of picking out S and saying that it is P, we say of reality as a whole that it is "S–P-ish," or as he later puts it "Reality is such that S is P" (Bradley 1922: 630). *This* analysis can deal with asymmetry, for it takes up into its predication not only the relation but the asymmetry of its context.

Russell argues that the monadistic and monistic theories of relations are the only two options for someone who believes that all relations are subject–predicate in form (Russell 1937: §212). But the accusation that Bradley holds all propositions to be subject–predicate in form is equally mistaken. For while he would admit that all judgments predicate or say something about reality, the question of what they do or how they function is different from any question concerning the logical structure of their content, and he certainly would not argue that we can reduce relational propositions to subject–predicate ones. Indeed quite the reverse; it was his view that subject–predicate ones are to be rejected precisely because they are relational – they involve a relation between subject and predicate – and on these grounds Bradley is as fierce a critic of subject–predicate logic as might be found anywhere.

Russell's position is that in addition to subjects and predicates, relations constitute a third *sui generis* category, too basic to reduce to anything else. It is simply the business of relations to relate, and we cannot ask how. But this would not satisfy Bradley. For him relations are part of our conceptual structure, not something we may passively accept as immediate or given in experience and, as such, the problem is not merely that we don't understand them but that they are trying to do something which by Bradley's lights is impossible; they try to bring things together into one single whole at the same time as holding them apart as distinct elements.

Perhaps Russell's most famous objection is that Bradley held what he calls "the axiom or doctrine of internal relations," the claim that all relations are internal (Russell 1956: 335). The terminology here calls for explanation: what are internal and external relations? Broadly speaking, the difference is that between thinking of a relation as either something more or less brought in from outside and placed between its terms, and thinking of it as something more or less bound up in the nature of those terms themselves. Thus what Russell's charge amounts to is the claim that all relations are grounded in or even reducible to the natures of their terms.

There are two levels at which one might respond to Russell's charge. At the most basic level it could be said, once again, that Russell has simply misunderstood Bradley's meaning. He accuses Bradley of saying all relations are internal, when it is in fact his view that there are no relations at all. For he argues that relations could not be made to work either internally or externally. The reasons he gives for this conclusion are precisely those which we have just considered, namely that external relations stand outside of, and make no real connection with, their terms, while internal relations lose themselves wholly in their terms, leaving us either with a term that has swallowed its own relation or a relation that has swallowed its own terms. Indeed, we can use this terminology to express Bradley's diagnosis of the fundamental problem. Internal and external are opposing notions, for concepts are hard-edged, and elements must fall squarely either within or outside their range. But a relation by its very nature strives to be *both* internal *and* external (Bradley 1935: 677); the relation in which things stand is no arbitrary accident but a function of their natures, and yet it is something separate from them both, something "between" them. Bradley laments the forced dichotomy. "The whole 'Either–or' between external and internal relations, to me seems unsound" (Bradley 1915: 238), he says. But he is stuck with it, for conceptual thought permits no middle path between belonging to a concept and falling outside of it. The one and the many remain forever opposed in thought and cannot be unified, and this is the sense in which for Bradley relational statements are trying to do something for which there is in conceptual terms simply "no room." A relational thought tries but inevitably fails to unite the diverse, and because it fails, not as measured against some higher purer standard, but simply in its own terms, as attempting something which its own nature undermines, Bradley thinks of it as self-contradictory. But note the direction of fit. Failure shows, not that things aren't the way thought is trying to tell us, but that thought just isn't up to the job of telling us how they really are.

But in an important sense it must be acknowledged that this is only half the answer. It cannot be the case that all relations are internal if all relations falsify reality, but Bradley does allow that some conceptions falsify more than others, and would agree that it is less inappropriate to view relations as internal than it is to view them as external (Bradley 1915: 312). To understand why he thinks this we must look to the stages of experience before and after the relational level, but for the moment let us just note the consequences of Bradley's argument thus far.

Consequences of the relational argument

Relations, then, are contradictory and cannot belong to reality. But relations are to be found everywhere. So anything which involves them will also be contradictory. Hence to abandon relations is, Bradley readily admits, to condemn "the great mass of phenomena" (Bradley 1897: 29). For instance, the very idea of a thing is bound up with that of relations – it is a complex of connected properties all inhering, perhaps, in some central point – and so if we cannot make sense of relations we cannot make sense of things either. Space and time are even more obviously relational, their loss entailing the loss of all motion and change too. A further important relation we must dismiss is causation, but perhaps the most worrying casualty of all is the notion of the self. Bradley rejects the idea of the self, for it too involves division and hence relation; for instance in its subject–object structure or between its various ideas, faculties or temporal stages. The ordinary world is then but a misleading appearance of a reality quite different from the way it seems.

Another important consequence is monism. The commonsense view of the universe as containing many distinct substances – pluralism – must be rejected; a non-relational world is a monistic world. But we need to be careful here, for what Bradley has in mind is not – as Russell once said (Russell 1959: 290) – some sort of homogeneous unity like that of Parmenides. For if, as we saw, relations both unite and divide their removal should no more imply unity than diversity. His Absolute is a many-in-one. It does not exclude difference, but it is *one*. There is no point in disguising the Hegelian flavour of this.

Pre-relational experience

Bradley is a firm adherent of a principle that most of us would accept, the coherence of reality: "Ultimate reality is such that it does not contradict itself" (Bradley 1897: 120). Hence if contradiction is found in our experience it must be something we have introduced; the mind in trying to grasp reality must have distorted it. If this is so, then we get back nearer to something like the truth, if we discount our troublesome contributions. In this way the contradictory realm of relational thought or experience points to something behind itself, to its origin in "feeling" or "immediate experience." There is more than an echo of Kant here.

"Immediate experience" and "feeling" are the technical terms Bradley uses to designate the basic experiential state in which reality is given or encountered. "The real" he says "is that which is known in presentation or intuitive knowledge. It is what we encounter in feeling or perception" (Bradley 1922: 44). However exotic their flower may be, that the roots of Bradley's thinking here are to be found in the tradition of British empiricism is seen in his further insistence that such experience is our only handle on reality; "Nothing in the end is real but what is felt" (Bradley 1915: 190). However, what he has in mind here is not simply the ordinary experience of everyday life, but rather something deeper which underlies that experience.

By calling it "feeling" or "experience," he wishes to protest against any more narrow or one-sided starting point, such as merely the experience of our senses. What Bradley has in mind here is a state that includes all types of sensation, emotion, will and desire – in short, anything of which we are in any manner aware (Bradley 1915: 189). By calling it "immediate," he wishes to stress that it is something presentational and pre-conceptual. Although it contains diversity, it is not broken up by concepts and relations. "It is all one blur with differences, that work and that are felt, but are not discriminated" (1935: 216, 1897: 90), he says. Notably, it is prior both to the distinction between self and not-self, and to the distinction between concept or knowledge and object or existence. It is a state as yet without either an object or a subject (Bradley 1897: 465).

Another important point to note about immediate experience is that it manifests itself filtered through what he calls "finite centres" (Bradley 1915: 410). These numerous (Bradley 1897: 468) centres of experience, closely identified in his mind with the indexical perspective of the "this" and the "mine" (Bradley 1897: 198) and thus impervious to each other (Bradley 1915: 173), are not to be thought of as objects existing in time or capable of standing in relation to one another; they are rather the raw data from which such objects and relations are built up as ideal constructions (Bradley 1915:

411). They are, we might say, the pre-conceptual experiential base from which we construct our entire conception of the world. In particular, finite centres are to be distinguished from selves. This is so in two respects. First, selves are objects that endure through time, and second, they are distinguished from their states. A finite centre, by contrast, has no duration and contains no subject–object distinction. For Bradley the self is something made out of, or abstracted from, a finite centre, and thus he allows that in so far as I think of myself as something developed out of a given finite centre, I may describe that centre as "mine" (Bradley 1915: 418), but it must always be remembered that the self which is thus developed is but an ideal construction lacking any ultimate reality (Bradley 1915: 248).

Although in some sense nearer to the truth than relational experience, immediate experience is not fully harmonious. And its lack of harmony leads it to break up and develop into the relational consciousness. The transition from immediate experience to relational thought results from the clash between the finitude of its feeling centres and its immediacy. It presents itself as a harmonious state, something that is no more than what it appears to be, a knowing and being in one. But in Bradley's eyes the finitude attributable to its manifestation through the "this" and the "mine" generates an instability which destabilises that harmony. Understanding finitude in the Hegelian manner as that limited from outside, the finite centre points beyond itself to a wider reality of which it is but a portion and against which it is contrasted. And thus enters the distinction between subject and object which is the hallmark of thought, and which spells the demise of the immediacy of feeling.

But too much talk of change or development should not lead us astray here, for Bradley is insistent that immediate experience is not left completely behind, but rather remains present in relational thought as a kind of foundation (Bradley 1915: 160, 175). Immediate experience provides us with the very experiential content that is subsequently conceptualised in relational experience, and its gives us an intuition of diversified wholeness against which our attempts to think the matter through are convicted.

Supra-relational experience

If the contradictions of thought point backwards to immediate experience, they also point forwards beyond themselves to the Absolute. The developmental process which caused the breach, left to continue, heals itself again. For it is the nature of thought to aim at truth, and in uncovering its own defects it at the same time shows what would be necessary to rectify them. Specifically it is seen that error arises precisely from the separation of things one from another, from which it follows that the more they are reconnected, the more things are returned in understanding to the context from which they were abstracted, the more holistic our vision becomes, and the closer we head to truth. By putting the jigsaw back together, we replace the pluralistic vision with a holistic one.

Bradley recommends connected and holistic thinking over separated and pluralistic schemes, but he insists that more healthy patterns of thought can never give a complete solution to our problem. For however much we try to compensate for it, and however much we are aware of doing it, it belongs to the very nature of thought to differentiate

– to separate one object from another, and all objects from the subject which thinks them. But to differentiate is to falsify. We divide A from B, but then add that of course A and B must be taken together. But they are still separate in thought. In the end argues Bradley, if the road to truth is the road of reconciliation, it must take us beyond thought, to an Absolute experience undifferentiated by concepts. It should thus be noted that Bradley has an importantly realist concept of the Absolute as something existing beyond (what he poetically describes as) thought's suicide.

For Bradley Absolute experience, experience driven by its own internal logic or engine to find a final consistency, contains all that is ultimately real. But what about all those elements of experience that get discarded along the way? Bradley designates these *appearance* and not (ultimate) reality, but what exactly does he mean when he says relations (and all those things that involve relations) are appearance, rather than reality? We might think this is to say they do not exist, to which we are likely to respond in a tone of commonsense indignation that surely such things *do* exist. But our indignation would be misplaced; Bradley does not, for a moment, want to deny that relations exist – nothing has been spirited away. In this respect his position is comparable to the doctrine of secondary qualities, which is not that objects don't really have colours, that colours don't exist, but rather that phenomenal colour is not a category applicable to ultimate reality. The reference to secondary qualities might suggest to us the metaphysical dualist's way of dealing with appearance, namely to think of it as mental representation (an idea or sense-datum) interposing between us and the world beyond, a kind of screen that gets in the way and prevents us from seeing things as they really are. However, Bradley's monism precludes any such move – his appearances are not in that sense appearances *of* anything. For Bradley, the Absolute *is* its appearances. They are its content. To call something unreal or appearance is to deny that it possesses genuinely independent being which, of course, covers everything except the Absolute. Seen falsely and picked out one by one, aspects of the world present a misleading face and must be called appearance, but seen truly as participants in an integrated whole, they are transformed together to form reality, or the Absolute. As Bradley puts it, "The Absolute, we may say in general, has no assets beyond appearances; and again, with appearances alone to its credit, the Absolute would be bankrupt. All these are worthless alike apart from transmutation" (Bradley 1897: 433). Ultimate reality is so far beyond conception that we could never think it, but at the same time it is all around us.

Appearance then for Bradley is a distorted vision or perspective on reality. It is a matter of taking something out of context and treating it as though it were fully and independently real. But distortion here is a matter of degree, hence Bradley believes that there is room for a theory of degrees of truth. It is a measure of the amount of transformation that would be required to turn appearance into absolute truth. It is in this sense that internal relations are truer than external ones.

Idealism

It will be noted that so far we have spoken only of experience; the felt directness of immediate experience, giving way to the plurality of relational experience, reconciling itself in the diverse-unity of Absolute experience. But is there not more to life than experience? Bradley insists that there is not. That is to say, he was an idealist.

Bradley's argument for idealism is nothing like as developed as his argument for monism. It might even be suggested that he just assumes it (Candlish 2007: 45) but that is problematic, for the kind of idealism he offers cannot be simply assimilated to other known types. There are (it might be suggested) two types of idealism. On the one hand, there is the Hegelian species of idealism, which identifies thought and reality. Quite what this means occupies Hegel scholars still, but need not be our worry here, since, for all Bradley was influenced by Hegel, it is clear that his idealism was not of this stripe. As he says of that view at the end of the *Principles of Logic*,

> It may come from a failure in my metaphysics, or from a weakness of the flesh which continues to blind me, but the notion that existence could be the same as understanding strikes as cold and ghost-like as the dreariest materialism. That the glory of this world in the end is appearance leaves the world more glorious, if we feel it is a show of some fuller splendour; but the sensuous curtain is a deception and a cheat, if it hides some colourless movement of atoms, some spectral woof of impalpable abstractions, or unearthly ballet of bloodless categories. Though dragged to such conclusions, we can not embrace them … They no more *make* that Whole which commands our devotion, than some shredded dissection of human tatters *is* that warm and breathing beauty of flesh which our hearts found delightful. (Bradley 1922: 590–1)

The other species of idealism is that best typified by Berkeley, who argues in anti-realist fashion that we can never pass outside the sphere of our own cognition, that we have no grounds for belief in anything beyond the ideas we encounter. While superficially Bradley might seem to be arguing like this, in the end his view is very different. Where Berkeley thinks that there cannot be anything beyond our knowledge, Bradley is quite clear that there is more to life than knowledge. He holds that reality is composed of a species of mind which is fundamentally non-cognitive (i.e. neither perceptual nor conceptual) and in this respect the idealism with which it comes closest is in fact that of Schopenhauer whose doctrine of the will presents a comparable species of non-cognitive mentality as forming the underlying constitution of reality.

References

Bradley, F.H. (1897) *Appearance and Reality*, 2nd edn, Oxford: Clarendon Press.
—— (1915) *Essays on Truth and Reality*, Oxford: Clarendon Press.
—— (1922) *The Principles of Logic*, 2nd edn, Oxford: Clarendon Press.
—— (1935) *Collected Essays*, Oxford: Clarendon Press.
Candlish, S. (2007) *The Russell/Bradley Dispute*, Houndmills, UK: Palgrave Macmillan.
Russell, B. (1937) *The Principles of Mathematics*, 2nd edn, London: George Allen & Unwin.
—— (1956) *Logic and Knowledge*, London: George Allen & Unwin.
—— (1959) *My Philosophical Development*, London, George Allen & Unwin.

Further reading

J. W. Allard, *The Logical Foundations of Bradley's Metaphysics* (Cambridge: Cambridge University Press, 2005) offers a helpful examination of the close relation between Bradley's logic and metaphysics. S. Candlish, *The Russell/Bradley Dispute* (Houndmills, UK; Palgrave Macmillan, 2007) gives a detailed analysis of the various exchanges between Bradley and Russell. W. J. Mander, *An Introduction to Bradley's Metaphysics* (Oxford: Clarendon Press, 1994) is an easy introduction to the main themes in Bradley's metaphysics. G. Stock (ed.), *Appearance versus Reality: New Essays on the Philosophy of F. H. Bradley* (Oxford: Clarendon Press, 1998) is a useful collection of essays on central themes.

18
WHITEHEAD
Process and cosmology

Peter Simons

Introduction

Alfred North Whitehead (1861–1947) occupies a remarkable position in twentieth century philosophy. Though he co-authored the seminal *Principia Mathematica* with his former student Bertrand Russell, and later supervised W. V. Quine, his influence on later analytic philosophy has been minimal, while in other circles his work enjoyed cult status. Largely ignored by professionals in his native Britain, he is respected in his adopted America, and receives interest in continental Europe. Trained as a mathematician, he moved into logic and the foundations of mathematics. In his fifties he began writing about the philosophy of science, physics and education, and at sixty-three emigrated to the United States, teaching as Professor of Philosophy at Harvard University for a further thirteen years. His chief work, *Process and Reality: An Essay in Cosmology* (1978 [1929]) has been compared, for length, difficulty and importance, to Kant's *Critique of Pure Reason*. This work – we will refer to it as *PR* – completed Whitehead's transformation into a metaphysician, and it is the focus of our attention.

PR crowned a flourishing period of metaphysical philosophy, but as analytic philosophy fell under the anti-metaphysical spell of logical positivism and linguistic philosophy, *PR*'s frankly speculative metaphysics came to seem outmoded. Its reception was not helped by Whitehead's often arcane terminology, the unclarity of crucial passages, and the off-puttingly abstract opening chapter. In America, with Whitehead on hand to expound his views in person, his influence blossomed, but in his native land he was largely written off. The process philosophy and theology that *PR* set in train frequently outdid the master in obscurity, and Whitehead's reputation suffered by association. He was also unfortunate that his work consistently fell into the cracks between mathematics, philosophy and physics.

In my judgement *PR* is the greatest single metaphysical work of the twentieth century. Despite its difficulties its message can be put clearly; despite Whitehead's shifts of interest it represents the culmination of a metaphysical odyssey he had pursued since his twenties; and despite its age we can take lessons from its content and method even today.

Early writings

Whitehead studied mathematics in Cambridge. In 1884 he submitted a dissertation on James Clerk Maxwell's epochal *Treatise on Electricity and Magnetism* (of 1873), which earned him election as a fellow of Trinity College. Maxwell's work is famous for proposing that electromagnetic waves radiate at the speed of light, and for the equations which draw electricity and magnetism together into a unified theory. Whitehead's dissertation was unfortunately not preserved: it might have given a picture of his earliest encounters with the themes of fundamental physical processes, space and time, to which his writings return throughout his career. The transmission of energy in electromagnetic radiation is very different from the picture of energy, found in Newtonian physics, as carried by moving material particles, and reflection on this may have led Whitehead to his criticisms of Newton and traditional mechanics.

Whitehead's first book was *A Treatise on Universal Algebra with Applications* (published in 1898), a systematic compendium of the algebraic revolution of the nineteenth century, covering Hamilton's quaternions, Grassmann's geometric calculus of extensions, and Boole's algebra of logic. Its principal focus is the algebra of geometry. He intended to continue the work but when his former student Bertrand Russell completed a first draft of *The Principles of Mathematics* in 1900 they found they had enough in common to pool their projects. The road to a common "Volume 2" was stony, being interrupted in mid-1901 by Russell's discovery of the paradox of set theory that bears his name. Their unexpectedly extended collaboration produced a three-volume epic: *Principia Mathematica* (1910–13). Its relevance for Whitehead's metaphysics is twofold. First, it schooled him as nothing else could in concocting new definitions and using symbolic logic to give rigorous proofs. Second, there was supposed to be a fourth volume of *Principia*, on geometry, which it was agreed Whitehead would write alone. For various reasons this was never completed, but the subject of geometry and its relation to reality drove much of Whitehead's later work.

Whitehead's interest in geometry showed itself in the publication of two textbooks, *The Axioms of Projective Geometry* (in 1906) and *The Axioms of Descriptive Geometry* (in 1907). But nothing from his early period so presaged his later metaphysical concerns as the remarkable sixty-page memoir "On Mathematical Concepts of the Material World" (1953 [1906]; MC), published in the *Philosophical Transactions of the Royal Society of London* in 1906. This memoir links his early interest in Maxwell, his *Principia* work on geometry, and his later work on space, time, physics and cosmology.

In MC, Whitehead put forward several different axiomatic models of a world of material entities in space and time, from each of which the principles of Euclidean geometry could be derived. Each concept is based on a number of different fundamental relations: the *essential* relation, the *time* relation, and the *extraneous* relation.

In the first, Newtonian concept, points of space are the field of the essential relation, and material particles the field of the extraneous relation. This is Newton's absolute space with its occupying matter. Whitehead disapproves of the dualism of space and matter, preferring a monistic account in which space and matter form a single field of entities. The next two concepts are monistic revisions of the first. For example in

Concept III the four-placed essential relation $R(a,b,c,t)$ means "the objective reals a, b and c stand in the R-relation at t." The points of this Concept are not static, but move, like particles. In Concepts IV and V the objective reals are not point-like but linear. The linear basic entities are used to define points as certain classes, anticipating White-head's later use of extensive abstraction. The preference for linear over punctual basic entities is related to Faraday's conception of *lines of force* as physically basic.

Each of the five main concepts is developed axiomatically, using a modified Peano notation which would become familiar only four years later with *Principia*, and so presented a challenge to which few contemporary readers could rise. The memoir was generally overlooked, but Whitehead thought it one of his best pieces.

Philosophy of nature

In working on the abortive fourth geometry volume of *Principia*, Whitehead intended to incorporate the new Lorentz–Einstein–Minkowski theory of relativity into his account of geometry. His criticism of Newton's dynamics was now clear. Newton's separation of an absolute space and time from its contingent filler, inert matter, consti-tuted an unacceptable "bifurcation of nature" embodying the "fallacy of simple location": the idea that material stuff is simply passively at a place at a time. Like Leibniz, Whitehead regarded matter as active and inseparable in reality from its spatiotemporal location. In expressing this he needed to take account of the revolutionary interweaving of space and time brought about by Einstein's theories of relativity and their formali-zation by Minkowski. Whitehead's response to the challenge was *An Enquiry Concerning the Principles of Natural Knowledge* (1925 [1919]; *PNK*), first published in 1919. This, the most polished of his middle-period works, is an attempt at "providing a physical basis for the more modern views" (vi) consonant with Whitehead's emerging philosophy. The result is a work juxtaposing lucid prose with sketched mathematical developments. The principle aim is to articulate a unified mathematical account of the related basic entities of nature, in such a way that both relativistic dynamics and classical geometry are adequately represented. It thus continues the thrust of MC, but in a less rigorous presentation.

To overcome the "bifurcation" and incorporate the interweaving of space and time, Whitehead takes the basic entities to be four-dimensional *events*, which was a step beyond Minkowski, whose world-lines represented the "everlasting careers" of material and electrical points. The challenge is to explain how events are related so as to give rise to the dynamics and geometry we expect. To do this Whitehead employs the idea of one event B's *extending over* another event A, or as we would say, event A's being *part of* event B. Whitehead rapidly sketches a formal theory of part and whole, or *mereology*, before proceeding to his new *method of extensive abstraction* for using events to define various geometrical entities. We can illustrate this method by the simple example of a spatial point. Ignore time, and just consider the events happening at one instant. Suppose we take one event, and find another which is part of it, then another which is a part of that, and so on without end, like an unending succession of nested Russian dolls. Suppose also that no event is a part of every one of the series, so they get ever smaller without limit. Intuitively, they converge to a spatial point. But we could have got to the same point by many such sequences. Whitehead cunningly shows how we can say that two such sequences co-converge, without actually mentioning the point. Any two co-convergent sequences give us the same point, but this is not a real thing nesting inside all the sequences: Whitehead turns the idea on its head and *defines* the point as the collection of all those co-converging sequences. The point is then a mathematical abstraction, not a real entity. All that really exists are the events, and "Every element of space or of time ... is an abstract entity formed out of this relation of extension ... by means of a determinate logical procedure" (1925 [1919]: 75). Using this method to define various other geometrical entities makes up the bulk of the book. But Whitehead knows that his events are unlike the familiar objects of everyday, so he explains that objects are not fundamental things, but items that can be "recognized" among certain sequences of events, intuitively, those that "involve" the object in question. While we name events after their participants, the events are more fundamental.

PNK replaced axioms by prose, perhaps to appeal to a wider readership, but Whitehead nevertheless failed to gain the attention of physicists, perhaps because the work was seen by them as too philosophical. *The Concept of Nature* (1920) repeated Whitehead's position less technically. Whitehead then published *The Principle of Relativity, with Applications to Physical Science* (in 1922), which unlike Einstein presented relativity theory within a Euclidean framework, separating the tensor of space–time from the tensor of gravity, whereas in Einstein these are unified. It showed Whitehead at the forefront of British reception of relativity theory and prepared to grapple with physicists on their own terms, but again they did not take it seriously, and it is now believed to have been empirically refuted, making predictions which diverged from those of Einstein. *Science and the Modern World* (1926; SMW), based on the Lowell Lectures delivered in Harvard, is a readable historical cruise through the after effects of the scientific revolution of the seventeenth century. It continues and deepens Whitehead's critique of post-Newtonian mechanistic materialism, deploring the various dualisms of mind and matter, science and art, mechanism and purpose that pervade the modern worldview. He traces the problems to what he calls the *fallacy of misplaced concreteness*, which consists in treating mathematical abstractions like instants of time or point-particles as if they were the realest things. Whitehead's aim is to replace mechanistic materialism by a new metaphysics true to our experience, which yields the right (modern) physical results, explains the applicability of mathematics, and satisfies his philosophical rejection of dualisms. The later chapters of *SMW*, added after the lectures, set about this task, plunging us into his mature metaphysical view, which Whitehead called the *philosophy of organism*.

The mature metaphysics: process and becoming

In 1924 Whitehead became a professional philosopher at the advanced age of sixty-three, with his appointment to a chair at Harvard. He loved America, and America loved him in return: he continued to teach until 1937, and his Sunday soirées in

Cambridge, Massachusetts, became legendary. After the lectures which became *SMW*, he was invited to give a 1927 series of Gifford Lectures in Edinburgh. Lord Adam Gifford (1820–87) had stipulated in his will that money from his estate be used to fund periodic lectures at the Scottish universities on natural theology. Whitehead had been much impressed by Samuel Alexander's 1917–18 Glasgow series, published in 1920 as *Space, Time and Deity*, and agreed. The result was published in 1929 as *Process and Reality*, and it is Whitehead's greatest philosophical work. Unfortunately it is also his hardest. The lectures were well attended at first, but dwindled to single-figure attendances, which Whitehead seems not to have noticed.

The first thing to note is that Whitehead seems, if we go by the title, to replace *events* as the principal items of his metaphysics by *processes*. This has misled many commentators. In fact there are no items in Whitehead's ontology called "processes." Rather the term "process" refers to the way in which the basic things – which still *are* events – come into existence and cease to exist. Whitehead calls this *becoming*.

The principal difference between the events of the nature philosophy and those of *PR* and afterwards is that the earlier events are complex: they have parts, their parts have parts, and so on without end: every event has some other event as a proper part, so there are no atomic events. The events of *PR*, however, are all atomic: they have no proper parts. To distinguish them from the earlier events, Whitehead renames them "actual occasions": "actual" because they are real. Apart from these atomic events, there is one other actual item in Whitehead's ontology, and that is God. Because God is eternal and not an event, Whitehead calls God and occasions taken together *actual entities*.

Why did Whitehead change his mind on whether events have parts? It turns on an argument in *SMW* (1926: 158–60), related to Zeno's Paradoxes. Recall that Whitehead rejected the idea of temporal instants as real entities: instants are abstract limits. So all times are finite in extent. Also there are no empty times or spaces: they are given with their occupants. Now imagine some event occurring. It cannot occur in an instant, since there is no such thing. So it occurs over an interval. But if the occurring has a first half, and this in turn has a first half, and so on, and an event cannot start unless its first instant occurs first, then no event can occur over an interval. Time becomes impossible. But time clearly is possible, so we must reject part of the reasoning. Whitehead rejects the view that an event which occurs over an interval comes into being gradually, instant by instant, as the interval unfolds. Rather the event *simply occurs*, and brings a small bubble of space–time into existence with it. This bubble has earlier and later parts, but the event itself is atomic. "There is a becoming of continuity, but no continuity of becoming … the ultimate metaphysical truth is atomism. The creatures are atomic" (1978 [1929]: 35). Each event "enjoys" a small bubble of space–time, and they cannot be separated, but they have different properties. Whitehead therefore transfers his mereology from events to spatiotemporal regions. The Zenonian argument must have been convincing to Whitehead, since it forced him to disjoin the continuity of space–time from the atomicity of its occupants, something he had previously opposed. As to the cogency of the argument, it seems to me that there is no absurdity in supposing that even miniscule events unfold continuously, and acquire new temporal phases as time goes by. Whitehead might as a matter of empirical fact be right that the most basic events are atomic, but it is not mandated by his argument. And while it is conceptually liberating to uncouple the parts of space–time from the parts of their occupants, it is not self-evidently correct.

If events do not unfold, why then, when they become, does Whitehead talk about "process"? Although events come about all at once, their becoming can be analysed in regard to their antecedents. This analysis Whitehead calls "genetic," since it comprises "stages" whose sequence is logical rather than temporal, and the analysis is essentially backward-looking. Every new event has its own universe, out of which it is generated. This universe comprises two kinds of thing. First, there are all the ideal kinds or universals, what Whitehead calls *eternal objects*. Being outside space and time, these are equally accessible to all events. Second, there are all the previous events which are accessible to the new event. This accessibility is restricted by the relativistic principle that no causal influence can travel faster than the speed of light. So the events accessible to a new event are all those in its backward light cone. The description of how events come to be on the basis of their antecedents is the central theme of Whitehead's metaphysics. Although in concrete detail it varies from one event to another, the general scheme of becoming is the same for all, so I call it the *basic cell* of Whitehead's metaphysics.

The key to understanding the basic cell is that events are what they are solely in virtue of their relations to other things. It is instructive to compare Whitehead's events with Leibniz's monads. The first difference is that Leibniz's monads are enduring things which have a history, whereas Whitehead's actual occasions are over and done in a flash. But more importantly, Leibniz's monads are as they are because of their qualities, and they do not depend on anything outside them, except God, for being the way they are. Leibniz denies that there is any real interaction between monads, describing them as "windowless." Whitehead's events by contrast are all window: they are as they are because of how they relate to other things. The first way in which they are is that they have certain qualities. But they have them not in themselves, as in Leibniz, but because they stand in a relation to certain eternal objects. This relation, which in traditional philosophy is called *instantiation*, in Whitehead is called *ingression*. Eternal objects ingress into individual events to make them what they are. Apart from the terminological difference from Plato, Whitehead's theory stresses two additional points. The first is that eternal objects are not actual or real in themselves, but only in so far as they ingress into actual events. In themselves they are nothing but pure potentialities for ingression. The second point is that for describing the genesis of events we should see the relation of ingression not from the eternal object's end of the relation but from that of the event. The genesis of the events is described in quasi-psychological terms. We imagine a would-be event striving to come into existence. It surveys all the eternal objects, is related to them by a relation Whitehead calls *conceptual prehension*. We might say the would-be event is "aware of" all the eternal objects. But it cannot be all ways, for example it cannot have an energy of 1 Joule and also an energy of 2 Joules. So it must "select" among the eternal objects those which are to ingress into it. The selection means it prehends some eternal objects positively and others negatively. Positive prehension Whitehead calls *feeling*. An event's feeling a universal is the same as the universal's ingressing into the event. But an event is determined as what it is not just by its relations to eternal objects, but also by its relations to all events in its universe. Whitehead again calls these relations "prehensions," but because the entities prehended are real he calls them *physical prehensions*. Again physical prehensions are positive or negative: a positive prehension of an event E by a becoming event B constitutes E's affecting the way B is when it becomes, so B being like E in some way, whereas if B negatively prehends E it becomes unlike E and E does not influence the way it is. Since influence can pass through events to later events, prehensions can be ramified to any degree of complexity, and each new event becomes what it is through the sum total of its prehensions. In general the physical prehensions have a far greater say in determining how an event is, conceptual prehensions being generally mediated by physical ones. Roughly speaking, like tends to engender like.

When an event comes to pass, it does so as a small burst of novelty in the world, integrating all the objects and events in its universe in a new synthesis which it embodies. Since no two events have the same universe from which to arise, each event is in some respect new. For this reason Whitehead thinks there is a supreme category which encapsulates the essence of the basic cell: he calls it *creativity* and describes it as *the category of the ultimate*. Creativity consists in a new individual (one) coming into being through a novel (creative) synthesis of its antecedents (many). As soon as an event comes into being, it ceases to exist, or "dies," and the quantum of space–time it brings with it is succeeded by others. Hence Whitehead describes time, in Locke's phrase, as a "perpetual perishing." But in coming to be, or becoming concrete (Whitehead also calls becoming "concrescence"), the event not only advances the world a little and enriches it with its novel character, in dying it becomes available for later generations of events to prehend: its influence lives on in subsequent events, in a way reminiscent of causal influence, though Whitehead uses the term "cause" with reluctance.

This is basically all there is to Whitehead's cosmology: the rest plays out the implications of the countless repetitions of the basic cell of becoming throughout time and space. The account is so schematic that it can fit parts of the life of the universe, what Whitehead calls *epochs*, which may differ in many respects from our own, for example in having more or fewer spatial dimensions, or different laws of nature. The term "process" then, paradoxically, refers principally to the atemporal genetic analysis of events, and Whitehead calls events *organisms* because his account of them is ecological, based on their relationships to their surrounding universes. Secondarily of course "process" can refer to the rich tapestry of happenings unfolding as ever new generations of events come into being.

Human beings and other enduring objects are obviously not events or even collections of events, so, as in his nature philosophy, Whitehead tries to explain what they (and we) are. Again he does so in terms of a kind of inherited order among families of (more or less) simultaneous events. Families of events may have what Whitehead calls a "social order": the social order of enduring objects like people is called "personal order."

The spatiotemporal arena which is advanced with novel events is subject to similar principles of part/whole that Whitehead employed in *PNK*, but now not events but their regions are what stand in those relations. Whitehead integrates his part/whole theory or mereology with the topological notions of connectedness and boundary, and so becomes perhaps the first to pursue what is now called *mereotopology*. Points and instants remain as abstract as before: Whitehead is concerned throughout to build his cosmology out of kinds of entities which can be experienced or perceived.

Perception, or rather its pre-conscious analogue, prehension, forms the cement out of which Whitehead's cosmos is built. Whitehead's use of psychological terms like "prehend," "feel" and "subject" is deliberate. Like Leibniz, he is a *panpsychist*, considering all actual entities to be in some way mental, if only at a rudimentary level. This marks him out from Alexander, who saw the mental as emerging from mere matter. Whitehead loses the categorial difference between the mental and the physical that besets Descartes, but the price of this is supposing that even electrons have feelings, just not the kind of conscious ones we know.

Whitehead rounds out his metaphysics, as befits a Gifford lecturer, with God. In Whitehead's scheme God has two aspects, or natures: a primordial nature, which consists in God's eternal characteristics, forming a repository for all eternal objects (which are potentialities, only actualized when something of their kind comes to be), and a consequent nature, in which God keeps pace with the evolution of the universe, providing a memory store for all actual occasions, including those that are no longer in existence, to retain a form of immortality beyond the more or less faint traces they leave in subsequent events. Whitehead's views, which are somewhat sketchily laid out in *PR*, became the fountainhead of a whole movement called "process theology," which has portrayed Whitehead as more of a theologian than he was – I personally regard the teleological or purposive aspect of Whitehead's metaphysics, including God, as a sentimental throwback that can be dispensed with.

Whitehead's God crowned his metaphysics, which retains elements of purpose even within the inanimate. In this as in many other respects Whitehead's metaphysics recalls that of Plato. He acknowledged this and declared that European philosophy "consists in a series of footnotes to Plato" (1978 [1929]: 39), not in the sense that Platonism dominated, but that Plato's many rich ideas, particularly those of his cosmology, the *Timaeus*, had been repeatedly taken up, echoed and modified throughout European history. The only cosmology to stand comparison with Plato's is that of the Scholium to Newton's *Principia*, a work whose title he and Russell had borrowed. But while Whitehead accepts that Newton's science was more advanced than Plato's, he regards Plato's cosmology overall as deeper and philosophically more satisfactory. It is in Plato's footsteps that he aspired to tread.

Speculative metaphysics and the categories

Metaphysics, the noblest of all philosophic enterprises, is the attempt to give an account of everything. Unlike the special sciences, metaphysics does not descend into detail for its own sake. Rather its job is to provide a universal framework within which anything whatever can take its place. That framework consists of a scheme of most general concepts or *categories*, within which all classifications of things are to be situated, together with a collection of general principles or *archai* which describe the way in which the things falling under the various categories are interrelated and interwoven.

Whitehead marked his awareness of these different basic things by distinguishing *four* conceptions of category. The category of the ultimate, creativity, epitomizes becoming as the creation of a new one from a prior many. It is intended to supplant Aristotle's first substance as the most important single metaphysical notion. But unlike substance, creativity is not an entity in the world. Not even God is the ultimate in Whitehead, since God is an entity. "In all philosophic theory," he writes, "there is an ultimate which is actual in virtue of its accidents" (1978 [1929]: 7). In Whitehead this is creativity, of which God is the first, non-temporal accident: Whitehead considered that Spinoza, Bradley and others wrongly elevated God to the position of the ultimate, which no actual thing could be. In taking the ultimate not to be an entity Whitehead is close to some pre-Socratic philosophers.

What others call "categories," most general classes of entity, Whitehead calls "categories of existence." They comprise actual entities (God and events) and eternal objects, but also prehensions, multiplicities (classes), nexūs (interlinked groups of events), subjective forms (roughly, perceptual complexes), propositions, and contrasts, which form an infinite class of kinds and are somewhat like Russell's types of propositional function. Of these, actual entities and eternal objects "stand out with a certain extreme finality" (1978 [1929]: 22). In addition, there are twenty-seven *categories of explanation*, which are not classes of things but sorts of general explanatory principles specific to Whitehead's cosmology. Finally there are nine *categorial obligations*, which are partly terminological, partly again explanatory principles. The first chapter of *PR*, "Speculative Philosophy," in which these categories and principles are listed, is one of the most dizzyingly abstract in all philosophy, and off-putting to most readers.

Despite this, the chapter repays patient study. Whitehead gave here perhaps the clearest account of the systematic role of metaphysics of any philosopher in recent centuries. He wrote, "Speculative philosophy is the endeavour to frame a coherent, logical, necessary system of general ideas in terms of which every element of our experience can be interpreted. By ... 'interpretation' ... I mean that everything of which we are conscious ... shall have the character of a particular instance of the general scheme" (1978 [1929]: 3). Whitehead's soaring ambition impelled him to attempt just such a system, covering everything, though the cosmology of *PR* was concerned principally with the physical universe rather than with biology, society, history, culture, art, religion or mathematics. Some of these topics he addressed in other late writings, especially *Adventures of Ideas* (1933). At the same time he was acutely conscious of his human and personal limitations, and mindful of the demise of Newton's cosmology, he warns "There remains the final reflection, how shallow, puny, and imperfect are efforts to sound the depths in the nature of things. In philosophical discussion, the merest hint of dogmatic certainty as to finality of statement is an exhibition of folly" (1978 [1929]: xiv).

Acknowledgements

I am indebted for discussion on Whitehead and relativity to Mr Ronny Desmet.

References

Whitehead, Alfred North (1920) *The Concept of Nature*, Cambridge: Cambridge University Press.

—— (1925 [1919]) *An Enquiry Concerning the Principles of Natural Knowledge*, 2nd edn, Cambridge: Cambridge University Press.

—— (1926) *Science and the Modern World*, Cambridge: Cambridge University Press.

—— (1933) *Adventures of Ideas*, New York: Macmillan.

—— (1953 [1906]) "On Mathematical Concepts of the Material World," in F. C. Northrop and M. W. Gross (eds), *Alfred North Whitehead: An Anthology*, Cambridge: Cambridge University Press, pp. 11–82; originally published in *Philosophical Transactions of the Royal Society* (Series A) 205: 465–525.

—— (1978 [1929]) *Process and Reality: An Essay in Cosmology*, corrected edn, edited by D. R. Griffin and D. W. Sherburne, New York: Macmillan.

Further reading

A. N. Whitehead, "On Mathematical Concepts of the Material World," *Philosophical Transactions of the Royal Society* (Series A) 205 (1906): 465–525; reprinted in F. C. Northrop and M. W. Gross (eds), *Alfred North Whitehead: An Anthology* (Cambridge: Cambridge University Press, 1953), pp. 11–82, offers five axiomatic cosmologies, still astonishing; *Science and the Modern World* (Cambridge: Cambridge University Press, 1926) accounts for why Newton's cosmology was wrong, and what to do about it; *Process and Reality: An Essay in Cosmology*, corrected edn, edited by D. R. Griffin and D. W. Sherburne (1929; New York: Macmillan, 1978) corrects the hundreds of typographical and other errors of the original – like Mount Everest, worth the effort; and *Adventures of Ideas* (New York: Macmillan, 1933), covering a wider range than *PR*, is the most accessible of Whitehead's late philosophical works. Victor Lowe, *Understanding Whitehead* (Baltimore, MD: Johns Hopkins University Press, 1962) is by Whitehead's student and his most balanced commentator; and Lowe's *A. N. Whitehead: The Man and His Work*, vol. 1: 1861–1910; vol. 2 1910–47, with J. B. Schneewind (Baltimore: Johns Hopkins University Press, 1985, 1990), is an insightful and sadly incomplete biography. Wolfe Mays, *Whitehead's Philosophy of Science and Metaphysics: An Introduction to His Thought* (The Hague: Martinus Nijhoff, 1977), shows the continuity of Whitehead's concerns, and the importance of MC, and strives to put Whitehead into plain terms.

19
HEIDEGGER
The question of Being

Herman Philipse

Many generations of readers, among them well-known philosophers such as Sartre and Levinas, have been intrigued by Martin Heidegger's most important book, *Sein und Zeit* (*Being and Time*), first published in 1927. The promise permeating the text that one may become a more authentic individual if one understands adequately Heidegger's philosophical analysis of human existence, offers an alluring prospect. Yet this "fundamental ontology of *Dasein* [being-there]," as Heidegger calls it, comprises merely one-third of the book as it was originally planned. In its initial setup, disclosed in section 8, there were to be six divisions of *Being and Time*, whereas the published fragment on human existence contains only two of them.

The work as a whole aims at raising anew an old question of philosophy, the so-called question of the meaning of being. On page 1 of the book, Heidegger introduces this question by a quotation from Plato's *Sophist*. He states that we do not have an answer to the question today, and that, consequently, we have to raise it anew. He also insists that he has to reawaken an understanding for the meaning of the question of being, since, allegedly, we are not perplexed nowadays at our inability to understand the expression "to be." But how can Heidegger pretend that we are not able to understand this expression? We are using the verb "to be" without difficulty of understanding, and linguists or logicians have analyzed its various uses.

There are quite a number of other interpretative problems concerning the question of being, which was to remain the focus of Heidegger's thought until his death in 1976. One problem is already apparent on the first page of *Being and Time*. Heidegger phrases his question in two radically different ways. According to one formulation, the question of being is concerned with the meanings of the verb "to be." The other formulation suggests that the question is about the meaningfulness of a phenomenon called Being (*die Frage nach dem Sinn von Sein*). Does Heidegger refer by this latter phrase to the question of being as raised by Plato and Aristotle, which was concerned with the ultimate constituents of reality? Or is he using "Being" as another name for God, as some schoolmen used to do? Surely these are distinct questions, which have to be answered by using different methods. And why does Heidegger think that time or temporality functions as a "horizon" of all understanding of being, as he asserts in section 5? What does this assertion mean?

Another problem emerges at the end of the published part of *Being and Time*, in section 83. Here Heidegger says that his philosophical analysis of human existence is merely a way or road (nur *ein Weg*), and that the aim is to develop the question of being as such. But if the question of being is not even developed in *Being and Time*, how should the reader know how to answer it? And why is a philosophical analysis of human existence needed in order to ask the question of being properly? When we read Heidegger's later works, mostly published after the Second World War, his question of being seems to become ever more mysterious. For example, he concluded his lecture series *Einführung in die Metaphysik* (*An Introduction to Metaphysics*), which he gave in the summer term of 1935 and published in 1953, by saying that the title "Being and Time" refers to something we can only know "in our questioning," and that "to be able to question means: to be able to wait, even a life long." Heidegger seems to be saying here that we should not attempt to answer the question of being, and that asking it in the right manner is some sort of waiting. Similarly, in his talk *Die Frage nach der Technik* (*The Question Concerning Technology*), given in 1953, Heidegger says that "questioning is the piety of thinking."

But do we at least know what Heidegger's question of being means? He seems even to deny this in many of his later works, since he says repeatedly that we live in "forget-fulness of being" (*Seinsvergessenheit*). In a television interview of 1969, the then eighty-year-old thinker stressed again that the question of being is not yet understood. He attributed this failure to understand the question not to us, but to the fact that we are "abandoned by being." Should we then give up all our attempts to grasp Heidegger's question?

If we want to understand a philosopher who is as enigmatic as Heidegger, we should not jump to conclusions and attribute ideas to him that we derive from our own philosophical background, such as pragmatism. Rather, we should give a properly historical and scholarly interpretation of Heidegger's works, based upon close reading of the German texts, which is informed by detailed knowledge of Heidegger's sources, such as Aristotle, Eckhart, Luther, Pascal, Kant, Hegel, Kierkegaard, Edmund Husserl and Oswald Spengler and of the philosophical and political situation of his time. Only after we have found out what Heidegger really meant, we can make up our mind about his views.

The formal structure of the question of being

Looking back on his career in 1963, Heidegger said that his first attempts to penetrate into philosophy had been guided by Franz Brentano's dissertation *Von der mannigfachen Bedeutung des Seienden nach Aristoteles* (*On the Several Senses of Being in Aristotle*, of 1862), which had been given to him on his eighteenth birthday in 1907. "If being is said in many ways, what then is the leading and fundamental meaning? What does to be mean?" From this retrospective reconstruction of the origin of Heidegger's question of being in his essay "Mein Weg in die Phänomenologie" ("My Way into Phenomenology"), we may infer that, like Aristotle's question of being, Heidegger's question has a bipolar structure.

One the one hand, "being" is said in many ways, as Aristotle stresses repeatedly in his *Metaphysics*. For example, the verb "to be" may be used to attribute accidental predicates to a subject ("Socrates is snub-nosed"), it may be used to stress that something is true ("Socrates *is* a great philosopher"), it may indicate that a subject is something potentially or actually, and, according to Aristotle, "to be" is used differently in each of his ten categories. Let us call this aspect of the question of being its pole of differentiation. However, Aristotle's question of being has a second pole, which is its pole of unity. In his *Metaphysics*, Aristotle attempts to reduce or to link all these different uses of "to be" to one fundamental sense, in which "being-a-so-and-so" refers to substances, that is, to particulars which can exist apart from other things, and, ultimately, to the divine substance.

Although the way in which Heidegger develops his question of being is different from Aristotle's, I propose that Heidegger's question of being has this bipolar structure as well. Both in his book *Being and Time*, and in the later works written from 1934 onwards, we find a pole of differentiation and a pole of unity in Heidegger's question of being. Interestingly, however, the contents of these poles in the early period differ from their contents in the later period, which lasts until Heidegger's death. As a consequence, we have to answer five questions regarding Heidegger's question of being if we want to understand it adequately: (1) What is the pole of differentiation in *Being and Time* and the works of that period? (2) What is the pole of unity in *Being and Time*? (3) How does Heidegger spell out the pole of differentiation in the later works? (4) What is the pole of unity in the later works? And finally, (5) How is the question of being in *Being and Time* related to the question of being in the later period?

The bipolar structure of *Being and Time*

To discover what is the pole of differentiation in *Being and Time*, it is best to study section 3 of that book. There Heidegger argues that within the totality of entities or beings we can distinguish different domains or regions, of which he mentions as examples history, nature, space, life, human existence, and language. These domains can become the subject matter of special sciences, and they are conceptualized in pre-scientific experience. Although in 1927 Heidegger is aware of recent conceptual revolutions in disciplines such as mathematics, physics and biology, he nevertheless holds that philosophy has the task of developing fundamental concepts for each of these regions of being in an *a priori* manner (*vorgängig*). By such a "productive logic," the philosopher would articulate for an entity in each of these domains the "fundamental constitution of its being," thereby laying the foundations of the special sciences. In other words, each type of entity has a different ontological constitution or mode of being, and the pole of differentiation of the question of being in *Being and Time* consists in articulating conceptually each of these modes of being.

Heidegger inherited this research programme of constructing "regional ontologies" from his teacher Edmund Husserl, and ultimately from Aristotle. Both Husserl and

Aristotle had assumed that reality is carved up into regions of essentially different kinds. Husserl believed, like Plato, that the philosopher can discern the essential structures of these regions of being without relying on extensive empirical investigations. The logical positivists rejected this research programme of an *a priori* philosophical foundation of the special sciences. They were aware of the fact that scientific revolutions could easily overturn allegedly *a priori* insights, and could unify domains that had appeared to be essentially different to philosophers who merely engaged in thought experiments. By endorsing Husserl's programme of constructing *a priori* regional ontologies, despite his awareness of scientific revolutions, Heidegger supported the foundational role of philosophy with respect to the special sciences, which was denied by logical positivists such as Carnap, Schlick and Reichenbach.

Heidegger's conservatism with regard to the foundational status of philosophy did not exclude him from being a philosophical revolutionary at another level. This becomes clear when we zoom in on Heidegger's analysis of human existence (Dasein) in *Being and Time*. I shall first interpret this ontology of human existence within the pole of differentiation of the question of being, that is, as a regional ontology of humanity. Let us take seriously for a moment Heidegger's thesis that all regions of being are essentially different. Let us also adopt for the sake of argument his view that each region has a separate set of fundamental concepts, by means of which the mode of being of entities within that region can be articulated. We might label these two theses, taken together, Heidegger's postulate of the regionality of being. As is clear from section 3 of *Being and Time*, Heidegger claims that life, nature and *Dasein* are each separate regions of being. His postulate of the regionality of being then implies that we cannot derive the fundamental concepts in terms of which our own human mode of being should be analyzed from other ontological regions, such as organic life or inanimate nature.

Heidegger contends, however, that this was exactly what philosophers of the past were doing when they analyzed human existence. For example, Aristotle conceptualized human existence in terms of "matter" and "form," concepts derived from the ontological region of artefacts. And Descartes conceived of human existence in terms of a physical mechanism, to which an immaterial mental substance was attached. Heidegger's postulate of the regionality of being implies that all these philosophical endeavours of the past are inadequate. He would also condemn our contemporary attempts to analyze human capacities in terms of metaphors derived from computer science, for example. This starting point explains the revolutionary nature of Heidegger's analysis of *Dasein* in *Being and Time*, which is reflected in the destructive–constructive architecture of the book. Heidegger intends to "destroy" the traditional categories of philosophers by showing that they are inadequate as a conceptualization of human existence, and to construct new categories for human life. These new categories he calls "existentialia" (singular: "existentiale"), to stress that they articulate the ontological structure of human *existence*. In short, Heidegger aims at revolutionizing the very conceptual apparatus in terms of which philosophers think about human life.

How can one create such new ontological categories? Heidegger answers that in everyday life (*Alltäglichkeit*) we already understand implicitly the human mode of existence. Consequently, we might articulate our own mode of being by interpreting or explicating conceptually our implicit self-understanding. Heidegger calls the method of constructing an ontology of human existence "hermeneutical," and his regional ontology is a "hermeneutics of *Dasein*." In this respect, Heidegger's philosophical programme is somewhat similar to that of Gilbert Ryle in *The Concept of Mind* (published in 1949), and it is significant that Ryle reviewed *Being and Time* in 1929. Both Heidegger and Ryle argue that Cartesian dualism is a deeply mistaken view of human existence, and they want to develop a more adequate conception. But there also is a crucial difference between them. Ryle focuses on misinterpretations of our ordinary psychological concepts and intends to "rectify the logical geography of the knowledge which we already possess" about ourselves. Heidegger has the ambition to create new concepts in order to construct an ontology of human existence, which, ultimately, would help us to become more authentic human beings.

One might illustrate this new ontology of human existence and its relevance to traditional philosophical problems by the fundamental existentiale of "being-in-the-world," which is the main theme of the first Division of *Being and Time*. Here, Heidegger argues that human beings are essentially in-the-world in the sense that they cannot but articulate their own personal identity in terms of worldly items, such as the town they are living in, the artefacts they are using, their social relations, the profession they have, the path in life they are envisaging, or the land they are inhabiting. The term "world" in this context does not stand for the sum of material particles, radiation, etc., which the physicist refers to as the "universe." Rather, it designates the structured whole of human institutions, practices, forms of life, and landscapes without which human existence cannot be imagined.

At the end of Division One, Heidegger argues that his new ontology of human existence shows the absurdity of the traditional problem of the external world, which had been raised by philosophers such as Descartes, Berkeley and Hume (*Being and Time*, §43a). Indeed, if we humans cannot but express our personal identity in terms of worldly items, such as our profession or our place of birth, how can one imagine that we might exist even though there were no world, as Descartes professed to do? Heidegger concludes that one should not try to answer the problem of the external world, but rather show that "the very entity which serves as its theme," to wit, the human being, "repudiates" this question.

However, Heidegger's contention that the traditional problem of the external world is an absurdity because it cannot arise on the basis of our everyday self-understanding, is faced with a pertinent objection. Although the problem cannot arise on the basis of our everyday self-understanding, this does not show that it is an absurdity. In fact, the problem is motivated by a scientific analysis of sense-perception, according to which our perceptual awareness of the world is the result of long and complicated causal chains. How can the perceiving subject know, one may wonder, that his perceptions are caused properly, that is, ultimately, by the objects of his perceptions? Traditional sceptics such as David Hume argued that the perceiving subject cannot offer convincing arguments to this effect.

Heidegger answers the objection implicitly in *Being and Time*, and his answer will bring us to the pole of unity of the question of being in that book. Using a terminology introduced by Wilfrid Sellars, one might say that according to Heidegger the problem of the external world does not make sense if raised within the "manifest image," that is, the world as we understand it in everyday life. But the problem makes sense, so the objector argues, if raised within the "scientific image," that is, the world as understood by scientists. Heidegger's global strategy for rebutting the objection is to argue that from an ontological point of view, the scientific image is merely secondary, whereas the manifest image is fundamental. Indeed, Heidegger claims that if one interprets the world in scientific terms, one "skips" (*überspringt*) many of its essential features, which are captured in our everyday understanding of the world.

In *Being and Time*, Heidegger borrows the conceptual tools for implementing this global strategy from Kant's transcendental philosophy. According to Kant, the transcendental subject constitutes the world as science sees it by processing the input of the senses in terms of Euclidean space, continuous time, and twelve categories, which are *a priori*. Similarly, Heidegger holds that the facts of science emerge only on the basis of an *a priori* conceptual framework (*Entwurf*), which we humans project on to the world. Whenever we project a scientific framework, such as that of mathematical physics, our understanding of the being of entities is transformed (*Being and Time*, §69b). In contradistinction to Kant, however, Heidegger holds that we humans always already live in a pre-scientific world, in which entities show up for us as tools, for example, and that the projected scientific images of the world impoverish our self-understanding. He stresses repeatedly that in our everyday pre-scientific understanding, the world shows itself *as it is in itself*.

In the published part of *Being and Time* this Kantian theme in the question of being functions as its pole of unity. Because all understanding of the being of entities is *Dasein's* understanding, which is projective in some sense, all regional ontologies should be understood against the background of the ontology of *Dasein*. This is why Heidegger argues in section 4 of *Being and Time* that regional ontologies have their foundation and motivation in *Dasein's* own ontical structure, so that the existential analytic of *Dasein* is a *fundamental* ontology. It follows that the ontology of *Dasein* in *Being and Time* can be read at two levels. On the one hand, it is a regional ontology of human existence, which belongs to the pole of diversity. On the other hand, it is a transcendental philosophy *à la* Kant, which functions as the foundation of all regional ontologies, and is the pole of unity. To what extent these two readings are compatible, is a question that cannot be discussed here.

The bipolar structure of Heidegger's later works

On 22 April 1933, Heidegger became rector of Freiburg University, and, having joined the Nazi Party with great pomp on the first of May, he was instrumental in the *Gleichschaltung* (forcing into the party line) of that university by the Nazi regime, which had seized power in Germany on 30 January 1933. Although Heidegger probably had the ambition to become a leading Nazi ideologist, he was compelled to abdicate as a rector a year later, and his career in the party came to nothing. From 1934 onwards, Heidegger started to develop what is now known as his later thought.

The literary form of Heidegger's later publications differs from that of *Being and Time*, which is a systematic philosophical treatise. After 1934, Heidegger mainly wrote lecture notes, essays, some dialogues, and a number of larger manuscripts, such as *Beiträge zur Philosophie* (*Contributions to Philosophy*, in 1936–8), the style of which resembles that of a religious revelation. These later works, mostly published after 1945, are concerned with a great number of different topics, such as Hölderlin's poetry, art, technology, Nietzsche, language, humanism, truth, Hegel, Anaximander, etc. But in all these works, the question of being plays a central role, explicitly or implicitly. As in *Being and Time*, the question of being has a bipolar structure, but its content is strikingly different from that in 1927.

The pole of differentiation in the later works is a peculiar philosophy of history, inspired by Hegel and Spengler, which in its turn influenced structuralists such as Foucault. As Hegel once said, philosophy is "its epoch comprehended by thought." Since one's epoch is the outcome of a historical development, both Hegel and Heidegger hold that the philosopher has to comprehend the preceding epochs as well. Heidegger professes that history can be divided into essentially different periods. Allegedly, each historical period is based upon what he calls a fundamental stance (*Grundstellung*) of humans to themselves and to the totality of beings, which is articulated by the metaphysics of that period. This fundamental stance determines the way everything shows up for each human being. By interpreting the metaphysics of historical epochs, the present-day philosopher can obtain a deeper understanding of history than ordinary historians are able to acquire. Let us say that he is able to grasp *deep* history. And since the consecutive fundamental stances in deep history determine how things show up for man in each epoch, that is, how things *are* in that epoch, whereas there are a number of different epochs starting with the Presocratics, Heidegger's philosophy of history is a pole of differentiation in the question of being.

Heidegger claims that we are now living in the historical epoch of technology, in which everything in the world shows up for us as raw materials for production, consumption and exploitation. He also claims that our technological epoch is the outcome of an inner logic of Western deep history, which started when Plato and Aristotle conceptualized everything in the terminology of "form" and "matter," that is, in a terminology derived from the domain of artefacts. Christianity fits into this logic, since it conceived of the universe as an artefact created by God. The logic of Western metaphysics allegedly culminates in the philosophy of Friedrich Nietzsche, who held that everything is a will to power. After the Second World War, Heidegger dismissed ethical criticisms of Nazism by analyzing them in a Nietzschean vein, as nothing but expressions of the will to power of democratic societies.

As is the case in the Catholic doctrine of deep history, according to which the Second Coming of Christ is slowly prepared in historical time, Heidegger unifies his philosophy of history by the formal scheme of an initial bliss or paradise, a fall, and the hope for a redemption. In a text on Anaximander, written in 1946, Heidegger speaks of an "eschatology of Being," and a "fate of Being" (*Geschick des Seins*). Playing with the kinship between the German words "Geschick" (fate), "schicken" (to send) and "Geschichte" (history), Heidegger suggests that a hidden event called Being sends humanity the metaphysical stances of deep history, which, taken together, form the history of metaphysics. This history as a whole from Plato to Nietzsche is interpreted as a fall (*Abfall*) or aberration (*Irre*), which mankind has to overcome. Heidegger professes that humanity can be rescued from this history of metaphysics by a saving event, a new arrival of Being, which his thought is meant to prepare. It is not difficult to diagnose the jargon of Heidegger's later philosophy of Being as structured by the logical grammar of Christian theology, deprived of its Christian contents. In the pole of unity in Heidegger's later works, the term "Being" figures as an analogue of the Christian word "God," although Heidegger stresses that Being is an event and not an entity.

The coherence of Heidegger's question of being

In a preface to the seventh edition of *Being and Time* (1953), Heidegger says he has omitted the designation "First Half," since after a quarter of a century the second half could no longer be added unless the first were to be presented anew. Yet he avers that "the road it has taken remains even today a necessary one, if our *Dasein* is to be stirred by the question of being." As was clear from section 83 of *Being and Time*, this road (*Weg*) is Heidegger's analysis of the ontological constitution of our human mode of being. The aim of that road is "to work out the question of being as such." Heidegger has always claimed that the entire "way of his thought" (*Denkweg*) was motivated by one and the same question of being. But how can that be the case, if the contents both of the pole of unity and of the pole of differentiation in the later works differ so drastically from those in *Being and Time*? How should one interpret the coherence of Heidegger's question of being?

There are two clues that can help us to solve this problem. One is that according to Heidegger, his later works are connected to *Being and Time* by what he calls *Die Kehre* (the turn). In German the term "Kehre" can be used to refer to a sharp bend in a road, but it is also part of words such as "Bekehrung" (conversion). Furthermore, it is interesting to note that in works published after the war, Heidegger drastically reinterprets the *existentialia* of *Being and Time*. For example, whereas the term "Entwurf" (project, projection) in that book refers to the active aspect of human life, the fact that we project ourselves into the future, Heidegger says in the "Letter on 'Humanism'," of 1946, that it is Being itself which pro-jects each human being into his ex-sistence. Such a reinterpretation of the *existentialia* had been predicted already in a talk called "Phänomenologie und Theologie" ("Phenomenology and Theology") of 1927, in which Heidegger argues that the ontological account of human existence in *Sein und Zeit* is a formal framework to be filled in by a theology which describes human existence as reborn in faith.

A second clue is contained in Heidegger's conception of authentic human existence in *Being and Time*. According to Heidegger, our relation to our own death is an important dimension of authenticity. He holds that the authentic attitude consists in an impassioned and anxious "freedom towards death." But why should anxiety be a hallmark of authenticity? Heidegger's arguments for his conception of an authentic relation to death are full of fallacies and conceptual confusions. But for someone acquainted with traditional Christianity, the rhetoric of his account of authenticity in *Being and Time* will be familiar. By stressing the fact that we should be anxious about our death, and that we are inauthentic if we stoically minimize its importance in life, the traditional Christian urges us to open our heart to God's grace. It is illuminating to read Heidegger's analysis of human authenticity in this light, and to assume that quite often, the term "Being" refers to God, as it did for Eckhart and other schoolmen.

Indeed, the question of being in 1927 and the question of being in the later works are related to each other by what may be called a "Pascalian strategy." As Blaise Pascal knew, rational arguments will rarely succeed in converting unbelievers to Christianity. This is why, in his *Pensées*, he applied a clever apologetic strategy, which consists of two stages. First, he gave a despondent analysis of human existence without God, showing that such an existence tends to flee from its unhappiness and is a mystery to itself. Second, he urged that revealed Christianity both solves the paradoxical mysteries of human life and contains the promise of eternal happiness. I suggest that one can read Heidegger's *Being and Time* as the first stage of such a Pascalian strategy, so that there is a third dimension to this book, apart from regional ontology and transcendental philosophy. If Heidegger says that the ontology of human existence prepares the reader to ask the question of being properly, he means that if the reader digests his ontology of *Dasein* and attempts to be authentic by adopting an anxious freedom towards death, he will open his heart to divine grace.

Since Heidegger adhered to a Lutheran conception of theology, according to which only someone who has received God's grace is warranted to say something theological, *Being and Time* could not contain the second stage of a Pascalian strategy. Indeed, Heidegger had to wait for divine grace before he could embark on it, and as he said in 1935, raising the question of being properly might mean that one has "to wait, even a life long." Initially, Heidegger was waiting for divine grace proffered by the Christian god. But in his rectoral address of 1933 he endorsed Nietzsche's dictum that God is dead, and at that time Heidegger also believed that Hitler revealed how things really *are*. Then, after the end of the rectorate in 1934, Heidegger started to develop his later philosophy of being, which may be seen as yet another version of the second stage of the Pascalian strategy. Rejecting the Christian god as an entity, Heidegger now holds that Being is a saving event, which sends us the epochs of our history, and which might liberate us from the reign of technology. No wonder, then, that Heidegger has attracted many followers who, once raised as Christians, lost their faith but are comforted by a philosophy that formally resembles the Christian view of the world.

Evaluation

What should we think of Heidegger's question of being, and, indeed, of his philosophical project? As far as the regional ontology of human existence is concerned, Heidegger is right in rejecting Cartesian dualism and scientistic reductions or eliminations of our everyday conception of ourselves. One might argue, however, that Heideggerian hermeneutics is not a reliable method for obtaining valid results. Instead of inventing new *existentialia*, one should focus on the existing conceptual networks in terms of which we express our knowledge about ourselves, and attempt to elucidate these networks if misunderstanding them creates philosophical problems. Furthermore, Heidegger's view that the ontological region of human existence is essentially different from the region of life in general might block fruitful attempts to understand aspects of human life on the background of biological evolution.

Like Kant, Heidegger devalues scientific knowledge in general by arguing that it is concerned merely with a phenomenal world constituted by a transcendental subject. This argument enabled both Kant and Heidegger to hold that from an ontological point of view religion is deeper than science, because allegedly religion is concerned with reality as it is in itself, as distinct from the constituted reality studied by science. But there are no good arguments for such an ontological devaluation of science. If a philosopher aims at determining the place of each human being in the world, he does well to do so against the background of modern cosmology and the theory of evolution.

Both *Being and Time* and Heidegger's later works are inspired by the Lutheran view that religion transcends human reason. This is why Heidegger rejects the canons of logic and scientific procedure in favour of what he calls "thinking," that is, an attempt to relate to Being. In the later works, Being is a post-monotheist analogue of the Christian god, who sends us humans our historical epochs. Unfortunately, however, Heidegger's later method of thinking by "listening to the voice of Being" is no more reliable than any old claim of a religious sect to have received a revelation. Heidegger's grandiose narrative of Western deep history as a continuous fall, and his prospect of a "saving event" that will deliver us, are nothing but a more abstract and abstruse version of the religious template of paradise, fall and redemption. To a philosopher who aims at acquiring reliable knowledge and conceptual insights, there is nothing to recommend these later views.

Further reading

For further reading, see Martin Heidegger, *Being and Time*, trans. John Macquarrie and Edward Robinson (Oxford: Blackwell, 1962); and *Basic Writings*, revised, expanded edn, edited by David Farrell Krell (London: Routledge, 1993). See also Charles Guignon (ed.), *The Cambridge Companion to Heidegger* (Cambridge: Cambridge University Press, 1993); Stephen Mulhall, *Heidegger and* Being and Time (London: Routledge, 1996); and Herman Philipse, *Heidegger's Philosophy of Being: A Critical Interpretation* (Princeton, NJ: Princeton University Press, 1998).

20
ANTI-METAPHYSICS II
Verificationism and kindred views

Cheryl Misak

Introduction

"Verificationism" is usually taken to refer to the core doctrine of logical empiricism or logical positivism. The position arose in the mid-1920s when a group of philosophers, physicists, mathematicians, social scientists and economists gathered around Moritz Schlick in Vienna and another gathered around Hans Reichenbach in Berlin. The impending war scattered the logical empiricists – Reichenbach, Rudolph Carnap, Carl Hempel and others went to America, where they quite literally changed the character of philosophy there. Schlick was shot dead in 1936 by a deranged student. Otto Neurath eventually ended up in England, joining A. J. Ayer, who had visited the Vienna Circle as young man and brought the view to England.

The aim of logical empiricism was to unify all inquiry under the umbrella of science. The verifiability principle did most of the heavy lifting: it required all of our beliefs and theories, if they are to be legitimate, to be verifiable by experience. Since metaphysics does not meet this test, aspersion is cast upon it.

But it would be a mistake to think that the anti-metaphysical thesis of verificationism came into being with logical empiricism. It is firmly rooted in thinkers such as David Hume (1711–76) and August Comte (1798–1857). All knowledge of the world, Hume argued, comes from experience. So an idea, if it is to be legitimate, must either be such that the opposite is inconceivable (allowing for the truths of geometry and arithmetic) or it must correspond to impressions, which are something like sensory experiences. Here is Hume making it clear that metaphysics will be in for a rough ride:

> When we run over libraries, persuaded of these principles, what havoc must we make? If we take in our hand any volume; of divinity or school metaphysics, for instance; let us ask: *Does it contain any abstract reasoning concerning quantity or number?* No. *Does it contain any experimental reasoning concerning matter of fact and existence?* No. Commit it then to the flames: for it can contain nothing but sophistry and illusion. (Hume 1975: 165)

Comte, who first made famous the term "positivism," does not begin with a Humean empiricist account of ideas or the contents of the mind. But he is just as clear about the fate of metaphysics. All domains of inquiry, Comte argued, start off in a theological, fictitious, or mythological stage, where we try to explain nature by an appeal to the rule of gods. This explanation is rejected as people discover that nature is ruled by laws. The gods are then depersonalized and become abstract metaphysical entities – essences or causes. But Comte argued that these too are beyond our reach. Metaphysics simply substitutes mysterious entities for mysterious gods. It is a primitive precursor of science and will disappear as science restricts itself to dealing with appearances.

So although the most well-known (and notorious) expression of verificationism came in the form of logical empiricism, verificationism can be found in many quarters. It can be argued that its founders include Hume, Comte, Berkeley, John Stuart Mill, Ernst Mach, Pierre Duhem, Albert Einstein, Bertrand Russell and, as we shall see below, the American pragmatists and the early Wittgenstein.

Charles Sanders Peirce and William James

American pragmatism originated in Cambridge, Massachusetts, in the early 1870s in The Metaphysical Club – an informal reading group in which Oliver Wendell Holmes, William James, Chauncey Wright, Charles Sanders Peirce and others thrashed out their views. But the name of the club, as Peirce made clear, is quirky. It was chosen "half-ironically, half-defiantly" "for agnosticism was then riding its high horse, and was frowning superbly upon all metaphysics" (CP 5.12 [Peirce 1931–5, 1958: Vol. 5, paragraph 12]).

At the heart of pragmatism is a kind of verificationist principle: "we must look to the upshot of our concepts in order to rightly apprehend them" (CP 5.4). To get a complete grasp of a concept, we must connect it to that with which we have "dealings" (CP 5.416); "we must not begin by talking of pure ideas, – vagabond thoughts that tramp the public roads without any human habitation, – but must begin with men and their conversation" (8.112).

Peirce thought that many metaphysical thoughts were such vagabond thoughts. William James agrees: his version of the pragmatic maxim has it making short work of many long-standing and seemingly intractable philosophical problems. "If no practical difference whatsoever can be traced, then the alternatives mean practically the same thing, and all dispute is idle" (James 1949 [1907]: 45).

Although Peirce's maxim is often taken to be a semantic principle about the very meaning of our concepts and although he sometimes does put it that way, it is not designed to capture a full account of meaning. Peirce's considered view is that the maxim captures an important aspect of what it is to understand something.

He takes his contribution to debates about meaning to be the identification of a third thing that someone needs to understand when they understand a concept. Not only does one have to know its connotation and denotation, but one has to know what to expect if beliefs containing the concept are true or false. If a belief has no consequences – if there is nothing we would expect would be different if it were true or false – then it lacks a dimension we would have had to get right were we to fully understand it. And without that dimension, it is empty or useless for inquiry and deliberation.

Peirce worried over what kinds of consequences counted – over what kinds of things we must expect from our beliefs – if they are to be legitimate. He amended the pragmatic maxim over the whole of his writing life. His first significant amendment acknowledged that it must be set out with a subjunctive, not an indicative conditional: the pragmatic meaning of "this diamond is hard" is not "if you scratch it, it will resist," but rather "if you were to scratch it, it would resist." Otherwise, diamonds stuck forever on the ocean floor would not be hard (CP 8.208). The practical effects that pragmatism is concerned with are those which *would* occur under certain circumstances, not those which *will* actually occur.

As his thoughts settled, he also made amendments regarding the nature of the required practical consequences. He occasionally suggests that they must be consequences for the senses – directly observable effects. But when he reflected on the matter, he was clear that he was not interested in narrowing the scope of the legitimate so severely. He thought, for instance, that some metaphysical inquiries were perfectly acceptable. In metaphysics, "one finds those questions that at first seem to offer no handle for reason's clutch, but which readily yield to logical analysis" (CP 6.463). Metaphysics, "in its present condition" is a "puny, rickety, and scrofulous science," but it need not remain so. It is up to the pragmatic maxim to sweep "all metaphysical rubbish out of one's house. Each abstraction is either pronounced gibberish or is provided with a plain, practical definition" (CP 8.191).

Peirce tries to divert our focus from sensory experience and direct it to a broader notion of experience. Experience, he argues, is that which is compelling, surprising, unchosen, involuntary or forceful. This extremely generous conception of experience is clearly going to allow for a criterion of legitimacy that encompasses more than beliefs directly verifiable by the senses. For one thing, Peirce thought that mathematical and logical beliefs were connected to experience in the requisite way. They have consequences in diagrammatic contexts – when we manipulate diagrams, we can find ourselves surprised. For another, he, like James and John Dewey, was willing to consider that ethics might be a legitimate domain of deliberation and inquiry.

Another issue that Peirce grappled with is whether the consequences in question were consequences for belief or consequences for the world. James took the former line, saying that the pragmatic maxim ought to "be expressed more broadly than Mr. Peirce expresses it" (1978 [1898]: 124).

James infamously argued in "The Will to Believe" that if a religious hypothesis has consequences for a believer's life, it is acceptable. Religious hypotheses, like all hypotheses, need to be verified. But the verification in question involves finding out only what works best for the "active faiths" or the lives of the believers:

> If religious hypotheses about the universe be in order at all, then the active faiths of individuals in them, freely expressing themselves in life, are the experimental tests by which they are verified, and the only means by which their truth or falsehood can be wrought out. The truest scientific hypothesis is that

which, as we say, "works best"; and it can be no otherwise with religious hypotheses. (1979 [1897]: 8)

The objection to this line of thought is that such experimental tests are relevant to the question of whether or not religion is good for human beings, but not relevant to the question of whether God exists. This is the very objection that Peirce ended up lobbing at James. Peirce, that is, sees that hypotheses about God's existence are hypotheses about the world. Hence they need empirical verification of the usual sort. (Mathematical hypotheses, in contrast, are about what Peirce called the "ideal world" and they require verification in diagrammatic contexts.)

A. J. Ayer thought that C. S. Peirce's pragmatic maxim was a direct predecessor of the verifiability criterion. He said that Peirce's position "allows no truck with metaphysics. Its standpoint is closely akin to that which was later to be adopted by the logical positivists. Peirce's pragmatic maxim is indeed identical ... with the physicalist interpretation of the verification principle" (Ayer 1968: 45). Ayer was not quite right about that, as Peirce offered a much broader account of experience than the verificationists ever envisioned, and he was very clear that he was talking about an aspect of meaningfulness, not the whole of it. But Ayer is right that Peirce and James argued that philosophical concepts divorced from experience and practice were spurious. Hence, much of metaphysics is spurious.

Ludwig Wittgenstein

Wittgenstein has often been taken to have been in league with the logical empiricists, much to his irritation and to the irritation of scholars of his work. One thing is certainly true – the logical empiricists were excited about Wittgenstein's early thought. They broke their habit of discussing a different work at each of their meetings and spent the whole of 1926–7 on Wittgenstein's *Tractatus*. And Schlick and Waismann, two mainstays of logical empiricism, met often with Wittgenstein to discuss philosophy. But the fit between Wittgenstein and the logical empiricists was far from perfect. Otto Neurath used to shout "Metaphysics!" during the logical empiricists' meetings whenever he thought he detected a whiff of metaphysical speculation. His interjections were so frequent when discussing the *Tractatus* that he at first interrupted continuously, then had the suggestion made that instead of his usual shout, he should instead hum "Mmmmm": to which he asserted that it would be more efficient if he simply said "Not M" on those occasions in which they were not misled by the *Tractatus* into talking metaphysics (Cartwright et al. 1996: 5–6).

Wittgenstein presented a "picture theory" of truth in the *Tractatus*, in which "The sense of a proposition is its agreement and disagreement with the possibilities of existence and non-existence of the atomic facts" (1955 [1918]: §4.2). Reality is the set of atomic facts or simple states of affairs and a true proposition is a picture of that reality. To understand what the truth of a proposition amounts to, you need to understand its structure. And meaningful propositions fall into one of two kinds of structure.

Tautologies are true or false, based on their form – for instance propositions of the form $p \vee \neg p$ are always true and propositions of the form $p \& \neg p$ are always false. These kinds of propositions are not dependent on contingent facts about the world. Indeed, they don't say anything about the world; they agree (or disagree) with every possible state of affairs.

Other meaningful propositions are structured as follows: "one name stands for one thing, and another for another thing, and they are connected together. And so the whole … presents the atomic fact" (1955 [1918]: §4.0311). Reality or the world is the set of these atomic facts or simple states of affairs and "[t]he proposition is a picture of reality" (§4.021). "The proposition *shows* how things stands, *if* it is true. And it *says* that they do so stand" (§4.022). A proposition "is like a scale applied to reality" (§2.1512), where "[t]hese connections are, as it were, the feelers with which the picture touches reality" (§2.1515).

The statements of metaphysics are not structured in either of these ways – they are not tautologies and they are not composed of simple statements which hook up to reality. In Wittgenstein's view, they are meaningless:

> The right method of philosophy would be this: To say nothing except what can be said, i.e. the propositions of natural science, i.e. something that has nothing to do with philosophy; and then always, when someone else wished to say something metaphysical, to demonstrate to him that he had given no meaning to certain signs in his propositions. (Wittgenstein 1955 [1918]: §6.53)

For Wittgenstein, "the limits of *language* … mean the limits of my world" (1955 [1918]: §5.62). There is no point in trying to go beyond what we can say via these two kinds of propositions.

The straightforward implication of this view is that most questions and answers put forward by philosophers are spurious – they arise from the fact that we fail to understand the logic of our language. Thus, "the deepest problems are really *no* problems" (Wittgenstein 1955 [1918]: §4.003). The proper role of philosophy is not to set out metaphysical theses that might be true. Rather, philosophers should concentrate on clarifying propositions.

Of the propositions of the *Tractatus* itself, which seem like statements that are not tautologies and not hooked up in the requisite way to the world, Wittgenstein famously says the following:

> My propositions are elucidatory in this way: he who understands me finally recognizes them as senseless, when he has climbed out through them, on them, over them. (He must, so to speak throw away the ladder, after he has climbed up on it.) (1955 [1918]: §6.54)

Frank Ramsey, Wittgenstein's brilliant contemporary and friend, thought that this was a bit of a cheat. Many think that he hit the nail on the head when he said "if the chief proposition of philosophy is that philosophy is nonsense … we must then take seriously that it is nonsense, and not pretend, as Wittgenstein does, that it is important nonsense!" (Ramsey 1931: 263).

Logical empiricism

Logical empiricism is largely responsible for what is now known as "analytic" philosophy, still the dominant methodology in philosophy. It was a brand of empiricism that took itself to have a new and important resource – the formal or symbolic logic that was developed in the latter part of the nineteenth century. It recognized only sensory perception and the analytic principles of formal logic as sources of knowledge.

The verifiability principle was at the heart of this project. In the hands of the logical empiricists, it was a semantic doctrine, holding that all meaningful sentences are reducible, via formal deductive logic, to statements that are empirically verifiable. Thus, no meaningful question is in principle unanswerable by science. Inquiry is unified, and progress is possible if all branches of inquiry are carried out in the same straightforward, logical, observational language. Domains of inquiry can achieve clarity and progress by having their theories symbolized in the language of logic and cashed out in observation. These deductive axiomatic theories, that is, are given empirical meaning by definitions which hook up the primitive terms in the formal language with observables in the world. Here we see why the logical empiricists were so interested in Wittgenstein.

Philosophy was to get with the program, put its theories in scientific language and render itself clear. Most of the age-old questions and their purported answers would be shown to be fruitless and meaningless, as they are not reducible to observation statements. They are not empirically verifiable and so they are "pseudo-propositions." Statements about essences, the Absolute, the thing-in-itself, etc., are quite literally meaningless. If science is the paradigm of rational knowledge, metaphysics is the scourge of it.

Ethics is imperiled as well. Statements about what is right or wrong either (i) are statements about what people actually approve of, not what they ought to approve of – that is, ethics is an empirical science; (ii) are meaningless; or (iii) express emotions or feelings. Hence the infamous "Boo–Hurrah" theory of ethics, on which to say that some act is odious is to say "Boo hiss!" to it and to say that some act is good is to say "Hurrah!"

The verifiability principle faced some formidable objections and was revised and liberalized in light of them. One set of objections centered around the strength of the verifiability required. If a meaningful statement is one that can conclusively be shown to be true or false, then there are few, if any, candidates for meaningfulness – it turned out that all kinds of discourses were in trouble on this stringent criterion. For instance, statements about the past, about the future, and about the mental states of others are not conclusively verifiable by observation and thus are swept away as meaningless on the strong verifiability criterion. Even the statement "blue, here, now," when presented with a patch of blue, is not conclusively verifiable. I might, for instance, be hallucinating or be suddenly colorblind. In order for the statement to carry certainty with it, it has to be reframed so it reads "it seems to me that blue, here, now." Hence, the statement "blue, here, now," if it is to be conclusively verified, is a statement about my mental state, not a statement about the world. And of course, the verifiability criterion was supposed to verify statements about the world, not statements about how the world seems to me.

Indeed, much of science seemed to fail the test. For instance, hypotheses about unobservable entities, such as subatomic particles, seemed not to be meaningful statements that were either true or false, but at best useful instruments. This instrumentalist view about the unobservable in science was held by Ernst Mach and is still held by, for instance, Bas van Fraassen. That is, the fact that these hypotheses were not verifiable by observation was not taken by all of the logical empiricists to be highly problematic.

What was most damaging were two problems for science – one about scientific laws and another about dispositional hypotheses. A scientific law is a universal generalization which ranges over an infinite domain and hence no finite number of positive instances will conclusively verify a law. Statements containing dispositional terms such as "soluble," "temperature," "mass," "heat" and "force" are analyzable only by counterfactual or subjunctive conditionals – "were x to be placed in water, then it would dissolve" or "were a thermometer to be in contact with x, it would register y degrees." First-order predicate logic is not capable of adequately characterizing counterfactual conditionals.

There were also important and related controversies about the very nature of the experience. With just a few exceptions – most prominently Neurath – the logical empiricists agreed that there is something given to us in experience that is raw or unencumbered by the observer's language, theories, or conceptual scheme. The problem was then to say just what that was. Some of the logical empiricists (the phenomenalists) held that observation reports are about private sensations and others (the physicalists) held that they were about public physical events. The problem for the phenomenalists was that it seems impossible to communicate such private qualitative content to others – the experiencer seems to be trapped in his or her own world. The problem for the physicalists was that they seemed to be grounding knowledge in something about which we could be mistaken. That is, they seemed to abandon the aim of epistemological security.

Many moves were made to liberalize the verifiability principle: not requiring conclusive verifiability; not taking verifiability to be the entirety of meaningfulness; extending deductive logic with inductive logic, etc. But tempering the criterion in these ways amounted to abandoning some of the very ideals of clarity, rigor and precision that drove the program. The reductionist program of analyzing meaningful sentences via logic and observational predicates seemed to collapse in light of the contortions required to save sentences that seemed to be worth saving.

Indeed, it was the reaction against this reductionist program which characterized post-positivist philosophy of science in America. Thomas Kuhn and Paul Feyerabend argued in the 1960s that science does not have the rational, deductive structure attributed to it by the logical empiricists. If we want to understand science, we must not try to rationally reconstruct it, but we must look to the historical or sociological development of theories or research programs.

The logical empiricists' program set the agenda for philosophy of science for decades and then was the received view against which philosophy of science rebelled. Despite that rebellion, the methods of the logical empiricists continue, for the most part, to be the methods of contemporary analytic philosophy. And of course, metaphysics has proven to be very tough indeed. It has survived all of the near-death experiences described here. Interestingly, it is an analytic metaphysics that is back in full force – a metaphysics that takes, if you like, the logical empiricists' methodology while rejecting its anti-metaphysical motivation.

References

Ayer, A. J. (1968) *The Origins of Pragmatism: Studies in the Philosophy of Charles Sanders Peirce and William James*, San Francisco: Cooper, Freeman & Co.

Cartwright, N., Cat, J., Fleck, L., and Uebel, T. (1996) *Otto Neurath: Philosophy between Science and Politics*, Cambridge: Cambridge University Press.

Hume, David (1975) *Enquiries Concerning Human Understanding and Concerning the Principles of Morals*, 3rd edn, edited by L. A. Selby-Bigge; rev. P. H. Nidditch, Oxford: Clarendon.

James, William (1949 [1907]) *Pragmatism: A New Name for Some Old Ways of Thinking*, New York: Longmans, Green & Co.

—— (1978 [1898]) *Essays in Philosophy* in *The Works of William James*, vol. 5, edited by F. H. Burkhardt, F. Bowers, and I. K. Skrupskelis, Cambridge MA: Harvard University Press.

—— (1979 [1897]) *The Will to Believe and Other Essays in Popular Philosophy*, in *The Works of William James*, vol. 6, edited by F. H. Burkhardt, F. Bowers, and I. K. Skrupskelis, Cambridge, MA: Harvard University Press.

Peirce, Charles Sanders (1931–35) *Collected Papers of Charles Sanders Peirce*, vols 1–6, edited by C. Hartshorne and P. Weiss, Cambridge MA: Belknap Press.

—— (1958) *Collected Papers of Charles Sanders Peirce*, vols 7 and 8, edited by A. Burks, Cambridge MA: Belknap Press.

Ramsey, Frank (1931) *The Foundations of Mathematics, and Other Logical Essays*, edited by R. B. Braithwaite, London: Routledge & Kegan Paul.

Wittgenstein, Ludwig (1955 [1918]) *Tractatus Logico-Philosophicus*, Oxford: Basil Blackwell.

Further reading

For further reading, see A. J. Ayer, *Language, Truth, and Logic* (London: Victor Gollancz, 1936); and his (ed.), *Logical Positivism* (New York: Free Press, 1959). See also August Comte, *The Positive Philosophy*, vol. 1, trans. A. Martineau (London: Trubner, 1875); Paul Feyerabend, *Realism, Rationalism, and Scientific Method: Philosophical Papers*, vol. 1 (Cambridge: Cambridge University Press, 1981); Thomas Kuhn, *The Structure of Scientific Revolutions* (Chicago, IL: University of Chicago Press, 1962); Cheryl Misak, *Verificationism: Its History and Prospects* (London: Routledge, 1995); and her "C.S. Peirce on Vital Matters," in Cheryl Misak (ed.), *The Cambridge Companion to Peirce* (Cambridge: Cambridge University Press, 2004); Thomas Uebel (ed.), *The Cambridge Companion to Logical Empiricism* (Cambridge: Cambridge University Press, forthcoming); and Bas van Fraassen, *The Scientific Image* (Oxford: Clarendon Press, 1980).

21
METAPHYSICS REVIVIFIED
Avrum Stroll

Introduction

It will be surprising to many philosophers, especially those raised in the heyday of logical positivism, to hear that there has been a resurgence of metaphysics in the past few decades. It will be surprising because of the generally bad press that metaphysics has had for much of the twentieth century, and even earlier. Hume, for example, ends *An Inquiry Concerning Human Understanding*, first published in 1748, with these words:

> If we take in our hand any volume – of divinity or school metaphysics, for instance – let us ask, *Does it contain any abstract reasoning concerning quantity or number?* No. *Does it contain any experimental reasoning concerning matter of fact and existence?* No. Commit it then to the flames, for it can contain nothing but sophistry and illusion. (Hume 1975 [1777]: 165)

As we move further into the twenty-first century, why has the prevailing attitude toward this form of philosophizing had such a reversal? I will suggest that there are two reasons: the identification of system building and metaphysics; and a different attitude that contemporary metaphysicians have toward science. But before discussing these changes, I would like to offer an explanation (it will obviously be too brief) of why metaphysics has been held in such low esteem for some time now. In my opinion, such an historical excursus is interesting in its own right. But more importantly, it will help pave the way for an account of the transformation that the profession has recently exhibited toward one of its main sub-disciplines.

There is no doubt that since the time of the ancient Greeks metaphysics has been one of the central fields of philosophy. Nearly all of the great philosophers from antiquity to the twentieth century have been metaphysicians. Even a partial list is impressive. It would include Parmenides, Plato, Aristotle, Plotinus, Augustine, Aquinas, Descartes, Hobbes, Spinoza, Leibniz and Hegel. But if we move into a more contemporary period, we can expand it to incorporate some unexpected names. An article in the current edition of the encyclopedia, *Wikipedia,* for example, gives a list of metaphysicians, past and present. It includes all of the historical figures mentioned above, as well as others, but also David Armstrong, Nicholas Rescher, Richard Rorty, Bertrand Russell, Wilfrid

Sellars, Donald Davidson, David Chalmers, Patricia and Paul Churchland and W. V. Quine.

Nearly all of these later thinkers are or were defenders of science, and many of them would be or would have been astounded to find themselves described as metaphysicians. But Russell would not have objected. He was a self-declared metaphysician, even though he argued throughout his career that the correct approach to the subject was "a scientific philosophy grounded in mathematical logic," a thesis that greatly influenced subsequent Anglo-American philosophy. His emphasis upon science and logic also explains why he praised Wittgenstein of the *Tractatus* and denigrated *Philosophical Investigations* and the later notebooks. Despite his commitment to a scientific philosophy, he proposed a variant of a classical pluralistic metaphysical system in his *Logical Atomism* of 1918.

> As I have attempted to prove in *The Principles of Mathematics*, when we analyze mathematics we bring it all back to logic. It all comes back to logic in the strictest and most formal sense. In the present lectures, I shall try to set forth in a sort of outline, rather briefly and unsatisfactorily, a kind of logical doctrine which seems to me to result from the philosophy of mathematics – not exactly logically, but as what emerges as one reflects: a certain kind of logical doctrine, and on the basis of this a certain kind of metaphysic. The logic which I shall advocate is atomistic, as opposed to the monistic logic of the people who more or less follow Hegel. When I say that my logic is atomistic, I mean that I share the common-sense belief that there are many separate things: I do not regard the apparent multiplicity of the world as consisting merely in phases and unreal divisions of a single indivisible Reality. (Russell 1986 [1918]: 178)

It is clear that Russell saw no incompatibility between metaphysics and science. In this respect, he reflected an ancient tradition. The early Greeks – Thales, Anaximander, Heraclitus and Democritus, *inter alios* – did not differentiate scientific and philosophical issues. Like later thinkers, they were interested in the nature of reality, but they thought that unassisted reason would allow them to discover its essential features. It was only after the Copernican Revolution, and especially after the celebrated experiments of Galileo, that a sharp division arose in which science and philosophy were seen as antagonistic to one another. The experimental method became a defining feature of this opposition. The attitude became even more pronounced in the Enlightenment, as the quotation from Hume illustrates. As Cheryl Misak indicates in her essay on verificationism in this volume (Chapter 20, "Anti-metaphysics II: Verificationism and Kindred Views"), the Vienna Circle (*der Wiener Kreis*) was one of the main sources of the disparagement of metaphysics. Yet, despite his avowal that he was a metaphysician, Russell was one of their major influences. They took his injunction that philosophy should be "scientific and grounded in mathematical logic" seriously. They were also influenced by Wittgenstein's *Tractatus Logico-Philosophicus*, which contained a form of scientism that they fully embraced. In §6.53, for instance, Wittgenstein had written the following:

The right method of philosophy would be this. To say nothing except what can be said, i.e, the propositions of natural science, i.e., something that has nothing to do with philosophy: and then always, when someone else wished to say something metaphysical, to demonstrate to him that he had given no meaning to certain signs in his propositions. This method would be unsatisfying to the other – he would not have the feeling that we were teaching him philosophy – but it would be the only strictly correct method. (Wittgenstein 1961: 151)

In that same work, Wittgenstein sharpened the opposition between sense and nonsense, relegating all philosophy and of course metaphysics to the category of nonsense. In §4.003 he wrote as follows:

Most propositions and questions, that have been written about philosophical matters, are not false, but senseless (*unsinnig*). We cannot, therefore, answer questions of this kind at all, but only state their senselessness. Most questions and propositions of the philosophers result from the fact that we do not under-stand the logic of our language … And so it is not to be wondered at that the deepest problems are really *no* problems. (*Ibid.*: 37)

Although he was never a positivist, Wittgenstein was also influenced by Russell. Wittgenstein said: "Russell's merit is to have shown that the apparent logical form of the proposition need not be its real form" (*Ibid.*: 37).

The influences of Russell and Wittgenstein

Russell's philosophy was a mix of British empiricism and logic. The members of the Circle, impressed by his distinguished contributions to logic, labeled themselves "logical empiricists" or more commonly "logical positivists." With these names they identified themselves with the empiricist movement of the Enlightenment and with the logical investigations of Frege, Russell and Wittgenstein. Although the positivists argued that logical and mathematical theorems were tautologies that have no factual content, and that any claim to be factually significant had to pass the verifiability test, their real commitment was to the form of scientism that Wittgenstein had expressed in *Tractatus Logico-Philosophicus*, §6.53. This was the principle that the only meaningful information human beings can attain about matters of fact derives from the natural sciences; and since metaphysics is not one of the natural sciences, it was therefore a form of nonsense. Not only was metaphysics so regarded but all nonscien-tific activity, such as history, literature, art, poetry and philosophy in general, was relegated to the same category.

Such a narrow, constricted view of any form of nonscientific intellectual activity was soon seen to be counterproductive. It was not only historians and persons in literature who objected to such a constraining view of meaningfulness, but even philosophers who were not metaphysicians began to have similar sentiments.

Ryle's dilemma

In his autobiography, published in 1970, Gilbert Ryle noted that even in the 1930s at the height of its influence, positivism was already seen as too constrictive. His objections were expressed colorfully, as follows:

> For by jointly equating Metaphysics with Nonsense and Sense with Science, it raised the awkward question "Where then do we anti-nonsense philosophers belong? Are the sentences of which *Erkenntnis* itself is composed Metaphysics? Then are they Physics or Astronomy or Zoology? What of the sentences and formulae of which *Principia Mathematica* consists?" We were facing what was in effect the double central challenge of Wittgenstein's *Tractatus Logico-Philosophicus* and the single central challenge of his future *Philosophical Investigations*. Neurath, Schlick, Carnap, Waismann, and for us, above all others, Ayer had undeliberately raised a problem the solution to which was neither in the *Logical Syntax of Language* nor yet in the *Tractatus*. We philosophers were in for a near-lifetime of enquiry into our own title to be enquirers. Had we any answerable questions, including this one?
>
> The conviction that the Viennese dichotomy "Either Science or Nonsense" had too few "ors" in it led some of us, including myself, to harbour and to work on a derivative suspicion. If, after all, logicians and even philosophers can say significant things, then perhaps some logicians and philosophers of the past, even the remote past had, despite their unenlightenment, sometimes said significant things. "Conceptual analysis" seems to denote a permissible, even meritorious exercise, so maybe some of our forefathers had had their Cantabrigian moments. If we are careful to winnow off their vacuously speculative tares from their analytical wheat, we may find that some of them sometimes did quite promising work in our own line of business. Naturally, we began, in a patronizing mood, by looking for and finding in the Stoics, say, or Locke, primitive adumbrations of our own most prized thoughts. But before long some of them seemed to move more like pioneers than like toddlers, and to talk to us across the ages more like colleagues than like pupils; and then we forgot our pails of whitewash. (Ryle 1970: 9–11)

Why scientism?

As I have indicated the members of the Vienna Circle went hook, line and sinker for the scientism that Wittgenstein had advanced in the *Tractatus*. It is this sort of scientism that impacted the analytic tradition that Ryle described. But why were so many twentieth century thinkers so influenced by science? At least part of the answer is the notable success that science has attained in the past four hundred years. It has produced a clearer and truer picture of the animate and inanimate features of the natural world than any scheme that preceded it. But its practical implications have been equally impressive. Science and technology working together have extended the lifespan of human beings, multiplied the food supply by orders of magnitude, and revolutionized communication. Many philosophers impressed by this record have argued, as Russell did, that philosophy should model itself on science. Hume, certainly one of the greatest philosophers of all time, was similarly influenced. He said that his ambition was to be the Newton of philosophy. It is thus not surprising that the subtitle of his major work, *A Treatise of Human Nature*, was: *BEING An ATTEMPT to introduce the experimental Method of Reasoning Into MORAL SUBJECTS*.

Despite the impact that science has made on philosophy a different attitude toward metaphysical speculation was beginning to set in even before World War II. As Ryle pointed out, anti-nonsense philosophers, like himself, were beginning to realize, even before World War II, that philosophy had a distinctive and autonomous role to play that was different from and yet compatible with the efforts of scientists to discern the basic features of the world. But in the 1930s they were still undecided about what that role should or even could be. However, in Ryle's statement we can find a hint. As he says, "Conceptual analysis seems to denote a permissible, even meritorious exercise."

Two factors leading to the resurgence of metaphysics

I mentioned at the beginning of this essay, that two factors have been responsible for the explicit resurgence of metaphysics in the past couple of decades. One of these is an emphasis on systematic philosophy, a matter that I will explore in detail in what follows. But in addition, many, though not all, analytic philosophers have developed a different attitude toward science. They no longer see science and metaphysics as incompatible, and I suggest that this is so because they see metaphysics as a species of traditional conceptual analysis. It is clear that even in the most hard-nosed scientific queries there are all sorts of conceptual infusions. Some of these ideas are confusions that create paradox and other sorts of infelicities, and conceptual analysis can help reduce or eliminate such confusions. Let me explain what I mean by conceptual analysis and why it is not inconsistent with science. I will pick a topic, as an illustration, that is in the forefront of philosophical concern today, namely the justification of abortion. As we shall see, it leads eventually to the mind–body problem and raises puzzles that go beyond anything science can deal with. The inference I draw from the example is that conceptual analysis and science are not in competition with each other.

We begin with the extreme right-to-life position. It advances the following considerations in support of its opposition to abortion. First, it argues that from the moment of conception, what has been produced is a human being, and that all human beings are persons. Second, it states that the unborn are innocent of any crime. Third, it contends that it is necessary to find a coherent set of principles – that is a defensible philosophy – that would justify killing the unborn. Fourth, it affirms that since similar cases must be treated in similar ways, such principles would justify the abortion of an innocent prenatal child only if they would also justify the killing of an innocent postnatal infant. Fifth, it holds that no considerations can be found that would justify the latter course of action, and, accordingly it concludes that no principles can be found that would justify the former. Therefore, abortion is never justified.

The pro-choice position attacks each of these premises and disagrees with the conclusion. But to bring out the special nature of a conceptual problem, I will simply concentrate on the first premise of the extreme right-to-life argument. It holds, as indicated, that from the moment of conception the unborn entity is both a human being and a person. Some advocates of the pro-choice position hold that not even the fetus is a person, although it has the potentiality of becoming one (Judith Jarvis Thomson, for example, has defended a variant of this position; see Thomson 1971: 47–56). This contention is supported by an analogy. Suppose – as many would agree – that cutting down an oak tree is, in a specific case, a bad thing to do. Yet those same persons might well agree that an acorn is not an oak tree, so destroying an acorn that eventually might become a tree is not identical with destroying a tree. According to this comparison, the zygote or even the fetus is like an acorn. It is not yet a person, with aspirations or a will; it is incapable of motion on its own, and lacks thought or intention. The prenatal entity is simply a mass of tissue, analogous to a benign growth. It can thus be excised and abortion can be thought of as analogous to a surgical procedure that eliminates an unwanted cyst or tumor.

This counterargument to the right-to-life thesis rests on an analogy, on the idea that the unborn is like an acorn. This analogy occurs in an early phase of the argument between these opposing approaches, but it already raises a conceptual question: "How good is the comparison?" It will be noted that the appropriateness of the analogy is not a factual or scientific question. It cannot be decided by a description of the scientific facts connected with conception. Both sides, I believe, would agree on those facts. They include such pieces of information as the following. The female germ cell, or ovum, is fertilized by a male germ cell, the spermatozoon. When this occurs, the cell possesses a full complement of twenty-three pairs of chromosomes, one in each pair from each partner. When fertilization first occurs, the resulting entity is called a "single-cell zygote." Within twenty-four hours, the single cell begins to divide. It acquires sixteen cells by the third day, and continues to grow as it moves through the fallopian tube into the uterus. During the first week, it implants itself in the uterine wall, and then is called a "conceptus." By the end of the second week, it is fully embedded in the uterine wall, and from this point until the eighth week, it is called an "embryo." Some human features appear by the fourth week – the embryo acquires a face and incipient limbs – and by the eighth week brain waves can be detected. From this point until birth it is called a "fetus."

These facts are not disputed by either side. The philosophical question is rather this: "When does the fertilized egg become a person?" But as one examines the facts they do not speak to that issue. Is a single-cell zygote a person? Is the fetus a person? Is neither a person? The scientific facts are silent with respect to these questions. The justification of abortion is thus not decidable by an appeal to the scientific facts. Whether an abortion is justified or not is instead a conceptual issue that may arise from religious or nonreligious perspectives. In many religions personhood occurs only when an entity develops a soul. But when is that? And what is the soul? Such questions are likewise not decidable by scientific means. The issue of whether the unborn entity is a person or not must thus be resolved in some other way, if it is at all possible to resolve it. This is the typical situation in dealing with metaphysical issues. Such issues typically turn on crucial premises that are conceptual, not scientific, in character. But whether such matters are decidable at all, even by conceptual analysis, remains an open question. It is the open nature of such questions that in a certain sense defines the sphere of metaphysics. It would seem that if scientific fact cannot resolve such issues, all that is left is argumentation and one of its major components, conceptual reasoning.

We can quickly deepen the issue. In the case of abortion, there is a perplexity about the relationship between bits of tissue and personhood. When do pieces of flesh become persons? If a person is not merely flesh, what is it? Is it some kind of nonmaterial entity, and if so, how can we identify it? Such questions give rise to one of the deepest and most intractable problems in the philosophical lexicon, the so-called "mind–body problem." Philosophers from the time of the Greeks to the present, theologians of all stripes, and ordinary persons have been puzzled about the relationship between personhood and the material constituents that constitute living objects. Where the Gospel according to St John states, "The word was made flesh" (John 1:14), we have a theological version of the problem. In my view, all philosophical problems are like the mind–body problem in being essentially conceptual in nature. As the example illustrates what science has to tell us about the unborn is not incompatible with what metaphysics has to say about that topic. So their compatibility is my first reason for arguing that metaphysics is back in vogue again.

My second reason is that there has recently been a slight modification in the characterization of metaphysics. The overall conception of metaphysics as an autonomous exploration of reality remains the same, but it has lately been given a specific twist that identifies it with the construction of systems. I can best illustrate such a change by taking a specific example, the recent work of Nicholas Rescher. Throughout his career, Rescher has been a strong supporter of science; but he has also distinguished science from metaphysics. In 2006, his metaphysics had, to a great extent, been devoted to differentiating these two varieties of exploration without seeing them as competitive. In a host of writings appearing since 1997, he has argued that since the end of the previous century, metaphysics has taken a form resembling the sorts of systems developed in the nineteenth century by Fichte, Hegel, Schelling, Schopenhauer and a host of "other princelings." But he also stresses that in the present century such systems will not be the products of individual "greats" but will involve many independent and often widely dispersed contributors working on themes of common interest. He calls such system building "disaggregated collaboration." He explains this concept as follows:

> Philosophy is no longer an intellectual enterprise of the "great thinker, great system" type familiar from the classical tradition. Systems are nowadays constructed like ant-hills rather than like pyramids that are the product of centralized direction. Unprogrammed and disaggregated collaboration among many workers distributively addressing large and complex projects has become the order of the day. And in every area of philosophy a literature of vast scope and complexity has emerged whose mastery is beyond the capacity of single individuals. Systematization is at work but rather at the collective level than at that of individual contributions. (Rescher 1997: 24)

Rescher's account of the current resurgence of metaphysics depends on two notions: the idea that systematic philosophy has returned to its traditional origins, and even more importantly that systematic approaches are necessary if theories that make sense in a particular area of philosophy are not to have untoward consequences in other areas of the subject. His view is that only systematization can eliminate such infelicities. His most recent thinking in this connection is contained in a letter he recently sent me:

> Working out the conceptual and substantive interconnectedness of philosophical issues will always lead us into metaphysics – and conversely. The possible world semanticist cannot ignore the metaphysics of possible worlds; the moral theorist cannot avoid free will, and the aesthetician cannot avoid abstract objects. Systematic philosophy and metaphysics are inseparably entangled.

Rescher's account of the resurgence of metaphysics

It will be noted in this passage that Rescher is stressing the conceptual aspects of philosophical inquiry as well as the interrelated nature of philosophical problems. The case of abortion is a good illustration of what he has in mind. Issues that are apparently central to a specific domain of philosophy, e.g., when the unborn develops into a person, quickly lead to bigger problems, such as the mind–body problem, a conundrum that has perplexed philosophers since time immemorial, but that has become *the* problem of epistemology since the time of Descartes. The conclusion he draws from the interconnectedness of philosophical thought is that metaphysics requires the abandonment of piecemeal endeavors, such as we find in the writings of G. E. Moore and J. L. Austin.

John Searle's account

Rescher is not the only distinguished scholar who sees the future as revitalizing an older tradition. John Searle ends a 2003 essay in which he predicts the return of systematic philosophy. As he says:

> What does philosophy look like in a post-epistemic, post-skeptical era? It seems to me that it is now possible to do systematic theoretical philosophy in a way that was generally regarded as out of the question half a century ago. (Searle 2003: 3)

In saying that "systematic theoretical philosophy is now possible in a way that was generally regarded as out of the question half a century ago," Searle, who was a student at Oxford in its post-World War II golden age, is clearly thinking of Austin, Urmson, Warnock, Pears and their colleagues, who favored piecemeal philosophy. In this respect his attitude toward the recent past is similar to Rescher's.

Yet they differ in an important respect. Searle's view about the non-incompatibility of science and philosophy is even stronger than Rescher's. Rescher sees the two as existing side by side, each concerned with its own methods and findings; but each as giving rise to differing results and understandings. Searle, in contrast, thinks that science will and should transform philosophy. He believes that many traditional philosophical issues are resolvable in principle by science. He says this about the mind–body problem, for instance:

> It seems to me that the neurosciences have now progressed to the point that we can address this as a straight neurobiological problem, and indeed several neurobiologists are doing precisely that. In its simplest form, the question is how exactly do neurobiological processes in the brain cause conscious states and processes, and how exactly are those conscious states and processes realized in the brain … It looks similar to such problems as: "How exactly do biochemical processes at the level of cells cause cancer?" and, "How exactly does the genetic structure of a zygote produce the phenotypical traits of a mature organism?"

I disagree with this form of scientism. I hold with Rescher that philosophy is essentially a conceptual activity, and accordingly that the sorts of factual problems science deals with are not at all comparable to the kinds of issues that philosophy has traditionally faced or will face. I am thus of the opinion that science and philosophy, and especially its important sub-branch, metaphysics, will continue to work in parallel, each having its own sphere of interest and that each will give rise to quite different sorts of findings. One can illustrate the difference by considering a classical metaphysical question: Is life after death possible? I have argued elsewhere (Stroll 2004: Ch. 2) that the answer is "yes." The issue is too complicated to be argued in full here, but the central point is easily surfaced: *Is a human being (i.e., a person) a complex entity consisting of a body and its various parts, and an element that is incorporeal and is generally called "the soul"?* The puzzles that this question generates form a virtually endless list. Here are a few of them: Is there such as thing as the soul and if so, what is it? If there is such a thing as the soul does it leave the body when a person dies, and is it immortal? Is reincarnation possible? Is the soul a distinctively human thing, that is, do animals lack a soul? Is there a difference between the death of the body and the death of the person whose body it is?

I should emphasize here the importance of Rescher's view that a problem that may turn up in one area of philosophy may have an impact in a different domain of the subject. As we have seen, the question of when personhood develops in the unborn is closely related to the question of what dies when a human being dies, an issue that has been debated since the time of Plato. The latter question is clearly not an empirical question, since if a person is more than his or her body, as Plato argued in the *Phaedo*, there can be no observable evidence about the nature of that which persists, if anything does, when a person dies. So whether postmortem survival is possible calls for argumentation and conceptual analysis, and in that respect it is like the question of when an unborn entity becomes a person. I must admit that I have some reservations about Rescher's thesis that conceptual analysis will inevitably lead to systematic philosophy. I suspect that piecemeal analysis will continue to be with us in the future. It has a long history that can be traced back at least to Plato's dialogues. In my view such an approach is central to philosophizing and I predict that it will always be an essential ingredient in philosophical practice. But I think Rescher is right in arguing that philosophical issues are synoptic and may have unexpected consequences in unanticipated areas of the subject.

Because of its conceptual components, metaphysical questions can never be wholly resolved by science. A list of such questions would certainly include the following: Does God exist? Is postmortem existence possible? Are human beings genetically determined, or is free will possible? Where did the universe come from, and what is it expanding into? What would an ideal society look like, and is such a society attainable? I believe that everyone is driven by the desire to find solutions to such queries. In my opinion they have a unique status: they are not scientific, historical, literary, moral, linguistic or aesthetic. The simplest name for them is "metaphysical." As I see the matter, they will exist side by side with science, and neither will supersede the other.

References

Hume, David (1975 [1777]) *Enquiries Concerning Human Understanding and Concerning the Principles of Morals*, edited by L. A. Selby-Bigge, 3rd edn, revised by P. H. Nidditch, Oxford: Clarendon Press.

Rescher, Nicholas (1997) *Profitable Speculations: Essays on Current Philosophical Themes*, New York: Rowman & Littlefield.

Russell, Bertrand (1986 [1918]) "The Philosophy of Logical Atomism," in *The Philosophy of Logical Atomism and Other Essays 1914–19*, edited by John G. Slater, London: Allen & Unwin.

Ryle, Gilbert (1970) "Autobiography," in O.P. Wood and George Pitcher (eds) *Ryle*, London: Macmillan, pp. 1–15.

Searle, John R. (2003) "Philosophy in a New Century," *Journal of Philosophical Research*, APA Centennial Supplement, pp. 3–22.

Stroll, Avrum (2004) *Did My Genes Make Me Do It? And Other Philosophical Dilemmas*, Oxford: OneWorld.

Thomson, Judith Jarvis (1971) "A Defence of Abortion," *Philosophy and Public Affairs* 1: 47–66.

Wittgenstein, Ludvig (1961) *Tractatus Logico-Philosophicus*, trans. D. F. Pears and B. F. McGuinness, London: Routledge & Kegan Paul.

Further reading

For further reading, see Paul M. Churchland, "Into the Brain: Where Philosophy Should Go from Here," *Topoi* (Fall 2006): 29–32; reprinted in *Neurophilosophy at Work* (Cambridge: Cambridge University Press); Richard M. Gale, *The Blackwell Guide to Metaphysics* (Oxford: Blackwell, 2002); J. Kim and Ernest Sosa (eds), *A Companion to Metaphysics* (Malden, MA: Blackwell, 2000); M. J. Loux, *Metaphysics: A Contemporary Introduction*, 3rd edn (London: Routledge, 2006); and Judith Jarvis Thomson, Symposium on Abortion, special issue of *Philosophy and Public Affairs* 1, no. 1 (1976).

Part II
ONTOLOGY
On what exists

INTRODUCTION TO PART II
Being and related matters

Ross P. Cameron

What is ontology? It's hard to say, without potentially begging the question against somebody. Quine said the ontological question could be asked in two words: "What exists?" But he won't find agreement on that with those, such as the Meinongians, who think that there are some things – such as unicorns, for example – that don't exist. Can we characterise ontology as the study of what there is, then? That would be acceptable to both Quine, since he thinks that that question is simply equivalent to asking what exists, and the Meinongian, who thinks that what exists is a proper sub-portion of what there is. But it's still not going to be acceptable to everyone. Some theorists are simply going to think that the English existential quantifier(s) are not up to the job of asking the ontological question: that while it might be true that there are tables and chairs, dogs and cats, persons and planets, the interesting ontological question is not about what there is but about what there *really* is, or what there is *fundamentally*. Tables and chairs, while they exist, cannot be said really to have *being*, thinks such a theorist. So is the ontological question about what has being? Again, Quine would be happy to say yes, since again, he will simply see "What has being?" as another way of asking what exists. But Meinong would no longer be happy, since he thought that there are things that don't have being (confusingly, these aren't simply the things that don't exist: some of the things that don't exist have being and others don't, thinks Meinong) – and surely these should still count amongst the subject matter of ontology.

It's probably a hopeless task to try to give a precise definition of ontology in a way that would keep every potential theorist happy; but the idea should be clear enough – ontology is concerned with questions *like*: What is there? What exists? What is there fundamentally? What has being?

But the ontologist does not aim simply at producing an ontological inventory: a mere list of what exists (or what there is, or has being, or is fundamental, etc.). She also wants to answer questions like: Is all of existence on a par, or do some things depend on the existence of other things? Are there important different kinds into which different things fall? If so, do the things of one kind exist in the same way as the things of another kind? Does existence come in degrees: are some things more real than others? Can what there is in the world simply be indeterminate? And of course, the ontologist will also be interested in how ontology connects to other areas in metaphysics.

As we saw, it's hard to give a nontrivial statement of the ontological question that ontologists would agree on; it's equally hard to give even a *partial* answer that isn't contentious. We might start with Descartes' *cogito*: if there's one thing I know for certain, it's that *I exist*. But not everyone accepts even this! Some (the compositional nihilists) think that there are only atoms – mereological "simples", lacking in proper parts – and hence that there aren't any humans. Could we all at least agree on the existence of the atoms then? No: for some are not prepared to rule out that the world is *gunky*: containing no atoms, but only smaller and smaller complex objects, each of which is further divisible, and so on to infinity (which raises an old question of Aristotle's: can there really be completed infinities in the world?). Still, almost everyone will agree that there are, now, *either* some complex objects *or* some simples (or both, of course), since that follows immediately just from the claim that there is *something*. And while the history of philosophy has included people who have denied that there is anything at all, it's fair to say that such a view is extremely unpopular. (Apart from anything else, if it were true there'd be no one around to believe it.)

So most of us can agree that there is something. The nature of the something, however, is hotly contested. Is it material or mental? Is the existence of any thing dependent on there being a mind that perceives it, as Berkeley thought, or is there a mind-independent external world of objects whose continued existence has nothing to do with their continuously being perceived?

The dominant trend in analytic metaphysics is realism about the external world: that there are some things whose identity and persistence is independent of mental activity. Furthermore, the current fashion is that this is all that there is: that not only was Berkeley wrong to think that everything is distinctively mental, Descartes was also wrong to think that even some things are distinctively mental. There may be minds but, think most modern ontologists, there is no distinctive category of the mental that minds belong to.

This last point bears elaboration. If there *are* minds, how can there not be a category of mental things? Well, there is a sense of "category" according to which there's a category of Fs (the category of tennis players with beards, for example) if and only if there are Fs (if and only if there are bearded tennis players, e.g.). If I talk about the category of bearded tennis players, you certainly know what I'm talking about, and you know the conditions a thing must meet to belong to that category: they must both have a beard and play tennis. But there is a strong sense that this category is entirely arbitrary: there's nothing *special* about bearded tennis players that demands that they be grouped together. We can choose to do so, but nothing about the world *demands* that we do so. Contrast this with, for example, the distinction between abstract objects (such as the number two, or the type *pop song*) and concrete objects (such as the two apples on my table or the CD of *Blood on the Tracks* that sits in my stereo). If there are such things as abstract objects, surely the world *demands* that they be grouped together and separated from the concrete objects. A society that talked about numbers and sets and about tables and planets, but that didn't recognise that the numbers and the sets belonged together in one category and that the tables and planets belonged together in another category, would be a society that failed to recognise something about the world; whereas a society that failed to distinguish bearded tennis players from those who are either beardless or who don't play tennis would not be missing anything important about the deep structure of reality.

If this is right, then the world comes pre-divided into *natural kinds*. Some objects just objectively belong together, and others don't. We can *choose* to group together the kettles and the beanbags – we can call them the "kettle-bags" – and it will be true that something is a kettle-bag if and only if it is either a kettle or a beanbag; but kettles and beanbags don't really belong together: not in the way that electrons, say, belong with one another. Electrons form a natural kind, but kettle-bags don't.

Metaphysics is about the fundamental structure of the world. If there are natural kinds, then one fact about the fundamental structure of the world is that some things belong together and others don't. One task for the metaphysician, then, is to say something about which of our predicates track these natural "joints" in the world. And there are other parts of our language – aside from the predicates – of which we can ask: are we talking here about an objective feature of the structure of the world, or are we merely imposing our own conceptual scheme on the world?

Consider tense. It is true that you are *now* reading this sentence and that you *were* reading the previous paragraph and that you *will* be finished with this introduction. But do these truths mark objective features of reality's structure? Is there a real distinction between the past, present and future, or is our grouping of events into these categories more like the grouping together of kettles and beanbags? (Those who say that reality itself makes this distinction are called "A-theorists" while their opponents are the "B-theorists." Philosophers have not always been particularly imaginative when it comes to naming their theories.)

Or consider modality. While you are in fact reading this book, you might never have picked it up. Indeed, it might never have been written. Reality might have differed in many respects – but not in every respect. No matter how things had been, 2 + 2 would still have been equal to 4, bachelors would remain unmarried, and you (if you existed) would still be a person (and not, say, a plate of scrambled eggs). Again: those are truths – but the question arises as to whether their truth says something about the deep structure of reality or about our way of describing it. Is the distinction between the necessary truths (those that couldn't have been false) and the contingent truths (those that could) like the distinction between electrons and non-electrons or like the distinction between kettle-bags and everything else? Would we be missing anything important about reality's structure if we failed to make it?

Or consider indeterminacy. Some sentences, it seems, just can't be classified as definitely true or definitely false. Is a man with a heavily receding hairline bald? Is a hundred grains of sand a heap of sand? It seems inappropriate to say either yes or no: such questions simply resist definite answers. It is *indeterminate* whether that man is bald or whether 100 grains of sand is enough to have a heap. Is indeterminacy a feature of the deep structure of the world? Orthodoxy says it is not: that while it is *true* that these claims are indeterminate, this isn't a fact about the structure of the world but a result of our using vague language to describe the world. But there are some dissenters to this orthodox view, who view indeterminacy as the A-theorist views tense: as a feature of fundamental reality, one that language *must* be able to talk about, lest we miss important features of the world.

Questions concerning the fundamental structure of the world have a huge bearing on what we should say regarding the ontology of the world. Suppose the A-theorist is right that there is a fundamental distinction between the present and the non-present. Does this have any bearing on what we should say as to the *existence* of present versus non-present entities? A presentist is one who thinks that the present time is privileged because it is the only time there is: there are no dinosaurs or Lunar colonies, thinks the presentist, even though there were dinosaurs and will be (we can suppose) Lunar colonies – what is real is only what is present. Other A-theorists admit past entities as well as present, but deny that there are any future entities; and others still admit past, present and future entities but nevertheless claim that the present entities are special.

This last view, the "moving-spotlight" view, might sound peculiar. If past, present and future entities all exist, *why* are the present entities privileged? What's so special about present things if it's not *existence*? *What makes it the case* that present entities are metaphysically privileged over the equally existent past and future ones?

The idea behind this objection is what motivates what many metaphysicians take to be a useful ontological principle: the truthmaker principle. This principle says that for any truth, there are some things in the world that *make* that truth true. This "making" isn't the kind of making that goes on when a sculptor makes a statue. The truthmakers don't *cause* the truth to be true, but rather *ground* the truth in question, in the sense that those things couldn't exist and the truth in question be false (whereas a cause *can* exist without its effects).

If the truthmaker principle is true, there is a tight connection between metaphysics, in general, and ontology, in particular. The metaphysician aims to discover the deep truths about the world; the truthmaker principle forces her to admit entities into her ontology to ground those truths. And so metaphysics in general will inform ontology; but this works both ways – if certain truths demand truthmakers that we don't want to believe in, we might have to rethink the truth of those propositions after all.

22
TO BE

Chris Daly

Discussions of being and existence concern a cluster of philosophical questions. The central question here is: "What is it for something to be?" A related question is: "What is the difference between something having being and something existing?" Answering this second question requires answering a still further question: "What is it for something to exist?" Moreover, as often in philosophy, various subsidiary but still important questions emerge in the course of tackling the central ones.

Besides their intrinsic interest, one source of motivation for these discussions is the issue of what kinds of thing exist. Do such kinds of thing as (for example) material objects, abstract objects, future individuals, or social institutions exist, and, if so, in what ways? Of particular interest here is the ontological argument for the existence of God. This argument claims that since the concept of God is a concept of a perfect thing, and since God would be less than perfect if he did not exist, then God must exist. A proper defence, or criticism, of that argument soon raises the questions mentioned in the opening paragraph.

Is there a difference between what has being and what exists?

Some philosophers (notably Quine) treat talk of what exists as interchangeable with talk of what is or of what has being. These philosophers think these phrases are merely stylistic variants on one another. There is no philosophically significant difference between "there are nine planets in the solar system," "there exist nine planets in the solar system," and "nine planets in the solar system have being." In slogan form: to be is to exist.

Other philosophers distinguish between what there is (i.e. what has being) and what exists. On this view, everything has being, but a thing may have being in one of two ways. A thing may have being and exist, or it may have being and subsist. The distinction between existence and subsistence is said to be exclusive (nothing can both exist and subsist) and exhaustive (everything either exists or subsists). As Russell put it, "For what does not exist must be something, or it would be meaningless to deny its existence; and hence we need the concept of being, as that which belongs even to the non-existent" (*The Principles of Mathematics* [1903: 450]). Russell thought that concrete things (roughly, things in space and time) have being and exist, whereas abstract things (roughly, things not in space and time) have being and subsist. Call Russell's view "the being theory" (for Meinong's quite different view, see Graham Priest's article "Not to Be," this volume).

One argument for the being theory arises from the problem of true negative singular existential statements. A singular existential statement says that some named or described thing exists. A negative singular existential statement says that a named or described thing does not exist. Consider the sentence "the current Czar of Russia does not exist." That sentence is not about something that exists. So what is it about? And how can it be true if it is not about something? The being theorist says that the sentence is about something that does not exist – namely, the current Czar of Russia – and the sentence is true because it says of that thing that it does not exist. This answer requires that there is something that does not exist; that something can have being without existing.

Another argument arises from another puzzle. If everything that can be talked about exists, then no sentence saying that a given thing exists will be false, and any true sentence saying that a given thing exists will be trivial. But there can be false existential sentences ("there existed chemical weapons in Iraq in 2003"), and not every true existential sentence is trivial ("Moses existed"). The being theorist's solution is to deny the antecedent of the conditional which states the puzzle: we can talk of things that have being but that do not exist.

An argument concerning talk about fiction draws the same conclusion. Sherlock Holmes was a famous detective. But Sherlock Holmes never existed. So there is something that never existed but was a famous detective. Another argument concerns intentional contexts. In the sixteenth century, allegedly the explorer Don Juan Ponce de Leon sought the Fountain of Youth. So there was something which Ponce de Leon sought. Unknown to him, however, the Fountain of Youth did not exist, but had being. A final argument concerns abstract entities, such as numbers, propositions and properties. Nominalism is often understood as the view that no abstract entities exist. Although there are good reasons supporting nominalism, there are also good reasons for talking about numbers and properties. One apparent solution is to maintain nominalism, but to allow that there are abstract objects (i.e. abstract objects have being). So saying (for example) that there is a prime number between four and six is not to say that a prime number between four and six exists. It is to say only that a prime number between four and six subsists.

The being theorist may have to take the distinction between being and existence as primitive. That move will not help those philosophers who say that they cannot understand the distinction. The issue then is whether the data that the being theorist cites – true negative singular existential statements, statements in intentional contexts, discourse about fictional characters or about abstract entities – can be satisfactorily accounted for without distinguishing between what exists and what has being.

Is there a difference between what is actual and what exists?

In discussions of modality (the study of possible and necessary truth), the word "actual" is standardly used in the following quasi-technical way. What is merely possible is non-actual. What is not only possible, but also the case at our world, is actual. Having agreed on this usage, however, there is a major philosophical disagreement about the relation between what exists and what is actual.

For some philosophers (the actualists) whatever exists is actual. Indeed, something is actual if and only if it exists. Since merely possible things are non-actual, these philosophers conclude that merely possible things do not exist. For example, there could have been talking donkeys, so talking donkeys are possible things. Nevertheless, talking donkeys are not actual things. It follows that they do not exist. Typically, actualists go on to say that there exist certain actual things (such as properties or set of sentences) which represent merely possible things (such as talking donkeys).

For other philosophers (the possibilists) whatever is merely possible exists. Indeed, something exists if and only if it is possible that it exists – that is, if and only if it is a possible thing. Since merely possible things are non-actual, these philosophers conclude that there exist some things that are not actual. For example, possibilists agree that there are no actual talking donkeys. But since it is possible that there exist talking donkeys, talking donkeys exist. They do not exist in our world, the actual world, but in other worlds. According to possibilists, the actual world is just one of a plurality of possible worlds. If something is actual, it exists in our world. But for something to exist, it does not have to exist in our world. Something exists if and only if it exists in some world. Talking donkeys are non-actual, merely possible, but existing things. Moreover, actualists take merely possible things to be the same kinds of thing as actual things. On this view, a merely possible donkey is a donkey that exists although it does not exist in the actual world.

The debate between the actualist and the possibilist is then a debate about whether there exist things other than actual things. Both sides agree that actual things exist. Both sides agree that for something to be is for something to exist. But the possibilist claims that there exist things which are not actual – namely, merely possible things such as talking donkeys or purple cows – whereas the actualist denies this. The possibilist may concede that his view is incredible, but he argues that nevertheless it gives the overall best account of modality. He claims, then, that the best account of modality requires that what exists consists not only in what is actual but also in what is not actual.

Are there different degrees of existence?

Some properties come in degrees. For example, the temperature and mass of things each admit of degree: some things have a higher temperature, or more mass, than other things. So if existence is a property, can it too come in degrees?

Some philosophers have thought that it can. Plato thought that some things fully exist whereas other things exist to less degree. According to Plato, only unchangeable things such as the Forms fully exist. Since physical objects are constantly changing, they are never anything permanently or exactly; they are in a state of becoming. So, Plato claimed, they exist to a lesser degree than the Forms. He further thought that souls have an intermediate degree of existence between the Forms and physical objects, because a soul is an enduring subject that has numerically different properties at different times. Similarly, F. H. Bradley thought that both truth and reality admit of degree, where to be real is to be a substance (i.e., a thing metaphysically capable of independent existence). The closer a judgement is to describing the whole of reality, the more true it is. And the larger a part of reality something is, the more real it is.

Other philosophers reject the view that things can exist to different degrees. For them, existence is an all-or-nothing affair. You cannot exist just a little bit, any more than you can be pregnant just a little bit. These philosophers might argue that the view that existence admits of degree falsely presupposes that existence is a property of things. For if existence is not a property of things, it is not a property of things that admits of degree. It is not clear, however, that Plato and Bradley's theories make that presupposition. The chief alternative to taking existence to be a property of things claims that (for example) for worms to exist is for the property of being a worm to have the property of being instantiated (i.e., to have the property of having an instance). Whether or not that alternative view is correct (see the section, "What is it to exist? How should existence claims be analysed?" below), note that Plato and Bradley could restate their theories in terms of that view. For the view could consistently say that the property of being instantiated admits of degree. Recall that Plato believed that souls exist more fully than physical objects. It is then open for Plato to express his belief in the following way: the property of being a physical object has the property of being instantiated to a lesser degree than the property of being a soul.

Plato's and Bradley's arguments can be challenged on other grounds. The premise that Forms cannot change, but physical objects can, does not entail that the Forms exist more fully than physical objects do. It is compatible with the premise that existence is an all-or-nothing matter, and that Forms, souls and physical objects all exist. The most the premise shows is that Forms, souls, and physical objects are different kinds of thing, not that they exist in different degrees. Bradley's argument relies on various idealist claims about reality which, if anything, are more questionable than the conclusion that he wants to draw. But it is one thing to find faults in the arguments for a given view, and another thing to show that the view is false. More needs to be done.

One ground for rejecting the view in question is that no justified account seems available of saying which things exist more fully than others do. Why should we rank things in the way that Plato does? Why not say that physical objects have a higher degree of existence than the Forms, because the former can change and the latter cannot? As for Bradley, since the local rubbish tip is a larger chunk of reality than you are, is it more real, more like a substance, than you are? Do people reach higher degrees of existence, the chubbier they get? And if Bradley did not mean "larger part of reality" in this literal-minded way, then what could he have meant by it?

Do things exist in different senses of "exist"?

Consider the following claims: "bodies exist," "minds exist," "numbers exist," and "universities exist." Set aside the question of which (if any) of those claims are true. Consider instead whether the word "exist" has the same meaning in each of those claims. Some philosophers (such as Aristotle and Ryle) think that it does not, and that "exist" is equivocal. If we say that minds exist, we are using the word "exist" in one sense, and if we say that bodies exist, we are using "exist" in another sense. "Exist" is equivocal just as the word "rising" is (consider "hopes are rising," "interest rates are rising," and "tidewaters are rising").

Other philosophers (such as Quine) think that "exist" occurs unambiguously in our examples. It is true that each of these claims differs in meaning. But these differences can be traced solely to the differences of meaning between the words "bodies," "minds," "numbers" and "universities." There is no need to suppose that "exist" has a different meaning in each of the claims. Quine's point can be developed as three worries about Ryle's thesis:

First, there seems to be no justifiable answer to the question of which things exist in which sense. If different things exist in different senses, it seems that we may as well say that knives exist in a different sense to that of forks. Moreover, given what Ryle says about the ambiguity of "exist," we may as well say that "thing" is ambiguous when we talk of mental things, physical things, fork-shaped things, or knife-shaped things. (Some philosophers, such as Putnam, do think that such words as "thing" and "object" are ambiguous, so they will not see the above comparison as a *reductio* of Ryle's view. They still need to specify the different senses that "object" and "thing" allegedly have.)

Ryle would presumably reply that it is things belonging to different categories which exist in different senses. But now we need an account of what a category is, of what categories there are, and of why one and the same thing cannot belong to more than one category at the same time. Ryle's envisaged reply is unsatisfactory for another reason: the supposition of fundamental categories in metaphysics does not obviously entail that things belonging to different categories exist in different senses. It seems consistent with the supposition to say that mental and physical things belong to different categories but exist in the same sense. So Ryle would need to make out why a thing's belonging to a given category has any bearing on the sense in which the thing exists.

Second, there are various informally valid forms of argument such as argument (A) below:

(A) (1) The number seven exists.
    (2) The University of Leeds exists.
    (3) The number seven and the University of Leeds are non-identical.
    (4) Therefore: at least two things exist.

Ryle is committed to denying that "exists" in (1) has the same sense as "exists" in (2). Either he has to deny that (A) is informally valid, although such a denial would be implausible. Or he has to explain the argument's validity by saying that (4) involves a yet further sense of "exists." Perhaps this sense could be defined disjunctively as: exist in the sense in which bodies exist or exist in the sense in which minds exist. But since such a sense of "exists" is available to us, it is not clear on what grounds Ryle thinks that (1) and (2) use different senses of "exists." It is open for us to say that they use the same sense of "exists," since we have seen how at least one shared sense can be defined. And how is it that a claim such as (4) can be true, without its specifying which of the (allegedly) many senses of "exists" it is using?

Third, we should draw distinctions only if there is some useful theoretical purpose in doing so. What is the purpose of introducing additional senses of "exists"? It seems *ad hoc* to introduce new senses of "exists" just to guarantee the informal validity of certain arguments. There is a variant of Ockham's razor, Grice's razor, which says that we should not multiply the senses of words unnecessarily. So if we can account for the informal validity of arguments such as (A) by taking "exists" to have a univocal sense, that is the view that we should take (unless there is prevailing reason otherwise).

What is it to exist? How should existence claims be analysed?

There are two principal answers to these questions. What we might call "the property account of existence" makes two claims: that existence is a property of everything that exists, and that "exists" is a predicate which ascribes existence to a thing. For example, just as redness is a property of everything that is red, so the property theory says that existence is a property of everything that exists. Likewise, just as "is red" is a predicate which can be correctly ascribed to every red object, so the property theory says that "exists" is (grammatically and logically) a predicate which can be correctly ascribed to everything that exists.

In contrast, what we might call "the quantifier account of existence" says that existence is not a property of individuals, but a property of properties, and that "exists" does not ascribe existence to a thing, but functions as a quantifier. This account is also often called "the Frege–Russell account of existence," after its original formulators. On this account, "exists" has the grammatical role, but not the logical role, of a predicate. A sentence such as "bird-catching spiders exist" is to be analysed as: "there exist bird-catching spiders." Using "$\exists x$" to mean *at least one thing exists that is such that*, we can symbolise the target sentence as: "$\exists x.x$ is a bird-catching spider." In this analysis, "there exists" has the logical role of the existential quantifier. In terms of our example, it ascribes the property of being instantiated to the property of being a bird-catching spider.

In Frege's system, the idea would be expressed as follows. The existential quantifier is a second-level concept under which first-order concepts fall. (Here, "concept" is Frege's term for a property). The concept of being a bird-catching spider is an example of a first-level concept. The existential quantifier maps that first-level concept to the truth-value True if and only if (iff) there exists an x such that x is a bird-catching spider.

Quine draws upon the quantifier view in devising his criterion of ontological commitment. Typically, a theory is originally formulated in a natural language. The theory is then to be reformulated in first-order logic (with identity). There is some leeway about how this can be done. Natural language sentences which are apparently about (for example) such things as sakes ("the sake of the nation") are to be paraphrased by sentences which lack the term "sakes." Any constants in the formalised theory are to be replaced with quantificationally bound variables. Sentences formed using these bound variables are true only if the variables have values. So those sentences are true only if there exist objects which are the values of the variables. Hence Quine's dictum, "to be is to be the value of a bound variable." A theory is ontologically committed to all and only those objects that it takes as values of its variables. That is, it is committed to the existence of all and only those objects that have to exist if the quantified sentences of the theory are to be true.

On the face of it, the property account and the quantifier account are each compatible with the being theory (and, on the face of it, they are each compatible with its negation). Those views are accounts of what existence is and what "exists" means. They do not exclude (or require) an existence/being distinction.

The property account says that everything that exists has the property of existence. But unless more can be said about that property, the property view seems unillumi-nating. It is a theorem of first-order logic with identity that, for every x, there is something that is x. So it is a point of logic that, if there is a property of existence, all and only things that exist have that property. Whether or not this consequence should be troubling for the property account depends upon whether we should expect every genuine property to have an interesting nature that can be discovered. Some philoso-phers deny that the property of truth has such a nature. If they are right, the property of existence would not be alone in this respect. Nevertheless, since the property account agrees that "$\exists x.x$ is a bird-catching spider" says that bird-catching spiders exist, it remains incumbent on the view to explain the connection between the (alleged) property of existence and the semantics of the existential quantifier.

In reply, the property theorist might argue that the quantifier phrase "there are" can be used in sentences without implying existence: consider such sentences as "there are things you believe in that don't exist" and "there are imaginary creatures." The existential import that "there are" has in other sentences might then be put down solely to conversational implicature. On this basis, the property theorist might argue that his account provides the correct analysis of existential sentences in ordinary language.

He might also argue that the existential quantifier can be analyzed in terms of the predicate "exists." Take the sentence "strawberries exist." The quantifier account analyses that sentence as: "$\exists x.x$ is a strawberry." Here the existential quantifier does double duty: it indicates the existence of things that satisfy the open sentence "x is a strawberry," and it specifies how many things satisfy that open sentence. The property theorist may reply that this conflates two distinct linguistic functions into "$\exists x$." On the property account, "strawberries exist" should be analyzed as: "$\exists x.x$ is a strawberry and x exists," where the variable "x" ranges over both things that exist and things that do not exist and are merely objects of thought (purely intentional objects).

The property account says that in a true sentence such as "the planet Venus exists," the descriptive name "the planet Venus" refers to a certain planet, and "exists" is a predicate that ascribes the property of existence to the object referred to. Now if there is a property of existence, is there also the negation or complement of that property – the property of non-existence? If so, does anything have it? If anything has that property, it will be a non-existent thing, such as the planet Vulcan. A sentence such as "the planet Vulcan does not exist" would then presumably require a parallel semantic analysis to "the planet Venus exists." That is, "the planet Vulcan does not exist" consists of a descriptive name referring to a certain planet, and the predicate "does not exist" ascribing the property of non-existence to the object referred to. But now the problem of true negative singular existential sentences returns.

What is the modal status of existence claims?

A final issue concerns whether all, some, or no objects exist necessarily. To set up the issue, we need to distinguish, for any F, between something's being contingently F and something's being necessarily F.

You are sitting down, but it is possible that you are instead standing up. That is, although you are sitting down, it is also the case that you could instead be standing up. In that sense, it is contingent that you are sitting down; you are contingently sitting down. Next, you are identical with yourself. It is not possible that you are not identical with yourself. That is, you are self-identical, and it is also the case that you could not fail to be self-identical. In that sense, it is necessary that you are self-identical; you are necessarily self-identical.

Now turn to existence. You exist. But it is possible that you did not exist. For it is possible that your parents never met. And if your parents had never met, you would not have existed. So it seems that although you exist, you might not have done. That is, it is contingent that you exist.

Consider the number two. Some philosophers say that the number two exists. If you agree with them, fine. If you do not, we can frame the relevant question in a conditional form. (This will not affect the point at issue). The question is this: given that the number two exists, could that number have not existed? To put it in an equivalent way: if the number two exists, could that number have not existed? Many philosophers think that the answer is "no." They say that the number two exists necessarily. Or, to return to our conditional way of posing the question, they say that if the number two exists, it exists necessarily.

Often in philosophy we are concerned with arguing about whether certain claims (say) "physical objects exist" or "the number two exists" are true. But here we are concerned with the modal status of such claims. That is, supposing that the claims are true, we are concerned with whether they are contingently true or whether they are necessarily true. And, similarly, supposing that the claims are false, we are concerned with whether they are contingently false or whether they are necessarily false. For example, some atheists think that the claim "God exists" is false, but that it could have been true. So they think that the claim expresses a contingent falsehood. Other atheists think that it expresses a necessary falsehood. To take another example, one philosopher of mathematics, Hartry Field, thinks that although the claim "the number two exists" is not true, it could have been true. That is, Field thinks that the number two does not exist, but that it could have existed. It contingently does not exist.

Let us consider the issue more generally. If you accept that claims have a modal status (and some philosophers, following Quine, do not) then there are three options:

(1) Some things exist contingently, whereas other things exist necessarily.
(2) Everything exists contingently. Hume seems to have thought that if you need experience to tell you the truth-value of a claim, then that claim cannot be a

necessary truth or falsehood. It has to be a contingent truth or falsehood, if it has a truth-value at all. Hume also thought that it is only experience which tells us whether any given thing exists (see Hume's *Enquiry Concerning Human Understanding*, §12 pt 3). It follows that all existence claims are contingently true or false, if they have a truth-value at all. That is, no existence claim is a necessary truth or falsehood. If an ice cube and the number two exist, they each exist contingently.

(3) Everything exists necessarily. This is the view of one contemporary philosopher, Timothy Williamson. Nothing can come into existence or go out of it. Although concrete objects often appear to come into existence, these are (necessarily existing) objects ceasing being abstract objects and becoming concrete objects. When concrete objects appear to cease to exist, these (necessarily existing) objects cease being concrete objects and become abstract objects.

Reference

Russell, Bertrand (1903) *The Principles of Mathematics*, Cambridge: Cambridge University Press.

Further reading

Michael Dummett, *Frege: Philosophy of Language*, 2nd edn (1973; London: Duckworth, 1981), chapter 3 and pp. 278–80, offers a sophisticated presentation and discussion of Frege's views on quantification. See pp. 92–101 of David Lewis, *On The Plurality of Worlds* (Oxford: Blackwell, 1986), for Lewis's distinction between what is actual and what exists; and p. 212, for Lewis's endorsement of the univocity of "exist." Lewis distinguishes his view from Meinong's, in "Noneism and Allism," *Mind* 99 (1990): 23–31; reprinted in Lewis's *Papers in Metaphysics and Epistemology* (Cambridge: Cambridge University Press, 1999), pp. 152–63. Colin McGinn, *Logical Properties: Identity, Existence, Predication, Necessity, Truth* (Oxford: Oxford University Press, 2000) chapter 2, contains a defence of the property view of existence. Terence Parsons, "Are There Non-existent Objects?" *American Philosophical Quarterly* 19, no. 4 (1982): 365–71, provides a very readable presentation of the view that there is a distinction between what exists and what has being. For Plato's views on degrees of reality, see pp. 34–5 of Plato, *Timaeus and Critias*, trans. D. Lee (Harmondsworth: Penguin, 1972). W. V. Quine, "On What There Is," in his *From a Logical Point of View: Nine Logico-Philosophical Essays*, 2nd edn (1953; Cambridge, MA: Harvard University Press, 1980), pp. 1–19, includes Quine's rejection of the distinction between being and existence, his advocacy of the quantifier view, and his account of ontological commitment; and see *Word and Object* (Cambridge, MA: MIT Press, 1960), p. 131, on the univocity of "exists," and pp. 238–43, for Quine's doctrine of ontological commitment. Also see Bertrand Russell *The Principles of Mathematics* (Cambridge: Cambridge University Press, 1903); *The Problems of Philosophy* (Oxford: Oxford University Press, 1912) (at the close of chapter 9, Russell claims that for anything to exist, it exists at a time; since he takes abstract entities, such as universals, to be timeless, he says that they do not exist but have being); and "The Philosophy of Logical Atomism," in *Logic and Knowledge: Essays 1901–1950*, edited by R. C. Marsh (1918; London: Routledge, 1992) (see lectures 5 and 6 for an informal presentation of the quantifier view of existence). See Gilbert Ryle, *The Concept of Mind* (London: Hutchinson Press, 1949), p. 23, for Ryle's view that "exists" is equivocal. A clear and sympathetic exposition of Quine's doctrines about existence and meta-ontology is Peter van Inwagen's "Meta-ontology," *Erkenntnis* 48 (1988): 233–50; reprinted in his *Ontology, Identity, and Modality: Essays in Metaphysics* (Cambridge: Cambridge University Press, 2001). Morton White, *Toward Reunion in Philosophy* (Cambridge, MA: Harvard University Press, 1956), chapter 4, is a chapter-length criticism of the view that "exists" is equivocal. Timothy Williamson, "Necessary Existents," in Anthony O'Hear (ed.) *Logic, Thought, and Language* (Cambridge: Cambridge University Press, 2005) offers an accessible exposition of Williamson's innovative view that everything necessarily exists.

23
NOT TO BE

Graham Priest

Introduction

It is wise, I suppose, to begin by saying something about the meaning of the words involved in the title of this essay, and especially, "to be." ("Not" is not entirely innocent either; but that is largely a different story.) For a start, though some philosophers are inclined to draw a distinction between being and existence (as we will note in due course), there seems to me to be little to be served by such a distinction. I will therefore take "is" and "exists" (and so "there is" and "there exists") to mean the same.

What, then, is it to exist? I am inclined to think that to exist is to engage in causal processes, or at least, to have the ability to do so. But this is not an analysis of the meaning of "exist": the claim that there are objects that take no part in causal interactions is not self-contradictory. I suspect that it is impossible to provide any analysis of "exist." Some concepts are so fundamental that it appears impossible to say anything much about their meaning, except give simple paraphrases. (The notion *set* is like this – collection, bunch, group.) And concepts don't come much more fundamental than existence.

One further preliminary word: following Priest (2005), I will write the particular quantifier, "some," as $\mathfrak{S}$, and not $\exists$. An important part of what will be at issue in this essay is precisely whether the quantifier must be read as "there exists." Notation should beg no questions. I stress, however, that the particular quantifier is to be taken as having its usual semantics. Given a domain of quantification, D, $\mathfrak{S}xA(x)$ is true just if something in the domain satisfies $A(x)$. Whether the things in D must be taken to exist is a further question.

The extremes

To matters of substance. Whatever "exists" and the quantifiers mean, there would seem to be three possibilities:

(1) Everything exists.
(2) Nothing exists.
(3) Some things exist and some things don't.

View (1) appears to be one of the earliest in philosophy. It is usually attributed to Parmenides (early fifth century BCE). In his poem *The Way of Truth* he tells us that one cannot countenance the non-existent: whatever can be investigated, spoken of, thought of, exists (Barnes 1982: Ch. 9). It also turns out that what exists is one thing, with some curious properties; but that is not an important part of the story here.

One naturally balks at Parmenides' view. Hasn't he heard of chimeras, false gods, fictional objects of stories? It would seem obvious that we can imagine, fear, desire, etc., things that don't exist. In reply, one imagines Parmenides saying, with a stamp of his foot, perhaps, "But, goddamit, if they are thought of, then they must be *there* to be thought of." But where, exactly? Non-existent objects exactly aren't in space or time, or they would enter into causal processes, and so would exist. At root, his claim would be that for a relation to hold between two objects, they must both exist. Well, that's certainly true for some relations, such as *kicking*, or *sitting on*, but why suppose that all relations are like this? To do so, would appear simply to be an unwarranted generalisation. *Prima facie*, objects can certainly have properties without existing – at least intentional ones, like *being thought of* or *being feared*, and status ones, such as *being possible* or *being impossible*, or, indeed, *being non-existent*.

Position (2) appears to have been taken by Gorgias, about 100 years later. In his lost text *What Is Not*, Gorgias claimed that nothing exists (Barnes 1982: 182–3). Gorgias provides more arguments than Parmenides. These are notable for their panache, but not for their persuasiveness (though this is not the place to go into them). It seems all too evident that some things exist – Australia, the Sun, pinot noir grapes. Well, Gorgias was a sophist (or maybe just a satirist of Parmenides; see Barnes 1982: 173). Few since him have endorsed the view that *nothing* exists.

The *via media*

So if the extremes of (1) and (2) seem implausible, we are left with (3). Some things, such as Australia and the Sun, exist. Some things, such as Father Christmas and Gandalf, do not. This was the dominant view in both ancient and medieval logic. Aristotle, for example, says: "one can signify even things that are not" (*Analytica Posteriori*, 92b29–30; translation from Barnes [1984]). And in *On Ideas*, 82.6, we have: "Indeed, we also think of things that in no way are … such as hippocentaur and Chimaera."[1]

The great medieval logicians were even more explicit on the matter (Read 2001; Priest 2005: Ch. 3, §7). According to standard theories of *supposition*, "some Ss are Ps" is true just if something that is actually S is P. However, the also standard doctrine of *ampliation* tells us that "some Ss will be Ps" is true just if something that is or will be S, is or will be P (symmetrically for past-tense sentences). So the domain of supposition is ampliated to a wider collection of objects: present and future ones. And the medievals had a very robust sense of reality. Future and past objects do not exist (though they will or did exist). It might be thought that we may identify existence *simpliciter* with existence at some time or other, as the medievals did not. But they go further. They held, applying the notion of ampliation again, that "some Ss can be Ps" is true just if something that is or could be S, is or could be P. The domain of supposition includes *possibilia*, things that do not exist (though they could do). Here, for example, is Buridan on the matter (Buridan 2001: 299): "A term put before the word 'can' ... is ampliated to stand for possible things even if they do not and did not exist. Therefore the proposition 'A golden mountain can be as large as Mont Ventoux' is true." The medievals standardly allowed that some verbs, notably intentional ones, ampliated the supposition of a term to an even broader class of objects. Thus, Marsilius of Inghen writes: "Ampliation is the supposition of a term ... for its significates which are or were, for those which are or will be, for those which are or can be, or for those which are or can be imagined" (Maierù 1972: 182). And at least for some logicians, what can be imagined includes *impossibilia* too. A standard medieval example of an object of the imagination is a chimera. On at least one understanding, this is an impossible object – having incompatible essences. Here is Paul of Venice (Paul of Venice 1978: 13): "Although the significatum of the term 'chimera' does not and could not exist in reality, still the term 'chimera' supposits for something in the proposition 'A chimera is thought of,' since it supposits for a chimera." We see, then, that medieval logicians took the middle way.

The way persisted into the nineteenth century. It was held by members of Brentano's phenomenological school, most notoriously, Alexius Meinong (Meinong 1904). Many, if not all, of our mental states are intentional. That is, they are directed towards objects. Meinong divided such objects into two kinds: those that are and those that are not. The objects that are not can be further divided into two kinds: the (merely) possible, such as Father Christmas, a golden mountain; and the impossible, such as a round square. The objects that are can also be divided into two: those that exist, properly speaking – these are objects in space and time, such as Melbourne and Meinong; and those that subsist (*besteht*) – these are abstract objects, such as numbers and propositions. A version of the view, too frequently confused with Meinong's, was held by Russell in the *Principles of Mathematics* (Russell 1903). Spatiotemporal objects exist; all the others (abstract, merely possible, impossible) subsist.

Parmenides makes a comeback

In the twentieth century, Parmenides' view made a comeback; indeed, it became the orthodox view. Of course, exponents of the modern Parmenideanism, do not subscribe to the sad view that Father Christmas really exists. Some way had to be found of understanding true claims which are *prima facie* about non-existent objects, which avoids this conclusion.

Thus, consider the (true) claim "Priest is thinking about Father Christmas." This cannot be understood as a relationship between Priest (an existent object) and Father Christmas (a non-existent one). If it is a relationship between two objects, the second must also exist. What, exactly, we take this to be, we might well debate. One natural candidate is a mental representation (whatever that is). Another is an individual concept, or a sense. (This was Frege's view in "Sense and Reference," in Geach and Black [1970: 56–78].) All such positions face problems with quantification. Thus, Priest is thinking about Russell, and Russell is a great philosopher. It follows that I am thinking about a great philosopher:

(1) &x(Priest is thinking about x and x is a great philosopher).

But that cannot be right. In the first conjunct, whatever "x" refers to, it is not a philosopher, great or otherwise. And in the second conjunct, "x" refers to a philosopher, not a mental representation, or whatever. Or again, Priest in thinking about Father Christmas, and Father Christmas does not exist. Hence it would seem that I am thinking of something that does not exist.

(2) &x(Priest is thinking about x and x does not exist).

But the "x" of the first conjunct refers to something that does exist. So this sentence is just plain false.

Another possibility is to refuse to take a sentence such as "Priest is thinking about Russell" at face value. Sentences reporting intentional states are not to be understood as stating a relationship between two objects. This was essentially Russell's view after he formulated his theory of descriptions (Russell 1905b). Using ι as a definite-description operator – so that one reads "$\iota x A(x)$" as "the x which satisfies $A(x)$" – sentences of the form $A(\iota x B(x))$ are to be understood as saying that there is a unique x satisfying $B(x)$, and it satisfies $A(x)$ too. And if we suppose that proper names are covert definite descriptions, we may apply this analysis to sentences containing these also. But this approach is beset with problems too. Leave aside the fact that names seem to behave quite differently from descriptions (e.g., they do not display scope ambiguities). Just consider the (true) claim "Priest is thinking about the greatest prime number." This becomes: there exists a unique x which is a prime number greater than all other primes, and Priest is thinking of it. This is false, since there is no greatest prime number. (For every prime, some prime number is a greater.)

An even more radical move (suggested in connection with perception in Ducasse [1942]) is to interpret a phrase such as "thinking of Father Christmas" as a simple monadic predicate, with no internal structure. Since there are an infinite number of things one can think of, this means that there will be an infinite number of semantically independent monadic predicates in the language. As such, it would be unlearnable. Since we do learn our natural language, this proposal therefore gets its semantics wrong. Perhaps more importantly, the approach also runs into problems with quantification. Neither (1) nor (2) makes any sense on this account. And suppose that you and I are both thinking about Russell. Then we are thinking about the same thing: &x(you are thinking about x and I am thinking about x). This makes no sense either.

Existence is not a predicate

Of course, there is much more to say about all the above matters. But what they suffice to establish is that Parmenides' comeback did not occur because people found clearly adequate ways to handle the natural objections to his position. Rather, what has driven the revival are problems taken to hold for the moderate view. The drivers are essentially three.

The first, and most important, is constituted around two claims:

ENP – Existence is not a monadic predicate of objects
EPQ – Existence is expressed by the particular quantifier.

Given EPQ, "some" just means "there exists," and "everything exists" is a logical truism.

ENP is usually attributed first to Kant, in his discussion of the ontological argument for the existence of God in the *Critique of Pure Reason* (Kemp Smith 1933: A592/B620ff.). In fact, Kant states that existence is a perfectly legitimate syntactic predicate. It is not a *determining* predicate. That is, for any concept *F*, to say that something is an *F* is the same as saying that it is an existent *F*.

It is by no means clear that Kant's claim is correct. Certainly, to say that something is an *F* and to say that it is an existent *F* are the same thing for some *F*s. If something is a $1 coin, it can be held, put in one's pocket, etc. These are causal interactions, and so the coin exists. To say that something is a $1 coin is to say that it is an existent $1 coin. (The converse is obvious.) But to say that something is an object of fiction (in the sense that the object occurs in a work of fiction), is by no means the same as saying that it is an existent object of fiction. Gandalf is an object of fiction, but not an existent one. Napoleon is an object of fiction (because of *War and Peace*), but also exists. But in any case, Kant's view is quite consistent with existence being a significant predicate. Kant himself points this out. He says: "When, therefore, I think of a being as the supreme reality, without any defect, the question still remains whether it exists or not" (*Critique of Pure Reason*, translation from Kemp Smith [1933: A600/B628]). Indeed, the judgment as to whether or not it exists is a synthetic one (A598/B626).[2]

More recently, many have taken ENP to be established by a claimed dissimilarity between pairs such as:

Tame tigers growl.
Tame tigers exist.[3]

The first sentence is ambiguous. It could mean that some tame tigers growl, that all do, or that generically they do. For our purposes, it is apt to consider the first of these. Then the logical form of this sentence is:

$$\mathfrak{S}x(Tx \wedge Gx)$$

The second sentence is not ambiguous. It means that there exist tame tigers; that is, some existent things are tame tigers. If we write the monadic existence predicate as *E*, this has exactly the same form:

$$\mathfrak{S}x(Tx \wedge Ex).$$

There is no dissimilarity of form – or even of truth value.

The particular quantifier

EPQ was first proposed by Frege. He explains (Geach and Black 1970: 48–9):

> I have called existence a property of a concept. How I mean this to be taken is
> best made clear by an example. In the sentence "there is at least one square
> root of 4," we have an assertion not about (say) the definite number 2, nor
> about −2, but about a concept *square root of* 4; viz. that it is not empty.

It is not clear that the reading of the quantifier is more than a *façon de parler*, however.
In a similar way, when a mathematician says that one group *can* be embedded in another,
this has nothing to do with possibility or permission. It is just a way of saying that
something (a function) satisfies a certain condition. So it would seem with "there is."
At any rate, Frege gives no *arguments* for reading the particular quantifier in this way
(see, further, Priest 2008a).

The matter is different with Russell. Russell endorses both ENP and EPQ, and defends
both in his *Lectures on Logical Atomism*. His central argument goes as follows (Pears
1972: 90):

> If you say "Men exist, and Socrates is a man, therefore Socrates exists," this is
> the same sort of fallacy as it would be if you said "Men are numerous, Socrates
> is a man, therefore Socrates is numerous," because existence is a predicate of a
> propositional function, or derivatively of a class. When you say of a proposi-
> tional function that it is numerous, you will mean that there are several values
> of *x* that will satisfy it … If *x*, *y*, and *z* all satisfy a propositional function, you
> may say that that proposition is numerous, but *x*, *y*, and *z* severally are not.
> Exactly the same applies to existence, that is to say that the actual things there
> are in the world do not exist, or, at least, that is putting it too strongly, because
> that is utter nonsense. To say that they do not exist is strictly nonsense, but to
> say that they exist is also strictly nonsense.

Russell asks us to compare two inferences:

Men exist	Men are numerous
Socrates is a man	Socrates is a man
Socrates exists	Socrates is numerous

and claims that the same sort of fallacy is involved in both. We are supposed to conclude
that the conclusion of the first is ungrammatical, as is that of the second. But the
analogy is lame. To say that men are numerous is indeed to say that many things are
men. In the right context, this is true, as is the other premise. The conclusion, however,
is *clearly* nonsense. The inference is therefore fallacious. The first argument, too, is
fallacious. But that is simply because it is of the form:

$$\mathcal{E}x(Mx \wedge Ex)$$

$$\underline{Ms}$$

$$Es$$

Note that the corresponding inference with a universal major premise:

All men exist

Socrates is a man
_____
Socrates exists

seems perfectly valid. (All the people in this story actually exist; Napoleon is in this story, so Napoleon is an actually existing person.) And the conclusion of both arguments, that Socrates exists, is perfectly grammatical. Compare: "Napoleon exists, but Father Christmas does not." Russell's argument does nothing to show matters to be otherwise.

Perhaps the most influential defence of EPQ was given some thirty years later by Quine in his essay, "On What there Is." Here, the view that the particular quantifier expresses existence – or, as Quine is wont to put it: "to be is to be the value of a bound variable" – is endorsed with panache. The full passage is worth quoting. Having argued that the use of predicates does not commit us to the existence of universals, Quine asks if there is nothing one can say which commits one to the existence of something. There is (Quine 1948: 12–13 of the reprint):

> I have already suggested a negative answer to this question, in speaking of bound variables, or variables of quantification, in connection with Russell's theory of descriptions. We can very easily involve ourselves in ontological commitments by saying, for example, that *there is something* (bound variable) which red houses and sunsets have in common; or that *there is something* which is a prime number and larger than a million. But this is, essentially, the *only* way that we can involve ourselves in ontological commitment: by our use of bound variables. The use of alleged names is no criterion, ... for I have shown, in connection with "Pegasus" and "pegasize," ... names can be converted into descriptions, and Russell has shown that descriptions can be eliminated ... To be assumed as an entity is, purely and simply, to be reckoned as the value of a variable.

The logic of the text is interesting. Quine argues that the use of names and predicates is *not* existentially committing; but there is absolutely no argument given as to why quantification *is* existentially committing. Quine simply *assumes* that the domain of quantification comprises existent objects – or what comes to the same thing, that the particular quantifier is to be read as "there is." No argument is given for this: it is stated simply as a matter of dogma. (So if neither names, nor predicates, nor quantifiers are ontologically committing, what is? To say that something exists, of course!)

Identity

The second driver for Parmenides' comeback concerns identity. In a famous passage of "On What there Is," Quine charges that non-existent objects have no well-defined identity conditions; but any entity must have such conditions, so the notion of a non-existent object is incoherent. But why should we suppose that non-existent objects have no well-defined identity conditions? Unfortunately, Quine mounts no arguments for this either. We simply find a string of rhetorical questions – many of which, incidentally, have very obvious answers.[4] Of course, the identity conditions of existent objects are a problem too. And pretty much any account of the identity conditions of existent objects that one can give can be applied with just as much plausibility to non-existent objects. For example, one can say that two objects are the same just if the one has a property iff (if and only if) the other does (the Leibniz condition of the identity of indiscernibles). Or, if distinct objects may, as a matter of chance, have the same properties in the actual world, then two objects are the same if, in every world, the one has a property iff the other does.

The only thing one cannot do for non-existent objects, as one might attempt for existent ones, is provide identity conditions in terms of spatiotemporal locations: they have none. Thus, one cannot say that they are identical iff they have the same spatial locations at all time. Of course, such identity conditions will not work for abstract objects either. So exactly the same point can be made about existent abstract objects.

In fact, attempting to provide spatiotemporal identity conditions is problematic even for objects that are in space and time. The medievals pondered how many angels could be on the head of a pin. This was because angels have no spatial extension, and so can exist at the same place. One standard answer to the question of how angels are to be individuated – offered by Paul of Venice (Conti 2007) – was in terms of individual essences (*haecceities*). Thus, to be Gabriel is to have the individual essence of Gabriel. Such an account of identity has also found favour in debates about transworld identity in modal logic, and can be applied just as well to non-existent objects. Or, a very different problem: a statue and a piece of clay may occupy the same spatial locations for all time; yet arguably they are not identical: one could exist without the other. A standard answer in this case, is to say that they are distinct since they may have different properties at worlds other than the actual. In this case, we are back to something like the transworld version of the identity of indiscernibles.

Which account of identity should be endorsed, we may, here, safely leave as a matter of debate. It suffices to note that problems about identity apply just as much to existent objects as non-existent ones. They therefore provide no leverage specifically against objects in the latter category.

Characterisation

The third driver for Parmenides' comeback surfaces in Russell's critique of Meinong's view, once Russell had jettisoned his own version of it in the light of the theory of descriptions (Russell 1905a). Russell's objections are essentially two. First, Meinong's view violates the law of non-contradiction, since the round square is both round and square. Secondly, the view validates the ontological argument for the existence of God – and anything else one can describe – since the existent so and so is both so and so and existent.

There are a number of things to note about the objection. First, the objection targets the characterisation principle: the thing that satisfies $A(x)$, satisfies $A(x)$:

CP – $A(\iota x A(x))$

This is a very natural feeling principle. An object has the properties in its characterisation; that is how we pick it out. Next, the CP is quite independent of the view that some objects do not exist. That some objects do not exist in no way commits one to the CP. Third, the unrestricted CP is acceptable to no one. It allows us to prove absolutely everything. Let B be any claim. Let t be $\iota x(x = x \wedge B)$. Then the CP delivers $t = t \wedge B$, from which B follows. Finally, everyone accepts *some* restricted version of the CP. Thus, on standard accounts of definite descriptions, including Russell's, we have $\ni!xA(x) \rightarrow A(\iota x A(x))$ (where the exclamation mark expresses uniqueness).

So what has Russell's objection to do with non-existence? The answer is that without some version of the CP, we would have, generally speaking, no way of establishing what properties non-existent objects have. If $\iota x A(x)$ exists, we can causally interact with it, and hence determine its properties. (At least, given the understanding of existence stated in the introduction. If there can be abstract existent objects, these are just as much a problem as non-existent objects.) If it does not, we cannot; we need something like the CP.

Meinong himself only ever gestured at a reply to Russell. Later friends of non-existent objects have gone various ways on the matter. One approach (endorsed, for example, by Parsons [1980] and Routley [1980]) is to distinguish between two kinds of vocabulary – characterising (or nuclear) and non-characterising (or non-nuclear). Only the first of these can be deployed in acceptable instances of the CP. Crucially, existence is not characterising, and maybe neither is negation. A major problem with this approach is to distinguish between the two kinds of vocabulary in a principled fashion. A more subtle, but perhaps more telling, worry is that we appear to be able to think of an object satisfying *any* description whatsoever, not just ones deploying characterising vocabulary. The object must, in *some* sense, have those properties, since it is *that* object we are thinking of.

Another approach is pursued by Zalta (1980).[5] Zalta distinguishes between two modes of predication, *instantiation* and *encoding*, the "is" of predication being ambiguous between them. Instantiation is the familiar notion, used when we say truly, for example, "Russell is a philosopher." Encoding, by contrast, delivers a way in which a non-existent object, in particular, may present itself. Thus, given any property, some object may present itself as possessing, and so encode, just that property. Encoding may be taken to satisfy the CP (though things are not quite that simple in Zalta's actual account); instantiation does not. If we use $\lambda x A(x)$ for the property corresponding to the conditions $A(x)$, ○ for instantiation, and ● for encoding, we may have the CP in the form

$\iota x A(x) \bullet \lambda x A(x)$, but not $\iota x A(x) \circ \lambda x A(x)$. "$\lambda$-conversion" holds for instantiation. That is, where y does not occur in $A(x)$:

$$y \circ \lambda x A(x) \leftrightarrow A(y)$$

But we are not guaranteed it for encoding. Hence, we cannot move from instances of the CP to their damaging consequences.

There is a certain feeling of artifice attached to the distinction between the two modes of predication, but once over this, the approach does avoid the problems noted so far. – Well, not quite. A version of Russell's paradox strikes. Let P be the property of encoding a property that is not exemplified, $\lambda x \mathfrak{S} Y(x \bullet Y \wedge \neg x \circ Y)$. Let t be the object that encodes this property. It is not difficult to demonstrate that t behaves inconsistently. (This was first observed by Clark [1978].) Zalta's reaction to the problem is to deny that every λ-term, in particular $\lambda x \mathfrak{S} Y(x \bullet Y \wedge \neg x \circ Y)$, denotes a property. λ-conversion cannot, therefore, be applied to it. This certainly avoids the contradiction, but does so at the cost of going back on the idea that for *any* guise, an object may present itself under that guise. We would certainly seem to be able to think of an object presenting under the guise P. (You just did.)

A third approach to the problem is to endorse but a single mode of predication, and a completely unrestricted CP, but say that the instances of the CP are not guaranteed to hold in this world (though they may); they are guaranteed to hold in some world or other (this is the approach followed in Priest [2005]). Thus, for example, an object was characterised by Arthur Conan Doyle as a detective with acute powers of observation and deduction, as living in Baker St, etc. The object does not satisfy this characterisation at the actual world: there has never been such a detective living in Baker St. But it does satisfy the characterisation at those worlds in which the stories which Doyle tells us are true. Of course, some characterisations are impossible, and even inconsistent; thus, we must suppose that not only are some worlds non-actual, but that some worlds are impossible.

This approach to the CP avoids all the problems we have met so far. Of course, it faces its own distinctive objections. For example, it obviously inherits any problems posed by the machinery of (impossible) worlds. Arguably, we have to deal with these for quite different reasons anyway. But all this is a can of worms too big to open here. (Criticisms of this approach to the CP can be found in Kroon [2008] and Nolan [2008], with a reply in Priest [2008b].)

Conclusion

As we have seen, the extreme views of Parmenides, that everything exists, and Gorgias, that nothing exists, are both *prima facie* implausible. The commonsense *via media*, that some things exist and that some things do not, was the predominant view in logic until the twentieth century. Things then changed. But this was not because a clearly acceptable way of rendering Parmenides' view more plausible was found. Neither was it because the *via media* was shown to be untenable. Perhaps, then, in the twenty-first century, common sense will reassert itself, and the twentieth century will come to be seen as something of an historical aberration.

Notes

1 The authenticity of this text is sometimes disputed. For a defence, see Fine (1993), from which the quote comes (p. 15).
2 Kant also rejects EPQ. In the table of categories (A80/B106), the categories of plurality ("some") and reality ("existence") are distinct.
3 The actual example comes from Moore (1936), who shows a characteristic ambivalence on the matter.
4 Thus, for example: How many merely possible men are in the doorway? Answer: none. Non-existent objects are not in space and time, or – *a fortiori* – doorways. For a discussion of the whole passage, see Routley (1982) and Priest (2005: Ch. 5).
5 Zalta often describes the non-existent objects as abstract, suggesting some form of Platonism, though this is not essential to his approach.

References

Barnes, J. (1982) *The Presocratic Philosophers*, revised edn, London: Routledge.
—— (1984) *The Complete Works of Aristotle*, Princeton, NJ: Princeton University Press.
Buridan, J. (2001) *Summulae de dialectica*, edited, trans. by G. Klima, New Haven, CT: Yale University Press.
Clark, R. (1978) "Not every Object of Thought Has Being: A Paradox in Naïve Predication Theory," *Noûs* 12: 181–8.
Conti, A. (2007) "Paul of Venice," in E. Zalta (ed.), *The Stanford Encyclopedia of Philosophy*; available: http://plato.stanford.edu/entries/paul-venice/
Ducasse, C. J. (1942) "Moore's 'The Refutation of Idealism'," chapter 8 of P. A. Schilpp (ed.), *The Philosophy of G.E. Moore*, Chicago, IL: Northwestern University Press.
Fine, G. (1993) *On Ideas: Aristotle's Criticism of Plato's Theory of Forms*, Oxford: Oxford University Press.
Geach, P. and Black, M. (eds, trans.) (1970) *Translations from the Philosophical Writings of Gottlob Frege*, Oxford: Basil Blackwell.
Kemp Smith, N. (trans.) (1933) *Immanuel Kant's Critique of Pure Reason*, 2nd edn, London: Macmillan & Co.
Kroon, F. (2008) "Much Ado about Nothing: Priest and the Reinvention of Noneism," *Philosophy and Phenomenological Research* 76: 199–207.
Lackey, D. (ed.) (1973) *Essays in Analysis*, London: Allen & Unwin.
Maierù, A. (1972) *Terminologia logica della tarda scolastica*, Rome: Edizioni dell'Atenio.
Meinong, A. (1904) "Gegenstandstheorie," in *Untersuchungen zur Gegenstandstheorie und Psychologie*, Leipzig; trans. into English as "The Theory of Objects," chapter 4 of R. Chisholm (ed.), *Realism and the Background to Phenomenology*, London: Allen & Unwin.
Moore, G. E. (1936) "Is Existence a Predicate?" *Proceedings of the Aristotelian Society, Supplementary Volume*, 15; reprinted as chapter 5 of A. Flew (ed.), *Logic and Language* (2nd series), Oxford: Basil Blackwell, 1961.
Nolan, D. (2008) "Properties and Paradox in Graham Priest's *Towards Non-Being*," *Philosophy and Phenomenological Research* 76: 191–8.
Parsons, T. (1980) *Non-Existent Objects*, New Haven, CT: Yale University Press.
Paul of Venice (1978) *Logica magna: secunda pars*, edited by F. del Punta; trans. M. M. Adams, Oxford: Oxford University Press.
Pears, D. F. (ed.) (1972) *Russell's Logical Atomism*, London: Fontana.
Priest, G. (2005) *Towards Non-Being: The Logic and Metaphysics of Intentionality*, Oxford: Oxford University Press.
—— (2008b) "Replies to Nolan and Kroon," *Philosophy and Phenomenological Research* 76: 208–14.

—— (2008a) "The Closing of the Mind: How the Particular Quantifier Became Existentially Loaded behind Our Backs," *Review of Symbolic Logic* 1: 42–55.

Quine, W. V. (1948) "On What There Is," *Review of Metaphysics* 48: 21–38; reprinted as chapter 1 of *From a Logical Point of View*, New York: Harper & Row, 1953.

Read, S. (2001) "Medieval Theories of Properties of Terms," in E. Zalta (ed.), *The Stanford Encyclopedia of Philosophy*; available: http://plato.stanford.edu/entries/medieval-terms/

Routley, R. (1980) *Exploring Meinong's Jungle and Beyond*, Canberra: Research School of Social Sciences, Australian National University.

—— (1982) "On What There Isn't," *Philosophy and Phenomenological Research* 43: 151–78; also as chapter 3 of Routley (1980).

Russell, B. (1903) *Principles of Mathematics*, Cambridge: Cambridge University Press.

—— (1905a) Review of *Untersuchungen zur Gegenstandstheorie und Psychologie*, by A. Meinong, *Mind* 14: 530–8; reprinted as chapter 2 of Lackey (1973).

—— (1905b) "On Denoting," *Mind* 14: 479–93; reprinted as chapter 5 of Lackey (1973).

Zalta, E. (1988) *Intensional Logic and the Metaphysics of Intentionality*, Cambridge, MA: MIT Press.

Further reading

On the Presocratics, see J. Barnes, *The Presocratic Philosophers*, revised edn (London: Routledge, 1982). On medieval logic, S. Read, "Medieval Theories of Properties of Terms," in E. Zalta (ed.), *The Stanford Encyclopedia of Philosophy* (2001) (available: http://plato.stanford.edu/entries/medieval-terms/); and G. Priest, *Towards Non-Being: The Logic and Metaphysics of Intentionality* (Oxford: Oxford University Press, 2005), chapter 3, §7. For the classical texts defending the contemporary view, see P. Geach and M. Black, (eds, trans.) *Translations from the Philosophical Writings of Gottlob Frege* (Oxford: Basil Blackwell, 1970), pp. 56–78; and D. F. Pears (ed.), *Russell's Logical Atomism* (London: Fontana, 1972), Lecture 5. On Quine and his critics, see W. V. O. Quine, "On What There Is," *Review of Metaphysics* 48 (1948): 21–38; reprinted as chapter 1 of *From a Logical Point of View* (New York: Harper & Row, 1953); R. Routley, "On What There Isn't," *Philosophy and Phenomenological Research* 43 (1982): 151–78; also as chapter 3). For modern defences of non-existent objects, see T. Parsons, *Non-Existent Objects* (New Haven, CT: Yale University Press, 1980); E. Zalta, *Intensional Logic and the Metaphysics of Intentionality* (Cambridge, MA: MIT Press, 1988); and G. Priest, *Towards Non-Being: The Logic and Metaphysics of Intentionality* (Oxford: Oxford University Press, 2005).

24
RAZOR ARGUMENTS
Peter Forrest

The appeal to simplicity

Often when Ockham's razor is invoked nothing more specific is intended than the general principle that simpler theories are on the whole more probable than less simple ones. Before considering the razor itself, it is worth examining first the more general principle, often called parsimony. Readers are warned, however, that simplicity is complicated, which is one reason for preferring more specific razor arguments.

Consider omphalism, the hypothesis expounded by Phillip Gosse in *Omphalos* (1857), that the universe was created by God in 4004 BC, complete with fake traces of earlier times, such as the fossil record. Any putative empirical evidence against omphalism, such as the direct naked-eye perception of the Clouds of Magellan some tens of thousands of years in the past, is question-begging. Nonetheless most of us judge omphalism to be highly improbable, and, if asked why, we might well invoke the name of Ockham, but Ockham's razor is, strictly speaking, the dictum that, "entities are not to be multiplied more than is necessary," and Gosse wielded the razor like Sweeney Todd. What is intended is rather that simpler theories are on the whole more probable. This may also be used to underpin the rule of inference to the best explanation. For other things being equal the simpler explanation is the better.

We may agree that the evolution is simpler than omphalism, but how do we characterise simplicity? Taking for granted the naturalness of the undefined terms in our language (e.g. a preference for "blue" over the artificial term "bleen," which applies to blue things before 2050 but to green ones thereafter) we could try considering the minimum number of bits of information required to state a proposition. Call this the *bit-complexity* of a proposition. It explicates the intuitive idea of complexity, provided we resist the temptation to define everything definable. Otherwise mathematical physics turns out to be more complicated than suggested by our intuitions – or at least those of mathematical physicists! Consider, for instance, the idea of velocity. We could define this as rate of change of location, which in turn requires a differential structure on space, usually characterised in terms of coordinate triples. Each coordinate is a real number and a real number is often defined as a Dedekind cut, a pair of sets of rational numbers, which are in turn thought of as equivalence classes of pairs of integers, and we could go on with the chain of definitions. When considering simplicity, however, we should avoid unpacking velocity in this way, and either treat it as a natural property or treat *relative velocity* as a natural relation.

Next we may start listing consistent hypotheses so that the earlier ones in the list are no more complicated than later ones, under the constraint that each hypothesis is inconsistent with all the previous ones. With a bit of ingenuity (aliens and angels are useful) we can come up with a large range of alternatives both to omphalism and evolution, and I find it plausible that if we allow really silly hypotheses there will be a countable infinity. So we may take them to be the first, the second and so on. The sum of the probabilities of all the hypotheses is equal to the probability that some hypothesis stateable in our language is correct. Call this the Universe's IQ (intelligibility quotient). Now consider the sum of the probabilities of all the hypotheses except the first n. Call this the PP(n) ("PP" stands for the probability of prolixity). The Universe has an IQ of no more than 100 per cent, so PP(n) tends to zero as n tends to infinity. That is, given any positive integer M, however large, there is some integer N such that for all n greater than N, PP(n) is less than 1/M. Hence the sum of the probabilities of the N simplest hypotheses is greater than IQ – 1/M. Especially if we grant that IQ is near 100 per cent this provides both an explication of and a justification for the principle that *on the whole* the simpler hypotheses are more probable.

We might well claim more. For initially we might think that either the probability of the hypotheses in the list decreases with every increase in complexity or the hypotheses all have equal probability. Assuming there is a countable infinity of hypotheses in the list the latter disjunct implies that IQ = 0, which is a tad pessimistic, and, more telling, a case of dogmatic scepticism. So, provided we require every hypothesis to be inconsistent with all the previous ones on the list we may suppose that the probability strictly decreases with complexity.

Unfortunately knowing that evolution is more probable than omphalism is not of much consequence. What if the probabilities are 40 and 39 per cent, respectively, or 0.25 and 0.24 per cent? Somewhat more significant would be knowing that evolution is a hundred times as probable as omphalism, because then we may reject omphalism. But even that is not especially encouraging: what if evolution has probability 0.1 per cent and omphalism probability 0.001 per cent? We would like to calculate probabilities from a combination of the evidence and the complexity, so that evolution turns out to be probable even though it is empirically equivalent to omphalism. To do this we need to assign probabilities to hypotheses prior to any evidence. The following method commends itself on the grounds of – note the reflexivity – its simplicity. Suppose the Universe has an IQ near 100 per cent. Then we would expect the number of hypotheses with bit-complexity n to increase exponentially with n. Hence for some unique constant c, between 0 and 1, we could assign *a priori* probability c^n to any theory of bit-complexity n (see Jeffreys 1961: 42, where c = ½). If readers do not like this derivation I challenge them to do better, but the point I want to make is not that this formula is correct but that if there is a correct formula it is totally useless. We do not and cannot perform probabilistic calculations on this basis, either consciously or unconsciously. (I am happy to concede there are parts of my brain much smarter than I am, but not *that* smart.)

As a consequence the general appeal to simplicity has limited use. Appeals to simplicity may be made fairly precise in statistics when we are considering the problem of fitting a curve to data. Apart from that they may be used to defend a preference for Darwin over Gosse against a mad-dog empiricist who always suspends judgement between empirically equivalent theories. If, however, they are used as an argument to try to convince an omphalist it invites the riposte that judgements of simplicity are subjective, in the sense of being up to the individual without guidance from agreed standards. The beauty of razor arguments, in the strict sense, is that not only are they far easier to understand, they are more objective than the general appeal to simplicity.

Ockham's razor: entities are not to be multiplied more than is necessary

William Hamilton named it after William of Ockham who said something equivalent ("Numquam ponenda est pluralitas sine necessitate," – plurality is never to be posited without necessity) and who used it to argue against abstract entities. And that remains one important application. For example, Hartry Field (1980) has argued that the sciences need numbers only as convenient fictions and so we should not believe they are real. For to be a realist about numbers if they are, as Field argues, redundant is to multiply entities more than is necessary.

Often Ockham's razor is used to argue against the position that there are things of two or more fundamental kinds by first claiming that we would not notice if one of the kinds did not exist, and then appealing to Ockham's razor against the redundant kind. The razor has been thus employed against the dualist thesis that things come in two kinds, the mental and the physical. For instance, George Berkeley argued in this way for subjective idealism, the thesis that so-called material objects are nothing but bundles of ideas in the minds of the observers. Although not his preferred argument, he says that it would be pointless of God to create both the mental and the material because the mental by itself would serve all the divine purposes. This argument is interesting for two reasons. The first is that it should make us ask whether the appeal to Ockham's razor is in fact based upon a conjecture about divine motives – hard for theists, harder for atheists. Many advocates of naturalism have significant reservations about any appeal to simplicity, even Ockham's razor (for a discussion, see Sober [2005]). The case made in the previous section that more complicated hypotheses are less likely, supports a negative answer: simplicity considerations need not depend on conjectures about divine motives. But if they do, so much the worse for naturalism, say I. The second point of interest is that Berkeley's argument is based on the "You would not notice the difference" thesis. I think we should reject that way of wielding the razor. For subjective idealists give more complicated explanations of the way things appear than do those who believe in a real physical world. Thus, the way the world looks from one point of view is correlated with the way that it looks from another to a far greater extent and in far greater detail than could be explained by divine providence. Such correlation is, however, just what we would expect if there is a material world.

With Berkeley occupying his customary role of awful warning I state the first of six qualifications to the way philosophers' use Ockham's razor.

(1) When it is enjoined not to *multiply* entities more than is necessary the word "multiply" means "hypothesise." If I *experience* things that do not help me understand, then I am not hypothesising them, so I should not invoke Ockham's razor to be sceptical about them. This might be the case with numbers: if you think you experience them when you are doing number theory, then the question of positing them as a hypothesis does not arise. But suppose you are positing numbers even though you have not experienced them and they do not help you understand what you have experienced. Then by Ockham's razor you should believe there are no numbers, and you have misunderstood if you retort that numbers are *necessary* beings so they are not being multiplied more than is *necessary*. For in the context of the razor, the word "necessary" means something like "not redundant in the best way of either interpreting or understanding appearances."

Another example worth thinking of here is a hallucination, such as those caused by tinnitus. In that case maybe something is experienced auditorily that makes the task of understanding the world a whole lot harder! But you should resist the temptation to deny its existence by appealing to Ockham's razor.

(2) Although Ockham's razor says that entities are not to be multiplied it is usually interpreted as telling us not to multiply *kinds* of entity. Consider the way a materialist might use Ockham's razor against the dualist, arguing that irreducibly mental properties, such as *qualia*, are redundant. Suppose that there are far fewer mental properties posited by dualism than there are neurophysiological properties. Even so it would be missing the point if the dualist replied to the razor argument stated above, "To be sure I posit a few more entities than you, but there is scarce 1 per cent difference between us in that regard." No, the defect is in positing two *kinds* of entity not one.

(3) Despite (2), we might note that on one theory there are infinitely many entities while on another, rival one, only finitely many, or more generally, but less precisely, that one theory postulates many times the entities that the other does. Relying on a version of Ockham's razor we might prefer the theory with fewer entities, provided it postulates no more kinds of entity. This version may be stated as the injunction not to multiply greatly the number of entities without necessity. It is a much weaker argument than the Ockham's razor as interpreted in (2), but maybe it is of some value. For instance, suppose you are a realist about space–time and, moreover you hold that every part of space–time is made up of points. Suppose also you hold that there is just the one universe (or at least that there are only as many universes as there are integers). There are discrete theories of space–time on which a region of finite volume contains only finitely many points. Hence there are no more points than there are integers. Contrast this with the standard position, namely that there is a point corresponding to every quadruple of real numbers – the coordinates. On this standard position, even if there is just the one universe and it is finite in size, there are more points than there are integers. Should that make us prefer the discrete theory, other things being equal? Maybe we should call this, rather weak, argument an application of Hamilton's razor, because his formulation of Ockham's razor lends itself to this, strictly numerical, interpretation.

(4) Most of us grant that there are very many kinds of entity: persons and other sentient beings; other living organisms; inanimate solid objects, portions of liquid, gas or plasma; molecules, atoms, subatomic particles. Many of us also believe in God, laws of nature, forces, and space–time; and many believe in properties, relations, sets and numbers. Are we all flagrantly opposed to the razor? I submit that in appealing to Ockham's razor we should consider only the most fundamental kinds. The reason for that is that when we have hypothesised fundamental kinds others will exist because of them and so do not need to be hypothesised. For instance, one theory of laws of nature, due to Dretske (1977), Tooley (1977) and Armstrong (1983), is that laws of nature are relations between universals. Assuming we already believe in universals we are not multiplying kinds of entity if we assert there are laws of nature but they are relations between universals and so themselves higher-order universals. In Armstrong's phrase, the laws of nature are then "an ontological free lunch." Like most free lunches, you only get this one if you have already bought something else. For example, the laws of nature are a free lunch only because Armstrong has hypothesised that relations between universals constrain their instances to be correlated – and that further hypothesis needs to be assessed as more or less probable.

(5) Ockham's razor arguments are good opening gambits, but they almost invariably invite the response that the putatively unnecessary kinds of entity are required for our best theory. For example Mark Colyvan (2001) has argued against Field that numbers in science are not just useful fictions, because in addition to facilitating inferences their use helps us understand the sciences.

(6) Like other appeals to simplicity including other razor arguments, no Ockham's razor argument is conclusive. At best they establish conclusions "beyond all reasonable doubt."

How sharp is the razor?

Thus qualified, I hope Ockham's razor is intuitive, in the sense that you tend to invoke it implicitly. As for many of our intuitions, however, we can have our *Hume moments* when we ask, "Why should I believe *that*?" In the case of Ockham's and other razor arguments the thought is "Why not just suspend judgement about redundant entities, instead of deciding, albeit inconclusively, that they do not exist?" (cf. van Fraassen 1980). Invoking the greater probability of simpler hypotheses does not exclude suspension of judgement.

Nonetheless I seek to undermine the "suspend-judgement" rule, as based upon a lack of imagination as to the redundant kinds. I want to make an unusual complaint against metaphysicians: we are too down to earth, too concerned to investigate only the likely hypotheses. If we spent more time developing hypotheses that violate Ockham's razor then it would be seen just how counterintuitive it is to deny the principle. In addition, the problem with all actual debates is that there is so often a counterargument from tradition or authority and the result of that is to make us reluctant to believe there are no things of the kind in question rather than suspend judgement. For instance, I think many philosophers are reluctant to believe there are no numbers because of their respect for the authority of mathematicians such as Kurt Gödel, who was convinced of their reality. Rather than debate the force of such appeals to authority it is better to present an example of the pure use of Ockham's razor, unsullied by such considerations, so as to show just how strange it would be to deny it. My first example is one of a number of *mongrel world* examples: the hypothesis is that the *world*, meaning all that is actual, contains parts (universes) in some of which materialism is correct but not idealism, and in others idealism but not materialism, and there are no dualist universes. I invite you to grant that my mongrel world hypothesis is one that any sensible person would dismiss as almost certainly false rather than suspend judgement about.

My other example is that of non-reductive pluralism, the position that there are many kinds of entity, none of which are more basic or fundamental than any other. These kinds might include those listed in (4) above, including persons, living organisms, inanimate macroscopic objects, subatomic particles, properties, relations, sets and numbers. I claim that there is a *prima facie* convincing argument from Ockham's razor against non-reductive pluralism, and that it would be silly to respond by suspending judgement.

Another objection to Ockham's razor arises from its seeming arrogance. Who are we to say there are not fundamental kinds of thing that we have never, and perhaps never will, think about? To that I reply that Ockham's razor applies primarily to any one given proposed kind of entity. But rejecting weird cases one by one is quite compatible with either suspending judgement about or even believing that there are many weird things going on. It is probable that the improbable happens on occasion.

Other razors

Here are some other razors, named more loosely than Ockham's: you can, no doubt, add to the list.

Hume's razor: necessities are not to be multiplied more than is necessary

In the case of modalities, simplicity is obtained either by minimising possibilities, and hence maximising necessities, or vice versa. It is the latter, which I call Hume's razor, that is intuitive. He assumed that the only necessities were conceptual ones, truths we understand the meaning of but just cannot grasp how things would be if they were false. To these we might add Kripkean necessities, where whatever is true at the actual world must, of conceptual necessity, be true at other, non-actual, worlds. Familiar examples in the literature are "Hesperus is the same planet as Phosphorus" and "Water is H_2O." Philosophers such as David Chalmers (1996: 136–8) treat all other proposed sorts of necessity as relative: something is necessary in this relative sense if it follows by strict necessity from some highly pervasive feature of the world. There are, however, mongrel world examples that show, I think, that some of these pervasive features are themselves necessary. Could there be a world composed of two otherwise similar universes, in one of which there are numbers but in the other there are none? No doubt, you reply that this is a silly question because if there are numbers they are not the sort of thing that could be localised to one of two universes. Quite so! But in that case I submit you are claiming as necessary a pervasive feature of reality, namely the non-localisability of numbers. In Chalmers' terminology such pervasive necessities are called *strong*.

Hume's razor may then be explicated as the injunction not to multiply strong necessities, bearing in mind the free-lunch principle that if some strong necessities explain others we do not have to count the others. For example if it is necessary that numbers are not localisable then it is necessary that it is necessary – and necessary that it is necessary that it is necessary, etc. – that they are not localisable, but this is not an additional cost.

An example in recent literature concerns David Lewis' thesis that an actual thing is just a possible thing that is spatiotemporally related to us (1986: Ch. 1). It follows that the actual world is not composed of two or more universes that are spatiotemporally unrelated. For on his theory, these universes would count as different possible worlds, so both could not be actual. "Whoever thought there was actually another universe spatiotemporally unrelated to ours?", you might ask. But Lewis' account of actuality has the further consequence that *necessarily* there are no two universes that are spatiotemporally unrelated to each other, because a "possible world" with two separated universes would not be one possible world but two. Rival theories of possibility do not have this consequence. Therefore Lewis multiplied necessities more than is necessary. Or so his opponents would say. Like all the other razor arguments this invites the response that the defect in question is outweighed by the other advantages of the hypothesis.

Leibniz's razor: brute facts are not to be multiplied more than is necessary

By a *brute* fact I mean one without further explanation. I call this Leibniz's razor because he is the best-known advocate of the principle of sufficient reason, the assertion that there are no brute facts. I could have called it Hudson's razor (see Hudson 2005: 12–13), but there are reasons for not naming anything after someone alive. One fact that even I, a Leibniz sympathiser, accept as brute is that there is something rather than nothing. That is to multiply brute facts – but not more than is necessary!

Among those who multiply brute facts even more but plead necessity, there is a tendency to restrict brutishness to the existence of various things: abstract objects (numbers, universals, real *possibilia*), God, the Universe; and laws of nature, for instance. If we thus restrict brute facts to existential ones, they can be kept to a minimum by Ockham's razor, and we might decide that we do not need Leibniz's razor as stated but instead claim that everything can be understood in principle in terms of what exists. Call this the existential understanding principle. It may in turn be derived from the truthmaker principle, which, in a weak version due to John Bigelow (1988: 123–34), states that all truths supervene on existential facts. The derivation requires the hypothesis that the supervenience in question is of the less fundamental on the more fundamental.

Should we, then, replace Leibniz's razor with the existential understanding principle? That replacement has, among other consequences, the following. There is no need to explain the non-existence of a kind of thing. Consider ghost-stuff, or ectoplasm, a form of subtle matter, portions of which have shape and size but which is not composed of particles. By Ockham's razor we should believe there is no ectoplasm unless its existence helps us understand what we experience. Should we also prefer a hypothesis that explains why there is no ectoplasm over one that just treats that as a brute fact? I suspect that intuitions vary in this case. Perhaps, then, you might decide that Leibniz's razor is redundant and to be replaced by Ockham's razor, existential understanding, and, I would add, Hume's razor. I argue below that redundancy does not matter, however, when it comes to razor arguments.

Reid's razor: counterintuitive theses are not to be proposed more than is necessary

This is not an appeal to simplicity, but is nonetheless a useful metaphysical razor, even though it might seem like an appeal to intuition to justify intuition. Its point is to commend the middle ground between rusted-on common sense and accepting everything that is advocated by orthodox science. The idea is that because science is ultimately based on intuitions we should not despise intuition on scientific grounds but that this does not stop us violating a few intuitions – as few as we can – if they conflict with science. Reid's razor is, I say, flagrantly ignored by popular expositors of science who measure their success in "Wow!" decibels. When it comes to the interpretation of general relativity and quantum theory Reid's razor might incline us towards more conservative interpretations *if* – a big "if" – they are otherwise adequate. Flat Universers are not Flat Earthers, and – beautiful though Hilbert spaces are – correct physics might just have something to do with particles, each with precise position and momentum.

Mill's razor: hypotheses should not be multiplied more than is necessary

I call this Mill's razor because it underlies the use of Mill's methods. The idea is that we should not propose one hypothesis to explain something and then propose another to explain something else if one of the two serves both explanatory purposes. As such it is an expression of the appeal to simplicity. Metaphysicians seldom violate Mill's razor – if anything being reluctant to posit enough hypotheses – but hypochondriacs often do.

Razors versus simplicity

"Razors are not to be multiplied more than is necessary," I hear you say. I disagree, for I am not suggesting that any of them are fundamental principles of a systematic theory of probable reasoning. Nor am I suggesting that someone capable of exquisite judgements of comparative simplicity need rely upon them when reasoning in private. They serve a useful purpose, however, when the attempt to use inference to the best explanation just results in disagreement about which explanation is best. What razor arguments do is to isolate a respect in which one hypothesis is better than another, rather than leaving the discussion with a subjective assessment of overall worth. And we have established something important if we can agree that there is a defect in a certain respect, for instance that Lewis' account of actuality does multiply necessities more than is necessary. Of course Lewis argued that his theory was better in other respects.

It could happen, though, that you prefer hypothesis A, which is clearly superior to hypothesis B in one or more respects but not clearly inferior in any. Then your opponent, who prefers hypothesis B, may still insist that all things considered hypothesis B is better. Often your opponent will insist that hypothesis B is *simpler* overall. There are, however, no procedures for deciding just which of two hypotheses is the simpler. For that reason the razors are not redundant. They provide us with the rules for debate. Thus, if your opponents argue that hypothesis B is simpler, without exhibiting a respect of simplicity they are committed to claiming a superior capacity to judge between theories. Well, we are not all equal when it comes to judging the overall worth of theories, so your opponents might perhaps be right. I appeal, however, to a razor from epistemology (Bacon's razor): "Do not multiply claims of superiority more than is necessary."

One advantage, then, in using razor arguments, rather than appealing to simplicity, is that the former are more objective in the sense that there is wide agreement as to when a razor, especially Ockham's is applicable. We all agree that Ockham's razor, if accepted, puts the burden of argument on those who defend the following: theism (as opposed to atheism); realism about properties and relations (as opposed to nominalism); realism about the subject matter of mathematics; realism about space–time (as opposed to the relational theory that seeks to paraphrase truths about space–time in terms of truths about spatiotemporal relations between objects); and realism about non-actual things, such as merely possible worlds. To be sure in all these cases a defence can be made, ones I myself consider successful, but at least the razor establishes the rules for subsequent discussion.

References

Armstrong, D. M. (1983) *What Is a Law of Nature?* Cambridge: Cambridge University Press.

Bigelow, John (1988) *The Reality of Numbers: A Physicalist's Philosophy of Mathematics*, Oxford: Clarendon Press.

Chalmers, David (1996) *The Conscious Mind: In Search of a Fundamental Theory*, New York: Oxford University Press.

Colyvan, Mark (2001) *The Indispensability of Mathematics*, New York: Oxford University Press.

Dretske, Fred (1977) "Laws of Nature," *Philosophy of Science* 44: 248–68.

Field, Hartry (1980) *Science without Numbers: A Defence of Nominalism*, Princeton, NJ: Princeton University Press.

Gosse, Phillip (1857) *Omphalos: An Attempt to Untie the Geological Knot*, London: John Van Voorst.

Hudson, Hud (2006) *Metaphysics of Hyperspace*, Oxford: Clarendon Press.

Jeffreys, H. (1961) *The Theory of Probability*, Oxford: Clarendon Press.

Lewis, David (1986) *On the Plurality of Worlds*, Oxford: Blackwell.

Sober, Elliott (2005) "Parsimony," in Sahotra Sarkar and Jessica Pfeifer (eds), *The Philosophy of Science: An Encyclopedia*, London: Routledge, 531–41.

Tooley, Michael (1977) "The Nature of Laws," *Canadian Journal of Philosophy* 7: 667–98.

van Fraassen, Bas C. (1980) *The Scientific Image*, Oxford: Clarendon Press.

Further reading

An excellent encyclopedia article on the general topic of simplicity is Alan Baker, "Simplicity," Edward N. Zalta (ed.), *The Stanford Encyclopedia of Philosophy* (available: http://plato.stanford.edu/entries/simplicity/). Peter Lipton, *Inference to the Best Explanation*, 2nd edn (London: Routledge, 2004) is the classic on inference to the best explanation. See also Elliott Sober, "Parsimony," in Sahotra Sarkar and Jessica Pfeifer (eds), *The Philosophy of Science: An Encyclopedia* (London: Routledge, 2005), pp. 531–41. Elliott Sober is an acknowledged expert on simplicity, especially in evolutionary theory and statistics; this article also exhibits his queasiness as a naturalist invoking simplicity. Paul Vincent Spade, "William of Ockham," in Edward N. Zalta (ed.), *The Stanford Encyclopedia of Philosophy* (available: http://plato.stanford.edu/entries/ockham/) is a good source for checking the historical origins of Ockham's razor.

25

SUBSTANCE

David Robb

A substance is a basic being, something at reality's foundation. What exactly this means is a matter of some controversy, one of several challenges the concept of substance presents. But even this simple definition reveals the topic's importance to metaphysics. Any attempt to discern the fundamental categories of being – a task of ontology – must inquire into the existence and nature of the most basic beings. And if there are substances, they will play an important explanatory role, for the most general structure and character of the world will rest on the nature of its foundation.

In thinking of substance as a basic being, I am picking up only one strand, albeit a dominant one, in the long and sometimes tangled history of the concept (Simons 1998; Robinson 2004), a history that goes back to the beginnings of Western philosophy in ancient Greece. Virtually all of the metaphysicians in the Western canon have something to say about reality's most fundamental beings, even if they do not always use "substance" to label them. Indeed, one source of the difficulties surrounding substance is that sometimes the term is used in other ways. For example, some philosophers think of a substance as an ultimate subject, something that *has* properties but is not itself a property of anything. This conception of substance can be found in Aristotle's *Categories* as well as Locke's *Essay* (at, e.g., Bk 2, ch. 23). A substance of this sort may be an ordinary object – a table, a human body, a planet – or, a bit more mysteriously, it may a component of an ordinary object, a *substratum* supporting the object's properties. Whether "substances" in this sense are also basic beings is an open question, and the answer turns on a number of difficult issues, some of which I will address in this entry. In any case, my focus throughout will be on substances conceived as (stipulated to be) basic beings. Whether the basic beings are ultimate subjects or something else is a matter for metaphysics to decide.

In what follows, it will be useful to divide the problem of substance into three questions. First is the question of *criteria*: What is it to be basic? What criteria must something meet to be at reality's foundation? Second is the question of *existence*: Are there any substances? It could turn out that once the criteria for being basic are made clear, nothing meets them. Alternatively, perhaps there must be substances: reality necessarily includes basic beings. Third is the question of *identification*: Supposing there are substances, which beings are they? Are they ordinary objects, such as tables and chairs, or more exotic entities, such as fundamental particles? Or might there be just one substance, such as the universe itself?

Criteria

Start with the most fundamental of these questions: What is it to be basic? In what sense are substances at reality's foundation? As a way of getting a handle on this question, consider first some beings that *prima facie* are *not* basic:

- *Trends*: There is currently a trend toward using more computer technology in the classroom. This trend is responsible for increased technology budgets at universities. But a trend doesn't look like a basic being, something at reality's foundation. Rather, as we might put it, a trend just consists of the various activities of individuals, institutions and the like.
- *Crowds*: A large crowd gathers on the National Mall in Washington, DC. The roar of the crowd can be heard miles away. Is this crowd a basic being? It seems not. After all, a crowd is nothing over and above some gathered people. If you were to list all of the relevant occupants of the Mall that day, you would list all of the people, one by one. But once you had done this, there would be no need to add "crowd" to the list.
- *Holes*: There is a hole in my left sock. I know this because I can feel it, and it was partly responsible for my getting a blister when I went jogging today. Nevertheless, it would be odd to think of a hole as a basic being. Rather, for there to be a hole in my sock is just for my sock to be torn a certain way. The hole exists, that is, but only in virtue of my sock's being torn.
- *Waves*: Surfers ride waves, and some waves are able to capsize sailboats. But is a wave basic, part of reality's foundation? Apparently not, for a wave is just the way some water is at a certain time. As we might put it, for there to be a wave (noun) on the ocean is just for the ocean to wave (verb). That's all there is to waves.

This is a motley list, to be sure, and there are others items one might add to it (Hestevold 1999). But this will do for present purposes. If these things aren't basic, why not?

One tradition has it that such questions should get *semantic* answers (Kneale 1939–40). Say that statements about *F*s can be "replaced by" statements about *G*s just in case the former can be translated into (or paraphrased by) the latter. So, for example, what we say about trends – e.g., "The trend is waning" – can, it seems, be replaced by a complex of statements only about the activities of individuals and institutions: trends needn't be explicitly mentioned at all. Similarly, perhaps anything we'd say about a hole can be replaced by statements about the object that has the hole. A substance, then, will be basic in the sense that statements about it *cannot* be replaced. For example, one brand of phenomenalism has it that sense-data are basic in this way: while anything we might say about the physical world can be translated into statements about momentary experiences, statements about the experiences themselves are semantically primitive.

Phenomenalism faces serious difficulties (Armstrong 1961: Chs 5–6), but to look at these would take us too far afield. More relevant to present purposes is whether semantic irreplaceability is the best way to understand basicness and thus substance. And the answer appears to be no. For one thing, translating or paraphrasing statements about non-basic beings has proved in some cases to be intractable. It's not at all clear, for example, that what we say about holes can be replaced by statements about ordinary objects such as socks (Lewis and Lewis 1970), or that what we say about trends can be replaced by statements about the activities of individuals and institutions. So it looks as if holes and trends have to count as substances on the present view, and this is the wrong result. Even setting aside such difficulties, there is a more fundamental problem: Translation is a relation among statements, while the basicness that concerns us is ontological, a feature of things in the world, whether or not it's reflected in our ways of speaking and thinking. So, for example, even if the phenomenalist were successfully to translate our talk about the physical world into a sense-datum language, this would say more about us – our conceptual scheme, our ordinary language – than about the world. Why should the structure of reality mirror these semantic relations? Metaphysics requires that we go deeper than this (see Dyke [2007] for discussion).

If semantic irreplaceability won't capture what it is to be basic, what will? Reflection on our list of non-basic beings provides a clue: all of them exist because something else does. A trend *consists of* the activities of individuals and institutions; a crowd is *nothing over and above* some gathered people; the hole in my sock exists *only in virtue of* my sock's being torn a certain way; a wave on the ocean *is just* some water waving. The italicized phrases attempt to get at the sense in which these things are not basic. And there are other more philosophical-sounding locutions one might use: the non-basic items have *borrowed reality* (Adams 1994: 335); they are *ontological parasites, not entities in their own right* (Chisholm 1976: 51). However one puts it, the idea is that a substance is not like this. A substance is not a parasite, does not have borrowed reality; a substance is a being in its own right.

Now these are just slogans: they do not amount to a theory of basicness. But they do point in the right direction, and this is toward a criterion of ontological *independence*. Such an understanding of basicness has a long history (Woolhouse 1993), and it looks promising. First, the dependence of some beings, and the independence of others, is a feature of reality itself, not merely of our language or concepts. Second, dependence and independence can secure the explanatory role for substance mentioned in the opening paragraph: What's basic should somehow explain what's non-basic. If the world has an ontological foundation, and if this metaphor is to have any meaning, then the whole of non-basic reality should somehow *rest* on it. If non-basicness is understood as dependence, and basicness as independence, we have taken one step closer to understanding this explanatory role of substance.

Now it may turn out, a bit disappointingly, that dependence and independence cannot be defined in any philosophically illuminating way. In that case, we would need to rest content with our examples and the slogans they inspire: dependent beings have borrowed reality, are ontological parasites, and so on, while independent beings (substances) are not like this. This would not be a disaster: these rough, intuitive notions may still be useful when addressing the questions of existence and identification. Alternatively, we might attempt informative definitions of dependence and independence (for discussion, see Lowe 1998: Ch. 6; Hoffman and Rosenkrantz 1997: Ch. 2). Such a project is beyond the scope of this entry, but it's worth briefly exploring a couple of strategies.

Start with a simple *modal* account: x is a dependent being just in case there's some y distinct from x such that necessarily, if x exists, then y does. The dependent beings – the ontological parasites – are those that require (necessitate) something distinct from themselves, while the independent beings are those that don't. Put another way, it's the ability to exist alone that's essential to being independent, and thus a substance. This gives the right result with our earlier examples of non-basic beings: A trend in higher education could not exist without various institutions (universities, etc.), but the trend is not the same as those institutions; the hole in my sock could not exist without my sock, but hole and sock are distinct; and so on.

Nevertheless, I doubt this simple modal account will do. One problem is that it precludes there being two necessarily existing substances – two gods, say – for if there were, each would necessitate the other, making each dependent, at least on the current modal understanding of dependence. I don't know if there could be two gods (or even one), but an account of basicness shouldn't rule them out. That is, however we spell out dependence and independence, the account should be general enough not to legislate on such a controversial issue as whether there could be two gods. *Prima facie*, there is no incoherence in such an idea, and the criteria for basicness should respect this. And in any case, there's a more general problem with a modal understanding of dependence. Modal relations are superficial: when they hold, it's in virtue of some deeper fact (Heil 1998). To define dependence in modal terms just invites a further question of *why* such modal relations hold. If a trend necessitates some institutions, or if a hole necessitates an object (such as a sock), we will still want to know what grounds this modal relation. And this looks like the problem we started with, the problem of understanding dependence. None of this is to say that modality will be useless for such a project – it's just that modal relations cannot be the whole story.

It is here that the "ultimate subject" understanding of substance mentioned earlier may enter the picture. Suppose we take the relation between a property and its subject to be the paradigm case of ontological dependence. To be an ontological parasite is to be a property of something else. An independent being, in turn, is not a property: it's an ultimate subject. Here ultimate subjects and basic beings coincide. Such a proposal allows for two necessarily existing substances: while each necessitates the other, neither is a property of the other. And by making the property–subject relation the relevant sort of dependence, the account begins to fill in the ontological details that a bare modal account lacks. Granted, it's not clear whether this proposal fits our earlier examples of dependent beings – Is a crowd a property of the people in it? Is the hole in my sock a property of the sock? – but perhaps the property–subject relation can be stretched to cover such cases.

Existence

However we end up explaining independence, we must confront our second question: Are there substances, so conceived? Maybe nothing qualifies: nothing is ontologically independent, a being in its own right.

Substance-denial can take a number of forms. The most extreme refuses to countenance the existence of anything at all; *a fortiori*, there are no substances. This particular
brand of nihilism has few adherents if any, however, and in any case would seem to be
quickly refuted by Descartes's *cogito*, on which I am certain that there is at least one
thing, namely myself (*Meditations*, Meditation 2). But even if *cogito*-style reasoning is
sound, it shows only that I exist. It does not show that I am a substance. A substance-
denier, then, may grant that something exists, but deny that there are any basic beings.
Reality on this view has no bedrock; nothing exists in its own right. The world is
instead a network of beings, each parasitic on other elements of the network. The
chains of ontological dependence in the network may eventually circle back on
themselves, resulting in a raft-like structure, or they might extend endlessly, resulting
in an infinite hierarchy of dependent beings. (One might object here that there's still
at least one substance on such a view, namely the network itself. But the network is
parasitic on its members, just as they are parasitic on each other.)

Such a picture of reality appears to be coherent, but it is nevertheless very implausible. One way to counter it – to show that there are substances – would be to point
to something we already have good grounds for believing in, and then show that it is
an independent being. In this case, the questions of existence and identification
would be answered at once. This is how Hume, for example, might proceed. While
Hume is skeptical of substance on a certain understanding of it, he's happy to allow
that perceptions – objects of our direct awareness – are substances in the sense that
they are ontologically independent (*Treatise*, Bk 1, pt 4, §5). Or consider Descartes,
who thinks he has grounds for believing that God, a perfect being, exists (*Meditations*,
Meditations 3, 5). Since independence is a perfection – to be a parasite would be a
limitation, a defect – Descartes has reason to believe that there is at least one
substance. In either of these cases, it would be useful to show as well that the substance
in question plays the appropriate explanatory role, that the non-substantial world in
some way rests on the substantial. Not surprisingly, then, Hume's view is friendly to a
form of phenomenalism, and Descartes believes – as do most traditional theists – that
everything depends on God.

If we cannot present to the substance-denier a clear example of a basic being, there
is an alternative strategy available. The idea is to postpone questions of identification
and try to show on general grounds that there must be substances, whatever they end
up being. Consider this line of argument: If a substance is independent, a being in its
own right, then existence is built into its very nature, its essence. This is the mark of a
necessary being, so a substance could not fail to exist. There are clear affinities here to
the ontological argument for God's existence, though there's no claim in this case that
a substance has any of the "personal" divine attributes, such as omnipotence or omniscience. Nevertheless, this argument, like the ontological argument, has problems. At
most it shows that *if* a substance exists, then existence is part of its essence. But whether
there is such a thing is the very point in dispute. Moreover, it's not at all clear that the
sort of independence required for being a substance precludes *causal* dependence – and
thus contingency – on some other being. Why couldn't a being in its own right have
been produced by something else? If this is possible, then a substance might very well

be contingent. In any case, this delicate issue is more properly addressed with the earlier question of criteria.

Another argument for substance, with an equally distinguished history, deserves more attention. It has some affinities with versions of the cosmological argument for God's existence, but again, there need be nothing divine about substance for the argument to succeed. The substance-denier, we're assuming, grants that something exists, but insists that everything is an ontological parasite. However, this looks impossible: A dependent being exists only in virtue of something else, "passing the buck" of existence. If this buck were passed without end, the regress would be vicious. So if nothing existed in its own right, if nothing were a substance, then nothing would exist at all (see Lowe 1998: 158, 171). (We here target an infinite hierarchy of parasitic beings, but similar remarks could be made against the "raft" conception of reality.)

Regress arguments of this sort are difficult to evaluate, but a structurally similar case will help to bring out their intuitive appeal. Suppose I am given a job to do, such as sweeping the floor. I "accomplish" this task by assigning it to my subordinate. But instead of sweeping the floor, my subordinate assigns the same task to his subordinate, and so on. Suppose this passing of the job proceeds *ad infinitum*. Even if the infinite series of assignments could be completed – suppose each takes half the time of the previous – it seems clear that the floor would not be swept. Since no one in the series does the sweeping – sweeps in his own right, so to speak – the job never gets done. The example seems relevantly like the regress of ontological parasites, except the "job" for them is simply existing. But the point remains: if existence were continually passed from one ontological parasite to the next, if nothing did the job (existed) in its own right, then nothing would exist at all.

One might object that the passing of orders takes time while the ontological dependence of a parasite is typically synchronic. It's not clear this is a relevant difference, however, and in any case, we can remove it by supposing that all of the sweeping orders are somehow given at once; even so, the floor still wouldn't get swept. A second objection says the sweeping analogy fails in a much deeper way: Existence is not an "accomplishment" or "job" to be done like sweeping. (And, the objector may add, the earlier metaphor of "borrowed reality" is similarly misleading.) To evaluate this worry would put us back into the question of criteria. If the existence of a non-basic being is *not* relevantly similar to a job that's passed to something else, then how are we to understand the parasitic nature of what's non-basic?

Identification

If the regress argument is sound, then there must be substances, independent beings. What are they? Which beings are fundamental in the required sense? At this point many options present themselves. They are the beings that would appear in any history of metaphysics: Plato's forms, Epicurus', atoms, Spinoza's God/nature, Leibniz's monads, Hume's perceptions, and many more. But a catalog of the options is not likely to be too useful for present purposes. So instead of attempting to single out the substances, I will explore a more general question of identification: Can a substance have parts? Answering this will not identify the substances definitively, but it may help to narrow the list of candidates.

It seems that a substance cannot have parts. After all, a complex object exists because its parts do. For example, a chair exists only because its legs, seat, and back exist (and are arranged a certain way). A complex object, then, isn't a substance, for a substance exists in its own right, not because something else does. So a substance must be simple, that is, without parts. An argument such as this seems to have moved Leibniz (Adams 1994: 334–5). Substances on his view are monads: simple, mind-like entities on which everything else in nature somehow depends. But whether or not substances are monads, the simplicity of substance is worth exploring. Is the above argument sound? It turns on two premises about parts and wholes.

The first premise says that a complex object exists because its parts do. On first glance, this looks self-evident. Indeed, the relation between a whole and its parts may be one of our clearest examples of parasitic existence, of borrowed reality. However, there are reasons to proceed slowly. For one thing, sometimes a whole can survive a loss of parts: the chair would still exist if it lost one of its legs, or if its seat were reupholstered. This seems to give complex objects a sort of autonomy over their parts. But this point is not especially damaging to the first premise. After all, a trend can survive the loss of one of its adherents, but trends are nevertheless clearly parasitic on the activities of such people. The fact that complex objects can lose or exchange their parts may call for refinement in the first premise, but we need not abandon it.

A more interesting challenge to the premise comes from examples in which, apparently, the parts of something depend on the whole they compose, reversing the normal direction of dependence. This seems to be how Aristotle understands the functional parts of living things (Gill 1989: 126–30). On his view, a hand depends for its identity, and so its existence, on the living body of which it is a part. If there is borrowed reality here, Aristotle would say, it comes from the whole and is bestowed on the part, not the other way around. Aristotle's position turns on some difficult elements of his metaphysics, but there are simpler examples making a similar point. An *eddy* is part of a river, but it nevertheless seems to be parasitic on the river, not the other way around (Campbell 1976: 30). The *top half* of an apple is a part of it, but couldn't exist without the apple (Lowe 1998: 162). Such examples deserve more attention than I can given them here, but I'll say this much: in cases such as the hand, the eddy, and the top half, there is a danger of confusing conceptual dependence with ontological dependence. We may not be able to think of a hand *as a hand* without thinking of it as part of a living body. Nevertheless, the body seems to be ontologically parasitic on the hand, among other parts. Something similar could be said about the eddy and the top half. If this is right, then the conceptual order of dependence, at least here, reverses the ontological order.

Consider now a second premise implicit in the argument: If something exists because its parts do, then it's not basic, doesn't exist in its own right. This premise also seems to be self-evident. No object is identical with any of its (proper) parts, and so if an object exists because its parts do, it is parasitic on something else and therefore not a substance.

However, while an object is distinct from its parts, it is not *wholly* distinct from them. A part of an object is, so to speak, bound up with the being of that object. And so it's not obvious that when an object depends on its own parts, this makes the object a parasitic being, disqualifying it from being a substance. Leibniz, for one, would not be moved by these doubts about the second premise. Through a spokesperson in one of his dialogues, Leibniz remarks, with characteristic color, "What does it matter whether the worm gnawing at me is within me or outside of me? Am I any less dependent on it?" (*Monadology*, in Leibniz 1989: 262). Such a reaction seems justified, especially when we consider our earlier examples of non-basic beings: While the water of a wave may not be, in any ordinary sense, part of the wave, the water is clearly *in* the wave. Despite this – in fact, *because* of it – the wave is a parasitic being. And more simply, a crowd is parasitic on its members; the fact that the members are parts of the crowd doesn't change this.

If substances must be simple, this will help with identification. It encourages, for example, some version of the ancient doctrine of atomism. While the true atoms of the world are no doubt quite unlike what Democritus or Epicurus ever imagined, the leading idea is the same: at the foundation of reality are simple beings. This still leaves open a variety of options, from the fundamental particles of modern physics to Leibniz's monads. It does, however, rule out at least some candidates. For example, the universe itself, which Spinoza identified as the *only* substance ("God" or "nature"), would appear to be excluded, since the universe has many parts. Spinoza apparently believed that God/nature is indivisible (*Ethics*, Pt 1, propositions 12–13), but his arguments turn on his own controversial metaphysical doctrines.

The simplicity of substance would also exclude ordinary objects from the category of substance, for tables, human bodies, planets and the like have parts. Earlier I said that basic beings and ultimate subjects may coincide, though now they seem to be coming apart. Ordinary objects, after all, look like ultimate subjects of properties, yet because they are complex, they are not ontologically independent, and so not basic beings. We might try to bring ultimate subjects and basic beings back into line by denying that ordinary objects really are ultimate subjects. Perhaps instead, ordinary objects are themselves properties of their parts. This would, no doubt, require some changes in how we usually think of objects, but revision of our ordinary thinking may be an inevitable consequence of metaphysics.

References

Adams, R. M. (1994) *Leibniz: Determinist, Theist, Idealist*, New York: Oxford University Press.

Armstrong, D. M. (1961) *Perception and the Physical World*, London: Routledge & Kegan Paul.

Campbell, K. (1976) *Metaphysics: An Introduction*, Encino, CA: Dickenson.

Chisholm, R. M. (1976) *Person and Object: A Metaphysical Study*, La Salle, IL: Open Court.

Dyke, H. (2007) *Metaphysics and the Representational Fallacy*, London: Routledge.

Gill, M. L. (1989) *Aristotle on Substance: The Paradox of Unity*, Princeton, NJ: Princeton University Press.

Heil, J. (1998) "Supervenience Deconstructed," *European Journal of Philosophy* 6: 146–55.

Hestevold, H. S. (1999) "Dependent Particulars: Holes, Boundaries, and Surfaces," in S. D. Hales (ed.), *Metaphysics: Contemporary Readings*, Belmont, CA: Wadsworth, pp. 415–23.

Hoffman, J. and Rosenkrantz, G. S. (1997) *Substance: Its Nature and Existence*, London: Routledge.

Kneale, W. (1939–40) "The Notion of a Substance," *Proceedings of the Aristotelian Society* 40: 103–34.

Leibniz, G. W. (1989) *Philosophical Essays*, edited, trans. by R. Ariew and D. Garber, Indianapolis, IN: Hackett.

Lewis, D. and Lewis, S. (1970) "Holes," *Australasian Journal of Philosophy* 48: 206–12; reprinted in D. Lewis, *Philosophical Papers*, vol. I, New York: Oxford University Press, 1983.

Lowe, E. J. (1998) *The Possibility of Metaphysics: Substance, Identity, and Time*, Oxford: Clarendon Press.

Robinson, H. (2004) "Substance," in E. N. Zalta (ed.), *The Stanford Encyclopedia of Philosophy*; available: http://plato.stanford.edu/entries/substance/

Simons, P. M. (1998) "Farewell to Substance: A Differentiated Leave-Taking," *Ratio* 11: 235–52.

Woolhouse, R. S. (1993) *Descartes, Spinoza, Leibniz: The Concept of Substance in Seventeenth-Century Metaphysics*, London: Routledge.

Further reading

For a clear, accessible introduction to Aristotle's views on substance, see C. Shields, *Aristotle* (London: Routledge, 2007) especially chapters 4 and 6; a version of the "sweeping regress" is on p. 282. Leibniz's views on substance can be found in G. W. Leibniz, *Philosophical Essays*, eds. and trans. R. Ariew and D. Garber (Indianapolis, IN: Hackett, 1989); see especially the *Discourse on Metaphysics* (Ch. 8), selections from the correspondence with Arnauld (Ch. 9), and the *Monadology* (Ch. 29). S. Levey, "On Unity: Leibniz-Arnauld Revisited," *Philosophical Topics* 31 (2003): 245–75, is a philosophically rich discussion of the Leibniz-Arnauld correspondence on substance. Contemporary views on substance include the following. States of affairs (fact-like entities) are basic beings: D. M. Armstrong, *A World of States of Affairs* (Cambridge: Cambridge University Press, 1997). Tropes (particularized properties) are basic beings: K. Campbell, "The Metaphysic of Abstract Particulars," *Midwest Studies in Philosophy* 6 (1981): 477–88. The cosmos is the one basic being: J. Schaffer, "Monism: The Priority of the Whole," *Philosophical Review* (forthcoming).

26
INTRINSIC AND EXTRINSIC PROPERTIES

Ross P. Cameron

Introduction

Consider two of my properties: my mass and my weight. There seems to be an interesting distinction between the reasons for my having these two properties. I have my mass solely in virtue of how I am, whereas I have my weight in virtue of both how I am and how my surroundings are. I have my weight as a result of the gravitational pull exerted by the Earth on a thing having my mass, whereas I have my mass independently of other things around me. If you change my surroundings, if you put me on the moon say, my weight will change, but my mass will stay the same.

We mark this distinction between properties by saying that mass is an *intrinsic* property, whereas weight is an *extrinsic* property. Intrinsic properties are those that an object has solely in virtue of how it is, independently of its surroundings. Extrinsic properties are those that are not intrinsic. My having a hand is intrinsic to me but my having a wife is extrinsic. Extrinsic properties include *being the tallest person* and *being watched by a Scotsman*, since having those properties depends on there not being someone taller, or there being a nosy Scot, in your surroundings. Intrinsic properties include properties like *being charged* and are also generally thought to include shape properties like *being square*.[1]

It is common to distinguish between global and local intrinsicness (see Humberstone 1996). A property is *locally* intrinsic to a particular thing if that thing has that property intrinsically, but it may be that other objects have that property extrinsically. For example, being such that there are dogs is plausibly locally intrinsic to every dog, but it is definitely not intrinsic to anything that is not a dog. Globally intrinsic properties, by contrast, are intrinsic to any possible thing that has them: they cannot be had extrinsically.

The distinction at work

To give an idea of the importance of the distinction I will illustrate its usage in a few key areas of metaphysics.

Change

I have undergone change during my lifetime. My mass used to be different from what it now is, as did my hair-colour. I also used to be such that the Berlin wall separated East Germany from West Germany, and I used to be such that a woman was the prime minister of the United Kingdom, yet I am these things no longer. But when I say *I* have changed it is my losing the former properties and not the latter ones that seems relevant. Why? Because the former are properties that are intrinsic to me, whereas the latter are extrinsic: I have "changed" in my being such that the Berlin wall exists not in virtue of undergoing any intrinsic change but purely in virtue of my surroundings changing. This seems to be an important distinction, and philosophers have marked the distinction by calling change in intrinsic properties *real change* and change solely in extrinsic properties *mere Cambridge change* (Geach 1969).

The problem of temporary intrinsics

The indiscernibility of identicals, also known as Leibniz's law, says that if *a* and *b* are identical then anything that is true of *a* is true of *b*. This is probably the most uncontroversial principle in philosophy, but despite its overwhelming plausibility it is not obvious how its truth is to be reconciled with the obvious fact that things change in their intrinsic properties over time. This is the problem of temporary intrinsics. Since the person currently (at time t^*) typing at his computer is identical to a certain child who is out playing (at time t), everything that is true of the former is true of the latter. But the child appears to have less mass than the person doing the typing; the child has light hair whereas the typist has dark hair; the child is (let us suppose) standing while the typist is sitting. These properties are incompatible: nothing can both have a mass m and have some greater mass, nothing can have both light hair and dark hair; nothing can be both standing and sitting. So how can the child and the typist be one and the same person?

Notice that the problem depends upon the persisting thing undergoing *real* change, a change in intrinsic properties, rather than undergoing mere Cambridge change. For suppose we put the problem thus: the child is not such that he has a wife, yet the typist is, so how can they be identical? The response seems obvious. All that is true of the child is that he does not have a wife *at time t*; but that is equally true of the typist. It is true of the typist that he has a wife *now*, at time t^*; but it is also true of the child that he has a wife at time t^*, he just didn't have a wife *then*. The problem arises in the case of intrinsic properties because an object does not seem to have its intrinsic properties relative to some time. Intuitively, I have the mass I have *simpliciter*; I do not have two different properties *being of mass* m *at time* t and *being of mass* m* *at time* t* (see Hawley [2001] and Sider [2001b] for discussion).

Truthmakers

Many metaphysicians have been tempted by the doctrine that (at least some important class of) true propositions are *made true* by some thing or things in the world: that truths have *truthmakers*. There has not, however, been agreement on just what truths require truthmakers, or what it takes for an object to be a truthmaker for some truth. The most popularly held view is that an object is only a truthmaker for a truth *p* if the object couldn't exist and *p* be false (see, *inter alia*, Armstrong [1997, 2004] and Fox [1987]). But truthmaker theorists are also mainly agreed that contingent predications need truthmakers, and these two doctrines together force us to make some heavy ontological commitments. Consider, for example, the truth that Socrates is snub-nosed. What makes it true? Not Socrates, if the truthmaker must necessitate the truth of the proposition, since Socrates could have existed and that proposition be false. We are forced to believe in something far more esoteric, such as the snub-nosedness of Socrates (a trope), or the state of affairs of Socrates being snub-nosed.

To avoid commitment to such things while respecting the truthmaker intuition, Josh Parsons (1999, 2005) proposed abandoning the view that the truthmaker necessitates the truth of that which it makes true. But what constrains when an object can be a truthmaker for *p* then? Parsons' answer was that an object O makes *p* true when the intrinsic nature of O suffices for the truth of *p*: that is, when the only possible worlds in which O exists and *p* is false are ones in which O has different intrinsic properties from the actual world.

Personal identity

A perennial problem in metaphysics is how to identify individuals across times and worlds. Given an object *o* existing at a time *t* (or world *w*), what makes this object identical to, or distinct from, object *o** existing at time *t** (or world *w**)? Let's focus on the temporal case. Criteria of identity across times – necessary and sufficient conditions for an object *o* at *t* to be identical to object *o** at *t** – have proven very hard to give. One big problem is that whatever criteria we lay down, it seems that there are possible situations in which two later objects bear the relevant relation to one earlier object, yet the logic of identity says that only of them can be identical to that earlier object.

For example, psychological continuity seems to be relevant to survival. Can we say, then, that it is a necessary and sufficient condition for *o** at *t** to be identical to *o* at *t* that *o* and *o** are psychologically continuous? Apparently not: it seems possible (perhaps as the result of a brain transplant) that there could be two people at *t** who are both psychologically continuous with *o*; and yet they can't both be identical to *o* unless they are both themselves identical, which they are not.

Such problems have led some (notably Parfit 1984) to a "closest-continuer" account of personal identity. The idea behind this is that it is a necessary condition for *o** to be identical to *o* that it bears the relevant continuity relation to *o*, and that it is sufficient for *o** to be identical to *o* that it bears this relation *provided* that there is no other candidate at *t** that also bears that relation to *o*.

Many have found such an account deeply unsatisfying, on the grounds that survival should be an *intrinsic* matter. On the closest-continuer account, whether or not *o* and *o** are identical does not depend just on what *o* and *o** are like but on whether or not there is something else in their surroundings which is continuous in the required sense with *o*; so whether or not *o* survives to be *o** depends on extrinsic factors concerning its surroundings, and many have found this uncomfortable.[2]

Analysis

It is all very well to make a list of paradigm intrinsic and extrinsic properties, but can we say *what it is* for a property to be intrinsic? Various attempts at analysing the concept have been given, and we will look at the most important analyses.

Intrinsicality as invariance over duplicates

David Lewis (1986: 61–2; and Langton and Lewis [1998]) defines a globally intrinsic property as one that never varies between duplicates across possible worlds (we will look at what it is for two objects to be duplicates below).

An immediate worry with Lewis' approach is that any property that is necessarily had, or necessarily lacked, by every thing will be intrinsic. If no two things can differ in whether or not they are F then, *a fortiori*, no two duplicates can differ in whether or not they are F. So, assuming that there are necessarily some abstract objects, *being such that there are abstracta* will come out as intrinsic according to this analysis. But intuitively, while this property might well be locally intrinsic to the abstracta, concrete objects have it in virtue of their surroundings containing abstract objects, and hence it should not count as globally intrinsic. Francescotti (1999) thinks this is sufficient to rule out Lewis' theory, but others, such as Sider (1993b), have been happy to reject the recalcitrant intuitions.

Another immediate consequence of this approach is that necessarily coextensive properties will either be both intrinsic or both extrinsic. If there are no two duplicates that differ in whether or not they are F, and if, as a matter of necessity, anything that is F is G and vice versa, then there are no two duplicates that differ in whether or not they are G; so F is intrinsic iff (if and only if) G is. But while *being massive* is intrinsic if anything is, *being massive or being within ten feet of a round square* might seem to be extrinsic, since whether or not something has it seems to depend on the presence or absence of round squares in the thing's near vicinity. But these properties are necessarily coextensive (since there couldn't be any round squares, something can only have the latter property if it is massive), and so both must be intrinsic or both extrinsic on Lewis' account.

Whether or not these two results seem like a reason to reject the analysis of intrinsicality as invariance over duplicates will depend largely on your favoured metaphysics of properties; in particular, it will depend on whether you think necessarily coextensive properties are identical or whether you individuate properties hyper-intensionally (which simply means that distinct properties can be necessarily coextensive). If necessarily coextensive properties are identical then neither of the above results looks bad. The latter result is obviously just what you'd expect: if F and G are identical then of course F is intrinsic iff G is – that is a straightforward consequence of Leibniz's law. And the former result becomes far less worrying as well. Sure, *being such that there are abstracta* might not wear its intrinsicality on its sleeve; but the illusion of extrinsicness only persists until you realise that this property is identical to the property *being self-identical*, which does wear its intrinsicality on its sleeve. Lewis (1986: §1.5) himself thought that the property *being F* was identical with the set of objects, in all the possible worlds, which are *F*. It follows immediately that necessarily coextensive properties are identical, so we can see why Lewis would not have thought the above consequences of his view to be problematic.

The second account of duplication

To grasp Lewis' analysis of intrinsicality we need to be told when two possible objects are duplicates. Lewis actually gave us two different definitions of duplication; we'll focus on his later definition first, which he proposed jointly with Rae Langton (Langton and Lewis 1998; cf. Zimmerman 1997) and which has received a lot of attention. The analysis relies on the thought that some properties are more natural than others. An in-depth discussion of this distinction is beyond the scope of this paper, but the idea is fairly easy to grasp: being blue is more natural than being blue before the year 2020 and being green thereafter; being charged is more natural than being charged or being a microwave oven. The natural properties are those that account for objective similarity in the world: they are the ones that "carve reality at the joints" (Lewis 1986: 59–60, 1983). The charged things all resemble one another in virtue of being charged, but there is no objective similarity uniting the things that are either charged or microwave ovens. (For a discussion of the notions of intrinsicness, naturalness and duplication see Sider [1993a].)

Langton and Lewis start from the intuitive thought that intrinsicality seems to have something to do with independence from surroundings; while the having of an extrinsic property can depend on what goes on outside of the bearer of that property, the having of an intrinsic property never depends on what things outside of the bearer are like. Indeed, the having of an intrinsic property seems not to depend even on whether or not there *are* any things outside of the bearer of the intrinsic property. This thought had led Peter Vallentyne (1997) to characterise the intrinsic properties as those that can be had by an object even if it exists unaccompanied (i.e. even if every contingent thing that exists is a part of that object), but as Lewis pointed out, this makes "being unaccompanied" an intrinsic property, when it is surely extrinsic. Lewis and Langton instead thought the crucial idea was possession of a property being *independent* of accompaniment, i.e. it can be had by an object *whether or not* it is accompanied.

A property *F* is independent of accompaniment iff the following four conditions are met:

(1) It is possible for an accompanied object to be *F*
(2) It is possible for an accompanied object to lack *F*
(3) It is possible for a lonely (i.e. unaccompanied) object to be *F*
(4) It is possible for a lonely object to lack *F*.

Now it won't do to say that what it is for a property to be intrinsic is for it to be independent of accompaniment. Consider the property *being lonely and spherical or accompanied and cubical*. This is an extrinsic property, seemingly, but it is independent of accompaniment: an accompanied cube can have it (satisfying [1]); an accompanied sphere can lack it (satisfying [2]); a lonely sphere can have it (satisfying [3]); and a lonely cube can lack it (satisfying [4]). But Langton and Lewis think that the notion of independence from accompaniment helps us define the notion of duplication. They first say that a property is *basic intrinsic* iff it is independent of accompaniment and is neither a disjunctive property nor the negation of a disjunctive property, where a disjunctive property is one that is non-natural (or at least, less natural than its disjuncts) but can be expressed by a disjunction of (conjunctions of) natural properties. The idea is that this will rule out properties such as *being lonely and spherical or accompanied and cubical*, because it will count as disjunctive. Duplicates are then taken to be things that don't differ in basic intrinsic properties, with the intrinsic properties remaining those that never vary over duplicates.

There are a number of potential problems with this analysis. Josh Parsons and Dan Marshall (Marshall and Parsons 2001) argued that the property *being such that there is a cube*, which is clearly not globally intrinsic, comes out as intrinsic on the Langton–Lewis analysis. It is independent of accompaniment: a lonely cube could have it, a lonely sphere could lack it, an accompanied cube can have it, and an accompanied sphere can lack it. And, while it has a disjunctive form, namely *being a cube or being accompanied by a cube*, neither disjunct looks more natural than the property itself, so it is not disjunctive. In that case it is basic intrinsic. But then every duplicate of a thing which is accompanied by a cube is also accompanied by a cube, which makes the property intrinsic, contrary to intuition.

Ted Sider (2001a) has argued that the Langton–Lewis analysis faces counterexamples from properties he calls *maximal properties*. A maximal property is a property F such that, roughly, large proper parts of a thing that is F are not F *because* they are *proper* parts of the thing that is F. Consider, for example, the property *being a rock*. Out of all the parts of some rock, the only part of it that has this property is the rock itself, and the reason certain of the other parts of the rock don't have this property is precisely that they are *proper* parts of the rock. *Being a rock* is a maximal property of things: it is only the largest rock part that has the property. *Being a rock* appears to come out as intrinsic according to the Langton–Lewis analysis. It is independent of accompaniment if anything is, and it does not appear to be disjunctive; hence it is intrinsic. But this looks like the wrong result, because there are proper parts of the rock that appear to lack the property *being a rock* only because there are some rock parts in their close surroundings. Consider the proper part of the rock Rock⁻, which is the rock minus a very thin outer layer of the rock's matter. Rock⁻ would be a rock if you chipped away that outer matter, and so the only thing that prevents Rock⁻ having the property *being a rock* is this outer matter surrounding it. And so the rock itself only has this property because there is no *further* layer of rocky matter surrounding it. Hence, the property *being a rock* is an extrinsic one, contrary to what the analysis says. (For further discussion, see Hawthorne [2001] and Weatherson [2001].)

The denial of necessary connections

It is worth considering the reliance of the Langton–Lewis analysis on a version of the Humean denial of necessary connections between wholly distinct contingent existents. Hume's doctrine is needed to ensure the possibility of worlds where things exist unaccompanied; if it is false then the Langton–Lewis analysis will give us some strange results. The most obvious case is if nothing can exist unaccompanied. In that case, there are no basic intrinsic properties, because clauses (3) and (4) of the definition of basic intrinsicality (above) will never be met. If there are no basic intrinsic properties, then any two possible objects are duplicates. (If there are no basic intrinsic properties then no two objects differ in their basic intrinsic properties.) In that case the only intrinsic properties will be properties had by every object as a matter of necessity, or lacked by every object as a matter of necessity. But that's obviously false. Now why might you think that no object can exist unaccompanied? Perhaps because you believe that whenever you have some thing you have the singleton of that thing, and the singleton of that singleton, and so on. Or perhaps you simply think there are limits as to how small the universe could have been. Perhaps you believe that God necessarily exists and necessarily would have created a race of intelligent creatures, but that he needn't have created the *same* creatures in each world. In that case there necessarily exists a plurality of contingent beings, and so nothing can exist unaccompanied. Now that is by no means a popular view amongst metaphysicians (or theologians for that matter), but you might think the question shouldn't be closed by our analysis of intrinsicality.

We don't have to look too far for more popularly held metaphysical claims that commit one to necessary connections of a sort that cause problems for the Langton–Lewis analysis. Consider, for example, universals. Many (see especially Armstrong 1997: §3.8) are Aristotelian about universals: they hold that they cannot exist uninstantiated. So while there is no thing that must exist for the universal to exist (since it can be instantiated by more than one thing), the universal must be accompanied by what instantiates it. It follows from the Langton–Lewis analysis that no property which can only be had by a universal is basic intrinsic. So take the property *being constituted from simpler universals* which can only be had by complex universals. It cannot be basic intrinsic, and so there can be a duplicate of a complex universal which is a simple universal. So it is not intrinsic to a universal whether it has simpler universals as constituents. This seems counterintuitive.

Or suppose substantivalism about space–time is a necessary truth; in particular suppose that it be necessary that there is some space–time but that it need not be the *same* space–time that exists in every world. Then nothing that is not a region of space–time can exist unaccompanied, since every other thing is necessarily accompanied by some space–time. In that case, the only basic intrinsic properties will be those that can be both had and lacked by regions of space–time. So, for example, if regions of space–time couldn't be massive, mass properties will not be basic intrinsic, in which case I could have had a duplicate with a different mass, and so mass is not intrinsic, contrary to intuition.[3]

The first account of duplication

Lewis' earlier definition of duplication (1986: 61) does not rely on any controversial modal claims like the denial of necessary connections. Lewis originally held that two objects are duplicates iff (i) they share all their perfectly natural properties; and (ii) there is a correspondence between the parts of each thing such that each part has the same perfectly natural properties as its corresponding part, and the parts of each thing stand in the same perfectly natural relations as the parts of the other thing.

The reason Lewis offered the second analysis of duplication was because this first analysis makes a number of questionable assumptions concerning naturalness.[4] The two most relevant assumptions are, first, it assumes that, as a matter of necessity, perfectly natural properties are intrinsic and, second, it has to assume that, necessarily, how a thing is intrinsically is determined completely by the natural properties it has. This is because the analysis rules out two possible objects sharing all their perfectly natural properties but differing in their intrinsic properties. Now one way to rule that out is to demand that the intrinsic properties are all perfectly natural; but if Lewis says this then he is saying that a property is intrinsic if and only if it is perfectly natural, since he has already said that all the perfectly natural properties are intrinsic. In that case we should doubt Lewis' claim to be analysing intrinsicality: he appears instead merely to have replaced the notion with perfect naturalness. But if there are intrinsic properties that are not perfectly natural, why would the intrinsic properties of a thing supervene on the natural properties of a thing? The supervenience claim would be secured if the natural properties of a thing (necessarily) determined *all* the properties of that thing. But that is a very strong modal assumption to be relying upon. Additionally, some philosophers simply find this talk of naturalness wholly mysterious; so how might we analyse intrinsicality without an appeal to the notion of naturalness?

Analysis in terms of essence

Our intuitive gloss on intrinsicality was that a property is intrinsic iff a thing's having that property is independent of its surroundings. The natural reading of this independence is modal: one should be able to make any possible changes to the surroundings of an object without changing its intrinsic character, but each extrinsic property should be changed with one or other possible alteration to the bearer's surroundings. It is this latter thought that goes awry if the Humean denial of necessary connections turns out to be false, precisely because some features of a thing's surroundings (and hence some of its extrinsic properties) cannot be altered. Should we be worried about this? Definitely, if we think that the Humean dictum is indeed false. But perhaps, even if we think it is true. After all, we are doing conceptual analysis here. Our ambitions are modest: simply to explain the concept of intrinsicality by appealing only to concepts we are happy to take as primitive (such as naturalness, perhaps). We might well worry if this modest goal makes lofty presuppositions regarding the extent of what is possible. At any rate, one might *prefer* it if we could analyse intrinsicality and stay neutral on whether or not there are non-Humean necessary connections.

If so, one might abandon the idea of construing the notion of independence involved modally. Instead, one might make appeal to the notion of *essence*. An intrinsic property is one such that it is no part of *what it is* to instantiate that property that the bearer stands in some relation to its surroundings.

The idea that there is a notion of essence that is not reducible to some modal notion has enjoyed a recent resurgence in metaphysics thanks in large part to the work of Kit Fine. Fine (1994) argued that while essential truths always give rise to necessary truths, a lack of essentiality need not result in possibility. For example, it is essential to Socrates to be human, and from this we can conclude that there is no possible world in which Socrates exists and is not human. Essence gives rise to necessity. However, it is not essential to Socrates to belong to his singleton – Socrates' nature has nothing to do with any set; but it does not follow that there is a possible world where Socrates exists and is not a member of singleton Socrates. It is necessary that when there is a thing, there is the singleton of that thing, even if it is no part of *what it is* to be a certain thing A that it belong to the singleton of A. The absence of essence does not entail possibility.

Suppose then we analyse the intrinsic properties as those properties such that it is no part of what it is to instantiate them that the bearer stand in some relation to its surroundings, and the extrinsic properties as those properties such that it is essential to the instantiation of them that the bearer stand in some relation to its surroundings. Then while it follows that, as a matter of necessity, if something has some weight (an extrinsic property) then it bears some relation to some thing in its surroundings (namely that some thing exerts a gravitational pull on it), it does not follow that something can have some mass (an intrinsic property) *without* bearing some relation to some thing in its surroundings, precisely because it might be necessary, for reasons having nothing to do with the nature of being massive, that massive things have certain things going on in their surroundings. So even if the denial of necessary connections is false – indeed, even if every truth turns out to be a necessary truth – we can still construe intrinsicality as independence from surroundings, provided this means essential and not modal independence.[5]

Notes

1 Although this is not wholly uncontroversial. While shape properties might be locally intrinsic to some things, they might be thought not to be locally intrinsic to others. Consider, for example, a hole: it seems to have the shape it has in virtue of its surrounding – in virtue of the topology of the thing it is a hole in. Also, in relativistic space shape is relative to inertial frame, and so may turn out to be extrinsic in general. (The topological features, though, may be intrinsic.) Lastly, see Hudson (2005: 111–13), who thinks that material objects have their shape extrinsically – in virtue of the shape of the regions of space–time they occupy, as opposed to the object occupying a region of that shape in virtue of being the shape it is.

2 For an excellent discussion of the complicated issues surrounding this topic see Hawley (2005). For a discussion of the modal version of the problem see Forbes (1985: Chs 5 and 6), Mackie (1987, 1989) and Garrett (1988).

3 As is often the case, whether this is a worrying example depends on one's whole metaphysics. Someone like Ted Sider (2001b: 101–13), who thinks that ordinary concrete objects like you or I, or the Taj Mahal or an electron, simply *are* regions of space–time, is going to have no trouble at all with this.

4 Lewis never actually came to think they were false, but he wanted to offer doubters an account that didn't make them.
5 Both Francescotti (1999) and Witmer et al. (2005) offer an analysis of intrinsicality that makes appeal to the notion of essence rather than modal notions. See Jenkins (2005) for a discussion of modal versus essential dependence.

References

Armstrong, David (1997) *A World of States of Affairs*, Cambridge: Cambridge University Press.
—— (2004) *Truth and Truthmakers*, Cambridge: Cambridge University Press.
Fine, Kit (1994) "Essence and Modality," *Philosophical Perspectives* 8: 1–16.
Forbes, Graeme (1985) *The Metaphysics of Modality*, Oxford: Oxford University Press.
Fox, John (1987) "Truthmaker," *Australasian Journal of Philosophy* 65: 188–207.
Francescotti, Robert (1999) "How to Define Intrinsic Properties," *Noûs* 33: 590–609.
Garrett, Brian (1988) "Identity and Extrinsicness," *Mind* 97, no. 385: 105–109.
Geach, Peter (1969) *God and the Soul*, London: Routledge.
Hawley, Katherine (2001) *How Things Persist*, Oxford: Oxford University Press.
—— (2005) "Fission, Fusion and Intrinsic Facts," *Philosophy and Phenomenological Research* 71, no. 3: 602–21.
Hawthorne, John (2001) "Intrinsic Properties and Natural Relations," *Philosophy and Phenomenological Research* 63: 399–403.
Hudson, Hud (2005) *The Metaphysics of Hyperspace*, Oxford: Oxford University Press.
Humberstone, Lloyd (1996) "Intrinsic/Extrinsic," *Synthese* 108: 205–267.
Jenkins, Carrie (2005) "Realism and Independence," *American Philosophical Quarterly* 42, no. 3: 199–211.
Langton, Rae and Lewis, David (1998) "Defining 'Intrinsic'," *Philosophy and Phenomenological Research* 58: 333–45, reprinted in *Papers in Metaphysics and Epistemology*, Cambridge: Cambridge University Press, 1999, pp. 116–32.
Lewis, David (1983) "New Work for a Theory of Universals," *Australasian Journal of Philosophy* 61: 343–77; reprinted in his *Papers in Metaphysics and Epistemology*, Cambridge: Cambridge University Press, 1999, pp. 8–55.
—— (1986) *On the Plurality of Worlds*, Oxford: Blackwell.
Mackie, Penelope (1987) "Essence, Origin and Bare Identity," *Mind* 96, no 382: 173–201.
—— (1989) "Identity and Extrinsicness: Reply to Garrett," *Mind* 98, no. 389: 105–17.
Marshall, Dan and Parsons, Josh (2001) "Langton and Lewis on 'Intrinsic'," *Philosophy and Phenomenological Research* 63: 347–51.
Parfit, Derek (1984) *Reasons and Persons*, Oxford: Oxford University Press.
Parsons, Josh (1999) "There is no 'Truthmaker' Argument against Nominalism," *Australasian Journal of Philosophy* 77, no. 3: 325–34.
—— (2005) "Truthmakers, the Past, and the Future," in Helen Beebee and Julian Dodd (eds), *Truthmakers: The Contemporary Debate*, Oxford: Oxford University Press, pp. 161–74.
Sider, Theodore (1993a) "Naturalness, Intrinsicality, and Duplication," Ph.D. dissertation, University of Massachusetts.
—— (1993b) "Intrinsic Properties," *Philosophical Studies* 83: 1–27.
—— (2001a) "Maximality and Intrinsic Properties," *Philosophical and Phenomenological Research* 63: 357–64.
—— (2001b) *Four Dimensionalism: An Ontology of Persistence and Time*, Oxford: Oxford University Press.
Vallentyne, Peter (1997) "Intrinsic Properties Defined," *Philosophical Studies* 88: 209–19.
Weatherson, Brian (2001) "Intrinsic Properties and Combinatorial Principles," *Philosophy and Phenomenological Research* 63: 365–80.
Witmer, D. Gene, Butchard, William, and Trogdon, Kelly (2005) "Intrinsicality Without Naturalness," *Philosophical and Phenomenological Research* 70, no. 2: 326–50
Zimmerman, Dean (1997) "Immanent Causation," *Philosophical Perspectives* 11: 433–71.

Further reading

The following are further readings (given in the order in which I think you should read them): Rae Langton and David Lewis, "Defining 'Intrinsic'," *Philosophy and Phenomenological Research* 58 (1998): 333–45, reprinted in Lewis, *Papers in Metaphysics and Epistemology* (Cambridge: Cambridge University Press, 1999), pp. 116–32 (this gives an excellent idea of the motivations for combinatorial accounts of intrinsicality, and offers a very clear analysis); *Philosophy and Phenomenological Research* 63 (2001) (this is a special issue of the journal devoted to Lewis and Langton's paper; it contains a number of excellent discussions [some of which are referred to above], together with replies from Lewis and Langton – crucial reading); Brian Weatherson, "Intrinsic vs. Extrinsic Properties," in E. N. Zalta (ed.), *The Stanford Encyclopedia of Philosophy* (2002) (available: http://plato.stanford.edu/entries/intrinsic-extrinsic/) (a continually updated encyclopaedia entry, that very clearly summarises the current state of play in the literature – pitched towards a somewhat more advanced level than this paper, highly recommended if you want to explore the issues in more depth); and Ross Cameron, "Recombination and Intrinsicality," *Ratio* 21, no. 1 (2008): 1–12 (in this paper I argue that one encounters a troubling circularity in attempting to justify combinatorial analyses of intrinsicality).

27

UNIVERSALS
The contemporary debate

Fraser MacBride

You can try this one at home

Hold up your hands. Say, as you gesture with the right hand, "Here is a hand," adding, as you gesture with the left, "Here is another hand." Have you not thereby proved *ipso facto* the existence of something common to both, viz. the existence of the property *being a hand*? That depends upon whether the conclusion really follows from these premises – whether from the fact that two things are hands it really follows that something else exists, a common property that makes them so.[1]

How does this "proof" strike you? If your initial response is a sceptical one, if it is *only* your hands that appear illuminated by the light of natural reason, then I hazard the diagnosis that you are predisposed to an *extreme* form of nominalism, a member of the family of doctrines according to which reality consists *solely* of particulars. I suggest in fact that you are inclined to admit only "concrete" particulars. You think that only such things as human beings and houses and cats and roads exist, things you can literally put your finger on. What makes it possible to identify concrete particulars in this way? The especially intimate connection to space and time they enjoy; the fact that a human being, say, during his or her lifetime, traces a unique and continuous path through space and time.

If, by contrast, the "proof" strikes you as compelling, compelling because it is not just your hands but also a further existing item, a property shared by both hands, that appears illuminated, then it is likely that you are predisposed to a version of realism, the family of doctrines according to which reality consists, in significant part at least, of universals. I suggest in fact that you are inclined to a moderate version of realism that admits universals alongside particulars. You think that alongside, say, the *many* things that are human beings there is the *one* common nature of which these concrete particulars partake; in this case, the common nature, the "one-over-many" of which they partake, is the universal *being a human being*. Such universals cannot be concrete in the manner of their instances. Universals gain a toehold in space and time because the concrete particulars upon which they confer a nature are located in space and time. But concrete particulars that partake of a common nature routinely trace a variety of different paths through space and time. Human beings literally run hither and thither. So the universal *being a human being*, determined to follow one as much as another, cannot enjoy the intimate relationship with space and time characteristic of its instances.

What of it? What does it matter whether you are a realist or a nominalist? It matters, in a sense, to your understanding of *everything*. Here is a fundamental fact that cannot have escaped your notice. The world that surrounds us is not a formless, undifferentiated morass. There is repetition. There are red things, square things, things 1 metre long, things that are human beings: the same colours and shapes and sizes and kinds repeated over and over again. Realists, to employ the jargon, "posit" universals – i.e. advance theories that are committed to the existence of such entities to explain how repetition arises in the world. According to realists, it is because different red things exhibit one and the same universal *redness* that the colour red is common to them. Nominalists disagree with realists because they believe that repetition may just as well be accounted for by theories that invoke only particulars. So they deny there is any need to posit universals.[2]

In presenting the case for realism to you as I have just done, nominalists will no doubt accuse me of grammatical sleight of hand. I have already spoken several times of things having a nature "in common." But nominalists declare this use of the phrase corrupting. It surreptitiously suggests that two different things have a nature in common in just the same way that you and I may have an old friend in common, i.e. by bearing a mutual relation to some third thing. Nominalists will warn that if you listen to this kind of talk for too long, universals will end up seeming as comfortable and familiar to you as old friends, despite the fact they are only acknowledged by us for purely theoretical reasons, which means they are not even acquaintances. So they will enjoin you not to listen to the realists but to attend to what they have to say instead. You do need to attend carefully, because what they have to say is brief; so brief that, intellectually blink and you may be unaware that any sort of account has gone by.

Here's their account. Of two red things it may be truly affirmed that they have something in common. There certainly *is* repetition in this sense. But that is *only* because they are both red. There's no third-party involvement, just two red things. And that's the end of the story.

To be absolutely fair, Quine, an arch nominalist, should be allowed to speak for himself:

> One may admit that there are red houses, roses and sunsets, but deny, except as a popular and misleading manner of speaking that they have anything in common ... That the houses and roses and sunsets are all of them red may be taken as ultimate and irreducible, and it may be held that [the realist] is no better off, in point of real explanatory power, for all the occult entities which he posits under such names as "redness."[3]

Of course realists are bound to disagree with Quine. Positing universals, they affirm, enables us to peer more deeply into the murky essence of things. Universals are multipurpose items; realists do not only posit universals to explain the presence of repetition in the world. Even a chaotic world may admit of random repetition amongst its elements, and ours is not a chaotic world. Our world is *not* akin to a jumble of letters strewn upon the ground but to a vast, sprawling, idiosyncratic narrative. Ours is a world where things are causally related, governed by the laws of nature, counted and measured, thought and talked about. It is to account for this complex web of more intimate relationships which bind our world together that realists also posit universals. To do so they posit universals on a monumental scale that would make a Victorian engineer go green with envy. A selection of the schemes proposed: structural universals the size of number series, potentially infinite systems of universals knit together with the algebraic organisation characteristic of the physical quantities, law-like connections between universals that settle from on high the arrangements of whatever things fall under them.[4]

We are already in a position to anticipate the most basic of accusations that nominalists level at their realist rivals: that of overweening explanatory ambition. No theory can avoid the use of concepts that, from the point of view of the theory, are "ultimate and irreducible." The analyses a given theory provides cannot proceed indefinitely. Eventually its explanations must terminate in concepts that, so far as the theory is concerned, are primitive. A metaphysician can no more effectively explain what the true and ultimate structure of reality is like without taking *something* as basic than a parasite can effectively survive by entirely consuming its host. According to nominalists, realists fail to appreciate the significance of this fact. So far from constructing a fundamental theory of reality based upon a judicious choice of primitives, they recklessly pursue an impossible ideal of analyses that leave nothing unanalysed. Are realists guilty as charged? Or is it nominalists who take too much for granted?

But that's not what I wanted to say

You may have responded to the purported proof with which we began our discussion in a number of other perfectly intelligible ways – in ways that are likely shaped by other philosophical commitments on your part. Perhaps you felt that whilst the version of realism outlined went too far, the nominalism sketched did not go far enough. Or you may have wished for a more extreme version of realism. Let me give you some more options to choose from.

The universals that realists invoke confer a *common* nature upon their instances because they are genuinely shared by the different instances that partake of them. So universals are not "divided" amongst their instances. An analogy may help us get clearer about what realists mean by this. The Brontë sisters belonged to the same family because they shared one and the same mother. It would be absurd to think that this was so because their mother was somehow divided between them – with Charlotte enjoying a maternal relationship with one part, her shoulder, whilst Emily enjoyed a maternal relationship with another part, her lap. Rather, it was the fact that they were offspring of the same mother – whole and undivided – that was responsible for their belonging to the same family. Analogously, it is the fact that two human beings are instances of the same universal – whole and undivided – that is responsible for conferring a common nature upon them.

This gives rise to a curious consequence that has driven many a philosopher into the arms of nominalism. Because it performs the role of conferring a nature whilst remaining undivided, the universal *being a human being* must be wholly, not partly, present in each of its instances. It must therefore be wholly present in each of the many different human beings that exist right now even though they are presently scattered over the face of the earth. But how spooky is that? There is nothing strange about one thing being wholly present in different places at different times (we move around all the time). Nor is there anything peculiar about one thing being partly present in different places at the same time (your feet at one end of the bed, your head at the other). But how can one thing be wholly present in different places at the same time? Is that not the prerogative of properly mythical creatures?

The realist may simply deny that the universals he or she posits are located in space and time, assigning them instead a purely abstract form of existence. But this threatens to be an ill-advised jump from the frying pan into the fire, making a mystery of how transcendent universals drawn from an abstract realm can confer a nature upon concrete particulars drawn from a realm of space and time.

Wary, for these or other reasons, of the universals that realists invoke, you may nevertheless be sceptical of the extreme nominalist claim that reality consists solely of concrete particulars. So whilst you are doubtful that there is a common property your hands both share (i.e. a universal), you are nevertheless certain of the fact that each of your hands *has* properties. If so, I suggest that you are prone to a *moderate* version of nominalism. Look at your hands again. You think that the left hand has a colour and a shape. You think that the right hand also has a colour and a shape. But these colours and shapes are as particular as the hands to which they belong, no more capable of being in different places at the same time – or, more generally, capable of repetition – than the hands themselves. After all, do you not see the colour of your left hand over there, whereas the colour of your right hand is over here? To distinguish them from the concrete particulars to which they belong, these properties are often called "abstract particulars" (although they are also called "tropes" and "moments").

It is important to avoid a misunderstanding here. Moderate nominalists declare that, for instance, the colour of your left hand cannot be shared by the right hand. This may sound as if moderate nominalists commit themselves to an absurdity, viz. that however subtly, or not so subtly, mismatched your hands may actually be, they are constitutionally incapable of matching in colour. But this is not the moderate nominalists' position.[5] It certainly is integral to their view that the colour of your left hand is one thing, the colour of your right another. However, that does not preclude the possibility of your left hand exhibiting a colour that *exactly matches* (exactly resembles) the colour of the right; even if, in such a circumstance, one of the colours (abstract particulars) that your hands actually exhibit would require to be replaced by another.

This is important to understand because of the role that resemblance amongst abstract particulars performs in the moderate nominalists' account of the fundamental and nonnegotiable fact that reality admits of endless repetition. Moderate nominalists cannot account for this fact, as realists do, by appealing to common natures; abstract particulars, by contrast to universals, cannot be held in common by different things.

But whilst they cannot be shared, abstract particulars can resemble one another. It is because the world is replete with abstract particulars that actually do resemble one another that repetition is to be found in the world. There are many different red things because there are many different abstract particulars that resemble the colour of the London bus passing by my office window. Whereas extreme nominalists take it as "ultimate and irreducible" that the houses and roses and sunsets (and London buses) are all of them red, moderate nominalists push their analysis of repetition a level deeper. It is not an un-analysable fact that different concrete particulars are red: they are red in virtue of their different properties (abstract particulars) resembling one another. But there is no underlying metaphysical mechanism responsible for making abstract particulars resemble one another. From the moderate nominalist point of view, resemblance amongst abstract particulars is "ultimate and irreducible," flowing ineluctably from their resembling, but nevertheless particular, natures; they resemble simply in virtue of what they are.[6]

Moderate nominalism occupies a position in logical space intermediate between extreme nominalism and moderate realism, thereby holding out the promise of avoiding their correlative excesses. But it may be that you are drawn towards a more left-field position. The moderate form of realism, which admits universals alongside particulars, is a "substance–attribute" ontology. It draws a distinction between a particular (a substance) and what is had by the particular (an attribute), i.e. a universal or universals. The persuasive force of moderate realism results from the fact that it thereby echoes the intuitive distinction between, say, an apple, and its sweetness, texture and odour. But be careful not to be hoodwinked. There appears to be a subtle process of conceptual alchemy that transforms what realists mean when they talk about particulars once universals are admitted. Their particulars no longer seem to be the familiar items of our ordinary experience, apples, hands, cars and so on; no longer the concrete particulars that are primitive and un-analysable from the point of view of many nominalist theories. Instead they are the result of a metaphysical subtraction. Realist-particulars are what remain of familiar things once their characteristics have been taken away: so-called "bare particulars," ordinary things minus every one of their universals.

Philosophers of an empiricist persuasion – from Hume onwards – have traditionally denied the possibility of bare particulars, because bare particulars appear to be inherently unknowable. We can only know of something by means of its characteristics, and bare particulars are supposed to lack characteristics. In response, philosophers of a more rationalist persuasion – from Leibniz to the present day – have maintained that bare particulars are perfectly knowable. Bare particulars are posited to serve as the "subjects," or "bearers," of characteristics. They are not without characteristics; they are simply the items in the world that *have* characteristics. This means that particulars are denuded *only* in thought, i.e. when considered in abstraction from every one of their characteristics. But in reality they are fully clothed by the characteristics of which they are the subjects. So "bare particulars" are none other than the familiar items of ordinary experience. They are the bearers of size, shape, taste, etc.; in other words, the cars, hands and apples about which we know as much as anything.

Perhaps you are persuaded by this. Nevertheless, you may still be left wondering whether there is really any theoretical necessity to admit the existence of a metaphysical residue left behind once the characteristics of a thing have been subtracted away. If so, then *extreme* realism may be the position for you. Extreme realists seek to demonstrate that bare particulars are theoretically superfluous by developing a "bundle" theory to replace the "substance–attribute" ontology implicit in more moderate versions of realism. Extreme realists deny that ordinary concrete things like apples and hands are composed of an underlying substance possessed of attributes. Instead ordinary things are merely confluences, or bundles, of universals. There is nothing hidden behind the sweetness and texture and odour of the apple, no bare particular that bears them; the apple is constituted entirely from the universals it exhibits.

Extreme realism is not for the faint-hearted. If there are no bare particulars, if ordinary things are only bundles of universals, then concrete things can only be different if they are constituted from different universals. But surely there could have been different things that exhibited exactly the same universals, two apples, say, with exactly the same shape, size, taste, etc.? If that really is the case then ordinary things cannot consist merely of confluent universals. Extreme realism thus appears committed to the extraordinary *a priori* claim that this cannot be the case. That however similar thoroughgoing investigation of the most exacting scientific kind may reveal two things to be, there must be *some* hidden universal that eludes examination with respect to which they differ.[7]

Now try this

Another exercise designed to test and challenge your understanding of the theories of reality we have developed so far: hold up your hands again. Say once more, as you gesture with the right hand, "Here is a hand," repeating, as you gesture with the left, "Here is another hand." Next place the right hand *on top of* the left hand. Now say, "Here are two hands related." Have you not thereby proved *ipso facto* the existence of something that relates them, viz. whatever it is that presently relates your right hand to your left?

One significant respect makes this proof different from its predecessor. The former proof sought to demonstrate the existence of a property, *being a hand*, whereas the latter seeks to prove the existence of a relation, *being on top of*. I am doubtful that an account of the distinction between properties and relations can be given in terms that do not ultimately presuppose it – the distinction is too basic to our understanding of the world to admit of any kind of reduction. Nevertheless, the distinction admits of elucidation and example. Whereas properties hold *of* a thing, relations hold *between* things – relations are borne by one thing to other things. Thus, the property *being a hand* holds *of* your right hand and also holds (independently) *of* your left hand. By contrast, the relation *being on top of* does not hold of your right hand, nor does it hold (independently) *of* your left. It holds, if it does, *between* them: the relation is borne by your right hand to your left hand. Similarly, whereas the property of *being a number* holds of 0 and also holds of 1, the relation *being less than* holds between 0 and 1 ($0 < 1$).

You may be tempted to elucidate the contrast between properties and relations in the following terms: whereas it takes a single thing to exhibit a property, it takes multiple things to exhibit a relation. But be careful not to overgeneralise from the present case. It is true enough that some relations require more than one thing to relate. Since one thing cannot be (wholly) on top of itself, the *being on top of* relation requires two distinct things for its exhibition. Similarly, two distinct numbers are required for the exhibition of the *being less than* relation. But the identity relation holds between a thing and itself, so the identity relation requires only a single thing for its exhibition (Socrates = Socrates). Of course you will not understand what has just been said about the property–relation distinction unless you already understand the relational constructions "holds of" and "holds between" in the right way, i.e. to indicate the contrast between the different ways in which properties and relations obtain. But this is just an indicator of the fact, already noted, that the property–relation distinction is far too basic to admit of reductive analysis.

Focus once more on the question that presently engages us: What, if anything, is responsible for relating your hands when one is on top of the other? If you are an extreme nominalist then your answer can be straightforward: nothing, yourself excepted, is responsible for relating your hands. There is no need to posit relations because the fact that your hands are related is "ultimate and irreducible," a feature of the explanatory bedrock. But if you are inclined towards the other views so far developed, your answer cannot be so straightforward.

The property–relation distinction may be fundamental, but this does not imply that if properties are admitted then relations must be admitted too (or *vice versa*). One may grant the force of the distinction whilst insisting only items that fall on one side of the distinction actually exist. Moderate nominalists and realists (moderate or otherwise) who have already granted the existence of properties – whether conceived as abstract particulars or universals – therefore face a strategic choice whose consequences will reverberate throughout their respective systems: to admit relations, or not to admit relations.

If realists admit relations, they are perforce universals. According to them, the relation that relates your hands, when one is on top of the other, will also be responsible for relating, say, the computer to the table. It is in virtue of being related by the same relation that your two hands are arranged in the same way as the computer and table. But if moderate nominalists admit relations, they must be as particular as the things they relate. There is the relation r_1, unique to your hands, in virtue of which one is on top of the other. There is also another relation r_2, unique to its bearers, in virtue of which the computer is on top of the desk. It is because of the bedrock fact that r_1 and r_2 closely resemble one another, that your hands exhibit the same arrangement as the computer and the table.[8] Alternatively, realists and moderate nominalists may refuse to admit relations, endeavouring instead to account for the (almost) undeniable fact – never say "never" where philosophers are concerned – that things are related and arranged in a variety of different ways, whilst acknowledging only the existence of properties.[9]

Whether particular or universal, relations are quite extraordinary creatures. Andorra is to the north of Barcelona. Knowing this helps us to locate these two towns. But where is the relation *being north of* to be found? It seems wrong-headed to locate the relation in Andorra or in Barcelona; after all, it relates *them*. So, somehow or other, *being north of* must be shared in some neutral way between them. It must share the divided locations of Andorra and Barcelona without itself being divided.

It may appear that if relations are universals then the fact that relations are capable of recurring in this way need present no special difficulty. After all, universals, if such exist, recur undivided amongst their divided instances. But relations, if they are universals, do not simply recur amongst their instances as, say, the non-relational universal *being square* recurs amongst square things, wholly present wherever square things are to be found. Consider three objects arranged thus upon a line:

A — — — B — — — C

Suppose that A is 1 metre from B, and B is 1 metre from C. Then *being 1 metre from* relates not only A to B but also B to C. So it must recur undivided not only amongst A and B, but also amongst B and C. Yet even though it is one and the same relation wholly present in each of these three locations, its recurrence in A has something to do with its recurrence in B that it does not have to do with its recurrence in C. Its recurrence in A and B makes for A being 1 metre from B, whilst its recurrence in A and in C does not – A is 2 metres, not 1, from C. This line of reflection may sound like a *reductio ad absurdum* of the doctrine that relations are universals, but it's not. What it shows is that facts about what things, and in which order, a relation relates are not reducible to facts about *where* a relation recurs. No wonder Russell was driven to declare that relations are "Nowhere and nowhen" (1912: 55–6).

We could learn to live with the differences that obtain between relations, ordinary particulars, and non-relational universals if relations were genuinely capable of the theoretical work for which they are posited – providing an account of how things, like your hands, are related – and there were no other way of getting the job done. But there's the rub. Are relations capable of doing the work for which they are employed? Must they be invoked to explain how things are strung together, literally and otherwise? Or can we make do with just properties instead?

Conclusion: take it to the next level

It's time to put my own cards on the table. To account for the fact that the world – both inner and outer – admits of repetition and order is a matter of singular intellectual significance. Moderate realists claim that *both* particulars and universals are required to account for repetition and order. Extreme realists disagree because whilst they affirm there are universals, they deny there are particulars, concrete things being merely bundles of universals. Nominalists, whether extreme or moderate, dissent from both realist parties. They claim there are particulars, whether concrete or abstract, but deny there are universals. Realists and nominalists are only able to disagree in these different ways because they agree upon a more basic assumption: that particulars and universals are fundamentally different kinds of entity. I am sceptical of many of the things that the different parties to the nominalist–realist dispute entreat us to believe. This is because

I am sceptical of the assumption they share; that there is a fundamental distinction to be drawn between particulars and universals.[10]

It is one thing to be doubtful that there are items falling on one side of the particular–universal distinction rather than the other. It's quite another thing to be doubtful of the distinction itself. But how can anyone be sure of it? Recall the manner in which the concept of a universal was introduced, as the "one" that unites the "many," the universal *being a human being*, for example, initially conceived as the one that unites the many particular human beings, Socrates, Plato and so on. This way of thinking is easily turned on its head. For we may equally well think of a particular human being, Socrates say, as the "one" that unites his "many" characteristics, *being Greek*, *being wise*, and so on. So even though universals have traditionally been distinguished from particulars by conceiving of the former as what unites the latter, this hardly suffices to show that the latter are different in kind from the former.

Perhaps you are tempted to think that if only time enough and labour were devoted to the task then philosophers would eventually light upon some more sophisticated elucidation of the particular–universal distinction that succeeded in characterising a metaphysical division written deep into the nature of things. But ask yourself the question, why are you convinced *a priori* that this must be so? Why think, in advance of such an investigation being undertaken, that reality admits of a simple binary division into exactly two classes, or categories, the particulars and the universals? Is this not like insisting *a priori* that the world be viewed solely in terms of black and white? Let us be wary. Let us not impose blinkers upon our theorising about reality.

Acknowledgements

I am grateful to the participants of my Birkbeck "Universals" seminar for their responses to the "director's cut." Thanks to Asunción Álvarez, Ross Cameron, and Mike Martin for comments on a penultimate draft.

Notes

1   This "proof of a universal" self-consciously seeks to parallel G. E. Moore's famous "proof of an external world" (1939), where he held up his hands to demonstrate the existence of things outside of us and thereby thought to put paid to external world scepticism. It is worth reflecting upon where the parallel breaks down and the significance of its so doing. Attempting to formalise these and the subsequent proof in the third section will help you get clear about what is at stake here.

2   One cannot do better here than reflect upon Russell's brief, but brilliant, exposition and defence of realism (see Russell 1912: Ch. 9). Once you've done that, compare Price's elegant defence of nominalism (in Price 1953: Ch. 1). You'll also need to take a look at Armstrong's (1978) influential treatment of the nominalist–realist dispute and the no-less-influential alternative that Lewis proposes in 1983.

3   See Quine's must-read paper, "On What There Is" (1948: 81), that, for better or worse, has done so much to shape the contemporary debate about universals. To get a good sense of what is at stake here, take a careful look at Hochberg (1978) and the exchange between Devitt (1980) and Armstrong (1980). I reflect further upon the debate about universals Quine initiated, in MacBride (2006).

4   See (e.g.) the mind-expanding Tooley (1977), Shapiro (1983) and Bigelow and Pargetter (1988).

5   Historically, this has been something that realists have often failed to appreciate. See G. E. Moore's (1923) influential, but nevertheless misguided, criticism of moderate nominalism.

6 See Campbell (1981) for an insightful introduction to moderate nominalism that takes inspiration from the work of D. C. Williams (1953). Compare Mulligan et al. (1984), where moderate nominalism is developed from a more "Austrian" perspective.

7 In his later career, abandoning moderate realism, Russell became a leading advocate of extreme realism (1948: 292–308). Van Cleve (1985) provides an illuminating discussion of a variety of objections to extreme realism.

8 The idea that relations ("moments of unity") are abstract particulars is to be found in Husserl. See Campbell (1990: 97–133), Mulligan (1998) and Simons (2002/3) for arguments for, and against, the existence of such relational items.

9 There is another position worth exploring, one usually credited to C. S. Peirce and seriously entertained by Russell: to admit relations but deny that there are any properties.

10 Following Ramsey's (1925) lead, I seek to undermine a variety of different versions of the particular–universal distinction in MacBride (1998 and 2005). See Simons (1992) and Lowe (2006: 101–18) for counterattacks to Ramsey-style scepticism about the particular-universal distinction.

References

Armstrong, D. M. (1978) *Nominalism and Realism*, vol. 1: *Universals and Scientific Realism*, Cambridge: Cambridge University Press.

—— (1980) "Against 'Ostrich' Nominalism: A Reply to Michael Devitt," *Pacific Philosophical Quarterly*, 61: 440–9.

Bigelow, J. and Pargetter, R. (1988) "Quantities," *Philosophical Studies*, 54: 287–304.

Campbell, K. (1981) "The Metaphysics of Abstract Particulars," in P. French, T. Uehling Jr, and H. Wettstein (eds), *Midwest Studies in Philosophy*, vol. 6: *The Foundations of Analytical Philosophy* (Minneapolis: University of Minnesota Press), pp. 477–88.

—— (1990) *Abstract Particulars*, Oxford: Blackwell.

Devitt, M. (1980) "'Ostrich Nominalism' or 'Mirage Realism'?" *Pacific Philosophical Quarterly* 61: 433–9.

Hochberg, H. (1978) "Nominalism, General Terms and Predication," *Monist* 71: 460–75.

Lewis, D. (1983) "New Work for a Theory of Universals," *Australasian Journal of Philosophy* 61: 343–77.

Lowe, E. J. (2006) *The Four-Category Ontology: A Metaphysical Foundation for Natural Science*, Oxford: Oxford University Press.

MacBride, F. (1998) "Where are Particulars and Universals?" *Dialectica* 52: 203–27.

—— (2005) "The Particular–Universal Distinction: A Dogma of Metaphysics?" *Mind* 114: 565–614.

—— (2006) "Predicate Reference," in E. Lepore and B. Smith (eds), *Oxford Handbook of Philosophy of Language* (Oxford: Oxford University Press, 2006), pp. 422–74.

Moore, G. E. (1923) "Are the Characteristics of Particular Things Universal or Particular," *Aristotelian Society Supplementary Volume* 3: 95–113.

—— (1939) "Proof of an External World," *Proceedings of the British Academy* 23: 273–300.

Mulligan, K. (1998) "Relations – Through Thick and Thin," *Erkenntnis* 48: 325–53.

Mulligan, K., Simons, P., and Smith, B. (1984) "Truth-Makers," *Philosophy and Phenomenological Research* 14: 287–321.

Price, H. H. (1953) *Thinking and Experience*, London: Hutchinson.

Quine, W. V. (1948) "On What There Is," *Review of Metaphysics* 2: 21–38.

Ramsey, F. P. (1925) "Universals," *Mind* 34: 401–17.

Russell, B. (1912) *The Problems of Philosophy*, London: Hutchinson.

—— (1948) *Human Knowledge, Its Scope and Limits*, London: Allen & Unwin.

Shapiro, S. (1983) "Mathematics and Reality," *Philosophy of Science* 50: 523–48.

Simons, P. (1992) "Ramsey, Particulars and Universals," *Theoria* 57: 150–61.

—— (2002/3) "Tropes, Relational," *Conceptus* 35: 53–73.

Tooley, M. (1977) "The Nature of Laws," *Canadian Journal of Philosophy* 7: 667–98.

Van Cleve, J. (1985) "Three Versions of the Bundle Theory," *Philosophical Studies* 47: 95–107.

Williams, D. C. (1953) "On The Elements of Being I," *Review of Metaphysics* 7: 3–18.

28
PARTICULARS
Herbert Hochberg

Differing about particularity

If one takes Abelard's attack on William of Champeaux to begin the great debate over the existence and nature of universals in the medieval period, then the debate began as one about *individuation* and the existence and nature of *particulars* (Abelard 1974: 58–61). Taking universal natures – species and genera – for granted, William faced the problem of accounting for the difference between two individuals, Plato and Socrates, of the same species, *humanity*. He did so, according to Abelard's account, by appealing to the different *accidents* of the particulars (Abelard 1994: 29–33). Socrates and Plato were held to differ in nonessential features like being snub-nosed, bald, short, etc. For what William seems to have claimed is that Socrates was to be construed – analyzed, as when one speaks of an *ontological analysis* – as being a complex of a nature, *humanity*, and various accidents, while Plato was another such complex involving the same nature but different accidents. It was as if the subject of the *predication* was the nature, *qualified by* accidents. This way of thinking apparently followed the construal of a genus, *animal*, as a substance or material (matter) modified by a *differentiating* form, *rationality* (and *mortality*), to yield the species, *man* (humanity). *Man* was thus *defined as* (or identified with) *rational animal.* William's purported Platonic realism was seen taking such a universal nature, common to Socrates, Plato and other humans, to exist and to be the *material substance* of such particulars.

Abelard attacked William's realism and developed an alternative view taking "whatever *is* is a particular" as a principle. Both his critical argument and his form of *nominalism* were to become classics, and variants would eventually be set out in the development of analytic philosophy in the course of the twentieth century (aided by "to be is to be the value of a variable"). Since the ordinary particulars, Plato and Socrates, were substances and were taken to be *substantially or materially* the same, being the same "in man," Abelard argued that accidents could not differentiate them. For one and the same substance, *humanity*, would simply have both sets of accidents – those of Plato and those of Socrates. Thus they would be *the same particular* individual, for the purported differentiating accidents cannot individuate them. Moreover, the view is incoherent, since some of the accidents of Plato are logically incompatible with the accidents of Socrates. In short, their *material* or *substantial identity* does not intelligibly allow for their accidental *particularity*. Abelard also applied this line of argument to the taking of genera as the *material* or *substance* for *differentiating forms* to yield the various species of the genus. Thus universals, as construed by William, are rejected as impossible or absurd (Abelard, *Glosses on Porphyry*, §28–31, in Abelard 1994: 29–31).

An early variant of Abelard's argument is found in Book 7 of Aristotle's *Metaphysics*, where Aristotle holds that only particulars are substances (are "one"). This is so, since a universal cannot be a substance, as it is *common* in that it naturally belongs to more than one thing. Thus, if it were a substance it would either be the substance of all the things that it is common to, which would then be *one* thing, or the substance of none. In his earlier writings, Abelard construed accidents as particulars or individual qualities in what is often taken to be Aristotle's manner – the *particular whiteness* of one piece of chalk being diverse from the *particular whiteness* of another piece of chalk of (*exactly*) *like* shade. He was thus, at one point, a "moderate nominalist" regarding accidents as characteristics that were particulars, not things common to diverse ordinary particulars. By contrast, extreme nominalism denies that there are attributes at all and takes true predications of the form "*x* is *f*" and "*y* is *f*" to simply reflect a relation between a common (linguistic) predicate and things the predicate is said to be "true of."

This latter view is found in Abelard's treatment of natures in his earlier writings, as he rejected them as universal *things* without recognizing particularized "substantial forms." Instead, he took the ground or "common cause" for the correct attribution of common linguistic predicates, like *is human*, to be the diverse particulars themselves and the "creative" activity of a particular act of understanding. The only universal involved in the correct attribution of *humanity* is a predicate phrase, "is human," a meaningful verbal item univocally applicable to many particulars. (To refer to different persons by the *same* proper name would be to use "*the* name" *equivocally*.)

Though Abelard had followed the more moderate and familiar medieval pattern that took *accidents* to be particulars, as in present day *trope theories*, he came to reject accidents as things, as he earlier rejected individual natures. The truth ground for "Socrates being white" as well as for "Socrates being a man" was simply Socrates, to whom we applied *universals*, construed as *meaningful* words. Such a view not only takes all existents to be particulars, but understands a particular to be an ordinary object and not a particularized characteristic. It thus dismisses all attributed characteristics in the extremist manner that would be resurrected in the twentieth century by W. Quine, N. Goodman and W. Sellars to dominate the analytic tradition.

Paradoxically, Abelard's later argument in *Theologica Christiana* against taking particular qualities as things appears to parallel Russell's well-known argument (Russell 1956a: 111–12) for relational universals (Abelard, cited in Marenbon 1997: 156–57, *Theologica Christiana*, 342: 2434 to 344: 2532). While Russell, arguing against particular qualities, assumed that relations were either particulars or universals, Abelard assumed that what exists is a particular. Thus both, to derive their conclusions, argued against the claim that existent relations are particulars by holding that particular qualities of the same kind would be *like* each other. Hence acknowledging them would force one to recognize the further likeness holding of diverse particularized likeness relations. But that gives rise to yet further particular likenesses *ad infinitum*. For Russell this forced the recognition of relations as universals (Hochberg 1980). For Abelard, since all accidents were likenesses, monadic accidents also led to such a regress. This is, in effect, a variant of a current argument against tropist accounts, which we will shortly consider, that forces the tropist to hold that diverse tropes of the same kind are of the same kind simply in virtue of themselves – what they are. While Abelard had earlier rejected relations as existents, but perhaps not all monadic accidents, he can be read as later rejecting all accidents as particular things, due to the purported regress.

Russell and Moore, besides arguing for universals, also argued that ordinary particulars could not be construed in terms of universals or complexes of universals, for numerical diversity and particularity of things could not be accounted for in terms of universal attributes. The idea, familiar in Scotus, is that neither attributes nor a nature can capture the *particularity* of a particular object – that a particular object is just that object and not one characterized in a certain way (Scotus, in Spade 1994: 101–103). Thus one finds the later thought experiment (modeled on Kant's example of a left and a right hand) that considers a space or "world" containing only two exactly similar spheres. We cannot, purportedly, *distinguish them* in terms of properties (including relations) – cannot give a description of one sphere that would not apply to the other. Hence one cannot construe a particular object as a complex or bundle of its properties.

While generally attributed to Max Black's paper (1952), the same argument is found earlier in a 1947 book by the Swedish philosopher Ivar Segelberg (1999: 160). The argument was directed against Russell's 1940 view that particulars are bundles of universal qualities. But Russell had not only considered the underlying pattern of the argument early in the century, he did so again in rejecting it in 1940 and 1948 (Russell 1941, 1951 [1948]). He took it up in the temporal rather than spatial case, and, instead of "identical" spheres, considered the possible "circularity" of time via the identity of "two" moments of phenomenal time. Such instants, on his view, were phenomenally temporal *particulars* construed as complete complexes of compresence of all simultaneously experienced qualities. Since the elements of such a complex were common qualities, the logical possibility of circularity resulted from indistinguishable particular instants of time. To meet the problems in the spatial and temporal cases, without special individuating *particulars* or *thisnesses* or "bare moments," he introduced locations and purported temporal phenomenal qualities (really the assumption that time was not circular). He apparently focused on the problem in terms of time since he took the space of the visual field to be *absolute* in that two circles (spheres) would be presented as *diverse* in being at different locations in visual space (one's visual "field").

Basic particulars

Suppose one introduces individuating bare particulars, as further components of the spheres, or takes the qualities to be particularized qualities (tropes). One can still not specify which sphere such individuating entities belong to, without already distinguishing the spheres, which we assume to be diverse to start with. All we may conclude from the case of the two spheres is that any purported definite description that we can give of "the one" will apply to "the other." Thus we cannot indicate by descriptions which sphere an indexical sign (name, label) would be taken to refer to. Likewise, we cannot say which sphere the supposed special individuating particulars belong to. This does not show that the spheres do not differ in that they do not stand in different relations (each to respective center points of the spheres for example) or that they do not have special individuating entities. It only shows that given the limitations imposed by the example we cannot form a definite description that will apply to one but not to both, though by assumption there are two. Black's discussion avoids the real philosophical issue involved and focuses on the lack of a basis for employing the "linguistic" diversity of different indexical signs to indicate the two objects. This points to a possibility not open in the case of the problem of universals, but misleadingly like the extreme move one finds in Abelard. The two spheres are just different without any "thing" making them different, for numerical diversity is indeed fundamental. This does not require that it be *carried* by special individuating entities like Gustav Bergmann's (1959) bare particulars. Moreover, one ultimately says about such purported entities that they are just diverse. It seems as if we start with diverse things and simply end up with further diverse things to "explain" diversity. In the case of the problem of universals, there is something further to be accounted for – the sameness of kind of diverse things (Hochberg 1965).

A basic issue was raised by both Moore (1901) and Russell (1956b [1911]). Russell argued that relations could not serve as individuating characteristics of particulars, since a relation could only be taken to ground the individuation of particulars if it is assumed to be irreflexive. The argument also followed a theme found in Scotus. Taking attributes, including relations, to ground particularity "presupposes" that the particulars are already distinguished as subjects for attributes, or as diverse, in order to be terms of the relation. In short, they are taken as *diverse particulars* in order to be diversified in terms of a relation *they* stand in. This leads to the point that *diversity* is basic, and it provides a motive for introducing either particular*ized*-qualities or special particular*izing* elements if one seeks a *ground of it* in special entities. Such elements have been taken as Bergmann's *bare particulars*, Russell's *substrata*, or Armstrong's *thin particulars* (2004: 105–6). They can then serve to *exemplify* or *combine with* the attributes of the ordinary object to form facts and/or the object. As simple particulars, they may be held not to have (exemplify) any specific property of the ordinary object *essentially* or *per se*, in the sense that any connection or tie to a property is a matter of fact – an atomic fact in a familiar sense – and not a matter of necessity. Yet, they are necessarily *particulars*, and not *universals*.

The issues about individuating particulars are found on the contemporary scene in the form of disputes about "transworld identity" in connection with modal contexts. For some, a so-called "possible world" with Socrates as Greek-nosed (rather than snub-nosed) "contains" a "counterpart" of Socrates, not Socrates (Lewis 1968). One easily sees such a view as a variant of a bundle analysis of ordinary particulars, since "counterparts" are such that any change of quality (Greek-nosed rather than snub-nosed, for example) results in a counterpart and not the *same* object. A counterpart, c, of an object, o, is basically something in some special relation to o but not numerically the same as o. Just think of Sartre's Humean-style bundle view of the self and one sees how he can write of meeting a "new" self or "stranger" in the mirror each morning. Alternatively, an individuating *bare* particular carries the burden of the "transworld" identity for others. S. Kripke's discussion clearly illustrates the implicit metaphysics of such a familiar pattern, despite his denial that he holds such a view (Kripke 1980: 52–3). The two alternative patterns of analysis are also found in the revival of the old disputes about continuants and identity through time. In place of questions about objects in different worlds, we have familiar puzzles about objects persisting through time in *this* world. Is Sartre, as a series of temporal stages, a different individual as *he* confronts himself in the mirror, while being one and the same individual in another sense, as a particular series of stages? Or is he one and the same "enduring" person – something that is always present, within or linked to each stage, as long as *he exists*? If he is a bundle, in the form of a series of the items of *his* history, then given the successive additions *he* is never literally one and the same series at any two "points." If *he* is a basic particular or substance that endures, then *he* is literally one and the same. And so the basic confrontation between attempts to analyze the *particularity* of particulars as complexes or bundles, without a special individuating factor, and views that take such attempts to fail, proceeds through various issues involving predication, indexical reference, modality, endurance, moments and places.

Particularized properties and their problems

Trope style theories were reemphasized in the Austrian school by Brentano and his students, in England by G. F. Stout, and, later, by Sartre. In one basic variant of a trope theory, ordinary particulars were construed as complex objects, ontologically analyzable into their qualities, which were taken to be simple particulars. Such a variant's supposed strength is that it can allow one to resolve two classic problems by avoiding universals as entities while also avoiding bare particulars to account for the diversity of ordinary particulars (Campbell 1990; Maurin 2004). Such views also share a theme with some bundle analyses that seek to avoid a *special relation* or *connection* between qualities and their *subjects* in terms of a supposedly unproblematic *part–whole* relation (a pattern found in major *idealists*, from Berkeley to Bosanquet and Bradley).

Since tropes are particulars, two ordinary particulars that are exactly alike, such as the two imagined spheres, do not have common constituent properties. The shape and color of the one are particulars that are diverse, though *exactly similar* to, the shape and color of the other. Since it is assumed that such individual attributes are *simple* particulars, their diversity supposedly need not be *accounted for*. The problem of accounting for the exact similarity of the tropes without appealing to universals is generally met in one of two ways. Two individual color qualities (tropes) are held to suffice to ground the truth of the judgment that they are exactly similar. It is purportedly a case of being an "internal relation," where what is meant is that the terms of the relation do not require, in Russell's terminology, a "relating relation" to relate them. In short, it is solely the existence of the two tropes, say w *and* w^*, that are required for the truth of "w is exactly similar to w^*." Just as two bare particulars are supposedly simply diverse *particulars* as they are diverse *simple* particulars, so two tropes, as exactly similar particular qualities, are held to be both simply similar and also simply diverse, since they are declared to be simply-diverse-particular-qualities. There is an obvious difference, however. Though the two tropes are simply diverse as numerically different particulars, the truth ground for "w is diverse from w*" is the existence of *both* w *and* w*, hence two logically independent claims have the same truth grounds.

One might hold that there is no problem, since a trope is not exactly similar to itself. But then one acknowledges that the phrase "exactly similar" is used as a transitive and symmetric, but not reflexive, verb or, alternatively, that the *internal relation* that it signifies is both symmetric and transitive but not reflexive, yet instantiated. By appealing to the contemporary exotic domain of "possible worlds," one may declare, invoking one's "metaphysical intuition," whatever that is, that there is no possible world in which w and w* are diverse but not exactly similar or are exactly similar but not diverse. For, given the existence of w *and of w**, both statements must be true, *given that* w *and* w* *are the kinds of things that they are – tropes*. It is, as it were, by their *nature*.

Given *two* particulars, it does indeed follow that they are diverse – that there are two of them. Likewise given the existence of *two* exactly similar tropes it does follow that they are diverse and exactly similar. What is at issue is what is packed into taking w and w* to be *two existents*. Consider a standard use of an existential quantifier and zero level constants and variables where "$(\exists x)(x = w)$ & $(\exists x)(x = w^*)$" is taken to express that there is a particular, w, *and* a particular, w*. That neither implies that w is a particular that is also an attribute of other particulars, nor that it is the case that $w \neq w^*$. Of course one can do two things. First, one can take variables of a certain kind to be used for particulars that are tropes, as well as certain iterations for tropes of the same kind – tropes understood in accordance with a certain philosophical account. Second, one can understand the schema one employs, as an explicatory tool in philosophical analysis and presentation, to be such that different primitive constant signs (proper names, basic predicates, etc.) are not assigned to (interpreted into) the same things (particulars of any kind, properties, etc.) and that they are all interpreted – that all signs of a certain kind in the schema in fact *represent*. Then, one can speak of it *following*, by the "logic" of the schema, including the interpretation rules, that $w \neq w^*$ and that w *is exactly similar to* w*. It is worth noting that if we consider all particulars as objects, and distinguish various kinds of particulars, ordinary particulars from tropes, then acknowledging the nature of a trope – of *being a trope* – has an interesting consequence.

It appears to be awkward, if not absurd, to consider such a nature in terms of a trope analysis and introduce special tropes that are particularized instances of *being a trope*. Thus, some advocates of tropes have claimed that it is simply w and w* that furnish the grounds for the truths that w and w* *are, are diverse*, and *are tropes*. Thus they follow the medieval pattern of Abelard and other "nominalists." The tropes themselves account, by *their natures*, for their diversity, their exact similarity, and their *being tropes* – without having natures that they are distinct from. A trope theorist can no more allow for the recognition of a *nature* of a trope, that is distinct from the trope, than Scotus could allow for the particularized nature of an object being *really diverse* from its *particularity* (*haecceitas*) or from the object, though the "three" were *formally diverse*. Hence his (in) famous "formal distinction" played its role. Trope theory is indeed a descendant of the Trinitarian accounts that created more than philosophical problems for their distinguished medieval adherents. It also employs the same move Abelard used when he took Socrates to be the truth ground for a variety of true statements about him, following the move extreme nominalists typically make (as F. MacBride has remarked [pers. commun., a conference in Geneva]). Interestingly, realists about universals need only face an apparent, but non-problematic, self-predication in accommodating universals of "universality" and "particularity."

Particulars: simples, complexes and facts

What is it to be a particular? Or, as some might put it, what distinguishes universals from particulars? Following an Aristotelian theme, a universal is often taken as what is (logically) predicable or predicable of many, while a particular is what is not so predicable, either in that it is not predicable at all or in that it is predicable of only one (a particularized quality on different variations of trope theory and senses of "predicable"). Thus Russell, in the 1940s, misleadingly held *common* qualities *in* bundles to be "particulars," since they were *contained in* complex particulars but not predicable of them. Particulars have also been characterized, not just as the bearers of properties, but as localized in space and time and perceptible. Universals, by contrast, have often been construed as non-spatial, a-temporal, abstract and apprehended by reason or cognition, not perception. The seemingly more "concrete" and down to earth particulars thus sometimes became the empirical objects that universals, as abstract "theoretical" objects, were introduced to explain – the latter being the basis for categorizing the former into collections (*natural* or otherwise).

The focus on the exemplification or instantiation connection (tie, relation, nexus), if one thinks of universal entities, rather than words, as having diverse particular instances, has been persistent. Russell, for example, spoke of considering things *from a logical point of view, a philosophical point of view,* and *a grammatical point of view* – in terms of "things" that were predicable and things that were not, what was spatial or temporal and what was not, and what was representable by a predicate expression and what was not. Being a predicable (thing) for Russell was also, at times, what could only occur in a basic fact of a certain logical form – monadic, dyadic, triadic, etc. – and such (atomic) facts could contain only one item in that predicable role. Particulars, by contrast, did not determine the logical form of the facts they were terms in, and any number could be present in an atomic fact. Thus universals, rather than particulars, could be thought to embody the logical forms of facts.

The problem posed by distinguishing particulars from universals in terms of a fundamental one-directional relation, tie or connection, has been raised from the time of the Greeks through the medieval period and into the modern and contemporary eras. While Berkeley's attack on material substance is standard fare, less attention has been paid to his rejection of the purported inherence of attributes (including powers) in material substances as senseless. The purported twofold incomprehensibility of bare particulars and exemplification contributed to the rejection of the particular-property-exemplification pattern by the British Absolute idealists and others and to the propounding of bundle theories, mereological sums and nominalism in various forms. Russell's bundle theories of 1940 and 1948 were complex, allowing for qualities to exemplify basic relations while *constituting* particulars, but not being exemplified by them (Hochberg 1996). But Russell, no more than Berkeley, avoided the need to *connect* elements to form a complex, whether one thinks of such complexes as facts or simply as unique complexes or bundles. Nor do trope theorists, with talk of parts and internal relations. Berkeley simply overlooked the issue, while Russell was often unclear about facts and particulars as *complexes*, and trope theorists disguise facts and universals as natured, diverse tropes, while declaring obviously complex entities to be simple.

From Aristotle's suggestion of prime matter as a ground of individuation for basic elements, to Scotus' *haecceitas*, and on to Moore and the early Russell arguing that there is a distinction between numerical and conceptual diversity, we have the classic move that introduces either strangely simple, yet natured, things or a unique, particularizing constituent – a bare particular or *haecceitas*. This is what others found unintelligible and led to various forms of bundle analyses of ordinary particulars.

Let "β" be an indexical sign or "name" of a white sphere and let W and S be the respective color and shape attributes. With x taken as the individuating *haecceitas* and C as Russell's compresence relation, we can construe the individual object, β, *as a fact*. This is an alternative to taking a fact to have x as a term, along with some attribute, as, for example, in the case of the fact that-x is W. The object β is then the fact such that x and the attributes W and S are *terms* of it. The relation C is construed as the relational attribute of (or "in") such a fact or object, and its logical form is that of a triadic (or a multi-grade) relation that takes an individuating "item" and monadic attributes as its terms. Alternatively, if one seeks to work out a view more in line with the rejection of such "individuators" or if one simply rejects the problem of individuation, β is simply the fact that W and S are compresent.

While the above pattern fits with recognizing that Russell's bundles of compresent qualities are really facts of compresence, one can say that both a traditional particular ground of individuation and universal attributes become terms of the fact that is the particular β, while the compresence relation is the only predicable *in* the fact. With or without individuators as entities, standard predications, such as "β is W," can now be said to be necessary in a specific sense. For the property W can be said to be a constituent of β. What that means, ignoring the slight complication posed by individuators, is simply that the statement "The unique fact of compresence that has only W and S as terms exists" is logically equivalent to "The unique fact of compresence that has only W and S as terms has W as a term." It is so by assuming Russell's account of definite descriptions. That such a description reflects the construal of the object as a fact with certain terms is part of the story. In a crucial and clear sense, however, what is stated is clearly not a necessary truth – for standard predications have been *replaced* by existential claims. And those are not, in any sense, necessary or logical truths (Hochberg 2001: 128–32). This simply exhibits a feature of bundle analyses of objects like β, and why it is sometimes said, in an imprecise sense, to be a "necessary truth" that the bundle composed of W and S contains W. Such an analysis of ordinary particulars and their connection to properties fits with a way of blocking the purported Bradley–Frege regress of facts, on an analysis that accepts particulars, properties and the logical form of exemplification. Take the problem to be that recognizing the fact that β is W supposedly forces us to acknowledge the additional fact that β is a term of the fact that β is W. However, as the key statement simply *reduces to* the claim that the fact that β is W exists, no further fact need be recognized.

Taking *particular substances* as facts of compresence that include an individuating *particular* as an entity that grounds the particularity of the ordinary object invites a question about such an entity, a "bare particular as *pure individuator*." One argues for there being such an item dialectically, as some put it, and, in so doing, employs a premise like: *diverse complex entities cannot share all constituents* – a claim analogous to standard theorems about mereological systems and sets. Just what kind of truth such a claim is raises one question. Another question arises when we consider that an individuating item x, the individuating item of the ordinary particular β, is referred to by way of referring to β. While that seems odd in that x is *identified* in terms of what it supposedly individuates, β, no circularity is involved, though it is perhaps one reason for the long-standing empiricist rejection of a particularizing entity.

The simple particular x does not exemplify the various properties of the ordinary object, β, and thus it does not serve as a unifying *substratum* nor as a *continuant* persisting through changes of attributes, roles traditional substrata played. It only serves as a mere, trivial in its way, marker or individuating item. But, such simple particulars, with individual things like β and Plato taken as facts or states of affairs, are the only simple or basic particulars. They are thus the only entities that are neither facts nor universal attributes and hence the only particulars, in one traditional sense of that term.

References

Abelard, P. 1974: *The Letters of Abelard and Heloise: Historia calamitatum*, trans. B. Radice, London: Penguin.

—— (1994) "From the *Glosses on Porphyry*," in Spade (1994), pp. 26–56.

Armstrong, D. M. (2004) *Truth and Truthmakers*, Cambridge: Cambridge University Press.

Bergmann, G. (1959) *Meaning and Existence*, Madison: University of Wisconsin Press.

Black, M. (1952) "The Identity of Indiscernibles," *Mind* 61: 153–64.

Campbell, K (1990) *Abstract Particulars*, Oxford: Oxford University Press.

Hochberg, H. (1965) "Universals, Particulars, and Predication," *Review of Metaphysics* 19: 87–102; reprinted in Hochberg (1984).

—— (1980) "Russell's Proof of Realism Reproved," *Philosophical Studies* 37: 37–44.

—— (1984) *Logic, Ontology, and Language*, Munich: Philosophia Verlag.

—— (1996) "Particulars, Universals and Russell's Late Ontology," *Journal of Philosophical Research* 21: 129–37; expanded in Hochberg (2001).

—— (2001) *Russell, Moore and Wittgenstein: The Revival of Realism*, Frankfurt: Hänsel-Hohenhausen.

Kripke, S. (1980) *Naming and Necessity*, Cambridge, MA: Harvard University Press.

Lewis, D. (1968) "Counterpart Theory and Quantified Modal Logic," *Journal of Philosophy* 65: 113–26.

Marenbon, J. (1997) *The Philosophy of Peter Abelard*, Cambridge: Cambridge University Press.

Maurin, A. S. (2004) *If Tropes*, Amsterdam: Kluwer.

Moore, G. E. (1901) "Identity," *Proceedings of the Aristotelian Society*, n.s., 1: 121–45.

Russell, B. A. W. (1956a) *Logic and Knowledge: Essays 1901–1950*, edited by R. Marsh, London: Allen & Unwin.

—— (1956b [1911]) "On the Relations of Universals and Particulars," in Russell (1956a), pp. 105–24.

—— (1941) *An Inquiry into Meaning and Truth*, New York: W. W. Norton & Co.; William James Lectures for 1940.

—— (1951 [1948]) *Human Knowledge: Its Scope and Limits*, London: Allen & Unwin.

Segelberg, I. (1999) *Three Essays in Phenomenology and Ontology*, trans. H. Hochberg and S. Ringström Hochberg, Stockholm: Thales.

Spade, P. (ed.) (1994) *Five Texts on the Medieval Problem of Universals: Porphyry, Boethius, Abelard, Duns Scotus, Ockham*, Indianapolis, IN: Hackett.

Further reading

G. Bergmann, *Realism: A Critique of Brentano and Meinong* (Madison: University of Wisconsin Press, 1967) is a meticulous but difficult study of the fundamental issues. N. Goodman, *Ways of World Making* (Indianapolis, IN: Hackett, 1978); and *Of Mind and Other Matters* (Cambridge, MA: Harvard University Press, 2004) are very readable and clearly argued presentations of nominalism and pragmatic-idealism. W. V. O. Quine, *From a Logical Point of View* (Cambridge, MA: Harvard University Press, 1953) is a classic of twentieth-century literature on the issues. For further reading, see also D. M. Armstrong, *A World of States of Affairs* (London: Cambridge University Press, 1997); R. N. Bosley and M. M. Tweedale, *Basic Issues in Medieval Philosophy* (Toronto: Westview Press, 2006); and H. Hochberg, "Moore's Ontology and Non-Natural Properties," *Review of Metaphysics* 15 (1962): 365–95.

29
COMPOSITION, PERSISTENCE AND IDENTITY

Nikk Effingham

Material objects

Unlike many other metaphysical categories, whether there are material objects is (idealism aside) uncontroversial. No wonder then that the metaphysics of material objects has become a febrile area of contemporary philosophy, as everyone (philosopher and non-philosopher alike) can make sense of, and have an interest in, the issues at stake. Three areas are mainly discussed: composition, persistence and identity (not that material objects are the sole subjects of these areas, nor do these areas exhaust the metaphysics of material objects). This chapter concentrates on how these areas help us answer questions about what material objects there are, and specifically examines the relationship, the *consanguinity*, between these areas.

Composition

The special composition question

My hand is a part of me; a star is composed of hydrogen and helium; conjoined twins overlap. These are *mereological* facts i.e. concerning the relation of wholes to their parts: my hand is related to me by parthood; a large number of hydrogen and helium atoms stand in the composition relation to the star; the two twins stand in the overlapping relation to one another.

These mereological relations have been formalised in *temporally relativised mereology*. Take as primitive the relation of temporally relativised proper parthood: "__ is a proper part of __ at time __." It is "proper part" that lines up with the English use of "part," whereas "part" in mereology has a technical meaning. A "mereological part" of a whole is anything that is either a proper part or improper part of that whole, where an improper part of a whole is just the whole itself. Because it is such a historically ingrained term in mereology, we will retain the proper/improper distinction here.

Next, define as follows:

x and y overlap at $t =_{df}$ there is an object both x and y have as a part at t.

So, given the technical definition, everything overlaps itself. Finally, define as follows:

The ys compose x at time $t =_{df}$ (i) each y is a part of x at t; (ii) no two of the ys overlap at t; and (iii) every part of x overlaps at least one of the ys at t (van Inwagen 1990: 29).

So you are composed of your torso, limbs and head (as well as such pluralities as your top half and bottom half, or all of your atoms); a table is composed of table legs and a table top; an amoeba is composed of organelles and cytoplasm. A question that has become popular amongst contemporary metaphysicians is this:

The special composition question (SCQ): Under what circumstances do the ys compose a further object?

In other words, when do little things come to compose bigger things? This intuitively takes place on some occasions (such as with you, the table and the amoeba), and we can say that any answer to the SCQ that misses out such things *underpopulates* our ontology. Similarly, there are cases where things intuitively *don't* compose e.g. intuitively there is no "Nikk-Bush" composed out of myself and George Bush (his atoms compose him, my atoms compose me, but our atoms don't, collectively, compose some four armed semi-Presidential freak of nature). Say that an ontology is *overpopulated* if it includes strange objects like Nikk-Bush.

If you want an answer to the SCQ that neither under- nor overpopulates, you will be hard pressed. Take a sample answer you might wish to consider:

Contact: The ys compose iff (if and only if) they are spatially contiguous.

If we take physics seriously, no objects ever truly touch; *a fortiori* objects never compose further objects; and Contact underpopulates. We could take spatial contiguity to just require objects being relatively close, but then we overpopulate the world. For instance, if I shake hands with George Bush there *would* be a Nikk–Bush object, on the grounds that we were now, loosely speaking, spatially contiguous. This is just one sample answer. Other allegedly sensible answers suffer similar counterexamples, failing to get by without either under- or overpopulating (van Inwagen 1990: 56–71; Markosian 2008: 348–52).

We can get an appropriate answer by making it very disjunctive, e.g. that the objects compose iff they are four table legs and a table top arranged tablewise *or* they are limbs, head and a torso arranged humanwise *or* they are organelles surrounded by pieces of cytoplasm *or* … well, you get the picture. Such an answer is of this form:

Serial: The ys compose iff either the ys are F_1s and are R_1 related, or the ys are F_2s and are R_2 related, or the ys are F_3s and are R_3 related, or …

Most people find Serial deeply unsatisfying (although see Lowe 2005b; Sanford 1993: 223–4; Thomasson 2007: 126–36). Compare with ethics. Rather than accepting utilitarianism or deontology, we could say an act is wrong iff it was a killing committed with no provocation *or* it was a man cheating on his loving wife *or* it was a non-starving man stealing bread, etc. One might reasonably worry that this wasn't an informative *answer* as to what counts as being morally wrong, instead just a list of our intuitions with disjuncts between them. *Mutatis mutandis* we might reasonably worry Serial isn't really an answer as to what counts as things composing either.

Given this difficulty of finding an informative answer that meets our population intuitions, many have tried quite different approaches to the SCQ.

Brutality

One such approach is *Brutality*: denying that there is an informative answer, and that instead what composes is simply a matter of brute fact (Markosian 1998). Brutality might fail to answer the SCQ but can now capture our intuitions about population: for every object that intuitively composes, Brutalists claim that it does (and does so as a matter of brute fact) and then deny that there are any cases of underpopulation or overpopulation (again, simply as a matter of brute fact).

- *First problem:* It would be remarkable if our beliefs about composition matched up with the brute facts. This is compounded, as our intuitions about composition aren't univocal, and there can be disagreements over whether things compose (for instance, you and I might disagree over whether a car and a caravan compose a further object when they are coupled together). If there are just brute facts, there is no principled way to resolve this disagreement, and only sheer prejudice would favour one view over the other. Indeed, one might suspect that actual cases where everyone does agree are only the result of anthropocentrism, and in principle we could disagree over anything composing. So how are we supposed to know what the brute facts are? (One move at this point is to take this epistemic barrier to heart and endorse *Mystery*, that there is no way to determine the correct answer to the SCQ (Markosian 2008: 358–9; Bennett, forthcoming), but presumably that is just as unsatisfying an answer as accepting Brutality).
- *Second problem:* Brutal explanations are to be discouraged (Hudson 2001: 22–5). Few think moral facts are inexplicably true, and that normative ethical theories are all doomed. We should think similarly of composition, accepting it only if all other answers were found wanting (which is, indeed, Markosian's argument for Brutality).

Nihilism and universalism

An alternative approach is to give up on meeting our intuitions about population and rely upon other motivations to find an answer to the SCQ. For instance, we might be worried about issues in vagueness, for like most other predicates "compose" seems to admit of borderline cases. But unlike most other predicates, whether things compose directly bears on whether certain things exist. So borderline composition results in vague objects, hovering between being and non-being, which many baulk at. One way to avoid this is to say that nothing ever composes (Hossack 2000: 426–9):

Nihilism: The ys compose iff there is one of them.

Given nihilism there are *no* objects with proper parts – every object is *mereologically simple*. So the only composition is when an object composes itself (which will never be vague for identity is, allegedly, not vague). Not that this is the only motivation for nihilism e.g. simplicity is a virtue and, trying to avoid the complexity of accounts like Serial and Brutality, we might be attracted by nihilism's simplicity (Markosian 2008: 347).

There are two varieties of nihilism. *Microphysical nihilism* is the view that the world is a sea of simples, where those simples are the tiny items of subatomic physics (Dorr 2005; Hossack 2000; Williams 2006). The second variety is *monistic nihilism*, whereby the world is just one big mereological simple *and that's it*. Monistic nihilism has been pinned on both Parmenides and Melissus, and has also had a recent resurrection (Horgan 1991; Schaffer 2007).

- *First problem:* Nihilism *radically* underpopulates for there are no cars, planes, tables etc. To solve this, nihilists introduce a *paraphrasing* strategy. Just as we assent to "the average man has 2.4 children" without thinking there exists some man who is average and has a grisly 40 per cent of a person as a child, nihilists assent to talk about composite objects without committing to those things existing. For instance, "There is a table over there" can be paraphrased (for the microphysical nihilist) as "There are simples arranged tablewise over there" (van Inwagen 1990: 98–114; Merricks 2001: 162–190; see McGrath [2005] and Uzquiano [2004] for problems). The monistic nihilist can make use of their own paraphrasing techniques in terms of the property distribution across the only thing that exists (Schaffer 2007: 181–3).
- *Second problem:* Given nihilism *we don't exist*. This triggers *cogito* style concerns that nihilism must be false given that we *know* that we exist. There hasn't been much discussion of this issue (the exception is Olson 2007: 180–210), although one move is to loosen the constraints on nihilism and allow that there are simples *and* composite organisms, such as you and I (van Inwagen 1990). How persuasive you find such a move, I leave up to you.
- *Third problem:* Microphysical nihilism demands the existence of microphysical simples. But are there such things? Perhaps science will discover that the microphysical structure of the world descends forever without "bottoming out" in simples. (Sider 1993; Ladyman and Ross 2007: 19–27; see Williams [2006] for a response).

An alternative to nihilism is to swing the other way:

Universalism: For any ys, then (if those ys do not overlap) those ys compose a further object.

"Overpopulation be damned!" cries the Universalist, as they overpopulate their ontology with hordes of strange objects like Nikk–Bush. This gross overpopulation has been a sticking point for many (Markosian 1998: 228, 2008: 344–5) for surely, the objection goes, it is just crazy to believe in these things. However, just as nihilists introduce a paraphrasing strategy, the universalist has a similar trick. Imagine you buy a six pack and put it in my fridge. You, truly, state that "All the beer is in the fridge." But imagine I questioned that statement. What of the beer remaining in the supermarket? Or in Estonia? What of the beer drunk throughout the 1800s? None of *that* beer is in the fridge. To resolve this dispute, note that both assertions contain a universal quantifier. We can say that in your case, context dictates that the quantifier ranges only over the beer you recently purchased. By talking about other countries and other times, I shift to a context where the quantifier in my sentence ranges over far more beer than that you just bought. So what we *both* say is true, but only in certain contexts (of which, the former context is most natural and the latter is a pedantic context). Universalists say the same of composite talk. Nikk–Bush exists, but normal contexts are such that we don't range over it and can (truly) deny that Nikk–Bush exists (just as you would deny you'd left any beer out of the fridge). When we do serious philosophy, the context changes, the domain of our quantifiers broadens, and it is now *true* that Nikk–Bush exists. This restriction strategy has proven popular (but see Korman [2008] for a response). Indeed universalism is by far the most popular answer to the SCQ (Armstrong 1989; Heller 1991: 49–51; Hudson 2001; Leonard and Goodman 1940; Lewis 1986: 211–3; McGrath 1998; Rea 1998; Sider 2001).

There are numerous motivations to believe universalism. Like nihilism it guarantees simplicity. It also renders composition non-vague, for it always takes place (Lewis 1986: 211–3; Sider 2001: 120–34; for responses, see Effingham, forthcoming; Merricks 2005; Smith 2006). It also goes some way to resolving the anthropocentric disagreements from "Brutality," above, for it now transpires that everyone is always right when they make assertions that things compose (and always wrong when they deny this) (see Sider 2008: 257–61). Finally, it is motivated on the grounds of the general utility it affords other philosophical theories (Hudson 2006: 636). For instance, in the early twentieth century it was traditional to rely upon universalism to explain plural predication (Leonard and Goodman 1940; Link 1998; Massey 1976) and to defuse problems in set theory (Goodman and Quine 1947; Leśniewski 1916). Whilst the former is no longer in vogue (McKay 2006: 19–54; Oliver and Smiley 2001), universalism still sees service for the latter (Lewis 1991).

Historical approaches

This does not exhaust the extant answers. There has been a surge of work in the connections between the history of philosophy and mereology, and there are now answers rooted in the works of Plato (Harte 2002) and Aquinas (Brown 2005: esp. 174). The eighteenth-century philosopher Jonathan Edwards also believed that what objects composed depends in some fashion upon the will of God, suggesting *Divine*: that the ys compose iff God wills that the ys compose (a similar answer is used by van Inwagen in the field of the composition of, not material objects, but organisations [van Inwagen 1995: 191–216]).

Doubtless other answers wait to be discovered, either in historical sources or elsewhere. This is good news, for given the problems we encounter finding an answer meeting our folk intuitions about population, unearthing alternative motivations (and answers to meet them) appears quite desirable.

Persistence

How things persist versus what things exist

Persistence is often phrased as a question about *how* things persist. So phrased, it makes it sound as if there is a deep mystery as to how an object persists from one moment to the next, and certainly it is not obvious that this is mysterious. So the question is somewhat murky. Indeed, the two answers to that question, perdurantism and endurantism, have themselves struggled to find a clear definition, so examining them won't necessarily clear up this murkiness. However, as will become in clear in the following subsection, the two sides do disagree over *what* things exist, and that is a readily intelligible disagreement. So I will stick to examining perdurantism/endurantism in light of their commitments to material objects. This might not be the end of the matter, for maybe there is more to those theories, but until the proponents of those theories are clear about what that extra ingredient might be, it is perhaps best not worried about.

Perdurantism/endurantism

Intuitively, things have spatial parts; e.g. one part of you is your heart. Perdurantists think things also have *temporal* parts; e.g. a part of you that is all of you from last week, and a distinct part that is all of you from next week. This might not make it clear what a temporal part is, and this was indeed an early objection from many philosophers (Chisholm 1976: 143; Geach 1972: 311; van Inwagen 1981: 133). Fortunately a more exact definition can be given:

> x is an instantaneous temporal part of y at $t =_{df}$ (i) x is a part of y at t; (ii) x exists at, and only at, t; and (iii) x overlaps at t everything that is part of y at t (Sider 2001: 59).

Perdurantism is then the claim that an object has an instantaneous temporal part at every instant that it exists at. Straightforwardly, this is a claim about what things exist, so perdurantism is a clear and crisp position. Endurantism, however, is less clear. Endurantists are unhappy with objects having temporal parts, often saying that objects must instead be "wholly present." However, just as people demanded we make clear what a temporal part is, the same has been said regarding "wholly present" (Sider 2001: 63–8). Whilst some definitions have been proposed (in terms of being multiply located [Gilmore 2007]; in terms of objects being extended [improper] temporal parts [Parsons 2007]; or otherwise [Crisp and Smith 2005]) none have, as yet, won popular support. But we can avoid discussion of that debate, for it is enough that endurantists are (generally) united in their opposition to the prolific population perdurantists commit to; i.e. the endurantist *denies* that there is an instantaneous object for every instant that a persisting object exists at. Indeed, this apparent overpopulation is itself an objection to perdurantism (Thomson 1983: 213; see Heller [1991: 16–19] and Sider [2001: 216–18] for discussion).

An exception can be found amongst *promiscuous endurantists*, who think they can have the prolific population and still be endurantists (Koslicki 2003: 121–2; Lowe 2005a; Miller 2005a). Given promiscuity, there would be an extra ingredient to perdurantism and/or endurantism. But if there is an extra ingredient, it is not obvious what it is. Moreover, most of those who are promiscuous go on to conclude that endurantism (promiscuously conceived) is, in fact, equivalent to perdurantism; i.e. the two theories are in fact two different ways of saying the same thing (Lowe 2005a; Lowe and Storrs-McCall 2006; Miller 2005b). Ergo there *can't* be an extra ingredient making them distinct, as they're the same! Given this, one might suspect that endurantism plus promiscuity is equivalent to perdurantism, solely on the grounds that (as I claim) being promiscuous with regards to what objects exist *is* what it is to be a perdurantist. So let us pass over the promiscuous endurantists, and take perdurantism and endurantism to be commitments to what objects there are.

Numerous arguments are mooted to decide between endurantism and perdurantism, such as using the theories to solve the paradoxes of coincidence (Sider 2001: 140–208; Hawley 2001: 140–75; Wasserman 2003a); the argument from temporary intrinsics (see Haslanger 2003; Lewis 1986: 202–4; Sider 2001: 92–8; Wasserman 2003b); arguments from special relativity (Balashov 1999; Gibson and Pooley 2006; Gilmore 2006; Hales and Johnson 2003); and even time travel (Effingham and Robson 2007; Gilmore 2007; Sider 2001: 101–9). I won't detail them here, concentrating instead upon how persistence meshes with the rest of the metaphysics of material objects.

Consanguinity I: composition and persistence

We have thus far only discussed composition *at a time*. Perdurantists are a mereologically greedy bunch though, usually demanding more than this, such that things from *different* times can compose, e.g. that all of my instantaneous temporal parts compose me. Such composition isn't temporally relativised, and perdurantists conscript *atemporal* mereological relations to do the job. The relations are analogous in all ways to those introduced under "The special composition question," above, except they are only dyadic, and aren't relativised to times. The perdurantist still retains temporally relativised parthood, but analyses it in terms of atemporal mereology:

> (P@T) x is part of y at t iff x and y each exist at t, and x's instantaneous temporal part at t is part of y's instantaneous temporal part at t (Sider 2001: 57).

Likewise (to avoid circularity) they offer a revised definition of instantaneous temporal part, equivalent to the one above, but in atemporal terms (by simply dropping the temporal relativisations from the first and third conjunct). It is not *necessary* for perdurantists to accept atemporal mereology and make these moves – indeed, Sider's definition of perdurantism was crafted to avoid just such a commitment – but most accept it anyhow. Endurantists, by contrast, have traditionally claimed not to understand "atemporal" parthood (which is why Sider gave the definition he did, as a fig leaf to such endurantists to make sense of perdurantism). Not that it is impossible for them to do so (see McDaniel 2004: 144; Hawley 2001: 29), although obviously they cannot go on to accept (P@T).

First, consider this new addition with regards to the perdurantist. Given (P@T) the answer to the temporally relativised SCQ will drop out of the answer to the atemporal analogue of the SCQ. However, answers to the temporally relativised SCQ don't easily map to answering its atemporal analogue.

Consider the sample "sensible" answer of Contact. Given Contact, composing objects have to be spatially contiguous, but no temporal parts are *spatially* contiguous so no temporal parts will compose. Temporal parts are spatiotemporally contiguous, but if we make *that* the criterion then this worsens Contact's overpopulation. Consider this: you can trace a continuous spatiotemporal path of one of my atoms back to the Big Bang, and from the Big Bang trace a path via an atom that ends up in George Bush. So whilst I and Bush aren't spatiotemporally contiguous, the two of us plus all the previous temporal parts of our smallest atoms *are* continuous (so we get a Nikk–Bush–past atom composite, which is just as bad as Nikk–Bush).

Microphysical nihilism doesn't fare so well either. Given nihilism, nothing has parts; *a fortiori* nothing has temporal parts. All that would exist would be *non-persisting* mereological simples. Whilst, technically, everything would still perdure (for everything would exist for a single instant, and have itself as an instantaneous [improper] temporal part) this is a pyrrhic victory. For instance, Parsons thinks enduring objects are just objects with no proper temporal parts: so the endurantist would say such objects endured. It's difficult to see what is left of the perdurantist enterprise if nothing persists and endurantists are comfortable with the world so described. Similarly, given monistic nihilism, the universe is a persisting simple, thus it has no temporal parts – *sayonara* perdurantism.

Universalism, though, is a popular position for perdurantists to accept (a notable exception being McCall [1994]). But even it has problems.

- *First problem:* Most perdurantists want to say that the properties an object has at a time are determined by the properties *simpliciter* an object's instantaneous temporal part at that time has; e.g. I am sitting now iff my instantaneous temporal part at this instant is sitting *simpliciter*. Now take the object composed of a turnip from throughout the year 1979 and all of Pavarotti's temporal parts from 1980–2007. Given this treatment of properties, that object was, in 1979, a turnip but was, from 1980 onwards, a tenor. So some tenor was once a turnip! In being obviously false, this commitment causes problems (see Varzi [2003] and Parsons [2005] for discussion).
- *Second problem:* We can construct weird objects that breach the laws of physics. For instance, that tenor–turnip managed to teleport instantaneously, being located in a

turnip field just before the stroke of midnight on New Year's Eve 1979 and then Italy the second after. But the laws of nature prevent this. Indeed, even weirder objects exist, for instance, given perdurantism and universalism, we can construct superluminal objects *contra* the laws of special relativity (Hudson 2005: 123–36; see Hawthorne [2006: 111–43] for a discussion of similar issues).

One lesson to draw is that we should look again at the less popular answers such as Divine, Mystery, Brutality, etc. (notably Edwards believed both Divine and perdurantism). Another lesson is that we need a totally new answer, but none is extant in the literature. A third lesson is that there is no univocal answer to the atemporal SCQ. Instead, there is one criterion for what objects compose at a time (using an answer such as Contact, universalism, etc.) and another criterion for what composes *across* time (Balashov 2005), although it's tricky to see what such a disjunctive answer could be (Hudson 2005). In any case, perdurantism has radical consequences for composition. Endurantism is less radical, for (even if they accept atemporal mereological notions) most endurantists will deny that any composition takes place other than at a time (for to say otherwise entails the existence of perduring objects, see McKinnon [2002: 294]).

Identity

Criteria of identity

Finally we come to the question of identity: under what conditions is x identical to y? Identity is tied into the ontology of material objects just as composition and persistence are. For instance, if $x_1, x_2, x_3 \ldots$ exist at times $t_1, t_2, t_3 \ldots$, then this fact alone won't settle what exists, for if those xs are all *identical* then it turns out that there is but one thing, persisting throughout the interval that has $t_1, t_2, t_3 \ldots$ as instants. Whereas, if they are all distinct, we have scads of objects, at least one for every instant just listed.

Problem scenarios about identity are well known from elementary philosophy lessons. If Leo has an accident and suffers total amnesia, is he identical to the person after the accident? If Chris and Malcolm have their brains placed in one another's body, who is Chris and who is Malcolm? If Jim is disassembled into his constituent atoms and reassembled on Mars, is the person we reassemble Jim? Nor does it end with people, as scenarios such as the ship of Theseus demonstrates. I'm not going to get bogged down recapping the literature here, instead turning straight to the relationship between identity, composition and persistence.

Consanguinity II: dissolution

There is an interesting way to dissolve these questions about identity if we accept the combination of perdurantism and universalism. Given that combination, for any putative disagreement about whether one object is identical to another there are always enough objects so *both* sides are right and are disagreeing only over what they think their words refer to. For instance, take the case of Leo suffering total amnesia. Given perdurantist–

universalism there is an object A, composed of all of Leo's pre-accident temporal parts. There is also an object B, composed of all and only the temporal parts of that guy after the accident. Given universalism, there is an object C, composed out of A and B. We can dissolve the disagreement over whether Leo survives the accident by saying that those who think he doesn't survive (i.e. think that A and B are both distinct people, whilst C is not a person but a composite object like Nikk–Bush that has persons as parts) mean one thing by "person," whilst those who think he does survive (i.e. think C is a person, whilst A and B are mere temporal parts of a person) mean something else. The dispute is merely over the *meaning* of "person," and so doesn't involve metaphysics at all. Compare to disputes over whether certain plots of land qualify as political states. There is vicious disagreement over whether Israel counts as a state or not, but that's not a *metaphysical* dispute, for all parties agree on the ontology – that the disputed plot of land *exists*.

Consanguinity III: kind relativisation

When it comes to identity, people have traditionally been willing to relativise the criteria of identity to different *kinds*. So one popular answer for people is that x is identical to y iff there is a chain of psychological continuity between x and y. But that won't work for tables (or mountains, or galaxies, etc.), for they have no psychological life, never mind a continuous one. Instead, such things have their own criteria.

But if we are willing to allow a disjunctive answer to the identity question, where the conditions of each disjunct are kind relativised, we come into tension with the reasons to give up on Serial, wherein relativising composition to kinds was discouraged. There are two lessons we can learn, either to look again at Serial (see Lowe 2005b: 516–17) or to be more critical of the traditional approach to identity (e.g. mimicking the moves in composition and, say, concluding identity facts are brute; see Merricks 1998).

Extreme consanguinity

I have detailed the close association of these three areas. Some philosophers, though, have gone one step further, claiming not just consanguinity between the areas, but that they are one and the same.

Composition as identity

Composition as identity (CAI) is the claim that the composition relation is the identity relation; i.e. when x is composed of the ys, x is identical to the ys (Baxter 1988a, b). As the whole is not distinct from its parts, CAI captures that intuition that objects are nothing "over and above their parts." But whilst it chimes with that folk intuition, it does violence to other intuitions.

- *First problem:* How can *one* thing be identical to *many* things? Isn't identity a one–one relation, not a one–many relation? (Merricks 2001: 21–8).

- *Second problem:* We must give up on Leibniz's law, for if x is one thing and is composed of many things, then (given Leibniz's law) x is both one thing *and* many things – an apparent contradiction (Lewis 1991: 87).
- *Third problem:* It is suitable only for perdurantists, as endurantists will either see it as trivial (identifying atemporal composition with identity, which for endurantists is uncontroversial, as they will say x is only ever *atemporally* composed by itself) or false (as identity is two place, and temporally relativised composition is three place, so it doesn't look like they can be identical).

Some philosophers try to avoid such problems by weakening CAI, claiming that composition is instead *analogous* to identity in certain ways (Lewis 1991: 81–7; Sider 2007). However, given this move the composite is now distinct from its parts and we've lost that respect CAI paid to the intuition that an object is nothing over and above its parts. So a weaker CAI will have to pay its way on some other ground.

Supersubstantivalism

CAI isn't the only twinning. Whilst it is wrong to think identity is the persistence relation that holds between an object and the interval it persists through (for there could be two *distinct* objects that persist through the *same* interval) there is a plausible claim in the same neighbourhood. We can say that all objects are identical to the regions of space–time they occupy. This is known as *supersubstantivalism*. Even though it has odd consequences, for instance that some spatiotemporal regions walk, talk and pay taxes, supersubstantivalism has found popular support amongst metaphysicians (Field 1984: 75n2; Sider 2001: 110; Quine 1995: 259) and scientists alike (Castelvecchi 2006; Sklar 1974: 221–4). Certainly the parsimonious ontology it offers, whereby there is only one category (space–time, with material objects as a subset of regions) rather than two (space–time and material objects as distinct sets of things), should make a metaphysician salivate. Again, though, it appears to be available only to the perdurantist, as space–time regions uncontroversially perdure (Sider 2001: 110–13).

References

Armstrong, David (1989) *Universals: An Opinionated Introduction*, London: Westview.
Balashov, Yuri (1999) "Relativistic Objects," *Noûs* 33: 644–62.
—— (2005) "On Vagueness, 4D and Diachronic Universalism," *Australasian Journal of Philosophy* 83: 523–31.
Baxter, Donald (1988a) "Many–One Identity," *Philosophical Papers* 17: 193–216.
—— (1988b) "Identity in the Loose and Popular Sense," *Mind* 97: 575–82.
Bennett, Karen (Forthcoming) "Composition, Colocation and Metaontology," in David Chalmers, David Manley, and Ryan Wasserman (eds) *Metametaphysics*, Oxford: Oxford University Press.
Brown, Christopher (2005) *Aquinas and the Ship of Theseus: Solving Puzzles about Material Objects*, London: Continuum.
Castelvecchi, Davide (2006) "Out of the Void," *New Scientist* 2564: 28–31.
Chisholm, Roderick (1976) *Person and Object*, London: Allen & Unwin.

Crisp, Timothy and Smith, Donald (2005) "'Wholly Present' Defined," *Philosophy and Phenomenological Research* 71: 318–44.

Dorr, Cian (2005) "What We Disagree about When We Disagree about Ontology," in Mark E. Kalderon (ed.) *Fictionalism in Metaphysics*, Oxford: Oxford University Press, pp. 203–33.

Effingham, Nikk (Forthcoming) "Universalism, Vagueness and Supersubstantivalism," *Australasian Journal of Philosophy*.

Effingham, Nikk and Robson, Jon (2007) "A Mereological Challenge to Endurantism," *Australasian Journal of Philosophy* 85: 633–40.

Field, Hartry (1984) "Can We Dispense with Spacetime?" *PSA* 2: 33–90.

Geach, Peter (1972) *Logic Matters*, Oxford: Blackwell.

Gibson, Ian and Pooley, Oliver (2006) "Relativistic Persistence," *Philosophical Perspectives* 20: 157–98.

Gilmore, Cody (2006) "Where in the Relativistic World Are We?" *Philosophical Perspectives* 20: 199–36.

—— (2007) "Time Travel, Coinciding Objects, and Persistence," *Oxford Studies in Metaphysics* 3: 177–98.

Goodman, Nelson and Quine, Willard (1947) "Steps Towards a Constructive Nominalism," *Journal of Symbolic Logic* 12: 105–22.

Hales, Steven and Johnson, Timothy (2003) "Endurantism, Perdurantism and Special Relativity," *Philosophical Quarterly* 53: 524–39.

Harte, Verity (2002) *Plato on Parts and Wholes: The Metaphysics of Structure*, Oxford: Oxford University Press.

Haslanger, Sally (2003) "Persistence through Time," in Michael J. Loux and Dean W. Zimmerman (eds.) *The Oxford Handbook of Metaphysics*, Oxford: Oxford University Press, pp. 315–54.

Hawley, Katherine (2001) *How Things Persist*, Oxford: Oxford University Press.

Hawthorne, John (2006) *Metaphysical Essays*, Oxford: Oxford University Press.

Heller, Mark (1991) *The Ontology of Physical Objects*, Cambridge: Cambridge University Press.

Horgan, Terence (1991) "Metaphysical Realism and Psychologistic Semantics," *Erkenntnis* 34: 297–322.

Hossack, Keith (2000) "Plurals and Complexes," *British Journal for Philosophy of Science* 51: 411–43.

Hudson, Hud (2001) *A Materialist Metaphysics of the Human Person*, Ithaca, NY: Cornell University Press.

—— (2005) *The Metaphysics of Hyperspace*, Oxford: Oxford University Press.

—— (2006) "Confining Composition," *Journal of Philosophy* 103: 631–51.

Korman, Daniel (2008) "Unrestricted Composition and Restricted Quantification," *Philosophical Studies* 140: 319–34.

Koslicki, Kathrin (2003) "The Crooked Path from Vagueness to Four-Dimensionalism," *Philosophical Studies* 114: 107–34.

Ladyman, James and Ross, Don (2007) *Every Thing Must Go*, Oxford: Oxford University Press.

Leonard, Henry and Goodman, Nelson (1940) "The Calculus of Individuals and Its Uses," *The Journal of Symbolic Logic* 5: 45–55.

Lesniewski, Stanislaw (1916) "Foundations of the General Theory of Sets," reprinted in S. J. Surma, J. T. Srzednicki, and D. I. Barnett (eds.) *Stanisław Lesniewski: Collected Works*, vol. 1, The Hague: Martinus Nifhoff, pp. 129–73.

Lewis, David (1986) *On the Plurality of Worlds*, Oxford: Blackwell.

—— (1991) *Parts of Classes*, Oxford: Blackwell.

Link, Godehard (1998) *Algebraic Semantics in Language and Philosophy*, Stanford, CA: CSLI Publications.

Lowe, E. Jonathan (2005a) "Vagueness and Endurance," *Analysis* 65: 104–12.

—— (2005b) "How Are Ordinary Objects Possible?" *Monist* 88: 510–33.

Lowe, E. Jonathan and McCall, Storrs (2006) "The 3D/4D Controversy: A Storm in a Teacup," *Noûs* 40: 570–8.

Markosian, Ned (1998) "Brutal Composition," *Philosophical Studies* 92: 211–49.

—— (2008) "Restricted Composition," in Theodore Hawthorne, John Sider, and Dean W. Zimmerman (eds), *Contemporary Debates in Metaphysics*, Oxford: Blackwell, pp. 341–63.

Massey, Gerald (1976) "Tom, Dick, and Harry, and All the King's Men," *American Philosophical Quarterly* 13: 89–107.

McCall, S. (1994) *A Model of the Universe: Space–Time, Probability, and Decision*, Oxford: Clarendon Press.

McDaniel, Kris (2004) "Modal Realism with Overlap," *Australasian Journal of Philosophy* 82: 137–52.

McGrath, Matthew (1998) "Van Inwagen's Critique of Universalism," *Analysis* 58: 116–21.

—— (2005) "No Objects, No Problem?" *Australasian Journal of Philosophy* 83, 457–86.

McKay, Thomas (2006) *Plural Predication*, Oxford: Clarendon Press.

McKinnon, Neil (2002) "The Endurance/Perdurance Distinction," *Australasian Journal of Philosophy* 80: 288–306.

Merricks, Trenton (1998) "There Are No Criteria of Identity Over Time," *Noûs* 32: 106–24.

—— (2001) *Objects and Persons*, Oxford: Oxford University Press.

—— (2005) "Composition and Vagueness," *Mind* 114: 615–37.

Miller, Kristie (2005a) "Blocking the Path from Vagueness to Four Dimensionalism," *Ratio* 18: 317–31.

—— (2005b) "The Metaphysical Equivalence of Three and Four Dimensionalism," *Erkenntnis* 62: 91–117.

Oliver, Alex and Smiley, Timothy (2001) "Strategies for a Logic of Plurals," *Philosophical Quarterly* 51: 289–306.

Olson, Eric (2007) *What Are We?* Oxford: Oxford University Press.

Parsons, Josh (2005) "I Am Not Now, nor Have I Ever Been, a Turnip," *Australasian Journal of Philosophy* 83: 1–14.

—— (2007) "Theories of Location," *Oxford Studies in Metaphysics* 3: 201–32.

Quine, W. V. (1995) "Naturalism; Or, Living within One's Means," *Dialectica* 49: 251–61.

Rea, Michael (1998) "In Defence of Mereological Universalism," *Philosophy and Phenomenological Research* 63: 347–60.

Sanford, David (1993) "The Problem of the Many, Many Composition Questions, and Naïve Mereology," *Noûs* 27: 219–28.

Schaffer, Jonathan (2007) "From Nihilism to Monism," *Australasian Journal of Philosophy* 85: 175–91.

Sider, Ted (1993) "Van Inwagen and the Possibility of Gunk," *Analysis* 53: 285–89.

—— (2001) *Four-Dimensionalism*, Oxford: Clarendon Press.

—— (2007) "Parthood," *Philosophical Review* 116: 51–91.

—— (2008) "Temporal Parts," in Sider, Theodore Hawthorne, John Sider, and Dean W. Zimmerman (eds), *Contemporary Debates in Metaphysics*, Oxford: Blackwell, pp. 241–62.

Sklar, Lawrence (1974) *Space, Time, and Spacetime*, London: University of California Press.

Smith, Donald (2006) "The Vagueness Argument for Mereological Universalism," *Pacific Philosophical Quarterly* 87: 357–68.

Thomasson, Amie (2007) *Ordinary Objects*, Oxford: Oxford University Press.

Thomson, Judith (1983) "Parthood and Identity across Time," *Journal of Philosophy* 80: 201–20.

Uzquiano, Gabriel (2004) "Plurals and Simples," *Monist* 87: 429–51.

van Inwagen, Peter (1981) "The Doctrine of Arbitrary Undetached Parts," *Pacific Philosophical Quarterly* 62: 123–37.

—— (1990) *Material Beings*, Ithaca, NY: Cornell University Press.

—— (1995) "Non est Hick," in Peter van Inwagen (ed.), *God, Knowledge and Mystery*, Ithaca, NY: Cornell University Press, pp. 191–216.

Varzi, Achille (2003) "Perdurantism, Universalism, and Quantifiers," *Australasian Journal of Philosophy* 81: 208–15.

Wasserman, Ryan (2003a) "The Argument from Temporary Intrinsics," *Australasian Journal of Philosophy* 81: 413–9.

—— (2003b) "The Standard Objection to the Standard Account," *Philosophical Studies* 111: 197–216.

Williams, Robbie (2006) "Illusions of Gunk," *Philosophical Perspectives* 20: 493–513.

Further reading

Ned Markosian "Restricted Composition," in Theodore Hawthorne, John Sider, and Dean W. Zimmerman (eds), *Contemporary Debates in Metaphysics* (Oxford: Blackwell, 2008), pp. 341–63, offers a contemporary survey of issues in composition. In persistence, Sally Haslanger, "Persistence through Time," in Michael J. Loux and Dean W. Zimmerman (eds) *The Oxford Handbook of Metaphysics* (Oxford: Oxford University Press, 2003), pp. 315–54, offers an in-depth introduction to the argument from temporary intrinsics; Ted Sider, *Four-Dimensionalism* (Oxford: Clarendon Press, 2001) covers the rest, including an extensive discussion of the paradoxes of coincidence. Cynthia MacDonald, *Varieties of Things* (Oxford: Blackwell,

2005) offers an introduction to identity over time. Nor are the above issues the only areas of consanguinity between the fields. See Katherine Hawley, "Principles of Composition and Criteria of Identity," *Australasian Journal of Philosophy* 84 (2006): 481–93, for more on the relationship between identity and composition; and Thomas Sattig "Identity in 4D," *Philosophical Studies* 140 (2008): 179–95, for a critical examination of how perdurantism bears on identity.

30
RELATIONS
John Heil

Recent years have witnessed renewed interest in the ontology of properties. Some philosophers shun properties altogether. Others embrace properties but differ on whether properties are universals or particulars (a.k.a. modes, individual accidents, tropes, abstract particulars). In most discussions of properties, relations are an afterthought. Perhaps relations are really kinds of property, "relational properties." Or maybe it is the other way round: properties are "monadic relations." The idea that properties are powers is increasingly popular. What then of relations? It is hard to see being a meter apart as a power. If it is not a power, what *is* it? If it is a power, what *has* it? Does it belong to the relata? Or does it subsist somehow *between* relata?

Such questions cry out for an account of relations. A satisfying account would be more than a purely formal characterization and more than an analysis of relational concepts. A satisfying account of relations must be *ontologically serious*. This means, among other things, refusing to rest content with abstract specifications of relations as, for instance, sets of ordered *n*-tuples. Such bloodless characterizations would satisfy only the mean-spirited and ontologically timid.

Relational worlds

Philosophical conceptions of relations occupy positions between two poles. At the one extreme are relation-phobes, those who regard relations as creatures of reason or as identifiable with objects' monadic properties. At the other extreme are lovers of relations, enthusiasts who regard relations as ontological bedrock, seeing other entities as constructed from relations. The middle ground encompasses pluralists happy to embrace both irreducible relations and non-relational monadic properties. As in most philosophical disputes of this nature, the middle ground has been, with few exceptions, occupied chiefly by theorists whose interests lie, not in ontology *per se*, but in its applications in particular domains.

Consider first the striking idea that relations are ontologically primary: monadic, non-relational features of the world are constituted by relations. A view of this kind is defended by C. S. Peirce and perhaps by contemporary advocates of "structural realism" (Ladyman 2007). Randal Dipert (1997) develops an austere ontology of relations, a conception of the "world as graph." On this conception, all there is to objects are relations into which they enter: if you have the relations, you have the relata.

The thesis is exciting, especially when you take seriously the perennially seductive thought that everything is what it is owing to ways it is connected to everything else. The difficulty is to get a grip on the ontology. It is hard not to think of relations as dependent on relata in the sense that, without the relata, there is nothing to relate. Suppose a and b stand in relation R (a and b are next to one another). Now subtract a and b, but leave R. You would do as well to subtract the cat and leave the smile.

This is too quick. Consider an example, due to Richard Holton (1999), who imagines a world, W_R, comprising four objects, A, B, C and D, wholly constituted by relations in which they stand to one another:

- A is directly to the left of B and directly above C;
- B is directly to the right of A, and directly above D;
- C is directly to the left of D, and directly below A;
- D is directly to the right of C, and directly below B.

We could represent W_R thus:

A •   B •
C •   D •

The labeled points, note, are meant only to help us visualize W_R. "There really is nothing more to A, B, C, and D than that given by the descriptions" (Holton 1999: 10). We get from our representation to W_R itself by erasing the points (and labels) while leaving the relations in place. The result is a world seemingly bereft of qualities and qualitied individuals. Might we make up the difference with relations? Or have we rather moved illicitly from the claim that a world could be given a purely relational *description* – via graph theory, for instance – to the much stronger thesis that this is *all there is* to the world? Such a move might be especially tempting to philosophers who start with scientific formalisms then attempt to extract an ontology directly from these. Carried to the extreme, the practice leads to Pythagoreanism: the world as number (Martin 1997).

The idea that relations could be fundamental, relata derivative, might strike you as preposterous. Relations seem to need something – something non-relational – to relate. As an argument, however, this expression of incredulity might fairly be counted as question-begging. It would be nice to be able to say more, to find a basis for the thought that relata are ontologically prior to relations.

One such basis becomes salient when you consider the individuation of objects and relations. Return to Holton's relational world. In the absence of dots or labels, what distinguishes the directly-to-the-right-of from the directly-above relation? How do we count instances of each relation? A purely relational world arguably lacks sufficient individuative resources. In this regard, purely relational worlds resemble "pure power" worlds, worlds in which objects' properties are exclusively powers to affect other objects by affecting those objects' powers. Powers are individuated in part by their qualitative effects, manifestations involving qualitative alterations (Unger 2006). More could be said on this topic, but I propose to move on to less contentious conceptions of relations.

Historical stage setting

For centuries philosophers took as their starting point Aristotle's categorization of relations as *accidents* – Socrates's whiteness, the sphericity of this ball – entities dependent on substances (*Categories*, 7). The thought is straightforward. Relations are clearly not substances, so they must be, if they are anything at all, accidents. As we shall see, this way of thinking about relations makes it especially difficult to accord them anything resembling a fundamental metaphysical standing and encourages anti-realist and reductionist impulses. Indeed, the history of philosophical discussion of relations divides conveniently into the period before and the period after the late nineteenth century. With important exceptions, relations were regarded with suspicion until philosophers working in logic and foundations of mathematics advanced reasons to doubt that we could provide anything like an adequate description of the world without employing a relational vocabulary (Russell 1903, chap. 26). To many philosophers this was reason enough to regard relations as ontologically fundamental: what is conceptually required is ontologically basic.

The historical record encompasses a proliferation of views on relations that emerged during the medieval period and thereafter. Here is a rough-and-ready taxonomy.

(1) *Flat-out anti-realism*: there are no relations; beliefs of the form "*a* bears *R* to *b*" are false.
(2) *Projectivism*: relations are creatures of reason, purely mental comparisons "projected" on to the experienced world.
(3) *Constrained projectivism*: Relations are creatures of reason, mental comparisons constrained by non-relational features of the world.
(4) *Reductionism*: relations are identifiable with non-relational features of objects.
(5) *Supervenience*: relations exist, but are somehow "dependent on and determined by" the relata and their monadic properties.
(6) *Modest realism*: truthmakers for relational predications are non-relational features of the world.
(7) *Hyper-realism*: relations are ontologically fundamental; the world includes, in addition to objects and their ("monadic") properties, relations.

Historians could certainly supplement and refine this list, but it will suffice for present purposes.

You might think it obvious that rejection of (1), flat-out anti-realism, requires something like (7), hyper-realism, or possibly (4), reduction. It was not always so. In particular, it was not so for medieval philosophers, many of whom contributed to the sizeable historical literature on relations. One way to understand various medievals is to see them as defending versions of all the other views (Brower 2005). One question, then, is whether a view such as (3) is *really* different from (4), (5) or (6). Perhaps (3) is a confusingly put attempt to express what (6) expresses and (5), too, is best understood as approximating (6). Perhaps philosophers have been driven to defend the remaining views in part owing to endemic confusion over what "realism about relations" requires.

Internal and external relations

The question whether all relations are "internal," whether some relations are "external," figured prominently in discussions of relations in the early part of the twentieth century. (Richard Rorty's entry on relations in the original 1967 *Encyclopedia of Philosophy* is devoted exclusively to the topic.) G. E. Moore (1919) characterizes internal relations modally: internal relations are relations essential to their relata. Suppose a and b are related R-wise. If R is an internal relation, a and b could not fail so to be related; otherwise R is external. Consider six's bearing the greater-than relation to five. It would seem impossible that six and five could fail to stand in this relation. Compare Simmias's bearing the taller-than relation to Socrates. Although Simmias *is* taller than Socrates, both Simmias and Socrates could have failed to stand in this relation: Simmias could have been shorter, Socrates taller.

Moore's discussion of the distinction emerges as part of an attack on F. H. Bradley (1893: Chs 2 and 3) to whom Moore ascribes the view that all relations are internal. Moore notes that a view of this kind implies that objects have all of their properties essentially: if Socrates has a bruise on his left shin, he could not have failed to have a bruise on his left shin. Why? A change in a single property of a single object changes relations among every object. Objects in Socrates's world would no longer be related in endless ways to bruised Socrates. So, whatever is, is what it is of necessity and could not have been otherwise. Although some philosophers, including Leibniz, have thought this, you might, following Moore, regard it as excessive.

Moore thinks Bradley is led to the thesis that all relations are internal by conflating two superficially similar principles:

(1) An object, a's, being P entails that, if some object, x, lacks P, then $x \neq a$.
(2) If an object, a, is P, then an object x's lacking P entails that $x \neq a$.

(Let a be Simmias and P be a "relational property," being taller than Socrates.) You could think of (1) as expressing the *indiscernibility of identicals*: if $a = b$, every property of a is a property of b and vice versa. In contrast, (2) expresses a much stronger thesis: if a has P, a could not have failed to have P. This would be true, if at all, only if P is an essential property of a. But not all of a's properties, and in particular not all of a's "relational properties," are essential to a. Bradley, Moore suggests, slides from the innocuous (1) to the implausible (2).

Before considering how Bradley might respond, a word about "relational properties." As Russell (1997 [1903]) notes, and Moore reiterates, ascribing a relational property to an object is an oblique way of asserting that the object stands in a particular relation. Simmias's possessing the relational property of being taller than Socrates is simply a matter of Simmias's being taller than Socrates. Relational properties are not kinds of property. To imagine that you might dispense with relations, replacing them with relational properties, is to engage in a linguistic subterfuge.

Relational properties aside, what, if anything, might be said in Bradley's defense? Bradley does indeed say that when you try to think of an object's being different from what it in fact is, you are not imagining *that* object, but only a qualitatively *similar* object, a *counterpart*. Thus, although we can apparently imagine Edward VII childless, when we do so, what we are imagining is someone very like Edward – an Edward counterpart – who is childless. This makes it appear that Bradley does indeed want to defend the thesis Moore ascribes to him, namely, that every object has all of its properties (including its "relational properties") essentially: no object could fail to have the properties it has or fail to enter into the relations into which it in fact enters.

One reason to doubt that this is Bradley's considered view, however, is that Bradley's arguments against relations go hand in hand with arguments directed against *qualities*, *non*-relational properties. Bradley insists that thoughts of qualities and relations alike are thoughts of impossible entities. (Think of an Escher drawing.) Qualities and relations belong to the realm of appearance. We are left with a single, undifferentiated substance: the Absolute. Because thinking is judging, however, and because judging involves predicating qualities and relations of substances, our very forms of thought prevent us from thinking clearly about reality, about the Absolute. Our representations of the world carry the seeds of their own destruction. The mistake is to confuse features of the apparatus we deploy in representing reality with features of reality itself. Characterizing Bradley as holding that all relations are internal, then, misses the mark (Candlish 2006: Ch. 6).

External relations and Bradley's regress

Whatever the merits of Moore's assessment of Bradley, the idea that every relation is internal possesses independent philosophical interest. Here is a simple way to think about internal relations.

(I) If R internally relates *a* and *b*, then, if you have *a* and *b*, you *thereby* have R.

Take six's being greater than five. If you have six and you have five, you *thereby* have six's being greater than five. God's creating a world in which six is greater than five requires only that God create six and five; six's being greater than five is, as D. M. Armstrong (1989: 56) puts it, *no addition of being*. Compare this with Simmias's being taller than Socrates. You could have Simmias and Socrates without its thereby being the case that Simmias is taller than Socrates. (Let me note in passing that, if (I) captures the notion of an internal relation, it will turn out that relations in a purely relational world are internal. Objects in such world are constituted by relations: if you have the objects, the relata, you have the relations.)

We seem obliged, then, to countenance two kinds of relation: internal, ontologically recessive relations, and ontologically substantive external relations. Following the medievals, we could say that internal relations are "founded" on monadic (non-relational) features of their relata: when an internal relation holds, it holds in virtue of non-relational features of whatever it relates. But what is the ontology of external relations?

Philosophical discussion of relations from Aristotle through the mid-nineteenth century could be viewed as a succession of attempts to *locate* external relations ontologically. Aristotle, as noted earlier, classifies relations as accidents. Accidents, unlike substances are dependent entities: ways particular substances are. Socrates's whiteness is *Socrates's* whiteness. Socrates could exist without being white, perhaps, but Socrates's whiteness could not exist without Socrates. Suppose Simmias is taller than Socrates: Simmias bears the taller-than relation to Socrates. *Where* is this relation? Not in Simmias, it seems, nor in Socrates, nor in both Simmias and Socrates. If the relation is located "between" Simmias and Socrates, it must either be a substance itself, not an accident, or be located in some other substance. Neither option appears viable. Leibniz puts it this way:

> The ratio or proportion of two lines L and M can be conceived in three ways: as a ratio of the greater L to the smaller M; as a ratio of the smaller M to the greater L; and lastly as something abstracted from both of them, that is to say as the ratio between L and M, without considering which is the anterior and which is the posterior, which the subject, which the object. In the first way of considering them, L the greater is the subject; in the second, M the smaller is the subject of this accident which philosophers call relation. But which will be the subject of the third way of considering them? We cannot say that the two, L and M together, are the subject of such an accident, for in that case we should have an accident in two subjects, with one leg in one and the other leg in the other, which is contrary to the notion of accidents. (1973 [1715]: Fifth Paper, §47)

Suppose *a* bears *R* to *b*. Where is *R*? Not in *a*, not in *b*, not in both *a* and *b*. Perhaps *R* is located *outside a* and *b*: between *a* and *b*. Such a view is hard to square with the idea that relations are *accidents*. What is *R* an accident *of*, if not *a* or *b*? If we turn *R* into a shadowy substance, it would appear that we would need another relation *R'*, to relate *a*, *R* and *b*. Now, however, the location question arises for *R'*. *R'* cannot be in *a*, in *b*, in *R* or in all three. Perhaps *R'* is between *a*, *b* and *R*? If so, we evidently require a *further* relation, *R''*, to relate *a*, *b*, *R* and *R'*. We are off on a regress. The regress is commonly called Bradley's regress because he (1893: 21) brandishes it in a campaign against non-substantial modes of being. The specter of a regress is all but guaranteed by traditional ways of thinking about relations, however. Versions were advanced by Aristotle, by Fakhr al-Din al-Razi, by Avicenna, by Aquinas, and by Scotus (see Weinberg [1965], pp. 78, 90, 93, 95 and 101, for references).

Reinhardt Grossmann (1983: Ch. 3), a champion of relations, contends that Bradley's regress assumes what is false: that relations need to be related to relata. *Relata* are related, not relations. This brings us back to the location problem. If relations are accidents, what are they accidents *of*? If they are not accidents, what might they be? Leibniz recommends seeing relations as creatures of reason. Relations are not "out there" but result from a mental act of comparing one thing with another.

> We are bound to say that the relation in this third way of considering it is indeed outside the subjects; but that being neither substance nor accident, it must be a purely ideal thing, the consideration of which is none the less useful. (1973 [1715], Fifth Paper, §47)

So one way to solve the location problem is to place relations in the mind. Does this mean that Simmias's being taller than Socrates is mind-dependent? That seems wrong. Perhaps, then, relations are located in, reducible to, or in some way constrained by properties of the relata. Plato hints at one such view (*Phaedo*, 102b7–c4). Simmias has the property of being-taller-than-Socrates; Socrates has the correlated property of being-shorter-than-Simmias; and this is all there is to Simmias's being taller than Socrates.

The properties in question, however, look dodgy. They must "point beyond" themselves in a peculiar way. Worse, we now have correlated properties of distinct substances (Simmias's being taller-than-Socrates and Socrates's being shorter-than-Simmias) but no clear explanation for the correlation. Worse still, Simmias could lose the property of being taller-than-Socrates without undergoing any intrinsic change whatever: Socrates might grow. It is easy to think that, although it is true that Simmias is taller than Socrates and Socrates is shorter than Simmias, what makes these statements true is not Simmias's and Socrates's possession of correlated relational properties, but their standing in the taller-than relation. We are back where we started. Locating relations in the mind appears unpromising, but so does locating them in the relata or mind-independently outside the relata. What options remain?

Founding relations non-relationally

Consider, again, internal relations, six's being greater than five, for instance. We have reason to think this relation is no addition of being: if you have six and you have five, you thereby have six's being greater than five. Traditionally, such relations were said to be "founded." The greater-than relation holding between six and five is founded on the respective "natures" of six and five; these natures are foundations of the relation in the objects. Another way of putting the point might be to say that the truthmakers for "six is greater than five" are six and five themselves. On this view, truthmakers for one class of relational truths are non-relational features of the world.

You might regard this as an ontologically satisfying account of internal relations, but what of external relations, Simmias's being taller than Socrates, for instance? For this relation to obtain, it is not enough for Simmias and Socrates to exist. Simmias and Socrates must have the right heights. Imagine that Simmias is six-foot tall and Socrates is five-foot tall. We now have Simmias's being taller than Socrates (and Socrates's being shorter than Simmias). Simmias is taller than Socrates owing to Simmias's being six-foot tall and Socrates's being five-foot tall, and six's being greater than five. The relation between Simmias and Socrates is derivative. Simmias's being taller than Socrates is founded on their respective heights. And these, you might think, are related internally.

Perhaps this is how it is with external relations generally. An external relation, R, holds between objects a and b, in virtue of a's being F and b's being G (F and G being non-relational properties of a and b), and F's bearing an appropriate internal relation to G. Again, the truthmakers for Simmias's being taller than Socrates are contingent, non-relational features of Simmias and Socrates. Further, (I), the initial breezy characterization of internal relations, can now be seen to apply quite generally: if you have the relata, you have the relation. The trick is to take care in specifying the relata. In the case of Simmias's being taller than Socrates, Simmias and Socrates are indirectly related; they are related via their possession of properties that are themselves directly – and internally – related. Again, we find relational truths being made true by non-relational features of the world. (Recent philosophers who defend versions of this thesis include Fisk [1972], Campbell [1990], Mulligan [1998], and Fine [2000].)

Might this approach extend to external relations across the board? What of two classes of paradigmatically external relations: causal relations and spatial and temporal relations? The plot thickens.

Causal and spatial relations

Philosophers commonly characterize causal relations as holding among distinct, temporally ordered events. One billiard ball's striking another causes the second billiard ball to roll across the table. The relation is presumed contingent: the cause might have failed to be followed by the effect; the effect might have occurred in the absence of the cause. Causes necessitate effects, perhaps, but only owing to contingent causal *laws*. Such a conception of causal relations renders them external through and through. Call this the orthodox conception of causation.

Consider an alternative picture, one that founds causal relations on objects' intrinsic features. Suppose objects interact as they do in virtue of their properties. And suppose properties are individuated by what objects possessing them *would* do. Events, on such a conception, are the mutual manifestings of reciprocal powers. Water's dissolving salt is a mutual manifestation of powers of the water, salt, and perhaps the surrounding atmosphere. This is a synchronic model of causation. There is succession: a state prior to the manifesting and the manifesting. But it would be wrong to think of the manifesting as a sequence in which a cause occurs, followed by an effect.

Some such picture is a natural one for anyone who takes seriously the idea that properties are powers. For our purposes, the important point is that, on such a conception, it is no longer obvious that causal relations are external. Given the powers – all the powers in play – you have the manifestations. This is certainly the direction in which philosophers attracted to an ontology of powers are moving. Others will resist abandoning the orthodox model. For them, causal relations will remain steadfastly external.

Two points are worth noting here. First, if it turned out that the orthodox conception made causal relations external and unfounded and *no other* relations were unfounded, this might itself afford a reason to revisit the orthodox picture. Second, the orthodox picture is in no way privileged; it is merely one substantive conception of causation among others. The point is worth mentioning because philosophers occasionally argue as though prevailing views are innocent until proven guilty. In philosophy, however, no theory enjoys a free pass.

Do not imagine that adopting an ontology of powers is the only way to ensure that causal relations are internally founded. Another strategy appeals to the general theory of relativity and provides a way of comprehending spatial and temporal relations as internal as well (see Campbell 1990: Ch. 5; Schaffer, forthcoming).

We find it easy to regard space as a kind of container, an insubstantial medium in which objects float, and through which they move. On such a conception, motion would be a matter of an object's successively occupying contiguous regions of space. We have long known, however, that space is not a faceless void. Space (or perhaps space–time) is curved and distorted by the presence of massive bodies. Space thus takes on the traditional role of a *substance*. This might be close to what Descartes had in mind for the material world (Bennett 2001: Chs 6, 7). The material world comprises a single extended substance. What we think of as material objects are in fact modes of this substance, local "thickenings" of space. Motion – the flight of a baseball over the fence, for instance – is not a matter of a substance's successively occupying contiguous regions of space. The baseball "moves" in the way a wave "moves" across the ocean, or your cursor "moves" across your computer monitor. The truthmaker for claims about the baseball's apparent motion is an evolving state of the world not itself in motion.

If objects – the particles, baseballs, trees, planets – are modes of space, their location is no longer contingent. The identity of a mode (an accident or, in current parlance, a trope) depends on the substance of which it is a mode. On the Cartesian model of space, a mode's identity is bound up with its location. Objects are like freckles. A freckle cannot migrate from your forearm to your back. The freckle's identity depends in part on its cutaneous location.

A Cartesian conception of space as a single extended substance does not square with everything physicists tell us about space–time, but it does put us in the ballpark. Perhaps all that exists is interpenetrating fields, each pervading space–time, each the locus of a fundamental force. Or perhaps there is but a single, unified field, *the* Field. In either case it is useful to see space–time or the Field as substances. Objects – tables, trees, the particles – are modes of these substances, wrinkles in the fabric of reality. On this picture, spatial and temporal location "supervene" on the modes in this sense: given the modes, everything's spatial and temporal location is thereby given. This model, too, ensures that causal relations are internally founded: truthmakers for causal claims are non-relational features of the world. It is hard not to think that physics is pushing us in this direction – towards Spinoza (see Martin 2008; Schaffer, forthcoming).

We are now in a position to appreciate the attraction of conceptions of relations according to which the deep truth about the world is utterly non-relational. Internal relations are ontologically trifling; apparent external relations can be shown to stem from internal relations among non-relational features of reality. A view of this kind solves the location problem by founding relations on unproblematic properties of relata while, simultaneously simplifying the ontology. The fact that it does this in a manner that well suits what physicists tell us about the world is a bonus.

What of the founding relation? Am I sneaking in a primitive unexplained relation in the midst of an account that purports to make relations dependent on non-relational features of the world? As noted earlier, you could construe foundational talk in terms of truthmakers. The claim that relations are founded amounts to the claim that truthmakers for relational claims are non-relational facts. Ah, but what of *truthmaking*? Are we not forced here at least to appeal to a fundamental relation, a relation holding between the world and some representation of the world, a truthbearer? Perhaps not. Truthmaking is a paradigmatic internal relation: if you have a truthbearer, a representation, and you have the world as the truthbearer represents it as being, you have truthmaking, you have the truthbearer's being true (Heil 2006).

Realism about relations

From the beginning, philosophers have found themselves pulled in different directions on the topic of relations. On the one hand, the ontology of relations appears hopeless. On the other hand, we are bound to deploy relational terms in describing the world. If you start with language, including the language of science, you will want to find a place for relations in your ontology. If you start with ontology, you will want to explain relations away.

Suppose I am right: relations are founded on internal relations, and internal relations are "no addition of being." If God makes Simmias six-foot tall and Socrates five-foot tall, God has *thereby* made Simmias taller than Socrates. Is this a version of anti-realism about relations? Does Simmias fail to be taller than Socrates? No, it is *true* that Simmias is taller than Socrates. Does it mean that the taller-than relation, or this instance of it, is identifiable with the monadic properties that found the relation? No. Indeed, it is hard to know what to make of such a suggestion. It means rather that the truthmakers for "Simmias is taller than Socrates" are non-relational features of Simmias and Socrates or, more generally, non-relational ways the world is.

It is tempting to formulate the fundamental question of the status of relations as the question whether relations, or some relations, exist mind-independently or whether they are mere creatures of reason. The question thus posed elicits confusion, however. Relations could be real, mind-independent, but no addition of being. You might distinguish three theses:

(i) *Hyper-realism*: relations are fundamental features of reality, truthmakers for relational claims.
(ii) *Antirealism*: relations are mere creatures of reason belonging only to the realm of appearance.
(iii) *Modest realism*: relations are real but no addition of being.

The mistake is to suppose that the denial of (i) lands you with (ii). My impression is that Aristotle, many medievals, and many philosophers who take relations to be non-relationally founded struggled to make just this point, but in different, and often confusing ways. Note that (iii) will sound paradoxical to anyone who thought (as many philosophers nowadays *do* think) that realism about relations requires that relations answer to relational predicates, thesis (i). This has led to a proliferation of views that obscure more than they reveal. My suggestion is that philosophers who have denied the existence of relations, philosophers who have sought to reduce relations to monadic properties of relata, and philosophers who have argued that relations are founded on non-relational properties of objects have had in mind more often than not something like modest realism. What they have lacked is a straightforward way of expressing the doctrine.

What about Peirce, Russell, Moore, Grossmann: the relation police? What Russell establishes (and Grossmann echoes) is that you cannot translate talk of relations into non-relational terms: relational predicates are indispensable. This cuts no ontological ice, however, unless you couple it with the idea that there must be a simple correspondence between predicates and fundamental features of reality. That idea, it appears, is a product of the linguisticizing of philosophy, something most ancient, medieval, and modern philosophers would have flatly rejected, something that would have struck them as hopeless.

References

Armstrong, D. M. (1989) *Universals: An Opinionated Introduction*, Boulder, CO: Westview Press.

Bennett, J. F. (2001) *Learning from Six Philosophers: Descartes, Spinoza, Leibniz, Locke, Berkeley, Hume*, Oxford: Clarendon Press.

Bradley, F. H. (1893) *Appearance and Reality*, London: Swan Sonnenschein & Co.

Brower, J. (2005) "Medieval Theories of Relations," in E. N. Zalta (ed.), *The Stanford Encyclopedia of Philosophy*; available: http://plato.stanford.edu/archives/fall2005/entries/relations-medieval/

Campbell, K. (1990) *Abstract Particulars*, Oxford: Blackwell.

Candlish, S. (2006) *The Russell/Bradley Dispute and Its Significance for Twentieth Century Philosophy*, Basingstoke, UK: Palgrave Macmillan.

Dipert, Randall R. (1997) "The Mathematical Structure of the World: The World as Graph," *Journal of Philosophy* 94: 329–58.

Fine, K. (2000) "Neutral Relations," *Philosophical Review* 109: 1–33.

Fisk, M. (1972) "Relatedness without Relations," *Noûs* 6: 139–51.

Grossmann, R. (1983) *The Categorial Structure of the World*, Bloomington, IN: Indiana University Press.

Heil, J. (2006) "The Legacy of Linguisticism," *Australasian Journal of Philosophy* 84: 233–44.

Holton, R. (1999) "Dispositions All the Way Round," *Analysis* 59: 9–14.

Ladyman, J. (2007) "Structural Realism," in E. N. Zalta (ed.), *The Stanford Encyclopedia of Philosophy*; available: http://plato.stanford.edu/archives/win2007/entries/structural-realism/

Leibniz, G. W. (1973 [1715]) "Leibniz–Clarke Correspondence," trans. M. Morris and G. H. R. Parkinson, in *Leibniz: Philosophical Writings*, edited by G. H. R. Parkinson, London: J. M. Dent & Sons.

Martin, C. B. (1997) "On the Need for Properties: The Road to Pythagoreanism and Back," *Synthese* 112: 193–231.

—— (2008) *The Mind in Nature*, Oxford: Oxford University Press.

Moore, G. E. (1919) "External and Internal Relations," *Proceedings of the Aristotelian Society* 20: 40–62; reprinted in *Philosophical Studies*, London: K. Paul, Trench, Trubner & Co.; New York: Harcourt, Brace & Co., 1922, pp. 276–309.

Mulligan, K. (1998) "Relations – Through Thick and Thin," *Erkenntnis* 48: 325–53.

Rorty, R. (1967) "Relations, Internal and External," in P. Edwards (ed.), *The Encyclopedia of Philosophy*, vol. 7, New York: Macmillan Co. and Free Press, pp. 125–33.

Russell, B. (1997 [1903]) "Asymmetrical Relations," chapter 26 of *The Principles of Mathematics*, London: Routledge.

Schaffer, J. (Forthcoming) "Spacetime, the One Substance," *Philosophical Studies*.

Unger, P. (2006) *All the Power in the World*, New York: Oxford University Press.

Weinberg, J. R. (1965) *Abstraction, Relation, and Induction: Three Essays in the History of Thought*, Madison: University of Wisconsin Press.

31
EVENTS, FACTS AND STATES OF AFFAIRS

Julian Dodd

Events, facts and our talk about them

When Alberto Contador won the 2007 Tour de France, the French public's response was, understandably, somewhat muted. (It had been a bad three weeks for professional cycling.) But notice that we could have made essentially the same point by saying this:

(1) The French public's reaction to *Contador's Tour de France victory* was somewhat muted.

Or this:

(2) The French public was not particularly enthused by *the fact that Contador won the Tour de France*.

The italicized words in (1) seem to name an event: a thing that happened. The italicized words in (2) appear to name a fact: a thing that is the case. But how should we distinguish events from facts? And why do entities of either kind deserve a place in our ontology: that is, our inventory of the kinds of thing there are? This essay addresses these questions.

The key distinction between events and facts has been introduced already. Events are things that happen, occur or take place: items such as Contador's victory, Cavendish's crash on Stage 1, and the playing of the Spanish national anthem at the victory ceremony. A fact, by contrast, does not happen, occur or take place; it is a *that* such and such is the case: something expressed by a true sentence and, as a result, the kind of thing canonically referred to by means of prefixing the said true sentence with "that" (or "the fact that"). But this is not the only relevant point of difference between events and facts. More can be gleaned if we follow Zeno Vendler (1967a) and Jonathan Bennett (1988) in, first of all, laying before us the variety of event-names and fact-names that we use, and then uncovering the different restrictions governing the insertion of event-names and fact-names within various types of host sentence. The thought is this: events and facts are, respectively, the things named by event-names and fact-names; so an examination of the kinds of container sentences that these names can enter into meaningfully will shed light on our concepts of event and fact and, in so doing, "give us a hint concerning their ontological status" (Vendler 1967a: 128).

With this strategy in place, we can begin by considering the phenomenon of nominalizing sentences: that is, turning complete sentences into noun-phrases. The results of this process – nominalized sentences (or, from now on "nominals") – fall into two kinds (Vendler 1967a: 127–31; Bennett 1988: 4–12). First, there are *perfect nominals*, such as

(3) Cavendish's crash on Stage 1,
(4) Rasmussen's press conference after Stage 17,

and

(5) The playing of the Spanish national anthem at the victory ceremony.

Contrasted with these are *imperfect nominals*: expressions such as

(6) (The fact) that Cavendish crashed on Stage 1,

and

(7) Rasmussen's giving a press conference after Stage 17.

Syntactically, the two types of nominal vary greatly (Bennett 1988: 4–6): only perfect nominals can be pluralized; only in a perfect nominal can a name be replaced by the definite or indefinite article; perfect nominals take adjectives in attributive position, whilst imperfect nominals take adverbs; and only imperfect nominals can be negated, tensed and modalized via auxiliaries. Such syntactic differences can be summed up by remarking that in perfect nominals the verb is "dead as a verb, having become a noun" (Vendler 1967a: 131); imperfect nominals, by contrast, are a case of "arrested development [because] the verb still kicks within the nominalised sentence" (Vendler 1967a: 131).

But what does this tell us about our respective ontological conceptions of events and facts? Arguably, quite a lot, once it is realized that imperfect nominals name facts and that events are only named by perfect nominals (Bennett 1988: 6–7). Given that (3)–(5) refer to events, and that (6) and (7) pick out facts, we can discern clear differences in the ways in which we think of events and facts by seeing how these nominals behave differently within certain sentential contexts.

Let us start with event-names. The acceptability of sentences such as the following reveals much about the way in which we think of events' relation to space and time:

(8) Cavendish's crash on Stage 1 happened suddenly on a stretch of road about 25 kilometres from Canterbury.

(9) The playing of the Spanish national anthem at the victory ceremony lasted about a couple of minutes, and was heard by all of those present.

(10) Rasmussen's press conference after Stage 17 was prolonged by his having to answer a series of embarrassing questions.

First, our folk concept of an event – the conception revealed to us by sentences such as (8)–(10) – has it that events are items that have a spatial location. (This is why, for example, in (9) and (10), it makes sense to speak of them as objects of perception.) Furthermore, the acceptability of (8)–(10) reveals that we think of events as occupying time by being *spread out* in it: that is, by having temporal parts. Whilst we think of material objects as enduring entities – things that persist by being wholly present at successive times – our talk of events as "lasting" (as opposed to "existing") for a certain period of time, and our talk of events as being "gradual," "sudden" or "prolonged," all suggest that we regard events as things that persist by virtue of having different temporal parts at different times.

When it comes to facts, P. F. Strawson points out that our everyday talk presents them as differing greatly from events. Facts, he says, "are not, like things or happenings [i.e. events] on the face of the globe, witnessed or heard or seen, broken or overturned, interrupted or prolonged, kicked, destroyed, mended or noisy" (1999 [1950]: 167). This remark essentially makes two plausible claims. First, attributions of spatial locations to facts have a forced, arbitrary air about them. Second, our talk about facts embodies the thesis that they do not persist as events do, by perduring. But neither, it seems, do we think of facts as persisting in the way in which material objects do, by enduring: facts, unlike enduring objects, are not described as "coming into existence" or "ceasing to be"; and we don't think of facts as having a history or anything like a life story. So facts, according to the nascent ontological conception embodied in our discourse about them, look to be the kinds of things that do not persist at all; and this encourages the thought that they are resolutely atemporal.

An ontology of events?

Whilst the kind of linguistic evidence appealed to by Vendler may provide "a hint" (1967a: 128) as to the ontological nature of facts and events, many philosophers will regard such hints as liable to be trumped by mature philosophical analysis. And there is even a breed of philosopher who will question the idea that events should have a place in our ontology at all. This section is devoted to assessing such scepticism.

Why think that the world contains events in addition to, say, material objects and the entities posited by the physical sciences? True enough, Cavendish crashed on Stage 1 of the 2007 Tour de France; but why should we think that saying this commits us to the existence, not merely of Cavendish, but of a thing that happened: an event?

Notice at once that the assumption here is that the existence of events is problematic in a way in which the existence of material objects is not. Someone asking why we should think that events exist is someone who presumes, with Horgan (1978: 28), that their existence must be *earned*: that is, that events are theoretical entities that should only gain admittance into our ontology, if there is a genuine theoretical or explanatory role that only they can perform. Typically, such a philosopher will be unswayed by the fact that our perceptual experience seems to present us with events; and, equally, she will be unmoved by the apparent ontological commitment to events that is found in our everyday talk. True enough, she might say, sentences such as (1) and (8)–(10) see us appearing to refer to events, and sentences such as

(11) Two crashes took place on Stage 1

and

(12) At least one of Cavendish's crashes was straightforwardly his own fault

appear to involve quantification over events; but she will argue that such sentences should not be taken at face-value, as long as we lack a sound theoretical reason for admitting events into our ontology. Until such a reason is found, we should continue to deny that events exist, whilst employing a strategy of paraphrasing away all apparent ontological commitment to them.

One way in which a friend of events can reply to such thinking is by taking up the sceptic's challenge of uncovering a genuine theoretical need that can only be met by positing events. Two such attempts to defend an event ontology in this way have been significant. The first claims that only events, and not facts, can serve as the *relata* of the causal relation. In other words, it is argued that we should replace reports such as this,

(13) The fact that there was a short circuit caused it to be the case that there was a fire,

with reports like this,

(14) The short circuit caused the fire.

But what could be wrong with a report such as (13)? A defender of the claim that events are the only causal *relata* is likely to press at least one of two charges. First, she may allege that (13) is illegitimate because facts, *qua abstracta*, are categorically unsuited to be causes: such entities cannot, after all, emit force and, as it were, push things around. Second, and drawing on the so-called "slingshot" argument (Davidson 1980a [1967]: 151–3), she could argue that "caused it to be the case that" in (13), since an extensional context, can only be truth-functional. If correct, this would mean that *any* true sentences can be intersubstituted *salva veritate* within the said context, and, hence, that *any* two facts can be causally related, which would be a *reductio ad absurdum* of the view of facts as causes.

Neither rationale for rejecting the thesis that facts can be causes is ultimately satisfying, though. When it comes to the first, Bennett disputes the premise that causal statements report relations between things that emit force and push things around. The things that do this are, he says, "*things* – elementary particles and aggregates of them – and not … any *relata* of the causal relation" (1988: 22). Consequently, since causal *relata* need not be pushers and shovers, there is no conceptual barrier to treating causes as facts. And when it comes to the slingshot argument – the argument that any extensional context must be truth-functional – philosophers are queuing up to explain why it is unsound (e.g. Neale 2001; Searle 1995: 223–6; Horgan 1978: 32–5).

Similar doubts also afflict the second prominent attempt to argue that events are needed to fulfil a certain explanatory role: Davidson's suggestion that an account of the logical form of sentences involving adverbial modification requires us to regard such sentences as involving quantification over events. Any cogent logical form proposal of such sentences should lay bare their structure in such a way as to explain the validity of certain adverb-dropping inferences: for example, the fact that

(15) Cavendish suddenly crashed 25 kilometres outside Canterbury

entails

(16) Cavendish suddenly crashed,

which, in turn, entails

(17) Cavendish crashed.

Davidson's ingenious logical form proposal for sentences such as (15) has two elements (1984 [1967]): such sentences are said to involve a hidden variable, bound by the existential quantifier, ranging over events; and adverbs are represented as predicates of events. In other words, (15)'s logical form is represented as

(18) $\exists e\,((\text{Crashed}(\text{Cavendish}, e))\,\&\,(\text{Sudden}(e))\,\&\,(25\,\text{kilometres outside}\,(\text{Canterbury}, e)))$,

a sentence that can be glossed as

(19) There was an event that was a crash by Cavendish, and which was sudden, and which was 25 kilometres outside Canterbury.

Neatly, with this proposal in place, the entailment of (16) by (15), and that of (17) by (16) is explained by nothing more than the fact that the truth of a conjunction entails the truth of its conjuncts.

Once more, though, this Davidsonian argument for the existence of events is contentious. First, there are certain kinds of adverbial modification with which Davidson's logical form proposal has trouble. Sometimes, for example, the kinds of entailment relations he was so keen to explain do not, in fact, obtain, as in

(20) Cavendish almost crashed.

(20) entails that Cavendish *did not* crash, not that he did. Likewise, Davidson's proposal cannot account for the behaviour of attributive adverbs: adverbs whose application to events is mediated by thinking of these events as being of a certain type. Contador, for example, travelled around France on his bike: his journey was certainly quick *qua* cycle-ride, but was slow *qua* a tour through France (since he did not use a car). Given that this is so, it cannot be right to represent the logical form of

(21) Contador toured France quickly

as

(22) $\exists(e)$ ((Toured (Contador, France, e)) & (Quick (e))),

since (22) presumes, falsely, that events can be fast or slow *simpliciter*.

As if this were not bad enough, another kind of logical form proposal is available which equally well accounts for the inferences Davidson can explain, and yet does so whilst avoiding a commitment to an event ontology. Romane Clark (1970) proposes that adverbs are not predicates of events, but *predicate modifiers*: items which, when attached to a predicate, yield a new predicate. As Horgan explains (1978: 46–7), if such an account can be made good, then there are two reasons to prefer it to Davidson's: first, it promises to cope with the non-standard adverbial modifiers that thwart Davidson; and, second, it does so whilst avoiding Davidson's counterintuitive claim that adverbial modification involves us in implicit quantification over events.

It is, then, far from easy to point to a genuine theoretical need that can only be met by positing events. But this just raises the question of whether an event ontology must stand or fall according to the success of such a project. For it is open to the friend of events to *deny* that events should only be admitted into our ontology once a cogent theoretical role has been assigned to them. An alternative methodological position is this: given our *prima facie* reference to, and quantification over, events in true sentences such as (1), (8)–(10) and (11) and (12), the existence of events is the *default position*: the position that should be accepted until it is defeated. It is up to the *enemy* of events to show *us* that we should forsake them. The existence of events is not contingent on demonstrating that they earn their explanatory keep.

No doubt, an eliminativist about events might try to paraphrase away all apparent ontological commitment to events. But this just raises the question of what, exactly, such paraphrase is supposed to show, even if successful. Suppose that we could come up with paraphrases of (11) and (12) which eliminated explicit quantification over events. It could yet be denied that it is the paraphrase, rather than the original sentence, that reveals our true ontological commitments: given that a sentence and its paraphrase have the same meaning – that what is said in an utterance of one is the same as what is said by an utterance of the other – who is to say that the original sentence does not, in fact, reveal the paraphrase's hidden ontological commitments? Once an event ontology has been claimed to be the default position, and once the strategy of paraphrase has been questioned in this way, the case for events looks stronger.

Events considered

Presuming that we remain unconvinced by claims that we should banish events from our ontology, we will now want to know more of their ontological nature. What kind of thing is an event? Two proposals have dominated the discussion.

According to Davidson (1980b, c [1969, 1970]), events are particulars – i.e. datable, locatable, unrepeatable entities – that are structureless in the sense that they may be referred to by nominals which make reference to different properties and particulars. Thus, for example, according to Davidson, one and the same event is referred to by "Cavendish's crash on Stage 1," "the first of Cavendish's crashes in the 2007 Tour de France," and even "the most disappointing event to date in Cavendish's professional cycling career." Jaegwon Kim (1980), by contrast, has it that events are property exemplifications: havings of properties by objects at times. If Kim is correct, then, although Cavendish's crash on Stage 1 is a datable, locatable, unrepeatable particular, it is, in fact, a structured individual that has Cavendish, the property of crashing, and the crash's time as constituents.

Who, then, is closer to the truth: Davidson or Kim? It is often supposed that Kim's account necessarily commits him to individuating events too finely. For if an event is an object's having a property at a time, then events are identical only if they have the same constituent objects, properties and times; and this, it is often claimed (e.g. Evnine 1991: 30–1) means that events described by making reference to distinct properties inevitably count as distinct. As Davidson himself puts it, it looks as if, according to Kim, "no stabbing can be a killing and no killing can be a murder, no arm-raising a signaling, and no birthday party a celebration. I protest" (1984 [1967]: 133–4).

Now, *if* such a fine individuation of events were an inevitable consequence of the view of events as property exemplifications, then we would, indeed, have a powerful objection to this view. But, as it happens, this consequence is not inevitable. As Bennett points out (1988: 93–4), we can accept that events are property exemplifications and, as a result, hold that a difference in any constituent makes for a different event, and yet do justice to the intuition that Brutus's stabbing of Caesar was the very same event as Brutus's killing of Caesar. Just as long as the stabbing of Caesar and the killing of Caesar are taken to be instances of the same *coarsely individuated* property F – and nothing in the view of events as property exemplifications rules this out – we can treat "Brutus's stabbing of Caesar" and "Brutus's killing of Caesar" as naming the same Kim-style event.

So, it turns out that what has come to be regarded as the standard objection to the conception of events as property exemplifications is, at best, an objection, not to this conception *per se*, but to Kim's own individuative proposal which he himself conflates with the property exemplifications view (Bennett 1988: 93–4). But having cleared up this matter, we are, nonetheless, left with (at least) two questions. First, how should we decide between Kim's and Davidson's respective ontological proposals? Second, how should we individuate events, given that Kim's own individuative proposal carves them too finely?

As one would expect, both questions are knotty. When it comes to the first, one might suppose that the conception of events as property exemplifications, once distinguished from the overly fine account of their individuation that Kim associates with it, has ontological economy on its side. For Kim-style events – the havings of properties by objects at times – are, to all intents and purposes, states of affairs; so, if there are good reasons for admitting states of affairs into our ontology, then we can have events for free. But as we shall see, the claim that the world contains states of affairs is itself controversial, and, besides this, positing states of affairs comes at a cost. Anyone committing themselves to states of affairs must explain what the *having* of a property by an object consists in; and therein lies a problem. Our talk of an object *a*'s having a property *F* is supposed to signal that *a* and *F* are unified in such a way as to constitute *a*'s *being F*: something that is the case. But if such talk introduces a relation – that is, the relation of *instantiation* supposedly holding between *a* and *F* – then a vicious regress is threatened instantly (Armstrong 1997a [1980]: 109). For the instantiation relation is just an additional (two-place) property, and so our problem now becomes how *a*, *F* and the instantiation relation can be unified; and so things will continue as we introduce further relations to try to glue together the ever-growing number of constituents. Somehow, we have to think of instantiation in non-relational terms; but, as will become clear presently, this is none too easy to do.

When it comes to the question of how events are to be individuated, two attempts to provide identity criteria have been particularly influential. First of all, Davidson (1980b [1969]: 179) famously suggested that events are identical just in case they have exactly the same causes and effects. A commonly expressed objection to this account of events' identity conditions is, however, that it is circular, even if true, and hence cannot work as a procedure for determining the truth of identity-claims concerning events. The causes and effects of events are themselves events, presumably. Consequently, applying Davidson's criterion would have us say that events *e* and *e** are identical just in case the events that are their respective causes are identical; but, applying Davidson's criterion once more, *e*'s causes are identical with *e**'s causes just in case they have the same effects; but since their effects include *e* and *e**, we have, alas, turned in a very small circle (Lombard 1998: 286–7).

In response to this objection, Davidson (1985: 175) came to adopt the other significant identity criterion for events that I shall discuss: Quine's (1960: 170, 1985). According to Quine, events are identical just in case they have the same spatiotemporal location. This account, though, faces two objections. First, one might wonder whether, by contrast with Kim's view on event individuation, it carves up events in too rough-hewn a manner. If a balloon were simultaneously to deflate and turn a deeper shade of red, it would follow, according to Quine, that its deflation and the change in its colour would be the very same event. Many would construe such a consequence as a counterexample to Quine's position (Lombard 1998: 283). Second, it has been suggested that Quine's criterion entails a false thesis concerning the ontological category in which events are found. For if events are individuated purely in terms of their spatiotemporal location, does this not entail that an event is really a material object? (Quine's criterion, after all, would certainly seem to be true of material objects.) Quine himself is willing to accept this consequence (1960: 170, 1985: 167): for him, the things we classify as events and as material objects differ only in degree, events being more heterogeneous and less unified than material objects. Most of us, I think, will feel a little queasy at this point, but I leave the reader to consider whether such a feeling has philosophical significance.

Facts, states of affairs, and true Thoughts

That there are such things as facts would seem to be enshrined in our everyday discourse. As we noted at the outset, we seem to use "that"-clauses (or "the fact that"-clauses) to refer to them, and we appear to quantify over them in claims such as these:

(23) At least one fact about the case cannot be explained by Watson's hypothesis.
(24) Most of the salient facts about the Tudors and Stuarts have been forgotten by Form 2B.

The existence of facts, no less than that of events, has the status of the default position. Naturally, an enemy of facts might seek to paraphrase away all apparent reference to, and quantification over, facts (Quine 1960: 246–8), but, as we saw in the case of events, it is unclear what the success of such a project would show; and, in any case, a friend of facts will insist that we should treat our apparent ontological commitment to facts at face value until it is demonstrated that facts are somehow unfit to grace our ontology.

So what is a fact? Two conceptions of facts have been dominant within analytical philosophy. The first kind of view – that associated with philosophers such as Russell (1958 [1918]), the early Wittgenstein (1922), and Armstrong (1997b, 2004) – has it that facts are entities in which objects and properties are united: *a's being F* (i.e. the fact that *a* is *F*), according to such philosophers, is the unity of the object *a* and the property *F*. Let us call facts thus construed *states of affairs* (Armstrong 1997b: 1). The second kind of view – that associated with Frege (1988 [1918]: 51) and Strawson (1999 [1950]: 37–8, 1998: 403) – has it that facts are not unified combinations of worldly objects and properties but true Thoughts, where a "Thought" is a proposition understood along Fregean lines: that is, a combination, not of worldly objects and properties, but of *ways of thinking* of such entities – things he calls "senses" (Frege 1952 [1892]: 57–62).

Which conception of facts is to be preferred? The defender of the conception of facts as states of affairs typically argues for her position by claiming that facts have to play a certain theoretical role which they could only play, if states of affairs. Three such arguments come to mind. The first, however – that facts could only act as causes, if construed as states of affairs (e.g. White 1970: 83) – can be given fairly short shrift, given our earlier discussion concerning causal *relata*. It is, of course, correct that a true Thought, since it is abstract, cannot emit force, push things around, and generally behave like an elbow to the ribs: but, given that states of affairs are abstract too, neither can states of affairs do this; and, furthermore, if Bennett (1988: 22–3) is right, then an entity can enter into causal relations, and yet *not* be an emitter of force. All of which suggests that an acceptance that facts can be causes commits us to no particular ontological conception of facts.

But what of the other two reasons for supposing facts to be states of affairs? The first such reason is that positing states of affairs is said to enable us to explain away what has become known as "the problem of instantiation": the problem of saying precisely what an object's having a property (or two or more objects entering into a relation) consists in. As we have already seen, instantiation cannot itself be a relation: if it were, the problem of how a and F came to be metaphysically glued together would just become the problem of how a, F, and the instantiation relation came to be so unified, and so on, ad infinitum. The moral of the story is that instantiation cannot be a relation, since, if it were, it would merely increase the number of entities requiring unification, rather than explain what such unity consists in.

Our problem, however, is to understand what else instantiation could be, if not a relation. And this is one of the reasons why an ontology of states of affairs might be helpful. For a tempting move is to deny that the problem of instantiation is genuine by treating states of affairs, and not objects and properties, as ontologically basic. On this view, objects and properties are not entities in their own right, but "vicious abstractions" (Armstrong 1997a [1980]: 109–10) from states of affairs. So, rather than digging too deep in trying to explain how an object can instantiate a property, we should accept that "[t]he instantiation of universals by particulars is just the state of affairs itself" (Armstrong 1997b: 119).

Coupled with this is an argument for treating facts as states of affairs provided by a recent growth area in contemporary metaphysics: truthmaker theory. Armstrong, indeed, proposes the following "truthmaker argument" (1997b: 113) for the existence of states of affairs (and, hence, for treating facts as states of affairs):

(25) Necessarily, if the proposition that a is F is true, then there is at least one entity in the world, α, such that α's existence entails that the proposition that a is F is true.

(26) Facts, construed as states of affairs, are best placed to be truthmakers.

So,

(27) Facts, construed as states of affairs, exist.

(25) is the so-called *truthmaker principle*, a principle that some truthmaker theorists (e.g. Armstrong 1997b, 2004) take to apply to every truth, and which others seek to restrict to some subset or other of truths (e.g. Mulligan et al. 1984). However, putting this local dispute to one side, it seems that states of affairs look well placed to fulfil this truth-making role. Presuming the proposition that a is F to be a contingent predication, neither the existence of a, nor the existence of F, nor the mereological sum of a and F can be the truthmaker of this proposition: each could exist and yet it not be true that a is F. By contrast, the state of affairs a's *being* F – the entity in which a and F are brought together (Armstrong 1997b: 116) – looks to be just the job. Since this state of affairs *just is a*'s

instantiating F, this entity cannot exist without a's being F, and so promises to play the truthmaking role perfectly. So, provided (25) is well motivated, and provided there is no other category of entity that can play the truthmaking function at least equally well, we have a powerful argument for the existence of facts *qua* states of affairs.

Once more, however, arguments that may strike us, at first blush, as convincing turn out to be controversial. To begin with, it may be disputed that positing states of affairs (and, hence, treating facts as states of affairs) enables us to bypass the problem of instantiation (Dodd 2000: Ch. 1). For it is not enough to be told that a and F are vicious abstractions from states of affairs; we need to know what this claim amounts to; and supplying a convincing explanation here is not easy. States of affairs are introduced as *things-having-properties* and *things-related-to-other-things* (Armstrong 1991: 190); to be, then, told that things and properties are mere abstractions from states of affairs looks circular. For this reason, it perhaps makes more sense to take the claim that objects and properties are "vicious abstractions" from states of affairs to mean, not that objects and properties are not entities in their own right, but merely that objects and properties are only to be found as the constituents of states of affairs. However, whilst making this move avoids the circle, it cannot help us to side-step the nature of instantiation. The problem of what it is for a to instantiate F has just been reformulated as the problem of how a and F can be brought together as constituents of a state of affairs. We seem to have relabelled the problem, not avoided it.

When it comes to the truthmaker argument for facts being states of affairs, objections could be raised against both of its premises. Some philosophers have questioned (26) – the claim that states of affairs are best placed to be truthmakers – on the grounds that there is another category of entity that is at least as well qualified for the job: tropes (Mulligan et al. 1984). Tropes are particularized properties that are unstructured entities: if a and b are both F, then, for the trope theorist, we have two properties, *the F-ness of a* and *the F-ness of b*; and the F-ness of a is not a complex consisting of a and the universal F, but a simple entity that cannot be understood in other terms. Clearly, if there are such things as tropes, then they would seem to form the basis of a powerful rival to a state-of-affairs-formulated truthmaker theory. First, tropes seem well qualified for the truthmaking role: if a's F-ness exists, then a must be F: the existence of the appropriate trope would seem to guarantee the truth of relevant proposition. And, second, because tropes are unstructured, we can treat tropes as truthmakers without being obliged to solve the kind of unity problem that we have seen afflict states of affairs. Perhaps these benefits are not as clear-cut as they seem (Dodd 2000: 8–9); but, for the time being at least, we can say that (26) is far from uncontroversial.

More significantly still, the same goes for (25): the truthmaker principle itself. Armstrong, truthmaker theory's most distinguished champion, admits that he does not know how to argue for it, preferring to claim that it is "fairly obvious once attention is drawn to it" (1989: 89). Others are not so sure (Lewis 1992, 2001; Dodd 2002). The proposition that a is F, if true, is true because a is, indeed, F. But why, for a to be F, must there be some entity whose mere existence guarantees this: some entity over and above a (and F)? Until we have a convincing answer to this question, the truthmaker theorist is unentitled to (25), and so the truthmaker argument for treating facts as states of affairs looks resistible.

This being so, we might become increasingly tempted by the Fregean position on facts. Presuming that we should include propositions in our ontology (Dodd 2000: Ch. 2), and presuming, further, that we should construe such propositions as Thoughts (Dodd 2000: Ch. 3), perhaps the way is clear to treat a fact as nothing more than a Thought that is true. On this line, facts do not form a distinct ontological category; they are just Thoughts that have the property of truth.

There is, I think, much to be said for this position (Dodd 2000: Ch. 4): not least that, given an ontology that already includes Thoughts, such an account has simplicity on its side. Once more, though, taking a stand in this area requires us to deal with a number of strenuously expressed objections. One such objection – that facts can only be causes if states of affairs (Kirkham 1992: 138; Searle 1998: 389) – has been dealt with already. But there are others. Is it not the case, for example, that we individuate Thoughts more finely than facts? The sentences

(28) Alberto Contador is Spanish

and

(29) The winner of the 2007 Tour de France is Spanish

express different Thoughts but, it is argued (Vendler 1967b: 711), express the same fact. And, why, if facts are true Thoughts, is

(30) True propositions are true

a truism, and yet

(31) Facts are true

absurd-sounding (Künne 2003: 10)? The defender of Fregeanism about facts must answer these, and other questions (Dodd 2000; Ch. 4), before she can rest easy. Here we have one final example of just how controversial are the available positions in the ontology of events, facts and states of affairs.

References

Armstrong, D. M. (1989) *Universals: An Opinionated Introduction*, Boulder, CO: Westview Press.
—— (1991) "Classes Are States of Affairs," *Mind* 100: 189–200.
—— (1997a [1980]) "Against 'Ostrich Nominalism': A Reply to Michael Devitt," in D. H. Mellor and A. Oliver (eds), *Properties*, Oxford: Oxford University Press, pp. 101–11.
—— (1997b) *A World of States of Affairs*, Cambridge: Cambridge University Press.
—— (2004) *Truth and Truthmakers*, Cambridge: Cambridge University Press.
Bennett, J. (1988) *Events and Their Names*, Cambridge: Cambridge University Press.
Clark, R. (1970) "Concerning the Logic of Predicate Modifiers," *Noûs* 4: 311–35.
Davidson, D. (1980a [1967]) "Causal Relations," in Davidson (1980), pp. 149–62.
—— (1980b [1969]) "The Individuation of Events," in Davidson (1980), pp. 163–80.

—— (1980c [1970]) "Events as Particulars," in Davidson (1980) 181–87.

—— (1980) *Essays on Actions and Events*, Oxford: Oxford University Press.

—— (1984 [1967]) "The Logical Form of Action Sentences," in *Inquiries into Truth and Interpretation*, Oxford: Oxford University Press, pp. 105–48.

—— (1985) "Reply to Quine on Events," in E. LePore and B. McLaughlin (eds), *Actions and Events: Perspectives on the Philosophy of Donald Davidson*, Blackwell: Oxford: 172–6.

Dodd, J. (2000) *An Identity Theory of Truth*, Basingstoke, UK: Palgrave.

—— (2002) "Is Truth Supervenient on Being?" *Proceedings of the Aristotelian Society* 102: 69–86.

Evnine, S. (1991) *Donald Davidson*, Oxford: Polity Press.

Frege, G. (1952 [1892]) "On Sense and Meaning," in *Translations from the Philosophical Writings of Gottlob Frege*, trans. P. Geach and M. Black, Oxford: Blackwell, pp. 56–78.

—— (1988 [1918]) "Thoughts," reprinted in N. Salmon and S. Soames (eds), *Propositions and Attitudes*, Oxford: Oxford University Press, pp. 33–55.

Horgan, T. (1978) "The Case against Events," *Philosophical Review* 87: 28–47.

Kim, J. (1980) "Events as Property Exemplifications," in M. Brand and D. Walton (eds), *Action Theory*, Dordrecht: Reidel, 159–77.

Kirkham, R. (1992) *Theories of Truth*, Cambridge, MA: MIT Press.

Künne, W. (2003) *Conceptions of Truth*, Oxford: Oxford University Press.

Lewis, D. (1992) "Armstrong on Combinatorial Possibility," *Australasian Journal of Philosophy* 70: 211–24.

—— (2001) "Truthmaking and Difference-Making," *Noûs* 35: 602–15.

Lombard, L. (1998) "Ontologies of Events," in S. Lawrence and C. MacDonald (eds), *Contemporary Readings in the Foundations of Metaphysics*, Oxford: Blackwell.

Mulligan, K., Simons, P., and Smith, B. (1984) "Truth-makers," *Philosophy and Phenomenological Research* 44: 287–321.

Neale, S. (2000) *Facing Facts*, Oxford: Oxford University Press.

Quine, W. V. (1960) *Word and Object*, Cambridge, MA: MIT Press.

—— (1985) "Events and Reification," in E. LePore and B. McLaughlin (eds), *Actions and Events: Perspectives on the Philosophy of Donald Davidson*, Blackwell: Oxford, pp. 162–71.

Russell, B. (1958 [1918]) "The Philosophy of Logical Atomism," in his *Logic and Knowledge*, edited by R. Marsh, London: Allen & Unwin, pp. 39–56.

Searle, J. (1995) *The Construction of Social Reality*, Harmondsworth: Penguin.

—— (1998) "Truth: A Reconsideration of Strawson's Views," in L. Hahn (ed.), *The Philosophy of P.F. Strawson*, Chicago: Open Court, pp. 385–401.

Strawson, P. F. (1998) "Reply to John R. Searle," in L. Hahn (ed.), *The Philosophy of P.F. Strawson*, Chicago: Open Court, pp. 402–4.

—— (1999 [1950]) "Truth," reprinted in S. Blackburn and K. Simmons (eds), *Truth*, Oxford: Oxford University Press, pp. 149–61.

Vendler, Z. (1967) "Facts and Events," in his *Linguistics in Philosophy*, Ithaca: Cornell University Press, pp. 122–46.

—— (1967b) "Causal Relations," *Journal of Philosophy* 64: 704–13.

White, A. (1970) *Truth*, London: Macmillan.

Wittgenstein, L. (1922) *Tractatus Logico-Philosophicus*, trans. C. K. Ogden, London: Routledge.

Further reading

H. Beebee and J. Dodd (eds), *Truthmakers: The Contemporary Debate* (Oxford: Oxford University Press, 2005) is a collection of contemporary essays, mostly sceptical, about truthmaker theory. R. Chisholm, "Events and Propositions," *Noûs* 4: 15–24, is a defence of the view, *contra* Davidson and Kim, that events are not particulars, but recurring entities. E. J. Lowe and A. Rami (eds), *Truth and Truth-Making* (Stocksfield, UK: Acumen, 2008) is a collection of classic papers and newer essays on truthmaker theory. A magisterial discussion of the varieties of slingshot argument is S. Neale, *Facing Facts* (Oxford: Oxford University Press, 2001). B. Taylor, *Modes of Occurrence: Verbs, Adverbs and Events* (Oxford: Blackwell, 1985), defends the thesis that events are a species of states of affairs.

32

POSSIBLE WORLDS AND POSSIBILIA

John Divers

Introduction

Possibilia are (supposed to be) possible things other than the actual things and, in particular, possible worlds other than the actual world. Talking in terms of *possibilia* has widely been supposed to offer some sort of advance in our philosophical thinking about modalities (such as various kinds of possibilities and necessities) and about certain kinds of abstract and intensional entity (such as propositions and properties).

Modality is cast as quantification over possible worlds. Possibility is correlated with what is the case at some world: that there might have been no humans corresponds to the existence of a possible world at which there are no humans. Similarly, necessity is correlated with what is the case at all possible worlds and impossibility with what is the case at none. Once modality is construed as quantification, absolute modality (perhaps logical or metaphysical) is naturally construed in terms of unrestricted quantification over all the possible worlds and various relative modalities (perhaps nomological or technological) are naturally construed in terms of quantification over appropriately restricted subsets of the worlds. Thus, the absolute impossibility of true contradictions would correspond with their holding at no possible worlds: but the merely relative, technological impossibility of intergalactic travel would correspond to its taking place at none of the possible worlds where technology is limited to that which humans have actually and presently contrived, but its taking place at some of those, more remote, possible worlds where technology outstrips our own, or the facts and laws of nature are more congenial.

Intensional entities are correlated with sets of possibilia. The propositions (e.g. *that donkeys talk*) are correlated with sets of possible worlds (those worlds at which donkeys talk) and the properties (e.g. *having a heart*) are correlated with sets of possible individuals (all those things, drawn from across all the worlds, which have a heart). Once the intensional entities are construed as sets of possibilia, intensionality appears as a kind of transworld-extensionality, since the identity (or difference) of intensional entities is determined exactly by the possibilia which are their members.

Beyond these primary applications to the cases of the overtly modal and the intensional, talk of possibilia has also been invoked in thinking about adjacent matters, such as counterfactual (and other) conditionals, essence and accident, supervenience, verisimilitude, reference and denotation, laws of nature, states of affairs, and causation.

Four fundamental, and related, kinds of philosophical issues are raised by talk of possibilia. First, metaphysical: what kinds of things are possible worlds and other possibilia supposed to be, and how do the possible individuals relate to the worlds in/at which they exist? Second, representational: how do possible worlds (in particular) represent things as being the case *at* them, or according to them? Third, explanatory: exactly what kinds of explanations of the modal and intensional do we take our talk of possible worlds to afford? Fourth, ontological: given a metaphysical and representational story about the nature of possible worlds, told without prejudice as to whether there (really) are such things, should we then go further and (really) assert, or believe in, their existence? Any comprehensive theory of possible worlds and possibilia would have to yield answers to all of these questions and such (putatively) comprehensive theories may be grouped in three recognizable kinds: Lewisian realism, other realisms, and non-realisms.

Lewisian realism

David Lewis's realism (genuine modal realism) is a belief in the existence of a vast infinity of possible worlds construed as alternate universes. The possible worlds (like our universe) are concrete individuals, and the possible individuals are the parts of those worlds. The worlds are those individuals which are spatiotemporally (and causally) isolated and closed: two individuals are parts of the same world if and only if (iff) they stand in some spatiotemporal relation to one another. Any individual that is part of any world is part of exactly one world. All and only the individuals are possible individuals, and all and only the worlds are possible worlds: there are no impossibilia. Among the things that exist, many do not actually exist – that is to say that they are not parts of the actual world. We rightly call our world and its parts "actual," but actuality is not an absolute attribute of any world. For "actual" is an indexical term, the reference of which varies from world to world: from the standpoint of any other world, that world is actual and our world is non-actual.

The worlds are so various that all possibilities (but no impossibilities) are represented across them. Worlds represent possibilities, things are the case at them, by having parts that have appropriate qualitative features. A world represents *de dicto* that – say – there are talking donkeys (at the world there are talking donkeys, or according to the world there are talking donkeys) by having parts that are talking donkeys. Thereby, there could have been talking donkeys. A world represents *de re* of – say – Hilary that she is blonde (at the world Hilary is blonde, according to the world Hilary is blonde) by having a part which is: (a) a counterpart of Hilary and (b) blonde. Counterpart relations are any relations of similarity, even those which are the resultant of similarity in many different respects weighted in different degrees. Generic truth-conditions are given for *de re* modal sentence types in counterpart-theoretic terms: "Descartes is necessarily a thinking thing" is true iff every counterpart of Descartes is a thinking thing. But which counterpart relation or relations are relevant to the interpretation of token sentences of that type is a matter of great variation – typically not determinate, and highly sensitive to many aspects of the context of tokening. Thus, *de re* modal contexts are typically referentially opaque (substitution of co-referential terms may alter truth-value) and *de re* modal sentence types are typically inconstant with respect to precise truth-condition and (*a fortiori*) truth-value.

The different kinds of explanation which Lewis intends in deploying talk of possibilia include conceptual analyses, ontological identifications and a semantic theory. Unrestricted quantification over all the worlds and all the individuals articulates analyses of our modal concepts which (it is claimed) take no modal concept as primitive. Various kinds of entities (propositions, states of affairs, meanings and events) are identified as certain kinds of property, and all properties – in turn – are identified with subsets of the (possible) individuals. A semantic theory for quantified modal logics is provided: a first-order theory of counterparts is stated; the formulas of quantified modal logic are translated into the language of the theory; validity is defined as theoremhood in the counterpart theory and determined accordingly. We ought to believe in the existence of genuine possibilia because the explanatory benefits of doing so offer a better ratio of theoretical benefits to costs than either giving up talk of possibilia altogether or of persisting with it under an alternative conception of possibilia.

Lewisian realism discussed

The first sort of criticism of Lewisian realism alleges failure to deliver the benefits promised. The complaint is that, even if we grant Lewis his ontology, the explanations built upon that ontology are either inaccurate or irrelevant.

Genuine realist analysis is alleged to fail in extension by determining as impossible (true at no world) that which (many find) pre-theoretically possible – for example, that there might have been nothing at all, or that there might have been spatiotemporally disconnected universes. However, the most persistent objection to the analytic ambition of genuine realism is that extensional accuracy of the analysis is bought at the price of circularity. The analysis succeeds only if Lewis can guarantee the possibility principle: it is possible that A iff at some world A. But accuracy here requires that the worlds (quantified over on the right-side) are all and only the *possible* worlds. So if the analysis is accurate it must (somehow) be circular in presupposing one of the modal concepts (possibility) that is supposed to be analysed away. However, even if extensional accuracy and non-circularity are granted, the relevance of Lewisian analyses is also an issue. Even if there are worlds (universes) enough to map or match exactly the range of possibilities, these other-worldly goings-on do not determine, constrain or constitute the modal truth – we know (*a priori*) that such goings-on are essentially irrelevant to the modal truth. This form of objection is most frequently applied to the specific case of the counterpart-theoretic analysis of *de re* modal claims: evidence is adduced in the form of a contrast between our (alleged) lack of concern for counterparts and our concern for *de re* modal facts about ourselves (how *we* might have done otherwise versus what someone else did). The capacity of counterpart theory to yield an adequate semantic theory of modal logics has been questioned, and particularly so in connection with relatively rich quantified modal logics.

The second sort of criticism talks up the theoretical costs of accepting Lewisian realism.

The proposal to quantify over non-actual individuals has been castigated as: outright inconsistent and contrary to analytic truth (there are things that don't actually exist), arbitrary in stopping short of further quantifying over impossible individuals, profligate in committing us to an ontology which is (in one sense) as big as could be and simply incredible in departing so far from the commonsensical and scientific views which are actualist about what there is.

The Lewisian deployment of worlds, in particular, also causes concern: on one hand, it is not entirely obvious what theoretical motive there is to single out worlds as a special kind among the possible individuals; on the other hand, trouble attends attempts to do so, since necessary conditions on being a world immediately set down how every world is and thereby exclude possibilities. If the worlds are (required to be) constituted by individuals in such-and-such relations, we are immediately drawn to consider whether there might have been no individuals and whether it might have been that no such relations were instantiated. The Lewisian principle of recombination seeks to characterize the extent of the worlds (and the extent of possibility) by prescribing that there are enough worlds so that, if we consider any individuals (a, b, c …) from any worlds, then for any numbers (m, n, k …), there is a world which contains m duplicates a, and n duplicates of b, and … . It has been alleged that this principle is paradoxical, in generating more worlds than there are on any initial hypothesis about their number.

It is often alleged acceptance of Lewisian realism would rationally constrain us to revise, unacceptably, our cognitive or ethical practices. Were we to take on board the ideas: (a) that the actual world is not ontologically special, and (b) that there are worlds in which the future fails to resemble the past, there are no exceptionless regularities, there are epiphenomena that leave no cognizable trace …, then we must surrender entitlement to procedures and inferences (induction, best explanation, Ockham's razor) which presume – one way or another – that our world is one of those which is cognitively nice rather than cognitively nasty. Were we to take on board that our actions never make a difference to the sum of utility in (unrestricted) existence – since our doing or not doing X will always be matched by the execution of the alternative action in another world – we would have to recognize the futility of our attempts to do right and acquiesce in non-deliberation and indifference.

Finally, it is objected that Lewisian ontology cannot be paired with an adequate epistemology, since the Lewisian conception of the modal facts renders them cognitively inaccessible to us. These facts (Lewis-construed) are not knowable by *a posteriori* warrant, since other worlds are (by definition) causally isolated from us. But nor are they knowable by *a priori* warrant, for if we can have *a priori* knowledge of existence at all, such knowledge cannot extend to the existence of concrete individuals, such as the dragons, Newtonian spaces, intelligent nonhumans, etc., in Lewisian ontology.

Ersatz realism

What unites all realists (in this context), and distinguishes them – Lewis included – from non-realists, is belief in the existence of a plurality of possible worlds. Realists who differ from Lewis in their conception of the nature of possible worlds are variously called abstractionist, actualist or ersatz realists. The use of the last term (Lewis's) is pejorative and, accordingly, contentious, but it is, in a sense, less misleading than the others. For one may be a non-Lewisian realist about possible worlds without thinking of them as abstract: they might be identified with sums of actual space–time points. Or one might believe that possible worlds exist and are abstract but also hold them to be non-actual, on the grounds that only the concrete is actual. However, ersatz realists (ersatzists) *typically* hold the conjunction: (a) every non-actualized possible world is abstract rather than concrete and (b) every possible world is an actually existing object. Thesis (b) is typically held as a corollary of generalized ontological actualism: (c) that (unrestrictedly) everything which exists actually exists. Further highly typical ersatzist theses are (d) that whatever entities had existed would, thereby, have actually existed; (e) exactly one of the possible worlds is distinguished from the others by being actualized; and (f) the actualized world is like all the other, non-actualized worlds, in being abstract. There are any number of ways of fleshing out this schematic description, but most issues can be illustrated by considering two paradigm instances of ersatz realism.

In Plantingan realism, the possible worlds are abstract entities – specifically, maximal possible states of affairs. States of affairs are conceived as unstructured entities (no parts or members) which represent: a world represents that Socrates is a carpenter, or it is true at a world that Socrates is a carpenter, when the world includes the state of affairs of *Socrates' being a carpenter*. Some such states of affairs are possible (could have obtained) like *Socrates' being a carpenter*; some are impossible (could not have obtained) like *Socrates' being a number*, and among the possible states of affairs some are actualized (do obtain) like *Socrates' being a philosopher*. For a world to include a state of affairs is for it to be the case that necessarily, if that world had obtained, then that state of affairs would have obtained. For a world to be maximal is for it to be the case that for every state of affairs, the world either includes that state of affairs (*Socrates' being a carpenter*) or its complement (*Socrates' not being a carpenter*). All states of affairs – maximal or not, possible or not – actually exist. Had things been otherwise, some other states of affairs would have obtained, but exactly the same states of affairs would have existed. The feature of obtaining or actualization is metaphysically primitive, and among those states of affairs that are possible worlds, exactly one is actualized (obtains) but remains, like all the others, an abstract object.

In linguistic realism, the possible worlds are taken as abstract entities – specifically, they are maximal consistent interpreted sentences. Maximal sentences are, naturally, conceived as structured entities: each is a set (conjunction) of basic sentences, and each basic sentence is itself a set (sequence) of words. A sentence represents that Socrates is a carpenter, by stating or entailing that Socrates is a carpenter: a world represents that Socrates is a carpenter, or it is true at that world that Socrates is a carpenter, by the world having as members basic sentences which entail that Socrates is a carpenter. The "words" of the worldmaking language are, typically, construed very extensively so as to maximize expressive power. In a "Lagadonian" language, we have (at least) a different name for each actually existing individual and for each actually instantiated property: the trick which achieves this is counting each of these individuals and each of these properties as a word that names itself. A sentence or a world is actualized by being true (*simpliciter*). A sentence is consistent just in case it could have been true. A sentence is maximal just in case, for every sentence S, it entails either S or not-S. Of the possible worlds (maximal consistent sentences) exactly one is actualized by being true, and it, like all the unactualized (false) and non-maximal sentences, is an abstract entity.

In general the explanatory aims of the ersatzist are far more modest than those of the Lewisian realist. In the matter of conceptual explanation, there is a generic obstacle to any actualist realist attempt to provide a modality-free analysis of the family of modal concepts. Typically, whatever the ersatzist takes her worlds to be, it seems that there will be some such things that represent impossibilities in whatever way the others are supposed to represent possibilities: thus, we might say, there are impossible worlds as well as possible worlds. So we cannot say, simply, that for something to be possible is for it to be the case at a world (in general) and must have a means of distinguishing, for that purpose, exactly the worlds that are possible. And, typically, the concession is made quickly by the ersatzist that this cannot be done without appeal to some modal concept which is unanalyzed (could have obtained, possibly true, etc.). In the matter of ontological identification, there is also a generic obstacle to matching Lewisian ambitions. For, typically, the ersatzist takes as a primitive constituent of her worlds at least one kind of intensional entity – e.g. states of affairs or properties. But that being so, there will be, in each case, at least one kind of intensional entity that is not apt to be identified (nontrivially) with any kind of construct out of the worlds or the world elements. However, these points, even if well taken, show only that the potential of ersatz realism to issue conceptual and ontological explanations is, in certain respects, limited. It has not been suggested that there is no such potential. Indeed, it would remain a legitimate ambition for the actualist realist to explain or unify the variety of modal concepts by appeal to a single primitive concept, and to explain or unify the variety of the intensional entities by appeal to a single primitive kind of intensional entity. Furthermore, ersatzists who acknowledge and embrace these limitations will also typically resist Lewisian claims to have (successfully) provided analyses without appeal to primitive modal concepts and to have (successfully) provided ontological identifications of intensional entities with sets of individuals. Ersatzists typically wish to lay claim to whichever semantic explanations are yielded by an application of standard (Kripkean) semantic theory for quantified modal logics. But in this case also, there is a generic obstacle to overcome. On the face-value reading of the Kripke semantic theory for propositional modal logics, its proponent is committed to the existence of a set of (many) possible worlds: but when the theory is enriched to cater for quantificational modal logics, the richer models bring further commitment to a set of all possible individuals. Thus, any ersatzist who would straightforwardly lay claim to the Kripke semantics must identify candidates to be – or to take the place of – the merely possible individuals which populate such a set. Plantinga takes as surrogates (in some sense) of possible individuals special properties – individual essences such that for each individual that might have existed (might have been actual), necessarily, that property would have been instantiated iff that individual had existed. One such individual essence, corresponding to actual individual Socrates, is (the property of) *being identical to Socrates* and the truth-conditions for modal sentences are modified accordingly: "Socrates is a carpenter" is true at a world w just in case, at w, an essence of Socrates and the property of being a carpenter are co-exemplified. The linguistic realist naturally takes the (surrogates for) the possible individuals to be singular terms, perhaps certain maximal descriptions, which can be constructed in the worldmaking language out of actually referring names (individuals) and predicates (properties).

Ersatz realism discussed

The ontology of ersatz realism does not include concrete possibilia – the talking donkeys, the dragons, etc. – and it appears otherwise safe and sane, since it includes categories of entity which are admitted (by many) on prior and independent grounds: properties, propositions, states of affairs, etc. However, it is one thing for us to assent to the existence of (say) properties and another thing altogether to assent, further, to the conjunction of that claim with a specific theoretical conception of the properties. Plantinga's theoretical conception of the various categories of abstracta is particularly demanding. First, the categories of states of affairs, property, proposition and set are *sui generis* and mutually exclusive: there is no question of any one of these categories being identified as a special case of the other. Second, the states of affairs and properties include the unactualized as well as the actualized – indeed, the unactualizable, as well as the actualizable. Thirdly, the states of affairs (at least) are unstructured simples: one might expect that certain sorts of relation hold between (say) *Socrates being wise and Socrates' being Greek* and *Socrates' being wise*, and that they do so in virtue of the structures of these states of affairs. Yet Plantinga cannot endorse this, since his states of affairs have no structure.

As illustrated above, ersatz worlds are characterized – one way or another – by a certain kind of maximality or all-inclusiveness: but these characteristics threaten paradox. To illustrate the problem, take it that the actualized world is, or corresponds to, the set of all true propositions, S. Let the size of S be k. We know, then, that there are 2^k subsets of S and that 2^k is bigger than k. But it appears that we can easily find distinct true propositions for each of these 2^k subsets – for example, in each case the proposition that the subset in question is a set. But then it appears that the size of the set of true propositions is at least 2^k, and that contradicts the hypothesis that the size is k. The challenge to the ersatzer is to restore consistency to her conception of worlds while continuing to ensure that the possible worlds (a) continue to represent all the possibilities that they should and (b) (collectively) form a set, as the Kripkean semantic theory of modal logics appears to require.

Representation by ersatz worlds is typically univocal. Unlike Lewis, the ersatzist does not invoke distinct kinds of representation, *de re* and *de dicto*: in particular, ersatz worlds typically do not represent (vicariously) by way of counterparts. This is reflected in the standard Kripke semantics, wherein one individual may be a member of the domain of distinct worlds (and thereby represents itself as existing at different worlds by being a member of the domain at both worlds). This semantical fact is the basis of the alleged problems of transworld identity and transworld identification. The former invites understanding as a metaphysical problem, but we must take care to avoid reading the metaphysical commitments of ersatzism too quickly off the semantic theory. For none of our ersatzists takes a world to be identical to the domain associated with it in the Kripke semantics. So nothing immediately follows from the semantic fact of overlapping domains about the worlds themselves overlapping by having common constituents. Once we are clear in asking a metaphysical question of transworld identity, the issue of whether possible worlds ever have common constituents falls out easily enough from any clear characterization of the nature of the ersatz worlds. In Plantingan realism the answer is, no: worlds have no constituents. In linguistic realism, yes: one actual individual, or actually instantiated property, can be a member of a worldmaking sentence when that sentence is a member of more than one world. The distinct, and broadly epistemic, problem of transworld identification concerns how we know that an individual, which is represented as existing at a world, is (say) Adam rather than Noah. After all, we cannot rely on identifying Adam by looking for an individual who is represented as having all of Adam's actual properties, for the point of the postulation of other worlds is precisely to represent Adam as he could otherwise have been. The standard reply is to deflate the alleged problem by pointing out that the ersatzist presents possible worlds in precisely such a way as to settle which (relevant) individuals are represented. Since we begin by presenting a world *as* a world at which *Adam* is thus and so, then if we have spoken of a (kind of) world at all, there is no question of whether such a world is one in which it is Adam who is represented. This point is often sloganized in saying that possible worlds are stipulated rather than discovered. But the slogan is potentially misleading, and quite seriously so. For the claim is not (or ought not to be) that the possible worlds themselves are stipulated into existence: their existence, on all relevant views, is independent of our (attempts to) talk about them. Neither is the claim (or neither ought it to be) that we present a world and then stipulate that it is possible – that it is a possible world rather than an impossible world. Again, on all relevant views, that a world is a possible world is independent of our (attempts to) talk about it.

Finally, Lewis confronts each version of ersatzism with a dilemma over representation. On one horn, the ersatzist allows us to understand how worlds are supposed to represent possibilities, but thereby demonstrates that their representational powers are inadequate. On the other horn, the ersatzist ensures against complaints of representational adequacy but only by invoking an obscure and unsatisfactory metaphysics of representation. Linguistic realism is confronted by the former horn. For even given all the actual individuals and actually instantiated properties as words of the worldmaking language, it seems: (a) that there are distinct possibilities that cannot be represented as distinct; and (b) there are alien possibilities (such as the instantiation of fundamental properties other than those which are actually instantiated) that cannot be represented at all. Plantingan realism is confronted by the latter, "magical" horn. Here, Lewis's dialectic is much more subtle and it is controversial exactly where the burden of his objection lies. However, and merely to advertise, at the heart of that dialectic is a further dilemma concerning the nature of the representation relation to which certain ersatzists are committed. If the relation is classified as internal, we have cognitive mystery: the ersatzist realist is crediting herself with the capacity to think of (grasp) relations while being unacquainted with them and possessing no identifying description of them. If the relation is classified as external, we have metaphysical mystery: the ersatzist is committed not only to unexplicated necessary connections between distinct things, but also to the further metaphysical thesis that the intrinsic natures of things can constrain the external relations in which they stand to other things.

Non-realism

Non-realists are those who do not believe in the existence of non-actual (or non-actualized) possibilia. The most interesting kind of non-realist is he who would, nonetheless, persist in talking as though possible worlds (or other possibilia) exist and claim to be explaining something in doing so. The non-realist territory is much less developed and explored than the realist territory, so here description of available positions is augmented by only a little critical commentary.

One general point that can be made about all non-realist approaches is that proper ontological applications of possibilia are simply not available to them: qua non-realist, one has no posibilia within one's ontological resources and so one has no possibilia from which to construct intensional entities (or, we might add, to be the truthmakers for any truth-bearers). Another general point is that each non-realist approach would appear to be available in both Lewisian and ersatzist versions: insofar as the specific version of non-realism leaves some aspect of the meaning of possible-world talk undetermined, the details might be filled out in either a Lewisian or an ersatzist way.

Quasi-realists about possible worlds attempt to situate use of the apparently descriptive discourse of possible worlds within a traditional non-cognitivist, and non-descriptivist, conception of modality. With a non-reductive conception of modal concepts deployed, perhaps some conceptual projects remain in quasi-realist play. But the most likely, and very limited, role that would appear to remain to possible-world talk is as some sort of device for calculating (not explaining or determining) which modal inferences are correct.

Various noneists and neutralists about quantification wish to construe apparently existential quantification over possibilia as particular quantification which is not existentially committing: there are possibilia but they do not exist. In this case, the gambit may well be that the various conceptual, ontological and semantic explanations proceed as in the relevant realist case(s) and that their explanatory force is not diminished even when the quantification is construed in noneist fashion.

Paraphrase approaches to possible-world talk (there is a possible world at which donkeys talk) are offered by both fictionalists (according to the Lewis fiction, there is a possible world at which donkeys talk) and modalists (it is possible that there is a world at which donkeys talk). In the modalist case, the provision of a full range of paraphrases is a nontrivial matter and inspires worry about whether the strategy can be applied to all relevant possibilia-sentences. In both cases, it is objected that some commitment to possibilia lurks somewhere within the proposal. But assuming that those difficulties can be overcome, the major question which hangs over these paraphrastic non-realisms is that of which explanatory benefits they preserve. It is one thing to earn the right to use the possibilia-sentences without incurring ontological commitment: it is another thing to show that the sentences in that usage can sustain any explanations of the kinds that realists offer of modal concepts, modal inferences or intensional ontology.

Finally, if possible-world talk is interpreted at face-value, exactly as a realist would interpret it, realism can be avoided by refusing to hold true any committing existential sentence. On one development of this approach, we would then invoke an alternate norm or value at which we aim when we indulge in this talk: we would expect to join with the realists in holding which worldly claims are correct, in assenting and dissenting, but explain that we are not claiming (to know) the *truth* of the sentences in doing so. The precedents for such views about other discourses include Field (1980) holding that the correct existential claims of mathematics are false but good for being consequences of conservative theories, and van Fraassen (1980) holding that the correct existential claims of microphysics are not known to be true, but good for generating empirically adequate theories. On another development, more promising for the agnostic than the disbeliever, one might eschew any secondary norm and persist with an account of oneself as aiming at the truth, while disciplining oneself only to hold true those worldly-claims that do not entail the existence of any mere possibilia. The prospects of this view are boosted when one considers the range of claims which translate as *non-existential* worldly claims – thus claims of necessity, impossibility, validity, would-counterfactuals. On either development of the face-value view, some promise of explanatory value lies with the consideration that the non-realist takes possible-world sentences (in her use) to have exactly the same conceptual content and truth-conditions as those assigned to them by the realist. So if it is these aspects of possibilia-sentences that do the work in realist hands, those sentences should do exactly the same work in the hands of the non-realist in whose account of the sentences those features are preserved. More definitely, it has been argued in some detail that the definitions and a substantial range of the results of Kripke semantics (with respect to validity, soundness, completeness, etc.) are available to one who asserts the standard theory within the constraints of agnosticism about non-actualized worlds.

References

Field, H. (1980) *Science without Numbers*, Oxford: Blackwell.
van Fraassen, B. (1980) *The Scientific Image*, Clarendon: Oxford.

Further reading

The recommended primary sources of the various views discussed are as follows: for Lewisian realism, D. Lewis, *On the Plurality of Worlds* (Oxford: Blackwell, 1986), as well as linguistic realism (chapter 3); for Plantingan realism, A. Plantinga, *The Nature of Necessity* (Oxford: Clarendon, 1974); for Kripkean semantics for quantified modal logic, S. Kripke, "Semantical Considerations on Modal Logic," *Acta Philosophica Fennica* 16 (1963): 83–94; for quasi-realism, S. Blackburn, *Spreading the Word* (Oxford: Clarendon, 1984), chapter 6; for noneism, G. Priest, *Towards Non-Being: The Logic and Metaphysics of Intentionality* (Oxford: Oxford University Press, 2005); for modalism, G. Forbes, *The Metaphysics of Modality* (Oxford: Clarendon, 1985); for fictionalisms, G. Rosen, "Modal Fictionalism," *Mind* 99 (1990): 327–54, and T. Sider, "The Ersatz Pluriverse," *Journal of Philosophy* 99 (2002): 279–315; and for agnosticism, J. Divers, "Agnosticism about Other Worlds: A New Antirealist Programme in Modality," *Philosophy and Phenomenological Research* 69 (2004): 659–84, and "Possible-Worlds Semantics without Possible Worlds: The Agnostic Approach," *Mind* 115 (2006): 187–225. For further and detailed discussion of the realist positions, and further references, see J. Divers, *Possible Worlds* (London: Routledge, 2002). For a more recent discussion of ersatz realism, see J. Melia, "Ersatz Possible Worlds," in J. Hawthorne, T. Sider, and D. Zimmerman (eds), *Contemporary Debates in Metaphysics* (Oxford: Blackwell, 2007), pp. 135–52. For discussion of various issues related to possible worlds, see D. Nolan, *Topics in the Philosophy of Possible Worlds* (Routledge: London, 2002).

33

MATHEMATICAL ENTITIES

Peter Clark

Introduction

Suppose for a moment that instead of a companion to metaphysics this was a companion to biology then this might well have been a chapter on biological entities. As such one would then have begun with a listing of the great forms of life, the prokaryotic organisms, the Protista (the eukaryotic organisms), the Fungi, the animals and the plants and then no doubt there would have been sections devoted to the great phyla of the five kingdoms of life. Perhaps each of the phyla would have been treated differently, reflecting the very great differences of constitution, of form and of function across each of the kingdoms of living things.

Interestingly such an approach to the topic of mathematical entities might well have been forced on an author for a volume on metaphysics written not so long ago, say in the early part of the nineteenth century, describing in the same way the inhabitants of the mathematical universe. Thus there would need to be a section on the great domain of the numbers, the natural numbers, the rational and real numbers, the complex numbers and their respective treatments in arithmetic and in analysis, both real and complex. There would also have needed to be separate treatments of geometry and of algebra which would have been thought of, following Kant, as resting on quite separate foundations. The foundations of arithmetic and number relying on temporal intuition, and not requiring an axiomatic formulation, while the foundations of geometry, the paradigm case of an axiomatic deductive science, relied upon a theory of spatial intuition and the possibility of constructions performed in, or guaranteed by, the pure form of outer intuition.

Equally while the numbers might well have been thought of as *objects* corresponding say to temporal instants, if *functions* had been treated they might well have been conceived, not as *objects* of any sort, but rather as operations, or mappings or transformations of some active kind, a mental performance of some sort or other which brought together in thought the object forming the argument of the function and the result of applying the function to the argument, its value. In short a *mathematica zoologica* of that time would have seen the mathematical universe as populated by many different *kinds* of entity, not just differing from each other in their properties or their characterisations but in their intrinsic, essential natures, of which the object–function distinction and the arithmetical–geometrical distinction were perhaps the most fundamental.

Furthermore the one outstanding characteristic of the fundamental mathematical domains of the natural numbers and of the continuum, that is, of their indefinite extensibility, their infinitude, produced in itself a very considerable difficulty, for that notion seemed inherently intractable. Locke writing in the late seventeenth century seemed to rule out giving any account of infinity as an object. He says,

> The clearest idea any mind can get of infinity, is the confused incomprehensible remainder of endless addable numbers, which affords no prospect of stop or boundary. [The infinity of number] lies in a power still of adding any combination of units to any former number, and that as long and as much as one will. (Locke, *Essays Concerning Human Understanding*, Bk 2, ch. 17, §9)

And Kant writing a century later makes a similar claim in giving his definition of an intrinsically infinite collection "the infinity of a series consists in the fact that it can never be completed through successive synthesis" (Kant 1973 [1787]: A426, B454, p. 397). How could there be an infinite object, or an object actually composed of infinitely many objects like a line segment, since any such collection would be incomplete and hence not an object? What was the real nature of such entities?

All this is in stark contrast to what we now regard as the answer to the question what mathematical entities exist? The working practitioner of classical mathematics can answer the question with one word – *sets*. Every mathematical entity is a set and all sets are objects, some of them being infinite objects. The question as to what mathematical entities exist is reduced to the question what sets are there, and the answer to that is provided by set theory, an explicit axiomatic account of set existence.

This brilliant intellectual achievement of the reduction of the whole of classical mathematics to set theory was essentially achieved in four steps. First the late nineteenth-century revolution in rigour established real analysis on the foundations with which we are now very familiar with completely clear notions of limit, continuity and differentiation, the second step was the formulation of a logic (quantification theory with multiple generality and quantifier dependence) sufficiently powerful to explicitly exhibit the validity of every valid mathematical inference, the third step was the formulation by Cantor of the theory of transfinite sets and the theory of ordinal numbers to "measure" them, and the fourth step was the formulation of a (consistent) explicit axiomatic set theory sufficiently powerful to establish the existence both of the fundamental mathematical domains and of the functions definable over them.

But why should what is after all in many ways a purely technical achievement in mathematics proper pose a metaphysical problem? The answer is that set theory, and consequently mathematics proper, is full of existence claims, from simple ones like, "there is a set with no members" and "there is a prime number between 17 and 21," to complex ones like "there is a function from the real numbers into the real numbers which is everywhere continuous and nowhere differentiable" and "there is a cardinal number which is the limit of the sequence of infinite cardinals $\aleph_i$ for i a member of the set of natural numbers." If we think that the theorems of mathematics are true and we understand the existential quantifier in the standard way, as we do in first-order logic, then there had better be objects which make the claims true. But these objects cannot be physical objects located in space and time. They must be abstract objects, but what sort of thing are *abstract* objects and how can we come to know them and succeed in referring to them if, however we might think of it, all our knowledge is derived ultimately from experience? Let us for the moment then boil this question down to the question what are sets and how do we come to know about them? Before we look at some answers we should briefly examine what a standard set theory claims in the way of set existence.

Zermelo–Fraenkel theory and the Zermelo hierarchy

What then does the mathematical universe contain as entities, given that everything therein is a set? There are a number of theories but let us stick to the one which standard mathematical practice usually embraces. The Zermelo–Fraenkel theory for pure sets, that is where the objects assumed to exist are only sets (there are no non-sets as individuals), can be formulated as eight explicit principles of set existence. The first axiom says that there is a set which has no members, the empty set. The second axiom, the axiom of extensionality, lays down the identity conditions for sets, and says that if two sets have the same members then they are identical. The third axiom says that there is an infinite set, that is, a set and hence a completed object containing all and only the natural numbers, ω. The fourth principle is the power set axiom, which says that given any set there is a set whose members are all and only the subsets of that set. The fifth principle is the axiom of union. This asserts that given any set x there is a set whose members are all the members of the members of x. The sixth principle is the axiom of foundation, which we can formulate here as the claim that the universe of sets is exhausted by the Zermelo hierarchy (of which more below). Then follow two axiom schemas which are really each an infinite list of axioms, the first is the separation principle, which says given any set x and a determinate property Φ there is a set whose members are all those members of x which have the property Φ. As noted above the schema is really an infinite list of axioms for we need a special axiom for each property Φ. Finally we need the replacement schema which says that if x is a set and F is a function then the collection of all $F(y)$ for y a member of x is also a set. Again this is actually an infinite list of axioms for we need a special axiom for each specific function F.

Given what we noted at the beginning of this essay it is of paramount importance to notice that every relation among sets x and y is in fact another set, another object, viz.: a subset of the set of all ordered pairs of members of x and y and that all functions F from x into y are themselves further sets and therefore objects, viz.: just those relations among x and y whose members satisfy the further condition that, for all $u \in x$, for all $w \in y$ and $v \in y$ (if $<u,w> \in F$ and $<u,v> \in F$ then $w = v$), where for any sets u and v, $u \in v$ means u is a member of v and $<u,w> \in F$ means that w is that object related by F to u.

A picture then of the set theoretic universe provided by the above axioms is given by what is called the Zermelo or cumulative hierarchy. Begin with the empty set as the zeroth level of the hierarchy and at each stage take the power set of the sets already obtained and continue indefinitely to iterate this operation. The number of sets so obtained remains finite (though immensely large) until the first infinite stage, that first stage after all finite stages (we know this stage exists because of the axiom of infinity); at that stage take the union of all the sets at earlier stages, that exists because of the axiom of union. Now we have a new collection and we can begin the iterative process again. The axiom of foundation tells us that any set which exists occurs at some stage in Zermelo hierarchy. The result of the reduction of mathematics to set theory which was a brilliant technical achievement is that every mathematical entity is a set lying somewhere in the hierarchy, and for most ordinary mathematical objects, pretty low down in the hierarchy at a level of iteration less than $\omega + \omega$. Could the whole hierarchy be a set? The answer is no, and we shall see why in the next section.

What are sets?

Having looked at what is required by way of set existence for mathematics we can ask what sort of entities they are and how we could come to know them. Cantor, the founder of set theory, certainly regarded any answers to those two questions as lying firmly within the purview of metaphysics. He wrote "The grounding of the principles of mathematics and natural science is a matter for metaphysics," and again, "The general *Mengenlehre* [set theory] ... belongs thoroughly to metaphysics" (Meschowski 1965: 512). More specifically, he says, "By a 'set' we understand any collection M into a whole of definite, well-distinguished objects of our intuition or our thought (which will be called the 'elements' of M)" (Cantor 1932: 282). One natural way of interpreting this remark is to consider the collection M of objects of our thought as the extension of a concept. If we can think or apprehend of the collection of objects as one, then it is natural to suppose that they all fall under a unifying concept and in falling under that concept, the collection is the extension of that concept. On this view then sets are the extensions of concepts and we come to know about them through our grasp of concepts. Something like this view seems to have been held at times by both Cantor and Dedekind.

In an early discussion in 1882 of the nature of sets Cantor formulates the conception as follows (Cantor 1932: 150):

> I call a manifold (a totality, a set) which belongs to some conceptual sphere well-defined, if on the basis of its definition and as a consequence of the logical principle of excluded middle it must be seen as internally determined both whether some object belonging to the same conceptual sphere belongs to the imagined manifold or not, as well as whether two objects belonging to the set are equal to one another or not, despite formal differences in the way they are given.

So there are conceptual spheres, perhaps to be thought of as very fundamental mathematical domains and concepts can be used to mark off sets of objects from those conceptual spheres, those sets being the extensions of the concepts over the objects in the conceptual sphere, in a manner in line with the separation principle mentioned above. It seems clear, however, that he did not think of the conceptual spheres as themselves being sets, for reasons we shall see later. Writing a year later, in 1883, he gives a particularly strong form of this view, for he insists that the concepts whose extensions we call sets can be formulated in the language of mathematics as laws or conditions. He wrote as follows (Cantor 1932: 204n1):

> *Theory of manifolds.* By this I mean a very extensive theoretical concept which I have only attempted to develop thitherto in the special form of an arithmetic or geometric *Mengenlehre.* By a "manifold" or "set" I understand in general any many which can be thought of as one, that is, every totality of definite elements which can be united to a whole through a law.

Similarly Dedekind remarks that a system "S" is completely determined (he uses the terminology of "system" rather than set) "when with respect to everything it is determined whether it is an element of S or not" (Dedekind 1963 [1888]: 45).

This natural, indeed Fregean, thought that sets are intimately connected with the extensions of concepts is, however, untenable; it is both far too narrow in one respect and far too broad in another.

It is too narrow because such a view will certainly not serve to generate sufficiently many sets, if the notion of Fregean concept is to be closely associated with the notion of predicate or of a condition formulated in a language which we can speak and in which we think and understand. As Cantor himself was very aware the problem arises because of the action of the separation principle and the power set axiom acting together (if we also add the axiom of replacement, then the combined action of all three will yield some very large sets indeed). The axiom of infinity in effect gives us, as a set, the collection of all natural numbers ω. But the power set axiom then tells us that the collection of all subsets of ω exists, and Cantor's theorem says that this is uncountable. But the expressions of the language of set theory or indeed of English or any natural language form a countable collection. So there must be very many sets – indeed the vast majority of them (subsets of the natural numbers) that have no characterising predicate in the language of set theory or indeed English. So if indeed the notion of a Fregean concept is tied to predicate in the language or law or articulable condition there will simply not be enough such concepts to go around. Perhaps in the spirit of Frege's realism this connection should not be made and we should think of Concept as another word for property or attribute, and then there is no reason to think that every property of the natural numbers should be describable by a condition in the language of set theory or indeed in any formal or natural language, but then the Cantorian conception of a set as a collection brought together in *thought* seems to fall away.

This conception is also far too broad in another respect. It certainly entails all the axioms given above but the trouble is it entails very much more, indeed everything! Frege's Basic Law V of his *Grundgesetze* (Frege 1893–1902) lays down that for any concepts F and G the object which is the extension of F and the object which is the extension of G are identical if and only if F and G are coextensive, that is if every object falling under F falls under G and every object falling under G falls under F. This principle entails the naïve comprehension schema, to the effect that every concept F has an extension and that an object falls under F when and only when it is a member of the extension of F. Now if we have a purely logical comprehension principle to the effect that if we have a condition formalisable in the language of set theory then that condition determines a genuine concept then the Russell condition of non-self membership – $\neg(x \in x)$ – determines a concept, so the Russell condition "being non-self-membered" falls under the universal quantifiers in the statement of Basic Law V and its entailment, the naïve comprehension schema. Russell's paradox immediately follows. (Let r be the extension of the Russell condition; then by the naïve comprehension principle, if r falls under the concept not self-membered, then it is a member of extension of the concept which is r, so it is self-membered. So it is self-membered after all. So it is a member of r and so by the principle in the reverse direction, it falls under the condition, so it is not self-membered and we have a flat contradiction.) Note immediately that all that follows in the set theory of Zermelo–Fraenkel that we adumbrated above, given the Russell condition, is that there is no universal set. For if there were we could use the separation schema to give us the subset of the universal set of all non-self-membered sets, this would then be the *set* of all non-self-membered sets and contradiction would result. So there is no universal set and the Zermelo hierarchy is not a set. Cantor called the extensions of such properties as the Russell property, inconsistent multiplicities. He remarks in a letter to Dedekind (Cantor 1932: 443–7),

> For a multiplicity can be such that the assumption that *all* of its elements "are together" leads to a contradiction, so that it is impossible to conceive of the multiplicity as a unity, as "one finished thing." Such multiplicities I call *absolutely infinite* or *inconsistent multiplicities*.

The extension of the concept "is self-identical" (the universal extension – absolutely everything) and the extension of the property "being an ordinal number" are, like the Russell collection, paradigm examples of "inconsistent multiplicities." They are certainly multiplicities, for things fall under their defining concepts, but they cannot be thought of as objects, they can't be thought of as a unity, as a single object, that is, as sets subject to the axioms of set theory. This is why Cantor, in the quotation given above, was reluctant to regard the fundamental conceptual domains from which certain definite sets could be split off as being the extensions of concepts, as being themselves sets.

Call the extension of a Fregean concept a class. Then what Russell's paradox shows is that not every class is a set, not every class falls under the quantifiers in the axioms of set theory. Those that do not are called *proper classes*, they unlike classes cannot be members. Some set theories entertain the existence of proper classes but ensure that they cannot be treated as sets. What is lacking, however, is a principled distinction as to why some classes form sets and some do not, as to why some classes can be collectivised into sets to form an object and why some cannot. It is for this reason as I mentioned above that Cantor would not have regarded the "conceptual spheres" out of which concepts then form sets (as envisioned in the quotation from 1882) as themselves being sets. Nevertheless the idea that determinate properties do form sets no doubt serves to motivate the separation principle, since it could be said that if we already had a *set* and concept definable over it then it was a straightforward logical fact that there was a subset of the given set satisfying the condition and hence another set, all of whose members where members of the given set that satisfied the condition.

Is there then a principled distinction between sets and proper classes, rather than the stark fact that if we treat a proper class as a set we will get a contradiction? One interesting suggestion, due to Ruth Barcan Marcus (1963) and Charles Parsons (1983), is the idea that set membership is a matter of necessity while the membership of proper classes is not. Let us recall that on any conception of set, a set is not a mereological fusion. A fusion of samples of water is not another sort of thing from the samples that go to make it up, it is another sample of water. But a set is always quite distinct from its members, it is another distinct object. It too may be a member of some other set but it is always distinct from *its* members. Certainly a set in some sense presupposes its members, it could not exist without the members of the set "first" existing and then being brought together to form the set. In this sense the set depends upon its members. It is this core idea which is at the heart of the iterative conception of set, that sets are in some sense built up in stages by collecting together sets constructed at prior stages. The difficulty is that the iterative conception must make clear what the relation of dependence or priority of set on its members is without appeal to constructive imagery (which is just that – imagery) and without appeal to a *temporal* metaphor of earlier and later stages. What is needed is an articulation of the metaphysical relation of dependency, no doubt one holding by necessity among sets and their members. We do not have space here to pursue this issue of dependency, but two interesting and rival accounts of it can be found in Potter (2004) and Boolos (1998a, b [1971, 1989]).

Abstractionism

There is another quite different way of thinking about certain basic mathematical domains, those fundamental conceptual spheres envisioned by Cantor, like the natural numbers and the real numbers, that is very closely related to the central Fregean solution to the problem of how numbers are given to us. Frege's programme was the result of an answer to the famous question raised in §62 of the *Grundlagen* (Frege 1884) viz.: "how then are numbers given to us, if we cannot have any ideas or intuitions of them?" The answer was "by explaining the senses of identity statements in which number words occur." That explanation was to be provided at least in part by what has come to be called Hume's principle: the claim that the cardinal numbers corresponding to two concepts are identical if and only if the two concepts are equinumerous. I say in part by Hume's principle because, as Frege had already argued in another context at §56 of the *Grundlagen*, whatever the merits of Hume's principle it can't explain the senses of identity statements in which number words occur of the form the number of F's is n, where n is not given in the form of "the number of G's, for some G. It could not resolve the Julius Caesar problem, on what basis do we recognise the falsity of the claim 'Julius Caesar = zero'?" Frege then adopted the explicit definition of number in terms of classes or extensions: "the number of F's is the class of all concepts G, equinumerous with F."

But this explicit definition, together with Basic Law V, the comprehension axiom for class existence, entails Hume's principle.

With Basic Law V in place, it looked as if Frege's programme could be carried out. In effect Frege showed that second-order logic, together with Basic Law V, entails Hume's principle and that that principle, together with axiomatic second-order logic, yields the Peano–Dedekind axioms for arithmetic. As such, the truths of arithmetic could be seen to be analytic; they could all be seen to be consequences of general logical laws, together with suitable implicit definitions (like Basic Law V, which implicitly defines the notion of an extension). Further arithmetic could be seen as a body of truths about independently existing objects – the finite cardinals – which were logical objects, logical in the sense that knowledge of which requires nothing beyond knowledge of logic and definitions. If this could be extended to the real numbers and other parts of mathematics, then a foundation for mathematics would have been established on which mathematics was presented as uncontaminated by empirical notions, presented as a body of truths in its full classical form and shown to be applicable to reality, since numbers are properties of properties which apply to reality. Of course as Russell and Zermelo showed, Basic Law V was inconsistent, but that fact, as has been pointed out by Wright, Boolos and Heck, in no way affects the validity of the deduction from Hume's principle in second-order logic of the Dedekind–Peano axioms. Wright and Hale argue that this fact alone can reconstitute the Fregean foundational programme for arithmetic, which they term neo-Fregeanism. They say (Hale and Wright 2001: 4),

> Neo-Fregeanism holds that Frege need not have taken the step which led to this unhappy conclusion [The appearance of the Russell contradiction]. At least as far as the theory of natural number goes, it is possible to accomplish Frege's central mathematical and philosophical aims by basing the theory on Hume's Principle, adjoined as a supplementary axiom to a suitable formulation of second-order logic. Hume's Principle cannot, to be sure, be taken as a definition in any strict sense – any sense requiring that it provide for the eliminative paraphrase of its definiendum (the numerical operator, "the number of …") in every admissible type of occurrence. But this does not preclude its being viewed as an implicit definition, effecting an introduction of a sortal concept of cardinal number and, accordingly, as being analytic of the concept – and this, the neo-Fregean contends, coupled with the fact that Hume's Principle so conceived requires a prior understanding only of second-order logical vocabulary, is enough to sustain an account of the foundations of Arithmetic that deserved to be viewed as a form of logicism which, whilst not quite logicism in the sense of a reduction of arithmetic to logic, preserves the essential core and content of Frege's two fundamental theses.

The claim of neologicism then is that (i) Hume's principle is a stipulation which gives the truth conditions of a restricted class of statements of numerical identity; (ii) the resulting explanation of the concept of number is complete, however, in that it suffices for the second-order derivation of the basic laws of arithmetic; (iii) the existence of numbers is something discovered and not stipulated (the platonism of Frege's original theory is preserved); (iv) our (*a priori*) knowledge of number is derived from a principle whose truth is a matter of stipulation; and (v) the close connection between number and concept is fully restored, since every sortal concept has a number associated with it on this account.

Abstraction principles, of which Hume's principle is a paradigm example, come in two types, conceptual abstractions and objectual ones, but all have the following form. There is a domain of entities, denoted say, by α, β, etc., and a relation R defined over them. Then an abstraction principle has the form

$$[(\Sigma\alpha) = (\Sigma\beta)] \leftrightarrow R(\alpha,\beta),$$

where $R(\ ,\ )$ is an equivalence relation among the α and β's. An abstraction principle may be called a logical abstraction when the relation $R(\ ,\ )$ is definable in purely logical vocabulary, e.g. equinumerosity among concepts or ordinal similarity among binary relations. Under the classical canonical interpretation in set theory $(\Sigma\alpha)$ is the equivalence class of α under the relation R (it is the set of all those things that are R related to α) and exists (where it does) in virtue of a set existence axiom. That is the existence and uniqueness of $(\Sigma\alpha)$ has in effect to be guaranteed by separate principles of set existence. Wright and Hale, however, argue that in certain cases logical abstraction principles can play the role of stipulations and if the relation on the right hand side of the iff is ever satisfied, then no further question concerning the existence of the $(\Sigma\alpha)$ need arise. Conceptual abstraction principles are those in which α's are concepts (as in the case of Hume's principle), and objectual abstraction principles are those in which the field of the equivalence relation comprises objects. In both cases and this is crucially so the abstracta, the $(\Sigma\alpha)$, are objects, so in the case of conceptual abstractions Σ acts as a type down operation, from concepts to objects.

Of course Wright and Hale do not argue that it is always legitimate to introduce abstracta in this way. Two examples of conceptual logical abstraction principles which fail to introduce abstracta are Basic Law V and what might be called Ordinal Hume which is the claim that $\forall(R)\forall(S)$ (Ord R = Ord $S \leftrightarrow R$ is similar to S). This has the form of an abstraction principle, since similarity is an equivalence relation among binary relations. But Ordinal Hume leads directly to the Burali-Forti paradox. Wright and Hale have, however, argued that there are general principles which can distinguish between good and bad abstraction principles and in any case, as is well known, there is no similar problem about Hume's principle, since it is known to be equiconsistent with real analysis. However, consistency problems are bound to arise for stronger abstraction principles, such as those employed by Shapiro (2000) and Hale (2001) (in their [independent] and very different construction of the real numbers, using cut abstraction, the principle that two cuts in the rationals are identical if and only if their upper bounds coincide).

While abstractionism is no doubt a metaphysically important contribution to the existence of fundamental mathematical domains and their epistemology there are considerable difficulties facing the idea, not least technically with respect to applying the idea to set theory itself, for there the obvious abstraction principle is just the notorious Basic Law V. The second difficulty is metaphysical in kind and is that to do with the stipulative character of abstraction principles and how that is to be consistent with the avowed platonism of abstractionism, that a stipulation, in effect an implicit definition, is sufficient to characterise a truth about a pre-existent domain.

The subject of this essay has been mathematical entities and in particular sets. I have concentrated primarily on this topic in classical mathematics because of its centrality in the practice of mathematics in the mathematical community. For the metaphysical issues surrounding constructive mathematics and foundational theories in mathematics the reader is referred to the further reading section.

References

Boolos, G. (1998a [1971]) "The Iterative Conception of Set," reprinted in *Logic, Logic and Logic*, Cambridge, MA: Harvard University Press, pp. 13–29.

—— (1998b [1989]) "Iteration Again," reprinted in *Logic, Logic and Logic*, Cambridge, MA: Harvard University Press, pp. 88–104.

Cantor, G. (1932) *Gesammelte Abhandlungen mathematischen und philosophischen*, edited by E. Zermelo, Berlin: Springer-Verlag.

Dedekind, R. (1963 [1888]) "Was sind und was sollen die Zahlen?" in W. W. Beman (ed.), *The Nature and Meaning of Numbers*, New York: Dover, 44–115.

Frege, G. (1884) *Die Grundlagen der Arithmetik, eine logisch-mathematische Untersuchung über den Begriff der Zahl*, Breslau: Koebner; trans. J. L. Austin, *The Foundations of Arithmetic: A Logico-Mathematical Enquiry into the Concept of Number*, Oxford: Basil Blackwell, 1953.

—— (1893–1902) *Grundgesetze der Arithmetik, begriffsschriftlich abgeleitet*, 2 vols, Jena: H. Pohle.

Hale, R. (2001) "Reals by Abstraction," reprinted in R. Hale and C. Wright, *The Reason's Proper Study: Essays Towards a Neo-Fregean Philosophy of Mathematics*, Oxford: Oxford University Press, pp. 400–20.

Hale, R. and Wright, C. (eds) (2001) *The Reason's Proper Study: Essays Towards a Neo-Fregean Philosophy of Mathematics*, Oxford: Oxford University Press.

Kant, I. (1973 [1787]) *Critique of Pure Reason*, trans. Norman Kemp Smith, London: Macmillan.

Marcus, R. Barcan (1963) "Classes and Attributes in Extended Modal Systems," *Acta Philosophica Fennica* 16: 123–36.

Meschowski, H. (1965) "Aus den Briefbüchern Georg Cantors," *Archive for the History of the Exact Sciences* 2: 503–19.

Parsons, C. (1983) "Sets and Modality," in *Mathematics in Philosophy: Selected Essays*, Ithaca, NY: Cornell University Press, 298–341.

Potter, M. (2004) *Set theory and Its Philosophy*, Oxford: Oxford University Press, 2004

Shapiro, S. (2000) "Frege Meets Dedekind: A Neologicist Treatment of Real Analysis," *Notre Dame Journal of Formal Logic* 4, no. 41: 335–64.

Further reading

The best introduction to modern mathematics itself is still Richard Courant and Herbert Robbins, *What Is Mathematics?* (Oxford: Oxford University Press, 1969). An informal and accessible account of some of the issues discussed here can be found in A. W. Moore *The Infinite*, 2nd edn (London; New York: Routledge, 2001). Michael Potter's *Reason's Nearest Kin* (Oxford: Oxford University Press, 2000) provides a sustained analysis of the problem of mathematical existence, from Kant to logical positivism, especially for arithmetic and real analysis. A standard and very readable introduction to set theory is Keith Devlin *The Joy of Sets, Fundamentals of Contemporary Set Theory*, 2nd edn (Undergraduate Texts in Mathematics) (New York: Springer-Verlag, 1993). An excellent source for articles on the topic of mathematical existence is S. Shapiro (ed.) *The Oxford Handbook of Philosophy of Mathematics and Logic* (Oxford: Oxford University Press, 2005). William Demopoulos's collection, *Frege's Philosophy of Mathematics*, is a fine source for both the revolution in rigour and the historical development of logicism. A thorough exposition of the problems of Cantorian set theory and its foundations can be found in M. Hallett, *Cantorian Set Theory and the Limitation of Size* (Oxford Logic Guides 1) (Oxford: Oxford University Press, 1984); and for especially the iterative concept of set, see M. Potter, *Set Theory and Its Philosophy* (Oxford: Oxford University Press, 2004). The *locus classicus* for neologicism is Crispin Wright's *Frege's Conception of Numbers as Objects* (Aberdeen: Aberdeen University Press, 1983). Abstractionism and its application to various areas of mathematics is very extensively covered in Roy T. Cook's collection, *The Arché Papers on the Mathematics of Abstraction* (Western Ontario Series in the Philosophy of Science, vol. 71) (New York: Springer, 2007). A full treatment of the general theory of abstraction principles can be found in K. Fine, *The Limits of Abstraction* (Oxford: Oxford University Press, 2000). An important modal nominalist theory is developed in C. Chihara, *Constructibility and Existence* (Oxford: Oxford University Press, 1990). Nominalist reconstructions of mathematics are fully discussed in J. P. Burgess and G. Rosen, *A Subject with No Object: Strategies for Nominalistic Interpretation of Mathematics* (Oxford: Oxford University Press, 1997). No study of the problem of mathematical existence should be undertaken without reference to Charles Parsons' work; see his *Mathematics in Philosophy: Selected Essays* (Ithaca, NY: Cornell University Press, 1983).

34
FICTIONAL OBJECTS
Richard Hanley

Fictional objects, such as fictional characters, are at once both utterly familiar and utterly mysterious. Anyone can name fictional objects: Pegasus, Sherlock Holmes, SpongeBob SquarePants and so on. Fictional objects that aren't usually described as *characters* include *kinds* of thing, such as unicorns, or dragons or Martians and *impersonal* individuals, such as the river Styx or Mount Doom or the Fortress of Solitude.

I'll restrict the discussion to characters because these are the fictional objects we tend to focus upon. We say some are better written than others, that some are smarter than others, that we like or dislike them, and that we do or don't want them to suffer or die. We say they are created by their authors, and we allow that other authors can then borrow them to serve as characters in new fictions. We compare them with ourselves and others we know. And, when pressed, we say they're nonexistent.

Can anything answer to all these uses of the notion of fictional characters – do they belong in our ontology? If so, then what – metaphysically speaking – are they? And if there aren't any such things, how can we explain all the talk that isn't really about "them"?

Quineanism vs. Meinongianism

Most theories of fictional characters employ a Quinean approach to meta-ontology, the tenets of which are set forward by Peter van Inwagen (1998):

(1) Being is not an activity
(2) Being is the same as existence
(3) Being is univocal
(4) Being is captured adequately by the existential quantifier of formal logic
(5) One's ontological commitments are indicated and exhausted by the existential quantifications one accepts.

Perhaps the easiest way into this approach is by examining the main competing view: Meinongianism.[1] Consider the *problem of non-existence*. Many negative existentials seem true, such as:

(N)   Holmes does not exist.

But this can seem puzzling on its face. Who or what doesn't exist? *Holmes*, of course! How can you even assert (N) without referring to Holmes? Moreover, isn't saying Holmes doesn't exist very different in meaning from saying Santa doesn't exist? The Meinongian treats "Holmes" as an ordinary proper name, which is properly translated into formal logic as an individual constant. So (N) says of the individual Holmes that it *is*, and that it doesn't exist. Holmes is a nonexistent individual, and Santa is another nonexistent individual, distinct from Holmes.

Meinongians, then, disagree with tenet (2), for there is more to *being* than *existence*.[2] They also disagree with tenets (4) and (5), since strictly the existential quantifier ranges only over existents! This leads van Inwagen to the suggestion that the Meinongian needs *another* quantifier in addition to the existential one. Van Inwagen (1977) then objects, "I confess I do not understand the words I have put into the Meinongian's mouth." Lycan (1979) likewise complains that "relentlessly" Meinongian quantification is "simply unintelligible," "literally gibberish" and "mere noise."

There are two forms the objection can take. The first is that the introduction of a second quantifier in addition to the existential quantifier cannot permit of meaningful interpretation. However, I think this form of the objection is ultimately unsuccessful. The Meinongian *needs* no extra quantifier and can regard "exists," not as a *quantifier*, but as a *predicate*. (N) can be rendered formally as "$(\exists x)[(x = h) \& \sim Ex]$." The Meinongian avoids contradiction by insisting that "$\exists$" is not an *existential* quantifier. "There is" doesn't mean "there exists," any more than it means "there flies."

Of course, a predicate can sometimes seem like a quantifier, because it can equivalently be understood as a restriction on the domain of quantification. Moreover, it is common enough to switch domains of quantification mid-sentence. In Lake Wobegon, Garrison Keillor assures us, everyone is above average in intelligence. But this might mean that *everyone in Lake Wobegon* (restricted quantification) is above *average* (less restricted – perhaps to the nation) in intelligence. Similarly, the Meinongian can say that *there are* (quantifying unrestrictedly over everything) things of which it is true to say *there are* (quantifying restrictedly, over existents) no such things.

Once the Meinongian makes it clear that they quantify unrestrictedly over *being* – over what *is* – then given their denial of tenet (2), they will reinterpret rather than deny tenets (4) and (5). They can also accept tenet (1) – being need not be an activity, even if existing is. Hence the real dispute seems to be over tenet (2), that being is the same as existence (I postpone discussion of tenet [3]).

This brings us to the second form of the objection, which is that the Meinongian is simply misusing language, since tenet (2) – that everything exists – is *analytic*. This form of the objection has all the advantages of "theft over honest toil," and the Meinongian can respond that linguistically competent folk are simply not sensitive to the issues at stake. First, what do they mean by "everything"? *Of course*, in addition to (N), the folk assert things like:

(N*) There is no such thing as Holmes.

But can we be sure they are not restricting quantification to existents, so that (N*) is equivalent to (N)?

And what do the folk mean by "exists"? I suspect they approach this by ostension. For starters, everything spatiotemporally related to us exists. But if they stop there, *by definition*, then thoroughly Platonic dualism doesn't even make it to false, and is instead mere noise. I believe Platonic dualism is *false*, not meaningless, and it seems unprincipled to hold Meinongianism to a stricter standard.

The view has a formal idiosyncrasy, however. For the typical Meinongian denies both the law of non-contradiction and its classical equivalent, the law of the excluded middle. Existent things obey these laws, but nonexistent things don't. It is not true that Holmes has type-O blood, and not true that Holmes doesn't have type-O blood. But in classical logic, if it's not true that Holmes has type-O blood, then it's true that Holmes doesn't have O-type blood. So Holmes arguably both does and doesn't have type-O blood – a contradiction. Meinongians needn't accept this consequence, given their rejection of classical logic, but the point is to believe in anything that is an object of thought, including impossible objects.

Perhaps the Meinongian will be charged with denying tenet (3). The solution may be to treat classical logic as the relevance logicians treat it: as holding only in certain domains (in this case, existents).

On balance, it may be better to avoid these sorts of problems.[3] Whether or not this is so, for the remainder of this article I'll consider only Quinean positions, those which accept tenets (1) through (5). Tenet (5), though, requires a little more examination.

Tenet (5)

One's ontological commitments are indicated and exhausted by the existential quantifications one accepts. Consider the sentence:

(C)   The average American owns 1.36 cars.

If (C) (which I just made up) isn't true, it's because the number isn't 1.36, but does commitment to (C) or something like it carry commitment to *the average American*? Tenet (5) gives us a method for answering this question for any sincere asserter of (C). The litmus test is: *do they paraphrase away when the ontological chips are down?*

For instance, for my own part, I will paraphrase away. (C) is just a convenient way of stating facts about the population of actual flesh-and-blood Americans and about the population of actual American-owned cars: it asserts that the ratio of the second to the first is 1.36.

Or consider:

(F)   This article is about fictional objects.

Does commitment to (F) commit one to fictional objects? Well, that's what this article is about. The Quinean approach does not claim that you can simply read off ontological commitment from the sentences one accepts. It recommends that you reduce such sentences to existential generalizations, but this will vary from person to person. For instance, one could be a Quinean and accept the average American, or Sherlock Holmes, into one's ontology as, say, an abstract thing.

The reduction in question will always appeal to other things you believe, and in particular to metaphysical beliefs, such as whether or not there are abstract things. It will also depend upon methodological principles, such as considerations of parsimony. All in all, the philosophical debate over fictional objects such as fictional characters is a wonderful example of the Quinean approach in action. As such, it can inform other debates in metaphysics, like those over mathematical, modal and moral objects.

The data

The role that fictions play in our lives and language can hardly be exaggerated. In addition to negative existentials, the data that challenge us to give an account of fictional characters are commonplace, and I have extracted all but one example from the *Wikipedia* page, "Sherlock Holmes" (Wikipedia 2008).

(1) Critical statements
   - Holmes first appeared in publication in 1887.
   - Writers have produced many pop-culture references to Sherlock Holmes, Conan Doyle or characters from the stories, in homage to a greater or lesser degree. Some have been overt, introducing Holmes as a character in a new setting.

(2) Fictional statements
   - Holmes can often be quite dispassionate and cold; however, when hot on the trail of a mystery, Holmes can display a remarkable passion, despite his usual languor.
   - Holmes is also proud of being British.

(3) Conative attitude statements
   - That's why I admire Holmes. But alas, I can only hope to be like Watson, one who follow his exploits as an observer. Both Watson and I want to be like him, but we can only be his friend (see Andersen 2006).

(4) "Carryover"
   - Sherlock Holmes' abilities as both a good fighter and as an excellent logician have been a boon to other authors who have lifted his name, or details of his exploits, for their plots.
   - In "The Adventure of the Greek Interpreter," Holmes also claims that his grandmother was the sister of Vernet, the French artist.

(5) "Mixed" statements
- In 2002, Holmes was inducted as an honorary fellow of the Royal Society of Chemistry.
- Readers of the Sherlock Holmes stories have often been surprised to discover that their author, Conan Doyle, was a fervent believer in paranormal phenomena, and that the logical, sceptical character of Holmes was in opposition to his own in many ways.

(6) Creativity
- Holmes is the creation of Scottish-born author and physician, Sir Arthur Conan Doyle.

Note that the sorts of sentences listed behave more or less classically in their logical relations. From "Holmes is proud of being British," you can deduce "Holmes is proud of something." From "Larry admires Holmes" and "Holmes is a fictional detective," you can deduce "Larry admires a fictional detective," and so on. Generally, the sorts of reasoning that apply to fictional characters seem just the same as those that apply outside of fiction.

One sort that is often overlooked is *counterfictional* reasoning. We concern ourselves not only with what *does* happen in a story, but what *would have* happened had things gone a little differently. Would marriage have ruined Holmes' career as a detective? Should Shylock have replied that Portia's reading of "a pound of flesh" was inappropriately narrow, and so have had his revenge after all? Should fornicating teenagers leave relative safety and venture out into the darkness when they hear a strange noise? We implicitly endorse all manner of "if it were such-and-such, then it would have been so-and-so" assertions about fictional characters and their actions, assertions which are often nontrivially true.

Responses to the data

Error theory

This is a position rarely taken in the literature. It's the view that denies the data. We talk as if there were fictional objects, making genuine assertions, so the data if true would commit us to fictional objects. But there aren't any such things as fictional objects, and the "data" are spurious.

One interesting but limited error theory is that of Colin Radford (1975), concerning our apparent conative attitudes towards fictional characters. According to Radford, we apparently admire, pity, and fear fictional characters – they really *move* us. But Radford is a *cognitivist* about emotions, though: to *truly* admire, pity or fear fictional characters, we would have to believe that they exist. Yet everyone knows that fictional characters don't exist! Radford's diagnosis is that we're behaving *irrationally* when we are moved by fictions, and we really *don't* admire, pity or fear fictional objects.

Quinean realism

Realists agree with error theorists that the data generally commit us to fictional characters, and so, when the ontological chips are down, they existentially quantify over fictional characters like Sherlock Holmes. The main tasks for the realist are to give an account of the nature of fictional characters and to explain (or explain away) the data in the light of that account.

There are, then, many varieties of realism. They disagree on questions such as:

(a) Are fictional characters abstract or concrete?
(b) Are they tokens (individuals) or types?
(c) Are they actual?
(d) Are they created or destroyed?

Realists need not hold that *all* the data commit us to fictional characters, and so can also disagree over which of the data so commit us. (In the list above, the mixed statement, "In 2002, Holmes was inducted as an honorary fellow of the Royal Society of Chemistry," is an excellent candidate for paraphrasing away, whatever one's views.) In practice, it is critical and fictional statements that realists most commonly turn to.

Anti-realism

Anti-realism agrees with error theory that there are no fictional characters but agrees with realism that the data are to be respected as often enough true or assertible. However, the anti-realist disagrees with both the error theorist and the realist in holding that the data do not commit us to fictional characters. When the ontological chips are down, anti-realists paraphrase such commitment away. But anti-realists who are also cognitivists will have difficulty avoiding an error theory about conative attitude statements.

Note the connection with *fictionalist* strategies elsewhere in ontology. For example, suppose it is claimed that the notion of a *person*, or of a *possible world*, is a convenient fiction. Presumably anyone making this claim is assuming that apparent reference to such things can be paraphrased away. But this seems to presuppose that anti-realism about fictions can be maintained. If it cannot, it is hard to see the point of a fictionalist strategy.

Desiderata

How to decide between anti-realism and the varieties of realism? One desideratum is ontological parsimony – it seems a bad idea to multiply types of entity beyond necessity. Another is semantic parsimony – not multiplying types of *meaning* beyond necessity. Another still is explanatory power: an explanation that gives a unified account of the data is to be preferred to a piecemeal approach; and explanations which capture *more* of the data are better than others.

The sad fact is that these desiderata are often themselves in competition, and every account has an implicit weighting of the desiderata, since each account tends to score better on some than others. Little wonder that reasonable people disagree!

The varieties of Quinean realism

Concrete realism

Lewis (1986) includes in his ontology non-actual possibilia that are every bit as kickable as actual persons. We cannot kick them, because they are not part of our world, but in non-actual worlds that contain a Sherlock Holmes, Holmes is a flesh-and-blood detective. Since truth in fiction is properly analyzed as truth at a set of worlds (Lewis 1978), there really is, there exists, a Sherlock Holmes. When we correctly assert that Sherlock Holmes doesn't exist, we implicitly restrict the domain of quantification to the actual world.

Although it is little discussed as a theory of fictional characters, Lewis's view has a number of advantages. First, it avoids the Meinongian problem of incompleteness. Each flesh-and-blood Holmes is a complete object, obeying the laws of excluded middle and non-contradiction. Second, those properties that are determinately Holmes's, such as being male, are genuinely *exemplified* by each Holmes in the worlds of the story. Third, and because of the second feature, at least some of the conative attitudes we take towards fictional characters are rather less puzzling on Lewis's view. Sherlock Holmes *is* admirable, really *having* many admirable qualities. Fourth, comparisons found in "mixed" statements, and counterfictional statements, are just special cases of the cross-world comparisons we routinely make in giving assertions about possibility.

The biggest disadvantage to Lewis's view is that most metaphysicians find Lewis's modal realism to be incredible. Also, Lewis must deny that authors literally create their characters: rather they choose them from amongst the possibilia. Far more common than Lewis's approach is what we can call *Quinean actualism*: the view that fictional characters are abstracta that exist in the actual world. There are three main varieties of Quinean actualism.

Characters as necessary, eternal types

First is another view that denies the genuine creativity of authors, since characters are *kinds* of thing. The main exponents of this view are Wolterstorff (1980) and Currie (1990), though Currie's view is more limited in scope, as we shall see.

The core idea is that fictional characters are kinds of *person*, and these kinds are real even if no actual person exemplifies them. Included in the kind HOLMES are properties such as being a detective, being male, and so forth. One advantage of this view is that kinds are things we (non-nominalists) already believe are actual. Another is that kinds are abstract, and so allow for incompleteness without contradiction. Being of type-O blood is not included in the HOLMES kind, nor is being of any other particular blood type. But Holmes certainly has a blood type – *that* is included in the HOLMES kind.

Arguably, the view also does justice to ordinary language. Talk of an actual person's character concerns the *way* that person is – what *kind* of person they are. (So a fictional character is a way a person might be, a kind of person, even if no one actually is that way.) But this must be weighed against an oddity, from the Quinean perspective: the names of fictional characters appear in subject position, and one would expect the Quinean reduction to employ an *individual* variable, existentially quantified over. To adapt Quine's famous dictum, one might reasonably hold that to be an *individual* is to be the value of a bound *individual* variable. On the kind view, there is no such individual at all.

Nevertheless, negative existentials can be paraphrased in a manner analogous to that which Quine (1948) recommends: by means of Russell's theory of descriptions. But there are two very different ways of doing this, since the kind incompletely specifies an object. (N) might be paraphrased as:

(N_1) Nothing instantiates all the properties included in HOLMES.

It seems a contingent fact that (N_1) is actually true. Or (N) might be paraphrased as:

(N_2) Nothing instantiates all and only the properties included in HOLMES.

Given that there cannot be incomplete objects, (N_2) is a necessary truth. This much would agree with Kripke (1980), who famously argues (for different reasons) that fictional characters necessarily are fictional.

An obstacle faced by any actualist view is the intuitive difference between critical and fictional statements. Consider that "Holmes is a fictional character" is true construed critically but false construed fictionally; while "Holmes is male" is true construed fictionally but false construed critically. Quinean actualists have a standard response: true fictional statements are not *predications* at all. Actualists postulate a relation between the abstract character and a property which is not exemplification or instantiation, but something else entirely. Van Inwagen (1977) calls it "ascription," but it is commonly called "holding" a property (as opposed to *having* it).

The kind view might accommodate cases of "carryover," too – this is Currie's reason for positing character kinds, which he calls "roles." Roles are more abstract kinds still than Wolterstorff's characters. One point in favor of roles is that several properties included in Wolterstorff's character kinds seem only *contingently* included. Consider that Holmes plays the violin. Couldn't he have played the viola instead, or no stringed instrument at all? Currie can say this is true, because playing the violin is not included in the Holmes role. Wolterstorff cannot say this, and so cannot accommodate carryover.

However, it seems even the more restricted notion of a role will suffer from the same difficulty. Couldn't I write a Holmes story in which *the* Sherlock Holmes never took up detective work at all? Or was in fact a Martian? It's hard to find any very distinctive properties are essential to the Holmes role.[4]

Conative attitude statements present a problem, too. If one is a cognitivist, there is perhaps indeed an object of one's admiration, pity or fear, but it seems the wrong kind of object. Perhaps the best the kind theorist can do is to say, for instance, that anyone who instantiated the Holmes character would be admirable, but this is difficult to square with cognitivism.

Finally, on the kind view, fictional characters come out actual but necessary and eternal. This runs counter to the intuition that characters are contingently created by their authors.

Characters as artifacts: contingent, created individuals

That last intuition seems to motivate a different Quinean actualism, according to which characters are after all created by their authors, and might not have existed at all. This view is endorsed in Howell (1983 and 1996), Levinson (1993), and in detail in Thomasson (1999).

I'll focus on Thomasson's view. According to her, fictional characters are human artifacts, differing from hammers and chairs in being *abstract* individuals. They are brought into existence when authors create works of fiction such as poems, novels, movies or plays. They *depend* upon these works, which are themselves abstract individuals brought into existence by authors creating *concrete individuals*, by writing manuscripts, and so forth. Ultimately, then, fictional characters are dependent upon "supporting" concrete objects.

There are advantages to this approach. First, fictional characters are *individuals*, and so satisfy the intuitive demand I mentioned earlier for a Quinean reduction to bound individual variables, as well as explaining why characters are available for other authors to borrow. I could write a story in which Holmes is a Martian, and it would still be *about* Holmes. No one ascribed characteristic *must* be preserved for carryover to succeed. That such individuals are *abstract* might raise eyebrows, but Thomasson is of the view that we need in any case to postulate abstract individual artifacts, such as works of fiction themselves, as well as products of other conventional acts, like marriages and other contracts.

The artifactual view does well also with modal intuitions about characters. Conan Doyle could have ascribed different properties to Holmes from the ones he actually did. Once he had *thought* of Holmes, so literally creating the character, Conan Doyle was free to rename him, or make him a duffer at the violin.

According to Thomasson, abstract individuals are not spatially located, and are therefore not available to enter into causal relations with utterances about them. But Thomasson appeals to companions in guilt: other abstract entities to which we refer, such as "works of music, kinds of car, scientific theories, or legal statutes." Fair enough – *if* we need to accommodate these things as non-spatial abstracta.

A deeper difficulty for the causal remoteness of fictional characters is its consequence for authorial creativity. Thomasson seems to propose a one-way epiphenomenalism, according to which authors, by bringing the supporting concreta into existence, literally cause the existence of fictional characters. And what of the persistence conditions of these abstracta? According to Thomasson, they exist only as long as we have concrete supporting entities such as copies of works.

Thomasson's fictional characters are in time, but are not in space. They are causally dependent upon concrete entities, but epiphenomenally. They are like concrete individuals, but also like Platonic kinds. They are *queer*, and I'm afraid I find it very hard to believe in them.

It is perhaps no surprise, then, that one of the main exponents of Quinean actualism, van Inwagen, sits on the fence about the nature of fictional characters, committed to their abstract nature, but officially neutral between kinds and individuals. Perhaps a new approach is called for.

Characters as "syncretistic" objects

Voltolini (2006) expands the kind approach, proposing that fictional characters are *composite* entities, thus adding a little of the flavor of the artifactual account, rendering fictional characters contingent. On one hand, there is a set of properties (those ascribed or held), and on the other hand, there is the process of storytelling, which instantiates a *process-type*. Voltolini proposes that a fictional character is constituted by both these abstracta, the property set and the process-type.

I find the proposal implausible. The idea is that the two abstracta – the property set and the process-type – may exist otherwise unrelated until the authorial act, which brings the new composite entity into being. Somehow, concretely instantiating the process-type, but not the property set, provides the metaphysical glue to bind the two abstracta into a new object. Add to this the fact that the view inherits another difficulty of the kind view – that the property set is essential to the character, and so Holmes necessarily is a detective, plays the violin, is named "Holmes," and so on – and the syncretistic account does not on balance seem an improvement on other Quinean actualisms.

Perhaps most interesting about Voltolini's approach is that it includes a new "ontological" argument for realism. It begins with Borges' well-known *Pierre Menard*. Voltolini relies on an intuition I readily grant: that even if lexically identical, Cervantes' and Menard's works are distinct. Voltolini then argues that the only possible way for the works to differ is in their fictional characters. Hence, since fictional characters enter into the identity conditions of fictional works, fictional characters exist if fictional works do.

Here are two short considerations against this argument. First, I think it is possible for a fictional work to contain no fictional characters at all, since I think it possible for a work of fiction to contain only *non*-fictional characters. Second, if there are fictional characters at all in Cervantes' and Menard's works – if realism is true – then my intuition is that they contain the *very same* fictional characters. I would argue in the reverse direction: since the works differ, but not in their fictional characters, then fictional characters do not generally enter into the identity conditions of the fictional works.

Anti-realism

The most common way to disavow fictional statements (by which I mean to regard them as neutral on commitment to fictional characters) is by means of a propositional operator – a *fiction* operator – as in "In *A Study in Scarlet*, Holmes is a detective." This is the intuitive difference between critical and fictional statements, since "In *A Study in Scarlet*, Holmes is a fictional character" is false.

This leaves two basic choices for an anti-realist. First, they might accept that critical statements commit us to abstract fictional characters, but deny that fictional statements do. This is an odd position on the face of it, since it posits an ambiguity (semantic or pragmatic) in fictional names like "Holmes" – in true critical statements, the name refers, and in true fictional statements, it doesn't. Then again, Quinean actualists are in a similar position with regard to the copula "is": in true critical statements, the copula denotes predication, and in true fictional statements, it doesn't.

The second option is a more unified account which denies that critical statements quantify over fictional characters. The most developed version of this view is Kendall Walton's (1990). According to Walton, we fiction consumers routinely engage in a vast game (or collection of games) of make-believe that I'll call the *Appreciation Game*. When you read a novel or watch a movie, or talk about them, you make-believe certain propositions, and some of these are clearly more appropriate than others: the way the fiction is put together, given the conventions governing how to put fictions together, *authorizes* certain sorts of making-believe and not others.[5] Some games are more or less direct, and in an authorized direct game, "Holmes is a detective" is appropriate, while "Holmes is a Martian" is not. Some authorized games involve more than one fiction, as when a character is borrowed by another author.

We also play more indirect games with fictions, and these are highly conventional, too, though not necessarily *authorized*. So we might play a game in which we compare the detective skills of Holmes and Poirot. Or we might engage in fairly high-level critical theory or philosophy, as in my writing the previous sentence.

Can we ever step outside the game, and simply make assertions? In a way. When we say things like "Holmes is a fictional character" we are stepping outside more direct games of make-believe and drawing attention to their make-believe status. And at least sometimes, we can make assertions about the various games we engage in. At bottom, Walton's Quinean approach is to quantify over the games and to disavow fictional character talk as disguised talk about the games.

When it comes to conative attitude statements, Walton has an ingenious cognitivist solution. Walton agrees with Radford that we don't *really* admire, pity or fear fictional characters. Rather, when such attributions are made, they are made *within* the Appreciation Game. We have real feelings, of course – Walton calls these *quasi-emotions* – for which objects are not required.[6]

The most common criticism of Walton's approach is that it fails to meet reasonable desiderata for explaining our talk about fiction. Consider two sentences from van Inwagen (2004): "Some novels have more chapters than others," and "Some novels have more characters than others." Thomasson and van Inwagen both complain that Walton must treat apparently analogous sentences like these very differently, and that it is much better to treat them alike. Thomasson writes,

> It always seems bad policy in a philosophy of language to offer different analyses of sentences of the same type, occurring in the same sort of context, just on the basis of the types of object they are purportedly about. (1999: 99)

This complaint has little force coming from Quinean actualists, however. Consider the sentences, "Holmes lived in Baker Street," and "Thatcher lived in Downing Street." The Quinean actualist treats both as true but denies that the second is ordinary predication, presumably because it's about a different type of object. Aren't they flouting their own principle?

The actualist might reply that the context is what justifies treating the sentences differently, but surely Walton can make the same reply and say that "Some novels have more chapters than others" occurs outside the Appreciation Game, while "Some novels have more characters than others" occurs inside it. I see no advantage to the actualist here.

Conclusion

As in the debates over mathematical, modal and moral objects, the main obstacle to realism about fictional objects is an argument from "queerness": the more a postulated object fits our intuitions about fictional characters, the more metaphysically queer it seems to be. But realism is not easy to abandon, especially in the light of commitment to critical statements.

On the other hand, anti-realism is not easy to abandon, either, especially in the light of commitment to negative existentials. And on both views the most troublesome data are fictional statements, and our conative attitudes concerning fictions. On either view, nothing *has* the properties we seem most invested in with regard to fictional characters, and so it's something of a mystery why we're so interested. Perhaps a more extensive error theory may yet be defended.

Notes

1 Proponents include Parsons (1980), Routley (1982), Priest (2005) and with qualification, Zalta (1983).
2 I am not here concerned with whether the terminology I use matches the Meinongian's own – Meinong himself, and some Meinongians, claim that some things have no being at all. The main point is that Meinongians quantify beyond existence.
3 I won't here explore other options, such as permitting truth values other than true and false.
4 Currie (2003) explains this result by appealing to considerations of the scope of modal operators: while it is true that necessarily, Holmes is a detective, it is also true that anything that is necessarily a detective is not Holmes.
5 Walton in my view needlessly stipulates that fictional names are (failed) singular terms rather than disguised definite descriptions, so that, for instance, neither "Holmes is a detective" nor "In *A Study in Scarlet*, Holmes is a detective" expresses a proposition *per se*. I will ignore this complication, since it makes little difference to the overall Waltonian strategy (though it does complicate the analysis of negative existentials). I also ignore Walton's misgivings about the term *authorizes*.
6 Currie (1990) has a similar but independent resolution, which also admits of a non-cognitivist interpretation.

References

Andersen, L. (2006) "Sherlock Holmes – Why I Admire Him," *September Destiny*; available: http://larry-andersen.blogspot.com/2006/08/sherlock-holmes-why-i-admire-him.html

Currie, G. (1990) *The Nature of Fiction*, Cambridge: Cambridge University Press.

—— (2003) "Characters and Contingency," *Dialectica* 57, no. 2: 137–48.

Howell, R. (1983) Review of *Nonexistent Objects*, by Terrence Parsons, *Journal of Philosophy* 80, no. 3: 163–73.

—— (1996) Review essay of *Mimesis as Make-Believe*, by Kendall L. Walton, *Synthese* 109, no. 3: 413–34.

Kripke, S. (1980) *Naming and Necessity*, Cambridge, MA: Harvard University Press.

Levinson, J. (1993) "Making Believe" (review of *Mimesis as Make-Believe*, by Kendall L. Walton), *Dialogue* 32: 359–74.

Lewis, D. K. (1978) "Truth in Fiction," *American Philosophical Quarterly* 15: 37–46; reprinted with postscripts in *Philosophical Papers, vol. 1*, Oxford: Oxford University Press, 1983, 261–80.

—— (1986) *On the Plurality of Worlds*, Oxford: Blackwell.

Lycan, W. (1979) "The Trouble with Possible Worlds," in M. J. Loux (ed.), *The Possible and the Actual*, Ithaca, NY: Cornell University Press, pp. 274–316.

Parsons, T. (1980) *Non-existent Objects*, New Haven, CT: Yale University Press.

Priest, G. (2005) *Towards Non-Being: The Logic and Metaphysics of Intentionality*, Oxford: Oxford University Press.

Quine, W. V. (1948) "On What There Is," *Review of Metaphysics* 2: 21–38.

Routley, R. (1982) *Exploring Meinong's Jungle and Beyond*, Atascadero, CA: Ridgeview.

Thomasson, A. L. (1999) *Fiction and Metaphysics*, Cambridge: Cambridge University Press.

van Inwagen, P. (1977) "Creatures of Fiction," *American Philosophical Quarterly* 24, no 4: 299–308.

—— (1998) "Meta-ontology," *Erkenntnis* 48: 233–50.

—— (2004) "Existence, Ontological Commitment, and Fictional Entities," in M. J. Loux and D. Zimmerman (eds), *The Oxford Handbook of Metaphysics*, Oxford: Oxford University Press, pp. 131–57.

Radford, C. (1975) "How Can We Be Moved by the Fate of Anna Karenina?" *The Proceedings of the Aristotelian Society* 49 (suppl.): 67–80.

Voltolini, A. (2006) *How Ficta Follow Fiction: A Syncretistic Account of Fictional Entities*, Dordrecht: Springer.

Walton, K. (1990) *Mimesis as Make-believe*, Cambridge, MA: Harvard University Press.

Wikipedia (2008) "Sherlock Holmes," *Wikipedia*; available: http://en.wikipedia.org/wiki/Sherlock_Holmes

Wolterstorff, N. (1980) *Worlds and Works of Art*, Oxford: Clarendon.

Zalta, E. (1983) *Abstract Objects*, Dordrecht: Reidel.

Further reading

T. Parsons, *Nonexistent Objects* (New Haven, CT: Yale University Press, 1980) is one of the first and best defenses of Meinongianism. A. L. Thomasson, *Fiction and Metaphysics* (Cambridge: Cambridge University Press, 1999) is the most comprehensive version of Quinean actualism, including an attempt to square it with more general metaphysics. K. Walton, *Mimesis as Make-believe* (Cambridge, MA: Harvard University Press, 1990) is the best defense of the anti-realist position, including a groundbreaking account of our emotional responses to fictions. For further reading, see also P. van Inwagen, "Fiction and Metaphysics," *Philosophy and Literature* 7 (1983): 67–77.

35
VAGUENESS
Elizabeth Barnes

Philosophical discussion of vagueness traces its origins back to at least the pre-Socratics. The Greek logician Eubulides is generally credited with stating the problem of vagueness in its classical form: the paradox of the heap. ("Heap" is "*soros*" in Greek – hence the term *sorites paradox*.) So the puzzle is an old one, and it remains a confusing one. In what follows, I'll first explain the basics of the problem and what it means to think that the problem is sometimes a metaphysical one (i.e., that there is "metaphysical vagueness" or "ontic vagueness"). I'll then outline some potential motivations for and objections to metaphysical vagueness.

The sorites paradox

Take some sufficiently large number of grains of sand (say 10,000) – that many grains of sand put together will give you a heap of sand. Now suppose you've got your 10,000-grain heap of sand in front of you, and imagine taking off a single grain of sand: is it still a heap? Of course. One grain of sand isn't going to make a difference between something's being a heap and its not being a heap. So if 10,000 grains of sand make a heap, then so should 9,999 grains of sand. But suppose you took another grain of sand off, and then another, and another, and so on. Eventually you would be left with a single grain of sand, and a single grain of sand is definitely not a heap. But what's happened here? We want to say a change has taken place, since we started with a heap (10,000 grains of sand is definitely a heap) but we ended up with a non-heap (1 grain of sand is definitely not a heap). Yet there's nowhere we want to locate the change: one grain of sand shouldn't make the difference to whether or not something is heap. Thus a change occurs, but at each step of the process we're inclined to say the change doesn't occur there. The change is a *vague* one.

Far more than just being a nifty puzzle, vagueness can easily be shown to be formally paradoxical (see Hyde 2005 for discussion of its various forms). To demonstrate the paradox with respect to a particular feature F, all we need is a series of objects $\{a_1 \ldots a_n\}$ and three basic claims:

(1) Fa_1
(2) $\sim\exists n(Fa_n \,\&\, \sim Fa_{n+1})$
(3) $\exists m(\sim Fa_m)$

These three claims are jointly inconsistent, but they each have a great deal of intuitive appeal. For the case of heaps, (1) is just the claim that, for some large enough pile of sand, that pile of sand is a heap. (2) says that taking away one grain of sand won't make the difference between whether or not something is a heap (i.e., in our series of sand piles that decrease by a single grain of sand, there aren't two adjacent ones such that the first is a heap and the second isn't a heap). And, finally, (3) just means that something in our series isn't a heap (which we think is obviously true, since we end up with a single grain of sand).

The basic phenomenon of vagueness, then, is this: for certain cases, we think that very small changes (like taking away one grain of sand) *can't* make a difference, but that big changes (like going from 10,000 grains to a single grain) *must* make a difference. Yet when you consider that a series of very small changes will add up to a big change, you realize that something's gone wrong.

There are many proposed solutions to this paradox in the literature, but I will not rehearse them here (Williamson [1994] offers perhaps the most comprehensive survey, but see also Keefe and Smith [1997]). I am, instead, going to focus on the *source* of the paradox. Specifically, I am going to focus on whether vagueness could ever be a *metaphysical* phenomenon.

Vagueness and indeterminacy

Before moving on, however, an important terminological clarification is in order. There is a difference between *vagueness* and *indeterminacy*. Indeterminacy (or more generically, "indefiniteness," as epistemicists are sometimes unhappy with the term "indeterminacy") is the basic phenomenon of *unsettledness*. If there's unsettledness with respect to p, things don't quite seem to be a p-way but also don't quite seem to be a not-p way, so that it seems inappropriate to categorically assert "p" or to assert "not-p."

Vagueness is that special form of indeterminacy which gives rise to the sorites paradox. Notice, though, that not all forms of indeterminacy will yield a sorites-like phenomenon. The indeterminacy often discussed in physics, for example, is not soritical, nor are certain famous cases of semantic indeterminacy (e.g., Field's example of Newtonian mass: the referent of "mass" as used in classical Newtonian mechanics is simply indeterminate between our current usage of "proper mass" and "relativistic mass," but this indeterminacy does not give rise to a sorites series – see Field [1973]). I take it that the more fundamental notion, for the metaphysician, is that of indeterminacy. The truly interesting question is whether the world itself could ever be such as to be fundamentally *unsettled*. Whether or not such unsettledness would then give rise to a sorites-style paradox is ultimately of secondary importance, though many of the examples below do involve sorites-like phenomena (see Williams [2008b] for further discussion of the terminological issues here).

Sources of vagueness and indeterminacy

Traditionally, philosophers have cited three potential sources of indeterminacy (and, as a result, vagueness): how we use our words (semantic indeterminacy), the limits of what we can know (epistemic indeterminacy/indefiniteness), and how the world is in and of itself (metaphysical indeterminacy). There aren't any major arguments to show that this trichotomy is exhaustive – there might well be other sources of indeterminacy and/ or vagueness which haven't yet been canvassed in the literature. And there's certainly no reason to think the trichotomy is exclusive. It seems plausible to think that, for example, there could be cases of vagueness which are partially semantic and partially metaphysical. The tripartite distinction is very common in the literature, though, and as it's both illustrative and useful I'll incorporate it in what follows.

The semantic view of indeterminacy maintains (in very simplified terms) that indeterminacy and the resulting sorites phenomena arise because of *semantic indecision*. For some parts of our language (numerical and logical vocabulary, for instance) we've decided very precisely what we mean. But for many or even most components of natural language – including, importantly, the paradigm cases of vagueness like "heap" – we're just not that exact. Our language use, in cases like "heap," is exact enough to pick out clear cases of heaps (10,000 grains) and clear cases of non-heaps (1 grain), but we just haven't made up our minds about what the precise boundaries of the term should be. That's why we encounter sorites-like phenomena: our language is decided enough to require that big changes make a difference, but too imprecise to differentiate small changes.

In contrast, a minority position on vagueness – *epistemicism* – claims (again, in very simplified terms) that our language use does determine exact truth conditions for all components of natural language: it's just that we're incapable of knowing what they are. So, in every context, our use of "heap" determines exactly how many grains of sand it takes to make a heap. But this is a fact that we must always remain ignorant of. This is because of so-called "margin-of-error" principles. Our language use in fact determines that n grains of sand is the smallest number that can compose a heap, but this might easily have been different; it could just as easily have been $n + 1$ or $n - 1$ that's the lowermost boundary. Because the facts might so easily have been different, and because we can't easily discriminate between such differences, we can never be *justified* in believing that the boundary is in fact located at n, and thus we can never *know* that the boundary is located at n.

Both of the above positions locate the source of indeterminacy and vagueness in our own conceptual scheme – how we use our words and what we can know, respectively. The metaphysical view of indeterminacy, in contrast, is the view that at least some cases of indeterminacy have their source in how the world is non-representationally. That is, we sometimes encounter unsettledness (perhaps with associated sorites-like phenomena) that arises in virtue of how the world is *in and of itself*, independently of how we think or talk about it.

Defining metaphysical indeterminacy and metaphysical vagueness

From here, the tripartite distinction in sources of indeterminacy gives us a useful way of categorizing the distinctively metaphysical cases of indeterminacy (one which will simply have to be amended with some additional permutations if the tripartite distinction turns out to be incorrect). We can say of metaphysical indeterminacy:

(MI) Sentence S is ontically indeterminate iff (if and only if), were all representational content precisified, there is an admissible precisification of S such that according to that precisification the sentence would still be non-epistemically indeterminate.

For metaphysical *vagueness* we then simply need to make a slight addition:

(MV) Sentence S is ontically vague iff: were all representational content precisified, there is an admissible precisification of S such that according to that precisification the sentence would still be non-epistemically indeterminate in a way that is Sorites-susceptible.

The thought behind these definitions is this: the vagueness/indeterminacy of a particular sentence is at least in part due to how the world is if that sentence could still be indeterminate (in a way that's not explained by what we know about it) even if we assigned precise truth conditions to every element of our language (i.e., even if we eliminated all semantic indecision). Basically, if language and thought aren't to blame then there's nowhere else to look – the source of the vagueness/indeterminacy must be the non-representational world (see Barnes [forthcoming b] for a detailed discussion of these definitional issues).

The Evans argument

But does this even make sense? The idea that at least some examples of sorites-like phenomena could have their source in the way the world is in and of itself (independently of how we represent it) has long been in philosophical disrepute. Metaphysical vagueness has been described as "not properly intelligible" (Dummett 1975) and "at bottom incoherent" (Horgan 1994). These days, though, many philosophers admit that metaphysical vagueness is at least coherent, it's still often seen as deeply objectionable.

There is not, however, a clear consensus as to *why* metaphysical vagueness is so objectionable. This is perhaps because there are many quite divergent arguments aimed at undermining the tenability of metaphysical vagueness. There is little consensus as to which is the best, but general agreement that at least some of them are effective.

I don't have the space here to rehearse all the major arguments against metaphysical indeterminacy (see Barnes [in prep.] for detailed discussion of these issues), but there is one argument that bears special mentioning because if it works it shows that metaphysical indeterminacy is not just objectionable, but in fact *inconsistent*. This is Gareth Evans' famous attempt to show that metaphysically indeterminate identity is impossible (Evans 1978).

Suppose, Evans argues, we have an object *a* which is indeterminately identical to some object *b*. We can assume, says Evans, that *a* is not indeterminately identical to itself, so it's determinate that *a* is identical to *a*. But this means that *b* has a property that *a* lacks – the property of being indeterminately identical to *a* (we know *a* doesn't have this property, because *a* is determinately identical to *a*, and we know *b* has it because the indeterminacy of identity between *a* and *b* was our starting assumption). From here we can simply apply Leibniz's Law and conclude that rather than being indeterminately identical, *a* and *b* are in fact distinct, since any two objects that differ in their properties are distinct. Yet this means that from the assumption (for any arbitrary *a* and *b*) that *a* and *b* are indeterminately identical we've managed to conclude that *a* and *b* are distinct: *reductio*.

Evans presents the argument formally as follows (with determinacy operators ∇ and Δ ranging over sentences, Δ meaning "determinately" and ∇ meaning "indeterminately"):

(1) $\nabla (a=b)$
(2) $\lambda[\nabla(x=a)]b$
(3) $\sim\nabla(a=a)$
(4) $\sim\lambda[\nabla(x=a)]a$
(5) $\sim(a=b)$ (from [2] and [4], by Leibniz's Law)

This is not a straightforward contradiction, but Evans then reasons that

> if "Indefinitely" and its dual "Definitely" ("Δ") generate a modal logic as strong as S5, then (1)–(4) and presumably Leibniz's Law can each be strengthened with a "Definitely" prefix, enabling us to derive

> (5+) $\Delta\sim(a=b)$

> which is straightforwardly inconsistent with (1).

The first and perhaps most important thing to point out about Evans' argument is that, even if successful, it is a *reductio* of metaphysically indeterminate *identities*, not metaphysical indeterminacy or metaphysical vagueness *per se*. Evans, and many others in turn, have tended to assume that metaphysical indeterminacy will entail metaphysically indeterminate identity, but this is arguably not the case (see Williams [2008a] for further discussion). So if Evans' argument is successful, it at best manages to rule out those particular forms of metaphysical indeterminacy which require metaphysically indeterminate identity.

For those interested in metaphysically indeterminate ontologies which do commit to vague identity, however, there are several salient options (canvassed in the extensive literature generated by Evans' argument) for resisting the argument. Many of these involve the rejection of classical logic or classical inference patterns (see, *inter alia*, Edgington 2000; Heck 1998; Parsons and Woodruff 1995), but such revisionary tactics are certainly not required (see Barnes [forthcoming a] for resistance in a classical setting). More significantly, perhaps, it is open for the defender of metaphysical indeterminacy to think that the argument itself is valid yet does not provide any evidence against metaphysically indeterminate identities. A crucial component of the argument (highlighted in Lewis [1988]) is that the names involved have no referential indeterminacy – they are rigid with respect to precisifications in the same way that names are, according to Kripke, rigid with respect to worlds. Their status as such is meant to follow from the focus of the argument on *metaphysical* (as opposed to semantic) indeterminacy, but Williams (2008a) shows that we can think that the terms in question are in fact referentially indeterminate, and furthermore that they are referentially indeterminate *because of the metaphysical indeterminacy in question*. If there is referential indeterminacy associated with the names, then the argument is unsound (the property abstraction steps – [2] and [4] – fail). The defender of metaphysical indeterminacy can thus avoid the proposed *reductio* without any need for revisionary logic.

Why locate indeterminacy in metaphysics?

There are, of course, further reasons for rejecting metaphysical indeterminacy and vagueness. But before discussing these it's helpful to discuss reasons for *accepting* metaphysical indeterminacy.

Why might you believe that indeterminacy is metaphysical? The answer will depend largely, if not entirely, on your ontological commitments. You must first decide what there is before you can weigh the evidence as to whether what there is might be indeterminate. Saying that things are indeterminate or vague is a characterization of how things are. So it's important to first make decisions about what kinds of things you think exist – only once those commitments are in place can you have good traction on the question of whether those sorts of things might admit of indeterminacy.

That said, there are certain ontological commitments which seem to lead quite naturally to forms of metaphysical indeterminacy/vagueness, and if these sorts of commitments are embraced you might have at least a prima facie argument that at least some cases of indeterminacy (and perhaps vagueness) are metaphysical in nature. Here are a few examples (though this list is by no means exhaustive):

(a) *Restricted composition*: If you believe in restricted composition, you think that some but not all collections of objects compose further, complex objects. There is an object (composed of organs, which are themselves composed of tissues, which are themselves composed of cells, and so on) that is my body, but there is not an object that is the sum of my left thumb and the rings of Saturn. Objects must cohere in a certain suitable way to compose a further object. Yet this can ostensibly lead to vagueness in what sorts of things should count as complex objects. Imagine a series of possible worlds, each containing two mereological simples. In the first world in this series, the simples are bonded together in a clear case of composition: they definitely compose a complex object. In the final world in the series, the simples are scattered at the far corners of the universe: they definitely do not compose a complex object. At each pair of worlds n and $n + 1$ in this series, the simples in $n + 1$ are farther apart than the simples in n, but they differ by an arbitrarily small distance. So the question becomes: Which world is the first world in this series that does not contain a complex object? The first world definitely does, and the last world definitely doesn't, so we know that a change occurs; but because the difference between each pair or worlds is so insignificant (like the difference between a single grain of sand in a heap), it looks wrong to locate the change at any particular point in the series. So what we're faced with here is a classic sorites series (small changes look like these shouldn't make a difference, but big changes obviously do), but one which appears metaphysical in nature – that is, it looks as though the best thing to say might be simply that it's metaphysically unsettled where the change takes place.

(b) *Moral realism:* Commitment to certain kinds of mind-independent normative facts might also give you reason to think that some indeterminacy/vagueness is metaphysical. Suppose, for example, that you think there is a moral difference between killing and letting die, and that this difference is not a matter of our beliefs, conventions, etc. (that is, it is a mind-independent fact about the world). It is fairly straightforward, however, to construct a series of cases, each differing only marginally from its neighbors, for which the first in the series is a case of killing and the last in the series is a case of letting die. It's tempting to think, due to the very "flexibility" of the normative issues in question, that there shouldn't be a sharp cutoff in this series between cases of killing and cases of letting die. That is, the transition between killing and letting die looks vague. Yet, if you're maintaining a robust realism about morality, the vagueness in question should plausibly be characterized as metaphysical in nature.

(c) *Personhood and personal identity:* You might also be led towards metaphysical indeterminacy or vagueness if you think that there are robust, mind-independent facts of the matter about whether something is a person. Imagine, for instance, that you divide the development of an organism from fertilized embryo to three-year-old child into instantaneous time-slices. At the first of this series of instants, the organism in question is (ostensibly) definitely not a person, and at the last it definitely is a person. Yet, again, it would be odd to say that there is a pair of instants, t and $t + 1$, neighboring one another in this series such that the organism is not a person at t and a person at $t + 1$. Any change that the organism can undergo in an instant seems too minute and arbitrary to ground the difference between whether or not something is a person. Or consider a case where a person undergoes drastic but gradual trauma which severely alters their personality. Such severe alteration might make it indeterminate whether the person left after the severe personality changes is the same person as the one we started out with. But it would be odd to say there's an exact instant where the personal identity facts suddenly change. So, again, we have series over which a metaphysical change takes place, yet there appears to be no place to locate the change – the transitions are vague. And, again, because of the nature of the facts in question, the vagueness seems plausibly described as metaphysical.

Critical consideration of the metaphysical view

The opponent of metaphysical vagueness, however, has several reasons for maintaining that the above cases (even assuming that we accept the ontology they presuppose) do not in fact give us good reason to believe in metaphysical vagueness. A common first objection put by those encountering cases like the above is that, precisely because the subject matter is metaphysical, there simply are precise facts of the matter about exactly where the (abrupt) transition in the series occurs, and we're simply ignorant of what those facts are. This is a natural (though by no means the only) thing to say if you are an epistemicist about vagueness in general, but it is also natural *only* if you are an epistemicist about vagueness in general. If you hold the more common semantic view of vagueness for classic cases like "heap," then a sudden switch to epistemicism just because the case in question is metaphysical (rather than obviously semantic) looks unwarranted. *Prima facie*, these cases exhibit the hallmark features of vagueness and indeterminacy – unsettledness, soriticality, borderline cases, etc. – so to assume, in contrast to the treatment of similar phenomena in other areas, that there simply must be sharp but unknown facts of the matter in the case of metaphysics is ad hoc. The only way to motivate such a difference in treatment would be to provide some sort of overarching argument that vagueness simply cannot be metaphysical, but such arguments do not appear readily available (see Barnes, in prep.).

The opponent of metaphysical vagueness can, however, claim that we have no reason to think the vagueness of the above cases is metaphysical, because there is quite obviously (at least on the assumption that epistemicism is false) a lot of semantic indecision involved in the terms we are using to describe the cases. Vagueness infects nearly all elements of natural language – certainly our terms "part," "kill" and "person" have a large degree of vagueness associated with them (indeed, as the above examples show). So surely the best and most natural explanation of the vagueness in the above cases is that we simply haven't quite made up our minds how to use the terms in question, and that this element of our language-use explains the phenomena (just as it does in more familiar cases like "heap").

But this is too quick. The claim of the defender of metaphysical vagueness was never (or at least needn't be) that there is no semantic vagueness involved in the above cases. Such a claim would be foolish, since (as stated above) vagueness infects nearly all elements of natural language. The friend of metaphysical vagueness is rather claiming that the semantic vagueness involved does not exhaustively explain the sorites-like phenomena, as it ostensibly does for cases like "heap." There is, in short, something more going on, something which cannot simply be explained by reference to our use of language.

The cases above are, *ex hypothesi*, matters which she takes with a level of ontological seriousness that is lacking in the more familiar examples of vagueness. We sort the world into heaps and non-heaps – i.e., the division between heap and non-heap isn't a natural one. But someone with the ontological commitments outlined in the cases above thinks that, as it were, the world sorts itself into complex objects, cases of killing or letting-die, and persons – facts of this sort hold independently of our thoughts and practices (they are facts about "joints in nature" or "natural kinds"). So there might well be vagueness in the words we use to *describe* such cases, but there is also room for an additional claim – the idea that the things themselves, in virtue of how they are mind-independently, do not admit of abrupt, arbitrary transitions or "sharp cutoffs." It is this idea (not the inability to recognize the semantic vagueness involved) that drives the diagnosis of metaphysical vagueness: that for certain special cases, you could get rid of the semantic vagueness in question and still encounter sorites-like phenomena (this, you will recall, is the basic definition for metaphysical vagueness given in [MV]).

The defender of a semantic-only view of vagueness, however, can agree that there is an intuitive pull towards metaphysical vagueness in these cases, while still maintaining that you should not, in the end, endorse metaphysical vagueness. For any commitment, *x*, you must always weigh up the evidence for *x* and the explanatory benefits of endorsing *x* against the *theoretical cost* of *x*. Thus, the opponent of metaphysical vagueness can agree that the above cases provide theoretical evidence for metaphysical vagueness and that positing metaphysical vagueness would do some explanatory work in such cases, but conclude that we should not commit to metaphysical vagueness, because the cost of such a commitment is too high.

There are several ways that the opponent of metaphysical vagueness might argue this, but I will cover only what are in my estimation the two most prominent and challenging (but see also Sainsbury [1994] and Lewis [1993] and Heller [1996]).

Theoretical uniformity

The first major worry, outlined in Eklund (2008), is that if we endorse metaphysical vagueness we must give up on the idea that vagueness is a uniform phenomenon. Since, Eklund argues, we have good reason to think that vagueness is uniform and we are already committed to semantic vagueness (as it is obviously prevalent in our use of natural language), a further commitment to a separate category of metaphysical vagueness is too great a cost. We should therefore assume that semantic vagueness can provide us with exhaustive explanations of sorites-like phenomena.

We must tread carefully with such an objection to metaphysical vagueness, though, because there are several distinct things that could potentially be countenanced in the demand that vagueness be a *uniform* phenomenon – many of which are perfectly compatible with the presence of both semantic and metaphysical vagueness. You could, for example, take the demand for uniformity to simply require that vagueness be given a uniform theoretical treatment. That is, you could think that all vagueness be handled according to, e.g., the precisificational structure laid out in standard supervaluationism (as in Fine 1975). But this is in no tension with vagueness sometimes having its source in language-use and sometimes having its source in the world, as a precisificational treatment is adequately suited to either and the basic mechanics of such a treatment are themselves utterly silent about the source of vagueness. Alternatively, you might think the uniformity of vagueness has to do with the concept – vagueness is, perhaps, a uniform functional concept characterized by certain cardinal features (sorites-susceptibility, instances of borderline cases, etc.). Yet, like any role-functional concept, it would still be open that the role-functional concept of vagueness has multiple realizers. That is, it would still be perfectly open that sometimes what fills the functional role we associate with vagueness is some portion of natural language, and sometimes what fills the very same functional role is some element of the non-representational world. Indeed, the only sense of uniformity which seems in open conflict with the existence of both semantic and metaphysical vagueness is uniformity in source: the idea that the phenomenon of vagueness must be uniform with regard to what sorts of things give rise to it. If such a notion of uniformity is what's intended by the above objection, however, then it needs independent defense to avoid obvious charges of question-begging. The defender of metaphysical vagueness obviously does not think that vagueness has a uniform source – indeed, it is one of the hallmarks of her position that she rejects such uniformity. So in the absence of independent argument that vagueness *must* have a uniform source, she has no reason to be swayed by the above argument from uniformity.

Metaphysical indeterminacy and logic

A second way of motivating the idea that metaphysical vagueness represents too great a theoretical cost is to claim that a commitment to metaphysical vagueness is too revisionary. The central charge, along these lines, is that metaphysical vagueness requires rejection of classical logic and semantics. Since, however, we have good reason to assume the truth of classical logic then any commitment which requires us to forgo it is simply too great a cost.

Certainly many ways of characterizing metaphysical vagueness have been couched in non-classical frameworks, and perhaps because of this metaphysical vagueness has become closely associated with non-classical logics. Options include "third-category" logical theories (which include an additional "neither" value, as well as the standard "true" and "false"), according to which it's metaphysically indeterminate whether p iff: it's neither true nor false that p (see, for example, Tye 1990). Degree-theory has also been popular among defenders of metaphysical vagueness; on this model, sentences which are metaphysically vague are assigned some value less than 1 (i.e., they are not "fully true") (see Rosen and Smith [2004] and Smith [2005] for discussion).

However, just as there are both non-classical and classical ways of theorizing about semantic vagueness, there are also both non-classical and classical ways of theorizing about metaphysical vagueness. Akiba (2004), Barnes (2006), Williams (2008a), Barnes (forthcoming b) and Williams and Barnes (in prep.) all give treatments of metaphysical vagueness within a fully classical setting. The common theme among these approaches has been to adopt a precisificational theory of vagueness, the basics of which simply have it that ΔP is true if P is true on all precisifications and ∇P is true if P is true at some precisifications but false at others. But add to this a correlation to modality: according to Akiba precisifications are like possible worlds, and according to Barnes and Williams they *are* possible worlds. Akiba (2004) and Williams (2008a) both use this basic setup to develop theories that apply a standard supervaluationist (as in Fine 1975; Keefe 2000; etc.) treatment to metaphysical forms of vagueness. As is common to most supervaluational approaches, they thus retain classical logic but reject the universal application of the bivalence principle of classical metatheory (indeterminate sentences, on this picture, are neither true nor false). As a result, they must reject various classical inference rules (though the extent to which the basic supervaluationist picture is revisionary is controversial [see Williams (2008b)]).

379

In contrast, Barnes (2006, forthcoming b) and Williams and Barnes (in prep.) develop a theory of metaphysical indeterminacy which preserves both classical logic and bivalence (their view is formally analogous to the fully non-revisionary semantics provided by the "non-standard supervaluationism" of McGee and McLaughlin (1994), though they have the advantage of not needing to explain how the notions invoked in the model can be understood in semantic terms – see Williamson (1994) for this criticism of the nonstandard supervaluationist treatment as applied to semantic vagueness). The central idea behind these fully classical views is that indeterminacy with respect to p is an unsettledness between two states: the truth of p and the falsity of p. But this is compatible with it being determinate that p has one or other truth value (those are the only two options) – determinately, p is either true or false (hence bivalence holds), but it's indeterminate *which* of those two truth values it has.

The idea that a theory of metaphysical vagueness *must* be logically revisionary is thus simply mistaken. There are certainly options for theorizing about metaphysical vagueness in a non-classical setting – and many of these non-classical frameworks have been popular among defenders of metaphysical vagueness. But the defender of metaphysical vagueness does not need to endorse non-classical logic. There are substantial ways of theorizing about metaphysical vagueness that operate within both a logic, and a metatheory, that is fully classical and requires no logical revision whatsoever. So the cost of revising classical logic is no argument against commitment to metaphysical vagueness *per se*.

Conclusion

To sum up, let's review the key points raised above. (i) That vagueness is sometimes metaphysical is a distinctive claim about the source of vagueness – namely that vagueness arises because of the way the world is, not because of how we represent the world or what we can know about the world. (ii) Contra Evans, locating vagueness or indeterminacy in the world itself doesn't automatically lead to contradiction. (iii) Whether you have reason to think that some vagueness or indeterminacy is metaphysical will depend on your ontological commitments – specifically, on what you take with ontological seriousness. (iv) Thinking that some vagueness or indeterminacy is metaphysical doesn't thereby commit you to thinking that *all* vagueness or indeterminacy is metaphysical. (v) Thinking that some vagueness or indeterminacy is metaphysical doesn't thereby commit you to thinking that vagueness can't have a uniform theoretical treatment. (vi) Thinking that some vagueness or indeterminacy is metaphysical doesn't thereby commit you to logical revisionism. None of (i)–(vi) will, of course, tell you whether *there is* any metaphysical vagueness. But they'll help you start asking the question with appropriate clarity.

References

Akiba, Ken (2004) "Vagueness in the World," *Noûs* 38: 407–29.
Barnes, Elizabeth (2006) "Conceptual Room for Ontic Vagueness," Ph.D. thesis, University of St Andrews.

—— (Forthcoming a) "Indeterminacy, Identity, and Counterparts," *Synthese*.

—— (Forthcoming b) "Ontic Vagueness: A Guide for the Perplexed," *Noûs*.

—— (In prep.) "What's So Bad about Ontic Vagueness?"

Dummett, Michael (1975) "Wang's Paradox," in Rosanna Keefe and Peter Smith (eds), *Vagueness: A Reader*, Cambridge, MA: MIT Press, pp. 99–118.

Edgington, Dorothy (2000) "Indeterminacy *de Re*," *Philosophical Topics* 28: 27–43.

Eklund, Matti (2008) "Deconstructing Ontological Vagueness," *Canadian Journal of Philosophy* 38: 117–40.

Evans, Gareth (1978) "Can There Be Vague Objects?" *Analysis* 38: 208.

Field, Hartry (1973) *Journal of Philosophy* 70, no. 14: 462–81.

Fine, Kit (1975) "Vagueness, Truth, and Logic," *Synthese* 30: 265–300.

Heck, Richard (1998) "That There Might Be Vague Objects (At Least So Far as Logic Is Concerned)," *Monist* 81: 274–96.

Heller, Mark (1996) "Against Metaphysical Vagueness," *Philosophical Perspectives* 10: 177–83.

Horgan, Terry (1994) "Robust Vagueness and the Forced March Sorites Paradox," in J. E. Tombelin (ed.), *Philosophical Perspectives*, vol. 8 of *Logic and Language*, Altascadero, CA: Ridgeview, pp. 159–88.

Hyde, Dominic (2005) "The Sorites Paradox," in E. N. Zalta (ed.), *The Stanford Encyclopedia of Philosophy*; available: http://plato.stanford.edu/entries/sorites-paradox/

Keefe, Rosanna (2000) *Theories of Vagueness*, Cambridge: Cambridge University Press.

Keefe, Rosanna and Smith, Peter (1997) *Vagueness: A Reader*, Boston, MA: MIT Press.

Lewis, David (1986) *On the Plurality of Worlds*, Oxford: Blackwell.

—— (1988) "Vague Identity: Evans Misunderstood," *Analysis* 48: 128–30.

—— (1993) "Many, but Almost One," in John Bacon, Keith Campbell, and Loyd Reinhardt (eds), *Ontology, Causality, and Mind: Essays in Honour of D.M. Armstrong*, Cambridge: Cambridge University Press, pp. 23–42.

McGee, Vann and McLaughlin, Brian (1994) "Distinctions without a Difference," *Southern Journal of Philosophy* 33: 203–51.

Parsons, Terrence and Woodruff, Peter (1995) "Worldly Indeterminacy of Identity," *Proceedings of the Aristotelian Society* 95: 171–91.

Rosen, Gideon and Smith, Nick (2004) "Worldly Indeterminacy: A Rough Guide," in Frank Jackson and Graham Priest (eds) *Lewisian Themes*, Oxford: Oxford University Press.

Sainsbury, Mark (1994) "Why the World Cannot Be Vague," *Southern Journal of Philosophy* 33: 63–82.

Smith, N. J. J. (2005) "A Plea for Things That Are Not Quite All There: Or, Is There a Problem about Vague Composition and Vague Existence?" *Journal of Philosophy* 102: 381–421.

Tye, Michael (1990) "Vague Objects," *Mind* 99: 535–57.

Williams, J. R. G. (2008a) "Multiple Actualities and Ontically Vague Identity," *Philosophical Quarterly* 58, no. 230: 134–54.

—— (2008b) "Ontic Vagueness and Metaphysical Indeterminacy," *Philosophy Compass* 3, no. 4: 763–88.

Williams, J. R. G. and Barnes, Elizabeth (In prep.) "A Theory of Metaphysical Indeterminacy."

Williamson, Timothy (1994) *Vagueness*, London: Routledge.

Further reading

Mark Heller, "Against Metaphysical Vagueness," *Philosophical Perspectives* 10 (1996): 177–83, gives an argument against metaphysical vagueness, based on the regress of higher-order vagueness. J. R. G. Williams, "Multiple Actualities and Ontically Vague Identity," *Philosophical Quarterly* 58, no. 230 (2008): 134–54, persuasively argues that genuinely ontically vague identity can involve referential indeterminacy, and thus that Gareth Evans' argument against ontically vague identity is unsound. J. R. G. Williams and Elizabeth Barnes, "A Theory of Metaphysical Indeterminacy" (in prep.) shows how a fully classical logic and semantics can be developed for metaphysical indeterminacy. An excellent, comprehensive overview of the problem of vagueness and its theoretical analysis is Timothy Williamson, *Vagueness* (London: Routledge, 1994).

36
MINOR ENTITIES
Surfaces, holes and shadows

Roberto Casati

Some entities have traditionally been considered major, relative to other, minor entities. Arguably, material objects are core or major ingredients of the content of our pre-reflective thought about the world; objects themselves, or other entities, such as subatomic particles or spatiotemporal worms, are core elements of reflective ontologies, here taken to include scientific ontologies. Still other entities are not so central. But the major/minor division is, of course, a disputable issue. That some entities are deemed metaphysically minor can be traced back to a matter of historical or psychological accident, given that entities such as material bodies and events, say, are labeled "major" purely because of their conceptual centrality, reflecting perhaps biological significance, or intrinsic complexity and interest. Some other criteria for minority may be invoked: surfaces, for instance, are lower dimensional entities, relative to material bodies; holes are characterized by their immateriality. Here we choose to stay with tradition and consider as minor some entities that are typically considered parasitic upon material bodies; from this viewpoint, key examples are surfaces, holes and shadows; other examples include waves and knots; from slightly different points of view, events and regions of space may as well be counted in.

Issues about the existence and the nature of these items can be quite general and concern entities other than minor ones. Thus, surfaces, holes and shadows are generally considered to be *dependent* entities. General issues about dependency (conceptual, metaphysical, semantic) are not specific to them, and, besides, dependency also applies to major entities (thus a material object is said to depend on its parts) and is thus not in itself a mark of the minor. Some metaphysical issues are however more idiosyncratic to our subject matter. What turns out to be interesting is the variety of ways in which these items turn out to depend upon other entities.

Minor entities are also interesting because their concepts can be usefully taken to constitute limit cases of certain key concepts. Holes, for instance, can be seen as degenerate bodies, i.e., as bodies deprived of material constitution. Surfaces are again, but on a different count, degenerate bodies – bodies with one spatial dimension stripped out. Studying holes and surfaces, under this view, is indirectly to study material bodies, their core sisters.

We shall consider three kinds of minor entities – surfaces, holes and shadows – as we take them as representative of classes of conceptual tensions and metaphysical complexities (although by no means the exclusive foci of these tensions and complexities). Surfaces are paradigmatic of a tension between concreteness and abstractness; holes, of a tension between space and objects – and shadows add a dynamic side to these both.

Surfaces

Surfaces exemplify a tension between the abstract and the concrete (Stroll 1988). They are intrinsically spatial entities as they mark the limits of a material object. At the same time the notion of a surface goes beyond a pure geometrical characterization, as it is also importantly *causal*, precisely because surfaces mark the outermost limits of objects. Surfaces are where action is first exerted on an object, and where the object first reacts. As a special case perceptual contact with an object is first and foremost perceptual contact with its surface: we see bodies, in the norm, by seeing their surfaces.

Setting aside complaints to the effect that the notion of a surface referred to in philosophical discussion is artificially made to lean towards the geometrical notion (aptly voiced in Austin's [1962: 100] phrase, "Where and what exactly is the surface of a cat?", intimating that the standards of precision that apply to the geometrical notion may simply not find application in the realm of ordinary objects), puzzles about surfaces arise from unresolved compromises between the abstract (spatial) aspect of the notion and the concrete (causal/material) aspect. On the one hand, if we touch or see a gold sphere (Galton 2007), we do indeed touch or see its surface, *and* we touch or see gold. Hence, one can conclude, both the sphere and its surface are made of gold. But if surfaces are to be two-dimensional entities, then no definite quantity of gold, no matter how small, can qualify for constituting a surface. The surface must be made of gold, but cannot. At this point we may try to force a solution within a scientific worldview and assume that the surface is – say – the outermost atom-thin layer of an object: only to end up with a one-atom-thick *film*, which then possesses *two* surfaces. If, on the other hand, one rather considers surfaces as abstract, lower-dimensional limits of objects, then one deprives them of the specific causal role they have; not being constituted of matter, they cannot be the element that supports the interaction with the world outside the object.

Another variation on the abstract/concrete theme concerns *contact* between bodies (Varzi 2007). A cube is superposed to a second cube; they touch, that is, the relevant surfaces are in contact. Surfaces are key explanatory ingredients of contact but the notion of a surface and the notion of contact are not obviously well aligned, as testified by the divergent accounts of their interrelation (a problem that affects boundaries of various types), when it comes to the dense structure of space, i.e., the property such that between any two points of space it is always possible to interpolate a third, distinct point. Consider our two abutting objects: how can they touch each other, if (a) the objects are topologically closed, that is, they have a boundary that is located at a definite point; and (b) between the points corresponding to the respective boundaries it is always possible to find countless many points? The worry about contact can be considered an artifact of a substantivalist conception of space, according to which space is a mind-independent, nonmaterial yet physical entity, irreducible to relations between objects in it. If space is entity-like, arguably all its parts, included points, are real, and the contact worry ensues.

Dramatic revisions of commonsense have been provided to address the worry. Bolzano (1851) dissolved the problem by claiming that one of the two bodies in contact possesses a surface and the other doesn't, a solution in line with a point-set topological account; in order to somewhat save ordinary intuitions it can be stated that it is just epistemically beyond reach which of the two bodies is surfaceless. Leonardo's view (1938: 75–6) was that there is one single surface dividing the two bodies, which belongs to neither of them. (It could also be claimed that that very one surface belongs to both, something that is allegedly made possible by the dimensionless nature of surfaces.) Finally, Brentano (1976) suggested that there are indeed two surfaces, one for each object, taking up no space, but spatially coincident (think of water as the surface of air, and air as seen from under water as the surface of water).

All these accounts appear quite revisionary, and this indicates the deep instability of intuitions about surfaces.

Holes

Both holes and surfaces are less abstract than numbers and less ephemeral than thoughts and dreams; but whereas surfaces cause concern because of their lower-dimensionality, holes are on this score more regular, as they have full three-dimensionality. Their puzzling features come from their being a type of privation.

Holes are *prima facie* conceptualized as *negative* entities, as they appear to be absences, or privations inflicted on an object. Much as this implicitly acknowledges the process behind many instances of hole formation, it does not contribute usefully to the discussion as it is not in itself transparent what absences amount to (and not all privations in this sense are holes, as we do not think of a hole in place of the missing hand of a vandalized statue: holes invoke a specific geometry).

Still the metaphor of privations can be usefully employed for characterizing some aspects of holes. Absences are typically *local*: Jimmy is earmarked as absent as he did not go to class, but the president of the United States is not so earmarked, although he did not go to class either, as he was not supposed to be there. If holes are absences or privations, they are indeed local privations of matter; a certain portion of matter was expected to be where the hole is. An arbitrarily chosen region of empty sidereal space does not count as an absence in this sense; hence it does not count as a hole. Holes are thus intimately tied to objects. At a minimum, holes are existentially dependent on the objects they are in. *Prima facie*, it looks as if *this* hole could not have been in *that* object.

The tie to objects could be taken to be so strong that holes are identified not with the empty regions of space they seem to create, but with material parts of the object itself – with what Lewis and Lewis (1970) called "hole-linings," the portions of the object that surround the hole. As there is a hole for each hole-lining, and there is a lining for each hole, the temptation may arise to identify holes with hole-linings, revisionary as the account may be. This would indeed amount to a materialist theory of holes, one that incidentally would dispel the worry with both absences and abstractions. Objections to this view include the fact that countless hole-linings line one and the same hole, and that some geometric and functional properties of holes cannot easily be rewritten as properties of hole-linings. The revision may well be metaphysically clean, but proves operationally impractical. At least as impractical as the hole-eliminativism recommended by Jackson (1977), according to which although holes are not to be identified with hole-linings, whatever we can say by making reference to holes we can equally well say by referring to hole-linings.

If not material parts of objects, holes could be "negative" parts (Hofmann and Richards 1985), albeit not of the holed objects itself, but of a theoretical entity which occupies the whole of the convex hull of a holed object, intuitively, the geometrical result of "wrapping up" the body and filling the whole content of the spatial region so defined. One (or more) parts of this super-object would coincide with its hole(s); these would be negative parts of the super-object, i.e., parts that correspond to a local privation of matter. The advantage of this conception is that holes are treated as any other part, and the simple framework for treating them is mereology, restricted to a specific domain. Intuitions about the super-object, however, are unstable: Is it material through and through, with negative parts as just abstractions, indicating operations performed locally on the matter the super-object is composed of? Or is it partly material and partly immaterial? In such a case the account comes close to the immaterial view of holes.

The immaterial view of holes holds that they are immaterial objects, whose notion is molded upon that of a material object up to the requirement of material constitution. Holes are then a subclass of ordinary objects – those that are not made of matter (a variant construal is that they are *made of* space, space being here considered as a peculiar sort of matter, as per substantivalist accounts). Their not being made of matter (or their insensitivity to matter) explains some of the particular intuitions about their identity: filling and emptying a hole does not change or destroy it; a screw is kept in place precisely by the geometry of the hole it fills; keeping the hole's geometric continuity up to topologically invariant deformation makes it survive, and so on. It should however be noted that material constitution overdetermines identity intuitions in the case of material objects (witness the puzzling reception of Theseus' ship or of statue/matter cases), whereas holes may take advantage of the fact that intuitions about their identity are principally controlled by functional properties – as they simply lack a material side. On other accounts the immaterial nature of holes could render other intuitions indeterminate, as happens with modal properties of holes. Thus we said that it is *prima facie* reasonable to claim that holes are individually existentially dependent on the objects they are in ("*this* hole could not have been in *that* object"), but as a matter of fact our modal intuitions could be insufficiently determinate precisely because holes are immaterial.

Of course, being recognized as immaterial, and coincident with regions of space, holes can be directly construed as (non-object) bounded regions of space; a view that is open to the objection that holes can move around, whereas regions of space cannot.

Finally, holes could be, not individual, but relations – between an object and a region of space.

An overarching *error account* of holes takes stock of some of these difficulties and proposals and must of necessity accompany some of them. Accordingly, holes would be illusions; mere projections of a cognitive apparatus that deploys readymade solutions to figure–ground problems and represents space as populated primarily by objects. The error account would add nothing philosophically interesting to a general projectivist construal of material entities – and there are indeed reasons to consider that material bodies themselves are mind-dependent – were it not for the fact that projectivism about holes could be paired with realism about objects, thereby circumscribing metaphysical oddity to a local matter of fact.

Shadows

Commonsense and pictorial practice distinguish between cast shadows, those that are projected on walls, and attached shadows, the dark side of objects (further complexities can be ignored here); let us just consider cast shadows. Shadows are usefully characterized, *prima facie*, as holes in light; they therefore inherit some of the metaphysically interesting features of holes, whereby the role of the material object host is now taken on by light. In particular, like holes, shadows are dependent entities; they have location, shape and size; and they have individuation principles that mimic those of holes (for instance, they can merge and split).

However, shadows have a couple of added complexities, due to the dynamic nature of light, and to the more structured system of their dependencies upon other entities (not only upon light itself, but also upon an obstacle that blocks light transmission, and upon a screen). Consider them in turn.

First, a shadow can only exist because an object, an obtruder, blocks light; the obtruder must be exposed to light. It may be left open where the cast shadow "begins," whether immediately beneath the lit up surface or immediately beyond the dark surface, i.e. whether the obtruder is spatially included or not in the shadow. (Is the interior of an object shaded by its lit-up surface?)

Second, a shadow exists insofar as light is locally missing. And as our spontaneous measure of light's presence or absence is perceptual, access to the light–shadow demarcation is typically constitutive of our attribution of shadow character to dark zones of our environment (this explains why we do not spontaneously conceptualize night as a shadow: we do not see the light night is carved into). However not all local deficiencies of light count as shadows: traceability back to an obtruder remains a necessary condition.

Now, if light is totally prevented from reaching the shadowed area (bar physical complications related to scattering) it is indeterminate whether this prevention will be exerted indefinitely in space or whether it will stop being exercised when the shadow is cast on a screen. There is here an intuition that the spatial features of shadows are supported by causal features, however broadly construed. Leonardo claimed (perhaps metaphorically) that shadows are carried around by "shadow rays," the negative counterpart of light rays; a modern variant suggests "shadowons," negative counterparts of photons (Talmy 1996: 115). If this were the case, then one could ask whether shadow rays penetrate objects or are stopped by them. After all, if a shadow ray is the privation of a determinate light ray, then shouldn't this privation extend as far as the light ray would have extended? (Notice the analogy with the above question of whether holes construed as negative parts belong to objects.)

A classical shadow puzzle arises from this indetermination. If in order for an object to cast a shadow, it must intercept light, and if the local absence of light is indeed stopped by the first screen encountered (the one on which we see the shadow projected), then it becomes indeterminate which of two serially interposed obtruders are responsible for shading a given area. The first in order of distance from the light source, call it A, is the one that intercepts light, but then it cannot cast its shadow through the second, B (Todes and Daniels 1975). From an observer situated at the screen, it is indeterminate whether the eclipsing body is A or B; and it is indeterminate whether it is A or B that is seen, assuming that their profiles visually coincide. Endorsing Leonardo's shadow rays only delays a resolution of the problem: a causal theory of perception must now accommodate "negative carriers." Sorensen (1999) ultimately denies the indeterminacy, and argues that A is casting the shadow and is seen as if it is the causal agent, the light blocker. Indeed, dimensions of indeterminacy abound for shadows, so much so that even the shadow/light distinction can be conceptually blurred: if the obtruder is a piece of green glass, its projection on the screen (a green expanse) can equally well be considered as a green shadow or as a green light spot (Casati 2002).

Conclusions

The entities described here are all superficial in the sense that they have to do with surfaces; this fact shows up in the analysis of their structure. Other minor entities will display other complexities (related to time, in the case of events). Minor entities are an enrichment of the ontology whose benefits appear to outweigh the costs in some cases (especially in terms of descriptive power, as it is hard to describe a superficial, perforated, and eclipsed world without referring to surfaces, holes and shadow). In other cases, the intrinsic difficulties encountered in the analysis of these entities may prove too taxing. A general, unified account of the metaphysically interesting features of the minor entities described here may be beyond reach given the peculiarities of each kind. Still, some of the tensions documented here may tentatively be ascribed to the fact that the concepts we use to deal with surfaces, holes and shadows each tap into different representational systems, and thus generate not obviously compatible representations of one and the same entity. The abstract notion of a surface could be tributary of a type of spatial representation that undergoes tighter constraints than the type of causal representation that, supposedly, underscores the material–causal conception of a surface. In the case of holes, a tension arises between holes considered as (almost) objects and holes considered as (qualified) regions of space, as well as from consideration of holes as the result of creating empty space by deleting a portion of an object. For shadows, these difficulties are compounded by the intuitive inscription of a strong causal component into the behavior of shadows. This component is likely to misfire when it comes to describing the "interaction" of a shadow with the surface it is cast upon – where the only fact of the matter is the absence of an interaction between *light* and the surface in question.

Thus, much as descriptions of reality in terms of minor entities can provide useful and poignant shortcuts (for instance, by avoiding complex references to the topological structure of the surface of a multiply perforated object), the underlying metaphysics requires fine-tuning and adjustments that may encounter hard-to-overcome conceptual limitations.

References

Austin, J. L. (1962) *Sense and Sensibilia*, edited by G. J. Warnock, Oxford: Oxford University Press.

Bolzano, B. (1851) *Paradoxien des Unendlichen*, edited by F. Pihonsk, Leipzig: Reclam; trans. D. A. Steele, *Paradoxes of the Infinite*, London: Routledge & Kegan Paul, 1950.

Brentano, F. (1976) *Philosophische Untersuchungen zu Raum, Zeit und Kontinuum*, edited by S. Körner and R. M. Chisholm, Hamburg: Meiner; trans. B. Smith, *Philosophical Investigations on Space, Time and the Continuum*, London: Croom Helm, 1988.

Casati, R. (2002) *Shadows*, New York: Vintage.

Galton, A. (2007) "On the Paradoxical Nature of Surfaces: Ontology at the Physics/Geometry Interface," *Monist* 90, no. 3: 379–90.

Hofmann, D. D. and Richards, W. A. (1985) "Parts of recognition," *Cognition* 18: 65–96.

Jackson, F. (1977) *Perception: A Representative Theory*, Cambridge: Cambridge University Press.

Leonardo da Vinci (1938) *The Notebooks of Leonardo da Vinci*, edited, selected trans. by E. MacCurdy, London: Reynal & Hitchock.

Lewis, D. and Lewis, S. (1970) "Holes," *Australasian Journal of Philosophy* 48: 206–12; reprinted in D. Lewis, *Philosophical Papers*, vol. 1, Oxford: Oxford University Press, pp. 3–9.

Sorensen, R. (1999) "Seeing Intersecting Eclipses," *Journal of Philosophy* 96 (January): 25–49.

Stroll, A. (1988) *Surfaces*, Minneapolis: University of Minnesota Press.

Talmy, L. (1996) "Fictive Motion in Language and 'Ception'," in P. Bloom, M. A. Peterson, L. Nadel, and M. F. Garrett (eds), *Language and Space*, Cambridge, MA: MIT Press, pp. 211–76.

Todes, S. and Daniels, C. B. (1975), "Beyond the Doubt of a Shadow: A Phenomenological and Linguistic Analysis of Shadows," *Dialogues in Phenomenology*, vol. 5 of *Selected Studies in Phenomenology and Existential Philosophy*, 203–16, edited by Don Ihde and R. M. Zaner, The Hague: Marinus Nijhoff.

Varzi, A. C. (2007) "Boundary," *The Stanford Encyclopedia of Philosophy*, Edward N. Zalta (ed.); available: http://plato.stanford.edu/archives/fall2007/entries/boundary/

Further reading

M. Baxandall, *Shadows and Enlightenment* (London; New Haven, CT: Yale University Press, 1995) offers a study of the pictorial representations of shadows, with a discussion of conceptual and taxonomical issues). N. Giralt and P. Bloom, "How Special Are Objects? Children's Reasoning about Objects, Parts, and Holes," *Psychological Science* 11 (2000): 497–501, provides empirical evidence of similar treatment of holes and objects in infants. R. Sorensen, *Seeing Dark Things* (Oxford: Oxford University Press, 2007) is an engaging and wide-ranging account of absences such as holes and shadows, discussing the threat they pose to standard accounts of perception. For further reading, see also R. Casati and A. C. Varzi, *Holes and Other Superficialities* (Cambridge, MA: MIT Press, 1994); and their edited, *Lesser Kinds*, special issue of *The Monist* (2007), including K. Miller, "Immaterial Bodies," pp. 349–81.

37

TRUTHMAKERS AND TRUTHBEARERS

John Bigelow

Throughout the twentieth century philosophers commonly asserted, with or without argument, that metaphysics was dead and buried. Towards the end of the century, however, signs emerged that metaphysics had never died after all, and many philosophers were once more not only doing metaphysics but explicitly owning up to it.

Quine contributed quite early to this return. His paper "On What There Is" (1953) includes the memorable motto "to be is to be the value of a variable." "To be" is a concern of metaphysics, and "the value of a variable" is a concern of the formal languages of modern logic; so Quine's dictum at least superficially seemed to draw "metaphysical" conclusions from reflections on language.

In Quine's wake came another idea broadly friendly to metaphysics: the bold but attractive *truthmaker thesis*. Like Quine's motto, "Every truth needs a truthmaker" at least superficially appears to draw metaphysical conclusions (the existence of "truthmakers") from reflections on language (the truth or falsity of "truthbearers").

The truthmaker thesis is worth exploring, for several reasons. Arguably, the thesis as first stated is false; but there may be near neighbours that are true and that deserve the same name. Furthermore, recourse to the truthmaker thesis is useful for the history of ideas. It aids understanding of many past philosophical theories, which it often seems tacitly to motivate and sustain. For a similar reason, the truthmaker thesis can be useful in advancing our own theories. It may enhance our understanding to ask *whether* we think a given hypothesis needs any truthmakers. And if not, then why not? And if so, then what might those truthmakers be like?

Truthmaking

In the world, there are things of the following two kinds. On the one hand, there are police officers and power poles and other things that are just *there*; and these things are not true or false, but simply exist. On the other hand, there are also such things as marks on pieces of paper (written statements, which police officers might sign, for instance), and these things not only exist in the world but are also "saying something," and so can be either true or false. We may call these things *truthbearers*.

"Truthmaker theories" hold that in order for any truthbearer to be true there must be something "outside the text," as we might say, that "makes" it true. If the truth is a truth about inanimate objects, then the world must contain those inanimate objects; if it is about a God then there must be a God; if it is about the way people conduct their lives, then there must be people and they must conduct their lives in that way; and so on.

To put this guiding idea slightly differently, "Truth supervenes on being" – meaning that there could not be any difference in what things are true unless there were some difference in what there is in the world. This "supervenience" version of the truth-maker thesis is slightly different from the "makes true" version, but it voices a very similar intuition: that some but not all of the things in the world are true-or-false, and that which of these truthbearers are true "depends" in some way on what there is.

Doubts

Some philosophers have found such truthmaker theses plausible. There is no consensus, however, on exactly what these theses actually *mean*. In particular, it is not clear in what sense a truthmaker is supposed to "make" a truthbearer true; the word in this context does not mean what it does when we say that a potter "makes" a pot, or that a police officer "makes" a mistake. Nor is there consensus on what it means to say that "truth supervenes on being," or whether this form of words adequately captures the relevant intuition.

Nor is there consensus on what sorts of *reasons* could be given for accepting such theses. Some might find them self-evident, or provable from self-evident premises. Others, however, would seek to support them by a kind of "inference to the best expla-nation."

There is no settled account of the history of truthmaker theses. For some early artic-ulations that themselves use the language of "truthmakers" and offer reflections on earlier historical background, see Mulligan et al. (1984), Fox (1987), and Bigelow (1988); and for early unpublished sources coming from C. B. Martin, see Armstrong (2004).

Despite continuing disputes over their meaning, justification and veracity, these truthmaker theses have been employed persuasively in justifying substantial theories concerning the fundamental nature of the world. They have been harnessed to hard metaphysical work.

Rhetorical force

Reality behind appearances

Roughly, philosophical idealists hold that only appearances in the mind exist. Yet if idealists are to speak not only of actual but also of merely *potential* observations (as perhaps they must), then it is fair, and rhetorically useful, to ask what truthmakers there could be for claims concerning such nonactual observations. Anti-idealists may object that only inanimate objects can supply the right kinds of truthmakers for them; and it is at least arguable that idealists cannot supply these, or even any satisfactory substitutes.

Inner life behind our actions

Philosophical behaviourists hold that when we talk about a person's thoughts, perceptions and feelings, this is really just a distinctive way of talking about patterns in their behaviour. Yet if behaviourists are to speak not only of actual but also of *potential* patterns of behaviour (as perhaps they must), then anti-behaviourists are entitled to ask what truthmakers there could be for claims about such merely potential behaviour. Plausibly, in some cases, conscious inner states can supply the right kinds of truthmakers; but philosophical behaviourists cannot supply these – nor, arguably, any adequate substitutes.

Things no longer present

According to one metaphysical theory, things that have no *present* existence – Abelard, for instance – lack existence altogether. It is a minimum requirement for truthmakers that they or their antecedents exist; but then, what can be the truthmaker for the intuitively unimpeachable truth that Abelard lusted after Heloise, if neither Abelard nor Heloise exists? The truthmaker theses therefore weigh heavily against this *presentist* theory. They lend support instead to *four-dimensionalism* – the theory that past and future things exist just as we exist *now*, each at its own temporal location in a four-dimensional manifold, just as things to the east and west of us all exist equally with, and in the very same way as, things that are *here* exist.

Universals and states of affairs

Truthmaker theses have also been used in justifying various species of metaphysical *realism*, of either Platonist or Aristotelian varieties, that affirm the existence of both "individuals" and "universals."

Suppose that an actual pig is some particular shade of pink; and then imagine the very same pig existing, but being a different shade of pink. Since it is the very same individual pig in both cases, the truthmaker for the truth about the pig's *actual* shade of pink cannot consist merely in the existence of this individual pig; it must somehow involve not just the pig but also this precise shade of pink. Arguably, if we were to accept the existence of this shade of pink, as a "universal," then that would help to supply the required difference in truthmakers that lies behind this difference in truths.

Some have gone further, and extended the argument to support, not only the existence of individuals and universals, but also of "facts" – or "states of affairs" – combining one or more individuals along with one or more universals, bound into some sort of "complex unity." If individual a has property F and b has G, then something is true that would not be true if instead a were G and b were F. A difference in truth demands a difference in truthmakers; but the required difference in truthmakers cannot consist in the mere existence of individuals a and b and universals F and G, since these all exist in both the actual and the possible alternative situation. The existence of "states of affairs" like "a's being F," however, might supply the required difference between these two situations. That they provide useful truthmakers furnishes one reason for believing in states of affairs.

"Diversals," tropes or qua-individuals

On the other hand, there have been some philosophers, of a more nominalist bent, who have recruited the very same truthmaker theses against the existence of universals, and *a fortiori* against states of affairs. Instead they propose a category that is distinct from both individuals and universals, but that provides truthmakers for the attribution of properties to individuals. Not all nominalists will take this course, but some will. It is ironic that this nominalist-friendly theory has no really satisfactory *name* for these truthmakers. They have been called *modes, moments, factors, property instances, abstract particulars*, and *tropes*. To contrast them with universals, it would be reasonable to call them *diversals*; but since established usage favours *tropes* above all alternatives, that is the term we will use here. To illustrate this rival theory, consider a donkey and a doormat.

Imagine a donkey and a doormat of exactly the same shade of brown. A realist about universals might first look at the donkey, and then turning to the doormat say: "There it is again – that very same precise shade of brown!" A realist about universals can say there is *one* thing (a shade of brown), which can be seen both in the donkey and in the doormat.

However, a realist about tropes may say that she sees first the brownness of the donkey, and then second the brownness of the doormat. The brownness of the doormat may still "exactly match" the brownness of the donkey, but on this rival theory the brownness of the donkey and the brownness of the doormat are numerically distinct, each located spatiotemporally in the world: the brownness of the donkey is in the paddock where the donkey is, and not on the doorstep where the doormat is; whereas the brownness of the doormat is on the doorstep where the doormat is, and not out in the paddock where the donkey is.

There is a second path open to a nominalist who affirms the truthmaker principle. Consider again the truth that the donkey is brown. In searching for a truthmaker for this truth, one path a nominalist might take would be to postulate the existence, not of any "property" (whether universal or trope), but of a new, concrete *individual* – which we might call "the donkey *qua* brown." This would be an individual that both is a donkey, and is *essentially* brown – that is, an individual that could not have failed to be brown except by failing to exist.

On this theory we have, in a sense, two donkeys. The donkey that "could have been another shade of brown" may then be said to *constitute* the "donkey *qua* brown."

Compare this to the theory that a lump of bronze may be said to *constitute* a statue. Constitution, it is said, is not numerical identity: just as the lump of bronze may continue to exist even after the statue ceases to be, so may the donkey continue to exist even after the donkey *qua* brown has ceased to be.

This postulated *qua*-individual may then be advanced as something whose sheer existence "makes" it true that the donkey is brown. This truthmaker, be it noted, is a concrete *individual*, rather than either a universal or an abstract particular. Thus, this theory respects the truthmaker principle without requiring an abandonment of nominalism.

Necessitation

Behind all of the above samples of philosophical argumentation – attacking idealism or behaviourism, or defending realism about universals and states of affairs, or about tropes or *qua*-individuals – lies the common assumption that a truthmaker's existence at least needs to *entail* the truth in question. If a certain ensemble of items (the proposed truthmaker) does not entail the truth in question, then it is agreed that some further item must be added so that the augmented ensemble does entail that truth.

To forestall confusion, note that the relationship between truths and truthmakers need not be one-to-one. We should speak of *a* truthmaker for a given truth, not of *the* truthmaker for that truth. Arguably, for instance, each and every penguin constitutes an equally satisfactory truthmaker for the truth "There are penguins." However, the truth that there are penguins does not entail the existence of any one penguin in particular. The relationship between truths and truthmakers is many–many and not one–one.

Nevertheless, our principle of *Necessitation* affirms that if any given item is to furnish a truthmaker, properly so-called, for any given truth, then the sheer existence of this truthmaker *would* need to entail the corresponding truth.

Maximalism

The thesis of *maximalism* asserts that "*Every* truth needs a truthmaker – there are no exceptions."

This thesis might be defended by appeal to a default truthmaker for any truth whatsoever: namely, the world as a whole. It might be maintained that if the world had been different in any way, no matter how minor, then this alternative possibility would have constituted a numerically different possible world from the actual world. Arguably then we can always fall back on "the whole world" as a truthmaker, if no other candidate can be found: anything that is true is, trivially, *entailed* by the existence of the actual world, since if it had not been true then what exists would have constituted another possible world rather than this one.

But this blanket recourse to "the world" as the truthmaker for every truth would threaten to render the truthmaker principle explanatorily vacuous. Idealists and behaviourists, for instance, could blithely meet the request for a truthmaker by saying that the truthmaker for their statements about potential experiences or potential behaviour will consist simply in the existence of a world "which is such that" these statements are true.

Does this constitute a devastating objection to the truthmaker principle? No. From the premise that a principle is *at least trivially true* we surely cannot show that it is *not true*, nor even that it is not also *interestingly* true. There are also ways of restoring metaphysical "punch" by *supplementing* the truthmaker principle. For instance, one could argue that if idealist or behaviourist theories cannot identify any plausible truth-makers *apart* from the near-vacuous "whole-world" truthmaker – whereas rival theories can identify some much more illuminating candidate truthmakers – then this counts in favour of the rival theories.

Furthermore, this whole-world defence of maximalism identifies the world as an individual of a very special kind: an individual for which every one of its properties is an *essential* property. On this theory, when we think of "the world as a whole," we need to think of this world "*qua* just as it is." This construes possible worlds as being like Leibnizian monads ("a different act, a different Adam"). Thus, if we defend the conjunction of maximalism and necessitation by appeal to "the whole world" as a truth-maker, we are not falling back on a mere triviality, but on what appears to be a substantial metaphysical thesis.

Logical constructions

So far we have cited no knock-down objection to maximalism. Nevertheless, an alternative theory is worth considering, according to which not all truths require specific truthmakers. The truths that do require their own truthmakers might be called *basic* truths. These basic truths can then be combined, using logical machinery, to yield many other, non-basic, truths. At least some of these non-basic truths would not need further truthmakers. Rather, as logically compound truths they inherit their truth-values from the truth-values of their constituent basic truths, *via* the logical machinery with which these constituents are stitched together. This picture matches some of the passages in Wittgenstein's *Tractatus* (1961 [1921]).

The key logical operators that motivate resistance to maximalism are those of *negation* and *universal generalization*. Consider negation. If it is true that there are *no* Arctic penguins, then maximalism seems to require there to be something whose existence *entails* that there are no Arctic penguins. The world must contain, as it were, a logically infallible Arctic-penguin-excluder. This is hard to swallow.

Universal generalizations are closely related to negation, because a universal generalization is equivalent to the denial of an existential claim: "*All* are thus" means "It is *not* so, that *some* are *not*." Consider the truth that *all* penguins are found outside the Arctic circle. What could be the truthmaker for this claim? Armstrong 2004, following Russell's lectures on logical atomism (1972 [1918]), appealed to a "totality fact" – sometimes memorably called "Porky" (echoing movies that ended with Porky Pig saying, "Th-th-that's all folks!"). Armstrong's colleague C. B. Martin argued for, as it were, many little Porkies, many little "absences," rather than one big "totality fact."

These theories of "totality facts" or "absences" should be compared with a rival.

Suppose someone asserts that there are Arctic penguins. Grant that this can be true only if it has a truthmaker. Imagine that you fail to find a truthmaker, so you *reject* the assertion "There are Arctic penguins." How do you reject this assertion? You do so by asserting its negation, which is equivalent to "*All* penguins live south of the Arctic circle." You assert this latter sentence, however, not because you think that it has a truthmaker, but rather, because you wish to reject its contradictory, because you think its contradictory lacks a truthmaker.

On this theory, a basic truth must have a truthmaker, and if it lacked a truthmaker it would lack truth; but its negation, if true, does not need a truthmaker. The negation, when it does get to be true, does so not because the world contains a truthmaker for it, but because the world does not contain a truthmaker for the proposition it is negating.

Theories of this kind that deny maximalism avoid the postulation of either absences or totality facts. They can, however, still preserve much of the spirit of the truthmaker principles – because they can still affirm the thesis that "truth supervenes on being."

Martin's objection to these theories is that they just shift the bump under the carpet. Any plausibility there may be in the truthmaker thesis carries over into a requirement that there must be *something* in the world in virtue of which any given basic truthbearer really does *lack* a truthmaker.

For this reason, there is no consensus on whether we should accept maximalism, or retreat to a weaker supervenience thesis together with a story about logical constructions.

Propositions or 2D-semantics

Consider the following objection to the truthmaker thesis:

> Does the existence of a particular penguin, Percy, entail the truth that there are penguins? Before answering, let us ask: What is the truth*bearer* for this truth? Suppose that the truthbearer, the thing that is either true or false, is the English sentence "There are penguins."
>
> Does the existence of Percy entail that this English sentence is true? No, surely not.
>
> The existence of Percy does not entail the existence of the English language, or even the existence of human beings. Still less does the existence of Percy entail that those English words mean what they do. Hence the existence of Percy does not entail that the English sentence "There are penguins" is true.

This objection demonstrates that the necessitation thesis could not be sustained, if it were to be interpreted as the claim that the existence of a given truthmaker entails all three of the following: (1) that a particular sentence exists, and (2) that this sentence has a particular meaning, and (3) that this sentence, with this meaning, is true.

There are, however, other ways of interpreting the necessitation thesis, under which it has at least some chance of escaping that sort of refutation. One option might be to say that the existence of a truthmaker will entail a truth, provided the relevant truth-bearer is taken to be, not a sentence in a natural language, but rather something more abstract: a "proposition."

Another strategy is also possible, which does not appeal to propositions. This alternative strategy appeals to one of the strands in what has been called "two-dimensional semantics." Suppose there is a sentence in the actual world (and *true* in the actual world), with a given meaning. Then ask whether the given sentence *would have been true*, if the world had been different in some specified way. This question is ambiguous. It could be asking whether this English sentence would still have existed, and also asking what it *would have meant* if the world had been different in the specified manner. Alternatively, it could be asking whether this sentence, in this actual world, with the meaning it has in this actual world, truthfully describes the state of affairs that obtains in a certain *other* possible world.

The necessitation thesis can thus be interpreted as requiring the following: If a sentence is actually true, there must be at least one truthmaker. The existence of this truthmaker must then "necessitate" this truth – in the sense that this sentence (in the actual world, with its actual meaning) truly describes *all* possible worlds in which that truthmaker exists. Quite plausibly it is this interpretation of the Necessitation thesis that captures its intended meaning better; and in any case, it is an interpretation that gives the thesis a chance of being true.

Disappearance theories of truth

Many philosophers have held that to say "It is *true* that the Alps are older than the Andes" is to say nothing more than "The Alps *are* older than the Andes." If it is true that P, then P; and if P, then it is true that P. This has led some to hold what might be called a "disappearance theory of truth." There is a large family of theories of this kind, with a variety of names ("the redundancy theory," "minimalism," the "disquotation theory," and so on).

Do these disappearance theories pose a threat to the truthmaker theses? It might seem that they deliberately eliminate the very subject matter truthmaker theories are intending to describe, namely, the conditions under which truthbearers are true.

Despite initial appearances, however, the truthmaker theses are not necessarily threatened by a disappearance theory of truth – because, paradoxically, truthmaker theses need not be essentially concerned with "truth" at all. The word "truth," in "Every truth needs a truthmaker," can be eliminated using standard "minimalist" techniques, leaving a very substantial thesis behind that does not make any appeal to the notion of truth.

Consider first the version of the truthmaker thesis that is clarified by the thesis of necessitation. Take as an example the truth that a certain donkey is brown. What does it mean to ask for a truthmaker for this truth? Suppose it were to mean something like this:

> If the donkey is brown, then there must be something in the world whose existence entails that the donkey is brown.

This falls under a schema:

> If P, then there must be something in the world whose existence entails that P.

Note that the words "true" or "truth" occur nowhere in this schema. Arguably, introduction of the word "truth" does little more than facilitate an alternative way of asserting the above schema, one which permits the elimination of the schematic letter P, by saying something like this:

> For *any truth*, there must be something in the world whose existence entails *that truth*.

This furnishes an alternative to invoking either propositions or two-dimensional semantics, in defending the truthmaker principle against objections trading on the contingency of existence for English sentences and other truthbearers.

Anti-necessitation truthmaker theories

Not all nominalists will accept the need for tropes, or *qua*-individuals, in place of universals. Some will reject the necessitation principle.

Compare a possible situation in which a donkey exists and is a given shade of brown, and another possible situation in which that very same donkey exists but has some other shade of brown. There is a difference in *truth* between these situations. What is the difference in *truthmakers* that accounts for this difference in truth?

Some nominalists might argue that all there relevantly is in the world is *the donkey*, so this donkey must supply the required "difference" between the two possible situations. Certainly this candidate truthmaker does not supply the required "difference" simply by *existing* in one situation and not in the other: no, it exists in both situations. Nevertheless, this donkey does supply the required difference, and it does this by *being different* in these two different possible situations.

That is, the donkey does exist in both situations: but it is a particular shade of brown in one situation, and not in the other. Hence the donkey is after all "a truthmaker" for the truth about the brownness of the donkey – because it is *this donkey* (or more precisely, *how this donkey is*) that makes it true, in the actual situation, that this donkey is this shade of brown.

The upshot is in fact a clarification of the issues, by way of distinguishing two distinct workable truthmaker theses worth considering:

- Every truth requires a truthmaker – *meaning* by "truthmaker" some *thing* whose *existence* entails the corresponding truth.
- Every truth requires a truthmaker – *meaning* by "truthmaker" something such that it is the *way* this thing is, which entails the corresponding truth.

These are indeed distinct theses. The second is of special interest because it is something that a nominalist could affirm without being drawn into any commitment to universals, or to tropes, or to any genuine plurality of *qua*-individuals.

Postscript on higher-order quantification

In exploring truthmaker theories, it is well to be mindful of the roots of set theory in the foundations of mathematics. Frege (1967 [1879]), and Russell and Whitehead (1927), began with a "higher-order logic," according to which the following two inferences are distinct, and both valid:

$$\frac{Fa}{\therefore \exists x.Fx \mathbin{\&} x = a} \qquad\qquad \frac{Fa}{\therefore \exists\varphi.\varphi a \mathbin{\&} \varphi = F}$$

The first says that when a thing *a* is thus-and-so ("is *F*"), *there is a thing* that is thus-and-so, and *a* is that thing. The second involves a higher-order quantification: it says that when a thing *a* is thus-and-so ("is *F*"), then *there is somehow* that the thing *a* is, and *being F* is *being that somehow*.

A prime intuitive motivation for the truthmaker principles may be that the above forms of inference are both valid; and both establish a deep connection between the *truth* of their premises and the *being* of the entities figuring in their conclusions. For Frege, the conclusion of the second is as "ontologically serious" as the conclusion of the first. Yet the conclusions differ in logical form, and the second should not be construed as *reifying* the "somehow" with which it is concerned.

Frege's set theory began with a "fifth axiom," now called *Naïve Comprehension*: for any description, there is a *set* containing all and only the things that fit that description. Let "*Fx*" abbreviate the claim that some *x* fits a given description. Then the following "second-order" inference is valid:

$$\frac{Fa}{\therefore \exists\varphi.\varphi a}$$

Naïve Comprehension, however, takes a different form:

$$\frac{Fa}{\therefore \exists y.(a \in y),}$$

where "*a* ∈ *y*" means that *a* is a member of the set *y*.

Naïve Comprehension entails a contradiction, and cannot be true. Its mistake lies in collapsing a second-order inference into a first-order one: it is a mistake to "reify," as a set of all sets, the *somehow* that a thing is, when that thing is a set. It does not follow simply from there being *somehow* that certain things are that there must be a certain reified *something* that is related to them all. Yet there are independent reasons for accepting not only the ontological commitments expressed by higher-order quantifiers, but also a first-order ontological commitment to a vast hierarchy of sets, along with sets corresponding to *many* higher-order ontological commitments, even if not all.

We can extend this argument beyond the "∈" of set membership to various other relations R, like "instantiates," or "has." It does not follow from there being *somehow* that all sets are that there is some *universal* that is instantiated by all sets, any more than it follows that there is a set that contains all sets as members. The truthmaker for "*a* is a set" could consist in nothing more than the individual *a* together with *somehow* that *a* is – without any need for a "universal" instantiated by *a*, or a trope that *a* has, or a "state of affairs" of *a*'s being a set, or a "*qua*-individual," of *a qua*-being-a-set, or any other first-order individual that might serve as a truthmaker.

Nevertheless, there may be independent support for postulating the existence of a great many sets, and sets of sets, even though their existence is not guaranteed by Naïve Comprehension. Likewise, there may be independent support for postulating many universals, tropes, states of affairs, and *qua*-individuals, even without any general truth-maker thesis. If their existence could *explain* enough, then it would be reasonable to believe in their existence – whether or not their existence would be required by an unrestricted truthmaker principle.

Arguably, the truthmaker theses, like Naïve Comprehension, are therefore not strictly true, and cannot furnish *a priori* proofs of any substantial metaphysical theses unaided. Yet they retain a role. *Asking* for truthmakers can be useful as a first step towards articulating substantial metaphysical theories, which may then be supported by such means as inference to the best explanation.

References

Armstrong, D. M. (2004), *Truth and Truthmakers*, Cambridge: Cambridge University Press.

Bigelow, John (1988) *The Reality of Numbers*, Oxford: Clarendon Press.

Boolos, George S. (1975) "On Second-Order Logic," *Journal of Philosophy* 72: 509–27.

Fox, John F. (1987) "Truthmaker," *Australasian Journal of Philosophy* 65: 188–207.

Frege, G. (1967 [1879]) *Concept Script: A Formal Language of Pure Thought Modelled Upon That of Arithmetic*, edited, trans. by S. Bauer-Mengelberg in Jean van Heijenorrt, *From Frege to Gödel: A Source Book in Mathematical Logic, 1879–1931*, Cambridge, MA: Harvard University Press; trans. of *Begriffsschrift: eine der arithmetischen nachgebildete Formelsprache des reinen Denkens*, Halle: Louis Nebert, 1879.

Morse, A. P. (1965) *A Theory of Sets*, New York: Academic Press.

Mulligan, K., Simons, P., and Smith, B. (1984) "Truth-Makers," *Philosophy and Phenomenological Research* 44: 287–321.

Quine, W. V. "On What There Is," in *From a Logical Point of View*, New York: Harper & Row, pp. 1–19; reprinted from *Review of Metaphysics* (1948).

Russell, Bertrand (1972 [1918]) *Russell's Logical Atomism*, edited by David Pears, London: Fontana.

Russell, Bertrand and Whitehead, A. N. (1927) *Principia Mathematica*, vol. 1, 2nd edn, Cambridge: Cambridge University Press; especially the preface and Appendix C.

Wittgenstein, Ludwig (1961 [1921]) *Tractatus Logico-Philosophicus*, trans. D. F. Pears and B. F. McGuiness, London: Routledge & Kegan Paul; originally published in *Annalen der Naturphilosophie*, with first English trans. in 1922.

Further reading

For further reading, see G. Frege, "Function and concept" (1891), in *Translations from the Philosophical Writings of Gottlob Frege*, 3rd edn (1953), edited by Peter Geach and Max Black (London: Blackwell, 1980), pp. 21–41 (original German published by Hermann Pohle, Jena); and "On Concept and Object" (1892), in *ibid.*, pp. 42–55 (original German published in *Vierteljahrsschrift für wissenschaftliche Philosophie* 16: 192–205). See also David Lewis, "Things *qua* Truthmakers," in H. Lillehammer and G. Rodriguez-Pereyra (eds), *Real Metaphysics: Essays in Honour of D.H. Mellor*, London: Routledge, 2003), pp. 25–42; and C. B. Martin, "How It Is: Entities, Absences and Voids," *Australasian Journal of Philosophy* 74 (1996): 57–65.

38

VALUES

Kevin Mulligan

We often refer to values and ascribe value properties. We refer to injustice and the sublime and say of one thing that it is valuable or of an action that it is evil. Or so it seems. But perhaps there are no values. If nihilism about values (sometimes called "axiological nihilism") is correct, then there are no tragedies, no murders, no sacrifices, no injustice, no costs, no goods, no evils, no vices, no ugly films, no mediocrity, no heroes, no geniuses, no saints and no heroic deeds. "And a good thing, too," say some. But of course they should not say this if axiological nihilism is correct. For then nothing is a good thing. Nihilism about values occupies one end of the spectrum of possible views about value (Mackie [1986: 15–41] argues for axiological nihilism about what he calls "objective" values). At the other end of the spectrum there is the view that there are values and objects which have positive and negative values; many of these values are what they seem to be, if experience and ordinary language are any guide, that is, monadic properties of their bearers which are not relative to persons or other animate creatures (Hartmann 1932). Another possibility is that nihilism is false but values are not what they seem to be. Perhaps a murder is just a type of action which is frowned on or is the object of other negative attitudes.

To understand and evaluate axiological nihilism and alternatives to it we should consider the internal structure of (what seems to be) the world of values and value properties and of closely related properties (the first to third sections below), the nature of the bearers of value properties (fourth section), and the relation between value properties and, for example, natural properties (fifth).

Values and value properties

Some objects, we say, have a positive value, others have a negative value, some are neither positively valuable nor disvaluable (they are axiologically indifferent), and some are more valuable than others. Some objects are valuable for you, some are disvaluable for me, some are more valuable for me than for you. If we compare these properties and relations with properties and relations such as ugliness, evil, elegance and being more unjust, then we may say that the former are "thin" properties and relations, and the latter "thick" properties and relations. The thick properties have more "content" than the thin ones. What is the relation between the two?

On one view, being ugly is a determinate of the determinable property of being disvaluable. The property of being ugly stands to the property of being disvaluable as the property of being red to the property of being coloured. Similarly, the relation of *being more unjust than* which holds between two actions, agents or situations is a determinate of the relation of *being more disvaluable than*.

Axiological properties and relations, thin and thick, are often said to divide into the intrinsic ones and the extrinsic ones. A pleasure sensation is intrinsically valuable, pain is intrinsically disvaluable. A pleasure sensation is also intrinsically valuable for its bearer. Sam's family mansion is intrinsically valuable for him but it is also extrinsically valuable for him – it is worth a lot of money. Intuitively, the value of an object is extrinsic if the source of its value is not to be found within the object and intrinsic if this is not the case. But the distinction between intrinsicness and extrinsicness is as difficult to characterise precisely here as elsewhere in metaphysics (see Chapter 26, "Intrinsic and Extrinsic Properties").

The sublime and injustice *are* values. If a symphony is sublime or an act unjust, then they *exemplify* value properties. Values stand to value properties much as numbers stand to number properties and colours to colour properties. In the case of each couple we may ask who wears the trousers: the values (numbers, colours) or the property of being valuable (being equinumerous, being red)? A common view has it that the properties of being good or beautiful are metaphysically more fundamental than Beauty or the Good, for example because values can be constructed out of, are abstractions from, value properties.

Values, like numbers and colours, stand in internal relations to each other. One such internal relation is the relation of axiological height or importance: justice is a higher value than charm, grace is perhaps just as high a value as elegance. These relations are internal relations because their terms must stand in these relations to one another. More contestable examples of internal relations between values are the claims that the vital values of health or life are higher or more important than the values of pleasure or well-being (a claim made by Nietzsche and denied by some utilitarians). Do all values stand in relations of height to one another? Not if some values are incommensurable – for example, the ideal of the English gentleman and that of the Japanese Bushido.

Suppose that the value of generosity is higher than that of pleasure. Does anything follow from such a claim about the relation between the value of one act of generosity and the value of several lifetimes of pleasure? If one thinks that a negative answer must be given to this and similar questions, then one may wonder what the content of claims to the effect that one value is lower than another could possibly be.

Normative properties

We may say of a particular action performed by Sam that it is *elegant* or *evil*, that he *ought not* to be doing what he is doing, that it is the *right* thing to do, that he is *obliged* to do it, that it is his *duty*, that he has *a right* to act as he does, or that it is *virtuous*. The different properties we ascribe in this way belong to one very large family which, for want of a better word, we may call *normative* properties. This family comprises value properties, the deontic property of oughtness, the properties of rightness and wrongness and the properties corresponding to the different vices (foolishness, cowardice) and virtues (wisdom, courage).

What are the differences between the members of the family of normative properties? What are their interrelations?

One type of value relation, as we have seen, is comparative: an object is more valuable than another object, or more valuable for someone than some other object; one deed is more shameful or unjust than another deed. Similarly, some people are more vicious than others. But, it is sometimes claimed, right and wrong, oughtness and obligatoriness do not admit of degrees. Thus Hume says that "right, and obligation admit not of degrees" (*Treatise*, Bk 3, pt 2, §6).

One difference between values and virtues, on one hand, and the other normative properties, on the other hand, is the variety of the former and the monotony of the latter. One taxonomy of values and value properties distinguishes sensory values, the pleasant and the unpleasant; vital values such as the values of health and life; aesthetic values such as the comic, the ugly, charm, elegance, the ridiculous and dumpiness; cognitive values such as the values of knowledge, truth, consistency and justification; the value of the right, to which we appeal to evaluate positive laws; the values of justice and freedom; the value of the holy and the ethical values of goodness and evil (Scheler 1973; cf. Hartmann 1932: Vol. 2). Similarly, there are many ethical and intellectual virtues and vices (courage, tolerance, temperance, vanity; clarity, thoroughness, narrow-mindedness). Do *oughts* and obligations exhibit a similar variety? There are different types of *ought* – for example, ethical, prudential, epistemic, linguistic, political and conventional *oughts*. That is not to say that "ought" is ambiguous. Nor is it obvious that the property of oughtness is a determinable property which can be specified in different ways. And whatever we say about how the variety of *ought* should be understood, this variety is less than that of values. Indeed we may think that all types of normative properties other than thick value properties and the properties corresponding to the different virtues and vices are thin properties.

Theories of ethics typically differ in the relative importance they attach to the different members of the family of normative properties. In Kantian accounts what we ought (not) to do ("the moral law") figures more prominently than in virtue ethics. In some utilitarian accounts of ethics the values of happiness, well-being or desire-satisfaction occupy centre stage. In phenomenological ethics, as in some utilitarian and consequentialist theories, values and value properties are taken to be more fundamental than other normative properties. On one view of virtues and vices, being virtuous and vicious are just value properties. But many accounts of ethical virtues do not make any such claim. They simply say that virtues are goods and vices are evils.

Goods come in many kinds. There are material goods such as land and immaterial goods, for example epistemic goods such as an education or a piece of information. Many goods form the object of economic exchanges. To be a good is to be a good for someone. Sam's generosity, like his health, is a good for Sam and for some of his friends. What is the relation between goods and values? One answer is that an object is a good for someone only if it is valuable or valuable for him.

Values and other normative properties

What is the relation between values and *oughts*? Consider

(1) Justice is valuable
(2) It ought to be the case that (justice is realised)

(2) employs the functorial "ought," which takes a sentence to yield a sentence. This is not the only type of *ought*. "Ought" frequently takes a predicate to make a more complex predicate, as in

(3) Sam ought to keep his promises
(4) Arguments ought to be valid

The "ought" in (2) and (4) is an *ought to be*. The "ought" in (3) is an *ought to do*. One view about the relation between (1) and (2) asserts both

(5) (1) iff (2)

and

(6) If (1) and (2), then (2) because (1).

(6) is an instance of the view that values ground oughts. (Leibniz, for example, defines what is permitted or allowed as what it is possible for a good man to do.) Another view is that (1) and (2) mean the same thing, express the very same proposition. Then (6) must be rejected. Another view reverses the direction of explanation in (6) and asserts that

(7) If (1) and (2), then (1) because (2).

This is an instance of the view that oughts ground values. Finally, there is the view that the use of the functorial *ought* is a fatal step in logic (Geach 1991), life and philosophy (Prichard 1912), the sort of expression only a politician would employ (Sidgwick called "ought to be" the political *ought*).

The bearers of value properties

Bearers of value properties seem to come in two kinds: they are either objects or states of affairs. A particular feeling of pleasure or a material good is valuable, and it is disvaluable *that* the state of affairs that Sam is unhappy obtains. On one view of states of affairs these are the sorts of things which contain properties and which either obtain or do not obtain. Then a state of affairs which obtains is a fact. (According to an alternative view a fact is just a true proposition.) Some philosophers think that the *only* bearers of value properties are obtaining states of affairs, that is, facts (Lemos 1994: 20–31). One argument to this conclusion begins with the claim that whenever value seems to be exemplified by an object, it is the exemplification of some non-axiological property by the object which makes it the case that value is exemplified. Then, the argument goes, what is valuable is the fact that an object exemplifies some non-axiological property: the fact that Sam exemplifies the property of feeling pain is what is disvaluable, not his feeling pain. To evaluate this claim we need to look in more detail at the theory of properties and at the connexion between axiological and non-axiological properties. But we may already note the apparent implausibility of the view that only facts can be the bearers of some ethical and many aesthetic value-properties.

Suppose Sam is ugly, and that what makes Sam ugly is certain features of his face. Is the fact that Sam exemplifies these features ugly? It is disvaluable, has a negative value, but is clearly not ugly. Facts, unlike objects, are never ugly or beautiful or graceful. Consider the ethical property of being evil and its opposite, (ethical) goodness. In many philosophical and non-philosophical traditions the bearers of these two properties are said to be persons. Of course, if a person is evil he is evil because of certain properties he has. But it is the person who is evil. If Sam is evil and evil because of a lifetime of cruelty, then it is certainly a bad thing that he has lived the way he has, but this fact is not evil.

Value properties and natural properties

What is the relation between value-properties and non-normative properties? Natural properties are one type of non-normative property. But what is a natural property? The properties appealed to by the best natural science is a popular answer. It is a striking fact that textbooks of cosmology and geology never need to ascribe value properties to anything. But Max Weber's famous assertion that the sciences are by nature value-free has been challenged (Putnam 2002). Poincaré thought that elegance was part and parcel of mathematics. Boltzmann remarked that elegance was a matter he preferred to leave to his tailor. The historian, it is sometimes claimed, has to evaluate. Psychologists and sociologists certainly ascribe evaluations to people. But such ascriptions do not commit one to the claim that anything has a value.

One distinction between value properties and natural properties has to do with what we might call the ontological status of these properties. One view of the ontological status of properties has it that properties are bearer-specific. On this view, if Sam is sad and Mary is sad, then Sam's property of being sad is numerically distinct from Mary's property of being sad. According to the main rival view, if Sam is sad and Mary is sad, then there is one property of being sad which each of them exemplifies. In other words, the property of being sad is not bearer-specific. (Bearer-specific properties are sometimes called "particularised properties" or "tropes" (see Chapter 28, "Particulars").) Friends of bearer-specific properties sometimes claim that these are parts of their bearers. Friends of the view that properties are not bearer-specific sometimes call them "universals."

There is a third view – *some* properties are bearer-specific and *some* are not. For example, a philosopher might think that psychological properties are bearer-specific but that the properties of numbers are not bearer-specific. Another example of the third view about the ontological status of properties is the claim that natural properties but not value-properties are bearer-specific. In one of the earliest and most influential contributions to twentieth century value-theory, G. E. Moore writes as follows:

> Can we imagine "good" as existing by itself in time, and not merely as a property of some natural object? For myself, I cannot so imagine it, whereas with the greater number of properties of objects – those which I call the natural properties – their existence does seem to me to be independent of the existence of those objects. They are, in fact, rather *parts of which the object is made up* than *mere predicates which attach to it*. If they were all taken away, no object would be left, not even a bare substance; for they are in themselves substantial and give to the object all the substance that it has. But this is not so with good (Moore 1966: 41; my italics)

Hochberg argues that Moore, in this passage and elsewhere, is thinking of natural properties as bearer-specific particulars which constitute their natural bearers, and of value properties as universals: "Goodness would not then be construed in terms of simple particulars like *this yellowness*. Rather, goodness is a *bona fide* universal. This may be the simple but striking difference between natural and non-natural properties. *Only nonnatural properties are universals*" (Hochberg 1969: 99).

That there is a gap between natural properties and value-properties is one of a series of claims made by Hume about the relation between natural and normative properties. Hume argues that we cannot deduce from matters of fact that some action is vicious or that one ought to do something (Hume, *Treatise*, Bk 3, §1, para. 1). Similarly, he says, it does not follow from the fact that an object has certain natural, spatial properties that it is beautiful.

Does the exemplification of natural properties imply that value-properties are exemplified? A large family of affirmative answers to this question makes extensive use of the relations of identity, reduction and supervenience, each of which has been understood in different ways (Jackson 1998). Thus it is sometimes argued that value-properties just are natural properties or relations, that, e.g., to be valuable is just to be the object of positive emotions and desires (which are taken to be natural properties and relations). Metaphysicians appeal to identity, supervenience and reduction, not only to specify the relation between natural properties and normative properties, but also to understand the relation between natural or physical properties, on the one hand, and psychological properties or colour properties, on the other hand (see Chapter 49, "Supervenience, Reductionism and Emergence"). But there are two accounts of the relation between natural properties and normative properties which are *specific* to these two families of properties. The first is the theory of *normative necessity*, the second is an account of value called "*neo-sentimentalism*."

To understand the first theory it is useful to consider one way of unpacking the intuition that there is a large gap between natural properties and value-properties. Suppose someone knows all the natural e.g. neurophysiological facts about feelings of pleasure and pain, knows everything there is to know about the nature of pleasure and pain. Does he thereby know that pain is a bad thing and pleasure a good thing? Is it part of the nature of pain to be a bad thing? Suppose someone knows all the natural facts about what goes on when x deliberately inflicts pain on y for fun. Does he thereby know that actions of this kind are evil? To give a negative answer to these and similar questions is to accept that it is not part of the nature of any natural object to exemplify any value-property. But Socrates necessarily exemplifies the property of being a man in virtue of his essence or identity. And whatever is coloured is necessarily extended in virtue of the nature of colour. Necessity which flows from essence in this way is what Kit Fine calls *metaphysical necessity* (Fine 1994).

If the exemplification of natural properties does not metaphysically necessitate the exemplification of value properties, one possibility is that natural and normative properties are connected by a distinct type of necessitation. According to Fine (2005) normative necessity does this job. Normative necessity is not rooted in the natures or essences of natural or any other objects. It is a type of *de dicto* necessity, unlike metaphysical necessity, which is *de re*. Friends of normative necessity include Sören Halldén (1954: Ch. 6), Husserl and Moore (Moore 1922). Moore's distinction between two types of necessity is the direct descendant of his distinction, described above, between the exemplification of value-properties and the inherence of natural properties (Hochberg 1969: 124).

Fine gives different examples of normative necessity from the family of normative properties: the badness of pain; the wrongness of war, if the pacifist is right; the connexion between making a promise and being obliged to keep it. Another possible example is one connexion between means and ends. Suppose x wants to F and only G-ing will ensure that Fx. Does it follow that x ought to want to G? If so, then it is the non-normative facts about x's desires and options which normatively necessitate the fact that x ought to want to G.

Are these examples equally plausible examples of normative necessity? It is sometimes claimed that if x promises to F, then he is obliged or bound to F in virtue of the nature of promises. But then the necessitation is metaphysical, not normative. Even if the fullest grasp of the nature of pain does not involve the information that is a bad thing, surely one who grasps what it is to be a promise must grasp that to promise is to incur an obligation. Perhaps the difference, if there is one, between the pain-badness case and the promise-obligation case is due to the fact that pain is a natural, psychological item, whereas promises belong to the category of social objects. For on some views of social objects, these have "deontic powers" built into them. Perhaps, too, the view that the promise–obligation connexion is an example of normative necessity overlooks the distinction between obligations and ethical duties. The obligations created by promises are not ethical duties for such obligations, unlike ethical duties, can be transferred from one person to another.

Suppose we grant that exemplification of natural properties normatively necessitates the exemplification of value-properties and so does this without any help from the essence of what exemplifies the natural properties or from the essence of these properties. What sort of connection, we might then ask, holds between properties *within* the normative sphere? Perhaps metaphysical necessitation is all we need once we have, so to speak, crossed the gap between natural facts and values with the help of normative necessity. If values are the most fundamental type of normative property, then perhaps war is wrong in virtue of its disvalue. Perhaps the ethical duty to keep one's promises holds in virtue of the nature of the obligations incurred by promising. Here are examples of what such a view might entail for three claims often made about connexions within the normative sphere. (1) If pro-attitudes towards what is valuable (admiration of courage) are themselves valuable, then this is the case in virtue of the nature of the pro-attitudes and of the values of the objects of these attitudes. (2) The utilitarian-consequentialist claim that what makes an action right is the value of the happiness or well-being produced by the consequences of this action should be understood to claim that rightness is metaphysically necessitated by psychological states and their values in virtue of the nature of these states and of their values. (3) We can also give a more precise formulation of a choice noted above – the choice between the view that values ground *oughts*, if anything does, and the view that *oughts* ground values, if anything does. The first view should add that values ground oughts in virtue of the nature of values. The second view should add that oughts ground values in virtue of the nature of *ought*. Which of the two views should be preferred? Consider the shamefulness (injustice) of some state of affairs. It seems plausible to say that such a state of affairs ought not to obtain because it is shameful (unjust) and that this is the case because of the nature of shamefulness (injustice).

The *second* account of the relation between natural properties and normative properties which is specific to these two families of properties is a popular theory of value which goes back to Brentano and Herbart and is now often called "the buck-passing theory" or "neo-sentimentalism": for an object to be valuable is just for it to be the case that some affective pro-attitude towards the object and its non-axiological properties is justified or appropriate (Scanlon 1998; Mulligan 1998; Rabinowicz and Rønnow-Rasmussen 2004; Dancy 2005; d'Arms and Jacobsen 2006). Neo-sentimentalism is not always understood as an account of the metaphysics of value. But if we do so understand it, then the value of an object is analysed in terms of (a) the non-axiological properties of the object; (b) psychological properties and relations; and (c) justification. But justification is often held to be at least partially constituted by deontic properties. For example, one might think that for x to have a reason to F is for it to be the case that he *may* F, that this is permitted. But then the neo-sentimentalist analysis of value avoids circularity only if deontic norms and values differ in nature. And the analysis is committed to the claim that deontic norms are more fundamental than values.

Values and formal properties

We noted that "oughts" can take both sentences (to make sentences) and predicates (to make predicates). In the former case, "ought," or more precisely "It ought to be the case that," is a functor. Functorial expressions express formal concepts. One part of logic, deontic logic, studies the relations between the deontic functors. Similarly, as we have seen, there are axiological functors, thin:

- It is valuable that p
- It is more valuable that p than that q
- It is more valuable for x that p than that q,

and thick,

- It is just/unjust/shameful/sad/unfortunate/ ... that p

Suppose that to each axiological functor there corresponds an axiological property. If the bearers of value are always states of affairs, then value properties are always formal properties. Although functoriality is sufficient for formality, it is not necessary. The property of being a whole and the relation of numerical difference are formal but not functorial. Thus if some bearers of value (for example, as suggested above, the bearers of ethical and aesthetic values) are objects, it might be the case that the non-functorial value properties of such objects are formal properties.

What is the relation between thin and thick value properties? One tempting view is that the thick values of facts can be resolved into thin values together with non-normative properties. A similar claim can be made about the thick value properties of objects. Let us consider the latter claim first. The shamefulness of a deed might be understood as made up of its disvalue and various natural properties of the deed or its being such that it tends to trigger shame reactions. Similarly, the injustice of an action might be broken down into its disvalue and its being a case in which equally needy people are treated unequally or its being such that it tends to trigger reactions of indignation. Whether or not one thinks that views of this type are correct for some or all thick value properties of objects, there is some reason for thinking that they cannot work for thick value properties of states of affairs. States of affairs have no natural properties. Their only properties are formal: they obtain, they do not obtain, they are possible, probable and so on. Thus if we want to decompose the thick value of a fact into a thin value and something else the latter should not be any property but a relation, for example, an intentional relation. We might say that the shamefulness of a fact consists in its being disvaluable and its tendency to trigger shame. And we might say of the injustice of a situation that it consists in its disvalue and its tendency to trigger indignation. One objection to this suggestion comes from the philosophy of emotions: shame cannot contribute to determining what shamefulness is, for shame is a reaction to (apparent) shamefulness; indignation cannot contribute to determining what injustice is, for indignation is a reaction to (apparent) injustice.

The assumption that axiological functors correspond to properties (have properties as their semantic values) may be rejected. Perhaps axiological functors, like the functor of negation ("It is not the case that ..."), have no semantic values. Then if the only bearers of value are facts, axiological nihilism is true. But it is sometimes claimed that, for example, the truth functor ("It is true that ...") expresses a concept and corresponds to a property, the truth property. Perhaps the same is true of axiological functors. Finally, the assumption that the thin property of being disvaluable is always a determinable property may be rejected. Some facts, perhaps the fact that Sam suffers, may be brutely disvaluable, they are not disvaluable in any particular way. But if the disvalue of some facts is not a determinable property we may think that the disvalue of facts is never a determinable property.

If some types of value are formal properties, this has one interesting consequence for naturalism. Let us say that metaphysical naturalism broadly conceived comprehends (a) axiological nihilism; (b) the view that the valuable is part of the natural; and (c) the view that value reduces to or supervenes on the natural. Then the project of naturalising value turns out to be very unlike the project of naturalising the mind (for example *qualia*) or colours and much more like the project of naturalising arithmetic, logical grammar or logic.

References

Dancy, J. (2005) "Should We Pass the Buck?" in T. Rønnow-Rasmussen and M. J. Zimmerman, *Recent Work on Intrinsic Value*, Berlin: Springer, pp. 33–44.

d'Arms, J. and Jacobsen, D. (2006) "Sensibility Theory and Projectivism," in D. Copp (ed.), *Oxford Handbook of Ethical Theory*, Oxford: Oxford University Press, 186–216.

Fine, K. (1994) "Essence and Modality," in J. E. Tombelin, *Philosophical Perspectives*, vol. 8 of *Logic and Language*, Altascadero, CA: Ridgeview, pp. 1–16.

—— (2005) "The Varieties of Necessity," in *Modality and Tense, Philosophical Papers*, Oxford: Clarendon Press, pp. 235–60.

Geach, P. (1991) "Whatever Happened to Deontic Logic?" in *Logic and Ethics*, Dordrecht: Kluwer, pp. 33–48.

Halldén, S. (1954) *Emotive Propositions*, Stockholm: Almqvist & Wiksell.

Hartmann, N. (1932) *Ethics*, trans. S. Coit, London: George Allen & Unwin.

Hochberg, H. (1969) "Moore's Ontology and Nonnatural Properties," in E. Klemke (ed.), *Studies in the Philosophy of G. E. Moore*, Chicago: Quadrangle, pp. 95–127.

Jackson, F. (1998) *From Metaphysics to Ethics: A Defence of Conceptual Analysis*, Oxford: Clarendon Press.

Lemos, N. M. (1994) *Intrinsic Value: Concept and Warrant*, Cambridge: Cambridge University Press.

Mackie, J. (1986) *Ethics: Inventing Right and Wrong*, Harmondsworth: Penguin.

Moore, G. E. (1922) "The Conception of Intrinsic Value," in *Philosophical Studies*, London: Routledge & Kegan Paul, pp. 253–75.

—— (1966) *Principia Ethica*, Cambridge: Cambridge University Press.

Mulligan, K. (1998) "From Appropriate Emotions to Values," *Monist* 84, no. 1: 161–88; special issue, *Secondary Qualities Generalized*, edited by P. Menzies.

Prichard, H. A. (1912) "Does Moral Philosophy Rest on a Mistake?" *Mind*, n.s., 21: 21–37.

Putnam, H. (2002) *The Collapse of the Fact/Value Dichotomy*, Cambridge, MA: Harvard University Press.

Rabinowicz, W. and Rønnow-Rasmussen, T. (2004) "The Strike of the Demon: On Fitting Pro-Attitudes and Value," *Ethics* 114: 391–423.

Scanlon, T. M. (1998) *What We Owe to Each Other*, Cambridge, MA: Harvard University Press.

Scheler, M. (1973) *Formalism and Non-Formal Ethics of Values*, trans. M. Frings and R. Funk, Evanston, IL: Northwestern University Press.

Further reading

An excellent recent anthology is T. Rønnow-Rasmussen and M. J. Zimmerman (eds), *Recent Work on Intrinsic Value* (Berlin: Springer, 2005). Recent good books on value are N. Lemos, *Intrinsic Value: Concept and Warrant* (Cambridge: Cambridge University Press, 1994); Graham Oddie, *Value, Desire and Reality* (Oxford: Oxford University Press, 2005); and M. J. Zimmerman, *The Nature of Intrinsic Value* (Lanham, MD: Rowman & Littlefield, 2001). Six classic or influential texts on values in phenomenology and analytic philosophy are (1) F. Brentano, *The Origin of the Knowledge of Right and Wrong*, trans. R. Chisholm and E. Schneewind (London: Routledge and Kegan Paul, 1969); (2) N. Hartmann, *Ethics*, trans. S. Coit (London: George Allen & Unwin, 1932), with three volumes, vol. 1 being *Moral Phenomena*; and vol. 2 being *Moral Values* (reprint, New Brunswick, NJ: Transaction, 2002–4); (3) G. E. Moore, *Principia Ethica* (Cambridge: Cambridge University Press, 1966); (4) W. D. Ross, *The Right and the Good* (Oxford: Clarendon Press, 1930); (5) M. Scheler, *Formalism and Non-Formal Ethics of Values*, trans. M. Frings and R. Funk (Evanston, IL: Northwestern University Press, 1973); and (6) G. H. von Wright, *The Varieties of Goodness* (London: Routledge & Kegan Paul, 1963). On intrinsic vs. extrinsic value, see M. J. Zimmermann, "Intrinsic vs. Extrinsic Value," in E. N. Zalta (ed.), *The Stanford Encyclopedia of Philosophy* (2007) (available: http://plato.stanford.edu/archives/spr2007/entries/value-intrinsic-extrinsic/); on intrinsic vs. final value, W. Rabinowicz and T. Rønnow-Rasmussen, "A Distinction in Value: Intrinsic and for Its Own Sake," *Proceedings of the Aristotelian Society* 100, no. 1 (2000): 33–51; on axiological parity and axiological (in)comparability, W. Rabinowicz, "Value Relations," *Theoria* 74 (2008): 18–49; and on thin vs. thick normative properties or concepts and their "entanglement," A. W. Moore, "Maxims and Thick Ethical Concepts," *Ratio* 19, no. 2 (2006): 129–47. Two of the more important topics *not* discussed in the entry are organic unity (axiological mereology) and degrees of value. See T. Hurka, "Two Kinds of Organic Unities," *Journal of Ethics* 2 (1998): 299–320; N. Lemos, *Intrinsic Value: Concept and Warrant*, pp. 196–200; and M. J. Zimmerman, "Virtual Intrinsic Value and the Principle of Organic Unities," *Philosophy and Phenomenological Research* 59, no. 3 (1999): 653–66.

Part III

METAPHYSICS AND SCIENCE

INTRODUCTION TO PART III
The study of nature

Robin Le Poidevin

The physical and social sciences raise all manner of philosophical problems. Some are methodological: What counts as a good explanation in the sciences? Some interpretative: Should we view scientific theory as an attempt to describe reality, or rather as an attempt to provide a series of useful fictions? Some epistemological: Insofar as we take science as descriptive of reality, how do we come to know about the unobservable entities or properties it postulates? But science also raises metaphysical problems. In the General Introduction we tried to characterise the difference between science and metaphysics, in terms both of subject matter and method, but we should not exaggerate the difference. There is a connection between them, or rather a series of connections.

One connection is historical: contemporary metaphysics and contemporary science had a common origin in early cosmological speculation, and what became well-developed scientific theories sometimes arose as a response to philosophical problems. One such case is atomism and the problem of change (see Chapter 1, "Presocratic Themes"). A key theme of early Greek philosophy was the paradoxical nature of change, leading some philosophers to deny its existence, thus driving a very large wedge between what experience and what reason told us concerning the nature of reality. As presented by Parmenides, what is problematic about change is that it seems to involve non-being: change is a coming-into-being from what was not. But, first, how do we even conceptualise non-being? What is it that we have in our minds? Second, how is it possible that non-being should give rise to being? The problem, we might note, is not immediately alleviated by distinguishing between, on the one hand, coming into being from nothing at all, and, on the other, changes in the properties of already-existing things. For even that second, "qualitative" change, involves the coming-into-existence of a property, or a state of affairs, that was absent before. The problem of change gave rise to some ingenious solutions, variations on the theme of combination and recombination. The basic idea was that there are permanent and unchanging elements in the composition of the cosmos, and different proportions and arrangements of these elements or components would give rise to different features. In one variant, the components were substances, like earth or water. But in the most sophisticated and influential theory, that of Democritus and Leucippus, all reality consisted of atoms in the void. The atoms themselves were eternal, unchanging and indivisible, but they could be arranged in different ways, and changes in these arrangements (which involved no changes in the existence or properties of the fundamental atoms themselves) would give rise to the changes presented in experience. Thus the only real changes were the relations between unchanging things. This idea, and its later more sophisticated incarnation, has been one of the most fruitful in the history of science. Although initially an abstract solution to a conceptual problem, it could be developed in sufficient detail for it to be put to use in explaining more specific phenomena.

Metaphysics and science also sometimes coincide in terms of their subject matter. It is true that the subject matter of metaphysical inquiry is generally at a more abstract level than the various subjects of the special sciences, but physics, like metaphysics, is concerned with the structure of space and time, cosmology is concerned with the universe as a whole, and psychology is concerned with minds. The list of topics that Aristotle discusses in the *Physics* as the concern of what he calls "the student of nature" captures very well the intersection of interests between science and metaphysics: time, change, place, void, cause and the infinite (and Aristotle's frequent mention of the soul in these discussions shows that the social sciences have not been left out entirely). Moreover, science employs certain fundamental concepts without those concepts necessarily being part of the subject matter of science. A particularly significant example of this is the concept of *law*. Chemistry may appeal to laws governing dissociation in solution, or of bonding, physics to laws of motion, or of energy transfer, biology to laws of inheritance, psychology to laws of associative learning, and so on (though whether talk of law has the same connotations in all these cases is a moot point). But it is not part of the scientist's job to study the notion of lawlikeness: that is a matter for the metaphysician or philosopher of science. The notion of law is one of three closely related concepts that we associate with scientific explanation, the other two being cause and disposition. All three appear to involve modality in some way or another: that is, they are concerned with the necessary and the possible. Laws say how things *must* be (though the sense of "must" here is not the logical "must" of "the conjunction of p and q must make it true that p"); causes are often held to necessitate (though again, in a non-logical sense) their effects, or the chances of those effects; and dispositions determine how things *would* behave in certain circumstances. So closely related are these three concepts, indeed, that we might wonder whether one of them is more fundamental than the others, so that talk of the other two can somehow be reduced to this basic one. Russell, for instance, takes the notion of law to be more fundamental than cause, so much more so, in fact, that he thinks that the notion of cause can be dispensed with altogether: "the reason why physics has ceased to look for causes is that, in fact, there are no such things" (Russell 1953 [1912–13]: 171). From his point of view, it is no loss, since we have no consistent notion of cause in any case. Diametrically opposed to Russell's view is Nancy Cartwright's: taken as universal generalisations, statements of scientific law are in fact false (since there are in real situations too many competing factors for the outcome of a situation to be exactly as the law says it should be). Rather than take law statements to be such generalisations, therefore, it is better to take them as capturing the causal powers of things, the causal contribution objects are disposed to make on the basis of the property mentioned in the statement (Cartwright 1983).

Thus, for Cartwright, causality and dispositions, but not the laws, form part of the bedrock of reality.

There are concepts, then, that we associate with science in general, and these can properly be the subject of metaphysical study. But science has a number of branches, each with its distinctive subject matter. Provided we take science to be attempting to describe reality, these different branches will, if they are successful, provide entirely consistent accounts of the world. But what do we infer from this? Is reality neatly divided into different areas, each studied by a different science, so that nothing said by one science could possibly contradict what is said by another science? Or is it rather (as seems more likely) that the sciences are often describing the same things, but from different angles, or at different levels of analysis? This second inference can in turn be taken in two ways: either the different sciences study distinct and unconnected properties of the same things, or the properties studied by one science may in some sense be constituted by the properties of another science. The second of these suggests a hierarchy of the sciences: at the bottom we have the science that studies the most fundamental entities and their properties (Democritean atoms, perhaps, or quarks), immediately above this we have the simplest non-fundamental entities and their properties (molecules, chemical processes), above this we have more complex systems (living things, genes) and at some point we reach the point a little lower than the angels (ourselves, and our conscious states). We can present this hierarchical arrangement in different ways. One way would be to take the laws of, say, biology, to be deducible from those of physics – deducible in principle, that is: in other words if we knew enough and had unlimited information-processing capacities. Alternatively, and more appropriately if one does not take law to be a fundamental notion, one might talk, as we did above, of the properties studied by one science as somehow constituted by those of a more fundamental science. But what is the exact nature of this relationship?

A key notion, which had its origins in moral philosophy, but which came to be used in the philosophy of mind in the 1970s and 1980s, and which is now being applied quite generally, is that of *supervenience*. Mental, social, chemical properties are sometimes said to supervene on physical ones. Supervenience is not, we gather, quite like any other relation: it is not identity, it is not composition, it is not mere necessary covariance. Is it then a new relation altogether? Or is it, in fact, just an umbrella term covering a disjunction of these relations? Whatever it is, many (though by no means all) philosophers take it to involve dependence of some kind: the supervenient properties depend upon, but do not determine, the subvenient ones. And many (though not all) philosophers take it to be in some sense a modal concept. Whatever else it is, it is certainly a very controversial relation, and it provides another instance of the way in which reflection on the sciences leads us to metaphysics.

A generation ago, it was a widely held assumption amongst philosophers that this hierarchical picture of the sciences was essentially correct, and that physics was the most fundamental science. This, in turn, was sometimes thought to imply that the other sciences did not raise any philosophical (and certainly no ontological) problems not already raised by physics. Consider this exchange between Hilary Putnam and Bryan Magee in the 1970s:

MAGEE: Are not philosophers of science open to the charge of being too physics-blinkered, and in particular of having paid too little attention to biology?

PUTNAM: Perhaps I can defend us against those charges by arguing that although theories in biology are of great scientific importance – Crick and Watson on the role of DNA in cell reproduction, Darwin's theory of evolution, and so on – they don't, by and large, pose important methodological problems that don't arise in physical science. I'm not sure you are going to agree with me.

MAGEE: I'm not. (Magee 1978: 235–6)

Although the point was made in terms of methodology, one suspects that it might as well have been made in terms of ontology. Magee's remark was prescient, for doubts about the hierarchical picture have increased, and the result has been the flourishing of philosophy of biology, philosophy of chemistry, "neurophilosophy," and so on, one of the key themes of which is that these sciences have their own ontologies, which deserve to be studied in their own right.

Finally, it is sometimes asserted that science delivers metaphysical results, that is, that particular scientific theories have consequences for metaphysical debate. To take one particularly prominent example, the special theory of relativity has been held to imply the falsity of a certain view of time, namely that time flows and that the present is in some way ontological privileged. Cognitive science has been held to imply that the self is in some sense a construction, not a real entity. And the success of neurophysiological studies of psychological states such as anxiety has been held to imply (or at least strongly suggest) that the mental is reducible to the physical. Thus we may have a process that reverses the historical connection between science and metaphysics: whereas, in the beginning, conceptual problems gave rise to empirical theories, so now empirical theories may give rise to revisions in our conceptual schemes. But against this it could be urged that metaphysics and science are doing quite different things. Metaphysics asks questions that have answers which, if true, are necessarily true. The questions that science asks, in contrast, have answers that are at best contingently true. So how can science resolve or affect metaphysical debate? In reply, it may be pointed out that we should not conflate two kinds of truth (the necessary and the contingent) with two kinds of route to truth (the *a priori* and the *a posteriori*): why should science not provide an *a posteriori* route to necessary truth? As we pointed out in the General Introduction, however, we need to be alive to the conceptual and metaphysical assumptions that inform our interpretation of empirical theory. How much are the metaphysical consequences we derive from a theory due to the metaphysical assumptions we bring to its interpretation? And, before we employ science in the service of revisionary metaphysics, we need to settle the interpretative issue mentioned at the beginning of this Introduction: Should we be realist about science? That is, should we take it as aiming at the correct description of reality? Or should we take an instrumentalist view, and take it as offering us useful models? Instrumentalism about science would appear to allow metaphysics total autonomy – provided, of course, that the considerations in favour of instrumentalism about science do not undermine metaphysics' claims to discern the true structure of reality.

References

Cartwright, Nancy (1983) *How the Laws of Physics Lie*, Oxford: Clarendon Press.

Magee, Bryan (1978) *Men of Ideas*, London: BBC.

Russell, Bertrand (1953 [1912–13]) "On the Notion of Cause," in *Mysticism and Logic*, Harmondsworth: Penguin, 1953, 171–96; originally published in *Proceedings of the Aristotelian Society*.

39

SPACE, ABSOLUTE AND RELATIONAL

Tim Maudlin

The problem

It is unavoidable in fundamental metaphysical disputes that the framing of the issue under discussion is likely to beg the question at hand. So I might begin this essay by saying that the topic is the nature of physical space, but one set of partisans will immediately object that there is no such entity as physical space, and *a fortiori* no nature of it. We must proceed with caution.

Let us therefore begin with the thesis that *the physical world has a spatial aspect*. That is, it is correct to say of some physical objects that they have particular geometrical shapes, and stand in various spatial relations to one another. If we accept this thesis, then two questions immediately arise: first, what *is* (in exact mathematical detail) this spatial structure and, second, what *has* this spatial structure. Various possible answers to the first question are easy to articulate: the spatial structure might be Euclidean, or it might be some non-Euclidean geometry of constant positive or negative curvature, or perhaps a Riemannian geometry of variable curvature. It could be continuous or discrete at a fundamental level. The mathematical elucidation of these various possibilities is a straightforward matter, and falls to the mathematicians rather than to philosophers.

But having the mathematical structures in hand leaves several foundational issues completely open. One question is what it means, exactly, to assert that the physical world has one of these spatial structures rather than another. This sort of question was taken up most extensively in the early twentieth century, with Hans Reichenbach's *Philosophy of Space and Time* (Reichenbach 1958) as *locus classicus*. Reichenbach argued that the attribution of geometrical structure amounts to claims about the observable behavior of certain physical bodies, denominated *rigid bodies*. According to Reichenbach, claims about, for example, the relative sizes of objects are given empirical content (which is to say, for him, given any content at all) only by reference to methods for measuring, and those methods in turn require the identification of rigid bodies. But since the notion of a rigid body is exactly that of a body that does not appreciably change its geometrical shape in normal circumstances, an evident circularity ensues. Reichenbach concluded that the geometrical structure of the world could only be settled together with an identification of rigid bodies (and, with this, propositions about the existence of "universal forces" that equally deform all bodies) as a package deal, it being possible for different packages to yield the same empirical consequences. Choice among these packages would then, according to empiricist criteria of meaning, be something like a matter of convention. That is, according to Reichenbach the physical world *per se* does not have any particular geometrical structure, rather the geometrical structure is just one element of a collection of propositions/definitions/conventions that face the tribunal of experience as a corporate body. So one strand of the logical empiricism of the early twentieth century held that the geometrical structure of the world is partly a matter of convention rather than an "objective" fact.

This line of thought seems to have largely evaporated nowadays, together with the empiricist criterion of meaning. The physical systems called "rigid bodies" (or, in the case of temporal structure, "clocks") do not really play any privileged role in modern physics, nor is it any longer thought that the meaning of all physical terms needs to be reduced to claims about the immediately observable properties of macroscopic objects. No physical system is *stipulated* to be rigid, or to be a good clock. In fact, no physical system is thought to be perfectly rigid or a perfectly good clock. Rather, all physical systems are treated as subject to the same laws of physics, and measuring sticks and clocks ought to be subject to the same physical analysis in terms of their microscopic physical components as all other composite objects. But the laws governing the microscopic parts – the fundamental laws of physics – are themselves specified in spatiotemporal terms. So contemporary approaches to the nature of space have turned from the analysis of clocks and rods to the analysis of fundamental laws: what sort of spatial structure is implied by the fundamental physical laws, and what is the status of this structure?

Already in the last paragraph, though, we can see an embarrassment for our topic. For modern physics – most obviously the theory of relativity but, as we will see, even Newtonian mechanics – does not postulate pure *spatial* structure so much as *spatiotemporal* structure to the physical world. In order that physics be brought to bear, we need to consider both time and space, not space alone. Indeed, in a straightforward sense the theory of relativity denies that there is any such thing as "the spatial aspect of the physical world." And given the way we initially exposited our topic, that would mean that, strictly speaking, according to relativity there is no subject matter for the analysis of the nature of space to address! (Even in the old-style Reichenbachian approach, it is essential to consider what happens when one *moves a measuring rod from one place to another*, or *sets a measuring rod in motion*, and these questions involve time as much as space.)

So a metaphysical treatment of space without time is really not possible, and anyone interested in "the nature of space" should begin by studying the theory of Relativity. But since this article in meant to be about space alone, and since Relativity will be treated elsewhere in this volume (Hawley, this volume), we will continue as best we can, making the appropriate *caveats*.

Newton and Leibniz

The traditional absolute-vs.-relational debate about the nature of space derives from the correspondence between Leibniz and Samuel Clarke (Alexander 1984). In the course of the correspondence, the issue arises whether Newton's philosophy respects Leibniz's principle of sufficient reason. Clarke asserts that it does, but that the relevant sufficient reason may sometimes be the mere will of God. As an example, Clarke notes that according to Newton's physics God would have had to make a choice about exactly how to locate the material universe in Absolute Space, and that such a decision could not be based on the intrinsic moral superiority of one way of locating it over another. That is, according to Newton an empty, infinite Euclidean space existed before the existence of any matter, and when God decided to create the material universe he made an essentially arbitrary choice among the infinitude of ways he could situate and orient the matter in this infinite space. The example of two possible material universes that differ only with respect to the location of the matter in the space (all relations among corresponding material elements being identical) has come to be known as a *Leibniz shift*, although it was Clarke who raised the example as a criticism of Leibniz's understanding of sufficient reason.

Leibniz, in a classic argumentative reversal, turns Clarke's own example against Newton. God, according to Leibniz, is so constrained by the principle of sufficient reason that he would be incapable of making an arbitrary choice between morally equivalent possibilities. Since the mere location and orientation of matter in Absolute Space would make no *moral* difference (neither of these possibilities is *better* than the other), God could not have created the world if creating it required such a choice. Hence, according to Leibniz, the existence of the material world refutes Newton's postulation of an Absolute Space that can exist independently of matter.

The question at issue here is not what the spatial structure of the world *is* but rather what that spatial structure *inheres in*. Newton and Leibniz agree that the relevant spatial structure is given by Euclidean geometry, but they disagree about what *has* that spatial structure. For Newton, it is the structure of Absolute Space, an entity distinct from material bodies. Material bodies stand in spatial relations to one another, but only in virtue of being located in regions of Absolute Space that bear exactly those spatial relations. Due to the symmetries of Euclidean geometry, different dispositions of matter in Absolute Space can exhibit identical spatial relations among corresponding pieces of matter. It is among these various distinct possibilities that God must choose.

Since Leibniz denies God the ability to make such a choice, he must deny that there are really distinct possibilities here. This is accomplished by a particular sort of relational analysis of spatial structure: the spatial aspect of the world is *nothing but* the set of spatial relations among material bodies. Since Leibniz-shifted worlds agree about all the spatial relations *among the bodies* (they disagree only about where the bodies are situated in Absolute Space), given Leibniz's account they do not really disagree about spatial structure at all. The supposed Leibniz-shifted distribution of matter in Absolute Space is not a distinct possibility from the unshifted situation, so God need not choose between them.

In addition to the appeal to the principle of sufficient reason, Leibniz makes an independent appeal to the principle of identity of indiscernibles. If we grant Absolute Space, then in some sense the shifted and unshifted distributions of matter would "look the same": the *qualitative appearance* of these worlds to their inhabitants would be identical. Leibniz concludes that we could therefore not have distinct ideas of these two possibilities, apparently on the thesis that the content of an idea must be specified in some qualitative way. It is not merely that a distinct, Leibniz-shifted distribution of matter is not *possible* (as would follow from his account of spatial structure) but that it is not *thinkable*.

How do these arguments stand up to scrutiny? One should first note that the whole discussion takes place under the assumption that the spatial structure is Euclidean: Euclidean space, being homogenous and isotropic, would admit of Leibniz shifts that move all the matter (by rotation or translation) while keeping the relative distances between objects the same. Were Newton or Leibniz to postulate a spatial structure that lacked the appropriate symmetries, it is unclear that the arguments could be formulated in the first place. So these arguments about what *has* the spatial structure are not entirely independent of questions about what the spatial structure *is*.

Second, neither the principle of sufficient reason nor the principle of identity of indiscernibles is known to be true. The apparently random behavior of, for example, atomic decay casts doubt on the former, whose use here requires dubious theological hypotheses in any case. The principle of identity of indiscernibles also lacks justification. And in this particular case, it seems clearly inapplicable. Supposing Newtonian Absolute Space to exist, and supposing it to have been *possible* for matter to have been distributed differently from the way it actually is in Absolute Space (by, say, everything being shifted 3 meters to the north), still these possibilities are not indiscernible: indeed, we would know which of the two obtains! So in whatever sense these possibilities are qualitatively identical, it is not a sense that would create some unknowable physical fact.

Since neither of Leibniz's arguments against Absolute Space establishes the untenability of Newton's theory, we still have on the table two radically different alternative accounts of the ontology that supports the spatial structure of the universe. According to Leibniz, the spatial aspect of the world is nothing but a set of relations among material bodies, so if there were no material bodies there would be no spatial facts at all. According to Newton, spatial structure is, in the first instance, the structure of Absolute Space, and hence exists independently of material bodies.

Newton's Scholium

Newton's arguments in favor of Absolute Space are found in the Scholium to Definition VII in the *Principia* (Newton 1962: 6–12). Newton there distinguishes true, absolute space, time and motion from their merely relative cousins. There are, of course, relative spatial relations among material bodies, relations between events and material clocks, and relative motions of things, but for Newton all of these are derivative matters. Just as there is Absolute Space, whose nonmaterial parts stand in geometrical relations to one another, so there is Absolute Time, which passes independently of the motions of material clocks. Newton's Absolute Space itself persists through time, so that Absolute Motion can be defined in terms of a body's changing location in Absolute Space.

Once again, we have found ourselves embroiled in questions not just of spatial structure but of spatiotemporal structure: motion, for Newton, involves both space and time. And so again we have drifted away from our announced topic – space – into the wider arena of space and time together. This widening of scope is unavoidable, since Newton's argument is directly an argument in favor of Absolute Motion and only derivatively (via the definition of Absolute Motion) for Absolute Space. The argument makes use of a bucket filled with water.

Newton points out that there are observable effects of certain kinds of motion: when the water in a bucket *spins* it climbs the sides of the bucket, forming a concave surface, and when it does not spin the surface is flat. So there is a real, verifiable physical distinction between these two states. But the relevant distinction does not coincide with the relative motion of the water and the bucket: sometimes the surface is flat when the water and bucket are at relative rest and sometime it is concave. Newton's explanation is the natural one: in the former case both the water and the bucket are not spinning, and in the latter case both are. But spinning *relative to what*? Not, evidently, to each other, or to any material object in their immediate environment. Newton suggests that the relevant spinning – the spinning that has observable effects – must be Absolute Spinning, a change of location in Absolute Space.

There have been two famous objections to Newton's inference. One, associated with Mach, observes that the phenomena still might be explained by appeal only to the relative motion of bodies: not the relative motion of the water to the bucket, or the water to the room, or even the water to the Earth (the bulging of the Earth at the equator and the Coriolis effect show that the Earth is, in some physically significant sense, spinning) but perhaps the relative motion of the water to the *fixed stars*. For whenever the surface of the water is concave it is spinning relative to the fixed stars: who's to say that it is not that relative motion which accounts for the effect?

The short answer to this objection is that it is merely the logical outline of a possible explanation of the effect, not an actual explanation. Newton's theory really does account for the phenomenon, while Mach points out only that all alternative theories have not been ruled out. But Mach does not offer such a theory, nor have any subsequent physical theories supported his conjecture. Even in general relativity there is a distinction between rotating and non-rotating bodies that makes no mention of the fixed stars, or of any material bodies relative to which the motion is defined.

The second objection is much more serious. It notes that the phenomenon Newton discusses does not depend on the Absolute Motion of the bucket (as Newton has defined it) but only on its Absolute Acceleration. Newton's law of motion is $F = mA$, and what the bucket demonstrates is that given this law the evident presence of forces indicates the (not immediately evident) presence of acceleration. But this gets us to Absolute Space only via a series of further inferences: acceleration is change in velocity and velocity is change of place, so Absolute Acceleration implies Absolute Velocity implies Absolute Place. This chain is a bit embarrassing for Newton because although his theory implies observable effects of acceleration, it also implies *no* observable effects of

Absolute Velocity: no mechanical experiment could indicate the Absolute Velocity of an inertially moving laboratory.

This tension has been resolved in the modern approach to space-time structure. If we think of the universe throughout its whole history as a four-dimensional object, then persisting bodies trace out trajectories (world lines) in this four-dimensional manifold. From this perspective, the acceleration of a body corresponds to a bending of its world line, and Newton's law of inertia just says that a body subject to no forces traces out a straight trajectory in space-time. The First and Second Laws together get rewritten, schematically, as $F = m\text{BEND}$, where "BEND" signifies a mathematical quantity that measures the curving of the body's trajectory. The definition of this quantity, as it turns out, does not require the identification of anything like Absolute Velocity or Absolute Place: it only requires that the spatiotemporal structure be rich enough to distinguish straight from curved trajectories, and to quantify the curvature. Newton postulated more spatiotemporal structure than he needed to make sense of his dynamical laws.

Details of various possible spatiotemporal structures and the physics they support can be found in Earman (1989: 27–40) and Sklar (1976: 194–210). Without entering into details, we can see that the question has again drifted from what has the spatiotemporal structure to what is the spatiotemporal structure. Although Newton's rotating bucket experiment is purported to refute a position like Leibniz's, according to which spatiotemporal structure is just a matter of relations among bodies, it does not in fact make direct contact with that issue at all. If Leibniz is unable to account for the phenomena, it is not because he locates the spatiotemporal structure in material bodies, but because the structure he postulates is not strong enough to do the physical work. Newton succeeds not because his Absolute Space is independent of matter, but rather because the individual points of his Absolute Space are postulated to persist through time, thereby defining a spatiotemporal structure rich enough to define his laws of motion. But, as we have seen, this structure is even richer than he needs: the laws of motion can be defined with less structure, so the persistence of points of space through time is physically otiose.

Are there any arguments that address the relational/absolute controversy directly, and do not devolve into questions about the mathematical particulars of the spatiotemporal structure?

The plenum

Even if a Relationist and an Absolutist settle on the same sort of spatiotemporal structure, they may end up with different explanatory resources. If the material contents of the world intuitively form a plenum, with no "vacuum," then it becomes hard to see how *physical* considerations could become relevant. The Absolutist may postulate a certain spatiotemporal structure of space–time itself, while the Relationist postulates the very same spatiotemporal relations among parts of matter, but if every supposed location in the Absolutist space–time contains some matter, then the difference in locutions will be hard to make out. Or rather, the Relationist and Absolutist may disagree about the class of distinct physical *possibilities* (the Absolutist will maintain that there is a distinct Leibniz-shifted physical possibility, while the Relationist denies this), it is not clear that this dispute about possibilities will have any bearing on the physical explanation of the actual world.

If the material world is not a plenum, though, the situation is quite different. Both the Relationist and the Absolutist must give truth conditions to the claim that there is a vacuum in some location: for the Absolutist, it means that there is a part of absolute space that is empty of all matter, while for the Relationist it means that there are certain pieces of matter such that *there is nothing at all* that bears a particular set of spatial relation to them. But the Relationist's lack of anything at all to quantify over "in the vacuum" restricts the sorts of analyses of spatial notions he or she has available.

Until now, we have not even asked the most fundamental question of both the Absolutist and the Relationist: what are the most basic spatial (or spatiotemporal) structures? It is often presumed that the fundamental spatial structure (whether between bodies or parts of absolute space) is a distance relation: any two elements have some distance between them, and the whole geometry is nothing but the set of these distances. But geometrical structure is not, in fact, specified in such a way. The mathematical object called a "metric" does not directly specify the distance between points: it rather allows one to integrate along a continuous curve to get a *path length*. And from these path lengths, distances can be defined: the spatial distance between two points is the minimal length of a continuous path that connects them.

The definition of distance in terms of path length has nontrivial consequences. Consider, for example, the triangle inequality: given any three points, the sum of the distances between two pairs of points is greater than or equal to the distance between the last pair. This inequality is an analytical consequence of the definition of distance given above: since conjoining a path from A to B with a path from B to C yields a path from A to C, and since the length of such a conjoined path is just the sum of the lengths of the paths conjoined, the length of the minimal path from A to C cannot be longer than the sum of the length of the minimal path from A to B with the length of the minimal path from B to C. If one were to start with *distance* as the primitive notion rather than *path length*, no such derivation of the Triangle Inequality would be forthcoming. Indeed, the physicist Julian Barbour, who has pursued relational formulations of physics with the greatest vigor, is reduced to postulating the Triangle Inequality (and an infinitude of other, more complex inequalities) as unexplained constraints on the distances among objects (Barbour 1999: 42; see also Maudlin 1993).

Once again the advantage that accrues to the Absolutist here does not derive from absolutism *per se*. Rather, it is because the Absolutist automatically has a plenum. Even if matter is only scattered in space, for the Absolutist all of the various continuous paths that connect a pair of points *exist* and have a determinate length. The Relationist, by contrast, can give truth conditions for the claim "there is a vacuum," but has no points in the vacuum or continuous paths running through the vacuum to quantify over. This is why a Relationist who admits the possibility of a vacuum must take the distance relation as primitive rather than derived.

But the notion of a vacuum and the corresponding notion of a plenum are only as clear as the notion of matter itself. For the Absolutist, there is a vacuum if there is space devoid of all matter, for the Relationist if there fails to be anything at all that bears certain geometrical relations to existent material bodies. But if we are unsure what constitutes a material body in the first place, then we will be unsure whether any vacuum exists. We have no problems in a Democritean physics of the Full and the Empty, but if a gravitational field or an electromagnetic field or a quantum field counts as matter, then a vacuum may not be even physically possible. In this case, the Relationist finds himself on even ground with the Absolutist again, able to replicate the Absolutist definitions of distance in terms of path length. And we are inclined to wonder, at this point, whether there is any contentful dispute between the two sides.

The hole argument

The most recent wrinkle in the absolute/relational debate is an argument inspired by some remarks of Einstein and formalized by John Earman and John Norton that goes by the name "the hole argument" (Earman and Norton 1987). The argument aims to show that an Absolutist (or, in alternative terminology a Substantivalist) about space–time will necessarily be committed to radical indeterminism in nature, at least if the laws of physics take a common mathematical form.

The hole argument applies only to space–time structure: there is no obvious form that concerns spatial structure alone. The "hole" is a delimited region of space–time, and the argument is intended to show that the Substantivalist must accept that for any physically possible state of the universe there exists an alternative, distinct state of affairs that perfectly agrees with the first outside of the hole, but disagrees with it inside. If true, then indeterminism follows: specifying the complete physical state of the world outside the hole, and the laws of nature, does not suffice to determine the exact state inside the hole.

The indeterminism at issue does not involve any *observable* property: if one accepts that different states inside the hole are possible, no observation or experiment would reveal which one was realized. Rather, the indeterminism involves only in which particular part of space–time various observable events occur. Since the particular parts are not *per se* observable, the different possibilities will be qualitatively identical. So this is not the indeterminism of quantum theory or dice tossing, where one can describe beforehand the various possible outcomes of an experiment, and can verify afterwards which actually occurred. Indeed, no one outside the hole could have the linguistic resources to specify various distinct possibilities inside the hole, and even if they could, people inside the hole could not determine which of the possibilities obtains. So this would be indeterminism of a particularly ghostly sort.

The hole argument depends on conceptualizing the world as a set of fields on a manifold called "space–time." The fields would include electromagnetic fields, matter fields, etc., and also *the metric field that specifies the spatiotemporal structure itself*. It will help to visualize a particular solution of the fundamental equations of physics as these fields painted on to an elastic sheet. The laws of physics themselves specify only *how the various fields are related to one another at each point (or infinitesimally small region) in the manifold*.

427

Take the elastic sheet and choose a closed region (the "hole"). Tack the edges of the hole down so that part of the sheet cannot move. Next, stretch the sheet (with the painted fields) inside the hole in some way. Looked at from above, the painted fields will now look different inside, and just the same outside. Finally, release the elastic sheet so it returns to its original shape *and paint on to this original shape the fields as they looked when the sheet was stretched*. The region inside the hole now has two images on it: the original and the distorted copy. These two images will evidently disagree about what the value of the "fields" are at particular points on the sheet inside the hole, although they agree completely outside.

Now if the laws of nature constrain only the relations of the fields at each point, then if one of these images satisfies the laws then the other will, since every point in one image has a corresponding point in the other where the field relations are identical. So there appear to be two distinct solutions to the laws of nature that agree outside the hole but disagree inside: radical indeterminism. Earman suggests that the way out of this indeterminism is to *deny the physical reality of the elastic sheet*, which is supposed to correspond to denying substantivalism about space–time. It is not evident what the resulting positive doctrine about spatiotemporal structure would be, and in particular whether it would be a recognizable form of relationism.

The exact form of the hole argument is rather complex, and there are several points at which it can be attacked. It turns on the claim that a particular ontological account of spatiotemporal structure commits one to specific claims about a mathematical construct (the "distorted" image): that it represents a situation that is both metaphysically possible and non-actual. Jeremy Butterfield has argued, using counterpart theory, that both mathematical models represent the same physical situation, not alternatives (Butterfield 1989), and I have argued that if the spatiotemporal structure of space–time is metaphysically essential to its parts, then one of the mathematical models does not represent a metaphysical possibility (Maudlin 1990). Other analyses of the argument can be found in Brighouse (1994), Hoefer (1996), Leeds (1995) and Rynasciewicz (1994). Suffice it to say that since issues of representation, ontology, modality and determinism all intersect in the hole argument, there is considerable fodder for philosophical analysis.

There is, at present, no agreed resolution of the absolute/relational debate. The inevitable extension of the argument to space–time, the obscurity of the physical nature of a "vacuum," and the unclarity of the significance of certain symmetries in the mathematical formalism all conspire to make it hard to even formulate clearly an Absolutist or Relationist version of contemporary physical theory. Given that it is no longer clear exactly what the argument is about, it is hardly surprising that it remains unsettled.

References

Alexander, H. G. (ed.) (1984) *The Leibniz–Clarke Correspondence*, New York: Barnes & Noble.

Barbour, J. (1999) *The End of Time*, Oxford: Oxford University Press.

Brighouse, C. (1994) "Spacetime and Holes," in D. Hull, M. Forbes, and R. M. Burian (eds), *PSA 1994*, vol. 1, East Lansing, MI: Philosophy of Science Association, 117–25.

Butterfield, J. (1989) "The Hole Truth," *British Journal for the Philosophy of Science* 40: 1–28.

Earman, J. (1989) *World Enough and Space–Time*, Cambridge, MA: MIT Press.

Earman, J. and Norton, J. (1987) "What Price Spacetime Substantivalism?" *British Journal for the Philosophy of Science* 38: 515–25.

Hoefer, C. (1996) "The Metaphysics of Spacetime Substantivalism," *Journal of Philosophy* 93: 5–27.

Leeds, S. (1995) "Holes and Determinism: Another Look," *Philosophy of Science* 62: 425–37.

Maudlin, T. (1990) "Substances and Spacetime: What Aristotle Would Have Said to Einstein," *Studies in the History and Philosophy of Science* 21: 531–61.

—— (1993) "Buckets of Water and Waves of Space: Why Spacetime Is Probably a Substance," *Philosophy of Science* 60: 183–203.

Newton, I. (1962) *Principia*, trans. A. Motte; revised by F. Cajori, Berkeley: University of California Press.

Reichenbach, H. (1958) *The Philosophy of Space and Time*, New York: Dover.

Rynasciewicz, R. (1994) "The Lessons of the Hole Argument," *British Journal for the Philosophy of Science* 45: 407–36.

Sklar, L. (1976) *Space, Time, and Spacetime*, Berkeley: University of California Press.

Further reading

J. Barbour, *The End of Time* (Oxford: Oxford University Press, 1999) is the most sustained recent attempt by a physicist to develop a completely relational account of space–time structure. J. Earman, *World Enough and Space–Time* (Cambridge, MA: MIT Press, 1989) is a technically sophisticated examination of the absolute/relational controversy, ending with a presentation of the hole argument; the work focuses on space–time rather than just space. M. Friedman, *Foundations of Space–Time Theories* (Princeton NJ: Princeton University Press, 1983) provides a general discussion of approaches to space–time ontology, with special attention to coordinate-free presentations of the physics (a more mathematically demanding work than Sklar, below). N. Huggett, *Space from Zeno to Einstein* (Cambridge, MA: MIT Press, 1999) contains a collection of classical texts on the nature of space, including Zeno, Newton, Leibniz and Clarke, Kant, Mach and Einstein, with useful commentary by Huggett. M. Jammer, *Concepts of Space* (Cambridge, MA: Harvard University Press, 1954) gives an account of the history of accounts of space from antiquity. A sustained argument against relationism with particular attention to the contingent features space can have that are independent of the material contents of space is found in G. Nerlich, *The Shape of Space* (Cambridge: Cambridge University Press, 1976). L. Sklar, *Space, Time, and Spacetime* (Berkeley: University of California Press, 1976) is the classic overview of both philosophical and mathematical issues surrounding accounts of the nature of space and space–time.

40
INFINITY AND METAPHYSICS
Daniel Nolan

Do space and time have limits, or do they go on infinitely? Are there smallest units of space, or time, or smallest divisions of objects, or can they be divided into infinitely many pieces? How are we to understand the infinities we find in mathematics? Metaphysicians since the Ancient Greeks have been fascinated by these questions and others about infinity.

Let us begin by considering a relatively familiar mathematical infinity. The counting numbers (1, 2, 3 …) go on infinitely: whenever you have such a number, you can always add 1. There is no greatest counting number, so the sequence has no end. When we consider the integers (… −2, −1, 0, 1, 2 …) we can see that this is a sequence that has no greatest member and also no least member – for any integer, no matter how low, you can always *subtract* 1 and get another integer. It is a sequence that is infinite in both directions.

There are some unusual features of these infinite series. One is that a part of the series can be the same size as the whole. Consider the sequence of even counting numbers (2, 4, 6 …) and the series of all counting numbers (1, 2, 3 …). The first, intuitively, only has "half" of the numbers of the second. However, they can be paired off one–one with each other. This is also true of the counting numbers and, say, the prime numbers – there are as many prime numbers as counting numbers. We can even assign a different counting number to each of the integers without leaving any out, if we order the integers in the right way. To illustrate,

Counting:	1	2	3	4	5	6	7 …
Even:	2	4	6	8	10	12	14 …
Primes:	2	3	5	7	11	13	17 …
Integers:	0	−1	1	−2	2	−3	3 …

Infinite collections can be split into non-overlapping infinite sub-collections, for example, by dividing the counting numbers into the odd and even numbers. The whole does not necessarily have more members than a part.

These results are curious, but it is easy to get used to them. Arithmetical infinities are not the only kind of mathematical infinity. In Euclidean geometry, lines (as opposed to line segments) go on in each direction without end, as do planes. Lines can be divided into line segments of greater and greater lengths, without end: and indeed there can be two divisions of a line, each adding up to an infinite length, which do not overlap.

As well as these sorts of infinities in the numbers and in geometry, we are used to infinities "in the small." Just as counting numbers can get larger and larger without end, so can fractions get smaller and smaller without end (just as there is no largest counting number n, there is no smallest fraction $1/n$). Between any two fractions there is another halfway between them, and there are infinitely many fractions between zero and one.

But what about infinities in the physical world? Even if mathematical infinities, of these familiar sorts, are well behaved, should we think the physical world can have those structures? Should we think that real space and time go on infinitely?

Space and time

The first issue of infinity about space and time that occurs to many is the issue about whether space and time extend infinitely. The consensus these days seems to be that this is an issue for cosmologists more than philosophers, though some philosophers still object to the idea that the past even *could* be infinite. (This is connected to the issue of an infinite regress of causes, discussed in the final section.) Of more philosophical interest is the question of whether space and time are infinitely divided: whether there are smaller and smaller regions or durations *ad infinitum*. This issue has been a traditional source of paradox.

Zeno of Elea is famous for a number of paradoxes about space and time, several of which use the infinite divisibility of space and time. Exactly what Zeno's arguments were and what they were intended to achieve remains a matter of controversy, so I will choose versions with more of an eye on illuminating issues of infinity than historical accuracy. Perhaps Zeno's most famous is the paradox of Achilles and the Tortoise. Swift Achilles and the very slow tortoise agree to have a race, and the tortoise is given a head start. Let us suppose the track is 100 metres long, and the tortoise has a 10-metre head start, and let us suppose Achilles travels 10 times faster than the tortoise. By the time Achilles has reached the tortoise's starting point, the tortoise has moved on to a new point (call it p_1). By the time Achilles reaches p_1, the tortoise has advanced again to a new point (p_2). And so on – no matter how many times Achilles reaches one of the ps, he has not yet caught the tortoise. He could only catch the tortoise, it seems, if he could reach the end of this infinite series: but the infinite series *has* no end. So Achilles can never catch up with the tortoise.

Obviously the above reasoning has gone wrong somewhere: fast runners *can* catch tortoises, even when the tortoises have a head start. We can even calculate when Achilles will catch the tortoise if we know their speeds; for example, if Achilles is travelling at 10 metres per second, and the tortoise 1 metre per second, Achilles will catch up with the tortoise after 1.1111111 … seconds. So what went wrong with the reasoning in the previous paragraph?

Zeno himself may have wanted to use the paradox to show that motion was an illusion, which would provide one "solution" to the puzzle. We could try denying that there is the infinite sequence of points p_1, p_2, p_3 and so on, and so deny a crucial assumption in Zeno's argument. But the most popular solution to the puzzle is to allow that, after all, Achilles can pass through the infinitely many p_n points in a finite time. Does that mean that we have to postulate an infinite series with a start and a finish? (Something I imagine Zeno would claim is just a contradiction in terms – a series with first and last members seems *finite*.) In one sense, yes, and in another sense, no. Since the infinity of points are all found in a line in a finite segment of space, we must be able to find a point after all of those points: the point where Achilles is adjacent to the tortoise comes after every point where he has not yet caught the tortoise up. In that sense the space where all the p_n are found has an end. However, we do not need a last p_n: *that* series of points will have no last member – it is just that as the time goes towards 1.11111 … seconds, the p_ns get closer and closer together. So the p_n series has no last member.

Another paradox of motion attributed to Zeno concerns the impossibility of an object starting motion in the first place. (Let me call this the "paradox of the arrow," though names for this paradox vary.) Consider an arrow fired at a target. Before it reaches the target, it must reach halfway. Before that, it must reach a quarter of the way, and before that, an eighth, a sixteenth, etc. Before the arrow can even get halfway to where it needs to go, it needs to travel through an infinite number of points. But that argument did not require us to focus on the target (or on arrows): anything that moves at all to another place would first have to make it to halfway, and before that a quarter … any mover has to complete infinitely many motions before it can get anywhere. So, Zeno concludes, motion is impossible.

One interesting thing about this second paradox is that it concerns an infinite series of points with a clear end (reaching the target, for example), but no beginning: no matter how far back we go towards the arrow's start, there are still midpoints it must reach before it can get any further. There is no first one of these points the arrow can reach – to have moved any distance the arrow must already have passed through many points (infinitely many, in fact). This matches the mathematical structure of the number line. There is no first fraction after zero, for example: pick any rational number to be the "first" and we can always find another one closer to zero by halving it. The application to physical space strikes some people as more troubling: how can an arrow start moving without there being a first place it moves to? But at least on the orthodox conception of space being made up of points at positive distances from each other, there is no such first place.

A third paradox of Zeno's (which I will call the "paradox of plurality") raises an interesting question about what space is like if it has infinitely many parts. Zeno invites us to consider what size the smallest parts are. If they are some positive, finite size, then when we add infinitely many of them together we will get an infinite magnitude. But if they are all of zero size (as points are often conceived of as being), then even adding together infinitely many of them will still give us zero. The first horn of the dilemma may not strike someone as particularly worrying: maybe space *is* infinite in size? The problem that makes it so uncomfortable is that the ordinary view of space has infinitely many points even in a finite region, such as the distance an arrow traverses to hit its target. Even if space as a whole is infinitely large, we do not want to say that the space on a typical archery range is infinitely large! Notice the same problem arises for time – time seems divisible into smaller and smaller intervals, so what are we to say about the smallest intervals, if any?

Perhaps this could motivate us to reject infinitely many parts of space after all. Indeed, some people believe that space is "granular" and only finitely many smallest pieces of space can be found in a space of finite magnitude. Another, slightly subtler response is to say that space has infinitely many parts, but no *smallest* parts – regions get smaller and smaller *ad infinitum*, just as we can find smaller and smaller distances from zero along the number line, but there are no zero-length points underneath. Or perhaps space has only a *potential* infinity of small parts – it *can* be divided smaller and smaller, but there are not already smaller and smaller regions corresponding to such divisions. Each of these alternatives to infinitely many zero-magnitude points will be discussed further below.

There is another answer available to someone who wants to maintain the orthodoxy of a space of points without positive finite size. This relies on the *kind* of infinity of points postulated in contemporary theories of space. According to standard theories of space, space is a *continuum*. It is dense (between any two points there is another) and complete, in a "no-gaps" sense (which has a variety of technical characterisations). Space has a structure like that of the real numbers, rather than just that of the rationals: there are lengths of $\sqrt{2}$ metres and π metres, as well as lengths expressible as ratios of integers.

Surprisingly, while the rational numbers and the real numbers are both infinite, there are strictly speaking more real numbers than rational numbers: the real numbers cannot be put in a one–one correspondence with the rational numbers. There are, in fact, many sizes of infinity in mathematics (infinitely many, in fact!). The size corresponding to the real numbers is often known as *continuum many*, while the size associated with the rationals (which is the same as for the counting numbers) is known as *countably many*.

When adding the sizes of finitely many non-overlapping regions together at once, the obvious thing to do is to assume the resulting larger region has the size which is the sum of the sizes of the smaller regions. A straightforward extension of this procedure covers adding countably many sizes together, and indeed on the standard picture the metric on space is *countably additive*. But it is less straightforward to extend this to the case of "adding" continuum-many regions – it cannot be done as limits of longer and longer finite sequences of addition, for example. When we want to know the size of a region made up of continuum-many distinct smaller regions, we cannot "add" the smaller sizes. Instead, the size of the large region is specified by a *measure* on the smaller regions, not by "addition."

Adolf Grünbaum (Grünbaum 1967) famously pointed out that this gives contemporaries another kind of response to Zeno's paradox of plurality. Zeno claimed that if we put together lots of things of size zero, the resulting size will be zero. But if we take a measure of a set of continuum-many size-zero points, the measure need not be zero. We can *agree* with Zeno that additions of zero (even countably infinite additions) always give zero, and nevertheless hold that a space made up of enough size-zero points is not itself of size zero.

The mathematical tools to make this distinction were not properly clarified until the twentieth century, so it is no surprise that Zeno did not consider this response. Suppose Zeno objected that this was mere mathematical trickery – we are still getting positive magnitude from putting together things of zero magnitude, even if the "putting together" is not addition. How is this any improvement? In response, we could say that the intuition that "putting together zeros" gives you zero is an intuition we have about addition – and we have conceded that addition does work this way. There are coherent models of measure theory that show us another way of "putting together." Of course, that by itself would not show that we can put together spatial points and get non-zero-sized spatial regions; but it does tend to undercut Zeno's argument that we *could not* get regions of non-zero finite size if we started from points.

A host of contemporary puzzles about the infinite divisibility of space and time, and what possibilities there are if actual infinities of objects are possible, have flowered in the second half of the twentieth century. These puzzles often go under the heading of "new Zeno." They include Thomson's Lamp (see the discussion reprinted in Salmon [1970]), Hilbert's Hotel (Gamow 1946), and many other fascinating scenarios introduced by José Benardete (Benardete 1964). Some have thought these raise new problems for the actual infinite (Craig 1979), but many have just drawn the conclusion that actual infinities can be used to generate surprising thought experiments.

Alternatives to continuous space and time

There are a number of alternatives to the view that space and time are made up of infinitely many points. You could believe that space and time are *granular*, and that there are minimum lengths and durations. If there are minimum lengths and times, the arguments of Zeno's given do not get off the ground: there is no guarantee that there will be any "halfway points" for the arrow to pass through, for example. (Consider an arrow that is only three spatial minima away from its target.) While the tortoise will have moved on from some places that it was when Achilles reaches him, there will be no guarantee that the tortoise will have moved on from all of them. (If Achilles moves 10 minima every time the tortoise moves 1, for example, if Achilles starts off 5 minima behind, the tortoise will not have moved when Achilles comes up level.)

Minimum spaces and times do bring with them puzzles of their own, however. Are speeds restricted to certain values, n minima of space per m minima of time? If someone moves 2 spatial minima per minimum of time, do they "jump"? After all, there is no instant of time for them to be in the middle space minimum. Shapes are also puzzling without continuous space. In standard geometry, the ratio of the hypotenuse of a right-angled triangle to the sides is often irrational: for example, when a right-angled triangle has the two sides of 1 metre, the hypotenuse will be $\sqrt{2}$ metres. But in a discrete space, it is hard to see how to get distances like $\sqrt{2}$ metres. Indeed, if we model discrete triangles by drawing a grid, and represent distances by the number of adjacent squares different squares are apart, then we get odd results if we draw a right-angled "triangle" with short sides of e.g. 5 squares long. If we allow squares that touch at a vertex to be adjacent, then the hypotenuse is 5 squares long! And if we insist that squares are adjacent only if they share a side, then the hypotenuse is 10 squares long! A model of space that treats 5 $\sqrt{2}$-metres as being either 5 metres or 10 metres comes with a serious cost. There are more sophisticated models of granular space: Forrest (1995) has an interesting though very technical discussion of a more plausible option.

What if space has smaller and smaller regions in it but it never grounds out in components of zero size (or parts without size at all, if you prefer to treat points as lacking volume altogether)? This picture of space is often called "gunky," connected to "gunk," the technical term for an object such that all of its proper parts have proper parts (i.e. parts other than themselves). The paradox of plurality, as presented, is blocked at the beginning: there are no "smallest parts" of space, on this view. The gunky view of space can allow that space has infinitely many parts of more than zero size, but they only add up to a finite amount because there are not infinitely many *non-overlapping* parts of the same finite size. In 1 metre of space, you can find 10 non-overlapping parts of 10 centimetres, or 100 of 1 centimetre or 1000 of 0.1 centimetre ..., but when you add up non-overlapping parts of the same size, you never get more than 1 metre. Since there are infinitely many parts, the gunk theorist has to agree that the arrow passes through an infinite sequence of distances before it hits the target, and that Achilles must run through infinitely many distances to catch the tortoise. The gunk theorist is a friend of infinity. Gunky space has been less discussed than its main rivals, but one worry about it is discussed under "Infinite-regress arguments," below.

Another option is to say that the infinite divisibility of space is only a "potential infinity." Insisting that infinities in the world are only "potential" is a tradition that goes back to Aristotle, and it is safe to say that this was the dominant tradition in the West until the twentieth century. A "potential infinity" could mean one of two things. The first is that there is, in fact, only a finitude, but it is just that this finite collection *could be increased* or *could be extended*. For example, one way for the counting numbers to be potentially infinite in this way would be if only finitely many of them exist but we can always extend the collection of counting numbers by adding 1. Another way, less connected with us and our adding activities, would be to think that there were only as many numbers as objects but that the highest number *could have been larger*, without finite limit, if extra objects had existed.

The other way to think about potential infinities is to think that there is indeed an infinite collection (regions of space, counting numbers, etc.), but that many members of that collection only have *potential existence*: they are not yet "actualised." For example, an Aristotelian might think that a point only has actual existence when it is a boundary of a real thing (e.g. when it is at the tip of the arrow) – those points at places where boundaries could be, but are not at the moment, could be considered *potential existents*. This version of potential infinities is not very popular today, since most philosophers dislike drawing this sort of distinction between kinds of existence.

Insisting that the divisibility of time or space is only *potentially* infinite is often offered as a solution to Zeno's challenges. It deals with the paradox of plurality: if space is not *made up of* any merely potential parts, either because there aren't any potential parts (on the first view), or they lack the "actual" existence needed to make up actual space (on the second), then the question of how these small bits can *make up* something finite does not arise. How potential infinities are supposed to address the paradox of the arrow is less clear. Aristotle seemed to deny that the "halfway points" the arrow had to pass through had actual existence. But completing an infinite series of passing through points with potential existence seems just as problematic. And if we interpret the claim that the halfway points have only "potential existence" as the claim that there are no halfway points *at all* (though there could be), we have to answer awkward questions about why the arrow does not ever get halfway to its target, since there's no halfway for it to get to. Saying infinities are only potential still leaves plenty of problems to deal with.

One interesting philosophical issue is which of the alternatives correctly describe space and time, or spatial and temporal things. But another interesting issue is which of these alternatives are coherent. If only one of these alternatives is coherent, (e.g. some finitists have suggested that only the granular view is possible), then surprisingly we can tell, without having to investigate the world, some important information about the ultimate structure of space and time. Or at least the only investigation we need to do is to notice that some things move, and other elementary observations of our everyday world. To decide whether there is a scientific question about whether the world contains continuous space, for example, we need to be as clear as we can about what the alternatives would amount to.

Infinite regresses in metaphysics

Infinities are often discussed when "infinite-regress arguments" are deployed to try to prove metaphysical conclusions. Perhaps the most famous infinite-regress arguments are those for the existence of a "first cause" – arguments often employed in an attempt to prove the existence of God. It is doubtful that a proof that there is a "first cause" would help very much in making the case for the existence of God – why suppose a first cause would be intelligent, or powerful, or beneficent, or have any other attributes commonly attributed to deities? But leaving aside theological concerns, the question of whether there is a first cause is interesting in its own right, and it would be surprising if armchair reflection about causation could establish that much about the origin of the universe.

There are dozens, if not hundreds, of versions of cosmological arguments. A simple form of the regress argument might go like this:

(1) Every natural thing has a cause.
(2) The chain of causes cannot go back infinitely.
(3) There can be no causal loops.
(4) Therefore every chain of causation must have a first cause at its beginning.

Presumably this "first cause" must be something that does not fall under the generalisation at (1): God is often offered as a candidate first cause that does not itself need a cause. Both premises (1) and (3) can be disputed, of course. Premise (1) is probably disputed more than premise (3): the idea that the Big Bang, or for that matter random quantum fluctuations, could "just happen" in an uncaused way remains a popular view.

For our purposes, though, the most interesting premise is (2). Why not think that there is a succession of cause and effect stretching back into the past without end? Of course, we might have specific evidence from cosmology that the world had a beginning (e.g. the Big Bang). But is there any principled philosophical reason to reject an infinite regress of cause and effect?

Two have traditionally been offered. One is the belief that there cannot be an "actual infinity," but only a potential infinity (see above). If the past is "actual," and we had an infinite regress of causes, we would have an infinite series of actual causes and effects already in existence. Those who claim actual infinities are incoherent will reject an actual infinity of past causes. Of course, this reasoning is only as good as that which supports rejecting actual infinities. (Interestingly, Aristotle himself, despite his rejection of actual infinities, did not object to an infinity of past causes. Aristotle seems to have thought that the past was not "actual" any more in the relevant sense: only the present was.)

The second reason to reject an infinite regress of cause and effect is that there is something incoherent in this infinite chain of dependence. However, the intuition that "the buck must stop somewhere" is hard to argue for. A defender of the claim could suggest that when we explain an effect by reference to its cause, for example, that explanation is somehow incomplete unless we explain the cause's occurrence as well: and if that in turn is explained by reference to a further cause, a further explanation is called for, and so on, and somehow there is something unsatisfactory unless that sequence comes to an end.

Of course, it is hard to see how such a sequence *could* end if we do insist that each cause is an unsatisfactory explanation until it itself is explained: any "first cause" will have this problem, and postulating a god as a first cause will not make the problem go away. Indeed, the challenge of trying to explain a god or that god's existence can seem even more intractable than explaining the Big Bang. Theists interested in using this sort of argument usually have some special pleading about how God is his own cause or explanation in the way that ordinary events and things are not, or that God is a necessary being and necessary beings do not need a further cause or explanation.

Other metaphysical infinite-regress arguments also rely on the idea that chains of dependence must ground out somewhere. Some people think that wholes depend on their parts – once you have the parts and the relations between them, nothing more is needed for the whole, whether we are talking about heaps of sand, tables and chairs, or human bodies. Some of them are tempted by a regress argument against the view that there is *gunk* (see above). If an object (or a region of space or duration of time) is made up of parts, and they are made up of parts, and so on for ever, then the whole structure will not "ground out" in ultimate parts that themselves have no proper parts. (Objects without proper parts are often called *simples* or *atoms*, though this use of "atom" is to be distinguished from the word's use in chemistry.) It should be clear how the infinite-regress argument would go.

If there is gunk, then the parts of objects have (proper) parts, and they have (proper) parts, and so on *ad infinitum*, without ever reaching a level of ultimate parts.

But this chain of dependence must ground out – it cannot go on for ever.

Therefore there is no gunk.

Here it is not infinity *per se* that is the problem: many of those who think gunk is impossible do believe in the possibility of an object made up of infinitely many simples (and so "infinitely divisible" in at least one good sense). It is rather the never-ending chain of parthood that is supposed to be the problem.

Others will want to deny that there is dependence of a whole on its parts. For example, one might think that the whole and its parts are equally well existing objects, and while they stand in a particularly intimate relationship, it does not follow that either is *dependent* on the other. Others may even want to think that parts sometimes, or always, depend on their wholes, and not vice versa. (Those who think dependence runs both ways will at least believe in the sort of dependence necessary for the argument above.)

Still others may be happy to concede that wholes depend on their parts, but be happy with infinite chains of dependence that do not "ground out" in partless parts that do not depend, in this way, on anything else. In the "first-cause" case, many are happy with the idea that there could be never-ending chains of causal dependence that do not stop with an uncaused cause. In the gunk case, many are happy with chains of part–whole dependence that do not "ground out" in partless parts (i.e. parts with no proper parts). Getting beyond this unease to a consideration that will convince their opponents, however, is a goal that has remained elusive.

Other topics

There are a number of other places in metaphysics where infinities play an important role, though there will be space to do little more than mention these topics. Readers who find these tastes particularly interesting can follow up the further references given below. In no particular order, other philosophical issues involving infinity include the following.

Are there *infinitesimal* magnitudes? An infinitesimal is less than any positive real number, but greater than zero. (Consistent mathematical models of infinitesimals have been developed, but they are not part of classical mathematics.) If infinitesimals have applications in the real world (e.g. there are infinitesimal distances or masses or objective chances), what impact does that have on standard theories (e.g. of space, time or chance)?

Some philosophers want to defend *strict finitism* – the view that there are not, and could not be, infinitely many objects. Strict finitists sometimes want to argue that there is something wrong with the concept of infinity, others just that it is unnecessary. One interesting question pursued by strict finitists is how much of our ordinary mathematical practice can be recaptured if there are only finitely many numbers or mathematical sets.

There are issues about infinities and abstract objects. How many possible worlds and possibilities are there? How many propositions are there? Presumably there are at least infinitely many of each, if they exist at all. But coming up with principles about the cardinality of these things is not straightforward.

Infinities come in different sizes. What is the largest size like, if there is one? (If there is not one, why does everything all together not get a size?) Georg Cantor, who first proved that there are infinities of different sizes, believed that there is a greatest infinity, the Absolute Infinite, which is not entirely understandable by us. Some contemporary "class theorists" believe that there are *proper classes*, collections too big to be sets. If proper classes are all of the same size, this would be the largest size.

Is God infinite? If so, in what sense? In some relatively mundane sense (e.g. being located at infinitely many locations in space or time, or being able to employ forces of infinite magnitude, or to do infinitely many different kinds of things), or in a special sense, or in both? If God is infinite in some distinctive sense, how is that sense related to the other mathematical and physical senses of infinity discussed here?

References

Benardete, J. (1964) *Infinity: An Essay in Metaphysics*, Oxford: Clarendon Press.
Craig, W. (1979) *The Kalām Cosmological Argument*, London: Macmillan.
Forrest, P. (1995) "Is Space–Time Discrete or Continuous?" *Synthese* 103, no. 3: 327–54.
Gamow, G. (1946) *One Two Three … Infinity*, London: Macmillan.
Grünbaum, A. (1967) *Modern Science and Zeno's Paradoxes*, London: Allen & Unwin.
Salmon, W. (ed.) (1970) *Zeno's Paradoxes*, Indianapolis, IN: Bobbs-Merrill.

Further reading

General: G. Oppy, *Philosophical Perspectives on Infinity* (Cambridge: Cambridge University Press, 2006) is perhaps the best book-length treatment of the role discussions of infinity play in contemporary philosophy, and certainly the most up to date (at the time of writing). It is worth consulting on most of the issues discussed in this article. A. Moore, *The Infinite* (London: Routledge, 1990) is a useful introduction to the history of debates about infinity, and contains a discussion more sceptical of theories of the infinite than this article. Zeno's paradoxes: Chapter 1 of R. M. Sainsbury, *Paradoxes*, 2nd edn (Cambridge: Cambridge University Press, 1995) contains a very accessible introduction to Zeno's paradoxes. This classic collection, W. Salmon (ed.), *Zeno's Paradoxes* (Indianapolis, IN: Bobbs-Merrill, 1970) contains not only important papers on Zeno's paradox, but an exchange between James Thomson and Paul Benacerraf about Thomson's Lamp. Chapters 12 and 13 of J. Barnes, *The Presocratic Philosophers*, revised edn (London: Routledge & Kegan Paul, 1982) contain interesting discussions of Zeno's puzzles in their historical context. J. Benardete, *Infinity: An Essay in Metaphysics* (Oxford: Clarendon Press, 1964) is a fascinating book for those intrigued by "New Zeno" paradoxes. Alternatives to continuous time and space: A philosophical introduction to treatments of space that is not infinitely divisible is J. Van Bendegem, "Finitism in Geometry," in Edward N. Zalta (ed.), *The Stanford Encyclopedia of Philosophy* (Summer 2002 edn) (available: http://plato.stanford.edu/archives/sum2002/entries/geometry-finitism/). See also P. Forrest, "Is Space–Time Discrete or Continuous?" *Synthese* 103, no. 3 (1995): 327–54. A good introduction to arguments about parts and wholes, including arguments about gunk, is H. Hudson, "Simples and Gunk," *Philosophy Compass* 2, no. 2 (2007): 291–302. Infinite-regress arguments: D. Nolan, "What's Wrong with Infinite Regresses?" *Metaphilosophy* 32, no. 5 (2001): 523–38. In this article I discuss infinite-regress arguments in general, and offer a reason to be suspicious of infinite regresses other than the reasons discussed above. Other topics: J. Bell introduces the history of infinitesimals and some of the debates about them in the history of philosophy in "Continuity and Infinitesimals," Edward N. Zalta (ed.), *The Stanford Encyclopedia of Philosophy* (Fall 2005 edn) (available: http://plato.stanford.edu/archives/fall2005/entries/continuity/). P. Grim, *The Incomplete Universe* (Cambridge, MA: MIT Press, 1992) raises an interesting series of size-related paradoxes about totalities of propositions, possibilities, mathematical objects and so on. Grim's own view is that these abstract objects do not form totalities at all. M. Hallett, *Cantorian Set Theory and Limitation of Size* (Oxford: Clarendon Press, 1984) is an excellent introduction to Cantor's own views about sets and cardinality, and the Absolute Infinite.

41

THE PASSAGE OF TIME

Eric T. Olson

Dynamic and static views of time

Time involves a kind of movement or activity. It does not stand still. It waits for no man. Sometimes it even flies. Poets liken time to a river, bringing fresh events and sweeping away old ones. Time is always passing.

The prosaic content of these sayings is that events change from future to present and from present to past. Your next birthday is in the future, but with the passage of time it draws nearer and nearer until it is present. Twenty-four hours later it will be in the past, and then lapse forever deeper into history. And things get older: even if they don't wear out or lose their hair or change in any other way, their chronological age is always increasing. These changes are universal and inescapable: no event could ever fail to be first future, then present, then past, and no persisting thing can avoid growing older. We call this process *time's passage*.

Passage is unique to time. It marks an essential difference between time and space, which are in other ways similar. Space doesn't pass. Things can move in space, but they can also stay put: there is no universal process of spatial change analogous to chronological aging or events changing from present to past.

So it seems, anyway. But time's passage is something of a mystery. Many philosophers see it as an illusion. Things can change in size or shape or temperature, they say, but nothing changes in any purely temporal respect, by becoming older or further past. Change takes place within time, but time itself doesn't change. Time merely separates events temporally, as space separates them spatially. This is the *static view* of time. The *dynamic view*, by contrast, says that time really does pass: the world is caught up in a process of purely temporal change.

For the past hundred years or so, the debate between the static and dynamic views has been the central battleground in the philosophy of time. Most of this chapter is about what the two positions come to and where the disagreement lies. The last two sections are about who is right.

Passage and tense

Time's passage follows from its division into past, present, and future. It seems, at least, that not all times are equal. One time – the present – is special. It may not differ in its content from the past or the future: history may judge the present entirely unremarkable, in that the same sorts of things go on now as before and after. But even if that is so, the present time and current events differ from non-present ones in a purely temporal way: they are going on *now*.

If we think of the whole of time spread out from earlier to later, we naturally imagine a boundary separating those times and events that are over and done with from those that are still to come. That boundary marks the present. But it doesn't stay where it is. Once it was in the Cretaceous period; later it was at 1640; now it is in the twenty-first century. It moves constantly towards the future, and every future event will one day coincide with it. The movement of this boundary is the heart of time's passage. If the boundary exists, its location must change, and the status of events as past, present, and future must change with it. The dynamic view will be true.

Of course, time's passage cannot literally be a kind of movement. Movement is change of spatial position, and the present can "move" only in time. It is at best a metaphorical sort of movement, akin to the rising of temperatures or prices. (Kinetic metaphors are common enough: think of "The government is moving to the right on crime.") The literal truth is simply that times and events change in their temporal direction and separation from the present.

So the division of times into past, present, and future leads to the dynamic view. We can see this in another way by reflecting on what philosophers call *tense concepts* (or "A-concepts"): *past, present, future*, and their more determinate forms such as *yesterday* and *next week*. They are by nature evanescent, and apply to things only temporarily. What is future cannot forever remain so, but must become present and then past. What is past always remains past, but its degree of pastness changes, from being only yesterday to being a month ago, and so on. Age is also a tense concept: to say that someone is 100 years old is to say that she was born 100 years in the past. And age too is evanescent. I can't remain 100 years old forever: within a year, if I'm still alive, my age must advance to 101. These changes are time's passage.

The tenseless theory

At this point things get more difficult. I have made the dynamic view sound like an obvious truism. Surely some events and periods of time are present; and none of them can avoid changing by becoming past. That change makes the dynamic view true. But then how can anyone seriously deny the dynamic view? It looks as if friends of the static view must say either that nothing is present (or past or future), or that some things *are* present, but they never become past. Neither option looks tenable. If nothing were present, why would we use clocks? Isn't their purpose to tell us what time is present? And no one can believe that your reading of this chapter will *always* be in the present.

To reject the reality of time's passage, it seems, is to deny the reality of time altogether. Call this the *basic challenge*:

(1) Some times are present.
(2) Whatever is present will one day become past.
(3) Thus, times change in respect of their presentness, contrary to the static view. The static view looks incredible.

Friends of the static view have a subtle and ingenious reply to this objection. They say that if (1) is understood as the dynamists understand it – as implying that the twenty-first century differs from other centuries in that it alone has the property of being present – then it is false. But there is another way of understanding (1), and (2) as well, according to which they are true, but do not imply (3), making them compatible with the static view. If the reality of time's passage sounds like a truism, that's because we have understood (1) and (2) as the dynamists do. But there is room for debate about whether this understanding is right.

Friends of the static view deny that the twenty-first century differs from other centuries in that it alone is present. Times and events do not have such properties as being present or being past. There *are* no such properties. Tense, like passage, is unreal. All times, as times, are equal. This is the *tenseless theory* (or "B-theory") of time. It is a natural ally of the static view.

The tenseless theory may appear to contradict (1), but it needn't. Tense can have a legitimate place in the content of our thought and talk, even if it is not a feature of temporal reality. The tenseless theory does not make it wrong to say that the twenty-first century is present. We can still call it present insofar as it is *our* century. Other centuries are present for others: for Descartes, the seventeenth century is present and the twenty-first century is in the future; and his temporal perspective is just as valid as ours. From the perspective of each time, *that* time is present, and earlier times are past and later ones are future. But no time is just plain absolutely present. There is no uniquely correct way of dividing times into past, present, and future.

This makes the current century's "nowness" analogous to the "hereness" of the earth. The earth is here for us, but far away for the Martians; and again, our perspective is not privileged. Every place is "here" at that place, but there is no absolute division of places into here and there. There is no such property as hereness, that some places have and others lack. All places, as places, are equal. Yet it is no mistake to say that the earth is here. The word "here" (without a pointing gesture) simply refers to the speaker's location. In the same way, on the tenseless theory, the word "now" refers to the time when it is uttered, written down, or thought. So the fact that you are now reading this chapter is not the fact that your reading takes place at the one moment of time that is absolutely present, but simply that your reading takes place at the time when you say or think, "I am now reading this chapter."

The reducibility of tense

These remarks suggest a way of eliminating tense from our thought and language. Your thought that you are now reading this chapter is true just in the case that it takes place during your reading. "Takes place," though grammatically present tense, is logically tenseless here, for the statement tells us nothing about where your reading is located relative to the present. (It's like saying that the Taiping Rebellion takes place in the nineteenth century.) And *during*, like *before* and *after*, is not a tense concept: what happens during or before or after what never changes. So we can say what makes it true that you are now reading this chapter in tenseless terms. Likewise, if I had a bath two weeks ago, we can describe this fact without tense by saying that I have a bath two weeks before the time of my writing this.

The basic rules are something like this:

- To say, at a time *t*, that *x* is present (or past, or future) is to say something that is true if and only if *x* is located at (or before, or after) *t*;
- To say, at a time *t*, that *x* is now *F* (or was *F*, or will be *F*) is to say something that is true if and only if *x* is *F* at (or before, or after) *t*,

where the final verb in each case is untensed. If these rules are correct, then tense concepts and words are eliminable in the sense that we can say all there is to be said, or describe all the facts, without them. This doesn't mean that we ought to stop using words like "now." The word "here" is also eliminable, in that we can describe all the facts without it – there are analogous elimination rules for statements such as "it's wet here" – yet "here" remains a useful word. Nor is the claim that our tenseless paraphrases have precisely the same meaning as the originals. It is merely that we can give the truth conditions for all statements in tenseless terms. Call this claim the *reducibility of tense*.

It is easy to see why the reducibility of tense goes together with the tenseless view. If the world is in itself tenseless, then we should expect tensed statements to be made true (or false) by tenseless facts, since those are all the facts there are; and it ought to be possible to describe these facts in tenseless language. Those tenseless descriptions will then give the truth conditions for the tensed statements. Conversely, if we can give tenseless truth conditions for tensed statements, we should expect the reason to be that the world is in itself tenseless.

Now recall the basic challenge: obviously some times are present, and whatever is present will one day become past; and this becoming past looks like precisely the sort of purely temporal change that the static view denies. But if we restate these obvious facts in tenseless terms, they no longer appear to imply any sort of temporal change. Our tense-elimination rules suggest that if we utter (1) and (2) at *t*, their truth conditions are these:

(1*) Some times are located at *t*.
(2*) For anything located at *t*, some time later than *t* is after it.

And although (1) and (2) may seem to imply that times change in respect of their presentness, (1*) and (2*) do not. They don't describe any sort of change at all. So if tense is unreal and therefore eliminable, the premises of the basic challenge are perfectly compatible with the static view. We can use tensed language, and have tensed beliefs, without committing ourselves to the reality of time's passage. The static view does not deny the obvious.

The tensed theory and the dynamic view

We began with time's passage, then moved to tense properties: presentness, chronological age, and so on. We can see now more clearly how these two themes intermingle. The static view rejects time's passage by denying that anything changes in its tense properties. In that case, we saw, there can be no tense properties in the world, for otherwise things would have to change in respect of them. So the static view entails the tenseless theory. This led in turn to the reducibility of tense, the claim that all statements have tenseless truth conditions.

The converse also holds: the tenseless theory entails the static view. If there are no tense properties in the world, there can be no purely temporal change. Suppose the Taiping Rebellion is past in 2020, present throughout 1852, and future in 1640, and that facts like these are all there is to say about its pastness, presentness, and futurity. (Likewise, my being 100 years old in 2008, 150 in 2058, and so on is all there is to say about my age; I have no age *simpliciter*.) Because events never change in respect of whether they are past, present, or future at a given time, there is no purely temporal change that they could undergo, and therefore no temporal passage. The only temporal property in respect of which something could change would be a tense property, such as being present – not present at some time, but present *simpliciter*. So the static view is true if, and only if, the tenseless theory is true.

Dynamists, by contrast, reject both the reducibility of tense and the tenseless theory. They deny that "now" is analogous to "here," and that tensed statements have tenseless truth conditions. They say that tense is woven into the fabric of temporal reality and not merely into the content of our thought and language: time is *in itself* divided into past, present, and future, and this division is in no way relative to times or observers. This is the *tensed theory* (or "A-theory") of time. If time's passage is real, there must be such properties as absolute presentness in respect of which things change: the dynamic view entails the tensed theory. And here too the converse holds: if there is a real and absolute division of times into past, present, and future, its location must change, and there will be genuine passage. So the dynamic view is true if and only if the tensed theory is.

Dynamic and static omniscience

I have described two pairs of views: the dynamic view and tensed theory, on the one hand, and the static view and tenseless theory, on the other. We can make this distinction more vivid by imagining an omniscient being. (To avoid certain complications, imagine her entirely detached from the world – not located anywhere in space or time, or at least not in *our* space or time.) She will know all the facts about the arrangement of objects and events throughout the whole of time: all about the roamings of the dinosaurs, the oil wars of our own age, the melting of the polar ice caps, and so on, and how these events relate to one another. Yet according to the tensed theory, she is not truly omniscient unless she also knows something else, namely which of these things are going on now, and which are past and which are yet to come. Otherwise her knowledge will be incomplete. And because what is present constantly changes – as the dynamic view has it – she cannot know this once and for all, but must constantly update her beliefs. She must know that you are now reading this sentence. But because that is true only for a moment, she must immediately reject it and start believing instead that you are now reading *this* sentence. And so it goes. If time's passage is real, omniscience would be a never-ending task.

On the tenseless theory, by contrast, our omniscient being needn't know any temporal facts beyond what happens at what date. She needn't know what events are present, any more than she must know what place is here. She needs no tensed beliefs because there are no tensed facts. And because the tenseless facts don't change – as the static view has it – she has no need to update her beliefs. She can know everything once and for all.

Why does time seem to pass?

I hope it is now clearer what the debate between the dynamic and static views is about. In the space remaining I will lay out a fragment of this debate. First a challenge for the static view.

The static view says that time does not really pass and the tenseless theory says that there is no absolute difference between past, present, and future. Defenders of this position have some explaining to do, because this is not how things appear. They need to explain why time *seems* to pass. They also need to say why the present seems to differ, as such, from other times, and why the past seems to differ from the future. And they will want to say what, if not passage, could distinguish time from space. How would a static time be anything more than just another spatial dimension?

Defenders of the static view say that time seems to pass because we need to change our tensed statements and beliefs to avoid error (Mellor 1998: 66). Suppose I say, correctly, that today is Monday. It would be wrong for me to say that yesterday, or tomorrow. The need to change what we say about something to remain correct ordinarily implies that whatever we're talking about is changing. If I need to change what I say about the temperature, then the temperature must be changing. So the need to change what I say about what day is present suggests that days change in their temporal properties – from being tomorrow to being today to being yesterday – in which case time really does pass.

But we can explain the need to update our tensed statements without positing time's passage. According to the reducibility of tense, my statement that today is Monday is true if and only if I make it on Monday. That explains why it's wrong to say it on

Tuesday. Not that my statement changes from true to false; rather, what I say on Monday is different from what I say on Tuesday, even though I express both in the same words. Compare the following: if we both say, "I am Eric Olson," we say different things, one false and one true.

Why does the past seem to differ from the future? For instance, what explains why we plan for the future but not for the past, and remember the past but not the future?

According to the static view, the apparent fact that we plan only for the future is really the fact that we plan only for times *after* our planning. This is due to the temporal asymmetry of causation: causes always precede their effects. This means that the effects of our planning will always occur after we make those plans. Since there is no point in planning for something we cannot affect, we plan only for what comes later. (The related fact that the future is "open" and the past "fixed" is really the fact that, at any time, we can affect only what happens after that time.) Memory, too, is a causal process: the memory of an event is an effect of it. So the apparent fact that we can remember only the past is really the fact that we can remember only things that occur before we remember them. This is all compatible with the static view, for what events occur before and after others never changes.

Why does the present seem different from other times? Why do we so naturally think of time as divided absolutely into past, present, and future? Well, the apparent fact that the present moment is special is really the fact that *any* time seems special at that time. This too is because of the temporal asymmetry of causation: the fact that at a given time we can affect only later events and remember only earlier ones, for instance. When you ponder the nature of the present, this temporal asymmetry gives the illusion that the time of your pondering is unique.

If there were a causal asymmetry in space, it would mislead us in the same way. If it were a law of nature that light never travelled southwards, everything to the south of you would appear bright during daylight hours, while to the north you would see only darkness. Your latitude would appear unique: it would seem to be the boundary between the illuminated part of the earth and the dark part. If you moved north, the darkness would seem to recede, so that more of the earth became bright. The boundary would appear to move, as if the dawn were following you. But this would all be an illusion. In reality there would be no boundary between the bright latitudes and the dark ones. They would all be equally bright. Nor would the overall pattern of illumination change as you moved. It is the same with the present.

If there is no such property as presentness, then clocks don't tell us what time has it. So what do they tell us? Looking at a clock tells you the time of your looking. Suppose you want to catch the noon train. Then each glance at the clock tells you how long that glance is before (or after) noon. So if the clock says 11:55 as you look at it, you can infer that your train leaves five minutes later, and act accordingly. That's what makes clocks useful.

What distinguishes time from space, if not time's passage? We have already noted that causes always precede their effects in time. Space has no such asymmetry: despite my imaginary story about light never moving southwards, causes can be equally above, below, north, south, east, or west of their effects. (*Why* time and space differ in this way is a good question, but they do.)

Another difference is that space, but not time, can have more than one dimension. Space has at least three dimensions; but there could not be a three-dimensional time.

We measure time and space differently – time with clocks, space with metre sticks. And they come in different units: time in seconds, space in miles. This difference is no mere convention, like the fact that we measure roads in miles and racecourses in furlongs. There is no non-arbitrary conversion from miles to seconds, as there is from miles to furlongs: we can't ask how many seconds long the Great North Road would be if its length were in time rather than in space. Time and space are simply different quantities, like mass and temperature.

More generally, time and space play different roles in physics. Power, for instance, is work divided by time, not distance: a powerful engine is one that can do a lot of work in a short time. The second law of thermodynamics says that the overall entropy or disorder of a closed system is greater at later times than at earlier ones – that's what makes it so hard to get spilled wine back into the bottle. No law of nature says that entropy is greater in one place than another. Swap temporal variables for spatial ones in physics, and in most cases you get nonsense.

None of these differences appeal to temporal passage.

How fast does time pass?

Finally, a problem for the dynamic view. It says that things change by becoming older or less future or more past. Now if a thing gets older or less future, it does so by a measurable amount: by a certain number of years or hours or seconds. And every such change takes a certain amount of time to occur. It follows that we can ask at what rate this change takes place. If a thing's temperature increases, it must increase at some rate: by a certain number of degrees per second. Just so, if my birth becomes more past, it must do so at some rate: by a certain number of seconds in a second. What is this rate?

Only one answer seems possible: time passes at one second per second – or some equivalent rate, such as sixty seconds per minute or twenty-four hours per day. I must get older by one second for every second I remain in existence. Time could not pass at two or at seventeen seconds per second.

This is odd. For one thing, the rate of any other change can increase or decrease: temperatures or prices, for instance, can rise faster or slower. But the rate at which time passes would be unalterable. For another, when something changes in any other measurable quantity, we can measure its rate of change; but we cannot measure the rate of time's passage. Clocks measure the amount of time separating two events, but they don't tell us at what rate that time elapses. For that we should need a chronological instrument analogous to a speedometer, and no such thing seems possible. In the passage of time a measurable quantity changes at an unmeasurable rate. If nothing else, time's passage would have to be radically different from any other sort of change.

But the real problem with time's passing at one second per second is that this is not a rate of change at all (van Inwagen 2002: 59). One second per second is one second divided by one second. And when you divide one second by one second, you get one. Not one *of* anything, just one. Dividing anything by itself, apart from zero, gives you

447

one. Sixty seconds per minute and twenty-four hours per day are also one, because sixty seconds is equal to one minute and twenty-four hours is one day. And *one* is not a rate of change. A thing can change at a rate of one mile per hour or one degree per second, but not at a rate of one. "One" cannot answer a question of the form, "How fast …?," but only a question of the form, "How many …?," or "What number …?" If we ask how many pigs are in the sty, "one" is a possible answer. But if we ask at what rate a certain process of change goes on – how fast the temperature is rising, say – the answer cannot be "one." Just so, if we ask at what rate things grow older, "one" is simply not an answer. So the dynamic view implies that time must pass at a rate that is not a rate, and that is impossible.

Dynamists need to argue that this reasoning is mistaken. They might say that one second per second really is a rate of change, even though it is equal to one (Prior 1993 [1968]: 37). Or they may argue that time passes without passing at one second per second – perhaps at no rate at all (Markosian 1993). But neither response looks promising (Olson, 2009).

References

Markosian, N. (1993) "How Fast Does Time Pass?" *Philosophy and Phenomenological Research* 53: 829–44.

Mellor, D. H. (1998) *Real Time II*, London: Routledge.

Olson, E. (2009) "The Rate of Time's Passage," *Analysis* 69: 3–9.

Prior, A. N. (1993 [1968]) "Changes in Events and Changes in Things," in R. Le Poidevin and M. MacBeath (eds), *The Philosophy of Time*, Oxford: Oxford University Press, pp. 35–46; originally published in Prior, *Papers on Time and Tense*, Oxford: Clarendon Press.

van Inwagen, P. (2002) *Metaphysics*, 2nd edn, Boulder, CO: Westview.

Further reading

Good introductions to the topic include (in roughly increasing order of difficulty) K. Seddon, *Time* (London: Croom Helm, 1987); R. Le Poidevin, *Travels in Four Dimensions* (Oxford: Oxford University Press, 2003), chapter 8; P. van Inwagen, *Metaphysics* (details above), chapter 4; and G. Schlesinger, *Aspects of Time* (Indianapolis, IN: Hackett, 1980). B. Dainton, *Time and Space* (Chesham, UK: Acumen, 2001), chapters 1–7 is a sophisticated but challenging overview. R. Gale (ed.), *The Philosophy of Time* (London: Macmillan, 1968); P. van Inwagen and D. Zimmerman (eds.), *Metaphysics: The Big Questions*, 2nd edn (Oxford: Blackwell 2008); and R. Le Poidevin and M. MacBeath (eds.), *The Philosophy of Time* (details above) are all useful anthologies. D. H. Mellor, *Real Time II* (details above) is the classic defence of the static view, though tough going for the uninitiated. A. N. Prior, "Thank Goodness That's Over," *Philosophy* 34: 12–17 (1959) sets out a famous argument for the dynamic view. J. M. E. McTaggart, *The Nature of Existence* (Cambridge: Cambridge University Press, 1927), vol. 2, book 5, chapter 33 (reprinted in Gale, Le Poidevin and MacBeath, and in van Inwagen and Zimmerman) gives a famous but notoriously difficult argument against it. C. D. Broad, *An Examination of McTaggart's Philosophy* (Cambridge: Cambridge Univerisity Press, 1938), vol. 2, pt 1 (reprinted in Gale and in van Inwagen and Zimmerman) defends the dynamic view against McTaggart. M. Tooley, *Time, Tense, and Causation* (Oxford: Clarendon Press, 1997) tries to combine the tenseless theory with the dynamic view (difficult).

42
THE DIRECTION OF TIME
D. H. Mellor

Formalities

The direction of time is the difference between being *earlier* than something and being *later* than it. The difference is not formal, since *earlier* and *later* are formally similar, each being the other's converse (any x is earlier than any y if and only if that y is later than that x) and both being transitive (if x is earlier/later than y, and y than z, then x is earlier/later than z). And if time is linear, i.e. if the passage of time returns nothing to its origin, *earlier* and *later* will also be irreflexive and asymmetrical: nothing will be earlier or later than itself, and nothing will be both earlier and later than anything else.

If anything does return to its origin, its world line (its path through space and time) will be a "closed time-like loop": global if time is circular and returns the whole universe to the Big Bang, local if the loop is the world line of a thing within it, like Dr Who's time machine TARDIS (Time and Relative Dimensions in Space), should backward time travel return that to its origin. In both cases *earlier* and *later* still share many formal properties, being now reflexive and symmetrical, since everything in a time-like loop is both earlier and later than itself and than everything else in the loop. And similarly in spatial loops, like the London underground's Circle line, where both clockwise and anticlockwise trains link every station to itself and to every other station.

But in both cases there are now formal differences too. For example, clockwise Circle line trains from Aldgate to Paddington go via Victoria, which anticlockwise trains do not. Similarly, going from earlier to later round circular time puts Cleopatra between the Big Bang and the Beatles, whereas going round from later to earlier puts the Big Bang between Cleopatra and the Beatles.

Extrinsic and intrinsic differences

Everyone agrees that time, whether linear or looped, is directed in a way that space is not. If so, *earlier* and *later* must differ in some substantive, non-formal way if the parallels noted in the first section, "Formalities," are not to give time's direction spatial counterparts. The difference between *earlier* and *later* must also be *intrinsic*, to distinguish it from substantive spatial differences, like that between *clockwise* and *anticlockwise*, which are merely extrinsic. For the Circle line direction from Paddington to Aldgate via

Victoria is only clockwise seen from above: seen from below it is anticlockwise; and in itself it is neither. No intrinsic non-formal feature distinguishes the two ways round a closed spatial loop, or the two opposed directions along an open spatial line: in both cases each is just the other's converse along a one-dimensional spatial path, with no substantive feature of the path itself telling us which is which.

I infer that, for time's direction to differ from that of any spatial dimension, it must follow from a substantive and intrinsic distinction between time and space, a distinction which, since it applies at all space–time points, must be local as well as global. These conditions set the tests that I think any adequate account of time's direction must pass: it must make that direction intrinsic, local and devoid of spatial counterparts.

The flow of time

The obvious account derives time's direction from its *flow*, i.e. from everything moving from the future to the past via the present. Theories that give this account I call *A-theories*, after McTaggart's (1908) distinction between an A-series of events ordered from past to future and a B-series ordered from earlier to later. And while different A-theorists credit A-series locations with different entailments – e.g. that only the present exists (Bourne 2006: Pt 1), or that only the past and present do (Tooley 1997: Ch. 2) – all that matters here is whether time flows at all (Oaklander and Smith 1994), a controversy about which I need only make two points. First, since the flow of time, if it exists, distinguishes time from space everywhere, it is, as required, both intrinsic and local. But second, it will still only give time its direction, by distinguishing *earlier* from *later*, if this distinction is derivable from that between *past* and *future*, not *vice versa*. That is why A-theorists think that "the intrinsic sense of a series of events in Time is essentially bound up with the distinction between past, present and future. A precedes B because A is past when B is present" (Broad 1923: 58). They are wrong: A-series locations are distinguishable only by how much earlier or later they are than the present: *yesterday* as one day earlier than *today*, for example, and *tomorrow* as one day later than it (Mellor 1998: Ch. 1.3). And so in general, *pace* Broad, the fact is that A *is past when* B *is present* because A *precedes* B, and not the other way round. An A-series is simply a B-series plus a present moment that, by mere definition, moves from earlier to later times rather than from later to earlier ones. But then even A-theorists need a B-theory account of time's direction to tell them what it is for a present to move from earlier to later times and not the other way. What might that theory be?

The expansion of the universe

B-theories of time's direction use an "arrow of time," a "process or phenomenon that has … a definite direction in time" (Savitt 1995: 1), such as the expansion of the universe (Zeh 2007: Ch. 5.3). But even if the universe expands for ever, this "cosmological" arrow cannot be intrinsic to time. For if it was, the universe could never stop expanding, since that would make the end of its expansion the end of time itself. But that is neither credible nor consistent with theories that take the universe's continued expansion to depend on a contingent balance of gravitational and other forces (Dainton 2001: Ch. 4.6), a contingency which requires time to have a logically independent direction that need not be reversed or destroyed if the expansion stops.

The cosmological arrow fails our other test, too, because it cannot give time a local as well as a global direction. For just as a child's growth is a fact about its whole body, not about any one of its cells, so the universe's expansion is only a fact about all of it, not about any point or thing within it. The expansion of the universe could only give time a local direction if events, like my typing of these words, could only occur successively, rather than simultaneously, while, and because, the universe continues to expand; and no one believes that.

Increasing entropy

Another arrow of time is provided by the fact that while all other forms of energy are completely convertible into heat, the converse is not true (Atkins 1986: 86). More precisely, let S be the entropy of a thing a, where S's changes are, when well-defined, given by

$$dS = dq/T,$$

where T is a's absolute temperature; and dq is a's net gain in heat from internal and external sources. Then while a is thermally isolated, i.e. while no heat is transferred into or out of it,

$$dS/dt \geq 0 \text{ (Denbigh 1955: 26)},$$

where t is time. In short, the entropy of a thermally isolated thing never decreases, so that if it is lower at t_1 than at t_2, then t_1 is earlier than t_2. This is the "thermodynamic" arrow of time.

The trouble with this arrow is that nothing is ever wholly isolated thermally, which is why the entropy of many things, including ourselves, can and often does decrease. The fact that these decreases have to be matched or exceeded by increases elsewhere only lets this arrow, like the cosmological one, give time a global direction, and then only because, by definition, there is nothing outside the whole universe for it to interact with. Nor does it help that if a thing *was* thermally isolated, its entropy would never decrease. For this can only be true, as a matter not of definition but of thermodynamic fact, if all world lines already have a direction for entropy to increase in, a direction that must therefore have a different basis. That is why, "when we … write $dS/dt \geq 0$, this is to take $+t$ as being towards 'the future' and $-t$ as being towards 'the past'" (Denbigh and Denbigh 1985: 15), a conclusion that is only reinforced in the statistical and quantum theories that have succeeded classical thermodynamics. For in these theories, the entropy of a thermally isolated thing has a non-zero chance of decreasing for a while, a chance it could not have if the thermodynamic arrow gave time a local direction.

Irreversibility

Neither these nor any of the other arrows listed by Zeh (2007: 5) gives time a direction that is both local and intrinsic. The real question about these arrows is not what links them to the direction of time but what links them to each other: why, for example, is the direction in which the universe expands that in which entropy increases? That is a good question, but it is not a question about the direction of time itself. To take a spatial analogue: "No one has seriously maintained that space is 'handed' … because of the *de facto* asymmetries between left- and right-handed objects. What then is supposed to make time different from space in this respect?" (Earman 1974: 32). What indeed? What tempts us to identify the direction of time with that of one of its arrows?

The best way to answer this question is to ask what proves that a movie is being played backward. Not how it shows things moving, for things can move in any direction; nor how people in it speak, since nothing rules out a language that sounds like a real language spoken backward. The real giveaway is its showing time's arrows pointing the wrong way: the universe contracting, or entropy spontaneously decreasing (as in the separation, with no energy input, of brine into fresh water and solid salt). It is because a movie that shows this *must* be running backward that we are tempted to identify time's direction with that of more or less irreversible processes.

To see why we should resist the temptation, consider the theory that positrons are electrons travelling backward in time, i.e. that the direction of time is reversed along the world lines of positrons (Reichenbach 1956: Ch. 30). The theory exploits the fact that positrons differ from electrons only in their charge being positive instead of negative, thus making positive charges, which attract electrons, repel them, and negative charges, which repel electrons, attract them. This makes a movie of electrons played backward look exactly like one of positrons played forward, just as a movie of positrons played backward looks like one of electrons played forward. But if the first similarity shows positrons to be electrons travelling backward in time, must not the second show electrons to be positrons doing so? But then which is it: which are the real backward time travellers, positrons or electrons?

Neither: the two particles simply have different properties, which is why movies of them differ when played the same way, whether forward (i.e. as shot) or backward. The fact that this difference happens to make either movie played backward look like the other one played forward is irrelevant. And as in this case, so in general: irreversible processes whose directions are not intrinsic to time – as its flow is – can tell us nothing about a direction of time that they must all presuppose. This is not to decry the questions they raise: the one noted above, of how independent their directions are, and the prior one of why they *have* directions, i.e. why they always or mostly go one way when no basic law of physics stops them going the other way. But answering those questions will not tell us what gives time itself its direction.

Seeing the direction of time

Perhaps nothing does. Why, after all, must time get its direction from something else, when the "directions" of increasing mass, size and other quantities do not? Why seek *The Physical Basis of the Direction of Time* (Zeh 2007), when no one seeks a "physical basis," i.e. a basis in something else, for differences between increasing and decreasing values of other quantities? It cannot be because telling which of two events is the earlier is harder than telling which of two things is the lighter or smaller: it is not. Seeing that a clock hand is moving clockwise, for example, includes seeing that its end passes nearby points in a certain order, e.g. that it passes the figure "1" *earlier* than it passes "2." If we could not see the time order of events, we could not see which way clock hands are moving, which we can.

Yet the direction of time that we perceive, and then use to distinguish reversible from irreversible processes, and to say which way the latter go, still needs a non-temporal basis. The reason lies in the fact, noted by Kant (1968 [1781]: Second Analogy) and others, that

> a succession of feelings, in and of itself, is not a feeling of succession. And since, to our successive feelings, a feeling of their own succession is added, that must be treated as an additional fact requiring its own special elucidation (James 1890: Vol. 1, 628–9).

For example, no single "feeling," i.e. experience, can tell me that my clock hand passes "1" (event *e*) earlier and not later than it passes "2" (event *f*). I need two: first the experience of seeing *e*, and then that of seeing *f*. Yet these two experiences are, as James says, not enough in themselves to tell me that *e* precedes *f*, since they will not tell me this if, when I see *f*, I have quite forgotten seeing *e*. This is why, if my seeing *f* does tell me that *e* preceded *f*, that is "an additional fact requiring its own special elucidation."

I think the elucidation is causal (Mellor 1998: Ch. 10.5): my seeing *f* will only make me see that *f* is later than *e* if it is *affected* by my having seen *e*. What the effect is, what produces it, and whether I am aware of it (i.e. whether, as James assumes, it is itself an experience) are immaterial; but an effect there must be. Of course the effect, whatever it is, will not ensure that what it makes my seeing *f* tell me, namely that *e* precedes *f*, is *true*, since it only links my perceptions of *e* and *f*, not *e* and *f* themselves. That is how, since light travels faster than sound, when I hear thunder seconds after I see lightning, my senses can tell me, falsely, that the thunder is that much later than the lightning. But all this shows is that here, as elsewhere, we should not believe everything our senses tell us.

How much can this causal account of how we perceive the time order of events tell us about their actual order? Well, since most if not all causes do in fact precede their effects – time *does* have a causal arrow – it does at least explain why the time order of our perceptions of events is the time order which these perceptions tell us, truly or falsely, that those events have. That is the causal basis of our perception, and hence of our conception, of the direction of time. But this is not enough to give the direction itself a causal basis; that requires another link between causation and time.

Causal and temporal order

The obvious candidate for the extra link we need between causal and temporal order is our inability to affect the past (some of which we can perceive) and to perceive the future (some of which we can affect). More precisely, and in B-theory terms, at any time t, we cannot affect anything earlier than t but may perceive it, and cannot perceive anything later than t but may affect it. And these are not two differences – between what we can and cannot affect, and can and cannot perceive – but one, since our perceptions are themselves effects of what we thereby perceive. What stops our senses showing us the future is the very fact that stops us affecting the past, namely, the fact that causes precede their effects, a fact that identifying time order with causal order immediately explains.

Time's causal arrow also shows how the positrons of the sixth section, "Irreversibility," differ from time-travelling electrons, by making a locally reversed time order entail a locally reversed causal order that positrons and electrons never exhibit. (For example, deflecting positrons at any time t only ever affects where they are after t, not before it.) Whereas when Dr Who's TARDIS travels back in time, its doing so automatically makes effects within it, that are later than their causes by TARDIS time, earlier than those causes by outside time.

Better still, the causal arrow explains special relativity's distinction between events that could be linked by things moving at or below the speed of light, which is what makes their space–time separation *time-like*, and events that could not, whose separation is *space-like*. This can be explained as follows (Mellor 1998: 108). If nothing causes a changeable property F of a thing a to change between a time t_1 and a later time t_2, then a's being F at t_1 can cause a to be F at t_2. This enables whatever causes a to be F at t_1 to be an indirect cause of whatever a's being F at t_2 causes, as when light made red by reflection from Mars causes us to see later that Mars is red. And if this is what transmits causation across space, then relativity's letting nothing accelerate to more than the speed of light makes light the fastest possible transmitter of causation. This in turn explains why the space–time separation of causally related events is always time-like, and why the time order of all events with time-like separations is the same in all reference frames. These two explanations, by making causation what distinguishes time from the spatial dimensions of space–time, and making time order coincide with causal order, are what make time's causal arrow intrinsic to time and therefore a credible source of time's direction.

Causation and time

Time's other arrows cannot begin to match this: none of them is both local and intrinsic to time; and none explains how we perceive (and conceive of) the direction of time, why we cannot affect the past or perceive the future, and what distinguishes time from space. Yet despite its long history (Robb 1914; Reichenbach 1956: Pt 2; Grünbaum 1968: Ch. 7), the causal theory is still often rejected (Lacey 1968) or ignored – it is not on Zeh's latest (2007: 5) list of time's arrows – for reasons I must therefore now outline and try to rebut.

(a) Because causal theories of time cannot define a cause as the *earlier* member of a cause–effect pair; they cannot use Hume's definition of a cause as "an object, *followed* by another, and where all the objects similar to the first are *followed* by objects similar to the second" (Hume 1975 [1748]: §60; my italics). But then this definition needs supplementing with a different theory of time order to account for *non*-temporal differences between cause and effect, for example, that causes explain their effects but not *vice versa*. One such theory is the A-theory:

> that past and present events and states of affairs are fixed ..., whereas at least some future ones are still to be fixed ... [and] if at any time A is fixed while B is still unfixed, B cannot be causally prior to A, because ... B [might] not occur. (Mackie 1974: 178)

How can B-theorists, who cannot use A-theories of how causes differ from effects, account for that difference? One way follows from Hume's counterfactual rewording of his definition: "... in other words where, if the *first* object had not been, the *second* never had existed" (Hume 1975 [1748]: §60; my italics). In other words, stripped of its temporal implications: if a cause had not existed, nor would its effects. This account of causation, which may or may not include a possible-worlds analysis of its counterfactuals (Lewis 1973), beats Hume's first definition hands down by making causation local (Lewis 1973: 558) but not – since a counter-factual does not entail its converse – symmetrical: it does not make effects as necessary for their causes as it makes causes for their effects. But nor does it make causation asymmetrical: it does not stop effects causing their own causes. And while a possible-worlds analysis of its counterfactuals may stop most of them doing so, it will not rule out backward causation altogether (Lewis 1973: 567). And although I take this to be a defect, most philosophers do not.

(b) Counterfactual theories, however, have trouble with causes that are not necessary for their effects, i.e. where "C causes E" fails to entail that E would not occur if C did not, as it often seems to do. Fred's smoking can, for example, cause his cancer even if he might have got cancer had he quit. What *can* handle these cases is a probabilistic theory of causation, provided its probabilities are not just the frequencies – e.g. the frequencies with which smokers and non-smokers get cancer – that Reichenbach (1956: §12) and others think they are. For these frequencies, like Hume's constant conjunctions, cannot apply to single events: Fred's cancer cannot be more or less frequently conjoined with his smoking or with his not smoking. Only theories whose probabilities are single-case chances (Mellor 1995: Chs 4–5), like Fred's chances of getting cancer if he smokes and if he doesn't, will make probabilistic causation give time a local direction.

(c) Some causes and effects seem simultaneous, as when "if I view as a cause a ball which impresses a hollow as it lies on a stuffed cushion, the cause is simultaneous with the effect" (Kant 1968 [1781]: A203). This, however, conflicts with laws like Newton's third law of motion, which implies, for example, that the momentum of each of two colliding things will cause the other's momentum to change. For that, if these causes and effects were simultaneous, would require each thing to have its changed and unchanged momentum at the same time, which is impossible (Le Poidevin 1991: Ch. 6). This is one of several incentives to try and explain away apparent cases of simultaneous causation, which I do in my *Real Time II* (1998: Ch. 10.3).

Modern physics may also allow causation across space-like intervals, provided it is either unmediated or mediated by *tachyons*, entities that always travel faster than light, which relativity allows. But the only evidence for this is quantum *non-locality*, where the result of one measurement fixes the result of another made at a space-like interval (Redhead 1983); and what this threatens is not the time order of cause and effect but only "the sense of locality that requires that correlation between space-like separated events always be factorable-out by a common cause" (Skyrms 1980: 127). In particular, since non-locality only links the *results* of measurements, not their being *made*, it does not enable faster-than-light signalling, that is, it does not turn the making of a measurement into an effective means of producing a specific result at a space-like interval. Yet it is a long-recognised implication of causation that causes *are* means to their effects in this sense (Gasking 1955; Mellor 1995: Ch. 7; Price 1996: Ch. 6), an implication that stops non-locality ruling out a causal distinction between time-like and space-like separations.

(d) Identifying time order with causal order seems to rule out backward causation, which is after all conceivable. But that is no objection to an identity proposed, not as a mere analysis of our concepts of causation and time, but as a substantive claim about causation and time themselves. Conceptual analysis of our causal discourse may be "… a guide to our main topic and an introduction to it; but it is not in itself our main topic, and with regard to that topic its authority is far from absolute" (Mackie 1974: 1). And anyway, as we saw in subsection (a), above, this identity does not rule out what we *call* backward causation, like that entailed by backward time travel: it merely makes it entail a local reversal of time.

Nor does identifying temporal with causal order rule out the time-like loops of the first section: identifying the *later* direction in them with that of causation does not make them impossible. Their possibility is indeed often inferred from Gödel's (1949) proof that a global loop is consistent with general relativity (Bourne 2006: Ch. 8) or Lewis's (1976) argument for the consistency of some local loops produced by backward time travel. I reject both inferences, for reasons given in my *Real Time II* (1998: Ch. 12), but either view is compatible with a causal theory of time.

(e) How can causation give the time order of events that are *not* causally related? My answer (Mellor 1998: 113) is that each space–time point is the location of many facts – about density, temperature, the intensity of electromagnetic and other fields, etc. – that *are* causally related to similar facts at other points. And all it takes for causation to fix the time order, if any, of two space–time points t_1 and t_2 is that some fact at t_1 (say) causes some fact at t_2, thereby making each fact at t_1 precede all facts at t_2, whether or not it causes them.

But if the time order of all facts at t_1 and t_2 follows from the causal order of only some of them, might not one fact P at t_1 cause a fact Q at t_2 while another fact R at t_2 causes a fact S at t_1, thereby making t_1 both earlier and later than t_2? Indeed it might, if the causal loops are possible that the causal theory makes backward time travel entail, as when TARDIS travels back in time from t_2 to t_1, with causation outside TARDIS making t_1 earlier than t_2, and causation inside it making t_1 later than t_2. If such loops are possible, as many philosophers suppose, it will also be possible for two space–time points to be both earlier and later than each other. Yet even if this is metaphysically possible, because "the openness of the causal chains [is] an empirical fact" (Reichenbach 1956: 37), and not the contradiction I think it is (Mellor 1998: Ch. 12.4), that openness may still, and I believe will, stop it ever happening in fact.

Conclusion

Inferring from subsections (a)–(e) that time *can* get its direction from its causal arrow, and from earlier sections that it *cannot* get it any other way, I conclude that time is indeed the causal dimension of space–time, with an intrinsic direction that it gets from that of causation.

References

Atkins, P. W. (1986) "Time and Dispersal: The Second Law," in R. Flood and M. Lockwood (eds), *The Nature of Time*, Oxford: Blackwell, pp. 80–98.

Bourne, C. (2006) *A Future for Presentism*, Oxford: Clarendon Press.

Broad, C. D. (1923) *Scientific Thought*, London: Kegan Paul.

Dainton, B. (2001) *Time and Space*, Chesham, UK: Acumen.

Denbigh, K. G. (1955) *The Principles of Chemical Equilibrium*, Cambridge: Cambridge University Press.

Denbigh, K. G. and Denbigh, J. S. (1985) *Entropy in Relation to Incomplete Knowledge*, Cambridge: Cambridge University Press.

Earman, J. (1974) "An Attempt to Add a Little Direction to 'the Problem of the Direction of Time',", *Philosophy of Science* 41: 15–47.

Gasking, D. (1955) "Causation and Recipes," *Mind* 64: 479–87.

Gödel, K. (1949) "A Remark about the Relationship between Relativity Theory and Idealistic Philosophy," in P. A. Schilpp (ed.), *Albert Einstein: Philosopher–Scientist*, La Salle, IL: Open Court, pp. 557–62.

Grünbaum, A. (1968) *Modern Science and Zeno's Paradoxes*, London: Allen & Unwin.

Hume, D. (1975 [1748]) *An Enquiry Concerning Human Understanding*, in *Enquiries Concerning the Human Understanding and Concerning the Principles of Morals*, 3rd edn, edited by L. A. Selby-Bigge and P. H. Nidditch, Oxford: Clarendon Press, pp. 5–165.

James, W. (1890) *The Principles of Psychology*, London: Macmillan.

Kant, I. (1968 [1781]) *Critique of Pure Reason*, London: Macmillan.

Lacey, H. M. (1968) "The Causal Theory of Time: a Critique of Grünbaum's Version," *Philosophy of Science* 35: 332–54.

Le Poidevin, R. (1991) *Change, Cause and Contradiction: A Defence of the Tenseless Theory of Time*, London: Macmillan.

Le Poidevin, R. and MacBeath, M. (eds) (1993) *The Philosophy of Time*, Oxford: Oxford University Press.

Lewis, D. K. (1973) "Causation," *Journal of Philosophy* 70: 556–67.

—— (1976) "The Paradoxes of Time Travel," *American Philosophical Quarterly* 13: 145–52.

Mackie, J. L. (1974) *The Cement of the Universe*, Oxford: Clarendon Press.

McTaggart, J. M. E. (1908) "The Unreality of Time," *Mind* 18: 457–84.

Mellor, D. H. (1995) *The Facts of Causation*, London: Routledge.

—— (1998) *Real Time II*, London: Routledge.

Oaklander, L. N. and Smith, Q. (eds) (1994) *The New Theory of Time*, New Haven, CT: Yale University Press.

Price, H. (1996) *Time's Arrow and Archimedes' Point*, New York: Oxford University Press.

Redhead, M. L. G. (1983) "Nonlocality and Peaceful Coexistence," in R. G. Swinburne (ed.), *Space, Time and Causality*, Dordrecht: Reidel, pp. 151–89.

Reichenbach, H. (1956) *The Direction of Time*, edited by M. Reichenbach, Berkeley: University of California Press.

Robb, A. A. (1914) *A Theory of Time and Space*, Cambridge: Cambridge University Press.

Savitt, S. F. (ed.) (1995) *Time's Arrows Today*, Cambridge: Cambridge University Press.

Skyrms, B. (1980) *Causal Necessity*, New Haven, CT: Yale University Press.

Tooley, M. (1997) *Time, Tense, and Causation*, Oxford: Clarendon Press.

Zeh, H. D. (2007) *The Physical Basis of the Direction of Time*, 5th edn, Berlin: Springer.

Further reading

B. Dainton, *Time and Space* (Chesham, UK: Acumen, 2001), chapters 1–8, provides a good introduction to the topics of this paper. For the flow of time, see R. Le Poidevin and M. MacBeath (eds), *The Philosophy of Time* (Oxford: Oxford University Press, 1993), pts 1 and 3; for time's non-causal arrows, S. F. Savitt (ed.), *Time's Arrows Today* (Cambridge: Cambridge University Press, 1995); and for causal theories of time H. Reichenbach, *The Direction of Time*, edited by M. Reichenbach (Berkeley: University of California Press, 1956), pt 2; and D. H. Mellor, *Real Time II* (London: Routledge, 1998), chapters 10–12.

43
CAUSATION
Michael Tooley

The concept of causation: alternative views

Accounts of the concept of causation can be divided up into four general types: direct non-reductionist, Humean reductionist, non-Humean reductionist, and indirect, or theoretical-term, non-reductionist accounts. This fourfold division, in turn, rests upon the following three distinctions: first, that between reductionism and non-reductionism; second, that between Humean and non-Humean states of affairs; and, third, that between states that are directly observable and those that are not. Let us, then, consider each of these distinctions in turn.

Non-reductionism versus reductionism

The non-reductionism-versus-reductionism distinction in this area arises in connection with both causal laws and causal relations between states of affairs, and it gives rise to a number of related theses. In the case of causal relations between states of affairs, a thesis that is essential to reductionism is this:

- *Basic reductionism with respect to causal relations:* Any two worlds that agree both with respect to all of the non-causal properties of, and relations between, particulars and with respect to all causal laws must also agree with respect to all of the causal relations between states of affairs. Causal relations are, then, logically supervenient upon the totality of instances of non-causal properties and relations, together with causal laws.

But while this thesis is an essential part of a reductionist view of causation, it is not sufficient, since this thesis can be combined with a view of causal laws according to which they obtain in virtue of atomic, and therefore irreducible, facts. What is needed, then, is a reductionist thesis concerning causal laws, and here there are two important possibilities:

- *Strong reductionism with respect to causal laws:* Any two worlds that agree with respect to all of the non-causal properties of, and relations between, particulars must also agree with respect to causal laws. Causal laws are, then, logically supervenient upon the totality of instances of non-causal properties and relations.

- *Moderate reductionism with respect to causal laws:* Any two worlds that agree both with respect to all of the non-causal properties of, and relations between, particulars and with respect to all laws of nature must also agree with respect to all causal laws. Causal laws are, then, logically supervenient upon the totality of instances of non-causal properties and relations, together with laws of nature.

What lies behind this strong-reductionism-versus-moderate-reductionism distinction? The answer is that while most philosophers who are reductionists with regard to causation tend to identify laws of nature with certain cosmic regularities, it is possible to be a reductionist with regard to causation while holding that laws are more than certain cosmic regularities: one might hold, for example, that laws of nature are second-order relations between universals (Dretske 1977; Tooley 1977; Armstrong 1983). Such a person would reject strong reductionism with regard to causal laws, while accepting moderate reductionism.

Each of these two reductionist theses concerning causal laws then entails, in conjunction with the basic reductionist thesis concerning causal relations, a corresponding thesis concerning causal relations between states of affairs:

- *Strong reductionism with respect to causal relations:* Any two worlds that agree with respect to all of the non-causal properties of, and relations between, particulars must also agree with respect to all of the causal relations between states of affairs. Causal relations are, in short, logically supervenient upon the totality of instances of non-causal properties and relations.
- *Moderate reductionism with respect to causal relations:* Any two worlds that agree both with respect to all of the non-causal properties of, and relations between, particulars and with respect to all laws of nature must also agree with respect to all of the causal relations between states of affairs. Causal relations are, then, logically supervenient upon the totality of instances of non-causal properties and relations, together with laws of nature.

To be a reductionist with regard to causation, then, is to accept the basic reductionist thesis with respect to causal relations, and either the strong or the moderate reductionist thesis with respect to causal laws. This then commits one either to the strong reductionist thesis or the moderate reductionist thesis with respect to causal relations.

A non-reductionist with regard to causation, accordingly, is one who rejects either the basic reductionist thesis concerning causal relations, or else both the strong and the moderate reductionist theses with regard to causal laws, or all of these.

Humean versus non-Humean reductionism

Within reductionist approaches, there is an important division. It is based upon the distinction between Humean and non-Humean states of affairs, which can be explained as follows. Let us say that an intrinsic property is non-Humean if and only if the analysis of that property involves an entailment relation between spatially or temporally distinct states of affairs. For example, suppose that water-solubility is viewed as an irreducible property of things, and is defined as follows: "P is the property of water-solubility" =def. "For all x, x's having P at time t and being in water at time t logically entails there is some temporal interval after t during which x is dissolving." Thus defined, water-solubility is a non-Humean property. Non-Humean states of affairs can then be defined as states of affairs that involve at least one non-Humean property, and Humean states of affairs as ones that do not involve any non-Humean properties (for a different definition of Humean states of affairs, see Lewis [1994, 474]).

Direct versus indirect non-reductionism with regard to causation

Non-reductionists with regard to causation, as we have seen, either reject the basic reductionist thesis concerning causal relations, or else both the strong and the moderate reductionist theses concerning causal laws. But there is a crucial divide within non-reductionist approaches, and it concerns the question of whether some causal states of affairs are directly observable. Direct non-reductionism claims that this is so; indirect, or theoretical-term, non-reductionism claims that it is not.

What causal states of affairs are, at least sometimes, directly observable, according to a direct non-reductionist approach to causation? Since it is not at all plausible that one can directly observe causal laws, the relevant states of affairs must consist of causal relations between states of affairs. Thus direct non-reductionism can be defined as a version of non-reductionism that claims that the relation of causation is at least sometimes directly observable.

Indirect, or theoretical-term, non-reductionism rejects this claim, maintaining either that the relation of causation is itself an irreducible, theoretical relation, or, alternatively, that causal relations logically supervene upon non-causal states of affairs, plus causal laws, and that the latter are irreducible, theoretical states of affairs. Either way, then, the relation of causation is not directly observable.

Direct non-reductionism

We can now turn to a consideration of the four general types of approaches to causation, beginning with direct non-reductionism. This view of causation involves four main theses: first, the relation of causation is, at least sometimes, directly observable; second, that relation is not reducible to non-causal properties and relations; third, the relation of causation is also not reducible to non-causal properties and relations together with causal laws – since such a reduction would entail that one could not directly observe the relation of causation; fourth, the concept of the relation of causation is analytically basic.

A number of philosophers have claimed that the relation of causation is observable, including David Armstrong (1997), Elizabeth Anscombe (1971) and Evan Fales (1990). Thus Anscombe argues that one acquires observational knowledge of causal states of affairs when one sees, for example, a stone break a window, or a knife cut through butter, while Fales, who offers the most detailed argument in support of the view that causation is observable, appeals especially to the impression of pressure upon one's body, and to one's introspective awareness of willing, together with the accompanying perception of the event whose occurrence one willed.

Suppose that it is granted that in such cases one does, in some straightforward sense, observe that one event causes another. Does this provide one with a reason for thinking that direct non-reductionism is true? For it to do so, one would have to be able to move from the claim that the relation of causation is thus observable to the conclusion that it is not necessary to offer any analysis of the concept of causation, that the latter can be taken as analytically basic. But observational knowledge, in this broad, everyday sense would not seem to provide adequate grounds for concluding that the relevant concepts are analytically basic. One can, for example, quite properly speak of physicists as seeing electrons when they look into cloud chambers, even though the concept of an electron is certainly not analytically basic. Similarly, the fact, for example, that sodium chloride is observable, and that one can tell by simply looking and tasting that a substance is sodium chloride, does not mean that the expression "sodium chloride" does not stand in need of analysis.

But might it not be argued in response, first, that, one can observe that two events are causally related in precisely the same sense in which one can observe that something is red; second, that the concept of being red is analytically basic, in virtue of the observ- ability of redness; and therefore, third, that the concept of causation must, for parallel reasons, also be analytically basic?

This response is open, however, to the following reply. If a concept is analytically basic, then one can acquire the concept in question only by being in perceptual or introspective contact with *an instance* of the property or relation in question that is picked out by the concept. One could, however, acquire the concept of a physical object's being red in a world where there were no red physical objects: it would suffice if things sometimes looked red, or if one had hallucinations of seeing red things, or experienced red afterimages. The concept of a physical object's being red must, therefore, be definable and cannot be analytically basic.

What is required if a concept is to be analytically basic? The answer suggested by the case of the concept of redness is that for a concept to be analytically basic, the property or relation in virtue of which the concept applies to a given thing must be such that that property or relation is immediately given in experience, where that is the case only if, for any two qualitatively identical experiences the property or relation must either be present in both or present in neither.

Is the relation of causation immediately given in experience? The answer is that it is not. For given any experience E whatever – be it a perception of external events, an awareness of pressure upon one's body, or an introspective awareness of some mental occurrence, such as an act of willing or a process of thinking – it is logically possible that appropriate, direct stimulation of the brain might produce an experience, E^*, that was qualitatively identical to E, but which did not involve any causally related elements. So, for example, it might seem to one that one was engaging in a process of deductive reasoning, when, in fact, there was not really any direct connection at all between the thoughts themselves – since all of them were in fact being caused instead by something outside of oneself. Causal relations cannot, therefore, be immediately given in experience in the sense required if the concept of causation is to be un-analyzable.

Let us now turn to objections to direct non-reductionism. The first has, in effect, just been set out. For if, for any experience in which one is in perceptual or introspective contact with the relation of causation, there could be a qualitatively identical, hallucinatory experience in which one was not in contact with the relation of causation, it would be possible to acquire the concept of causation without ever being in contact with an instance of that relation. But such experiences are logically possible. So the concept of causation must be analyzable, rather than being analytically basic.

Second, it seems plausible that there is a basic relation of causation that is necessarily irreflexive and asymmetric, even if this is not true of the ancestral of that relation. If either reductionism or theoretical-term non-reductionism is correct, one may very well be able to explain the necessary truths in question, since the fact that causal concepts are, on either of those views, analyzable means that those necessary truths may turn out to be analytic. Direct non-reductionism, by contrast, in holding that the concept of causation is analytically basic, is barred from offering such an explanation of the asymmetry and irreflexivity of the basic relation of causation. It therefore has to treat these as a matter of synthetic *a priori* truths.

Third, direct non-reductionism encounters epistemological problems. Thus, features such as the direction of increase in entropy, or the direction of the transmission of order in non-entropic, irreversible processes, or the direction of open forks often provide evidence concerning how events are causally connected. In addition, causal beliefs are often established on the basis of statistical information – using methods that, especially within the social sciences, are often very sophisticated. Given an appropriate analysis of the relation of causation, one can show why such features are epistemologically relevant, and why the statistical methods in question can serve to establish causal hypotheses, whereas if causation is a basic, irreducible relation, it is not at all clear how either of these things can be the case.

Humean reductionism

The two most important present-day types of Humean reductionist approaches to causation are, first, accounts in which counterfactual conditionals play the crucial role, and, second, accounts based upon probabilistic relations of a Humean sort.

Counterfactual conditional approaches

This first reductionist approach involves analyzing causation using subjunctive conditionals. John L. Mackie (1965) was the first to advance such an approach, but the best-known and most fully developed version is that of David Lewis (1973b, 1986). Lewis's basic strategy involves analyzing causation in terms of a narrower notion of causal dependence and then analyzing causal dependence counterfactually: (1) an event *c* causes an event *e* if, and only if, there is a chain of causally dependent events linking *e* with c; (2) an event g is causally dependent upon an event f if, and only if, had f not occurred, g would not have occurred.

Counterfactual approaches to causation are exposed to a number of objections. One involves overdetermination, where two events, c and d, are followed by an event e, and where each of c and d would have been causally sufficient, on its own, to produce e. If it can be true, in such cases, both that c causes e and that d causes e, then one has a counterexample to Lewis's counterfactual analysis.

A second objection involves cases of preemption. These are cases where there is some event c that causes e, but where there is also some event d that did not cause e, but that failed to do so only because the presence of c prevented it from doing so.

Initial discussions of preemption focused on cases where one causal process preempts another by blocking the occurrence of some state of affairs in the other process, and a variety of closely related ways of attempting to handle this type of preemption were advanced, involving such notions as fragility of events, quasi-dependence, continuous processes, minimal-counterfactual sufficiency, and minimal-dependence sets (Lewis 1986; Menzies 1989; McDermott 1995; Ramachandran 1997).[1] But none of these approaches can handle the case of trumping preemption, advanced by Jonathan Schaffer (2000), where one causal process preempts another without preventing the occurrence of any of the states of affairs involved in the other causal process.

Third, there is the problem of explaining the direction of causation. One possibility is to define the direction of causation as the direction of time, but neither Mackie nor Lewis favored that approach: both thought that backward causation is logically possible. Mackie's main proposal for analyzing the direction of causation appealed to the direction of irreversible processes involving the transmission of order – such as with outgoing concentric waves produced by a stone hitting a pond. Lewis advanced a related proposal, in which the direction of counterfactual dependence, and hence causal dependence, is based upon the idea that events in this world have many more effects than they have causes. Both suggestions, however, seem unsatisfactory, since the relevant features are at best contingent ones, and it would seem that, even if the world had neither of these features, it could still contain causally related events.

A final objection, and the most fundamental of all, concerns the truth conditions for the counterfactuals that enter into the analysis. One familiar approach to counterfactuals maintains that the truthmakers for counterfactuals concerning events in time involve causal facts (Jackson 1977). Such analyses cannot of course be used in an analysis of causation, on pain of circularity. Accordingly, Lewis formulated his analysis of causation in terms of counterfactuals whose truth conditions are a matter of similarity relations across possible worlds (Stalnaker 1968; Lewis 1973a). It can be shown, however, by a variant on an objection advanced by Bennett (1974) and Fine (1975), that this account of counterfactuals does not yield the correct truth-values in all cases (Tooley 2003). Moreover, the same type of counterexample also shows that an analysis of causation based on such conditionals will generate the wrong truth-values in the cases in question.

Probabilistic approaches

Among the more important developments in the philosophy of causation since the time of Hume is the idea, partly motivated by quantum mechanics, that causation is not restricted to deterministic processes. This has led several philosophers to propose that causation itself should be analyzed in probabilistic terms.

The central idea is that causes make their effects more likely. This idea can, however, be developed in two rather different ways. The traditional approach, advanced by Hans Reichenbach (1956), I. J. Good (1961–2) and Patrick Suppes (1970), focuses upon types of events and involves the notion of positive statistical relevance. According to this notion, an event of type C is positively relevant to an event of type E if and only if the conditional probability of an event of type E, given an event of type C, is greater than the unconditional probability of an event of type E. The basic idea, then, is that for events of type C to be direct causes of events of type E, a necessary condition is that the former be positively relevant to the latter.

But do causes necessarily make their effects more likely? Consider two types of diseases, A and B, governed by the following laws. First, disease A causes death with probability 0.1, while disease B causes death with probability 0.8. Second, contracting either disease produces complete immunity to the other. Third, in condition C, an individual must contract either disease A or disease B. (Condition C might be a weakening of the immune system.) Finally, assume that individual m is in condition C and contracts disease A, which causes his or her death. Given these conditions, what if m, though in condition C, had not contracted disease A? Then m would have contracted disease B. But if so, then m's probability of dying had he or she not contracted disease A would have been 0.8 – higher than the individual's probability of dying given that he or she had contracted disease A. So the claim that lies at the heart of probabilistic approaches – that causes necessarily make their effects more likely – cannot be true.

Humean reductionism and the direction of causation

In addition to objections against specific Humean reductionist accounts, there are also general objections that tell against all such accounts. One, for example, concerns the question of what Humean facts determine the direction of causation. For while Humean reductionists have advanced various suggestions, some arguments seem to show that no such account can possibly work. One argument, for example, appeals to the idea of a very simple world consisting of a single particle. Such a world would still involve causation, since the existence of the particle at a later time would be caused by its existence at an earlier time. But since such a world would be time-symmetric as regards Humean facts, the events in it would not exhibit any non-causal patterns that could provide the basis for a Humean reductionist account of the direction of causation.

Non-Humean reductionism: objective chance approaches to causation

Traditional probabilistic approaches, in analyzing causation in terms of statistical relations, offered a Humean reductionist account of causation. Recently, however, an alternative type of probabilistic approach to causation has been suggested, one that involves analyzing causation in terms of propensities, or objective chances. At least some objective chances, however, are non-Humean properties of events, as is shown by the earlier water-solubility example. An analysis of causation that involves objective chances is therefore a non-Humean reductionist account.

Several philosophers – including Rom Harré and Edward Madden (1975), Nancy Cartwright (1989) and C. B. Martin (1993) – have both advocated an ontology in which irreducible dispositional properties, powers, propensities, chances and the like occupy a central place, and maintained that such an ontology is relevant to causation. Usually, however, the details have been rather sparse. But a clear account of the basic idea of analyzing causation in terms of objective chances was set out in 1986, both by D. H. Mellor and by David Lewis, and then, more recently, Mellor has offered a very detailed statement and defense of this general approach in his book *The Facts of Causation* (1995).

Mellor's approach, in brief, is roughly as follows. First, he embraces an ontology involving objective chances, where the latter are ultimate properties of states of affairs, rather than being logically supervenient upon causal laws together with non-dispositional properties, plus relations. Second, he defines chances as properties that satisfy three conditions: (1) the necessity condition (if the chance of P's obtaining is equal to one, then P is the case); (2) the evidence condition (if one's total evidence concerning P is that the chance of P's obtaining is equal to k, then one's subjective probability that P is the case should be equal to k); (3) the frequency condition (the chance that P is the case is related to the corresponding relative frequency in the limit). Third, chances enter into basic laws of nature. Fourth, Mellor holds that even basic laws of nature need not have instances, thereby rejecting reductionist accounts in favor of a non-reductionist view. Fifth, any chance that P is the case must be a property of a state of affairs that temporally precedes the time at which P exists, or would exist. Finally, and as a very rough approximation, a state of affairs c causes a state of affairs e if and only if there are numbers x and y such that (1) the total state of affairs that exists at the time of c – including laws of nature – entails that the chance of e is x; (2) the total state of affairs that would exist at the time of c, if c did not exist, entails that the chance of e is y; and (3) x is greater than y.

This account is open to four main objections. First of all, there is the objection that the whole idea of non-Humean properties, and so of non-Humean states of affairs, appears incoherent. This is clearest if one considers causal laws involving objects of one type, S, giving rise to objects of some other type, T. If an object of type S has some dispositional property that makes it the case that it will give rise to an object of type T, and if that dispositional property is an intrinsic property of objects, then an object's having that intrinsic property logically entails that there will be an object of type T at a later time. But how can this be, given that an intrinsic property of an object is one that an object can possess even if there are no other objects that exist at any time or place?

Second, this account necessarily involves Stalnaker–Lewis counterfactuals, and, as was noted earlier, such a closest-worlds account of counterfactuals is unsound.

Third, a number of objections can be directed against the view that objective chances are ontologically ultimate properties. For example, imagine that the world is *deterministic*, that every temporal interval is divisible, and that all causation involves continuous processes. Let t_1 and t_2 be any two times, and let C be some possible property of x. Then there are an infinite number of moments between t_1 and t_2 and for every such moment, t, it must be the case either that x at time t_1 has an objective chance equal to 1 of being C at time t, or that x at time t_1 has an objective chance equal to 1 of not being C at time t. But then, if objective chances are ontologically ultimate, intrinsic properties of things at a time, it follows that x at time t_1 must have an infinite number of intrinsic properties – indeed, a non-denumerably infinite number of intrinsic properties.

This view of the nature of objective chances involves, accordingly, a very expansive ontology indeed. By contrast, if objective chances, rather than being ontologically basic, supervene on categorical properties plus causal laws, this infinite set of intrinsic properties of x at time t_1 disappears, and all that there need be is a single, intrinsic, categorical property – or a small number of such properties – together with relevant laws of nature.

Fourth, there are objections to the effect that, even given this view of objective chances, the resulting account of causation is unsound. Here one of the most important objections is that, just as in the case of attempts to analyze causation in terms of relative frequencies, it can be shown that the crucial claim that a cause raises the probability of its effect remains unsound when one shifts from relative frequencies to objective chances.

General objections to reductionism

In addition to objections directed specifically either against Humean reductionism or non-Humean reductionism, there are also general objections that bear upon reductionism in any form, since they are directed against the basic reductionist thesis that causal relations are logically supervenient upon the totality of instances of non-causal properties and relations, together with causal laws. For example, assume that indeterministic laws are logically possible and that, in particular, it is a basic law both that an object's acquiring property P causes it to acquire either property Q or property R, but not both, and that an object's acquiring property S also causes it to acquire either property Q or property R, but not both. Suppose now that some object simultaneously acquires both property P and property S and then immediately acquires both property Q and property R. The problem now is that, given that the relevant laws are basic, there cannot be any non-causal facts, including ontologically ultimate dispositional facts, that will determine which causal relations obtain. Did the acquisition of P cause the acquisition of Q, or did it cause the acquisition of R? On a reductionist approach, no answer is possible. Accordingly, it would seem that causal relations between events cannot be logically supervenient upon causal laws plus non-causal states of affairs.

Indirect, or theoretical-term, non-reductionism

Direct non-reductionism with regard to causation is, as we saw earlier, deeply problematic. There is, however, a very different form of causal non-reductionism, according to which causation is a theoretical relation between events. This approach to causation involves finding postulates that serve to define implicitly the relation of causation. One suggestion here (Tooley 1990), for example, starts out with postulates for causal laws that say, very roughly, that the *a posteriori* probabilities of effects are a function of the *a priori* probabilities of their causes, whereas, by contrast, the *a posteriori* probabilities of causes are not a function of the *a priori* probabilities of their effects. Then, when one adds the further postulate that causal laws involve the relation of causation, the result is an implicit definition of the relation of causation. That implicit definition can then be converted into an explicit one by using one's preferred approach to the definition of theoretical terms. So, for example, if one adopted a Ramsey/Lewis approach, the relation of causation could be defined as that unique relation between states of affairs that satisfies the relevant open sentences corresponding to the postulates in question.

The most common objection to theoretical-term non-reductionism, advanced by Huw Price (1996: 154) and others, is that such an approach makes causal relations epistemically inaccessible. But given that we can have justified beliefs about other theoretical states of affairs, it is not clear why things should be different in the case of causation if causal states of affairs are treated as theoretical. Moreover, the objection seems especially problematic in the case of a non-reductionist approach that brings in probabilistic relations, since then different causal hypotheses will generate different predictions concerning statistical relations involving non-causal states of affairs. It would then seem that nothing more than the use of Bayes' theorem will be needed to determine the probability that a given causal hypothesis is true.

Note

1   This is evident in the following passages:

> An event is *fragile* if, or to the extent that, numerically the same event could not have occurred at a different time or in a different manner. (Lewis 1986: 196)

> An event *e quasi-depends* on event *c* if and only if, while *e* is not counterfactually dependent upon *e*, *e* and *c* belong to a process *p* which is such that in the vast majority of processes that are identical with *p* with regard to their intrinsic character, the event *e** that corresponds to *e* is counterfactually dependent upon the event *c** that corresponds to *c*. (Lewis 1986: 205–6)

> A set C of events is a minimal, counterfactually sufficient condition of event *e* if and only the following three conditions are satisfied: (i) set C is a counterfactually sufficient condition of *e*, where this means that, given the occurrence of all of the events in set C, *e* would have occurred, regardless of what other actual events failed to occur; (ii) no subset of C is a counterfactually sufficient condition of *e*; (iii) no actual event *r* that is distinct both from *e* and from all the members of C is such that both (a) there is a proper subset C* of C such that the union of C* and {*r*} is a counterfactually sufficient condition of *e*, and (b) there is a proper subset C* of C such that the union of C* and {not-*r*} is a counterfactually sufficient condition of *e*. (McDermott 1995: 533–5)

A non-empty set of events, S, is a dependence set for an event e, where e is not a member of S, if and only if, had none of the events in S occurred, then e would not have occurred. If, in addition, no proper subset of S is a dependence set for e, then S is a minimal dependence set for E. (Ramachandran 1997: 270)

References

Anscombe, G. E. M. (1971) *Causality and Determination*, Cambridge: Cambridge University Press.

Armstrong, David M. (1983) *What Is a Law of Nature?* Cambridge: Cambridge University Press.

—— (1997) *A World of States of Affairs*, Cambridge: Cambridge University Press.

Bennett, Jonathan (1974) "Counterfactuals and Possible Worlds," *Canadian Journal of Philosophy* 4: 381–402.

Cartwright, Nancy (1989) *Nature's Capacities and Their Measurement*, Oxford: Clarendon Press.

Dretske, Fred I. (1977) "Laws of Nature," *Philosophy of Science* 44: 248–68.

Fales, Evan (1990) *Causation and Universals*, London; New York: Routledge.

Fine, Kit (1975) "Critical Notice – *Counterfactuals*," *Mind* 84: 451–8.

Good. I. J. (1961–2) "A Causal Calculus," Pts 1 and 2, *British Journal for the Philosophy of Science* 11: 305–18, and 12: 43–51.

Harré, Rom and Madden, Edward H. (1975) *Causal Powers*, Oxford: Blackwell.

Jackson, Frank (1977) "A Causal Theory of Counterfactuals," *Australasian Journal of Philosophy* 55: 3–21.

Lewis, David (1973a) *Counterfactuals*, Cambridge, MA: Harvard University Press.

—— (1973b) "Causation," *Journal of Philosophy* 70: 556–67; reprinted, with postscripts, in *Philosophical Papers*, vol. 2, Oxford: Oxford University Press, 1986.

—— (1986) "Postscripts to 'Causation'," in *Philosophical Papers*, vol. 2, Oxford: Oxford University Press, pp. 172–213.

—— (1994) "Humean Supervenience Debugged," *Mind* 103: 473–90.

Mackie, John L. (1965) "Causes and Conditions," *American Philosophical Quarterly* 2: 245–64.

Martin, C. B. (1993) "Power for Realists," in John Bacon, Keith Campbell, and Lloyd Reinhardt (eds), *Ontology, Causality and Mind*, Cambridge: Cambridge University Press, pp. 175–85.

McDermott, Michael (1995) "Redundant Causation," *British Journal for the Philosophy of Science* 40: 523–44.

Mellor, D. H. (1986) "Fixed Past, Unfixed Future," in Barry Taylor (ed.), *Contributions to Philosophy: Michael Dummett*, The Hague: Nijhoff, pp. 166–86.

—— (1995) *The Facts of Causation*, London: Routledge.

Menzies, Peter (1989) "Probabilistic Causation and Causal Processes: A Critique of Lewis," *Philosophy of Science* 56: 642–63.

Price, Huw (1996) *Time's Arrow and Archimedes' Point*, Oxford: Oxford University Press.

Ramachandran, Murali (1997) "A Counterfactual Analysis of Causation," *Mind* 106: 263–77.

Reichenbach, Hans (1956) *The Direction of Time*, Berkeley; Los Angeles: University of California Press.

Schaffer, Jonathan (2000) "Trumping Preemption," *Journal of Philosophy* 97, no. 4: 165–81.

Stalnaker, Robert C. (1968) "A Theory of Conditionals," in Nicholas Rescher (ed.), *Studies in Logical Theory*, *American Philosophical Quarterly* (Monograph 2), Oxford: Blackwell, pp. 98–112.

Suppes, Patrick (1970) *A Probabilistic Theory of Causality*, Amsterdam: North-Holland Publishing.

Tooley, Michael (1977) "The Nature of Laws," *Canadian Journal of Philosophy* 7, no. 4: 667–98.

—— (1990) "The Nature of Causation: A Singularist Account," *Canadian Journal of Philosophy* 16 (suppl.): 271–322; special issue, *Canadian Philosophers*, edited by D. Copp.

—— (2003) "The Stalnaker–Lewis Approach to Counterfactuals," *Journal of Philosophy* 100, no. 7: 321–27.

Further reading

For further reading, see Aristotle, *Physics*, Book 2; Wayne Davis, "Probabilistic Theories of Causation," in James H. Fetzer (ed.), *Probability and Causation: Essays in Honor of Wesley Salmon* (Dordrecht: Reidel, 1988), pp. 133–60; Daniel M. Hausman, *Causal Asymmetries* (Cambridge: Cambridge University Press, 1998);

Germund Hesslow, "Two Notes on the Probabilistic Approach to Causation," *Philosophy of Science* 43 (1976): 290–2; and David Hume, *A Treatise of Human Nature* (London, 1739–40); and *An Enquiry Concerning Human Understanding* (London, 1748). David M. Armstrong and Adrian Heathcote, "Causes and Laws," *Noûs* 25 (1991): 63–73, is a defense of the thesis that causal necessitation is identical with nomic necessitation, and that this is a necessary, but *a posteriori*, truth. P. Dowe, *Physical Causation* (New York: Cambridge University Press, 2000) offers a defense of a conserved quantities account of causation. Phil Dowe and Paul Noordhof (eds) *Cause and Chance* (London; New York: Routledge, 2004) contains essays on the relation between causation and probability. Ellery Eells, *Probabilistic Causality* (Cambridge: Cambridge University Press, 1991) offers a detailed exposition of a probabilistic approach. Douglas Ehring, *Causation and Persistence* (New York: Oxford University Press, 1997) gives a defense of a singularist conception of causal relations, based on a theory of trope persistence; and David Fair, "Causation and the Flow of Energy," *Erkenntnis* 14 (1979): 219–50, an exposition of a contingent identity theory of causation. David Lewis, "Counterfactual Dependence and Time's Arrow," *Noûs* 13 (1979): 455–76 (reprinted, with postscripts, in *Philosophical Papers*, vol. 2 [Oxford: Oxford University Press, 1986]), addresses the problem of the direction of counterfactual dependence; "Causation as Influence," *Journal of Philosophy* 97, no. 4 (2000): 182–97, revises his earlier counterfactual account of causation; *The Cement of the Universe* (Oxford: Oxford University Press, 1974) gives a careful exposition of a reductionist approach to causation; and *Counterfactuals* (Cambridge, MA: Harvard University Press, 1973), an exposition of a similarity across possible worlds approach to counterfactuals. Wesley C. Salmon, *Scientific Explanation and the Causal Structure of the World* (Princeton, NJ: Princeton University Press, 1984) takes a reductionist approach, combining the idea of causal processes with a probabilistic account of causal interaction; and "Probabilistic Causality," *Pacific Philosophical Quarterly* 61 (1980): 50–74, critically examines probabilistic approaches to causation. Ernest Sosa and Michael Tooley (eds), *Causation* (Oxford: Oxford University Press, 1993) is an anthology of contemporary discussions of causation, plus a bibliography. Galen Strawson, *The Secret Connexion: Causation, Realism, and David Hume* (Oxford: Oxford University Press, 1989) defends non-reductionism and challenges the standard reductionist interpretation of David Hume's approach. Michael Tooley, *Causation: A Realist Approach* (Oxford: Oxford University Press, 1988) offers a defense of a non-reductionist view, arguing that causation is a theoretical relation between events. See also his *Time, Tense, and Causation* (Oxford: Oxford University Press, 1997) (reprinted in a revised, paperback edition in 2000); and "Probability and Causation," in Phil Dowe and Paul Noordhof (eds), *Cause and Chance* (London; New York: Routledge, 2004); and Philip von Bretzel, "Concerning a Probabilistic Theory of Causation Adequate for the Causal Theory of Time," *Synthese* 35 (1977): 173–90; and James Woodward, *Making Things Happen – A Theory of Causal Explanation* (Oxford: Oxford University Press, 2003). Georg Henrik von Wright, *Explanation and Understanding* (Ithaca, NY: Cornell University Press, 1971) offers a defense of the view that the concept of causation is to be analyzed in terms of the idea of action.

44
LAWS AND DISPOSITIONS
Stephen Mumford

Evidently there is at least some order and predictability to be found in the world. According to some, this order has an explanation in terms of the world being law-governed. Regularity is thus explained in terms of laws of nature that determine the events occurring in the world or the regular associations that can be found between properties, or between natural kinds and their properties. The source of such laws remains philosophically controversial, however, and it is even controversial that there are any real laws of nature at all. One problem seems to be that while the empirical sciences are concerned with the phenomena and may be happy to call something a law merely because there is some statistical correlation or other regularity to be found, metaphysicians usually require a law to be something more substantial that perhaps underlies and explains any correlations to be found. They tend to think that some regularities could be pure coincidences and that there is a distinction to be drawn between an accidental and genuinely law-like regularity. If they think this, they will seek a metaphysical theory of laws as lying beyond the observable phenomena, and the fact that science often speaks of laws of nature does not determine conclusively that the world is literally law governed.

It should be apparent that this issue concerns the most fundamental features of the way our world works. Do things happen in our world just by accident or do they happen because a law determines them? Do they happen because something else determines them? The latter option has come to prominence recently due to the emergence, or re-emergence, of an ontology of real causal powers, in which it is claimed that powers or dispositions do much of the work previously attributed to laws. There is thus real debate and at least three strong but opposed explanations of the fundamental workings of reality. I will describe and assess each of these three main options. They are the law-governed account of the world, the Humean lawless account, and finally the powers account.

Let us first, however, consider the sort of phenomena under investigation. We accept certain claims of science to have the status of laws. Some of these are very famous and well-known, such as Newton's laws of motion and the law of gravitational attraction. The laws of motion state how material bodies will move. The law of gravitational attraction tells us that the force of attraction between two bodies is a function of their masses and distances apart. But these are just laws of physics. Other sciences employ laws, such as in chemistry, where the laws tell us how different elements combine; and in biology, where there are putative laws about how genes combine. In some areas of knowledge, such as economics, psychology or sociology, it is controversial whether there are genuine laws to be found. Their status as sciences may depend on whether they genuinely discover laws.

Laws of nature

The idea of nature being law-governed may well have its historical roots in theism (Ruby 1986). Nature was at one time widely regarded as God's creation and just as he was thought to have made moral laws, in the form of the Ten Commandments, he was thought to have made natural laws. Even now, scientists such as Stephen Hawking say that if we understand all the laws of nature, then we will know the mind of God (Hawking 1988). The idea is that instead of having constantly to intervene to keep the world in an ordered state, God could simply have set in place laws that do the work for him. Because the mind of God was understood to be perfect, these laws would be simple and efficient. There would be no unnecessary duplication or redundancy among them. The three laws of motion in Newtonian mechanics reflect this economy as Newton (1934 [1687]) attempted a system of laws that was both simple, with the fewest laws possible, but strong, able to explain as much of nature's workings as possible.

If we are not theists, should we still utilize the historically theological notion of a law of nature? Can we accept, for instance, that there can be such laws without a lawmaker? Many metaphysicians have said that there can be. The natural sciences suggest that there are real natural laws, irrespective of God's existence, and a metaphysics ought to be able to explain what they are. There is far from a consensus on this, however. Some metaphysicians say that we can, and should, develop a metaphysics that does not require substantial laws of nature, and one philosopher has explicitly criticized realists about laws for seeking a surrogate for God in their law-governed view of the world (Carroll 1994).

The most metaphysically thorough attempt to construct a naturalistic account of laws is the so-called DTA theory, named after Dretske (1977), Tooley (1977) and Armstrong (1983), who developed similar accounts simultaneously but independently. What unites their theories is the idea that laws are relations of necessitation holding at the level of universals. Previous accounts said that laws somehow bound groups of particulars. A law would say something such as "if this is a raven, then it is black." In logical form, law statements would be universally quantified conditionals such as $\forall x \, (Fx \rightarrow Gx)$. The innovation of the DTA theory was to argue that the law should be seen as something that holds between the properties, F and G, rather than between the particulars that bear those properties. The law would hold between ravenhood and blackness, for instance, if those were genuine properties. Furthermore, the DTA theory is a claim that there is a nomological relation of necessity that holds between these properties. Thus, in Armstrong's version, the logical form of a law statement is $N(F,G)$, where N is a higher-order relation of natural necessitation that takes properties such as F and G as its relata. The law could thus be stated in terms of ravenhood necessitating blackness.

There are numerous claimed advantages of this theory over a regularity theory. A regularity is about only the actual things that are F, and it does not therefore support counterfactuals. We would usually think, however, that any theory of laws that deserves the name ought to have laws that support counterfactuals. It ought to allow that if this thing that is not actually F were F, then it would also be G. $\forall x\,(Fx \to Gx)$ cannot support this claim. But if the law instead holds directly between the universals involved in the law, then it would support the relevant counterfactual. Being F naturally necessitates being G, so if anything were to be F then it would be G. It should be clear, therefore, that $N(F,G)$ entails $\forall x\,(Fx \to Gx)$, though the entailment does not hold in the opposite direction.

This allows us to distinguish, as a further advantage of the theory, between accidental and genuinely law-like regularities. A famous case in the literature concerns every moa bird dying before the age of fifty. It is supposed that every bird of this now-extinct species died at a young age, though not because of anything in its genetic makeup. Rather, it died mainly because of some virus that just happened to sweep though the population. One bird could have escaped the virus only to be eaten by a predator on the day before its fiftieth birthday. In such a case, something of the form $\forall x\,(Fx \to Gx)$ would be true but it is implausible, so the proponents of the DTA view claim, that there is a law of nature at work. The theory can distinguish cases of accidental and genuinely law-like regularities, therefore, on the basis that while a universally quantified conditional is true in both instances, only in the latter case is something like $N(F,G)$ true.

The DTA theory comes at the price of accepting a realist theory of universals, though some think that in any case there are independent reasons for being a realist about universals. We have to accept that F-ness and G-ness are real features of the world. Armstrong has basically an Aristotelian theory of immanent universals whereas Tooley's realism is more Platonist. Nominalism is to be rejected as that view accepts an ontology only of particulars. There would thus be a natural association between nominalism and a theory of laws (if the nominalist wants any laws at all) as universal quantifications over classes of, for instance, resembling particulars. The particulars that are F would be just a class of resembling things rather than particulars that instantiate a real universal F. But if we accept the reality of universals, there are payoffs. In the first place, we would have an explanation of why laws of nature are genuinely universal, holding at all times and places, without exception. In the theory of universals, a property or relation is identical in every instantiation. Universals are a genuine identity that runs through many different possible particulars. Thus where a is square and b is square, squareness is some genuine feature to be found, fully present, in both a and b. Now $N(F,G)$ is a relation and thus itself a universal. It is a higher-order relation in that its relata are themselves universals. But relations, as universals, must be identical in every instance. In other words, if $N(F,G)$ holds in just one case of F and G, it holds in all cases. Genuine laws cannot, thus, be spatiotemporally limited.

In Armstrong's version of the theory, there is a further, rather spectacular payoff. Because he is an immanent realist about universals, all universals must be instantiated at least once, at some time and place in the history of the world. The law $N(F,G)$ is itself a universal so it too must have at least one instance. What would count as an instance of N(F,G)? It cannot be simply that some particular thing is both F and G. That would not be enough as it would be an instance simply of the conjunctive universal F&G. The instances must instantiate not just the F and the G but also the natural necessitation between them. Armstrong sees that the most likely candidates for the instantiations of laws of nature are particular causal sequences, where some particular being F causes that same particular to be G in virtue of the F and G. We thus arrive at a satisfying interdependence of the notions of law and cause. For something to be a cause of something else is for that sequence to instantiate a law. And what it is for something to be a law is for its instances to be causal sequences.

It should be noted that Armstrong has worked to produce variants on the basic nomological form. There could thus be laws that relate distinct particulars, where something being F necessitates that something else is G. There can be functional laws, probabilistic laws and laws that allow for exceptions. He offers theories of each, still within the basic terms of laws being higher-order relations.

What, though, are the weak points of such a theory? It has provoked many criticisms, mainly over the nature of the natural necessitation relation, N. It was said by some to be an *ad hoc* and *sui generis* relation (Mellor 1980). It is a relation that is defined as playing a certain role: of necessitating a regularity. But merely saying that there is something that plays this role is no evidence that it is real, nor is it an explanation of how the role is played. Armstrong tried to address this problem by saying that if being F necessitates being G in one instance, then it must do so in every instance. Why, though, should we believe that, even in one case, being F necessitates being G, in virtue of F and G? Armstrong believes that we get an idea of laws through experiencing their singular instances in causation. This is a very controversial part of his theory. He thinks that through our own bodily experiences, of being subject to forces and pushes, and initiating the same, we can experience causation directly and thus know that the world contains this kind of natural necessity. Humeans, and many others, deny that the world contains such necessity and that we have any such experiences.

Humean views

Hume (1739–40) looked, and professed he could not find, the kind of necessity in the world that realists about laws claim. He did not deny that regularity could be found, or constant conjunction as he called it, but denied that we had any legitimate reason to believe in necessity underlying or causing such regularity. In seeking empirical evidence of such necessity, however, his examples were mainly confined to visual cases, where he saw merely one thing followed by another.

This Humean view spawns an account of laws that is an entirely different way of looking at the world to the realist view considered thus far. David Lewis has been the leading philosopher to have developed a Humean metaphysic, Hume having not thought of himself as a metaphysician. As Lewis says, in the Humean view, the world is a patchwork of unconnected facts or events. This is known as the Humean mosaic: the individual mosaic tiles representing Hume's distinct existences. There is no necessitation between any of the tiles: they just occur or exist, without there being anything that makes them occur or exist.

What can we say of laws of nature if the world really is constructed this way? There is a basic Humean theory of laws and then a more sophisticated version that Lewis himself develops. The basic theory is known as the regularity theory. On this view, the laws are just the regularities to be found among the world. The law would be nothing more than that everything F is also G, for instance that all unsupported objects fall to the ground or that human beheading is invariably associated with death. The temptation in these cases is to think that there are laws, of physics and biology, that make it the case that one thing regularly follows another. But this is to assume some kind of necessity in the world of which, according to Humeans, we have no evidence. Instead, we might think of mosaic tiles having been shaken up in a bucket and then thrown across the floor at random. Were that to happen, we could well find that there are patterns, formed of such randomness. Perhaps whenever there is a blue, square tile, there is a red, round tile to be found next to it. There is no reason why there is this regular pattern to be found in the mosaic: it is just there. So it is, the Humean thinks, for regularities to be found in the world at large. Beheading and death just happen to be regularly associated because that's the way the world's events occur. Whenever there is a beheading, there is death, but we cannot say that one kind of thing necessitates the other.

As a theory of laws, however, this metaphysically minimal view may have some attraction. A scientist, after all, does not worry about whether there is any necessity that makes a regularity. Their job is merely to report the regular associations they find in nature. A law is just about what invariably follows what. And where science does attempt to explain such regularities, it does so in terms of further, more fundamental regularities (e.g. all decapitated animals die). When we get to those fundamental regularities, however, no one can offer further explanation. They are simply the case: brute facts of regularity. The Humean view could well claim, therefore, consistency with the scientific use of laws.

Lewis (1973: 72–7) has offered a more sophisticated version of the regularity view in what is known as a Best Systems account of laws. He noticed that laws tend to come in interconnected, integrated systems, with explanatory relations between lower- and higher-level laws. For Lewis, the laws of nature would be the regularities that could form the axioms (for fundamental laws) or theorems (for non-fundamental laws) of the best possible systematizations of the total world history. All the world's events could in theory be organized into a deductive system in the same way as the logical systematization of mathematics by Russell and Whitehead (1910–13). The best possible systematization would be one whose axioms had the optimal combination of simplicity and strength. A system would be stronger the more of the world's history it could produce. A system would be simpler the fewer axioms it contained. The best system or systems is that or those with the right balance between these two assets of strength and simplicity (two systematizations could tie for first place). The laws in Newton's *Principia* can be understood very much in this way. Newton even calls his three laws of motion his *axioms*. He is looking for the fewest, simplest assumptions from which we could deduce as much as possible about the way material bodies actually move.

On this sophisticated Humean view, the laws are still regularities. It is just that they are the regularities that would be the axioms of the best possible systematization(s) of the world. But they are regularities nevertheless and are thus subject to some of the same concerns as the basic regularity theory. These regularities cannot govern the workings of nature: they are merely reports, summaries or systematizations of nature. That may be well and good – it is just a statement of the Humean view – but it does of course have the implication that, fundamentally, Humean laws do not explain anything. Stating that everything that is F is also a G does not explain why everything that is F is G. Laws thus lose their explanatory role. They also lose their predictive role so the theory invites the problem of inductive scepticism. We would only be able to know all the strict regularities once we knew all the world's history, and we cannot know that until the very end of the world. The things we may have so far taken to be regularities may not be so, as our experience could be of some temporally limited unrepresentative sample of things that are F. It may be that all the things that have been F thus far have also been G but that from next year, Fs that are not G start to occur. There is nothing to rule this out because, on this view, there is no necessity in what follows what. Any inductive inferences we make are based on the small sample (compared to the world's totality) we have observed, and we have no reason to assume that the unobserved cases will be like those observed.

This is a consequence of accepting the basic Humean view. We may have thought that the events that occur in the world are in part a consequence of the laws of nature: that they are law-governed. But Humeanism sees things the other way round. This is explicitly acknowledged by Lewis, who refers to his position as *Humean supervenience*. The laws, and much else besides, supervene on the Humean mosaic. The history of events determines the laws of nature rather than vice versa.

Dispositions

There is a third way of understanding the workings of the world that denies both the Humean view in which nothing makes the regularity of the world and the laws view in which regularity is produced by external laws of nature. This is the view that there are real dispositions or causal powers at work in the world.

The notion of a disposition is familiar from examples such as fragility, elasticity and solubility, which are commonplace, macroscopic dispositions, the sort which even non-philosophers will talk about and attribute, as properties, to objects. A disposition is understood to somehow contain within itself the possibility of some further property, and this further property would manifest itself when all the conditions are right. Hence fragility is a disposition to break easily when dropped, elasticity is a disposition to stretch when pulled and solubility is a disposition to dissolve when in liquid. Importantly, however, dispositional properties can be possessed or instantiated even when they are not manifesting themselves in these further properties.

According to some, many or even all properties have this kind of dispositional aspect. That something is hard, or spherical, or magnetic, seems to suggest the possibility of some further behaviour when that thing is in a certain kind of situation. Spin, charge and mass, for instance, which are arguably among the most basic properties of fundamental particulars, all seem to have a dispositional nature.

If one were to accept real dispositional properties into one's ontology, then it opens up the prospect of a new account of the way the world works. Instead of having external laws of nature governing the actions of the particular things, those things would instead be naturally disposed towards behaviour of a certain kind in virtue of their properties. For this reason, it is sometimes said that the dispositional ontology makes particular things *active* in the sense that their properties will naturally produce certain kinds of behaviour without needing additional laws that somehow are capable of directing their actions. The alternative – a world with governing laws of nature – supposes that things are essentially passive, containing no principle of activity within themselves and subject entirely to the direction provided by the laws. As has already been indicated, however, it is questionable how governing laws of nature are ever able to do their work. Some account would have to be given of how the law, which is some kind of general fact or rule, is able to determine the behaviour of any particular. Armstrong's realism about laws probably comes closer than any to answering this question, though it depends on acceptance of his theory of universals.

Even if one is able to construct a plausible and acceptable account of how the law is supposed to relate to its instances, there is a further issue that the dispositionalist raises. For Armstrong, and almost all theories of laws, the laws of nature are contingent. Although in the realist view they determine, and some might say necessitate, what happens in the world, it is contingent exactly what it is that they necessitate. The laws of nature could have been different. And although the regularity view of laws denies that laws determine anything, it is certainly in agreement with the view that the regularities are contingent. This contingency is something that the dispositionalist denies. The causal role of a property, understood as its dispositions to behave, is essential to it: it is the major part, if not all, of what the property is. The causal role of a property could not vary and the property remain the property it is. Its role is thus understood as necessary.

There are three main variants on this dispositional ontology currently on offer. While they are in agreement on the basic ontology, they differ over the detail of how to treat laws. In Bird's view (2007), the laws of nature are accounted for by these essential relations between dispositions and their manifestations. Laws can be understood as basically about properties, in agreement with the DTA view. The law of gravitational attraction, for instance, is a law that says a gravitational force between two objects is a function of masses and distances apart. Coulomb's law says something similar about charges. Mass, distance, charge and attraction are all properties, and they can all be understood dispositionally. According to this version of dispositional essentialism, such laws provide the essences of such properties. Gravitational mass would not be the property it is unless it played exactly this role, for instance, in attracting other objects in precisely this degree in this kind of space. This makes all the laws strictly necessary. The gravitational law could not have been an inverse cube law, instead of an inverse square law, because then it would no longer be a law involving our properties of mass and distance and our space.

Ellis (2001) adds to his ontology a rich metaphysic of natural kinds and argues that they have essential properties. He thinks that this is where the laws of nature are chiefly to be found. Although he accepts the ontology of causal powers – another term for dispositions – and is against the idea of there being external laws of nature governing essentially passive particulars, he thinks that as well as there being natural kinds of event and property, there are natural kinds of object. Many laws will be about such kinds of object and their essential dispositional properties. Electrons, for instance, are essentially negatively charged. In any possible world in which there are electrons, they are negatively charged. Anything we imagine that is not negatively charged, is thus not an electron.

While these two forms of dispositionalism attempt to construct the laws from elements within the dispositional ontology, Mumford (2004) instead argues that dispositions offer an alternative to laws, urging that laws of nature are redundant in our ontology. This view is thereby in agreement with the Humean view that there are no external, governing laws of nature, but also in disagreement with the Humean view that the world is a world of pure contingency and there is no explanation for the world's regularity. Those who believe in laws typically suggest that unless there were laws, nature would be irregular and chaotic. The dispositional ontology would show that this is not the case. Things are disposed to behave in a certain way of necessity, so laws are not something that needs to be added to nature to make it work. That would be just as well, as we have already seen some reason to think of laws as being a part of an implausible metaphysic. There are difficult questions for the laws theorist to face about how laws do their work and whether they can truly be contingent. We need not solve these problems if real dispositions do all the work for which we thought we needed laws. Speaking purely metaphysically, laws of nature could thus be eliminated. This would be consistent with retaining law-talk in a scientific, empirical sense. Such laws may be just the regularities, but for the dispositionalist metaphysician it is the natural causal powers of things that are productive of those regularities.

This view also comes at a price. One would have to accept the ontology of causal powers, which those of a Humean inclination are loath to do as they think they introduce precisely the kind of necessary connection in nature that Hume went to lengths to deny. Causal powers may be thought of as mysterious and unobservable or mere theoretical posits. The view is not merely metaphysical, however. Philosophers of science such as Cartwright (1999) think that science is best interpreted as uncovering the causal powers of things. Metaphysics and philosophy of science have converged on the same idea.

Summary

The popular conception of nature as something whose actions are governed by contingent laws of nature is just one alternative. There has been a robust metaphysical defence of such a view in the form of the DTA (Dretske, Tooley, Armstrong) theory of laws. But there are at least two more conceptions of the world. The Humean view, that there is no necessity in nature, has remained plausible, partly due to Lewis's sophisticated version in the Best Systems view. Laws of nature are understood as the simplest set of assumptions from which the history of the world would result. The third alternative is to see the workings of nature as necessitated, though not by laws of nature. Instead, there are real causal powers that make necessary the dispositional behaviour of things. Each of the three alternatives has difficulties to face. The laws view needs to provide a plausible account of how the laws actually do their work, of governing the actions of particular objects from outside them. The Humean view posits a world of complete contingency, which many will find implausible. The laws, such as they are, supervene on what actually happens in the world, rather than the other way round. Such laws therefore offer no real explanation of the world's history, and nor does anything else they offer. The dispositionalist view asks us to accept an ontology of causal powers which many, especially Humeans, think introduces far too many necessary connections into the world.

As I indicated at the beginning, this issue concerns one of the most fundamental questions in the whole of human understanding: how the world works. It is rather disconcerting then that philosophers have not been able to settle on a solution.

References

Armstrong, D. M. (1983) *What Is a Law of Nature?* Cambridge: Cambridge University Press.

Bird, A. (2007) *Nature's Metaphysics*, Oxford: Oxford University Press.

Carroll, J. (1994) *Laws of Nature*, Cambridge: Cambridge University Press.

Cartwright, N. (1999) *The Dappled World*, Cambridge: Cambridge University Press.

Dretske, F. (1977) "Laws of Nature," *Philosophy of Science* 44: 248–68.

Ellis, B. (2001) *Scientific Essentialism*, Cambridge: Cambridge University Press.

Hawking, S. (1988) *A Brief History of Time*, London: Bantam Press.

Hume, D. (1739–40) *Treatise of Human Nature*, Oxford: Oxford University Press.

Lewis, D. (1973) *Counterfactuals*, Oxford: Blackwell.

Mellor, D. H. (1980) "Necessities and Universals in Natural Laws," in *Matters of Metaphysics*, Cambridge: Cambridge University Press, pp. 136–53.

Mumford, S. (2004) *Laws in Nature*, London: Routledge.

Newton, I. (1934 [1687]) *Principia Mathematica*, Cambridge: Cambridge University Press.

Ruby, J. (1986) "The Origins of Scientific 'Law'," in F. Weinert (ed.), *Laws of Nature*, New York: De Gruyter, pp. 289–315.

Russell, B. and Whitehead, A. N. (1910–13) *Principia Mathematica*, 3 vols, Cambridge: Cambridge University Press.

Tooley, M. (1977) "The Nature of Laws," *Canadian Journal of Philosophy* 74: 667–98.

Further reading

A. Bird, *Nature's Metaphysics* (Oxford: Oxford University Press, 2007) contains a detailed presentation of a dispositionalist view of laws. D. M. Armstrong, *What Is a Law of Nature?* (Cambridge: Cambridge University Press, 1983) is a lucid, much-discussed attempt to defend real and governing laws of nature. J. Carroll, *Laws of Nature* (Cambridge: Cambridge University Press, 1994) argues for the centrality and irreducibility of laws. D. Hume, *Treatise of Human Nature* (Oxford: Oxford University Press, 1739–40) is still the classic source of the regularity view. M. Lange, *Natural Laws in Scientific Practice* (Oxford: Oxford University Press, 2000) gives a thorough and detailed philosophical interpretation of laws as understood in science. S. Mumford, *Laws in Nature* (London: Routledge, 2004) argues in favour of powers rather than laws as being the ultimate explanation of the world.

45

DETERMINISM AND PROBABILITY

Philip Percival

Determinism

(i) "Determinism" has been identified with the doctrine that all non-initial events have causes (Hospers 1997: 154–5), and with the doctrine that the (entire) future is predictable in principle (Popper 1982: 1–2). In contemporary philosophy, however, it is usually taken to be the view that each "global" state (i.e. of the entire world) determines, in combination with laws (i.e. determines "nomically"), the world's later states.

More precise formulations vary. Earman (1986: 13) requires nomic determination of earlier states, as well as later ones, and takes a global state to be a momentary state on a simultaneity plane through the entire world, and determinism to be true iff (if and only if) the world is deterministic; but Lewis (1999: 31–3) takes a global state to be a temporally extended initial segment of the entire world up to some moment, and determinism to be true iff the laws are such that each possible world at which they hold – each "nomically" possible world – is deterministic. These definitions are not equivalent: the laws could be such that global states nomically determine later states without nomically determining earlier ones; initial segments could nomically determine all subsequent states though momentary states do not (e.g. if there is delayed action at a distance, as in Poincaré's special relativistic theory of gravity [Earman 1986: 69]); and only Lewis's definition renders determinism true just in case it is nomically necessary. One must choose, therefore, or adopt a compromise.

Lewis's definition is favoured by the fact that future-directed nomic determination by segments is better suited to the debate regarding determinism's impact on human freedom: the arguments of incompatibilists such as van Inwagen (1975, 1983) and Kane (1998: Chs 4–5) concern the view that the world's state up to and including some moment nomically determines its later states. Against this, a definition that renders determinism physically necessary if true is uneconomical; moreover, nomic determination by states on simultaneity planes, rather than by initial segments, is more central to foundational studies in the philosophy of physics (in part because of Earman's influence).

I shall compromise. Let a "global momentary state" be a state on a simultaneity plane through an entire (metaphysically) possible world, and let two such worlds w and w^* "split" iff (i) w has a global momentary state s that is a duplicate of some global momentary state s^* of w^*, but (ii) the entire later segment of w from s onwards is not a duplicate of the entire later segment of w^* from s^* onwards; and let a possible world be "deterministic" iff, among possible worlds having exactly its laws, none splits from it. Then "determinism" is the doctrine that the world is deterministic.

(ii) Most contemporary philosophers hold that determinism is an empirical hypothesis to be evaluated by science. Almost all take laws for granted, but some deny that there are laws (van Fraassen 1989; Mumford 2005). Earman's (1993) impatience with scepticism about laws is understandable, however, since any internal weakness in the notion of law is an infection brought on by metaphysical speculation far removed from scientific practice. In the first instance, the quest of e.g. Planck (1959: 195), Hawking (1988: 156), or Penrose (2005) for "the ultimate laws" is the mundane aim of finding better alternatives to certain equations. The notion most suited to scientific practice, therefore, must at least approximate Lewis's (1999: 39–43, 231–6) "best-system" analysis, according to which laws are the regularities entailed by the best of all possible scientific theories. The transition from "better" (than Einstein's field equations, etc.) to "best" (among all possibly true theories) is far from trivial, but even so, to avoid irritating the scientific community needlessly, anti-Humeans should agree that there are laws before insisting on something Humeans refuse to grant – that laws are metaphysically necessary (Shoemaker 1998; Black 1998), or that laws are grounded in something contingent but more fundamental (Armstrong 1983).

In any case, all parties may ask questions of the form "assuming the laws are such and such, is determinism true?" More particularly, let putative laws L concerning properties Q be "deterministic" iff, among possible worlds that conform to L, no world has a global momentary state that is in complete agreement regarding Q with some global momentary state of another world unless the two worlds' later segments are in complete agreement regarding Q. Then all parties may ask "assuming the laws are deterministic, is determinism true?" The answer is "maybe." That the laws are deterministic is neither necessary nor sufficient for determinism: it is not necessary because laws that are not deterministic might combine with each *actual* global momentary state to determine the world's subsequent states; and it is not sufficient because, among worlds the laws of which are exactly the deterministic laws L concerning properties Q, splitting may occur with respect to any contingent property that does not supervene on Q.

Whether the putative laws of our best theories are deterministic is nevertheless relevant to determinism. Although Newton is often thought to have introduced a deterministic worldview that went unchallenged, scientifically, until the advent of quantum mechanics, his laws are not deterministic. No state of a system nomically determines subsequent states unless outside interference is ruled out. But because Newton's laws place no limit on velocity, they permit outside interference – by so-called "space invaders" (from spatial infinity) – even when the system comprises the entire world (Earman 1986: 34). Special relativity avoids this difficulty provided it is interpreted as holding that the velocity of light is an upper bound. It is not so interpreted by tachyon enthusiasts, however, and in any case special relativity itself is prevented from being deterministic by additional considerations. It allows different ways of slicing up a world (given its denial of absolute simultaneity), including some that yield simultaneity planes that are not "future Cauchy": for each plane, for some point in its future, there is a possible causal path through the point that cannot be extended backwards so as to pass through the plane. Clearly, a momentary state on a plane that possesses this property cannot nomically determine subsequent states: some point in the state's future could be affected by a causal process the state cannot register. Special relativity even fails to be deterministic if the issue is confined to slicings the global simultaneity planes of which *are* future Cauchy: space invaders are not the only counterexamples to the claim that Newton's (putative) laws are deterministic, and "supertask" counterexamples apply equally to relativistic mechanics (Perez Laraudogoitia 1996, 1998; Norton 2003 describes a different kind of counterexample).

General relativity stretches the conceptual framework behind naïve views of determinism and deterministic law still further: among possible worlds at which it holds, some worlds have space–times that cannot be sliced into global simultaneity planes, while others, though they can be so sliced, cannot be sliced into global simultaneity planes that are future Cauchy (Earman 1986: 172–8). Moreover, even with respect to possible worlds that can be so sliced, general relativity is not deterministic: for each such possible world w and global simultaneity plane s of w, there is a non-duplicate possible world $w*$ the segment of which up until $s*$ duplicates the segment of w up until s. This need not be because of a "hole" argument to the effect that in $w*$, the space–time points of some region $R*$ in $s*$'s future are a permutation of the space–time points in the corresponding region R of w (Earman and Norton 1987): although the space–time of each mathematical model of general relativity can be permuted in this way, the model that results from the permutation might be thought not to represent a different possible world (Butterfield 1989). Rather, it is simply because general relativity allows space–time the option of cutting out: w and $w*$ are not duplicates, because either w *ends* some time after s, while $w*$ continues on, or vice versa (Earman 1986: 180–1).

(iii) That these non-probabilistic theories are not deterministic illustrates the fact that "indeterminism" – the view that determinism is false – is not inseparably bound to the truth of theories that are probabilistic, such as statistical mechanics and quantum mechanics (*pace* Giere 1973: 475). In contrast, except in trivial cases, a probabilistic theory is indeterministic. One pressing question, therefore, is whether the employment of probabilities in contemporary scientific theories is *consistent* with determinism (assuming these theories correct). The answer might be thought obvious: *of course* the mere fact of a theory's being probabilistic does not render it incompatible with determinism. A more illuminating answer is that the matter depends on what is meant by "probability."

Probability

In the standard mathematical theory – but not always in non-standard theories surveyed by Hajek (2001: 372–6) – probability is defined over certain subsets, called "events," of a set of "outcomes." The theory no more specifies probabilities than arithmetic specifies the number of sheep in Australia; it offers no definition of probability, and even "outcome" and "event" are employed as terms of art. To apply it, therefore, probabilities must be established independently. Implicitly, this involves an interpretation of "probability."

An interpretation must say which kinds of set have probabilities. Lewis's (1986: Ch. 19) account is perhaps most economical: "outcomes" are possible worlds, "events" are sets of possible worlds, i.e. coarse grained propositions, and the probability of a particular event e proper, such as the Battle of Waterloo, is the probability of the proposition that e occurs. This account is rejected e.g. by those who deny that probability can be ascribed to particular events, however. An interpretation must also specify the circumstances under which sets have probabilities. In this regard some "monists" hold that probability is exclusively epistemic (de Finetti 1937); others, that it is exclusively non-epistemic (Reichenbach 1938: Ch. 5). "Pluralists," who reject monism, hold that there are at least two kinds of probability (Carnap 1945; Lewis 1986: Ch. 19; Mellor 1969; Howson and Urbach 1989).

In part to illustrate pluralism's motivation, but mainly to focus the discussion, two kinds of circumstance in which probability claims are made should be distinguished. In the first, a trial T (such as firing electrons at a barrier) has been performed many times on a setup S (such as a two-slitted barrier behind which there is a detector screen) and regularities in the resulting data are observed that are "statistical" in the following sense: (i) they pertain to the relative frequencies with which nomically possible results E_i of T occur; (ii) the relative frequencies of E_i stabilised as the number of trials increased (perhaps around some number r_i); and (iii) in practice, no result of any one performance of the trial was predictable. In such circumstances, a common response is to employ the language of probability, and to assert some such claim as e.g. "the probability of a trial T on setup S resulting in E_i is r_i." In the second kind of circumstance, in contrast, *prima facie* no repeatable trials are involved. For example, having lost his credit card for the first time, Smith concludes his reflections by saying "it probably fell from my pocket when I ran for the train." While one might seek to test the probability claim made in the first kind of circumstance, the occurrence of "probably" in Smith's claim is a distraction to further investigation: he might seek further evidence, but only regarding whether or not his wallet fell from his pocket when running from the train; the thought of obtaining further evidence as to whether *probably* that's what happened would not occur to him.

The notion of probability employed in the first kind of circumstance is often called "statistical probability," but I shall follow increasingly common practice by calling it "chance." Typically, pluralists claim that the notion of chance is distinct from the notion of probability employed in the second kind of circumstance: they hold that probability claims made in the first kind of circumstance purport to be objective in a way in which those made in the second kind of circumstance, being epistemic, do not. This claim is peripheral to metaphysics, and I shall not engage it directly. Epistemic probability cannot be ignored completely, however. Among realists about chance, pluralists typically give epistemic probability a central role in the epistemology of chance (Lewis 1986: Ch. 19; Howson and Urbach 1989: Ch. 9). Moreover, anti-realists about chance typically place epistemic probability at the centre of their accounts of the role chance plays in science and elsewhere.

Realism about chance holds that chance is real. It divides into a thesis about content – roughly, that typical chance claims represent the world as being a certain way independently of us – and a thesis about the world itself – roughly, that the world makes some such representations true. As in debates over realism regarding e.g. meaning or morals, it is hard to sharpen such theses satisfactorily. This leads to "quietist" complaints to the effect that disputes between realists and anti-realists are insubstantial. Perhaps in this, as in other areas, in the final analysis realists and anti-realists about chance must both appeal to primitive sentential operators "it is factual as to whether" and "it is in reality the case that" (Fine 2001).

Realist theories of chance fall into various categories. Those of most importance to metaphysics are: frequency vs. nonfrequency; single case vs. non-single case; Humean Supervenient vs. non-Humean Supervenient; and propensity vs. non-propensity.

(i) The frequency theory holds that chances are defined over "attributes" relative to populations, and that the probability of A relative to Z is defined in terms of the relative frequency with which A occurs in Z. Different versions place different constraints on populations and offer somewhat different definitions.

"Finite" frequentism allows Z to be finite, and defines the chance of A relative to finite Z as the relative frequency of A in Z. But in von Mises's (1981) frequency theory chance always coincides with the *limiting* relative frequency of A in what he calls a "collective," i.e. a population Z such that (i) Z is infinite; (ii) Z is ordered; (iii) the relative frequency with which A occurs in Z tends to a limit; and (iv) A occurs randomly in Z. The first three conditions are illustrated by the following series:

$$(A) \quad 1, 0, 1, 0, 1, 0, 1, 0, 1, 0, 1, 0, \ldots$$

In (A) the limiting relative frequency of 1 is ½, since the relative frequency with which 1 occurs in successive initial segments generates a sequence (B):

$$(B) \quad 1, \tfrac{1}{2}, 2/3, \tfrac{1}{2}, 3/5, \tfrac{1}{2}, 4/7, \tfrac{1}{2}, 5/9, \tfrac{1}{2}, 6/11, \tfrac{1}{2}, \ldots,$$

and (B) converges to ½. (A) is not a collective, however, since 1 and 0 do not occur randomly: 1 occurs in every odd-numbered position. Indeed, since no series specified by any such rule as "the nth member is 1 iff n is odd, 0 otherwise," it follows that if collectives exist, they do so independently of our ability to construct them. This does not trouble platonists (like von Mises); but to constructivists, who hold that only "constructible" mathematical objects exist, the notion of a collective is untenable.

Even platonists might think von Mises's appeal to collectives defeats his express purpose of providing foundations for a science of chance: actual populations of concrete objects that are infinite and suitably ordered are far less prevalent than the chance claims science makes. For example, although e.g. science assigns a chance ½ that a radium atom will decay in 1,600 years, there is reason to think the set of radium atoms finite. In an attempt to avert the ensuing danger that tying chances to limiting relative frequencies renders many of science's chance claims false, von Mises resorts to "hypothetical" frequentism: there is a chance r of the result in a trial T on setup S having attribute A iff either (a) T is repeated infinitely often and the results form a collective in which the limiting relative frequency of A is r; or (b) T is repeated finitely often, and *were* it repeated indefinitely the results *would* form a collective in which the limiting relative frequency of A is r.

Many critics object that this attempt to avert the danger fails: even condition (b) is met too rarely. Jeffrey (1992: 192ff.) takes (b) to require a collective that would result were T performed infinitely often, and then objects that there is none. But this interpretation is at odds with von Mises's insistence that chance is a species of randomness. A more charitable interpretation construes (b) as stating that for some number r, had the trial been repeated indefinitely, some collective *or other* in which the limiting relative frequency of A is r would have resulted. Others claim that even this weaker requirement is met too rarely: there are *no* such counter-factual limiting relative frequency facts. In so far as the ground for so doing is the thought that whenever the chance of a result of a trial T on setup S having attribute A is r, it *could* happen that the trial T is repeated indefinitely without the limiting relative frequency of A being r, in which case it is not true that were T repeated indefinitely the limiting relative frequency of A would be r (Lewis 1986: 90), then the response should be that the question is begged: this thought presupposes that the chance r of the result of a trial T on setup S being A is a *nonfrequentist* "single-case" chance r of the result of *each* trial T on S being A.

A "single-case" theory of chance holds that chance pertains to particular events, such as the result of *this* repetition of trial T being A (e.g. *this* coin arching through the air being about to land heads on *this* toss). It is dismissed by von Mises, who holds that chance is "meaningless," except in so far as it pertains to a kind of event relative to a population (or "reference class"), and that each particular event determines different collectives in which the relevant limiting relative frequencies vary: each repetition of a trial T (e.g. tossing this coin) is also a repetition of a trial that is more specific (e.g. tossing this coin five feet in the air) and of one that is more general (e.g. tossing *a* coin). Most frequentists follow him in this, but Salmon (1979: 197) is an exception: he suggests that one among the many (actual and counterfactual) populations to which a particular repetition of a trial belongs can be singled out as having a unique status – namely, the one that is "broadest" among the "homogeneous" populations. In hypothetical frequentist terms, on this proposal the chance that the result of *this* repetition c of trial T will be A is the limiting relative frequency A would have were the trial T^* performed indefinitely, where T^* has all and only the properties of c to which the counterfactual limiting relative frequency is sensitive. Nonfrequentist advocates of real single-case chance denigrate this proposal: there is no ontological basis for conferring a special status on any one population. Many of them take frequentism's fundamental weakness to be its inability to accommodate genuinely single-case chance.

(ii) A single-case theory of chance is nonfrequentist just in case it holds that chance r other than 0 or 1 of the result of a trial T being A does not entail a limiting relative frequency r of A in infinitely many repetitions of T: A might chance *never* to occur. The most influential theory of this kind is Lewis's (1999: 233–6) "best system" analysis of chance. Its express purpose is to reconcile chance with Humean Supervenience, the doctrine that everything actual supervenes on a "subvenient" base B of which the following is true: (i) B comprises all matters of particular fact constituting the possession by individual points of certain perfectly natural monadic intrinsic properties, and the bearing of spatiotemporal relations between these points; and (ii) all combinatorially possible ways of points' possessing these properties are metaphysically possible. The analysis assumes that these properties neither include nor involve chance. Its fundamental notions are the proposition H_{tw}, which captures the segment of the subvenient base in w that extends up to and includes t, and the proposition T_w, which exactly captures the laws of chance at w. It assumes that chance is temporal, in that the chances change over time as events chance to happen, and invariably determined by history and law: in w, at t, a proposition p has chance $\mathrm{Ch}_{tw}(p)$ equal to r iff $\mathrm{Ch}_{tw}(p) = r$ is entailed by $H_{tw}T_w$ (an assumption Fisher [2006] denies). Its aim is to exploit this assumption so as to define chance $\mathrm{Ch}_{tw}(p)$ in terms of *law* of *chance* i.e. in terms of T_w (and H_{tw}).

The analysis is an extension of Lewis's best system analysis of deterministic law, according to which for all worlds w whose laws are deterministic, the laws at w are the regularities entailed by the deductive system that, with respect to w, is "better" than others when judged by the criteria of strength and simplicity (the eligible deductive systems being systems the primitive vocabulary of which refers only to perfectly natural properties). To extend this analysis to (laws of) chance, deductive systems that are only partially interpreted are allowed to compete: it would defeat the purpose if the best system used the concept of chance (or any concept that presupposes chance), so eligible systems are allowed to employ an uninterpreted constant f. Although the main role of f is to pick out what are in fact the laws of chance at w, it also serves to provide an additional criterion, "fit," by which the competition is judged.

- The best system analysis of chance (and law)

(a) For all propositions p, worlds w, times t, $\mathrm{Ch}_{tw}(p) = r$ iff there is a constant f such that
  (i) f occurs uninterpreted in some theorems of an otherwise fully interpreted deductive system $S(f)$.

(ii)   That the probability axioms hold for f is a theorem of $S(f)$.

(iii) $f(p, t) = r$ is entailed by the conjunction of $S(f)$ and H_{tw}.

(iv)   A proposition $f(p_w) = s$ is entailed by $S(f) - p_w$ being the world-proposition true just at the world w; a system $S^*(f)$ "fitting" w to degree n iff $S^*(f)$ entails $f(p_w) = n$.

(v) $S(f)$ is "best" with respect to w – a system $S^*(f)$ being "best" with respect to w iff $S^*(f)$ is better than other systems when evaluated with respect to w by the criteria of strength, simplicity and fit.

(b) For all regularities R and worlds w, R is a law at w iff R is a theorem of the fully interpreted system S that results when, in the system $S(f)$ that does best at w, f is interpreted as chance.

One might think that this analysis conflicts with the fact that the pattern of non-chance matters of local fact displayed by the entire world might mislead as to the chances: the fully interpreted system S obtained from the best system $S(f)$ is just the system most highly confirmed by the evidence; it could be false (Briggs, forthcoming). But like the analogous worry directed against hypothetical frequentism above, this thought begs the question when presented as an objection. Two technical problems are more pressing. The first is the problem of fit: if the criterion of fit is to do any work, $f(p_w)$ must be positive in the system $S(f)$ that does best with respect to w, in which case $Ch_w(p_w)$ must be too; but $Ch_w(p_w)$ cannot be expected to be positive, given the standard mathematical theory of probability – and while Lewis's response is to say that it could be positive in a non-standard theory in which chances are permitted infinitesimal values, this response is vulnerable to the further worry that it is impossible for a partially interpreted system's fit $f(p_w)$ with respect to w to be both infinitesimal and best (Elga 2004; Percival 2006; but see Herzberg 2007). The second technical problem is that the analysis presupposes atemporal chances $Ch_w(p_w)$: atemporal chances are problematic in themselves – Lewis (1986: 91) himself says "I do not think … we have some timeless notion of chance"; moreover, no satisfactory account of their relation to temporal chances Ch_{tw} – and hence of the relation between the uninterpreted functions $f(p_w, t)$ and $f(p_w)$ appealed to in the analysis – has been given (Percival 2006).

A problem of "undermining" is deeper. A possible future F_{ti} is undermining with respect to a world w iff (i) at w, at t, F_{ti} has a positive chance r of coming about (i.e. $H_{tw}T_w$ entails $Ch_{tw}(F_{ti}) = r$); and (ii) given w's history until t, F_{ti}'s coming about is inconsistent with w's laws of chance T_w (i.e. $H_{tw}F_{ti}$ entails $\neg T_w$). The best system analysis generates undermining in this sense: for some world $w = H_{tw}F_{tw}$, the laws T_w determined by the best system $S(f)$ for w combine with H_{tw} to give a positive chance at t, in w, to a future F_{ti} so radically different from w's future, F_{tw}, that with respect to the world $w^* = H_{tw}F_{ti}$ some other system $S^*(f)$ is best (the laws T_w^* determined by S^* being incompatible with T_w).

Lewis takes the main problem undermining poses to be the difficulty of reconciling it with normative personalism. Normative personalism holds that there are "personal" probabilities in that (i) there are beliefs, or belief-like states – "credences"

– having degrees (one claimed justification being that the strengths of these states can be measured numerically e.g. by betting behaviour under certain strict conditions); (ii) for each rational agent b the function Cr_b that captures b's credences' degrees is "coherent," in so far as it satisfies the axioms of the standard mathematical theory of probability (claimed justifications being representation theorems to the effect that coherent credences are implicit in rational preferences (Maher 1993: Ch. 1), or Dutch-book theorems to the effect that incoherent credences are committed to bets that are certain to lose (Howson and Urbach 1989: Ch. 3); and (iii) a sense of "probability" can be captured in terms of credence (as e.g. in a rule "assert 'probably q' only if your credence in q is higher than your credence in $\neg q$"). Lewis's pluralism consists in the fact that he endorses normative personalism but denies that personal probability (i.e. rational credence) is chance.

Some personalists deny there are synchronic constraints on rational credence other than coherence – they are sometimes called "(extreme) subjective Bayesians" – though almost all personalists admit an additional *diachronic* normative principle stating that credence Cr_{old} should be updated, in the light of new certain evidence E, by setting $Cr_{new}(p)$ equal to $Cr_{old}(p \mid E)$. But Lewis claims that a further synchronic constraint is provided by an internalist normative connection between rational credence and (credence in) chance that he holds *a priori*. It is convenient to focus not on the constraint itself, which Lewis calls the "Principal Principle," but on a consequence of it, namely

- The Principal Principle reformulated (PPR)
  $$Ch_{tw}(p) = Cr_0(p \mid H_{tw}T_w)$$

PPR says that for all possible worlds w, propositions p, and times t, the chance $Ch_{tw}(p)$ at t in w of p is equal to reasonable initial credence $Cr_0(p \mid H_{tw}T_w)$ in p conditional on the conjunction of w's history until t, H_{tw}, and its laws of chance T_w; Cr_0 is "initial" because prior to the acquisition of *any* empirical evidence about *anything*, and "reasonable" in that, for all propositions E, every non-initial credence function obtained from Cr_0 by conditionalising on E is rational.

PPR entails that no future F_{ti} is undermining: if in w, at t, $H_{tw}F_{ti}$ entails $\neg T_w$, then $F_{ti}H_{tw}T_w$ is inconsistent, in which case $Cr_0(F_{ti} \mid H_{tw}T_w) = 0$ (by the coherence of Cr_0); but if F_{ti} has positive chance r of coming about, PPR requires that $Cr_0(p \mid H_{tw}T_w) = r$. Since the best system analysis engenders undermining, it is therefore incompatible with PPR. Lewis's (1999: 245–6) response is that chance thus analysed satisfies a principle that approximates PPR – namely

- The New Principle
  $$Cr_0(p \mid H_{tw}T_w) = Ch_{tw}(p \mid T_w),$$

and that since nothing else comes close to so doing, the analysis is vindicated.

This response is most straightforwardly construed as being to the effect that the best system analysis is a satisfactory *explication* of chance that replaces an old concept by a superior close relative. Lewis seems to intend that it be construed as being more ambitious, but either way it does not address the fact that undermining can force rational agents into states of mind that seem absurd: if F_{ti} is undermining with respect to w, an agent certain of both the course of history H_{tw} and the theory of chance T_w must give credence 1 to the proposition that there is a positive chance of F_{ti} coming about, but credence 0 to the proposition that F_{ti} does come about. Nor can Lewis consistently hold that no feature of the world comes closer to satisfying PPR than does chance as defined by the best system analysis: letting the feature this analysis defines be "LCh_{tw}," it follows, given Lewis's New Principle, that a further chance function, $L*Ch_{tw}$, defined as LCh_{tw}, conditional on the laws T_w of chance – i.e. so that $L*Ch_{tw}(p) = LCh_{tw}(p \mid T_w)$ – satisfies PPR exactly (Shaffer 2003).

Many critics complain that Lewis's preoccupation with the tension between undermining and normative personalism ignores deeper, strictly metaphysical problems. The peculiarities of undermining are of a different order to the peculiarities of Lewis's treatment of counterfactuals under determinism, i.e. according to which, had any one actual event not occurred, the laws would have been different. In undermining (at w), it is the laws T_w themselves that, in combination with the initial history segment H_{tw}, accord some chance $Ch_{tw}(F_{ti})$ to events F_{ti} with which they are inconsistent (given H_{tw}). This is highly irregular: the law is not usually so generous to those who contradict it! Correlatively, whereas undermining renders the laws of chance dependent on what chances to happen, the true order of dependency might be thought the opposite: what happens depends on the laws (even if, because determinism is false, dependency on laws falls short of determination). Moreover, undermining weakens the sense in which chance events are possible: if F_{ti} is undermining with respect to w, it only occurs in worlds $w*$ whose laws T_{w*} differ from the laws T_w of w, or whose history H_{tw*} differs from the history H_{tw} of w (in violation of what Bigelow et al. [1993] call the "Basic Chance Principle").

Of those basically sympathetic to the best system analysis, some (including Lewis) bite these bullets, claiming that chance turns out to have metaphysical features that were not anticipated, while others try to avoid undermining, either by modifying the analysis piecemeal (Hoefer 1997) or by abandoning realism about the laws of chance (Halpin 1994; Ward 2005). In contrast, more hostile critics argue that any analysis of chance that is guided by Humean Supervenience is bound to go wrong – either because chance is not Humean Supervenient, or because nothing is so supervenient (i.e. on account of the subvenient base being wrongly characterised). Some turn to a "propensity" theory of chance.

(iii) A propensity is a kind of disposition or tendency. "Full-blooded" propensity theories take chances to be identical to propensities; "modest" propensity theories take chances to be grounded in propensities, but not identical to them.

Although the dispute as to whether propensities are dispositions or tendencies is in part terminological, the way in which tendencies contrast with dispositions is important. A disposition, such as fragility, is a property that has a manifestation condition, such as subjection to certain impact forces, and a display, such as shattering. The relation between the manifestation condition and the display has been thought to be counterfactual dependence, but in reality it is weaker: an object might have a disposition even though it is not true that were the manifestation condition met, the disposition would be displayed; in "finkish" cases, the meeting of the manifestation condition might cause the object to lose the disposition before display occurs (Lewis 1999: Ch. 7). If a tendency is to be construed as a weakened disposition, therefore, its distinguishing feature is most naturally taken to be a further weakening of the relation between manifestation condition and display: even in cases that are not finkish, the manifestation condition of a tendency might be met without a display. Some propensity theorists do not construe tendencies in this way, however: they do not think of tendencies as having manifestation conditions (*pace* Eagle 2004). A better model for tendency in their sense is the property an object has in virtue of possessing a disposition that, although activated on account of its manifestation condition being met, has yet to display. I will reserve "tendency" for the weakening of such a property, and distinguish this usage from the previous one by calling a weakened disposition a "tendency$_d$." Crucially, tendencies (and tendencies$_d$) may have various strengths.

The single-case nonfrequentist propensity theories of Mellor (1969) and Giere (1973) illustrate the importance of distinguishing tendencies from tendencies$_d$. Mellor's theory is modest and takes propensities to be dispositions: a propensity is a disposition of a setup, the manifestation condition of which is the performance of a certain kind of trial on the setup, and the display condition of which is the trial's possession of the property that the chances of its various possible outcomes are thus and so. Apparently in contrast, Giere's theory is full-blooded and takes propensities to be tendencies: a chance $Ch(A) = r$ is a tendency of a setup towards a result A, the strength of which is r. Thus characterised, the two theories appear incompatible. But while they are commonly taken to be so (e.g. Eagle 2004: 378–83), the apparent differences are terminological. First, Mellor's theory does not exclude Giere's view that chances are tendencies: trials may have tendencies of strengths r_i towards results A_i. Second, Giere's view does not exclude Mellor's theory that setups possess dispositions displayed as chance-distributions. In Mellor's terminology, "setups" are physical objects such as coins and experimental arrangements such as a barrier with two slits behind which is a detector screen, while "trials" on setups include e.g. tossing a coin and firing a beam of electrons. It would be absurd to interpret Giere as attributing tendencies to setups in this sense, however: if there is a ½ chance/tendency of this coin, which is arching through the air, landing heads, there is no chance of its landing heads after it is buried in concrete immediately afterwards; to attribute a tendency ½ of landing heads to the coin itself is to confuse tendencies with tendencies$_d$. When Giere employs the term "tendency" he does not speak of tendency$_d$ (*pace* Eagle). In his terminology, "setups" are "random experiments" – i.e. Mellor's trials. A random experiment does not have a manifestation condition; one can expose the fragility of a glass by dropping it, but there is not much to be done with a random experiment except conduct it.

A propensity theory need not be nonfrequentist. Like Popper (1959), Howson and Urbach (1989: 221) characterise and defend a full-blooded version of it that is a species of hypothetical frequentism: "[chances *are*] dispositions of repeatable experiments to generate convergent relative frequencies when repeated indefinitely." Indeed, unlike Popper, Howson and Urbach attribute this version of the propensity theory to von Mises himself. Their presentation of the theory is incoherent, however. A repeatable experiment is a type, and a type only has a disposition if at least some of its tokens do: the brand-X hairdryer has a disposition to ignite – a design flaw – only if at least some hairdryers of this design have it (or would have it were the hairdryer manufactured). But since the idea of a *token* of a repeatable experiment having a disposition to generate convergent relative frequencies upon being repeated indefinitely is absurd – tokens are not repeatable – it follows that no repeatable experiment can have it either.

A better formulation of the theory Howson and Urbach have in mind identifies chance with a disposition of a setup on which a trial might be performed: its manifestation condition is the performance of infinitely many trials on the setup; its display condition is a relevant limiting relative frequency. This formulation is better placed to accommodate the fact that actual setups are liable to disintegrate before infinitely many trials can be performed upon them than is the original version of hypothetical frequentism: it can hold this fact to be mere finkishness; the disposition is nomically incompatible with its manifestation condition. More worrying, however, is the disposition's sheer oddity. A disposition the manifestation condition of which is being dropped a hundred times and the display of which is breaking into an average of thirty pieces is extraordinary (in the absence of a disposition to break into thirty pieces when dropped). But why couldn't a vase have such a disposition if e.g. a coin can have a disposition to land heads randomly with limiting relative frequency of one-half when tossed indefinitely?

Propensity theory need not be opposed to Humean Supervenience either: dispositions have been thought Humean Supervenient, and, obviously, tendencies (and tendencies$_d$) might be thought so too. In effect, Eagle (2004) builds a failure to satisfy Humean Supervenience into the notion of tendency (and of tendency$_d$), as do many others. But while theorists who identify chances with tendencies are typically hostile to Humean Supervenience, so doing distorts the debate. Just as Humean Supervenience theorists sympathetic to the propensity view must choose between frequentist and nonfrequentist species of it, so too must they choose between modesty and full-bloodedness. If they opt for the latter, they must decide whether chances are dispositions, tendencies$_d$ or tendencies.

The most distinctive version of propensity theory is nevertheless a full-blooded nonfrequentist single-case theory that identifies chances with tendencies while denying that tendencies are Humean Supervenient. Its two main variants oppose Humean Supervenience in different ways: the first accepts its characterisation of the subvenient base and the contingency of the laws of tendency, but denies that tendency supervenes on non-tendency; the second rejects its characterisation of the subvenient base, and in so doing takes the laws of tendency to be necessary.

Both variants of the theory must explain how tendencies relate to other properties. The first claims that tendency is *sui generis* and only contingently related to them; on one formulation it is a relation (of varying strengths) between universals, and therefore a weakening of the contingent necessitation relation invoked in Armstrong's theory of laws under determinism. The second claims that tendency is a relation that holds between properties non-contingently, and that even its strength in individual cases is essential to, and hence part of the essences of, its *relata*. One rationale offered for this claim begins by observing that for the laws to be contingent, and for all mathematically possible combinations of subvenient properties to be metaphysically possible, properties must retain their identities across possible worlds in which such recombinations and variations in the laws are realised; it then objects that to suppose properties capable of so retaining their identities involves an untenable doctrine of "quiddities." (Lewis's [forthcoming] reply to Black's [2000] objection to this effect is discussed in Shaffer [2005].)

In denying Humean Supervenience, both variants of propensity theory drive a wedge between chance and the pattern woven by the distribution of subvenient properties at points. Lewis (1994) objects to so doing that no feature of the world divorced from the pattern of property instances could play the *a priori* normative role chance plays in constraining credence (in the manner captured by PPR or some such principle). As Hall (2004) complains, Lewis does not explain why he thinks it impossible for such a feature to play this role. If Lewis's objection is that a non-Humean Supervenient feature that normatively constrains credence would be metaphysically "queer" in the way Mackie holds moral properties as conceived by the moral realist to be queer, the response must be that making the feature Humean Supervenient wouldn't render it less queer. If his objection is that if chance is not Humean Supervenient no chance–credence normative constraint can be derived from more fundamental normative constraints on initial credence functions, the likely response must be that there is no hope of such a derivation if chance is Humean Supervenient either. (In contrast, Howson and Urbach [1989: 227–8] argue that the corresponding hypothetical frequentist credence–chance principle has a Dutch-book justification.)

Propensity theories that identify chances with non-Humean Supervenient tendencies are more vulnerable to objections that are less ambitious, but more metaphysical. The fact is that thus conceived, chance satisfies no one. Since it is compatible with the absence of even statistical regularities, it cannot provide ontological explanations of the kind opponents of Humean Supervenience insist upon. In practice, therefore, the status of determinism is not metaphysically neutral vis-à-vis Humean Supervenience. Under determinism, the rejection of Humean Supervenience offers *some* prospect of grounding the world's apparent regularities (in natural necessities). Given indeterminism, this prospect vanishes. It is a remarkable fact that when the prospect of having to abandon determinism is taken seriously, opponents of Humean Supervenience seek consolation in a species of realism about chance. Whether or not necessitation is superglue, non-Humean Supervenient chance is starch.

The status of determinism and chance

If determinism is true, and the laws $T_@$ of the actual world @ are deterministic, every proposition p entirely about a time later than t is either entailed by $H_{t@}T_@$ or incompatible with it; in that case either $Cr_0(p \mid H_{t@}T_@) = 1$ or $Cr_0(p \mid H_{t@}T_@) = 0$, from which it follows, given the credence–chance principle PPR, that either $Ch_{t@}(p) = 1$ or $Ch_{t@}(p) = 0$. For this and similar reasons, most theorists have held that realism about (non-trivial) single-case chance is incompatible with determinism (Loewer's [2001] attempt to reconcile the two being an exception to which Shaffer [2007] replies). Accordingly, most would accept that quantum mechanics is incompatible with determinism *if* it is committed to realism about single-case chance.

Even if quantum mechanics does have this commitment, it does not follow that we have reason to believe single-case chance real and determinism false, however: perhaps constructive empiricism is correct, and the most science requires is belief that quantum mechanics' chance claims are empirically adequate (as van Fraassen [1980] argues, although his own account of what it is for chance claims to be empirically adequate is frequentist).

In any case, quantum mechanics is not *committed* to even realism about chance. As practiced in the laboratory, orthodox quantum mechanics has two components: a non-probabilistic law that governs the evolution through time of microphysical systems – the laws of the ψ-function – and a rule by which to extract from a ψ-state probabilistic predictions regarding the outcomes of measurements upon a system in a ψ-state – Born's rule. Establishing the status and nature of Born's rule – and, correlatively, the nature of the probabilities it generates – is one of the central tasks of an "interpretation" of quantum mechanics. While some interpretations are naturally construed as being committed to realism about single-case chance – namely, "collapse" interpretations, and, in particular, collapse interpretations that do not bind collapse to the process of measurement (Frigg and Hoefer 2007) – other interpretations are not so construed. Bohmian mechanics, for example, which stands to quantum mechanics as classical mechanics stands to statistical mechanics, is not *naturally* construed as involving a commitment to realism about single-case chance. Nor is the many-worlds interpretation. Indeed, some personalists (Bayesians) have argued that such interpretations – and even collapse interpretations! – should be construed as not involving so much as a commitment to realism about chance. In so doing they afford anti-realists about chance who are not constructive empiricists hope of showing due respect for science.

Like frequentist realists, anti-realists about chance can turn the tension between determinism and realism about single-case chance into an objection: they too can argue that since observed statistical regularities provide our strongest reason for making chance claims, and since the notion of a statistical regularity is neutral as to whether determinism is true or false, the notion of chance must be similarly neutral (Salmon 1977; Howson and Urbach 1989).

Whereas the instrumentalist variant of anti-realism about chance holds that realism about chance is right about our representations, but wrong about the world – a position envisaged by Giere (1973) and in effect endorsed by van Fraassen (1980:

Ch. 6) – the more popular non-instrumentalist variant holds realism about chance wrong about our representations: our chance-claims do *not* purport to represent an objective feature of the world. In this respect, contemporary anti-realism about chance echoes the "classical" theory of Laplace (1951). Laplace defines probability as the proportion, among "cases" that are "equipossible," of cases that are "favourable," i.e. where equipossible cases are the cells of a partition of the space of epistemic possibilities between which an agent is indifferent, in the sense that he or she has no reason to predict one cell rather than another. Classical probability is clearly epistemic: both the space of epistemic possibilities, and the partitions to which indifference applies, are relative to a knowledge state.

Modern theories of probability evolved from two kinds of critique of the classical theory. The critique that led to the theories that have been my primary concern focused on what the classical theory had to say about chance, while a second critique focused on what it had to say about rational judgement and decision making under uncertainty. The second kind of critique engendered not just personal probability, but also "inductive" probability, i.e. a conditional probability function $P_1(q\,|\,p)$ (supposedly) capturing degrees to which propositions p provide inductive or evidential support for propositions q.

Realists about chance who are pluralists acknowledge chance and epistemic probability, but insist that their natures are entirely different (normative connections between them notwithstanding). In contrast, non-instrumentalist anti-realists about chance hold that the notion of chance is to be explained in terms of personal or inductive probability or both. One promising anti-realist strategy begins with the thought that chance is "objectified" credence (Jeffrey 1983: Ch. 12; Skyrms 1977).

References

Armstrong, D. (1983) *What Is a Law of Nature*, Cambridge: Cambridge University Press.

Bigelow, J., Collins J., and Pargetter R. (1993) "The Big Bad Bug: What are the Humean's Chances?" *British Journal for the Philosophy of Science* 44: 443–62.

Black, R. (1998) "Chance, Credence, and the Principal Principle," *British Journal for the Philosophy of Science* 49: 371–85.

—— (2000) "Against Quidditism," *Australasian Journal of Philosophy* 78: 87–104.

Briggs, R. (Forthcoming) "The Big Bad Bug Bites: Anti-Realist Theorists about Chance," *Synthese*: DOI 10.1007/s11229-007-9290-6.

Butterfield, J. (1989) "The Hole Truth," *British Journal for the Philosophy of Science* 40: 1–28.

Carnap, R. (1945) "The Two Concepts of Probability," *Philosophy and Phenomenological Research* 5: 513–32.

de Finetti, B. (1937) "Foresight, Its Logical Laws, Its Subjective Sources," in H. Kyburg and H. Smokler (eds), *Studies in Subjective Probability*, New York: John Wiley, pp. 97–158.

Eagle, A. (2004) "Twenty One Arguments against Propensity Analyses of Probability," *Erkenntnis* 60: 371–416.

Earman, J. (1986) *A Primer on Determinism*, Dordrecht: Reidel.

—— (1993) "In Defense of Laws: Reflections on Bas van Fraassen's *Laws and Symmetry*," *Philosophy and Phenomenological Research* 53: 413–19.

Earman, J. and Norton, J. (1987) "What Price Substantivalism? The Hole Story," *British Journal for the Philosophy of Science* 38: 515–25.

Elga, A. (2004) "Infinitesimal Chances and the Laws of Nature," *Australasian Journal of Philosophy* 82: 67–76.

Fine, K. (2001) "The Question of Realism," *Philosophers' Imprint* 1: 1–30.

Fisher, J. (2006) "On Higher-Order and Free-Floating Chances," *British Journal of the Philosophy of Science* 57: 691–707.

Frigg, R. and Hoefer, C. (2007) "Probability in GRW Theory," *Studies in History and Philosophy of Modern Physics* 38: 371–89.

Giere, R. (1973) "Objective Single-Case Probabilities and the Foundations of Statistics," in P. Suppes, L. Henkin, A. Joja, and Gr. C. Moisil (eds), *Logic, Methodology and Philosophy of Science IV*, Amsterdam: North-Holland Publishing.

Hajek, A. (2001) "Probability, Logic, and Probability Logic," in L. Gable (ed.) *The Blackwell Guide to Philosophical Logic*, Oxford: Blackwell.

Hall, H. (2004) "Two Mistakes about Credence and Chance," *Australasian Journal of Philosophy* 82: 93–111.

Halpin, J. (1994) "Legitimizing Chance: The Best-System Approach to Probabilistic Laws in Physical Theory," *Australasian Journal of Philosophy* 72: 317–38.

Hawking, S. (1988) *A Brief History of Time*, London: Bantam Books.

Herzberg, F. (2007) "Internal Laws of Probability, Generalized Likelihoods and Lewis's Infinitesimal Chances – A Response to Adam Elga," *British Journal for the Philosophy of Science* 58: 25–43.

Hoefer, C. (1997) "On Lewis's Objective Chance: 'Humean Supervenience Debugged'," *Mind* 106: 321–34.

Hospers, J. (1997) *An Introduction to Philosophical Analysis*, 4th edn, London: Routledge.

Howson, C. and Urbach, P. (1989) *Scientific Reasoning: The Bayesian Approach*, La Salle, IL: Open Court.

Jeffrey, R. (1983) *The Logic of Decision*, Chicago: University of Chicago Press.

—— (1992) *Probability and the Art of Judgment*, Cambridge: Cambridge University Press.

Kane, K. (1998) *The Significance of Free Will*, Oxford: Oxford University Press.

LaPlace, P. S., de (1951) *A Philosophical Essay on Probabilities*, New York: Dover.

Lewis, D. (1986) *Philosophical Papers*, vol. 2, Oxford: Oxford University Press.

—— (1999) *Papers in Metaphysics and Epistemology*, Cambridge: Cambridge University Press.

—— (Forthcoming) "Ramseyan Humility," in D. Braddon-Mitchell and R. Nola (eds), *Naturalism and Analysis*, Cambridge, MA: MIT Press.

Loewer, B. (2001) "Determinism and Chance," *Studies in History and Philosophy of Modern Physics* 32: 609–20.

Maher, P. (1993) *Betting on Theories*, Cambridge: Cambridge University Press.

Mellor, D. H. (1969) "Chance," *Proceedings of the Aristotelian Society Supplementary Volume* 43: 11–36.

Mumford, S. (2005) "Laws and Lawlessness," *Synthese* 144: 397–413.

Norton, J. D. (2003) "Causation as Folk Science," *Philosophers' Imprint* 3: 1–22.

Penrose, R. (2005) *The Road to Reality: A Complete Guide to the Laws of the Universe*, London: Vintage.

Percival, P. (2006) "On Realism about Chance," in F. MacBride (ed.) *Identity and Modality*, Oxford: Oxford University Press.

Perez Laraudogoitia, J. (1996) "A Beautiful Supertask," *Mind* 105: 81–3.

—— (1998) "Some Relativistic and Higher-Order Supertasks," *Philosophy of Science* 65: 502–17.

Planck, M. (1959) *The New Science*, vol. 3 of *Complete Works*, New York: Meridian.

Popper, K. (1982) *The Open Universe*, London: Hutchinson.

Reichenbach, H. (1938) *Experience and Prediction*, Chicago: University of Chicago Press.

Salmon, W. (1979) "Propensities: A Discussion Review," *Erkenntnis* 14: 183–216.

Shaffer, J. (2003) "Principled Chances," *British Journal for the Philosophy of Science* 54: 27–41.

—— (2005) "Quidditistic Knowledge," *Philosophical Studies* 123: 1–32.

—— (2007) "Deterministic Chance?" *British Journal for the Philosophy of Science* 58: 113–40.

Shoemaker, S. (1998) "Causal and Metaphysical Necessity," *Pacific Philosophical Quarterly* 79: 59–77.

Skyrms, B. (1977) "Resiliency, Propensities, and Causal Necessity," *Journal of Philosophy* 74: 704–13.

van Fraassen, B. (1980) *The Scientific Image*, Oxford: Clarendon Press.

—— (1989) *Laws and Symmetry*, Oxford: Clarendon Press.

van Inwagen, P. (1975) "The Incompatibility of Free Will and Determinism," *Philosophical Studies* 27: 185–99.

—— (1983) *An Essay on Free Will*, Oxford: Clarendon Press.

von Mises, R. (1981) *Probability, Statistics and Truth*, New York: Dover.

Ward, B. (2005) "Projecting Chances: A Humean Vindication and Justification of the Principal Principle," *Philosophy of Science* 72: 241–61.

Further reading

For further reading, see E. Nagel, *The Structure of Science* (London: Routledge, 1961) Chapter 10 and S. Shoemaker, "Causality and Properties," P. van Inwagen (ed.), *Time and Cause* (Dordrecht: Reidel, 1980), pp.109–35. D. H. Mellor, *Probability: A Philosophical Introduction* (London: Routledge, 2005); D. Albert, *Time and Chance* (Harvard: Harvard University Press, 2001); D. Albert, *Quantum Mechanics and Experience* (Harvard: Harvard University Press, 1993); and (advanced) W. M. Dickson, *Quantum Chance and Non-Locality: Probability and Non-Locality in the Interpretation of Quantum Mechanics* (Cambridge: Cambridge University Press, 1998).

46
ESSENCES AND NATURAL KINDS

Alexander Bird

Introduction

Essentialism as applied to individuals is the claim that for at least some individuals there are properties that those individuals possess essentially. What it is to possess a property essentially is a matter of debate. To possess a property essentially is often taken to be akin to possessing a property necessarily, but stronger – although this is not a feature of Aristotle's essentialism, according to which essential properties are those properties a thing could not lose without ceasing to exist. Kit Fine (1994) takes essential properties to be those that an object has in virtue of its *identity*, while other essentialists refer (as Fine also does) to the *nature* of an object as the source of its essential properties. It is sometimes important to distinguish the essential properties of a thing and the "full" essence of a thing. The latter is the set of the essential properties of a thing, when that set necessarily *suffices* to determine the thing's identity. One might hold that something has essential properties without agreeing that it has an identity-determining essence.

Essentialism was largely in abeyance during the first two-thirds of the twentieth century thanks to the domination of analytic philosophy by anti-metaphysical logical empiricism and the linguistic turn. The rehabilitation of essentialism owes much to the development of a formal apparatus for the understanding of modality more generally, thanks to C. I. Lewis, Ruth Barcan Marcus, and Saul Kripke. Kripke's discussion of essentialism both about individuals and also about natural kinds brought essentialism to wider philosophical prominence. Natural kind essentialism, which finds its modern genesis also in the work of Hilary Putnam, claims that natural kinds have essential properties: to say that possession of property P is part of the essence of the kind K implies that, necessarily, every member or sample of the kind K possesses P. Essentialism about individuals has been linked to thinking about natural kinds by the contentious claim that one of the essential properties of any entity is that it belongs to the natural kind (or kinds) it actually belongs to.

In this chapter I shall first outline certain claims and arguments concerning essentialism concerning individuals (second section). I shall then (third section) introduce the notion of a natural kind in more detail before discussing natural kind essentialism (fourth section).

Essentialism concerning individuals

A simple account of essentialism concerning individuals takes a's essential properties to be precisely those a possesses necessarily (reading "$\Box p$" as "necessarily p"):

>   (N) a possesses F essentially $\leftrightarrow \Box Fa$.

The implications in (N) may be challenged in both directions. Considering the right-to-left implication, as Kit Fine (1994) emphasizes, it is not the case that if $\Box Fa$, then a possesses F essentially. Anything is such that 2 + 2 = 4, and necessarily so, but being that way is not an essential property of every object; it is essential to the singleton set containing Socrates that it contains Socrates, but while it is a necessary truth concerning Socrates that he is a member of that set, that truth is not any part of Socrates' essence.

The left-to-right implication in (N) is rarely challenged in modern metaphysics, but, it should be noted, is not required by Aristotle's essentialism:

>   (A) a possesses F essentially $\leftrightarrow \Box$ (a loses $F \rightarrow a$ ceases to exist).

The Aristotelian idea that a property F is essential to a when a cannot lose F without ceasing to exist is consistent with the possibility that a might never have acquired F. Some properties are persistent, in that once acquired, they are possessed at all later times, so long as the possessor continues to exist: "existing on 1 January 2008" is an example, "being born in Boston" (see Brody 1967) is another, as is "being a butterfly." The persistent properties just mentioned can be acquired but might not have been: many things existent on New Year's Day 2008 might have ceased to exist during 2007; the mother of an unborn child might have decided to have her baby in Cambridge rather than Boston; the caterpillar may have died before metamorphosis (we are assuming here that metamorphosis involves a persisting individual). All persisting properties are essential according to (A), but as these examples show, they are not necessary properties of their bearers. The first two may suggest that (A) is too liberal in what it allows to be an essential property, and indeed (A) allows to be essential properties those which Fine rejects, since necessary properties are trivially persistent properties. Note that (A) also makes existence an essential property of any existing thing. While this may require some tightening up of the right-to-left implication of (A), for example, by reference to an entity's nature, the Aristotelian would still claim that an entity might acquire a nature that once acquired cannot be lost. Aristotle himself thought that an embryo is not itself a human but becomes a human; but once human, something cannot cease to be human without ceasing to exist. Similarly, and less contentiously, the caterpillar becomes a butterfly, but once a butterfly cannot cease to be a butterfly without ceasing to exist.

As it happens, most contemporary discussions of essentialism assume (N) – which is not to say that contemporary arguments for essentialism cannot be transformed to support a more exacting notion of essence, such as Fine's. Kripke argues for *F*'s being an essential property of *a* by eliciting our intuitions that *a* could not lack *F*. But since the relevant property *F* is in each case something that is plausibly part of *a*'s nature or is relevant to *a*'s identity, then *F* is at least a candidate for an essential property by Fine's standards.

Kripke argues for the essentiality of (a) origin; (b) composition or substance; and (c) character or kind. We will review these arguments in turn.

In responding to a passage from Timothy Sprigge (1962), Kripke raises the question: could a person, the Queen for example, have had different parents from those she actually had? Kripke is careful to distinguish (implicitly, Sprigge was not) this modal question from an epistemic question: could we discover that the Queen's parents are not the people we thought them to be? The answer to the latter question might, perhaps, be *yes*, but that does not answer the modal question: given that it is in fact true that the Queen's parents were George VI and Elizabeth Bowes-Lyon, would it have been possible for the Queen, that very same woman, to have had different parents, say Mr and Mrs Truman (the thirty-third president of the United States, Harry S. Truman and Elizabeth Virginia Truman, *née* Wallace)? Kripke's answer is that while we can imagine that the Queen never became Queen, we cannot imagine her having different parents or being born from a different sperm and egg. Thus, more generally, a person's origin, being born of those parents and from that sperm and egg, are necessary properties of that person. By (N), origin is essential to a person – and since origin, arguably, concerns a person's identity or nature, origin may plausibly be regarded as essential by Fine's more exacting standards (for a defence and elaboration of the essentiality of origin, see McGinn [1976]).

Essentiality of origin is not limited to persons or even to living creatures. Kripke asks of a particular wooden table: could it have been made from a different block of wood or even from a block of ice from the river Thames? For example, the presidential desk in the Oval Office is constructed from planks from the ship HMS *Resolute*. Could that very same desk have been constructed from wood from different planks from different trees or even from kevlar? The kevlar desk is intrinsically different from the actual presidential desk. But the desk made from wood from different planks need not be. Could that desk have come from material of completely different origin, even if intrinsically identical to the actual desk? (Likewise Forbes points out that we can conceive of scientists constructing a zygote [fertilized egg] intrinsically just like that which grew into Queen Elizabeth II. Given that she did not in fact come from such a zygote, could she have done? Essentiality of origin says *no*.)

Kripke's claim does not rest upon intuition alone – he does offer the following (much-discussed) supposed proof. Consider some source material suitable for a wooden desk like the presidential desk, say a certain selection of planks from the USS *Rattlesnake*. Could the very same presidential desk, the one now sitting in the Oval Office, have been made from the *Rattlesnake* planks rather than the *Resolute* planks? Here is an argument as to why not. Consider a world like ours, except that in addition to the making of the presidential desk (call it "P-desk"), another, intrinsically identical desk is made from the *Rattlesnake* planks (call this "Q-desk"). Clearly P-desk and Q-desk are different desks. Now consider a third world, in which no desk is made from the *Resolute* planks, but a desk is made from the *Rattlesnake* planks. That would be Q-desk, and since Q-desk is not P-desk, the desk made from the *Rattlesnake* planks is not P-desk. So P-desk, the actual presidential desk, could not have been made from the *Rattlesnake* planks, nor, for the same reasons, from any other hunk of matter that is entirely distinct from the matter from which it was actually made.

The issues of the *substance* (composition) and the *kind* (nature) of an individual are clearly related to that of origin, but essentiality of substance and kind are not immediate corollaries of the proof just given. For the latter depends only on the *identity* of the originating matter. The presidential desk originates essentially from those planks in HMS *Resolute*, but if those planks could have had a different composition, such as kevlar, then the presidential desk would also have had a different composition. Kripke notes that it is the *original* composition and kind of the desk that are at issue here, not the Aristotelian question of whether it could change in certain ways. (Perhaps the same desk could fossilize over time and so no longer be made of wood, or it may, with some small adjustments consistent with retaining its identity, become some other piece of furniture and no longer a desk – yet it may still be true that it must have started out as a desk made of wood.) Kripke does not offer an argument for the essentiality of original composition. However, it is intuitively highly plausible that a plank of wood must have had as its source some tree or other woody material and could not have been made in a kevlar factory. So for the planks at least, it seems as if they must originate from a certain stuff (wood). And if the essentiality of the identity of origin is true, then the presidential desk must be *made* from wood (whatever it may subsequently become).

Even if it is true that the presidential desk must have come from those planks and be made (originally) of wood, a further pair of questions would be whether it must be a desk, and whether it must originally have been a desk. Thus we have considered so far (i) the essentiality of identity of origin, and (ii) the essentiality of composition and original composition; now we are considering (iii) the essentiality of *kind* and of *original kind*. Again the last two are distinct. It could well be that the desk could retain its identity without remaining a desk – perhaps some president might order it to be turned into a drinks cabinet with a few modifications. It might be correct to say, "that cabinet was once the presidential desk." Still, it might also be true that the cabinet must have been a desk once. One might doubt whether the cabinet would be that very thing, had it been fashioned directly from the planks of HMS *Resolute*. Although the claims of essentiality of (identity of) origin and the essentiality of (original) kind are distinct, in this case at least the driving intuitions may be related. For the discussion of the origin of the desk in those planks from HMS *Resolute* generated the result that the desk must originate with those planks, not simply that it must originate with those molecules (which need not be arranged as planks). Arguably therefore, the intuition that this item must have started life as a desk has the same source – it must have originated from that matter arranged desk-wise.

In the case of the desk, a change of kind seemed possible – it could become a cabinet and remain the same thing. In other cases, however, kind seems essential in addition to original kind. As noted, this is a different question from whether it is possible to lose one's kind. It may not be possible for Augustus to stop being a god, once he has become one, although it was merely contingent that he became a god at all. A caterpillar need not have become a butterfly, but having done so, she must remain a butterfly until death. Of course, if belonging to kind K is essential to x then x cannot cease to be of kind K. Are there cases where it is essential to x that x is of kind K?

A very strong claim of this sort is that it is essential to every item x and for every *natural* kind K, that if x is of kind K, then x is essentially of kind K. The butterfly case may seem to be a counterexample. But in such cases there seems to be room for denying that "caterpillar" and "butterfly" are kinds at all – perhaps they should be regarded as *phases* along the lines of "child," "adolescent," "adult" (to pass through puberty is not to change one's natural kind). The intuitive case for essentiality of kind appears, at first sight at least, quite compelling. The human prince could not have been a frog; it seems that being human he must necessarily be human. Similarly for other kinds: could this gem, a diamond, have been quartz, this nugget of gold have been a lump of lead, or the moon have been a star? Negative answers are at the very least plausible.

The fact that essentialism renders fairy tales and dreams of transmutation impossible is no objection, since the denial of an essential truth need not be incoherent. And in the transmutation case, what essentialism rules out is not the production of gold from lead but rather the continued existence of any items made of lead through the process of transmutation (they cease to exist and are replaced by gold items). However, to concede that x is human → □ x is not a frog, is not to agree that x is human → □ x is human. The process of speciation allows individuals to become members of new species – when a species divides into two species, the old species ceases to exist, hence its members change their kind. In an actual process of transmutation, such as beta decay, there is good reason to maintain that the individual nucleus retains its identity while changing the element it instantiates.

We have discussed whether individuals might have certain sorts of essential properties – we have not yet addressed the question of whether they have full essences, i.e. sets of essential properties that necessarily distinguish the individuals. One might think that although it is essential to Castor and Polydeuces that they have Zeus and Leda as their parents and that they come from such-and-such an egg, if they come from one and the same egg (i.e. if they are monozygotic "identical" twins), then there is no further property that distinguishes one from the other in all possible worlds. However, Graeme Forbes (1985) argues that to make sense of identity across possible worlds, we need essences. For without essences we could imagine a non-actual possible world where everything true in the actual world of Castor is true of Polydeuces and vice versa; intuitively, that would not be a different world at all. One could avoid this by appealing to basic facts about identity. But what sort of facts would these be? One might expect such facts to be grounded in some ontological feature of the world, such as the properties of things. Duns Scotus' proposal for such an individuating property asserts that each individual has a *haecceity* – a non-qualitative property that is necessarily possessed by exactly that individual (e.g. the property of being Socrates). Forbes argues for a more attractive but more ambitious view according to which individual essences are grounded in non-haecceitistic qualitative properties.

Natural kinds

We find it intuitively natural to classify objects and samples of stuffs into kinds. Many such classifications seem to us to be natural, corresponding to divisions that exist in nature, distinguishing, for example, bees from wasps, bits of gold from bits of silver, and perhaps also cases of cholera from cases of bubonic plague. One might maintain that the appearance of naturalness is merely appearance, and that the classifications in question are no more objectively natural than, say, divisions of motor vehicles by manufacturer, engine size, or style. The latter view is *conventionalism* about kinds and is related to constructivism (constructionism) more generally in the philosophy of science.

Those who take the more intuitive, naturalistic approach, agreeing with Plato that such classifications do, sometimes at least, "carve nature at the joints" are faced with the question: what is it in nature that makes such classifications genuinely natural? It cannot merely be that the members of a kind are objectively similar, by sharing some natural property. For it is possible for objects to share a natural property without forming any kind: the class of positively charged objects is too heterogeneous, including as it does all protons and positrons, sodium ions and hydronium ions, balloons that have been rubbed on a jumper, and so on. Likewise the class of objects of mass 1 kilogram all share a natural property without forming a kind. J. S. Mill makes this point, remarking that white things do not form a kind. Mill and others have allied kinds to induction – natural kind classifications are those that permit induction. But that again does not, as it stands, distinguish natural kinds from the sharing of some natural property – we can make inductions concerning positively charged objects, objects 1 kilogram in mass, and white objects, respectively.

More promising is the idea that natural kinds are particularly *rich* sources of inductive knowledge – they are marked by the confluence of several natural properties, such that membership of the kind can be inductively inferred from knowledge that a particular possesses some subset of those properties, which in turn permits an inductive inference to the remainder of the properties associated with the kind. An organism may readily be identified as a tiger – a member of the species *Panthera tigris* – on the basis of casual visual inspection. That allows one to infer that the organism is a vertebrate, carnivorous, sexually reproducing, viviparous, and so forth. According to Richard Boyd's (1999) *homeostatic property cluster* view of kinds, kinds involve clusters of properties as just described, and for good reason. Natural mechanisms ensure that individuals frequently have most or all of the properties in the cluster, but infrequently or never have just several of the properties.

Biological species were, until Darwin, the paradigm of a natural kind. However, deeper understanding of species – especially in the light of evolution – has cast doubt, for many philosophers of biology, on the claim that species are natural kinds. First, there is no set of intrinsic properties such that possession of these properties is necessary and sufficient for species membership. Almost any characteristic property of a member of a species can be lacked by some member or other, and this goes even for genetic properties – there is no genotype all and only common frogs (*Rana temporaria*) have. Furthermore, a creature may have all the characteristic properties of a kind yet fail to be a member of that kind – a creature that evolved on another planet to be the intrinsic duplicate of some common frog will not be a member of *Rana temporaria*. Thus species membership is not an intrinsic property of an organism.

Many philosophers of biology have responded to this fact by denying that species are natural kinds, asserting instead that species are individuals (Ghiselin 1974; Hull 1976). Furthermore, this allows one to say that species evolve, since individuals can change, but natural kinds, being abstract entities, cannot. But these reasons need not be taken to be decisive. Perhaps the membership of some natural kinds is not an intrinsic matter. It may be that the belief that it is intrinsic stems from the view that natural kinds have essences, and that essential properties should be intrinsic. But as we have seen above, the essential properties of individuals need not be intrinsic; perhaps they need not be for kinds either. As regards the point about evolution, the evolution of species is a matter of changes in the frequency of certain genotypes within the population, which is consistent with a variety of views about the ontology of natural kinds. Note, for comparison, that the frequency of various isotopes of an element may change over time without that showing that the chemical elements are not natural kinds.

The discussion of the preceding paragraph assumed that natural kinds are abstract objects, and furthermore implicitly assumed that natural kinds have essences. I shall now address the first of these two matters and then turn to the issue of natural kind essentialism in the fourth and final section of this chapter.

One should, *prima facie*, distinguish two claims: (i) there are natural divisions among things into kinds; (ii) there are entities that are the natural kinds. The latter is an ontological claim about the existence of certain things. The former is a claim about the grouping and differentiation of things in a natural fashion. A much older and more prominent debate over the nature of properties divides realists who think that properties are certain entities, universals, from nominalists who think that there are no such entities. Most (property) nominalists think that there are genuine and natural similarities and differences between things. Likewise a natural kind nominalist may reject conventionalism without buying into the analogue of realism for natural kinds, a belief in natural kinds as entities. One reason why the distinction between (i) and (ii) has not been so prominent for natural kinds as for properties is that it is common to express the rejection of conventionalism by saying "there are natural kinds," which has an implicit quantification over natural kinds, and hence an ontological commitment. Another is the fact that the term "realism" in connection with natural kinds has tended to be used to denote the rejection of conventionalism. In both respects the impression is given that positive answers to (i) and (ii) are to be conflated. (For these reasons I suggest that we differentiate between *strong realism*, which is the ontological commitment to the existence of natural kinds as entities, and *weak realism* [or *naturalism* about natural kinds], which is the view that there are objectively natural divisions of things into kinds).

Given the analogy between ontological strong realism about natural kinds and realism about universals, one might wonder whether arguments for the existence of universals can mutate into arguments for the existence of natural kinds. It seems not, however. Arguments for realism about universals claim that without universals we are unable to explain the similarity and difference we find between things. The analogous argument for natural kinds would claim that we need the existence of natural kinds to explain the perceived natural groupings of things. But there does not seem to be any explanatory deficiency here. For example, the homeostatic property cluster view of natural kinds is able to explain the groupings of things into kinds by appealing to properties alone, and without the addition of kinds also.

A commitment to natural kinds as entities requires, therefore, a different argument. One such argument, I suggest, starts from the observation that natural kinds are widely regarded as having essences. As was remarked at the outset, essentialists typically take essential properties to concern the identity or nature of a thing. But only genuine existents have an identity or nature – in which case, essentialism about natural kinds commits one to their existence. In the next section, we examine the claim that natural kinds do indeed have essential properties.

Natural kind essentialism

Natural kind essentialism may be understood in a stronger form that implies strong realism about kinds – there are entities that are natural kinds and these have essential properties (and possibly full essences also) – or in a weaker form that is *prima facie* compatible with natural kind nominalism: there are *a posteriori* necessary truths concerning the extensions of natural kind predicates. Most discussions of natural kind essentialism have assumed only the latter. Above I mentioned the view that the natural kind to which an individual belongs is an essential property of that individual. This claim is not implied by essentialism about the natural kinds themselves. One might think that an individual may change its kind from K to L, yet hold that so long as it is a member of the kind K, then it must also have certain properties that are nontrivially entailed by membership of K. For example, it may be necessary that a frog has certain (possibly extrinsic) properties in virtue of being a frog, but that may not prevent some creature ceasing to be a frog as the result of some speciation event (e.g. were *R. temporaria* to split into two daughter species).

Recent discussions of the view that natural kinds have essences have the work of Kripke (1971, 1980) and Putnam (1975) as their origin. Their arguments are intertwined with arguments in the philosophy of language concerning reference and designation. I shall briefly discuss this context, partly to make it clear that the arguments for essentialism are not in every case corollaries of the arguments in the philosophy of language, and can be stated independently of them.

One of Kripke's central concerns is to refute a conception of the reference of proper names and natural kind terms which maintains that reference is achieved in virtue of the referent satisfying a certain content (e.g. a description or sense) that constitutes the meaning of the term in question, in such a way that this content is grasped or understood by a competent user of the term. With respect to proper names – let one such name be a – Kripke proceeds by taking some plausible content for the meaning of a – let that content be Φ – and then shows that Φa is (i) not necessary; (ii) not analytic; and (iii) not knowable *a priori*. Hence Φ cannot be the meaning of a – and by extension all other candidate meanings will fail these tests too. Kripke's diagnosis of the failure of candidate meanings to pass the test of necessity is not simply that a proper name has no meaning but also, more positively, that a proper name functions so as to designate the same individual in every possible world where that individual exists. Because a particular can, across possible worlds, lack the properties of the sort that would make up Φ, Φa is not necessary. A term that designates the same individual in every possible world is a *rigid designator*. If "a" and "b" are rigid designators, then "$a = b$" asserts a necessary truth.

Now let us turn to natural kinds. As Kripke points out, many interesting discoveries in science are theoretical identities concerning natural kinds, for example that water is H_2O, that gold is the element with atomic number 79, that lightning is electricity, heat is molecular motion, light is a stream of photons, and so forth. According to Kripke, these theoretical identities should be understood as identities involving rigid designators and so are necessary truths. Arguably they tell us the essences of the relevant kinds: the essence of water is that it is H_2O. This approach raises a number of questions. What does rigid designation amount to for natural kind terms? What are the referents of natural kind terms such that they can be involved in identities? What shows that "H_2O" and "element with atomic number 79" are rigid designators, given that they look like descriptions? Can "lightning is electricity" really be an identity, given that not all electricity is lightning (and likewise for the claims about light and about heat)?

However, not all grounds for natural kind essentialism flow from the rigidity of the terms in theoretical identities. One may appeal to certain modal intuitions we have. Thus in Putnam's famous Twin Earth thought experiments, we are asked to consider Twin Earth, a planet like Earth except that where Earth has water, Twin Earth has a substance that has every superficial appearance of water, but a radically different molecular constitution, XYZ. Although XYZ appears to be very much like water, it would not *be* water. Although Putnam's account concerns the extension of thoughts about water, the core appeal to intuition and its metaphysical import are independent of semantic considerations. The metaphysical import is that having molecular constitution H_2O is, necessarily, a necessary condition for being water. Since the considerations in question are those that concern what it is to *be* water, this necessary truth asserts an essential property of water. Whether being constituted by H_2O is *the* essence of water depends on whether being thus constituted thereby suffices for being water, and Putnam's thought experiment does not yield an answer to that question. The answer rather depends upon whether one is willing to regard ice and water vapour as water and whether a single molecule of H_2O is water. One complication for such discussions is that "water" is a vernacular term as well as one that seems to pick out a natural kind, and discussion of the latter can be infected by considerations emanating from the former.

Earlier I considered a criticism of the view that species are natural kinds that assumed that natural kinds have intrinsic essences, whereas species do not. Kripke does mention

biological kinds. He does argue that a creature with a very different internal constitution (e.g. a robot) could not be a cat, even if it was very cat-like in appearance and
behaviour. Nonetheless, having some intrinsic essential properties is consistent with
having others that are not, in which case the essence of the kind would not be intrinsic.
Kripke does also argue that some creature could lack many of the superficial properties
that we take to be characteristic of being a tiger, yet could be a tiger nonetheless. It may
be implied that the creature is a tiger in virtue of some hidden internal properties, such
as genetic constitution – but we saw above that this is biologically and metaphysically
implausible. Cladism in biological taxonomy takes biological taxa to be defined by
shared common ancestry. Thus membership of a taxon, such as species, is an extrinsic
property. As discussed in the second section "Essentialism concerning individuals,"
Kripke himself argues that individuals can have extrinsic properties essentially – origin
for example. Cladism, when allied with essentialism, extends this to biological kinds
also (see McGinn 1976; LaPorte 2004).

References

Boyd, R. (1999) "Homeostasis, Species, and Higher Taxa," in R. A. Wilson (ed.), *Species: New Interdisci-
plinary Essays*, Cambridge: MIT Press, pp. 141–85.
Brody, B. A. (1967) "Natural Kinds and Real Essences," *Journal of Philosophy* 64: 431–46.
Fine, K. (1994) "Essence and Modality," in J. Tomberlin (ed.), *Philosophical Perspectives*, vol. 8 of *Logic and
Language*, Atascadero, CA: Ridgeview, pp. 1–16.
Forbes, G. (1985) *The Metaphysics of Modality*, Oxford: Oxford University Press.
Ghiselin, M. (1974) "A Radical Solution to the Species Problem," *Systematic Zoology* 23: 536–44.
Hull, D. (1976) "Are Species Really Individuals?" *Systematic Zoology* 25: 174–91.
Kripke, S. (1971) "Identity and Necessity," in M. K. Munitz (ed.), *Identity and Individuation*, New York: New
York University Press.
—— (1980) *Naming and Necessity*, Oxford: Blackwell.
LaPorte, J. (2004) *Natural Kinds and Conceptual Change*, Cambridge: Cambridge University Press.
McGinn, C. (1976) "On the Necessity of Origin," *The Journal of Philosophy* 73: 127–35.
Sprigge, T. (1962) "Internal and External Properties," *Mind* 71: 197–212.

Further Reading

The classic text of modern essentialism is Kripke's *Naming and Necessity* (Oxford: Blackwell, 1980), along
with Putnam's "The meaning of 'meaning'," in *Mind, Language and Reality: Philosophical Papers*, vol. 2
(Cambridge: Cambridge University Press, 1975), pp. 215–71. Kripke's origin essentialism is developed by
McGinn, while individual essences are promoted in Forbes's *The Metaphysics of Modality* (Oxford: Oxford
University Press, 1985). An excellent recent discussion of essentialism is Penelope Mackie's *How Things
Might Have Been* (Oxford: Oxford University Press, 2006). Joseph LaPorte gives a very clear introduction to
the key issues surrounding natural kinds and kind essentialism in *Natural Kinds and Conceptual Change*
(Cambridge: Cambridge University Press, 2004). Brian Ellis develops a metaphysics for science based on
essentialism in *Scientific Essentialism* (Cambridge: Cambridge University Press, 2001). For a general introduction to natural kinds and to natural kind essentialism, see Alexander Bird and Emma Tobin, "Natural
Kinds," in E. N. Zalta (ed.), *The Stanford Encyclopedia of Philosophy* (2008) (available: http://plato.stanford.
edu/).

47
METAPHYSICS AND RELATIVITY

Katherine Hawley

Isaac Newton gave us a theory about how objects move, forces interact, and gravity operates. Centuries later, Albert Einstein transformed physics, first with his special theory of relativity (SR) and then with his general theory of relativity (GR). SR tells us how objects move when they are unaffected by gravity; GR generalises the account to include gravity.

According to SR, Newton was more-or-less right about how objects move at ordinary speeds: that's why his theory was successful for so long, and why it continues to be useful. But SR comes into its own when accounting for the surprising behaviour of objects moving near the speed of light (300,000 kilometres per second, or 186,000 miles per second). Despite ignoring gravity, SR in its turn is usually successful: this is because, as GR tells us, over shortish distances gravity has much less influence than other forces. But GR comes into its own when accounting for the surprising nature of the universe on the grand scale, where local forces become negligible, and gravity is crucial.

Why should metaphysicians take a particular interest in all this? Modern physics has many specialist subfields, including biophysics, geophysics, quantum cryptography, and the study of chaotic systems, but these typically do not feature in a *Companion to Metaphysics*: Why do theories of motion and gravity raise distinctively philosophical issues?

The theories of relativity show how motion and gravity are deeply connected with the fundamental nature of space and time. As we will see, SR threatens our ordinary distinctions between past, present and future, whilst GR suggests that space and time are not just the neutral stage upon which events take place, but are themselves actors in the drama. Questions about space and time, and about the persistence and motion of material objects have always been central to metaphysics; many of the great philosophers – Aristotle, Descartes and Leibniz for example – contributed significantly to what we now think of as the science of physics, whilst some of the greatest physicists – including Newton and Einstein – thought deeply and philosophically about the metaphysical nature of space, time, force and motion.

This is a realm in which it can be difficult to draw a sharp distinction between metaphysics and physics. It can be difficult to know what is a matter of straightforward empirical fact and what is a matter of legitimate philosophical disagreement: how much philosophy is built into the usual understanding of the physics? We are travelling through border country, and will need our wits about us.

Special relativity

The relativity of simultaneity

From a metaphysical point of view, the most significant consequence of SR is the *relativity of simultaneity*, the idea that, for many pairs of events, there is no objective fact of the matter as to whether the events occurred at the same time, or different times. It is not just that we can't find out whether the events happened at the same time – sometimes there is simply nothing to find out. Or so the usual story goes.

Suppose I am sitting in the middle of a moving single-carriage train, and I throw two balls at the same time with the same effort in two different directions, towards the driver at the front of the train and the guard at the back. We would expect the balls to reach the guard and the driver at the same time: after all, they each have the same distance to travel, and I threw them at the same speed.

What does this look like from the ground outside the train? From this perspective, the train carries the guard forward to meet the ball I throw at him. The other ball has farther to travel, since the train is carrying the driver away from it. But nevertheless the guard and the driver get bumped on the head simultaneously, because the ball I throw at the driver travels faster than the one I throw at the guard: it is already travelling quite fast in that direction, because of the motion of the train, and my throw only increases its speed. (This addition of velocities explains why jumping from a moving car is more painful than stepping out of a stationary one.)

Commonsense tells us that how fast each ball is moving depends upon our frame of reference: from the frame of reference centred on the train, each ball has the same speed, while from the frame of reference centred on the surrounding countryside, the balls have different speeds. No puzzle there. But experiments show that light violates this commonsense principle: it travels at the same speed with respect to every non-accelerating frame of reference, as does other electromagnetic radiation, like X-rays, infrared, and radio waves.

Suppose I send a radio message to the driver at the front and to the guard at the back. From my perspective – the frame of reference centred on the train – the driver and the guard receive the message simultaneously. After all, their messages each have the same distance to travel, and each travels at the same speed.

What does this look like from the ground outside the train? From this perspective, the train carries the guard forward to meet his message, and carries the driver away from hers. But the driver's message doesn't travel any faster than the guard's: like light, radio signals travel at the same speed with respect to every non-accelerating frame of reference. The driver's message travels farther, at the same speed, so it arrives after the guard's message.

According to the frame of reference centred on the train, the messages are received *simultaneously*, but according to the frame of reference centred on the surrounding countryside, the guard's message is received *before* the driver's message. (And suppose you are on a train overtaking mine: from your perspective, my train is moving backwards, the driver is moving towards her message and the guard moving away from his, so that the guard's message is received *after* the driver's.) Are the messages received simultaneously? Different frames provide different answers to this question, and SR gives us no reason to take any one frame of reference to be more fundamental than the others.

This relativity of simultaneity does not apply to all pairs of events. If two events happen simultaneously at the same place – like the events of my sending a signal to the driver and my sending a signal to the guard – then they are simultaneous with respect to every non-accelerating frame of reference. Moreover, if there is time to send a signal between two events, then their temporal order is fixed: there is no frame of reference according to which the guard receives his message before I send it. Nevertheless, there are plenty of events whose temporal order is frame-dependent.

Pre-relativistic commonsense suggests that we can classify events by the time at which they occurred. In principle at least, I could write down the sequence of events which make up my life history, one on each page of a notebook, then fill up the rest of each page with all the other events which were going on at that time. For example, as I was being born, Elvis was playing Las Vegas, and a Neil Young live album was announced in New York. But the relativity of simultaneity undermines this picture. Although there is a frame of reference according to which all these events occurred simultaneously, there are other frames according to which Elvis's show was over before I was born, and others in which I was born before his show began. SR gives us no grounds for picking one privileged frame, no grounds for preferring one division of events into "simultaneity groups" rather than another.

Past, present and future

The relativity of simultaneity seems to undermine the distinction between past, present and future. After all, which events are present *now*, as you read this paragraph? Well, all those events, near and far, which are simultaneous with your reading this paragraph. If simultaneity is a frame-dependent matter, then whether some distant event is past, present or future is also a frame-dependent matter.

This poses a problem for metaphysical theories which give particular significance to the distinctions between past, present and future (see Chapters 4, 6, 41 and 42). Perhaps the most radical of such theories is *presentism*, the view that only presently existing objects and events are real. For presentists, temporal distance has a significance that spatial distance does not. Spatially distant objects and events on the Moon are less accessible to me than are the ones here in my office, but nevertheless Crater Tycho exists as fully as my desk does. We might say that Crater Tycho does not exist here in my office, as a way of saying that it is not located here, but this doesn't mean the crater is somehow unreal. In contrast, for presentists, temporally distant objects and events which do not exist now simply do not exist at all.

Other philosophers, whilst they accept that past and future objects and events exist, believe nevertheless that there are objective, metaphysical differences between these: events change as they move from the future, through the present, and on into the past.

The relativity of simultaneity looks like a major problem for all these theories, though I shall focus on presentism in what follows. If there is no frame-independent fact of the matter about which events are simultaneous with your reading this paragraph, then there is no frame-independent fact of the matter about which events are now present. So, according to presentism, there is presumably no frame-independent fact of the matter about what exists.

How can presentists respond? The most drastic option is to give up thinking that all present events and objects exist and focus only on I–here–now: after all, there is no indeterminacy about what is happening right here, right now. This is self-centred in the extreme.

A slightly less drastic option is to stick with the idea that only what is present exists, accept that presentness is frame-dependent, and so conclude that which events have the special status is a frame-dependent matter. This might not sound too bad, but it is important to understand how strange this view really is. First, a frame of reference is not a rich conceptual scheme, a culture or worldview; it's just a possible set of coordinates, like latitude and longitude. Second, frames of reference are multitudinous. A frame is often introduced by mentioning an object (e.g. a train) which is stationary with respect to it. But that is just a matter of convenience: there can be a frame of reference even if nothing is stationary with respect to it, just as there can be a viewpoint in the mountains even if nobody is standing there looking out. Right now, you are in many, many, *many* frames of reference, with a different velocity in each (and thus you have many different "takes" on what's present).

To soften the blow, presentists might argue that, although there's no privileged frame of reference underpinning objective, universal facts about simultaneity, there is at least a privileged frame of reference for you right now – the one according to which you are stationary right now. But even this slightly more modest view has peculiar consequences. Suppose you are on the station platform, and I travel past in a train; our eyes meet, and our hearts flutter. Because we're at rest according to different frames of reference, some events which are present-with your heart flutter are not present-with mine: suppose the bellow of a bison in Boise is one of these events. If presentism is correct, then the bellow exists-with your flutter but does not exist-with mine. So my flutter and the bellow both exist-with your flutter, but my flutter and the bellow do not exist-with each other. This might make you question whether we're still discussing existence: we might have expected existence-with to be *transitive*, to use the jargon.

None of these options for presentism look very promising, especially if presentism is supposed to vindicate our ordinary ideas about the passage of time and the immediacy of the present. (A further option is to look beyond SR for empirical evidence of a privileged reference frame; more on that story later.)

Faced with these problems, some presentists have questioned whether their metaphysical claims can really be refuted by a scientific theory. SR tells us that simultaneity is frame-relative, and that the laws of physics do not pick out one frame as being more fundamental than all the others. We could accept this yet still wonder whether there might nevertheless be a privileged frame of reference, one which is undetected by the laws of physics. This frame would have no empirical, scientific significance but could be the ground of unique, objective simultaneity, and thus, for the presentist, of unique, objective facts about what exists.

Accepting SR does not logically compel us to give up the idea of a privileged frame of reference. But many people – both philosophers and physicists – think that the philosophical reasons to believe in such a frame are far outweighed by our empirical grounds for thinking it does not exist. Why? First, there is the idea that if there were a privileged reference frame, this would show up in our best scientific theories: unlike, perhaps, God, beauty or morality, this is just the sort of thing you'd expect science to tell you about. Second, there is the idea that an empirically undetectable distinction between past, present and future, whilst not incoherent, cannot form the basis of a philosophical theory which is supposed to explain or vindicate our pre-theoretical ideas about time and existence. To this, presentists may respond that worries about the relativity of simultaneity only arise over very long distances or very short periods, so it is no wonder that our pre-theoretical ideas about time and existence are not sensitive to these concerns.

The relationship between presentism and SR is fraught but fascinating. The nature of time and existence are themselves central philosophical concerns, of course, but this debate is also a battleground for methodological issues about human knowledge: what is the relationship between science and philosophy, between the empirical and the *a priori*? Above all, can we infer that something – like a privileged reference frame – does *not* exist from the fact that it is *not* mentioned in a successful scientific theory?

Persistence and the relativity of simultaneity

How do material objects persist through time? Or, as it is often put, how can a single object exist at several different times? Perdurantism is the view that material objects persist through time by having different temporal parts at different times, just as they extend through space by having different spatial parts in different places. In contrast, endurantism is the view that material objects persist through time by being wholly present at each of several times. For endurantists, temporal persistence is quite different from spatial extension.

In their standard formulations, both perdurantism and endurantism presuppose that persistence is a matter of existing – somehow or other – at more than one moment in time. But what is a moment in time? Commonsense suggests that we can divide history into groups of simultaneous events, events which happen at the same moment. Yet the relativity of simultaneity undermines this picture, and thus the very notion of a moment: the grouping (or "foliation") of events differs according to different frames of reference. How does this affect perdurantism and endurantism?

As usually formulated, perdurantism invokes a distinction between spatial and temporal parts, a distinction which is undermined by the relativity of simultaneity. But

511

the theory is also a species of "four-dimensionalism," the view that objects are stretched out through the four dimensions of space–time, not just the three dimensions of space. Given relativity, the claim that persisting objects are four-dimensional becomes more fundamental than the claim that they have temporal parts. Talk of temporal parts and spatial parts can be replaced by talk of spatiotemporal parts, and then the claim that a persisting object has a different temporal part at every time at which it exists can be replaced by the claim that it has a different spatiotemporal part for each part (or "subregion") of the whole region it occupies. Which of these are temporal parts – rather than spatial parts – is a frame-dependent question.

What about endurantism? It certainly looks as if, unlike perdurantism, endurantism presupposes a significant distinction between space and time, a presupposition which is threatened by the relativity of simultaneity. But philosophers have disagreed about whether this is a fatal problem for endurantism, or whether there is a way of adapting the theory to fit with SR.

Endurantism is a "three-dimensionalist" theory: it claims that objects are stretched out in the three dimensions of space, but move in their entirety through time. The pre-relativistic picture is that an enduring object "sweeps out" a four-dimensional region by being successively wholly present at each momentary subregion of it; in contrast, a perduring object would simply fill up the whole four-dimensional region. In this respect, enduring objects are like universals (see Chapters 2, 5 and 27), which are wholly present in each of several different locations.

The difficulty is to specify what counts as a "momentary" sub-region of an enduring object's four-dimensional region, given the relativity of simultaneity. One promising option is to acknowledge that which subregions are momentary is a frame-dependent matter, but claim nevertheless that an enduring object is wholly present at any subregion which is momentary according to some frame of reference or other. On this account, an enduring object is not wholly present at every subregion of its four-dimensional region: some subregions will be temporally extended according to every frame of reference. Other subregions will be momentary according to some frame of reference, yet, intuitively, be occupied by a spatial part of the enduring object, not by the whole object itself.

If we adopt this notion of endurance, enduring objects are wholly present at very, very many different subregions of their four-dimensional region, and many of those wholly occupied subregions will intersect with one another. This picture does not seem incoherent, but it does raise questions about the initial motivations for endurantism, just as relativity-friendly versions of presentism raise questions about motivations for that theory. Endurantism begins with an apparently natural picture of spatially extended objects sweeping majestically through time, and it can be hard to recognise that natural picture in this story of multi-location.

General relativity

Gravity is what makes the apple fall down from the tree, what enables us to step outdoors without flying off into space. Magnetic forces draw the compass needle towards the pole, and we might think of gravity as a force which draws material objects towards each other, affecting the way they move. Newton told us that the strength of the gravitational attraction between two objects depends upon how much mass each has, and how far apart they are (the less their mass, or the farther apart they are, the less the mutual attraction).

This pre-relativistic story takes gravity to be a kind of direct connection between spatially distant objects, a connection which is somehow generated by their mass, and which pushes or pulls the objects in one direction or another. Einstein's GR (general theory of relativity) replaces this picture with one according to which an object's mass has an impact on the shape of space itself, and thus, indirectly, on the ways in which other objects move about in space.

It can be difficult to imagine space itself having a shape, partly because "shape" often means "outline," and it is hard to see how something could have an outline unless it is an element of a bigger system. But we can begin to grasp the idea by thinking about the shape of a two-dimensional surface, like a trampoline. Initially, the trampoline is flat, with two parallel lines running from one end to the other. If we mark three different points on the trampoline and connect each point to the other two, using straight lines, the resulting figure is an ordinary triangle, with internal angles adding up to 180 degrees. If we place lightweight table-tennis balls at random on to the trampoline, they will lie scattered across the surface. Now suppose we place a heavy bowling ball on to the trampoline, stretching out the material and creating a deep well. What happens? The lightweight balls roll down into the well, gathering together at the bottom. The triangle is distorted, and its angles no longer add up to 180 degrees. The parallel lines are no longer parallel; the one nearer the well is more severely affected than the other.

We observers see this as a change in the three-dimensional shape of the two-dimensional trampoline. But the change would also be apparent to creatures living on the surface itself. Having been surprised by a sudden convergence of table-tennis balls, an ant would find that parallel lines now look divergent, that it has farther to travel to get from one side of the trampoline to another, and that what used to be a detour may now be the shortest path (one which avoids the bottom of the well).

In respect of our own four-dimensional space–time, we are like ants, not trampolinists: we cannot step outside and observe the varying shape of space–time, but we can observe how objects move, and make other measurements which confirm Einstein's theory of gravity.

Relativity of simultaneity again

Faced with the fact that SR does not isolate a privileged perspective on simultaneity, some presentists have hoped to find a privileged reference frame in GR. (Endurantists who are uncomfortable with the "relativistic" version of their view might share this hope.) Cosmologists using GR believe that the universe is expanding, and that the distribution of matter everywhere is becoming less dense as a result of this expansion. This seemingly inexorable move from denser to less dense gives us the option of taking events to be simultaneous if they occur in regions of equal density.

This strategy for rescuing presentism and straightforward endurantism raises two important issues. First, the expansion of the universe is thought to be a contingent fact. There are other ways things might have turned out – consistent with GR – according to which the universe is in a "steady state." Are presentism, endurantism and absolute simultaneity therefore contingent facts about the world, not even physically necessary? Or is the expansion perhaps a contingent empirical sign of an underlying necessity? Second, it is not clear whether this highly sophisticated idea from fundamental physics can really vindicate the commonsense ideas about time and persistence upon which presentism and endurantism are supposed to be built. (This is very like the question I raised at the end of the first section.)

Substantivalism and relationalism

Metaphysicians have long argued about whether space and time are entities in their own right, or whether they are mere abstractions from concrete objects and events. Could there be space and time if there were no objects and nothing ever happened? There is consensus that, given relativity, we can no longer talk about three-dimensional space and one-dimensional time, and must instead talk about four-dimensional space–time. But there is no consensus about whether GR favours substantivalism, the view that space–time is a genuine entity, or relationalism, the view that space–time is nothing over and above the events occurring in it (see Chapter 39).

As we have just seen, GR invokes the shape of space–time itself to explain why objects move as they do, why the apple falls, why we can walk around on the surface of the Earth. Space–time is no longer just an inert, neutral backdrop against which objects and forces interact; it is an element in that interaction. In this way, GR points towards substantivalism about space–time.

Yet, as we shall shortly see, the "hole argument" points in the opposite direction, indicating that substantivalists are committed to the existence of physical facts which go beyond anything required by GR. (In this respect, the hole argument is like the argument against presentism from the relativity of simultaneity, according to which presentists are committed to facts which go beyond anything required by SR.)

Suppose you had to describe the room you're in right now. You could describe the various objects in the room, and then describe how they are related to each other ("there's a monkey and a toy car, and the monkey is sitting in the car"). Asked to describe the whole universe, we could say "there's a bunch of space–time points, they have such-and-such spatiotemporal arrangement, and matter and energy are distributed amongst them thus-and-so." The bunch of points is the "manifold," their spatiotemporal arrangement is the "metric," and the distribution is the "matter field." GR tells us how the metric is related to the matter field, how the shape of space–time is related to the distribution of objects.

Now, how does the traditional substantivalism–relationalism debate translate into these terms? What do substantivalists affirm and relationalists deny? Perhaps substantivalists should claim that the manifold of points exists independently of the events happening at those points, whereas relationalists should deny this.

If substantivalists rashly accept this characterisation of their position, then relationalists can pounce. Suppose we have the manifold of points, arranged with their metric and their matter field. Would things have been different if the points had been reshuffled, keeping the metric and the matter field constant? If the points are independently existing entities, as substantivalists think, then presumably any reshuffle makes a difference. But GR tells us that many reshuffles make no detectable difference at all. The points themselves don't seem to differ in their intrinsic properties: they don't have tiny labels that would enable us to keep track of them if they were switched around. So substantivalists are committed to facts in addition to those recognised by GR – facts about which points are where.

(This criticism of substantivalism is known as the "hole argument" because, as a special case, the points in a given region – known as the "hole" – could be reshuffled without affecting what happens before, after or around that region.)

Substantivalists need to reconsider what they are substantivalists about. If they take space–time to be just the manifold, the bare collection of points, they will be committed to undetectable facts, but they may be on safer ground if they take space–time to be the manifold together with the metric, i.e., the collection of points together with the way in which they are arranged with respect to one another. If this more complex entity is replaced by an alternative manifold-plus-metric, this would certainly make an empirical difference.

What sort of entity is a manifold-plus-metric? Different "sophisticated substantivalists" have developed this idea in different ways, but one option is to think of each space–time point as having its relations to other points essentially, so that the points exist together in a web of mutual dependence. It seems clear that substantivalists can escape the hole argument in this way.

What's not so clear is whether sophisticated substantivalism is really distinct from relationalism. The more that GR gives a quasi-causal, dynamical role to the manifold-plus-metric, the more difficult it is to draw a line between material things (which relationalists accept) and space–time itself. What's so special about the spatiotemporal properties of a point, in contrast to its other properties, like those which fix how much mass or charge is there? Why think the spatiotemporal properties of a point are essential to it, whilst its other properties are not?

As we saw with the debate surrounding SR, presentism and endurantism, the collision of ancient metaphysical problems and modern scientific theories can be highly fruitful, even though science rarely gives us a straight answer to a metaphysical question. Substantivalists, presentists and endurantists are all forced to rethink their theories, to consider what motivates them, what is central and what is peripheral to their views. If this rethink does not kill the theories, it may make them stronger.

Acknowledgements

Many thanks to Craig Bourne, Joseph Melia and Robin Le Poidevin for comments on an earlier draft. This work was supported by a Philip Leverhulme Prize, which I gratefully acknowledge.

Further reading

Craig Bourne, *A Future for Presentism* (Oxford: Oxford University Press, 2006) defends presentism, considering both the objection from SR and the possible impact of GR. Barry Dainton, *Time and Space* (Chesham, UK: Acumen, 2001) introduces a wide range of issues about time and space, including the impact of relativity. Ian Gibson and Oliver Pooley, "Relativistic Persistence," *Philosophical Perspectives* 20 (2006): 157–98, offers a comprehensive study of the impact of relativity theory on theories of persistence, with useful references. Carl Hoefer, "The Metaphysics of Space–Time Substantivalism," *Journal of Philosophy* 93 (1996): 5–27, defends substantivalism against the hole argument. Leo Sartori, *Understanding Relativity* (Berkeley: University of California Press, 1996) is a gentle introduction to the physics of relativity. Simon Saunders, "How Relativity Contradicts Presentism," in Craig Callender (ed.), *Time, Reality and Experience* (Cambridge: Cambridge University Press, 2002), pp. 277–92, gives a clear statement of the case against presentism. E. N. Zalta (ed.), *The Stanford Encyclopedia of Philosophy* (available: http://plato.stanford.edu/) is a very useful online resource. Relevant articles in the encyclopaedia include "Being and Becoming in Modern Physics," by Steven Savitt; "Time," by Ned Markosian; "Temporal Parts," by Katherine Hawley; "The Hole Argument," by John Norton; "Newton's Views on Space, Time and Motion," by Robert Rynasiewicz; and "Space and Time: Inertial Frames," by Robert DiSalle. Some of these articles are more introductory than others, but all provide useful references, both to the general literature and to other articles in the encyclopaedia.

48
METAPHYSICS AND QUANTUM PHYSICS
Peter J. Lewis

Quantum physics confronts contemporary metaphysicians with a fascinating and frustrating puzzle. It appears to be telling us something novel and surprising about the nature of the physical world, but it is hard to pin down exactly what it tells us. In large part, this is because quantum physics presents us with a particularly striking example of underdetermination; there are several quantum theories that are at least arguably consistent with the observed data, and which seem to entail very different ontologies. So while quantum mechanics is clearly revolutionary, it is unclear what form the revolution takes.

The following is a summary of several recent debates over the ontology of the quantum world, and an attempt to sketch some lessons about how we should approach the task of extracting metaphysical conclusions from quantum physics. The first section lays out the bare bones of the "standard" theory of quantum mechanics and introduces the measurement problem, which is widely taken to show that the standard theory is inadequate. The second section summarizes three of the major theories that have been developed in response to the measurement problem and discusses the metaphysical implications of each. The final section concerns the nature of the underdetermination problem facing us and what we should do about it.

Standard quantum mechanics

The most readily visualizable mathematical representation of the quantum mechanical state of a system is the wavefunction. For a system consisting of a single particle, the wavefunction $\psi(x, y, z)$ at a time can be expressed as a function of the three spatial coordinates x, y and z. There are other representations, and ease of visualization is no guarantee of special ontological status, but let us proceed on the (perhaps hopeful) assumption that the wavefunction is not unduly misleading as a picture of the reality behind quantum phenomena. This wavefunction evolves over time according to the Schrödinger equation, which resembles a classical wave equation. Hence the term "wavefunction"; wavefunction evolution resembles the mathematical representation of ripples on a pond, or the ripples in the electromagnetic field that constitute light waves. If one takes this mathematics as a description of the underlying reality, it looks like quantum mechanics describes the fundamental stuff of the world as consisting of some kind of wave.

But how does this wave-like evolution represent the state of a system consisting of a single *particle*? In outline, the standard story is as follows. Suppose that the particle is initially located inside some small region of space. This is modeled by taking the wavefunction to be some function that is large only within this region; typically, a narrow Gaussian (bell curve) is assumed. That is, the implicit rule linking wavefunction amplitude and particle location is that the particle is located in a given region if (and only if) almost all the wavefunction amplitude is concentrated in that region. (The requirement that *all* the wavefunction amplitude be contained in the region is usually taken to be too strong, since a wavefunction that is so contained will immediately evolve to one in which a small proportion of the amplitude lies outside the region.) One then derives the final state of the system at some later time from this initial state using the Schrödinger equation. So far, this sounds just like classical physics; one takes an initial particle position, and applies a dynamical law to obtain the final particle position. But there is a crucial difference; generally, in the quantum case, the final wavefunction does not have almost all its amplitude concentrated in any small region, but is instead spread over regions corresponding to every possible final position. In such a state, the above rule does not assign the particle *any* final position; nevertheless, the particle is observed to be somewhere.

The standard solution to this puzzle is that the wavefunction *collapses* on measurement. That is, the wavefunction evolves according to the Schrödinger equation until a measurement occurs, at which time the Schrödinger dynamics is suspended, and a different, incompatible dynamical law takes over. According to this new law, when the position of the particle is measured, the wavefunction instantaneously jumps to a state in which the amplitude is concentrated in one of a set of regions. The set of regions is determined by the details of the measurement; each region corresponds to a distinct outcome. The region to which the collapse occurs is a matter of pure chance, the probability of a collapse to a particular region being given by the proportion of the squared amplitude of the pre-measurement wavefunction contained in that region.

A further feature of the wavefunction, which will be taken up in the second section, under "Spontaneous collapse theories," is that the wavefunction for a system consisting of more than one particle does not occupy ordinary three-dimensional space. For a two-particle system, the wavefunction $\psi(x_1, y_1, z_1, x_2, y_2, z_2)$ at a time is a function of *two* sets of spatial coordinates, one for each particle. That is, the wavefunction for two particles occupies a six-dimensional space, in which each point corresponds to a *configuration* of the two particles. Similarly, the wavefunction for n particles occupies a $3n$-dimensional space, in which each point corresponds to a configuration of the n particles. For such a system, according to the standard theory, a measurement induces a collapse into a region of this configuration space, where as before, each region corresponds to a distinct outcome of the measurement.

Unfortunately, the standard theory just described is unacceptable as it stands. The problem is that according to the standard theory, measurements proceed according to a different dynamical law from non-measurements. First, this is problematic because "measurement" is a vague term, so the standard theory does not make unambiguous predictions. Second, measurements are presumably physical processes like any other, in which case they cannot in principle introduce any new physical laws. Hence a simple stipulation of what counts as a measurement, while it might solve the first problem, does not address the second. The various modifications to the standard theory that have been proposed in response to the measurement problem are sufficiently distinctive to warrant consideration as different physical theories. In particular, they at least appear to presuppose very different underlying ontologies. Some of the main options are described in the following section.

Three alternatives

Spontaneous collapse theories

The alternative theories that are closest in spirit to the standard theory are spontaneous collapse theories. They attempt to complete the standard theory by providing a precise account of wavefunction collapse that does not make essential reference to measurement; collapses are postulated to be spontaneous events, governed by a new law of nature. The paradigm example is the GRW theory (Ghirardi, Rimini and Weber) (Ghirardi, Rimini et al. 1986). According to this theory, each particle has a very small probability per unit time of undergoing a collapse, in which the wavefunction is multiplied by a narrow Gaussian in the coordinates of that particle. The location of the centre of the Gaussian is a matter of chance, with a probability distribution given by the square of the pre-collapse wave amplitude. Otherwise, the wavefunction obeys the Schrödinger equation.

No mention is made of measurement – so how does the GRW theory ensure that measurements have outcomes? The key is that the kinds of devices that we humans use to display the results of measurements are relatively large, containing of the order of 10^{27} particles. For any single particle, the chance of it undergoing a collapse in (say) the next hour is vanishingly small – which is important, because all our observations of microscopic systems consisting of just a few particles show them to obey the Schrödinger equation. But for a macroscopic object like the pointer on a measuring device, it becomes overwhelmingly likely that *one* of the particles that make it up will undergo a collapse, even in a tiny fraction of a second. The collapse assigns that particle a location, and because the locations of the particles in a solid object are well correlated, it thereby assigns a location to the macroscopic object as a whole. So provided that measurements always involve the location of a macroscopic object, the GRW theory ensures that measurements always have outcomes.

What are the metaphysical consequences of this theory? Like the standard theory, it is indeterministic; for a given particle, the occurrence of a collapse and the point on which that collapse is centred are both matters of pure chance. It is often maintained that quantum mechanics shows that there are genuine ontic chances in the world – that chance is not just a matter of ignorance – and the GRW version of quantum mechanics supports this assertion.

The other thing we might hope to glean from the GRW theory is the nature of the fundamental stuff of the world, but here matters are somewhat murky. Again like the standard theory, the GRW theory is just a theory of wavefunction evolution, so it is natural to take it as implying that there is nothing but a wave at the fundamental level. One might conclude on this basis that there are no particles, or one might argue that particles supervene on the wave distribution. But in either case, there is a further problem with taking the wave alone as fundamental, namely that the wavefunction of the universe occupies a $3n$-dimensional space, where n is the number of particles in the universe. Some are prepared to bite the bullet; Albert asserts that if the GRW theory is true, then the apparent three-dimensionality of our world is an illusion (Albert 1996). Further, he argues that the illusion can be explained by the fact that the dynamical laws obeyed by ordinary medium-sized objects take a particularly simple form when expressed in three dimensions, so we should expect organisms like us to represent the world to themselves as three-dimensional. By contrast, Monton argues that Albert's derivation of apparent three-dimensionality fails, because there is no fact of the matter about which of the $3n$ wavefunction coordinates is associated with which of the supervenient particles, and hence no fact about which three-dimensional particle configuration supervenes on a given wave distribution (Monton 2002). Furthermore, Monton argues that even setting aside this technical problem, giving up the *actual* three-dimensionality of the world is too great a metaphysical cost to bear, given that other theoretical options are available (Monton 2004).

The other theoretical options involve supplementing the $3n$-dimensional wave ontology with a three-dimensional ontology. The most influential proposal along these lines involves the postulation of a mass density distribution evolving in three-dimensional space, in addition to, and determined by, the $3n$-dimensional wave distribution (Ghirardi et al. 1995). The idea here is that the arrangement of ordinary objects in three-dimensional space supervenes on the mass density distribution, but the mass density distribution does not supervene on the wave distribution; rather, the evolution of the latter directs the evolution of the former. Hence the actual three-dimensionality of the everyday world is recovered (by explicit postulation), although there is also a higher-dimensional entity operating behind the scenes, playing a causal and explanatory role. It remains controversial whether a "two-layer" ontology of this kind is really necessary (Lewis 2004).

Hidden variable theories

Hidden variable theories constitute a second major class of solutions to the measurement problem. They differ from the standard theory and spontaneous collapse theories in eschewing collapse altogether; according to hidden variable theories, the wavefunction always evolves according to the Schrödinger equation. Instead, hidden variable theories take the wavefunction to be an incomplete representation of the physical state of a system, and supplement it with variables representing further properties of the system. The paradigm example of a hidden variable theory is Bohm's theory (Bohm 1952). According to Bohm's theory, the extra variables represent the positions of the particles in the system. The motions of the particles are determined by a new dynamical law, which gives the velocity of each particle at a time in terms of the wave distribution and the positions of all the other particles at that time. Essentially, then, the wave distribution can be viewed as pushing the particles around, much like the electromagnetic field pushes charged particles around.

How does this ensure that measurements have outcomes? It does so by stipulating that the positions of the particles determine our measurement results. While the wavefunction at the end of a measurement will typically be spread all over configuration space, the particles have determinate locations (in three-dimensional space). Hence the fundamental ontology according to Bohm's theory is fairly clear; the ordinary objects we observe supervene on the arrangement of Bohmian particles (in three-dimensional space), and the wavefunction (in $3n$-dimensional space) operates behind the scenes to direct the evolution of the particles. So to describe the positions of the particles as "hidden variables" is misleading, since it is the particle positions that we directly observe in the world, and the wavefunction that is hidden from us (Bell 1987: 128). In fact, some have sought to interpret Bohm's theory as positing only particles at the fundamental level, with the wavefunction serving as a law directing the motion of the particles (Dürr et al. 1997). However, since laws presumably do not change over time, the possibility of such an interpretation remains contingent on the vindication of a version of quantum mechanics in which the wavefunction is unchanging.

The most notable feature of Bohm's theory is that it is entirely deterministic; the wavefunction and particle positions at one time determine the wavefunction and particle positions at all other times. There are no ontic chances in Bohm's theory, and probabilities arise due to ignorance alone. It is an assumption of Bohm's theory that the particles are initially distributed at random, with a probability distribution given by the squared wavefunction amplitude. It then follows from the Bohmian dynamics that our measurement results will also be distributed according to the squared wavefunction amplitude, just as in the standard theory. Essentially, in making measurements, we are finding out about the initial particle distribution. Not all hidden variable theories are deterministic; for some, the dynamical law by which the hidden variables evolve is probabilistic. But even so, Bohm's theory stands as an important counterexample to the claim that quantum mechanics shows that there are ontic chances in the world.

Many worlds theories

The simplest and most radical response to the measurement problem is to assert that standard quantum mechanics without wavefunction collapse constitutes a complete physical theory (Everett 1957). The challenge is to explain how such a theory can account for our measurement results. The problem, recall, is that at the end of an experiment, the wavefunction is not concentrated in a single region of configuration space – corresponding to a single measurement result – but is spread over regions corresponding to every possible measurement result. The many worlds proposal is that every possible measurement result actually occurs. Why, then, does it appear to us as if exactly one result occurs? The proffered explanation is that each measurement outcome occurs in a distinct *world*, so an observer (in a world) sees exactly one result.

This, of course, raises a host of metaphysical questions, the most pressing of which concerns the status of these worlds. On what basis can we assert that each result occurs in a distinct world? Early versions of the theory took it that the basis of this assertion had to be additional theory – that the structure of worlds had to be explicitly added to standard quantum mechanics. That is, it was proposed that the physical world – the universe – literally splits into a number of copies when a quantum measurement occurs, with one copy for each possible outcome (DeWitt and Graham 1973: v). But this just raises the measurement problem all over again; world splitting on measurement is arguably no better than wave collapse on measurement (Lockwood 1989: 226).

So more recently (and perhaps more in the spirit of Everett's original paper), advocates of many worlds theories have instead insisted that the "worlds" are really just a way of speaking about the wavefunction (Wallace 2003). That is, there is a single physical universe, represented by a wavefunction that always evolves according to the Schrödinger equation. A quantum measurement is simply a process that correlates a microscopic property – say, the location of a particle – with a macroscopic property – say, the position of a pointer on a dial. Each possible measurement result corresponds to a particular pattern in the universal wave distribution, and in the absence of any collapse process, the wave distribution after a measurement consists of all these wave patterns superposed. But it can be shown that the patterns corresponding to macroscopically distinct states of affairs hardly interact. Hence each such pattern can be regarded as its own "world", and each "world" contains a unique measurement result. So while the physical universe as a whole does not split, the history of that universe, in ordinary macroscopic terms, has a branching structure, with different measurement results appearing on different branches.

According to this theory, "worlds" and their contents supervene on the wave distribution. Hence this theory, like the GRW theory, posits the fundamental nature of the world as wave-like, and the discussion above concerning the dimensionality of the wavefunction is equally applicable here. More notable, however, is the fact that the supervenient entities, including people, have a branching structure. That is, whenever a quantum measurement occurs, the person observing the measurement splits into many copies, each seeing precisely one measurement result. This is certainly a surprising result for the metaphysics of persons! It means, for example, that debates over Parfitian fission (Parfit 1971) are no mere academic exercise.

Unlike the GRW theory, the many worlds theory is entirely deterministic; the genuine chance in the former lies entirely in the collapse process. But since quantum mechanics still makes its predictions probabilistically, the many worlds theory needs an account of the meaning of these probabilistic predictions. The obvious move is to endorse a subjective, epistemic account, like that described above for Bohm's theory; probabilities reflect our ignorance about future measurement results. But in the case of the many worlds theory, it is not clear that such an account is available. If an observer branches into successors who see each possible measurement result, then there is a straightforward sense in which she is *certain* to see each result, and hence if she is fully informed, it looks like an assignment of probabilities other than 1 to the various possible results is inappropriate. Much recent work has gone into describing an appropriate sense of ignorance or uncertainty for many worlds contexts (Saunders 1998; Vaidman 1998; Wallace 2006), but these arguments have been challenged (Lewis 2007a). Alternatively, one might think that the many worlds theory motivates a revisionary account of probability, according to which an agent may attach subjective probabilities (other than 0 and 1) to outcomes, even in the absence of uncertainty (Greaves 2004).

Underdetermination

The previous section is far from exhaustive; many other attempts to solve (or dissolve) the measurement problem could be mentioned, and many of them have equally radical metaphysical consequences. But the three theories outlined so far provide plenty of material to illustrate the striking underdetermination that faces us in trying to take quantum mechanics as a guide to metaphysics. Suppose we want to know whether there are genuine ontic chances in the world. We naturally look to fundamental physical theory for the answer, and we find that some versions answer "yes" and others answer "no." Furthermore, they differ over whether the world is fundamentally wave-like or particulate, whether it exists in three dimensions or more, and on whether history is linear or branching. And note that these versions of quantum mechanics are not mere philosopher's constructions – they are at least in some sense genuine contenders for the correct quantum theory.

What should we do in the face of this underdetermination? The obvious answer is "wait and see"; if theory is underdetermined by evidence, then we should wait for new evidence to break the tie. In some cases, this seems exactly the right strategy. For example, since wavefunction collapses are, in principle, empirically detectable, there may be experiments that could verify or falsify the GRW collapse process. Leggett (2002) has championed such an experimental research program, but technical difficulties stand in the way of receiving a definitive result any time soon. Furthermore, no such experimental strategy is available to distinguish Bohm's theory from the many worlds theory, since (at least at first blush) they make exactly the same predictions. But Bohm's theory and the many worlds theory apparently offer radically different metaphysical pictures; according to the former, particles are fundamental and history is linear, whereas according to the latter particles are emergent and history is branching. Here, then, we seem to have an example of underdetermination *in principle*. Does this mean that the fundamental nature of the physical world is beyond empirical discovery – that it must remain forever unknown, or must somehow be divined by non-empirical means?

Fortunately, such unpalatable conclusions are not (yet) forced on us, because there are ways that a theory can fail other than by direct conflict with observation. First, a theory can be rejected because its theoretical assumptions conflict with those of some other well-established theory, even if it doesn't make any false empirical predictions.

This fate threatens the GRW theory and Bohm's theory; in each case, the new dynamical law of the theory assumes instantaneous action at a distance, whereas special relativity apparently rules it out (Bell 1987: 132, 206). Of course, it is not a foregone conclusion that it is the quantum mechanical theory, rather than special relativity, that must yield in the face of this conflict (Bell 1987: 110). Still, it is an advantage of Everett's theory that it is apparently consistent with relativity.

Second, a theory can be rejected because its theoretical assumptions are more-or-less directly shown to be false. This fate might befall any of the three theories we have considered. The GRW theory, for example, presupposes that distinct measurement outcomes differ in the position of one or more macroscopic objects, since only this situation produces a high probability of a wave collapse. But this assumption can be challenged; for example, measurement outcomes displayed as distinct images on a television screen may differ only in the energies of a small number of fluorescent atoms (Albert and Vaidman 1989). In such cases, the wavefunction typically remains spread over several distinct outcome regions even at (what one usually takes to be) the end of the measurement, and hence the GRW collapse mechanism fails to ensure that measurements have determinate outcomes. One might try to defend the GRW theory by arguing that the television image is not the end of the measurement (Aicardi et al. 1991); otherwise, the theory cannot be taken as adequate to our experience.

Similarly, Bohm's theory presupposes that distinct measurement outcomes differ in the position of at least one particle, since measurement results are taken to supervene on particle positions. But this assumption, too, might come under suspicion, since it seems *prima facie* that one could use (e.g.) the energy of a particle as a record of a measurement result. In this case, it is not clear that the failure of this assumption would make Bohm's theory inadequate to our *experience*; rather, it leads to internal inconsistencies in the theory's description of the particle trajectories (Barrett 2000). Again, the assumption might be defended (e.g. Barrett 2000), and the success of such a defence is required if Bohm's theory is to be retained.

The many worlds theory is more flexible in this regard; according to the standard contemporary version, no presupposition is made concerning precisely which physical properties form the basis of measurement results. But the many worlds theory, too, relies on controversial assumptions, notably concerning probability. To yield probabilistic predictions that agree with standard quantum mechanics (and hence with observation), the many worlds theory must presuppose that the squared amplitude of a branch can be understood as its probability. But as noted in the previous section, this can be challenged on the grounds that every branch actually occurs. Unless the standard assignment of probabilities to branches can be defended, the many worlds theory is inadequate to our experience, since it fails to explain the observed relative frequencies of measurement outcomes.

Considerable theoretical work is required, both in physics and in philosophy, to resolve these issues. If we are lucky, this work will leave just one coherent, empirically adequate theory. But we might not be so lucky; perhaps both Bohm's theory and the many worlds theory (or their relativistic variants) can successfully capture all the phenomena. In that case, the conclusion that there are substantive questions about the ontology of the physical world that are beyond the reach of empirical methods may be forced on us.

But there is another possibility worth considering, namely that despite the apparent differences in their underlying ontology, Bohm's theory and the many worlds theory are in some sense the *same* theory. Deutsch (1996), for example, has argued that since all the branches of the wavefunction are present in Bohm's theory, it too entails that every outcome of a measurement actually occurs, and hence Bohm's theory is just the many worlds theory, disguised by the presence of some entirely superfluous particles. However, a Bohmian might not concede that a wavefunction branch is necessarily a *world* containing actual measurement results (Lewis 2007b). The converse position – that the many worlds theory is a Bohmian theory in disguise – has not been seriously defended, although Bell has speculated along these lines (1987: 97, 133).

Conclusion

What, then, does quantum mechanics tell us about the fundamental nature of physical reality? At the moment, not very much. There are several approaches to quantum mechanics, any or none of which might yield an acceptable physical theory. According to some approaches, the world is deterministic, and according to others it is indeterministic. According to some there are particles at the fundamental level and according to others there are only waves (in a high-dimensional space). According to one, the contents of the universe, including people, are constantly branching into multiple copies. The question of which theory is correct is in part a matter of empirical investigation by experimental physics. But in part it is a matter of theoretical investigation, by both physicists and philosophers, since it is not clear what the phenomena are that must be captured by an empirically adequate theory, and it is not clear what each theory entails about the phenomena. It is not even clear how many distinct theories there are. In the meantime, any metaphysical claim of the form "Quantum mechanics shows that …" should be treated with suspicion.

References

Aicardi, F., Borsellino, A., Ghirardi, G. C., and Grassi, R. (1991) "Dynamical Models for State-Vector Reduction: Do They Ensure That Measurements Have Outcomes?" *Foundations of Physics Letters* 4: 109–128.

Albert, David Z. (1996) "Elementary Quantum Metaphysics," in J. Cushing, A. Fine, and S. Goldstein (eds), *Bohmian Mechanics and Quantum Theory: An Appraisal*, Dordrecht: Kluwer, 277–84.

Albert, David Z., and Vaidman, Lev (1989) "On a Proposed Postulate of State-Reduction," *Physics Letters* A 139: 1–4.

Barrett, Jeffrey A. (2000) "The Persistence of Memory: Surreal Trajectories in Bohm's Theory," *Philosophy of Science* 67: 680–703.

Bell, John S. (1987) *Speakable and Unspeakable in Quantum Mechanics*, Cambridge: Cambridge University Press.

Bohm, David (1952) "A Suggested Interpretation of Quantum Theory in Terms of 'Hidden Variables'," *Physical Review* 85: 166–93.

Deutsch, David (1996) "Comment on Lockwood," *British Journal for the Philosophy of Science* 47: 222–28.

DeWitt, B. S. and Graham, N. (1973) *The Many-Worlds Interpretation of Quantum Mechanics*, Princeton, NJ: Princeton University Press.

Dürr, D., Goldstein, S., and Zanghì, N. (1997) "Bohmian Mechanics and the Meaning of the Wave Function," in R. S. Cohen, M. Horne, and J. Stachel (eds), *Experimental Metaphysics*, Dordrecht: Kluwer, pp. 25–38.

Everett, Hugh (1957) "'Relative State' Formulation of Quantum Mechanics," *Reviews of Modern Physics* 29: 454–62.

Ghirardi, G. C., Grassi, R., and Benatti, F. (1995) "Describing the Macroscopic World: Closing the Circle within the Dynamical Reduction Program," *Foundations of Physics* 25: 5–38.

Ghirardi, G. C., Rimini, A., and Weber, T. (1986) "Unified Dynamics for Microscopic and Macroscopic Systems," *Physical Review* D 34: 470–91.

Greaves, Hilary (2004) "Understanding Deutsch's Probability in a Deterministic Multiverse," *Studies in History and Philosophy of Modern Physics* 35: 423–56.

Leggett, A. J. (2002) "Testing the Limits of Quantum Mechanics: Motivation, State of Play, Prospects," *Journal of Physics: Condensed Matter* 14: R415–R451.

Lewis, Peter J. (2004) "Life in Configuration Space," *British Journal for the Philosophy of Science* 55: 713–29.

—— (2007a) "Uncertainty and Probability for Branching Selves," *Studies in History and Philosophy of Modern Physics* 38: 1–14.

—— (2007b) "Empty Waves in Bohmian Quantum Mechanics," *British Journal for the Philosophy of Science* 58: 787–803.

Lockwood, Michael (1989) *Mind, Brain and the Quantum*, Oxford: Blackwell.

Monton, Bradley (2002) "Wavefunction Ontology," *Synthese* 130: 265–77.

—— (2004) "The Problem of Ontology for Spontaneous Collapse Theories," *Studies in History and Philosophy of Modern Physics* 35: 407–21.

Parfit, Derek (1971) "Personal Identity," *Philosophical Review* 80: 3–27.

Saunders, Simon (1998) "Time, Quantum Mechanics and Probability," *Synthese* 114: 373–404.

Vaidman, Lev (1998) "On Schizophrenic Experiences of the Neutron or Why We Should Believe in the Many-Worlds Interpretation of Quantum Theory," *International Studies in the Philosophy of Science* 12: 245–61.

Wallace, David (2003) "Everett and Structure," *Studies in History and Philosophy of Modern Physics* 34: 87–105.

—— (2006) "Epistemology Quantized: Circumstances in Which We Should Come to Believe in the Everett Interpretation," *British Journal for the Philosophy of Science* 57: 655–89.

Further reading

David Z. Albert, *Quantum Mechanics and Experience* (Cambridge, MA: Harvard University Press, 1992) is a lucid and engaging introduction to the measurement problem and its solutions. John S. Bell, *Speakable and Unspeakable in Quantum Mechanics* (Cambridge: Cambridge University Press, 1987) is a collection of classic papers, both technical and non-technical; Bell's insights into the nature of quantum mechanics are invaluable. Michael Lockwood, *Mind, Brain and the Quantum* (Oxford: Blackwell, 1989) gives a defense of a version of the many-worlds theory and an exploration of its consequences for the metaphysics of mind. Tim Maudlin, *Quantum Non-Locality and Relativity* (Oxford: Blackwell, 1994) is a clear introduction to the difficulties of reconciling quantum theories with relativity. Huw Price, *Time's Arrow and Archimedes' Point* (Oxford: Oxford University Press, 1996) offers an accessible exposition of the difficulties facing hidden-variable theories, and an exploration of backwards causation as a potential solution.

49

SUPERVENIENCE, REDUCTION AND EMERGENCE

Howard Robinson

The nature of the problem

Any physical thing can be described in a variety of ways and at a variety of "levels." We might, using the language of ordinary discourse, characterize something as a rose. But one might also describe it in the language of certain of the sciences. The biologist will describe it in one way, a chemist in another and a nuclear physicist in another. Each of these descriptions will have its own vocabulary, invoking entities and properties at least some of which will be missing from the other forms of discourse. But we are happy to accept all the various discourses as capable of being used to say things which are true and we have no doubt that, in some fundamental sense, it is the same thing – the same chunk of physical reality – about which all of them are being used to talk. The core issue of this chapter is how we are to understand the relationship between the different discourses and their ontologies if we are to make sense of the idea that they in some sense have the same subject matter.

The most ambitious claim is that one of these ways of talking is basic – usually this is assumed to be the most fundamental form of physics – and that all the rest (which, putting aside our informal discourse, are termed the special sciences) are somehow *reducible* to this basic science. We shall see that the correct account of reduction is itself very controversial. Philosophers who want to avoid talk of reduction (for reasons that will emerge) often resort to claiming that the higher levels *supervene* on the lower ones. This means that there is no higher-level difference without a lower-level one – for example, no biological difference without a chemical difference and no chemical difference without a difference at the level of physics. This supervenience relation is meant to articulate the nature of the dependence of higher on lower levels without a need to deploy any tighter notion of reduction.

Emergence is the opposite of reduction. Properties and behaviour are emergent at higher levels with respect to the lower if they cannot be reduced to the properties and laws manifested by the lower-level objects. Because emergence is the obverse of reduction, however, what counts as emergence depends largely on what account of reduction one accepts. As we shall see, the strongest sense of emergence, is associated with the idea that the world is not "closed under physics" – that is, that what happens at all macro levels cannot be thought of as simply the necessary product of objects at the basic level following the laws uncovered by an ideal fundamental physics: more macroscopic levels manifest behaviours or other phenomena which, in principle, could not have been predicted from physics.

To avoid confusion when discussing these topics, it is necessary to distinguish what might be called the analytic from the substantive or ontological issues that might be at stake. Some objects are uncontroversially "purely physical." This applies, for example, to any inanimate material object and probably to vegetable life, which is living but mindless. Nevertheless, such things will satisfy physical, chemical and biological descriptions, and the issue of how to understand the relation between these descriptions and their ontologies will arise, even though, on an intuitive level, one takes there to be no substantive ontological issue. Other questions are taken to be more substantive. The issue of whether mental states can be reduced to physical ones, for example, is not usually regarded as a question about how different levels of description are to be harmonized, but about whether mental states differ radically in kind from physical states. So the question "can the other special sciences in general be reduced to physics?" and the question "can mental states be reduced to physical states?" are importantly different. The latter is closer to the following: Whatever the relation is between the physical special sciences and physics, (for we do not think that these raise serious ontological issues) can the relation between mental and physical ascriptions be treated in a similar way, whatever that may be, or is the mental–physical relation seriously different from the others?

Different theories of reduction

The following line of thought has intuitive appeal. If physicalism is true for a certain domain, then it should be possible, in principle, to give what is, in some sense, a total description of that domain in the vocabulary of a completed physics. To put it in the material, not the formal, mode, all the properties that there *ultimately* are, should be those of the basic physical entities. But there are many ways of talking truly about the world other than that couched in the vocabulary of physics; and there are, in some obvious sense, many properties that the world possesses that are not contained in that physics. These higher order predicates and properties are expressed in the other (or so-called *special*) sciences, such as chemistry, biology, citology, epidemiology, geology, meteorology, and, if physicalism holds for the mind, psychology and the supposed social sciences – not to mention our ordinary discourse, which often expresses truths that find no place in anything we would naturally call a science. How does the fundamental level of ontology – which we are presupposing to be captured ideally in physics – sustain all these other ontologies and make true these other levels of discourse?

The logical positivists had a simple answer to this question. Any respectable level of discourse was reducible to some level below it and ultimately to physics itself. The kind of reduction of which they were talking has a *strong form* and a *very strong form*. According to the very strong form, all respectable statements in the special sciences and in ordinary discourse could, in principle, be translatable into statements in the language of physics. In the end, therefore, all truths could be expressed using the language of physics. This strongest form of reduction can be summarized as

(1) *"Translation" reductionism:* For the concepts of any special science, there is a speci-fication of definitional necessary and sufficient conditions for their satisfaction, which is expressed in the concepts of some more basic science and, ultimately, in the concepts of physics. Because the concepts of the sciences can be expressed in the terms of physics, so can the laws.

Early Hempel and Carnap exemplified this approach. The former, for example, said of psychology, "All psychological statements which are meaningful ... are translatable into statements which do not involve psychological concepts, but only the concepts of physics. The statements of psychology are consequently physicalistic statements" (Hempel 1980 [1935]: 18). This does not apply to psychology alone, but to all the sciences, natural and social. After listing some of these he says, "Every statement of the above-mentioned disciplines, and, in general, of empirical science as a whole ... is translatable, without change of content, into a statement containing only physicalistic terms, and consequently is a physicalistic statement" (*ibid.*: 21). Carnap tells us what "physical language" is: "The physical language is characterized by the fact that state-ments of the simplest form ... express a quantitatively determinate property of a definite position at a definite time" (1995 [1934]: 52). In other words, physicalistic statements ultimately attribute measurable quantities to spatiotemporal locations. He concludes, "On the basis of [this account] our thesis makes the extended assertion that the physical language is a universal language, i.e. that every statement can be translated into it" (*ibid.*: 55). Such a reduction to physics would not be possible, for most sciences, in one step. In the case of biology, for example, the hope would be to provide a translation of biological statements using only the language of chemistry, and chemistry would itself have been given a translation into "physics-ese," thus completing the process for biology.

This form of reduction was soon perceived to be impossible. The idea that a statement in economics, for example, means the same as a statement about the behaviour of particles, or even about the behaviour of macroscopic bodies is impossible to believe. In the case of a human science like economics, this problem might be thought to stem from the *substantive* irreducibility of human consciousness and, hence, psychology. But it is hard to see how a statement in genetics, for example, could be said to mean the same as something cast in the language of physics. The motivation for this theory is clear, however, for if statements in a special science are just shorthand for statements in the idiom of physics, it is clear how they could be about the same subject matter and involve no inflation of ontology.

Because of the obvious implausibility of the *very strong* translation form of reduc-tionism, a merely *strong* form was adopted. This is the version of reductionism most often cited, and it asserts that there have only to be scientific laws (called "bridging laws"), not sameness of meaning, connecting the concepts and laws in a higher-order science with those in the next lower, and ultimately with physics. So the concepts and laws of psychology would be nomically connected with those of some biological science, and these, in turn, with chemistry, and chemistry would be nomically reducible to physics.

(2) *"Nomological" reductionism:* This consists in the provision of non-definitional nomological necessary and sufficient conditions for being F in terms of some lower-level discourse, ultimately physics.

So "reducible to," in this sense, meant that the entities and properties invoked in the non-basic discourse were *type identical with* certain basic structures. For example, our ordinary concept *water* is reducible to the chemical type H_2O, and this chemical molecule always consists of the same atomic arrangements. This pattern makes it easy to understand intuitively how the existence of water and the truths of sentences referring to water need involve nothing more than the existence of things in the ontology of physics. With the help of these bridging laws, the theory or science to be reduced can be derived from the theory or science to which it is to be reduced. Nagel (1961) is the classical source for such a theory:

> when the laws of the secondary science … contain some term "A" that is absent from the theoretical assumptions of the primary science … [a]ssumptions of some kind must be introduced which postulate suitable relations between whatever is signified by "A" and traits represented by theoretical terms already present in the primary science … With the help of these additional assumptions, all the laws of the secondary science, including those containing the term "A," must be logically derivable from the theoretical premises and their associated coordinating definitions in the primary discipline. (1961: 353–4)

Despite the fact that Nagel here calls these bridging assumptions "coordinating *definitions*," he does not think them to be normally analytic; they are essentially empirical.

> The assumptions … are empirical hypotheses, asserting that the occurrence of a state of affairs signified by a certain theoretical expression "B" in the primary science is a sufficient (or necessary and sufficient) condition for the state of affairs designated by "A" … the expressions designating the two states of affairs must have identifiably different meanings. (*ibid.*: 354–5)

But not all concepts in the special sciences, let alone ordinary discourse and the social sciences, can be fitted into this pattern. Not every *hurricane* that might be invoked in meteorology, or every *tectonic shift* that might be mentioned in geology, will have the same chemical or physical constitution. Indeed, it is barely conceivable that any two would be similar in this way. Nor will every *infectious disease*, or every *cancerous growth* – not to mention every *devaluation of the currency* or every *coup d'etat* – share similar structures in depth. Jerry Fodor, in his important article, "Special Sciences" (1974), correctly claims that the version of reductionism expressed in (2) requires that all our scientifically legitimate concepts be *natural kind* concepts and – like *water* – carry their similarities down to the foundations, and that this is not plausible for most of our useful explanatory concepts. It is particularly not plausible for the concepts of psychological science, understood in functionalist terms (that is, even without bringing in dualism), nor for the concepts in our lay mentalistic vocabulary. All these concepts are *multiply realizable*, which means that different instances of the same kind of thing can be quite different at lower levels – in their "hardware" – and that it is only by applying the concepts from the special science that the different cases can be seen as saliently similar at all. Whereas you could eliminate the word "water" and speak always of "H_2O" with no loss of communicative power, you could not do this for "living animal," "thought of the Eiffel Tower," "continental drift," etc.

Supposing the failure of type reductionism, even for non-controversially physical objects or domains, where does that leave us in the task of articulating how the different scientific descriptions apply to the same piece of physical reality? Fodor's answer is that though thoughts of the Eiffel Tower will not be type-identical with any neural state, let alone any atomic configuration, each such thought will be token-identical to some neural and atomic state. The same will apply to hurricanes, cases of an infectious disease, and anything else from the ontology of a special science. Token identity is what maintains the sameness of ontology.

We have so far been discussing the type–type reductions of Carnap (1995 [1934]) and Nagel (1961) as expressed in (2), and treating them as definitive of reduction in the philosophy of science. This, too, is Fodor's assumption. He considers, that is, that his own theory of token identity, is a non-reductive theory. Indeed, many philosophers who boast that they are non-reductive physicalists in the philosophy of mind have the nomological model of reduction in mind when they reject the label. Davidson (1970, 1993) is a prime example of such. Token identity, on this account, sustains something which is not reduction. But the definitions of reduction provided by Kemeny and Oppenheim (1956) and Oppenheim and Putnam (1958) seem to be wholly consistent with the token identity that Fodor advocates. The requirements for reduction there provided are these: given two theories T_1 and T_2, T_2 is said to be *reduced* to T_1 if and only if

(a) The vocabulary of T_2 contains terms not in the vocabulary of T_1.
(b) Any observational data explained by T_2 are explained by T_1.
(c) T_1 is at least as well systematized as T_2.

These criteria are satisfied without type reduction. All that this definition requires is that a particular explanatory task performed by T_2 – namely the explanation of observable data – be performed also by T_1. Suppose that every observable physical state of affairs were explicable by reference to basic physics *in principle*; then, all other physical sciences would be reducible to physics, irrespective of the availability of bridging laws or type reductions. It is important to notice that Kemeny, Oppenheim and Putnam do not require that every kind of explanatory task performed by T_2 be performed by T_1, but only that all the observational data be explained. It is not required that the point or purpose of the reduced science be equally well served by physics.

So the token identity propounded by Fodor as a form of non-reductionism, and what Kemeny, Oppenheim and Putnam call reduction, are quite compatible.

There is a relation between base and special sciences that satisfies what Fodor, Putnam, Kemeny and Oppenheim all require, and that is that the base should be *a priori* and conceptually sufficient for all that supervenes on it.

That there is such a strong sufficiency of the base for the higher levels in the case of physics and the special sciences is intuitively plausible. Let us suppose that meteorology is a nomically irreducible science. There is no logically possible world which, at the level of physics, is just like one in which a hurricane is destroying a village, but in which there is not a hurricane destroying a village: the physics base is *a priori* sufficient. There is no need to invoke some elusive conception of supervenience here: in the broadest sense of "logically possible," there is no possible world with the same physical base as the given one and no hurricane; the relation is one of entailment in the strongest sense. The same would apply to any special science in a realm in which there were no occult or immaterial features. If, for example, some version of functionalism were correct about the mind, having the atoms arranged just as they are on earth would be logically sufficient – though not necessary, for there might be other ways of making minds – for the existence of conscious beings.

The version of reductionism just developed might be described as *the* a priori *sufficiency of the base*: that is,

(3) "A-priori-*sufficiency-of-the-base*" *reductionism*: the next level down, and, ultimately, the world as characterized by physics, is conceptually and *a priori* sufficient, but not necessary, for the higher-level states. This is the situation between physics and all the special physical sciences that are not reducible in senses (1) or (2).

The reductionism defined in (3) is equivalent to what David Chalmers (1996) calls "logical supervenience." Logical supervenience occurs when there is no logically possible world in which higher-level facts vary whilst lower-level facts remain constant. This contrasts with *natural supervenience*, which is typified by a causal, and therefore contingent, dependence of one level on another, and which allows logically, but not naturally or nomically, possible worlds in which the supervenience does not hold. Stating the point in terms of the *a priori* sufficiency of the base explains *why* there is this logical supervenience – why there is no logically possible world in which the higher-level varies without the lower – namely that there is a clear entailment between the two.

Using the jargon of contemporary philosophy of mind, we can say that it is sufficient for the reductionism of type (3) that there is no *explanatory gap* between the different levels of the special sciences. This contrasts with what is claimed by dualists, who deny that there is an *a priori* sufficiency of the base, or any logical supervenience, and that there is an explanatory gap in the relation between matter – specifically the brain – and consciousness.

Non-reductive conceptions

Because reduction is mainly associated in philosophers' minds with versions (1) and (2), which make the base both sufficient *and necessary* for the special sciences, the theory that it is only sufficient is often treated in terms of the concept of supervenience. Supervenience is defined as the impossibility of variance at the higher level without difference at the lower. Put simply in this way, there is no explanation of *why* independent variation should be impossible and supervenience obtain, in a given case, for that they cannot vary independently is stated as a bare fact – albeit sometimes as a "metaphysically necessary" one. The definition provided in (3) explains why supervenience holds, namely that there is an *a priori* or conceptual sufficiency for the higher truths in the base.

Getting clear about the *a priori* or conceptual sufficiency of the base is important for avoiding confusion about the various senses in which the concepts of the special sciences can be deemed "irreducible" or "emergent." We can distinguish between things that are *merely explanatorily* irreducible and things that are *substantively* irreducible.

(4) *(Mere) explanatory irreducibility:* This is the situation for all discourse with causal explanatory force, which is not nomically reducible to the base, but for which the base is conceptually – *a priori* – sufficient.

A hurricane is strictly constituted by the things physics describes, and that is why there is no problem about attributing causal power to hurricanes. A hurricane is *nothing but* the action of physical particles, though talk about hurricanes is not nomically reducible to physics. This is the situation for all the physical special sciences. This kind of weak explanatory irreducibility is the natural concomitant of (3). The reductionism of type (3) talks in general about the relation between two ontological levels; (4), specifically about explanation. If we focus on properties, we have

(5) *Weak property emergence:* This is the position of a property in a special science with independent explanatory value, but conceptually sufficient conditions in the physical base.

A nominalist approach to such properties is *prima facie* plausible, because it is plausible to see them as just different, higher-order *ways of describing* the base subject matter. This contrasts with

(6) *Real property emergence.* This is the status of a property with no conceptually sufficient conditions in the base for its exemplification.

This is the status allowed to emergent properties by those who believed in emergent evolution. It is also the status allowed to psychological properties by anyone who allows the conceptual possibility of zombies. It involves the rejection of reduction as in (3) above. In the philosophy of mind, it is a realist version of a dual aspect theory of mind.

In fact, most of the debate about supervenience and "soft" materialism in the philosophy of mind has concerned an attempt to create a weak version of (6):

(6_w) *Real but supervenient property emergence*: This is the status of a property with no conceptually sufficient conditions in the base for its occurrence, but with some stronger dependence on that base than the merely causal and contingent.

This is the relation that most people who describe themselves as "non-reductive physicalists" in the philosophy of mind seem to favour. This is not the place to discuss this issue, but the annexation of the term *reduction* to (1) and (2), and the consequent failure to notice (3), has led to much confusion about what "non-reductive" physicalism amounts to (see Robinson 2001).

The limitations of type-(3) reduction

I hope that I have given a plausible account of the different senses of "reduction," shown why my sense (3) is the only credible one, and explained how the notions of supervenience and emergence orbit around one's notion of reduction. I now want to investigate some limitations of reductionism (3) and see what their consequences might be.

Fodor thinks that the weak reductionism that I express in (3) – and which he denies is a form of reduction – is no threat to physicalism, because each instance of a higher-order concept will be identical with some structure describable in terms of basic physics, and nothing more. This token reductionism is all that physicalism and the unity of the sciences require: type reduction is unnecessary. I shall now try to explain why, contrary to appearances, this may be wrong.

Fodor is quite right to think that the very same subject matter can be described in irreducibly different ways and still be just that subject matter. What, in my view, he fails to do is to explain how this is possible. Now this might seem a strange request: Why should it be deemed at all problematic that one portion of the world can be characterized in various ways? Why one might think that there is an issue here can be brought out by contrasting Fodor's view with the more traditional forms of reduction. What they would make possible is a "bottom-up" explanation of how the more macroscopic features arise and why they are just a function of the base ontology. In so far as the special sciences merely translate statements in physics, as in reductionism (1), or express the same natural kind or essence, as in (2), they add nothing real to the base. But in (3) there is a "top-down" interpretation of the base, so the special sciences do not encapsulate either the meanings or the real essences of the base physics. They are, I would claim, more like a perspective from outside on the same subject matter.

What is the solid content of calling the special sciences a "perspective from outside"? The special sciences tend to be marked by three features. (i) They are selective: their subject matter is only part of the world. So that, whilst everything physical consists of the basic entities of physics, only some of the world consists of the entities that concern chemistry, less is living and hence biological; cytology concerns only cells; and so forth. (ii) Many, if not all, the special sciences are teleological or interest-driven. This is clearly true for certain special sciences, such as meteorology, which exists only because of a practical concern with the weather, but it is also more generally true. The flow of physical events has no natural beginnings and ends between the Big Bang and the Apocalypse, if there is such, but we are interested in marking things off as the beginnings and ends of processes that concern us. All processes that we mark off as the beginnings and ends of non-atomic entities come into this category, so the whole of biology, and hence the medical sciences are like this. (iii) Many of the entities involved are Gestalt-like phenomena. What I mean by this is that there is no exact similarity between them physically, but they are *seen as* similar from a certain perspective or for a certain purpose. Entities in physics are analogous to a perfectly circular object, which needs no interpretation to be taken as a circle: those in irreducible special sciences are like a series of discontinuous dots or marks arranged roughly in a circle which one sees as circular. Two hurricanes, for example, are not perfectly similar and would present themselves as a kind only to someone with an interest in weather: plate tectonics exists only given an interest in the habitability of the earth. This is not, of course, to say that these entities are invented. There are, in Dennett's phrase, "real patterns" out there, but, like *Gestalten*, they are reified as being of a certain kind by an interpretative act.

These three features – selection, the reading-in of a teleology, and the reification of certain patterns to create the ontology of the special sciences – show that Fodor's "non-reductive" theory (what I have called reductionism [3]) presupposes a perspective on the subject matter, which is the viewpoint from which these interpretative acts take place. The stronger forms of reductionism enable one to understand the special sciences in the light of physics without the addition of such interpretative perspectives: that is why I called them "bottom-up" theories. But the perspectival approach, involving a view from outside the subject matter seems to give the interpreting mind an irreducible role in the creation of these sciences. Fodor's theory appears to be essentially dualistic. It seems that the same portion of the physical world is being viewed from outside in a variety of ways for a variety of purposes.

One might be tempted to take this last claim metaphorically, and as simply pointing out that it involves a contrast between the subject matter and its interpretation. But it is more than metaphorically dualistic. It can avoid a literal dualism of mind and body only if the interpretative perspective can be treated as part of the physical realm being interpreted. This concerns the ontological status of the mental acts that constitute such interpretation. These are amongst those psychological states described by propositional attitude psychology. But propositional attitude psychology is one of those special sciences which is, at best, reducible only in a Fodorian way: it meets no more than the standards of type (3), with no translational or nomic reduction. Indeed, it was with this science in mind that Fodor introduced his theory. The science of psychology is, therefore, itself something that emerges as an interaction of real patterns and interpretation: the external perspective cannot be eliminated.

References

Boyd, R., Gasper, P., and Trout, J. (eds) (1991) *The Philosophy of Science*, Cambridge MA: MIT Press.

Carnap, R. (1995 [1934]) *The Unity of Science*, Bristol, UK: Thoemmes Press; originally published by Kegan Paul in 1934.

Chalmers, D. (1996) *The Conscious Mind: In Search of a Fundamental Theory*, New York: Oxford University Press.

Davidson, D. (1970) "Mental Events," in L. Foster and J. W. Swanson (eds), *Experience and Theory*, London: Duckworth, pp. 79–101.

—— (1993) "Thinking Causes," in J. Heil and A. Mele (eds), *Mental Causation*, Oxford: Clarendon Press, pp. 3–17.

Feigl, H., Scriven, M., and Maxwell, G. (eds) (1958) *Minnesota Studies in the Philosophy of Science*, vol. 2: *Concepts, Theories, and the Mind–Body Problem*, Minneapolis: University of Minnesota Press.

Fodor, J. (1974) "Special Sciences, or the Disunity of Science as a Working Hypothesis," *Synthese* 28: 77–15; reprinted in Boyd et al. (1991), pp. 429–41.

Hempel, C. G. (1980 [1935]) "The Logical Analysis of Psychology," in N. Block (ed.), *Readings in Philosophy of Psychology*, vol. 1, London: Methuen, pp. 14–23; originally published in French in 1935.

Kemeny, J. and Oppenheim, P. (1956) "On Reduction," *Philosophical Studies* 7: 6–19.

Nagel, E. (1961) *The Structure of Science: Problems in the Logic of Scientific Explanation*, London: Routledge & Kegan Paul.

Putnam, H. and Oppenheim, P. (1958) "Unity of Science as a Working Hypothesis," in Feigl et al. (1958), pp. 3–36; also in Boyd et al. (1991), pp. 405–27.

Robinson, H. (2001) "Davidson and Non-Reductive Physicalism," in C. Gillett and B. Loewer (eds), *Physicalism and Its Discontents*, Cambridge: Cambridge University Press, pp. 129–51.

Further reading

N. Cartwright, *The Dappled World* (Cambridge: Cambridge University Press, 1999) and the Dupré and the Gallison and Stump volumes, below, discuss or defend the radical disunity of science. This is an important position that space has prevented me from discussing. D. Charles and K. Lennon, *Reduction, Explanation and Realism* (Oxford: Clarendon Press, 1992) is a good collection of original essays, discussing the application of reductive ideas to a wide range of disciplines. See also John Dupré, *The Disorder of Things* (Cambridge MA: Harvard University Press, 1993); and Peter Gallison and David J. Stump (eds), *The Disunity of Science* (Stanford: Stanford University Press, 1996). The article by E. R. Scerri and I. McIntyre, "The Case for the Philosophy of Chemistry," *Synthese* 111 (1997): 213–32, disputes the view, often held, that chemistry at least is reducible to physics in a fairly strong sense.

50
BIOMETAPHYSICS
Barry Smith

Historical background

Aristotelian realism

While biology has spawned many of the problems that have shaped the discipline of metaphysics since its inception, current advances in the biological sciences are disclosing hitherto unimagined dimensions of complexity in the processes of life, to a degree which poses challenges to standard metaphysical ways of thinking. In what follows, I shall show how metaphysical ideas nonetheless continue to play a role in biological science, focusing my attentions in particular on problems of biological classification.

In the time of Linnaeus, familiarly, biology was still rooted in a recognizably Aristotelian view of classification. Before articulating this view, it will be useful to begin by distinguishing two meanings of "classification," (1) as a division or sub-grouping of the entities in reality; and (2) as an artifact created by humans. The common Aristotelian–Linnaean view of the classification of organisms can be summarized in these terms as follows:

(a) There is a fixed division of the totality of organisms into subgroups called *species* (sense 1), which obtains independently of the activities of scientists. This division is permanent in virtue of the fact that to each species there corresponds an ahistorical essence, a property or group of properties severally necessary and jointly sufficient for an organism to belong to that species. (An assumption of this sort still prevails today in many areas of physics and chemistry, for example in the classification of quarks or of the chemical elements.)

(b) This division forms one level in a hierarchy, which has the structure of a directed acyclical graph (the "tree of life"), whose nodes (*taxa*) are ordered by the relation of inclusion culminating in a single maximal root node (*organism* or *living thing*). All taxa on any given level in the hierarchy are disjoint (they share no common instances and also no common subtaxa). All instances of taxa on lower levels inherit those properties which hold of all instances of the including taxa above them. Each node in the hierarchy below the root has exactly one including node on the next higher level (the principle of *single inheritance*).

(c) There exists a single classification (sense 1) of the biological realm, which scientists attempt to reproduce in the form of a single, correct representation (sense 2). To achieve this goal, they seek to identify organisms that are exemplary or prototypical for each given species. Differences between and changes in organisms of a single species are noted, but they are regarded as being of secondary significance.

Darwin and beyond

Already in the eighteenth century, biologists had begun to move away from the essentialist idea of fixed species, and Darwin's decisive achievement consisted in establishing a framework for understanding how new species can come into existence (have *origins*) in time. As mutation and the non-prototypical thereby come to occupy roles at the centre of biological science, all of the other mentioned aspects of the traditional approach to classification are to different degrees called into question. Already (though not consistently) Darwin saw the notion of species as a matter of mere fiat determination on the part of biological theorists: "I look at the term species as one arbitrarily given for the sake of convenience to a set of individuals closely resembling each other" (Darwin 1988; 39; cf. Stamos 2007). More recently, competing approaches to biological science on the part of taxonomists, evolutionary biologists and molecular biologists have brought competing conceptions of the goal of species classification and of the nature and status of species, and some have embraced pluralist views according to which there is no single division on the side of reality to be reflected in our classifications.

The impact of the mentioned changes should not be overestimated. The tree of life conception still serves as overarching framework for the understanding of evolutionary history, and even though the simple branching-tree conception breaks down for bacteria and other microorganisms because of the prevalence of lateral gene transfer, most taxonomists still see the totality of organisms as susceptible to a division into taxa that look very much like traditional species, even if the rationale (or rationales) for division is nowadays quite differently conceived. The major competing species concepts still broadly agree in the classifications of organisms they dictate in areas of overlap (though what is, for example, subspecies in one may be species in another).

Moreover, while most philosophical attention to biological classification has been focused on the classification of organisms, the classificatory concerns of contemporary biologists extend much further. Already Linnaeus had proposed a classification of diseases (Linnaeus 1763), and efforts are, as we shall see, increasingly directed towards the creation of standardized classifications (called "ontologies") of entities such as genes, proteins, cells, anatomical structures, or biochemical networks and pathways.

The species problem

What is a species?

A large number of different conceptions of species have been advanced in recent years (Ereshefsky 1992), including for example definitions based on shared environments, on cohesion, or on intraspecies recognition. Three families of definitions are of particular importance:

- On *similarity-based (phenetic) species definitions*, a species is a totality of organisms possessing certain predefined properties. Traditionally all species definitions were of this type. For Linnaeus organisms were classified according to differences in the form (shape) of their reproductive apparatus. Currently, similarity-based definitions often include the factor of similarity of DNA of individuals or populations.
- On *phylogenetic species definitions* a species is a lineage of one or other sort, which is to say a totality of organisms extended over time and linked by parenthood relations to a common ancestor.
- On *biological species definitions* a species is a totality (a population or aggregate of populations) of interbreeding organisms. It is a persisting material object that is delineated by the ability of its constituent organisms to reproduce naturally in such a way as to yield fertile offspring.

Particulars, collections and classes

The above provides us with some examples of how species are conceived by influential communities of biologists. But it does not yet tell us how species, on such conceptions, are to be understood metaphysically. In answering this question we shall adopt the following terminological conventions:

- A *particular* is an entity which exists in space and time and which is involved in causal relations. Particulars are divided into *continuants*, entities (things, objects) which endure through time, and *occurrents*, entities (processes, changes) which occur or take place in time. An organism is a particular continuant; an organism's life is a particular occurrent. In the course of its life each organism undergoes changes of various sorts, including gaining and losing parts.
- A *collection* is a continuant particular comprehending at any given time a number of simultaneously existing continuant particulars as its parts and linked together via certain relations, for example of spatial proximity. A collection – for example the collection of stickleback fish in this pond – is a concrete, historical entity, similar in this respect to a single organism. And just as a single organism may survive the gain and loss of cells, so a collection of organisms may survive the gain and loss of members.
- A *class* (for our purposes here) is an entity that results from the grouping of other entities, whereby the latter are not required to be entities that exist simultaneously. The class of tiger beetles, for example, is the grouping of all tiger beetles which exist, have existed and will exist in the future. Classes as thus conceived do not endure through time while gaining and losing members. Their members may exist in time and undergo changes of various sorts, but the class abstracts away from all such temporal differences. Thus the members of the class of beetles are indeterminately eggs, larvae, pupae and adults.

The biological approach to species

Species as classes and as collections

All three families of species-definitions are in one or other form compatible with both collection- and class-based views of species. However, both similarity-based and phylogenetic definitions have tended to go hand in hand with a view of species as classes.

Because of the growth in predominance of population-based approaches to the study of biological phenomena, it is the biological approach to species as articulated by Ernst Mayr (1942) that comes closest to enjoying consensus status among contemporary biologists, and it is this approach that will occupy us in what follows. Species are seen as collections; thus they are continuant particulars made up of organisms as parts. Each species is a cohesive population (aggregate of populations) that maintains its integrity over time in virtue of highly sensitive intraspecies recognition systems which promote actual gene flow within the species and inhibit gene flow without. Species on this view are not lineages (any more than individual organisms); rather, they form lineages when viewed in terms of their development over time.

Species and particulars

The most crucial element of the biological approach from our present perspective is the thesis to the effect that species are particulars, a thesis first advanced by Ghiselin (1974) and then by Hull (1976). Mayr accepts this thesis, though he objects to the specific formulation given to it by Ghiselin and Hull:

> There is no doubt that there is a real difference between a spatio-temporally unrestricted class characterized by its definition (its essence), and a spatio-temporally restricted item with internal cohesion. It is only that the designation "individual," chosen by Ghiselin and Hull, is rather unfortunate. I refer to such items as "particulars" or, when involving living organisms as "populations." They have, indeed, all the characteristics ascribed to them by Ghiselin, except that the use of the name "an individual" for 5 billion humans is rather absurd. (Letter to Peter Simons, 15 January 1993)

The thesis that species are *cohesive scattered continuant particulars* represents a radical departure from traditional views according to which species are *natural kinds* (like *oxygen* or *gold*) with organisms as particular instances. If each species is a particular, then it does not make sense to speak of species terms as figuring in statements of natural laws, any more than it would make sense to speak of "Arnold Schwarzenegger" or "Belgium" as figuring in such statements.

But just as the *class* of organisms – like the class of cells or the class of proteins – forms a natural kind, so also does the *class* of species. For just as there are natural laws governing the class of organisms, so also there are natural laws governing the class of species.

Such laws are typically statistical. One example is this: *species formation typically requires antecedent geographical isolation.* A statistically typical speciation event occurs when a species is divided into two separate sub-collections which over time develop into two reproductively isolated populations. One species is replaced by two, in a process analogous to the splitting of an amoeba. The totality of organisms after species separation is then like the totality of living material in the two amoebae that result from splitting: each is a purely historical entity that forms no biologically significant unity. On the view of Ghiselin, something similar applies to all higher taxa – all are purely historical entities that do not function as cohesive units. This suggests also one potential resolution of what some see as a fatal flaw in the biological approach, namely that it can be applied only to organisms which reproduce sexually. The solution is to treat asexual taxa, too, as purely historical entities (Ghiselin 2002: 157). Thus where some would argue that a mix-and-match of different species views is needed to cope with the peculiarities of organisms of different types (a phylogenetic view, for example, to cope with bacteria), Ghiselin can maintain a unitary view, and thus preserve the capacity of species to figure in natural laws (1997).

Mereology and set theory

Species as sets

Species are, on the biological approach, like cells and organisms. They exist in time and undergo changes in the course of time. They are cohesive material actors firmly rooted in the nexus of cause and effect. Despite this, there are some, such as Kitcher (1984) and Guenin (2008), who have defended a view of biological species as sets. This view is in line with assertions often found in introductory textbooks of set theory, according to which collections such as "a pack of wolves, a bunch of grapes, or a flock of pigeons are all examples of sets of things" (Halmos 1960: 1). As Simons has noted, such remarks imply that "one can be chased, attacked and even eaten by a set, oneself eat a set and absorb vitamins from it, press a set and make wine out of it" (Simons 2005). The cognitive dissonance sparked by such implications rests on the fact that all standard attempts to specify axioms for the theory of sets rest on a view of sets as entities which exist outside the realm of time and change. Sets, as defined by these axioms, cannot evolve. Species evolve. Hence species are not sets.

Kitcher's response is to argue that there is committed here what he calls "the fallacy of incomplete translation" (Kitcher 1984: 310–11). This is because "a species evolves" is left untranslated. To complete the translation we need to bear in mind that each set-theoretically conceived species is a union of subsets – call them "time slices" – comprising, for each given time, all the organisms belonging to the species alive at that time. On Kitcher's view, "a species evolves" is then shorthand for *the frequency distribution of properties across one time slice will differ from the frequency distribution of properties across a later time slice*, and similarly for other assertions involving apparent reference to species changing over time, such as "this species branched into two species" or "that species became extinct" (Guenin 2008: 107).

Note that Kitcher is not here telling us what species (entities which, on standard views, evolve, speciate, become extinct, etc.) *are*. Rather, he is offering a proposal to replace the familiar species notion with another, different notion. As Guenin puts it, "expressions in terms of sets more accurately describe selection than does talk of species changing."

One advantage of the language of set theory is that it provides us with a well-understood common logical framework within which we can clearly and rigorously formulate what might otherwise be opaque claims pertaining to species and their instances, as well as to biological entities of other sorts. Against this, however, is the fact that the conception of species themselves as sets cannot do justice to those aspects of the biological approach which rest on the view of species as particulars, entities which not only evolve but also do a variety of other things, including crossing mountains, replenishing the earth, and so forth. This requires a view according to which species have organisms not as *members* in the set-theoretic sense but as *parts* in the sense of mereology (Simons 1987). Can we, then, formulate a compromise framework in which we can enjoy the advantages of both the set-theoretic and the mereological approaches?

Species, sets and biological classification

A framework along these lines has been most prominently advocated by John Dupré, who argues that two distinct approaches to species are required, one for the study of evolution, which demands a view of species as particulars exactly as adumbrated by Ghiselin, and one for classification, where in addition, as Dupré sees it, a pluralistic view is required, which allows for a mixing and matching of species concepts (Dupré 2001).

Understandably, given his interest in biology as a science, and in natural laws, Ghiselin responds in negative tones to Dupré's proposal: "The idea here is that there should be one way of ordering nature for evolutionary research, another for classification, perhaps with classification adapted to the needs of the aquarium trade" (Ghiselin 2002: 159). We should beware, however, of assuming that every supplementation of the strictly mereological approach to species must involve an avowedly promiscuous pluralism of the sort defended by Dupré. A more acceptable strategy would be to see set theory, not as an ontological alternative or supplement to mereology-based particularism, but rather as an ontologically neutral linguistic framework within which to formulate the classificatory implications of biological research in a rigorous and consistent way.

It can provide us, for example, with the means to enhance the strictly mereological formulation of the particularist view of species by allowing us to capture the sense in which species are totalities of *organisms* rather than of *cells* or of *molecules* – the sense in which species, on the biological approach, are thus properly referred to in terms of *populations*. The problem here is that, in contrast to set-membership, parthood is transitive – so that there is a sense in which mereology washes away the differences between parts at different levels of granularity. Every part of me – my cells, my teeth, my digestive tract – is also a part of the species of which I am a part. Yet my teeth are not human beings.

The language of set theory provides us with a means of resolving this problem in a way that leaves the underlying ontology unchanged. Briefly, we can define for each nonempty set A a corresponding *mereological fusion*, which is what results when we imagine the members of A as being put together to form a whole. In symbols: the fusion σ(A) is the maximal whole all of whose parts overlap with some member of A. For any species S as conceived on the biological approach, we can then create a series of designations of such mereological fusions, each of which recognizes the parts of S at a certain specified level of granularity. Most prominently, these include

(i)   σ({x | *part_of*(x, S) & *instance_of* (x, *organism*)})
(ii)   σ({x | *part_of*(x, S) & *instance_of* (x, *cell*)})
(iii)   σ({x | *part_of*(x, S) & *instance_of* (x, *molecule*)})

where the terms *organism*, *cell* and *molecule* refer to the corresponding natural kinds. Only (i), it seems (or better: some modified version of [i], in which account is taken of time) represents a generally applicable candidate to *be* the species S; for only (i) does not leave mereological gaps. ([ii] leaves out bones, hair and other parts of organisms of higher species which are not made of cells; [iii] leaves out parts, such as the cavity of the bladder, not made of molecules.)

The future of biometaphysics

We referred earlier to attempts by contemporary biologists to create standardized classifications of entities such as proteins, cells, or pathways. Such work is playing a crucial role in helping to organize the massive quantities of data now being made available through high-throughput experimentation techniques in functional genomics and related areas, to the degree that the activity of classification is itself enjoying something of a renaissance in biological science. The most successful example in this regard is the Gene Ontology (GO), a collection of three cross-species classifications (of *molecular functions*, *biological processes* and *cell components*) now applied in many areas of biological and biomedical research to promote the integration and comparison of data deriving from the study of genes and gene products in organisms of different species. The GO has proven useful, especially in research on so-called "model organisms," which are studied experimentally for purposes of drawing implications for our understanding of human health and disease (Gene Ontology Consortium 2006). The GO is now supporting efforts (a) to establish for each type of biological entity that mode of classification which best conforms to our current scientific understanding; and (b) to create on this basis an orthogonal suite of interoperable representations of biological reality employing a common formal framework. Interestingly, these efforts are drawing on both biological and philosophico-ontological expertise (Smith et al. 2007). Their goal is to ensure that we will be able to harvest maximal benefit from the biological information resources of the future.

We already face enormous challenges in assimilating the huge amounts of life science data being made available to researchers, and there is an increasingly urgent need to ensure that these data work well together. The language of set theory – or better: one or other modified language honed to possess more useful computational properties

(Rubin et al. 2008) – is beginning to provide the framework within which classifications of organisms, diseases and molecular functions can be made to work together in ways useful for research. The need for such a framework creates at the same time, however, a strong practical argument against pluralistic approaches of the sort favored by Dupré. For the mentioned challenges would become even more intractable were different research groups addressing the same biological phenomena each encouraged to employ their own classifications in a spirit of tolerance and diversity.

References

Darwin, Charles (1988) *On the Origin of Species*, vol. 15 of *The Works of Charles Darwin*, edited by P. H. Barrett and R. B. Freeman, Cambridge: Cambridge University Press.

Dupré, John (2001) "In Defence of Classification," *Studies in the History and Philosophy of the Biological and Biomedical Sciences* 32: 203–19.

Ereshefsky, Marc (ed.) (1992) *Units of Evolution: Essays on the Nature of Species*, Cambridge, MA: MIT Press.

Gene Ontology Consortium (2006) "The Gene Ontology (GO) Project in 2006," *Nucleic Acids Research* 34 (database issue): D322–D326.

Ghiselin, Michael T. (1974) "A Radical Solution to the Species Problem," *Systematic Zoology* 23: 536–44.

—— (1997) *Metaphysics and the Origin of Species*, Albany, NY: SUNY Press.

—— (2002) "Species Concepts: The Basis for Controversy and Reconciliation," *Fish and Fisheries* 3: 151–60.

Guenin, Louis M. (2008) *The Morality of Embryo Use*, Cambridge: Cambridge University Press.

Halmos, Paul R. (1960) *Naïve Set Theory*, Princeton, NJ: Van Nostrand.

Hull, David (1976) "Are Species Really Individuals?" *Systematic Zoology* 25: 174–91.

Kitcher, Philip (1984) "Species," *Philosophy of Science* 51: 308–33.

Linnaeus, Carolus (1763) *Genera Morborumin Auditorum Usum*, Uppsala, Sweden: C. E. Steinert.

Mayr, Ernst (1942) *Systematics and the Origin of Species from the Viewpoint of a Zoologist*, New York: Columbia University Press.

Rubin, Daniel L., Shah, Nigam H., and Noy, Natalya F. (2008) "Biomedical Ontologies: A Functional Perspective," *Briefings in Bioinformatics* 9: 75–90.

Simons, Peter M. (1987) *Parts: A Study in Ontology*, Oxford: Clarendon Press.

—— (2005) "Against Set Theory," in J. C. Marek and M. E. Reicher (eds), *Experience and Analysis*, Vienna: HPT & ÖBV, pp. 143–52.

Smith, Barry, Ashburner, Michael, Rosse, Cornelius, Bard, Jonathan, Bug, William, Ceusters, Werner et al. (2007) "The OBO Foundry: Coordinated Evolution of Ontologies to Support Biomedical Data Integration," *Nature Biotechnology* 25, no. 11: 1251–5.

Stamos, David N. (2007) *Darwin and the Nature of Species*, Albany, NY: SUNY Press.

Further reading

For further reading, see Ernst Mayr, "The Ontological Status of Species," *Biology and Philosophy* 2 (1987): 145–66.

51

SOCIAL ENTITIES

Amie L. Thomasson

The social sciences study social entities, including social facts (e.g. the fact that there is a crisis in the housing market, or that Hong Kong was returned to Chinese rule), social actions (e.g. the dissolution of parliament, the invasion of Poland), and social objects (e.g. the Magna Carta, Microsoft). But social entities are not merely the concern of social scientists – they are also the focus of most of our daily concerns, as we consider which courses to enroll in, worry about the status of our bank accounts, apply for new drivers' licenses, rent apartments, and organize dinner parties.

Social entities seem to differ from merely natural objects like sticks and stones in an important respect, however: they are, in some sense, human constructions and would not exist without human habits, practices, beliefs, and/or agreements. Thus, as Finn Collin puts it, "It is a truism that the reality in which the human species lives is of humankind's own making ... Human beings make their own world" (1997: 1).

The fact that social entities depend on human beliefs and intentions for their existence raises metaphysical questions about them that do not arise for mere natural objects. If we in some sense just make these things up, should we consider them to be genuine parts of our world at all – or should we consider them just as illusory as the creatures in the stories we make up? As John Searle puts it, we have a "sense that there is an element of magic, a conjuring trick, a sleight of hand in the creation of institutional facts out of brute facts," so that "In our toughest metaphysical moods we want to ask ... are these bits of paper really *money?*... Is making certain noises in a ceremony really *getting married?* ... Surely when you get down to brass tacks, these are not real facts" (1995: 45).

Yet despite their apparent mind-dependence, social entities exhibit certain hallmarks of real entities: first, there is much about them that we apparently do not know, but require serious investigations – including those of tax collectors, courts of law, and the social sciences – to discover. And such discoveries at least purport to present objective knowledge, just as those of the natural sciences do. Second, although social entities are in some sense made up by us, we typically encounter them as being independent of our will, even coercive of us. I cannot, simply by willing alone, make it the case that I am not in debt, or that Barack Obama is not president. It is predominantly this independence from our will that led Emile Durkheim to declare that we must study social phenomena "objectively as external things," as "the most important characteristic of a 'thing' is the impossibility of its modification by a simple effort of the will" (1994 [1938]: 438–9).

Thus three central puzzles arise regarding social entities: (1) How can human beliefs and intentions create new facts, events and objects? As Berger and Luckman put it, "How is it possible that human activity should produce a world of things?" (1966: 18). (2) How can these mind-dependent social entities ever be unknown, potential objects of objective knowledge and discovery? (3) Given their mind-dependence, how can social objects be independent of our will, even coercive of us?

I address these puzzles in turn below. I begin in the first section by discussing the ways in which human intentionality may create social reality. I then go on in the second and third sections to suggest how understanding the different ways social reality is created enables us to unravel the latter two puzzles, explaining how such social entities may be open to objective discoveries and independent of our will.

The creation of social entities

What are social entities? I began by saying that they are the entities studied by the social sciences, though this may hardly be considered a definition. Social *facts* have been more often considered than social entities more broadly considered, and attempts to define "social fact" have generally been aimed at distinguishing them, on the one hand, from mere natural entities, and, on the other, from mere private, personal, or psychological entities. As we have already noted above, social entities differ from natural entities insofar as the former, but not the latter, would not exist without human habits, beliefs, and/or agreements. (Of course some anti-realists hold that all objects are in some sense mind-dependent – but even they must acknowledge a difference between that and the dependence of the many aspects of the social world created by the practices or agreements of the people who participate in it. For further discussion, see Devitt [1991: 246–9]).

But this does not yet distinguish social entities from individual psychological states and their products (such as personal wishes, hallucinations, or actions). To make this distinction, the distinctively *social* is typically identified with the *collective* (Collin 1997: 5), and so, e.g., Searle defines "social fact" as "any fact involving collective intentionality" (1995: 26). More broadly, we can think of social entities as entities that depend on collective intentionality. The dependence here is not just causal – it's not just that social entities are causally brought into existence by collective intentions (as Mount Trashmore was created by city workers jointly covering over an old landfill). Instead, the dependence of social entities on collective intentionality is a metaphysical or conceptual matter: given the very idea of money, or a school, or real estate, it clearly doesn't make any sense to think that such things could exist without collective human (or other intelligent) intentions. By contrast, it does make sense to think that a mountain could exist without any collective human intentions, so Mount Trashmore is not a social entity, even though it happens to have been brought into existence by teams of humans working together to serve a common goal.

But what, exactly, is collective intentionality? "Intentionality" is a feature of mental states that are *of* or *about* something, and so not only intentions (in the sense of intending to do something), but also beliefs, desires, hopes, fears, and the like are mental states with intentionality. We often attribute intentional mental states to social groups, e.g. when we say that the Calvinists believe in predestination, the Smiths want a larger home, or the Bears hope to win on Sunday. But there has been little agreement about what exactly it takes for beliefs, desires, etc., to count as *collective*. Searle (1995: 26) takes collective intentionality to be a certain "we" form of intentionality, consisting in each individual having thoughts of the form (e.g.) "we intend" (rather than "I intend"). Others (e.g. Bratman 1993) have taken collective intentions to involve individual beliefs and intentions that are interrelated in specified ways (involving certain intentions about the others' intentions in conditions of common knowledge). By contrast, Margaret Gilbert proposes understanding collective intentions not as intentions of individuals at all, but rather as the intentions of plural subjects formed when individuals undertake a certain kind of joint commitment (Gilbert 1989). Others still (Tuomela 2003: 154) have suggested distinguishing a range of different kinds of collective intentionality relevant to the existence of different parts of social reality. Here I will leave to one side debates about how to understand collective intentionality.

If social entities are any entities that depend on collective intentionality then there are as many kinds of social entity as there are ways of depending on collective intentionality. While making no claim to being exhaustive, below I will provide an overview of some importantly different categories into which social entities may fall.

Provided we accept that everything depends on itself, the most basic social entities are collective intentional states themselves and facts about what is collectively believed, desired, accepted, or valued in a given social group. Collective intentions may also form the basis for collective actions – given the right kind of collective intentions, the movements of a number of individual people may amount to performing a collective action, e.g., building a house.

Given the need for stability and the importance of being able to predict each other's actions and coordinate our behaviors, such collective actions tend to fall into repeated patterns – via what Berger and Luckmann (1966: 53) call "habitualization." Where activities are habitualized, we can develop collective conceptions of certain "types" of actions and of actor, simplifying social interaction by leading to mutual expectations about forms of behavior (Berger and Luckmann 1966: 54). When these expectations become normative, having implications for how participants *ought to* behave, we reach the level of social reality Raimo Tuomela (2003: 152) has called "social practices," e.g. the Midsummer Feast, the Saturday lesson, and corresponding social roles, e.g. the carver at the feast, the teacher of the lesson.

But social entities are not limited to our collective intentions and practices themselves; as Searle has pointed out, a far greater range of social entities may be constructed by using collective intentions and actions to impose new social features on "brute" physical objects. On Searle's account mere *social* facts may be created when we assign new functions to old material entities, e.g. assigning this log the function of serving as our bench. The more interesting cases, however, are those of *institutional* facts, which arise when we collectively impose upon some entity a new function which (unlike being a bench) it could not perform solely in virtue of its physical features – as, for example when we impose upon a river the function of serving as the boundary of our territory (1995: 38–9). These are the so-called "status functions" that, according to Searle, are the hallmarks of institutional reality. Status functions may be iterated – e.g. we may assign this person the status of being citizen, and then assign this citizen the status function of being president. But all status functions, on Searle's account, ultimately confer new deontic powers – enablements and requirements – on individuals (e.g. the president is given the power to sign legislation into law).

On Searle's account, we impose status functions on objects by collectively accepting constitutive rules. Whereas "regulative" rules (such as "drive on the right side of the road") merely regulate preexisting activities, constitutive rules are rules where the relevant activity is in part "constituted" by following those rules – e.g. you must be following a certain set of rules to be playing chess, to be filing a lawsuit, or to be earning credits towards a university degree at all. Searle describes the basic form of constitutive rules as "X counts as Y (in context C)." The "X" term may stand for an individual (token) item, as, e.g., we may accept that this river counts as the boundary between our nations, or it may stand for any item of a certain type as, e.g. we accept that any pieces of paper of this pattern issued by the Bureau of Printing and Engraving count as twenty-dollar bills, and thereby assign any and all pieces of paper that meet those conditions the status function of serving as money – a function their mere physical nature alone does not enable them to fulfill (1995: 44–6).

As I have argued elsewhere (2003a), we should actually consider these as two different sorts of rule for creating institutional reality: cases of the first type involve adopting a *singular* rule, of the following form (where "S" names some social feature): of a particular (preexisting) object a, we (collectively) accept (Sa), e.g. of this river, we accept that it counts as the boundary of our territory. Cases of the second type involve adopting a *universal* rule: that, for any x, we accept that if x meets certain conditions C, then Sx. In either case, the object only continues to serve this new function as long as we continue to accept the corresponding constitutive rules, so, e.g., pieces of paper meeting conditions C continue to count as money only as long as we continue to accept the relevant constitutive rule. Such constitutive rules enable us to endow preexisting objects with new social features – either one at a time (using singular rules), or wholesale (using universal rules). In fact, Searle argues, no new objects are involved in institutional reality at all; "rather, a new status with an accompanying function has been assigned to an old object" (1995: 57).

But although Searle's story explains how preexisting entities like rivers and pieces of paper may acquire new status functions, it can't explain how new social entities such as laws, companies, and religions may be constructed. For there is no constitutive rule that assigns to some preexisting physical object or objects the function of serving as an antismoking law, as Microsoft, or as the Anglican Church. These things cannot be understood simply as preexisting physical objects with new status functions, since they are not physical entities at all – indeed we might call them "abstract" social objects.

To account for the creation of abstract social objects, I have argued (2003a), we must allow that constitutive rules may take a third form: *existential* rules involve collectively accepting that, if certain conditions obtain, then *there is some (new) entity x such that*

Sx. These constitutive rules, unlike those of the first two forms, are existence-introducing, since they allow that the obtaining of certain conditions counts as sufficient for the existence of a new social entity. Thus, for example, we accept that if congress votes with a majority in favor of a bill and the president signs it, then a new law is created. That law, however, is not identical with any piece of paper the president signs (it may continue to exist even if that paper is destroyed), nor with any member of congress or action of any such member. Similarly, constitutive rules ensure that if the relevant paperwork is filed, a new company may be created which is not identical to its founder, its board of directors, or any of the paperwork used in setting it up. Broadening the range of constitutive rules in this way enables us to explain how collective intentions may create, not only new social facts (involving old material objects), but also new social objects such as laws, corporations, etc.

All of these entities are in some sense intentionally created – either individually (via a singular rule) or by acceptance of universal or existential rules that lay out conditions for what it takes for objects to have that social feature, or what it takes for such a social object to be created. Call these "constructed social entities." Constructed social entities exhibit what Searle calls "self-referentiality" (1995: 32): for there to be entities of the relevant social kind, there must be collective intentional states *about* that social kind – either designating certain entities as belonging to that kind, or laying out principles for there being something of the kind.

But it is important to note that there are a great many social entities that are not intentionally created – even though they depend on collective intentionality. Basic social entities such as collective intentions themselves (e.g. a collective fear of being attacked by a lion) are not constructed in the above sense (Tuomela 2003: 161). Moreover, such social entities as racism, economic recessions, class systems, and gender-biased power structures are typically not intentionally created (either directly or indirectly) by accepting constitutive rules about entities of that kind – indeed they may exist even if they are not *intentionally* created at all, making it more natural to speak of them as *generated* rather than *created* or *constructed* (Thomasson 2003a).

Such unintended social entities emerge as the byproducts of more basic social and institutional facts, especially when considered on a large scale (or as Andersson puts it, at the "macro level" [2007: 113]). So, for example, all particular acts of hiring, firing, establishing wages and granting promotions, involve institutional facts that must be constructed, according to constitutive rules regarding what counts as a hiring, etc. But these may fall into patterns that constitute a case of a gender-biased system, without such a system being intentionally created by anyone. In such cases we clearly have entities that, at some level, depend on collective intentionality (since the individual acts of hiring, firing, etc., each depend on collective acceptance of constitutive rules involving those concepts), but they do not depend on collective intentions *about* gender bias at all (Thomasson 2003a). As a result, unlike intentionally constructed entities, they do not exhibit self-referentiality and may come into being without the intentions or knowledge of members of that society. (Tuomela [2003: 129] draws a similar distinction between "primary constructively social" entities and other social entities not directly constructed.)

Social entities as objects of knowledge

Armed with the above understanding of some of the ways social entities may come into being, we can now see at least four ways in which social entities may be *discoverable*, despite the fact that they all ultimately depend on collective intentionality.

First, there is always room for discovery of facts about societies *other than our own*, for although social entities depend on collective intentionality, the relevant intentional states of course needn't be *universally* held. So although what counts as money, or as sacred, or as legally required, may depend on what participants *regard as* money, as sacred, or as illegal in their society, these facts nonetheless require substantive discovery by outsiders – leaving plenty of room for the discoveries of historians, cultural anthropologists, archeologists, and the like.

The trickier part is understanding how we may potentially make discoveries about *our own* society – especially those parts of it that we intentionally *construct*. We do have certain kinds of privileged knowledge about our own social constructions (see my 2001, 2003b). For example, where a social fact (e.g. that this river is our boundary) is created using a singular rule, then it can't be unknown, since it must be collectively accepted to exist at all. More generally, given the self-referentiality discussed above, constructed social entities cannot exist unless certain facts about entities of that type are collectively accepted, e.g. there cannot be money without either directly accepting certain objects as money, or accepting universal or existential rules about what counts as (there being) money.

Nonetheless, where social entities are constructed by accepting universal or existential rules (rather than singular rules), individual (token) entities of that type can still exist unknown – yielding a second way in which social facts may be available for discovery. For although we have to collectively accept general rules about the conditions under which there are entities of that kind, it's possible that no one knows that those conditions are met. So, for example, members of a society may collectively accept that if anyone pulls the sword out of the stone, that person counts as their king – and yet it may remain unknown to them that a foreigner has passed by and pulled the sword out, and thus unknown that they have a (rightful) king (see Searle 1995: 32).

A third, more interesting, opportunity for discoveries about the social entities we construct concerns what we might call "higher-order" facts about social reality, that is, not first-order social facts themselves, but facts about how those very social facts came into existence, and what continues to give them their legitimacy. On the above understanding, social facts come into existence through certain forms of collective agreement, and someone counts as king, for example, only if he is collectively accepted as king, or certain rules are collectively accepted that entail that he is king. But while collective acceptance is fundamental to the existence of such institutional facts, that doesn't mean that there must be collective awareness that *that's all there is* to establishing and maintaining these institutions (Searle 1995: 21–2, 47). On the contrary, as Berger and Luckmann (1966: 92ff.) point out, our most important social institutions typically undergo a process of *legitimation* – devising (sometimes false or mythical) justifications for the existence of social institutions and for their being the way that they are, in order to ensure conformity. Thus, e.g. the legitimation may involve saying that this man is king *because* he was appointed by God, covering over the fact that he is actually only king because of collective acceptance of him as king. Similarly, marriages exist if there are certain collectively accepted procedures that lay out what counts as a marriage, and those procedures are sometimes followed. But legitimations may cover this over by treating marriage as a union blessed by God, as the only acceptable or most effective means of rearing children, etc. This opens room for what is often called "critique" in social sciences, where that involves showing up these legitimating stories and uncovering the real basis for various social institutions, often by demonstrating their actual history and showing what functions they really serve in society.

The fourth and perhaps richest area for potential discoveries is regarding those social entities that are generated as byproducts rather than being constructed. So although money, presidents, and drivers' licenses may not be able to exist without people accepting certain things (or sorts of thing) *as* money, presidents, or drivers' licenses, the same is not true for economic cycles, patterns of human settlement, or gender-based discrimination in the workplace. These social entities may exist without anyone having any thoughts at all about economic cycles, settlement patterns, or gender discrimination – indeed the very concepts needed to describe such things as recessions, racism, and gender discrimination may not be possessed by societies in which they are commonplace (see my 2003a). Nonetheless, they still depend, at bottom, on individual social facts (about transactions, habitation, employment) that exist only given collective acceptance (either of those facts or of constitutive rules that, combined with the basic facts, generate them).

Finally, it is worth emphasizing that despite the fact that social entities depend on collective intentionality, our discoveries about them may nonetheless be *objective* knowledge. Searle makes this point by distinguishing two senses of "objective." In the *epistemic* sense, we may speak of *judgments* as objective or subjective – they are objective if there are "facts in the world that make them true or false [which] are independent of anybody's attitudes or feelings about them" (1995: 8). In the *ontological* sense, we may speak of entities being objective if their "mode of existence is independent of any perceiver or any mental state" (1995: 8). Social features of the world are ontologically subjective, since their existence always at some level depends on collective intentionality. But judgments about the social world – e.g. about the state of the economy, or the status of Sam's drivers' license – may nonetheless be epistemically objective, since their truth or falsehood is not just a matter of people's attitudes or feelings about them. Sam may refuse to believe that his drivers' license has been suspended, but that does not make the problem go away, and politicians may refuse to accept that we are in a recession without that having the least impact on the fact itself. This is possible quite simply because the collective intentions on which these facts depend are not our own attitudes or feelings about those very facts. The facts about the economy, for example, depend on our collective acceptance of certain rules regarding what counts as money, what counts as buying and selling stock, etc. – but they do not depend upon our collective beliefs *about the state of the economy* (we may all be wrong in thinking that the economy is doing just fine – or we may even fail to have any general opinions about the economy at all, each just focusing on our own financial transactions).

Social entities as independent of the will

Social facts, as Durkheim observed, have "coercive power, by virtue of which they impose themselves" on us, independent of our will (1994 [1938]: 433), and it was this which, on his view, marked them out as "thing-like" entities distinct from mere products of our own imagination or fantasy. There are a number of different senses in which social entities may be said to be "coercive" of us. The first, weakest, sense is that they exist independently of our individual wills, and (in Durkheim's phrase) can't be modified "by a simple effort of the will" (1994 [1938]: 439). In stronger senses, social entities may be said to be coercive of us insofar as they may shape what it is that we will or desire (e.g. encouraging girls to desire motherhood over career success), or provide resistance against or punishment for pursuing our desires. The impact on our wills isn't always negative: social entities also *enable* us to form certain intentions or desires we would not otherwise have had, such as the desire to qualify for the Olympics, or to receive a Ph.D., but this again suggests their *independence* from our wills.

While these are all interesting and important issues for the philosophy of society, given space constraints here I will focus simply on the weakest sense, since it is the fact that social facts, like natural facts (e.g. that water freezes at 0 degrees Celsius) cannot be modified by a simple effort of the will that (according to Durkheim 1994 [1938]) gives them their "thing-like" status.

Once we see that social entities depend on *collective* intentionality, it is easy to see why they typically cannot be modified by any *individual's* effort of the will. For whatever account of collective intentionality we adopt, it is clear that the *collective* intentions on which our social practices, institutions, and the like depend may persist in the absence of any individual's intentional states. Yet it also seems that social entities often can't be modified by a simple collective "effort of the will." A society may come to collectively lament the high proportion of its population in jail or the wretched state of the economy, without the public will alone being able to make the offending facts go away. (This of course is not to deny that certain forms of collective action could help change these facts.)

Here again a variety of avenues for explanation are available, according to the differences in social entities involved. Social facts may not be altered by a simple collective effort of the will if they are facts that are constructed by accepting universal or existential constitutive rules – instead, either the rules themselves must be changed, or the conditions that, when combined with the rules, yield the social facts, must be changed. So if there is a constitutive rule to the effect that those convicted of three crimes count as sentenced to life in prison, a simple effort of the collective will cannot change the prison population – instead, either the relevant constitutive rule must be changed, or the underlying conditions (about how many people are multiple offenders) must be changed.

It is even more difficult to willfully alter social facts that are generated as byproducts of constructed social entities. Thus, e.g., the state of the economy is a byproduct of a great multitude of intentionally conducted transactions – but while any of those trans-actions might be modified by willful efforts of the parties involved, the overall state of the economy is not responsive to individual or collective desires *about it* at all, since it is independent of these. It can, at best, be modified very indirectly, by our undertaking many other individual transactions (e.g. consumers spending, the Federal Reserve lowering interest rates) that we hope will help.

The social world is puzzling since it seems to be at once a human creation, and something that may be unknown to us, and even coercive of us. The way to unravel these puzzles, as we have seen, lies in understanding the different ways in which social entities may be created, and the different senses in which they may depend on human intentionality. A proper ontology of the social world may thus help us see how, despite their dependence on human intentionality, social objects may show up to us as genuine, discoverable, and even recalcitrant parts of our world.

Acknowledgements

Thanks to Åsa Andersson and Andrew McGonigal for helpful comments on an earlier draft.

References

Andersson, Åsa (2007) "Power and Social Ontology," Ph.D. dissertation, University of Lund, Sweden.

Berger, Peter L. and Luckmann, Thomas (1966) *The Construction of Social Reality*, New York: Anchor–Doubleday.

Bratman, Michael (1993) "Shared Intention," *Ethics* 104: 97–113.

Collin, Finn (1997) *Social Reality*, London: Routledge.

Devitt, Michael (1991) *Realism and Truth*, Oxford: Blackwell.

Durkheim, Emile (1994 [1938]) "Social Facts," reprinted in Michael Martin and Lee C. McIntyre (eds), *Readings in the Philosophy of Social Science*, Cambridge, MA: MIT Press, pp. 433–40; excerpted from *The Rules of Sociological Method*, trans. Sarah A. Solovay and John H. Mueller; edited by George E. G. Catlin, New York: The Free Press, 1938.

Gilbert, Margaret (1989) *On Social Facts*, New York: Routledge.

Searle, John (1995) *The Construction of Social Reality*, New York: The Free Press.

Thomasson, Amie L. (2001) "Geographic Objects and the Science of Geography," *Topoi* 20, no. 2: 149–59.

—— (2003a) "Foundations for a Social Ontology," *Protosociology* 18–19: 269–90.

—— (2003b) "Realism and Human Kinds," *Philosophy and Phenomenological Research*, 67, no. 3 (November): 580–609.

Tuomela, Raimo (2003) "Collective Acceptance, Social Institutions, and Social Reality," *American Journal of Economics and Sociology* 62, no. 1: 123–65.

Further reading

For discussion of why mind-dependent social entities should nonetheless be considered "real" parts of our world, see my "Geographic Objects and the Science of Geography," *Topoi* 20, no. 2 (2001): 149–59; and "Foundations for a Social Ontology," *Protosociology* 18–19 (2003): 269–90. For a clear overview of the debates about collective intentionality, see Deborah Tollefsen, "Collective Intentionality," in James Fieser and Bradley Dowden (eds), *The Internet Encyclopedia of Philosophy* (2004) (available: http://www.iep.utm.

edu/c/coll-int.htm). For an account of deontic social powers (imposing enablements and requirements), see John Searle, *The Construction of Social Reality* (New York: The Free Press, 1995), 100ff. For arguments that we must broaden our understanding of social powers beyond mere deontic powers, see Åsa Andersson, "Power and Social Ontology" (Ph.D. dissertation) (University of Lund, Sweden, 2007), chapter 5.

52
THE MENTAL AND THE PHYSICAL
Louise Antony

Introduction

There are many different kinds of things in the natural world. For example, there are stars and planets, mountains and rivers, plants and animals. While all these things are different from each other in lots of interesting ways, they are also similar to each other in fundamental ways: they are all made (ultimately) out of the same kind of stuff, and they are all subject to certain basic forces. Physics, roughly, is the science of what all these things have in common. "The physical" is a term that signifies the domain of the science of physics. "Physicalism" is the doctrine that all concrete objects and phenomena lie within the domain of physics. These definitions are overly simple and somewhat tendentiousness, but they'll serve our purposes.

The doctrine of physicalism, so understood, must be compatible with the observation, recorded above, that there are differences as well as similarities among the things that exist. The claim that, e.g., mountains and plants are both physical things cannot mean that there are no important differences between mountains and plants. However, commitment to physicalism does require commitment to a certain view about how such differences arise. According to physicalism, the properties that distinguish physical objects of one kind from physical objects of another kind are all – somehow – due to differences in the arrangements and interactions of the fundamental physical elements that constitute things of each kind. The devil here is in the details: how, exactly, are the properties of large-scale objects and substances supposed to be "due to" the arrangements of their parts? There are at least two different models for such a relationship. (Again, I oversimplify.)

The first is *reduction*: it is exemplified by the relation between the macroscopic substance property WATER, and the micro-structural property H_2O. All and only water turns out to have this particular chemical makeup. But the relationship between the two properties is not merely correlative, it is *explanatory*. The fact that water is composed of two hydrogen atoms bonded to an oxygen atom in a particular way explains why the substance we recognize as water possesses the properties we observe it to possess: why it is liquid at room temperature, why it is odorless, why it is potable (and, indeed, necessary for life), why salt dissolves in it, and why heavy objects can float upon it. All in all, the property of BEING H_2O is an excellent candidate for telling us what it is *to be* water, for being the *essence* of water. The terms "water" and "H_2O," in that case, pick out not two separate properties, but one. Water has been "reduced to" H_2O.

The second relationship is *realization*. This is a relationship that holds, not between two properties at different levels of aggregation, but rather between properties at different levels of *abstraction*. Realization involves functional or structural properties, like ION or CELL, properties that capture abstract dimensions of similarity among things that may vary considerably in their composition. The more abstract property is said to be "higher-order" because it is the property of having some other property that fits certain specifications. A lower-order property that meets the specifications (or by extension, a thing that possesses such a lower-order property) is said to "realize" the higher-order property. Thus, ION can be defined as an atom or molecule that has a positive or negative charge as a result of losing or gaining a valence electron. Examples of its realizer properties are PEROXIDE (O_2^{2-}) and AMMONIUM (NH_4^+). Typically, a higher-order property has more than one distinct realizer property, or at least the potential to have more than one. In these cases, we say the higher-order property is *multiply realizable*.

So we can refine our definition of physicalism: physicalism is now the doctrine that every property of every concrete thing is either a fundamental physical property, reducible to a physical property, or realized in a physical property. Is physicalism, so understood, true? The doctrine seems overwhelmingly plausible in connection with inanimate, natural objects (try not to think about artifacts for the moment). We understand the molecular structures of many kinds of substance, and can explain how structures of these various sorts give rise to observable properties like color and texture, and to behavioral dispositions, like conductivity and solubility. Physicalism also seems plausible when we consider plants and simple animals. While the phenomenon of life was once a mystery from the physical standpoint, we now have a very detailed understanding of the way that cellular building blocks constitute plant and animal structures, and of how the molecular properties of cells enable them, and the organs they compose, to function. We can also explain, in physicalistic terms, the appearance, structure, and behavior of many complex animals: we understand the bio-physics of animal flight, and the molecular bases of sexual reproduction and biological inheritance. On the basis of past success like this, physicalism looks like a good bet.

However, there is one phenomenon – displayed most floridly, if not exclusively, by human beings – that threatens to spoil the physicalist picture. That phenomenon is mentality. There are two features of the mental that make it singular: *consciousness* and *intentionality*. In what follows, I'll survey the problems posed by these phenomena, as well as the available physicalist responses. None of these seems fully adequate. However, I contend, neither does any non-physicalist alternative. My conclusion, then, will be unsatisfying: we still do not know exactly how mentality fits into an otherwise physical world.

Consciousness: subjectivity and *qualia*

An individual who possesses mental states is not merely an object in the world; she is, additionally, the *subject* of experiences. There is (in the apt words of Thomas Nagel [1974: 219]) some "way it is like to be" a psychological being. A conscious subject has a *perspective* on the world, a *viewpoint*. Having a perspective is not simply a matter of having spatiotemporal location. All physical objects are located in space and time, but it's hardly the case that all physical objects have perspectives – the vast majority do not. Nor is having a perspective simply a matter of being some particular object rather than some other. Again, everything has an identity, but only subjects experience themselves *as existing*. But being some particular object and existing at some particular time and place seem to be the only "locational" or "individuative" things about an object that can be specified in the terms of physical description; if "having a perspective" cannot be constructed out of these, it's difficult to see how this property could be explained reductively.

Subjectivity gives rise to epistemological asymmetries – peculiar differences in the way things can be known. To begin with, there is the *first-person/third-person* asymmetry. As a subject, I can know the contents of my own mind directly, just by introspecting. I cannot, however, know anyone else's thoughts or feelings in this same, unmediated way, nor can they know mine. We must all infer each other's mental states from their facial expressions, their behavior (including, importantly, their verbal behavior), their circumstances. Any adequate physicalist treatment of the mind will have to explain how individuals have "privileged" epistemic access to their own thoughts.

There is a second, related, asymmetry between the way I know my own mind and the way I know things about the physical world, including things about my own body. René Descartes, in his *Meditations on First Philosophy* (1985 [1641]), made this vivid. He pointed out that I can coherently pretend that none of the physical objects in my external environment exist by imagining that all of the sensory experience that leads me to believe in them is being produced in me by an evil genius, bent on deceiving me about the character of my world. It is possible for me to imagine that this deception extends even to the existence of my own body; that while I seem to see my limbs, or to feel the intake of my breath, these sensations actually correspond to nothing at all. However, Descartes continued, there is one thing that I cannot coherently imagine being deceived about, and that is my own existence. In order for me to be the victim of any of these other deceptions, I must at least exist. Insofar, then, and as long as I am the subject of some mental state, my own existence is certain.

What follows from this? Descartes argued as follows: if I can be certain that I exist even while doubting that my body exists, then I am, in effect, conceiving of myself as existing independently of my body. But if a state of affairs is conceivable, then it is possible. Hence, it's possible for me to exist without my body. But if it's possible for one thing to exist without some other thing, then those two things must in fact be really distinct from each other, even if they both happen to exist in actuality. Hence, I – the subject of my mental states – must be actually distinct from my body. This position is known as *substance dualism*; I'll discuss its merits and limitations shortly.

A second thing that makes consciousness puzzling from a physicalist point of view is the fact that conscious experience possesses *qualitative character*. To be the subject of experiences is to have things *seem to be* some particular way or other. When conscious beings with the power of sight look at colored objects, they have experiences with very specific and definite characteristics. There is a distinctive way that red things look and a different, equally distinctive way that green things look. The same thing is true about experiences in other sensory modalities: the sound of a flute is different from the sound of a car engine, and so forth. Emotions, like anger and contentment, have distinctive qualitative characters, and so do episodes of pleasure and pain.

Now it might be thought that at least this aspect of consciousness can be explained reductively. After all, a great deal is now known about the biophysical and neurological processes that correlate with the kinds of experience I've mentioned. We know, for example, that the difference between seeing something as red and seeing it as green has to do with differential patterns of firings by specialized cells in the retinas of the eyes. Flutes produce different patterns of vibrations in the air than do car engines, differences to which the tympanic membrane in our ear is sensitive. Anger and contentment are correlated with different kinds of hormonal and somatic states; pain involves the activity of specialized nerve cells; and pleasure, the presence of specific chemicals in the brain. Although there are gaps in our understanding of all these processes, we can at least see how reductive explanations might go. Why not simply identify having an experience with being in a particular neurophysiological state?

The view suggested, the "identity theory," was advocated by U. T. Place (1956), Herbert Feigl (1958), J. J. C. Smart (1959) and others in the mid-twentieth century. These philosophers appealed to general methodological considerations in defense of the view. If qualitative states are regularly correlated with particular types of neuro-physiological states, then we must either identify them with the physical states or admit irreducibly mental states, states that would be inexplicably correlated with the physical states, and that would stand outside the reach of natural laws governing everything else in the world. Rather than admit such "nomological danglers," and the peculiar, special-purpose laws needed to describe their relationship to the physical states with which they were perfectly correlated, it would be more economical to identify qualitative states with brain states, just as we identified WATER with H_2O. Today, we could add that specific reductive accounts of sensory processes have even proven successful in explaining aspects of the formal structure of qualitative experience: why, for example, we experience red as being more similar to orange than to green, or why we hear tones separated by an octave as in unison rather than as in harmony.

Such identifications would, moreover, be explanatory: they'd explain why things that happen in and to our bodies affect our mental states, and also how our mental states can affect things in the physical world. Here we have an important consideration against Cartesian substance dualism: if mind and body are distinct substances, how is causal interaction possible between the two? This problem was familiar to Descartes; it was raised by his own correspondent, Princess Elizabeth of Bohemia (Kenny 1970). The problem was particularly acute if one maintained, as Descartes did, that bodies are mechanisms. Consider a case in which I hear a sound and turn toward it to see what it was. If the body is a mechanism, then presumably the sound's striking my eardrums was causally sufficient for the activation of a chain of nervous activity, which was in turn sufficient to cause the contractions of muscles that culminated in the turning of my body. If that's so, where in the causal chain was there room for an intervening mental event? If there were such an intervening event, how could it have made any causal difference, given the sufficiency of the preceding physical events? And if a mental event can make no causal difference, why think that it's even there?

Despite all the points in its favor, however, the identity theory still fails to address what is really puzzling about the qualitative character of experience. While the biophysics of color vision can explain why a ripe Beefsteak tomato looks *different* to me than does the grass on a well-tended golf course, it cannot explain why the physical process associated with the tomato experience is *reddish* while the grass experience is *greenish*. Why does the firing of C-fibers have a stabbing character, while the uptake of endorphins feels floaty? As eighteenth-century philosopher John Locke (1979 [1690]: Bk 2) put it, it's as if God first created all the physical processes, and then gratuitously added subjective, qualitative aspects to some of them, randomly attaching the reddish character to this one, or the stabbing character to that one.

The problem is not that we haven't discovered, or don't understand the physical processes correlated with particular qualia; it's that we don't understand why those particular correlations should hold. Worse yet, we seem unable even to conceive what an explanation of these correlations would look like, what sort of addition to the physicalist story would be satisfactory. There is, in the words of Joseph Levine, an "explanatory gap" between the physical and the qualitative (Levine 2001).

Thinking once more about knowledge provides another way of appreciating the radical contingency of the connection between the facts about our physical makeup, and the facts about our qualitative states. Frank Jackson (1982) proposed the following thought-experiment. Imagine a brilliant vision scientist, Mary, who is brought up in a completely black-and-white environment. (We can suppose that some expedient prevents her from seeing the colors on her own body.) Mary, we are to suppose, has learned *everything* there is to know about the physics, biology and psychology of color perception. She has also been instructed in common facts about color: the colors of various everyday objects, the emotional or poetic associations people have with color, the effects of various colors on various creatures (so if red really does excite bulls, Mary will be told this). Mary knows, in short, every physical fact there is to know about color. Now what will happen if Mary is allowed to leave her black-and-white environment? What if the first thing that Mary sees, upon her emergence is a red rose? Clearly, she will be surprised. "So *this* is what it's like to see red," she'll think. Mary has *learned something new*; she was unable to infer from what she already knew about color what it would be like to see red. But since Mary, by hypothesis, had known *all* the *physical* facts there are about color, it follows that what she now knows is not a physical fact.

Physicalist responses to this, what is now known as the "Mary Problem," have typically taken issue with the conclusion that Mary, in this situation, comes to know a new *fact*. Rather, they contend, she has come to know an old fact – that roses are red

– in a new way. To understand and evaluate this line of response, we need to look at the *realization* approach to mentality.

Functionalism

I argued earlier that the identity theory could not provide an account of the connection between particular kinds of brain states and the qualitative mental states with which they are correlated. But there's another problem with the identity theory. If we simply identify mental states with states of the human nervous system, then we rule out the possibility that a differently constituted creature could have a mind. We certainly seem to be able to make sense of such a possibility, as the robustness of the science fiction industry attests: our stories and movies overflow with thinking aliens and sensitive robots. However *unlikely* it is that we will ever encounter an android like *Star Trek*'s Data or a Kryptonian like Superman, such individuals are certainly *conceivable*. If so, then our concept of MIND is more like CELL than like WATER; minds are multiply realizable.

The fundamental idea here is that the relationship between mind and brain, or mind and body, is a matter of the *level of abstraction* at which we consider things, and it's an idea that can be credited to a group of philosophers and psychologists called *behaviorists*. These included the philosopher Gilbert Ryle (1949) (and later, W. V. Quine [1960]) and the psychologist B. F. Skinner (1953). Ryle argued that it would evince logical confusion either to say, as dualists did, that the mind is a distinct entity from the brain, or, as the identity theorists did, that the mind is identical to the brain. To make either claim would be to commit a *category* mistake – to improperly compare items belonging to different logical categories. Consider a university: it would be wrong to identify the university with the buildings, faculty and students that constitute it at any one time, but it would equally wrong to think that the university was therefore somehow an additional, separate entity, existing alongside all these other things.

Ryle's view, then, was that both dualists and identity theorists erred in treating mental states and events as if they were discrete elements in the causal chain of events leading from environmental circumstance to behavior: they were identical with neither particular physical events in such chains nor separate "ghostly" events with mysterious properties. Rather, our attribution of mental states, Ryle argued, signifies our apprehension of patterns of *behavior*. To say that someone was *hungry*, for example, is not to attribute to the individual some kind of causally efficacious psychic event or inner drive, triggered by a lack of food, and triggering, in turn, efforts to obtain some. Rather it is to evince confidence that the person, *if* presented with food, *would* accept and consume it. The "logic" of psychological attribution and explanation, therefore, is tacitly conditional in form. In principle, Ryle claimed, all talk of mental states could be eliminated in favor of claims about how people would behave were certain circumstances to obtain. On the empirical side, Skinner argued that the only legitimate subject for a science of psychology would be the patterns of contingency among physical stimuli, behavior (or "operants") and the observable consequences of that behavior.

Behaviorism, then, is less a theory of what the mind is, and more a theory of what the mind *isn't*; it is, for that reason, usually considered to be a form of *eliminativism* – a theory according to which all reference to minds and the mental could be eliminated without any loss to our understanding of the world. My point in bringing it up here, in the context of realization theories of mind, is to point out that it offered us a way of seeing how MIND could be a *functional* property, and thus a multiply realizable property. If all it is to have a mind is to display certain patterns of behavior, then there is no reason in principle why a creature made of very different stuff from us could not also be counted as having one. Behaviorists were on to something in holding that mentality could be analyzed and explained in terms of a functional relationship; they were wrong, however, in thinking that such an analysis could make do without any reference to mental states.

Consider the case of hunger. Ryle says that what it means to say that someone is hungry is, *inter alia*, to say that if he is offered food, he will eat it. But we can think of many cases in which it would be true to say that someone is hungry and yet the person does *not* eat food that is offered. A person could, for example, be deliberately fasting, for religious or political reasons. Or, a person could believe that the proffered food is poisoned ("ick – carbs!"). Or, he could be a stubborn philosophy student who just wants to prove behaviorism wrong. Whether a hungry person eats depends not only on the availability of food, but also on what *other mental states* he is in: on what else he wants, and on what he believes. Mental states turn out to be ineliminable – because independent – variables in the equation relating behavior to circumstance.

Taking this point to heart, philosophers David Lewis (1972) and David Armstrong (1981), proposed a different way of defining mental states in functional terms. According to their view, called *analytical functionalism*, one could specify mental states in non-mental terms by abstracting them from the mentalistic generalizations and explanations that abound in ordinary life. Back to hunger: it's a truism that a hungry person will be disposed to eat if offered food unless he believes that the food is poisoned, or unless he has a compelling desire to forego nourishment, or .... Abstracting, we can get a fragment of a *joint* definition of all the mental states mentioned: hunger, belief, and desire are those mental states related to each other in the complicated way specified in the truism. To get a complete definition, we would need to list all the truisms about mental states, and then abstract from all of them together. We would still be left, after such an operation, with an ontological commitment to mental states, contra Ryle. But in treating mental states as abstract functional states, we would be honoring at least Ryle's insight about the relation of mind to body.

A different form of functionalism was proposed by Hilary Putnam (1967). Putnam argued, at the dawn of the revolution in information technology, that there was a powerful analogy between human minds and *computers*. Due to the work of mathematician Alan Turing (1936–7), it was known that any computational device, as well as many other mechanical devices, could be characterized by what's called a *machine table* – an abstract and systematic specification of each of the internal states of the device in terms of the inputs to the device, the outputs from the device, and the relations of that state to other internal states. For example, here is Ned Block's machine table for a simple (and anachronistically inexpensive!) vending machine (Block 1978):

Inputs	State A	State B
Nickel	Shift to State B; emit nothing	Shift to State A; emit a Coke
Dime	Remain in State A; emit a Coke	Shift to State A; emit a Coke and a nickel

If we think of the inputs to the machine as stimuli and the outputs as behavior, we can see that the table's definition of the machine's internal states is quite analogous to the functionalist's proposal for defining mental states. We can even, if we like, think of the machine as having mental states: State A would be the state of WANTING A DIME, and State B the state of WANTING A NICKEL.

Computers are realizations of complex machine tables – programs, or software, in effect – in electronic circuitry, but their machine tables can, in principle, be realized in any kind of stuff whatsoever. Why not, then, in brain tissue? Why not think of the mind as a kind of computer, as "software" running on neurological "hardware"?

This suggestion of Putnam's neatly dovetailed with burgeoning research in artificial intelligence and with the infant science of cognitive psychology, which, inspired by Noam Chomsky's computational approach to human language (1965, 1975), sought computational models of a variety of cognitive and perceptual processes. According to this approach to the mind, we need more than the commonsense platitudes about mental states on which the analytical functionalists rely. We need to do empirical research to determine precisely what computations the mind is performing in the course of perceiving, thinking, and acting in the world. The form of functionalism inspired by the computer analogy is therefore called *scientific functionalism*.

But what does all this have to do with the Mary problem, with which this whole discussion began? Remember: the anti-physicalist believes that Mary comes to know a *nonphysical fact*, while the physicalist insists that she merely comes to know a physical fact *in a new way*. We are now in a position to say exactly what this proposal might mean. According to scientific functionalism, the nature of a mental state is given by a complex functional specification. Qualitative states, in general, will be very complex and finely detailed functional states. Let's call the mental state occupied by a normal observer looking at a red rose "SR" (for "seeing red"). Mary, while she is still in her black-and-white room, learns what this complex functional description is – that is, she learns a fact we can express this way: "to see red is to shift into functional state SR." Of course, learning is itself a mental state, so when Mary acquires knowledge of this fact – the fact that to see red is to be in state SR – she is occupying some other functional state, which we can call "K(SR)" ("Knowing the functional description of the mental state, 'seeing red'"). But crucially, the functional state K(SR) is *not* the same functional state as SR – to know a functional description is not at all the same thing as actually satisfying the functional description. Mary knew, in one way, what it is to see red before she left her room – she knew what would have to be true of her, or anyone else, to be experiencing red. When she left the room, she came to know "what it is to see red" in a different way – she came to satisfy the functional description.

Putnam argued that functionalism could exploit this distinction to explain the first-person/third-person asymmetry. It could be, first of all, that it's part of the functional profile of conscious states of mind that being in such a state causes one to say – to oneself, or perhaps right out loud – "I am in state such and such." Pain, for example, is a state such that one is apt to cry out or exclaim when one is in it. Nothing more is required to explain my "privileged access" to such states; my "access" is guaranteed by my simply being in the state. However, I obviously cannot get access to *your* mental states in this same way, since *I* cannot be in *your* functional states. (As Thomas Nagel once quipped, this is no more mysterious than the fact that *I* cannot get *your* haircuts.) For me to know what you are thinking or feeling, I have to learn *that* you are in some particular functional state. And as in Mary's case, this will put me in a very different functional state from the state of being in that functional state myself.

Functionalism, in my opinion, offers the physicalist her best hope of solving the problem of consciousness. But I must admit that there are, as Ned Block put it in his now-classic essay, "Troubles with Functionalism" (1978). Ironically, it turns out that functionalism's biggest selling point – its treatment of mental states as abstract – is also its greatest liability. As I've been at pains to emphasize, there are no in-principle limits to the kinds of physical system that could satisfy a functional description. But in that case, Block says, let's imagine that we arrange for all the citizens of China to cooperate in realizing the (enormously complicated) machine table that characterizes some particular conscious person. Would we want to say that the *nation of China* is (insofar as the good citizens keep up with their individual assignments) *conscious*? We can even imagine things organized so that the Chinese people's efforts together run a gigantic robot (now known affectionately as a "Block-head"), whose patterns of behavior, by design, will match precisely its human model's.

And now we come full circle. What the Block-head seems, intuitively, to be missing, is *subjectivity*. It's hard to believe that there is anything it is like to be such a thing, that just because the internal states of the Block-head bear a formal similarity to those of a conscious creature, the robot feels pain or sees red.

John Searle argues, in another classic essay (1980), that systems like the Block-head are missing something else as well – *intentionality*. And that brings us, finally, to the second property that makes mentality problematic for physicalism.

Intentionality

Many mental entities and events, like thoughts, seem to be *about* other, (typically extra-mental) things; they *represent* or *stand for* things beyond themselves. We tend to identify and individuate thoughts in terms of this representational or intentional content. This relation of one thing's being about another was termed "intentionality" by the German philosopher Franz Brentano (1973 [1874]). So central to the phenomenon of mentality did he regard intentionality that he called it "the mark of the mental" – the feature that distinguishes mental phenomena from non-mental ones. Today it is controversial whether all mental phenomena are intentional, but it's perfectly obvious that many are. And representation is a relation that does not seem otherwise found in nature. It's true that there are *indication* relations that hold among non-mental things: because fire reliably causes smoke, and because it's (pretty much) the only thing that does, the existence of smoke is a good indication that a fire does or did exist. But genuine representation differs importantly from indication.

Thoughts can represent things that do not, never did, and perhaps never could exist. It is easy to think about the Fountain of Youth, as, apparently Ponce de Leon spent a good deal of time doing; but nothing in nature could *indicate* it, since it is not and never has been there to be indicated. It's very handy to be able to form thoughts about things that don't exist. This ability allows us to desire, and subsequently to create or invent, things that otherwise would not exist. (It also allows us to search fruitlessly – *vide* poor de Leon, so perhaps it's a mixed blessing.)

The ability to think of things that don't exist is, in fact, a special case of a more general feature of intentionality that sets it apart from natural indication relations – what Jerry Fodor (1987) calls "robustness" and what Joseph Levine and I (Antony and Levine 1991) have called *separability*: Genuine representations can be caused to be tokened by many things other than those that constitute their contents, unlike natural indicators, which work because they can only occur as the causal consequences of the things they indicate. Separability makes memory possible, but it also makes possible *mistakes*.

Intentionality involves *normativity*, another anomaly from the physicalistic point of view. Some mental states – perceptual states and beliefs – represent things *as being a certain way*. Insofar as they do this, they are *normatively evaluable*. It makes sense to consider such questions as whether one's memory or mental image of a thing is accurate, and whether one's belief that such-and-such is the case, is true. In contrast, it makes no sense to ask whether smoke is an apt or accurate representation of fire. We can ask whether it's true that smoke really does indicate fire – but this is really a question about how probable it is that fire has occurred, given that there's smoke. Not only are some individual thoughts normatively evaluable, but whole sequences of thoughts are as well. Reasoning can be logical or illogical, cogent or haphazard. Our actions can be assessed in light of our beliefs and desires for their rationality. No other set of entities or sequence of states in nature appears to be subject to such normative assessment. (Arguably, the full range of phenomena we categorize as normative – ethical and aesthetic value as well as cognitive value – enter the world of nature only through or with mentality. But since these other forms of value raise metaphysical issues above and beyond those raised by mentality *per se*, I will not discuss them further.) Donald Davidson (1970) argued that this one fact made it impossible for mental states like beliefs and desires to be reductively explained in terms of physical states. We'll see.

The essential role of intentionality in our mental life provides another explanation of the failure of behaviorism. Human intentional behavior is not influenced directly by external circumstances; rather, everything is mediated by our *representation* of those circumstances. Oedipus's decision to marry his mother is inexplicable unless and until we realize that he thought of her *as* Jocasta, and not *as* his mother. The crucial stimulus was not Jocasta herself, but Oedipus's representation of her. This argues for taking representations seriously, as elements in the causal etiology of behavior. But how, given the strange properties representations display, can that be done?

Jerry Fodor was, along with Putnam, an early advocate of the computational model of mind. But Fodor took the computer metaphor further than Putnam did. He argued (Fodor 1975) that the computational models that were showing signs of success in psychology – Chomsky's theory of language acquisition, for example – involved computational processes defined over structured symbols. They presuppose, in other words, a computational language. If human thought is computation, then, human thought must be conducted in a medium of computation – a "language of thought." Mental representations, on this view, would be actual physical entities – presumably realized as patterns of neuronal firing – that would possess, like a public, spoken language, both syntax and semantics.

The syntactic properties of this "Mentalese" could explain two things: first, it answers the question that Cartesian dualists cannot, namely, how thoughts can cause actions. Beliefs and desires are, on this picture, different functional relations to the physically realized mental sentences; for a belief and desire to combine to produce action is for there to be a causal process involving the physical realizers of the representational contents of those mental states. The second thing the model can explain is the fact that thoughts can stand in rational relations to each other, and for that matter, to actions. The logical properties of propositions – the properties in virtue of which the propositions stand in logical relations to each other – can be encoded in the syntax of the sentences that express them. Computers are devices the causal operations of which are designed to be sensitive to the syntactic properties of the symbols they manipulate. The hypothesis, then, is that the mind is a naturally occurring computer, structured so as to perform operations that are sensitive to the syntactic properties of its "machine language," and hence to the logical properties of the propositions they express. I have argued (Antony 1989) that the language-of-thought hypothesis thus provides a fully adequate answer to Davidson's contention that the normativity of the mental cannot be explained in terms of physical processes.

Syntax, however, is one thing – what about semantics? This question brings us back to the argument of Searle's I alluded to in the previous section. Searle asks us to imagine a man, a monolingual speaker of English, who sits in a room and carries on a peculiar job. At various times he is passed a piece of paper on which Chinese characters are written. As he receives each message, he looks up the sequence of characters in a large manual. Next to each sequence is another sequence, which the man copies on to another slip of paper and passes back to someone waiting to receive it. Now as it turns out, each slip of paper contains a sensible message in Chinese, and the sequence the manual matches with each sequence is a sensible response. To a Chinese speaker looking at the situation from the outside, it appears that the man inside is carrying on a perfectly reasonable conversation; however the fact is that the man does not understand the slightest bit of these exchanges. He is simply manipulating what are to him meaningless symbols.

This, according to Searle, is all that a computer can do: manipulate meaningless symbols. Because the operations of the machine are sensitive only to the *formal* features of its computational language, the machine is necessarily blind to whatever *meaning* the symbols may have. Thinking, Searle concludes, cannot just be a computational process, and minds can not be just mechanisms. Intentionality, according to Searle, is a *biological* phenomenon, a causal power of the *brain*, just as digestion is a causal power of the stomach and intestines. This is not to say, Searle insists, that there could not be alien minds or even artificial minds. There could conceivably be minds made of something other than brains; it's just that whatever substance that is, it would have to replicate the causal powers of human brains, and not just their form.

Fodor, along with many other philosophers (Searle 1980), have found fault with Searle's argument. Fodor contends that Searle is confusing the claim that computers perform *formal operations* on symbols with the claim that they perform operations on *formal symbols*. Computationalism is committed to the former claim, but not to the latter. Actual computers operate with a purely formal language – the only "meanings" its symbols have are meanings that we, the designers and users – impute to them. The intentionality of such languages is therefore *derived* from human action and intention. But the meaningfulness of the symbols of Mentalese is hypothesized to be *original*, the result of some kind of systematic, natural connection between the representations and things in the world.

That leaves only the small matter of explaining what in the world such a systematic natural connection might be, and how in heaven's name it might be established. The project of figuring this all out is known as the "naturalization problem." I have space here only to outline the basic approaches.

Fodor's own approach (1987) is the causal covariance approach, following a proposal of Denis Stampe's (1977). I explained above the reasons why intentional representation cannot be simply identified with the natural indication relation. Nonetheless, Fodor believes that indication must be the raw material of genuine representation. What's needed, he argues, is a way of distinguishing, from among all the possible causes of a given type of representation, those causes that involve the *content* of the representation. So suppose that we have a mental representation of the form "horse," and suppose that tokenings of "horse" are caused by horses, but also by cows on dark nights. Both patterns of causation will be lawful, but there is, Fodor maintains, an asymmetry: the causal connection between cows-on-dark-nights and tokenings of "horse" is dependent on the causal connection between horses and tokenings of "horse." Intuitively, the idea is this. The only reason you think "horse" in response to a cow on a dark night, is that you think it's a *horse*. If "horse" stopped being causally connected to horses, it would also stop being causally connected to cows on dark nights. However, it could easily happen that the "horse"/cow-on-dark-night connection breaks without the connection between "horse" and horses being disturbed; this would be the case, for example, if you acquired night-vision goggles which you were careful to use in pastoral settings.

A second approach, the teleological approach, also tries to exploit asymmetries in patterns of causal relations, but the relata are different. Here the strategy is to look to conditions in either the phylogenetic (Millikan 1984; Dretske 1995) or ontogenetic (Dretske 1988) history of the organism under which its representational system developed. The idea is that the representation's *function* for the organism is what determines which of the various factors that causally prompt tokening of the representation count as the *content* of the representation. An example from Ruth Millikan illustrates. A frog, as we find it, has a system of tracking black dots in its visual field; once it locates such a dot, the frog snaps at it. It turns out that snapping at black dots has proved advantageous for the frog because the black dots are pretty much all nutritious flies. Since it is the black dot's being a fly that explains how the frog's representational system enhances the frog's fitness, we are warranted in treating the property FLY as the content of the frog's dot-tracking representation, rather than the property of being a BLACK DOT. In any case in which the frog tokens the representation in the absence of a fly (say, in the presence of a BB), the frog is counted as having made a mistake.

A third approach to naturalizing semantics looks to the functional profiles of the representational elements themselves. The intuition here is that what determines the representational content of a mental state is, first of all, its relation to sensory inputs and behavioral outputs, and second, its connections with other representational states. So what would give an internal state the representational content "horse," would be such things as the following: a propensity to be tokened in response to perceptual contact with horses, a propensity to cause such behavior as saying (assuming certain other mental states are in place) "there's a horse," and finally a propensity to cause the tokening of other representational states, like those with the content "animal" or perhaps "mammal." This functional profile is called the "conceptual role" of the symbol, and this approach to the naturalization problem is called, accordingly, "conceptual role semantics." Gilbert Harman (1982) and Ned Block (1986) have both defended versions of conceptual role semantics.

There are other proposals and many variations of the proposals I've described. All of these proposals harbor difficulties, which advocates of competing views have been effective at pointing out. And there are many philosophers who are quite convinced that no proposal for naturalizing intentional content could possibly work. One of these, ironically, is Hilary Putnam, who repudiated the computational model of mind only a decade after proposing it (Putnam 1987). Suffice it to say that no one has succeeded in demonstrating to the satisfaction of everyone else that intentionality can be reduced.

Where does this leave physicalism? As I warned the reader earlier, I have to be equivocal. The problems for the doctrine posed by the phenomenon of mentality are serious, and may be intractable. But it's important to remember that a refutation of physicalism is not the same thing as a positive account of mentality. Dualism has problems of its own, some of which I pointed out above. But here's its main problem: dualism explains nothing. We have no better idea of how subjectivity could attach to an immaterial substance than to a material one. As David Lewis pointed out, an immaterial thing is just another thing. Facts about nonphysical phenomena are still the kinds of facts you could "learn in school" – not at all what Mary needed more of in order to know what it's like to see red. Intentionality, it seems to me, becomes more mysterious, not less, if mental representations are not physically realized – all the non-mental representations we know of are physical: signs, pictures, words and so forth. When we say a physical symbol "stands for" something else, at least it can really *stand*. What can nonphysical symbols do?

Who knows?

References

Antony, L. (1989) "Anomalous Monism and the Problem of Explanatory Force," *Philosophical Review* 98 (April): 153–87.

Antony, L. and Levine, J. (1991) "The Nomic and the Robust," in B. M. Loewer and G. Rey (eds), *Meaning in Mind: Fodor and His Critics*, Oxford: Blackwell.

Armstrong, D. (1981) *The Nature of Mind*, Brisbane: University of Queensland Press.

Block, N. (1986) "Advertisement for a Semantics for Psychology," *Midwest Studies in Philosophy* 10: 615–78.

—— (1978) "Troubles with Functionalism," in Wade Savage (ed.), *Minnesota Studies in the Philosophy of Science*, vol. 9: *Perception and Cognition: Issues in the Foundations of Psychology*, Minneapolis: University of Minnesota Press, pp. 261–325.

Brentano, F. (1973 [1874]) *Psychology from an Empirical Standpoint*, New York: Humanities Press.

Chomsky, N. (1965) *Aspects of the Theory of Syntax*, Cambridge, MA: MIT Press.

—— (1975) *Reflections on Language*, New York: Pantheon.

Davidson, D. (1970) "Mental Events," in L. Foster and J. W. Swanson (eds), *Experience and Theory*, New York: Humanities Press, pp. 79–101.

Descartes, R. (1985 [1641]) *Meditations on First Philosophy*, in *The Philosophical Writings of Descartes*, vol. 2, edited, trans. J. Cottingham, R. Stoothoff, and D. Murdoch, Cambridge: Cambridge University Press, pp. 1–62.

Dretske, F. (1995) *Naturalizing the Mind*, Cambridge, MA: MIT Press.

—— (1988) *Explaining Behavior: Reasons in a World of Causes*, Cambridge, MA: MIT Press.

Feigl, H. (1958) "The Mental and the Physical," in H. Feigl, M. Scriven, and G. Maxwell (eds), *Minnesota Studies in the Philosophy of Science Series*, vol. 2: *Concepts, Theories and the Mind-Body Problem*, Minneapolis: University of Minnesota Press, pp. 370–497.

Fodor, J. (1975) *The Language of Thought*, Hassocks, UK: Harvester Press.

—— (1987) *Psychosemantics*, Cambridge, MA: MIT Press.

Harman, G. (1982) "Conceptual Role Semantics," *Notre Dame Journal of Formal Logic* 28: 242–56.

Jackson, F. (1982) "Epiphenomenal Qualia," *Philosophical Quarterly* 32: 127–36.

Kenny, A. (trans., ed.) (1970) *Philosophical Letters*, by René Descartes, Oxford: Clarendon Press.

Levine, J. (2001) *Purple Haze: The Puzzle of Consciousness*, Oxford: Oxford University Press.

Lewis, D. (1972) "Psychophysical and Theoretical Identifications," *Australasian Journal of Philosophy* 50: 249–58.

Locke, J. (1979 [1690]) *An Essay Concerning Human Understanding*, edited by P. Nidditch, Oxford: Oxford University Press.

Millikan, R. (1984) *Language, Thought, and Other Biological Categories*, Cambridge, MA: MIT Press.

Nagel, T. (1974) "What Is It Like To Be a Bat?" *The Philosophical Review* 83: 435–50.

Place, U. T. (1956) "Is Consciousness a Brain Process?" *British Journal of Psychology* 45: 243–55.

Putnam, H. (1967) "The Mental Life of Some Machines," in H.-N. Castaneda (ed.), *Intentionality, Minds, and Perceptions*, Detroit, MI: Wayne State University Press, 177–200.

—— (1987) "Computational Psychology and Interpretation Theory," in *Artificial Intelligence*, New York: St Martin's Press.

Quine, W. V. (1960) *Word and Object*, Cambridge, MA: MIT Press.

Ryle, G. (1949) *The Concept of Mind*, London: Hutcheson.

Searle, J. (1980) "Minds, Brains, and Programs" (with commentaries and author's replies), *Behavioral and Brain Sciences* 3: 417–57.

Skinner, B. F. (1953) *Science and Human Behavior*, New York: Macmillan.

Smart, J. J. C. (1959) "Sensations and Brain Processes," *The Philosophical Review* 68: 141–56.

Stampe, D. W. (1977) "Towards a Causal Theory of Linguistic Representation," *Midwest Studies in Philosophy* 2: 42–63.

Turing, A. R. (1936–7) "On Computable Numbers, with an Application to the *Entscheidungsproblem*," *Proceedings of the London Mathematical Society*, Series 2, 42: 230–65.

53

THE SELF

John Campbell

Historically, the voluminous literature on what the self is (in the analytic tradition) stems from two basic puzzle cases. The first is Locke's example of the prince and the cobbler. The second is Williams' idea that it might be possible to print off multiple versions of a single person. This article reviews positions on what the self is. I begin by separating positions on what the self is from those on a different subject: the most illuminating ways to draw distinctions between types of self-knowledge.

Ways of knowing vs. what the self is

Our knowledge of ourselves seems to be special in a number of ways. We usually take it that there is some special access we have to our own minds, for example, or to our knowledge of our own actions, or our own past. The notion of "the self" is sometimes used, not as a term standing for an object of a particular type, but in a way that has to do with one special type of knowledge or another. For example, in an influential paper the psychologist Ulric Neisser (Neisser 1988) distinguished between five types of self-knowledge. One type is provided by perception: ordinary vision, for example, does not tell you just about the things in your environment; it also tells you where you are with respect to them and whether you are moving or stationary. Neisser referred to this as knowledge of "the ecological self," the self triangulated back from perception of the environment. He contrasted the "ecological self" with the "interpersonal self," knowledge of which depends on affective or emotional perception; the "extended self," knowledge of which depends on memory and anticipation; the "private self," which depends on knowledge that our experiences are exclusively our own; and the "conceptual self," knowledge of which is based on social and broadly cultural knowledge.

It is a vivid literary figure to say there are different "selves" here. But not much weight should be put on the figure. The "self" is what one refers to when one uses the first person. Our ordinary use of the first person, "I," seems to be a referring use: when someone says, "I am *F*," there is something, the self, on whose being *F* or not being *F* the truth or falsity of the proposition depends. We ordinarily take it there is a single thing that has all the properties attributed to Neisser's various "selves"; there are not, ultimately, five different things here. If, for example, I say, "I, a Navajo, now walk towards you," I have combined the ecological and the cultural selves. But the thing walking is not something different from the Navajo. Neisser's distinctions between types of self-knowledge do not undermine the use of a single term to refer to the single individual that has self-knowledge in all those five ways.

Moreover, it has to be emphasized there is good reason for the importance theorists give the notion of the self. You use the idea in formulating your own plans. More generally, civilization, as currently practiced, seems to depend on the idea. Everything from the most rudimentary social relations through legal contracts and responsibilities to taxation and death duties seems to depend on our knowing what we are talking about when we say that Y at time t_2 is the same person as X at time t_1. Analysis of this idea of the self would therefore seem to be a fundamental topic. However, these notions of the "ecological self" and so on are not meant to take that kind of weight. They are mere reflections of distinctions between kinds of self-knowledge. And our interests might suggest many different, equally valid ways of distinguishing between types of self-knowledge.

Philosophers have sometimes suggested that one's knowledge of oneself is so special we have to give a quite unusual characterization of the self to explain the possibility of self-knowledge. For example, Dennett proposed we distinguish "person" and "self," and say each person has a self; or perhaps in some cases, more than one self (Dennett 1992). The "self" is, then, not a concrete object, but something else: a "center of gravity" of a narrative one constructs about oneself. Just as the center of gravity of Moby Dick is the narrator Ishmael, so "the self" is the center of gravity of the non-fictional, autobiographical narrative of a person. This line of thought leads to some difficulty in explaining just what a "self" is, if it is not the same thing as the person telling the story. Dennett's own view is that the self is a "fiction," or perhaps an "abstract object." The trouble with this is that whether fictional or autobiographical, narrative is representational, a kind of discourse. While it makes some intuitive sense to speak of "Ishmael" as the center of gravity of Moby Dick, we are talking about the referential devices used to identify the narrator. Similarly, the "center of gravity" of the stories one tells about one's own life is one's use of "I," a referential device. This use of "I" in turn refers to the non-fictional, concrete person telling the story. The various narratives people have about their own lives are characteristically fragmented. The stories a single person tells about their own life may be plural, being apparently disjoint, and interrupted, with many gaps in the record (Allbright 1994). But we characteristically take it that uses of "I" across the autobiographical narratives of a single person all refer to one and the same person. There is an overarching principle of plot construction for autobiographical narratives, however plural and disjoint. All these stories concern a single individual, referred to throughout by means of the first person. So typically, we insist on a certain overarching coherence of plot: that all these stories could relate to the career of a single concrete individual. We need the notion of the narrative, the discourse. We need the notion of the person, the concrete object whose discourse it is. We do not need any further notion of "the self." It is not obvious there is any metaphysically significant distinction to be drawn between self and person.

The first basic case: the prince and the cobbler

Usually, if you look round a room to see how many people are there, you count the human beings. Still, a lot of science fiction depends on the presumption that we can make sense of the idea that members of other biological species could be people, even if we're skeptical about whether any of the other species on earth are people. We acknowledge the possibility. So, you might think, a person is just a member of a suitable biological species, and for Y at time t_2 to be the same person as X at time t_1 is just for Y to be the same animal as X. This view is currently known by the title of "animalism" (see Snowdon 1995; Olson 1997). It is plainly a plausible view. The great majority of the literature on personal identity is based on reflection on a single example, Locke's case of the prince and the cobbler (Locke 1975). The exact construal of Locke's text is a subtle and interesting question. Here I am going to focus only on the most common and influential way of understanding the example. On this way of reading it, the example involves a morning when the body in the palace, a body that is clearly the prince's, wakes up with all the apparent memories of a humble cobbler, down to a drunken brawl in a tavern on the previous evening. This body exhibits no evident memory of the prince's life. Simultaneously, an irate figure awakens in the gutter. It is the body of the cobbler, but it has all the apparent memories of the prince's life. The natural description of the situation is that the prince and the cobbler have swapped bodies.

The first reason why Locke's example is important is that it seems to show animalism is mistaken. It is the same human being that wakes up in the palace as was there yesterday. But it's a different person. So sameness of animal and sameness of person cannot be the same. How then are we to explain what personal identity consists in?

Notice that the example is not an argument for dualism. It does not help to postulate nonphysical stuff with thoughts, memories and so on. For suppose there are nonphysical souls. Then the prince's soul and the cobbler's could swap memories. If people can swap bodies, they can swap souls too.

What does sameness of person come to? A first reaction to the story of the prince and the cobbler is that we should say something like the following:

- *The memory criterion*
  Y at time t_2 is the same person as X at time t_1 if and only if Y at t_2 remembers seeing and doing what X at t_1 saw and did.

What is it to remember something? Here is one shot at a definition:

- Y remembers a past experience if
  (a) Y seems to remember having an experience
  (b) Y did earlier have that experience
  (c) Y's apparent memory is causally dependent, in the right kind of way, on that past experience.

This already means there is a problem with the memory criterion. The criterion has to deliver a verdict as to whether Y at t_2 is the same person as X at t_1. Suppose Y at t_2 seems to remember meeting the governor. Suppose X at t_1 did then meet the governor. Does Y at t_2 remember doing that? Only if Y is the person who met the governor at t_1. Whether Y remembers depends on the question of identity. So we can't appeal to memory in explaining what it is for Y at t_2 to be identical to X at t_1.

Sydney Shoemaker proposed that what we need, to address this problem, is a notion of "quasi-memory." The idea of quasi-memory is just like the idea of ordinary memory except that it misses out the condition that the person doing the remembering has to be the same as the person who had the original experience. So we could define it like this:

- *Quasi-memory* – Y quasi-remembers a past experience if
  (a) Y seems to remember having an experience
  (b) Someone did earlier have that experience
  (c) Y's apparent memory is causally dependent, in the right kind of way, on that past experience.

This is Derek Parfit's (1971, 1984) way of explaining Shoemaker's notion of quasi-memory; I use this formulation because it is so easy to see the intended relation between this notion and the ordinary notion of memory. We might now try explaining personal identity in terms of quasi-memory. But the immediate trouble is that merely having a quasi-memory that derives from an experience of X's is by no means sufficient for identity with X.

Suppose it's the year 3000. The current practice of bringing back holiday photos has all but vanished. It has been replaced by a more vivid way of letting people know about your trip. Everyone these days has a slot machined in their head while they are still young. I do not have the technical vocabulary to explain exactly how it all works, but here is the upshot. Suppose I come back from my visit to the Taj Mahal and want to explain to you what it was like. Rather than showing you a photo and saying how that doesn't really give a proper sense of its size, I can do the following. I extract from my head a "brain slide" that holds my memory-impression of the Taj Mahal. And I drop the slide into the slot in your head. Now you have an impression of the past scene that couldn't be discriminated from my impression of the scene. You can't be said to remember that evening, because you weren't there. But you have something that is quite like a memory of the scene. It does not meet the above definition of "memory," but it does meet the definition of "quasi-memory." It is a quasi-memory of the scene. But though you now can be said to quasi-remember my trip to the Taj Mahal, you can't be said to be identical to the person who saw it that moonlit night.

If we bear in the mind the case of the prince and the cobbler, though, there is a natural way to pursue the definition. Suppose that having dropped one slide into your brain, I get a bit carried away. I drop into your head slides from the entire vacation. Laughing maniacally, I don't stop there. Soon I am having to remove areas of your brain that hold your memories to make way for the quasi-memories. And I keep them pouring in, until my body isn't holding any memory traces at all. Plainly, this is an alarming scenario, and not just because of all these holiday snaps. After a bit there is something radically different about the process here. I am no longer merely passing you quasi-memories. I have invaded your body, leaving my own, and I am now using your body as a host. You have been destroyed in the process, you no longer exist. This suggests that we might say

- *Quasi-memory criterion*
  Y at t_2 is the same person as X at t_1 if and only if the overwhelming majority of Y at t_2's quasi-memories derive from what X at t_1 saw and did.

This is Sydney Shoemaker's analysis of personal identity (Shoemaker 1970). You can see why this seems plausible. The notion of "overwhelming majority" is not exact, but in that it seems to match our ordinary notion of personal identity. It is not easy to say at exactly which point in the above process I have destroyed you and taken over your body. But that the transition happens seems like the natural thing to say. The case is after all just a variant of Locke's case of the prince and the cobbler. (For an excellent further review of the issues in this section and the next, see Noonan [2003].)

The second basic case: printing off

Still, the idea that persons are simply members of a suitable animal species is not simply finished off by these considerations. In Locke's case, there is just one later version of the prince. Williams (1956–7) pointed out that there seems to be no reason why we couldn't have "printing-off" of people. We could have many descendants of an original self, all with an equally good title to being identical to the original. Suppose we take the case in which one person, Charles, turns up in the twenty-first century with what are, so far as we can tell, quasi-memories relating to the life of Guy Fawkes. We acknowledge that he is not mad, that these memory-impressions do indeed causally derive from the life of Guy Fawkes. We say that Guy Fawkes has been reincarnated. But it could now happen that Charles' brother Robert also shows up with a similarly persuasive collection of quasi-memories, all also deriving from the life of Fawkes. There has been printing-off; he has been reincarnated twice. Williams' suggestion seemed to be that to avoid this kind of puzzle, we should stick with the conception of the identity of the self as equivalent to sameness of the body. The trouble is that "printing-off" of bodies also seems possible. Consider fission, where one person divides into two, like an amoeba. The two successors just as distinct from one another as are Charles and Robert. Suppose we call them Lefty and Righty. Lefty and Righty may each be so related to the original that (a) had Righty not existed, we would have been happy to say that there was only one person in existence all the way through; and (b) had Lefty not existed, we would have been happy to say there was only one person in existence all the way through.

When we have fission, does the original person continue to exist after the fission? On the face of it the answer is no, because (a) there is no reason to say that the original is identical to Lefty rather than Righty, or to Righty rather than Lefty; and (b) we can't say that the original is both Lefty and Righty, because the original is only one person and Lefty and Righty are two different people. One thing can't be identical to two different things. Derek Parfit famously argued that nonetheless, what happens in fission is just as good as ordinary survival, from the point of view of the original person (Parfit 1970, 1984).

For a proponent of the memory criterion, in ordinary survival, what the continued existence of the original person comes to is the existence of memories and other psychological states causally connected to the condition of the original person. In fission, there is a plethora of future psychological states causally linked to the psychological states of the original person. How can this burgeoning be a failure to survive? Yet as we just saw, there is, after fissioning, no one around who can be said to be identical to the original person. So survival is one thing, and the existence of anything identical to the original person is another. Survival, not identity, is what matters.

I began by saying that the notion of the identity of the self seems to be basic to civilization. Certainly survival is something we care about. But what is it to survive? On our present analysis, what we care about in survival is the prolongation of a particular series of quasi-memories. But if we could have the propagation of a series of quasi-memories without there being a single continuing self, wouldn't that be enough to have all that one cares about in survival? That is exactly what happens in a case of fission. After fission there is no-one around who is identical to the original person. But the stream of quasi-memories is propagating abundantly into the future. On the face of it, on this analysis, fission ought to be preferable to ordinary survival.

There is a problem with this line of thought. The problem is that we do not care only about the propagation of quasi-memories. We care about their truth. The question of truth or falsity is not a matter of indifference for quasi-memories. And for many quasi-memories, there is a self-directed aspect to their content. When I remember scenes from my earlier life, I remember them as involving me. As Paul McCartney put it, "Well that was me, Royal Iris, on the River Mersey beatin' with the band, that was me." Suppose, however, that Sir Paul were to undergo fission. The two fission products, Sir Paul 1 and Sir Paul 2, would each have quasi-memories of that earlier life. But would either of them have the right to say, "That was me"? Evidently not. The whole point of a fission case, as we have explained them so far, is that we have what matters in survival without identity. But if we do not have identity, then neither product has the right to say "that was me." For it to be me that did that, I have to be identical to the person who did it.

The concern to survive may seem so primal that this kind of consideration is neither here nor there. I once read, as an example of how strong is the will to survive, of a soldier who had been burned alive in a tank. His skeleton was found with its hands on the exit port, gripping the sides and trying to force his body through. In this kind of case, you might think that concerns with what memories or quasi-memories might be around after the event are not truly central.

Nonetheless, a concern with the narrative of our life is of basic concern to most of us, even if it is not always explicitly to the front of our minds. One sharp way to bring this out is to consider what goes on with people who suffer some arbitrary calamity, such as the amputation of a limb after a car crash. A characteristic remark that people make in such a case is, "Why me? This doesn't make any sense." This kind of case brings out the demand for a kind of narrative sense that often goes unexpressed because ordinarily the demand is reasonably well met. Very often we do manage to work with narratives of our lives that do make reasonable sense. But that is always open to sharp challenge.

It seems arguable that much of the importance we assign to personal identity is correlative with the importance of narrative as a way of making sense of all that is going on. The important point to grasp here is that this does not mean that the availability of narrative constitutes the sameness of the self. Suppose we consider again Dennett's proposal that there is no more to the self than the construction of a narrative: the self is a "center of narrative gravity." Now if that is how we think about it, then the two fission products should be able to construct narratives going all the way back to the original self. We have here two long narratives, and thus just two selves, each the "center of gravity" of their narrative. But in fact that is not how we think of it. Before the fission there was only one person there, not two. After the fission, neither product is identical to the original. So neither has the right to say, "that was me." This means that both have to distance themselves from their quasi-memories. Once they understand the situation, they will realize that their quasi-memories are indeed reliable guides to what happened, but not to who it happened to or who was doing it. Their relation to their quasi-memories will thus be very different from our ordinary relation to our autobiographical memories, which typically constitute the narrative of a single self. The construction of our memory narratives demands, rather than constitutes, the sameness of the self.

The first person

Discussion of the self is framed by the idea that whatever else it is, the self is what our uses of the first person refer to. When Sally says, "I am in pain," the self is the referent of her use of the term "I." However, a number of philosophers have argued that uses of the first person do not refer to anything at all (see, e.g. Anscombe 1975; Hume 1973). If that is right, you cannot pursue philosophical problems about the self by providing an account of the reference of "I," for it has no reference. Rather, you can only characterize the various ways the first person is used, the kinds of knowledge it figures in expressing, links between the first person and action, and so on.

The idea that the first person does not refer seems absurd on first encounter. Statements using "I" are true or false. How could there be such a thing as the truth or falsity of the statement "I am in pain," if that use of "I" did not refer? And anyhow, when a first-person statement is made, there is always a concrete object around, the human being, which is a candidate, anyway, for referent of the term.

The issues here are more far-reaching than that superficial reaction suggests, however. We can bring this out by contrasting the way the first person works with the way in which a perceptual demonstrative term like "that tree" works. A perceptual demonstrative is a term like "that tree," used to refer to a currently perceived tree, on the basis of that perception of it. So suppose someone says to you, "that tree has been scorched by a fire." How would you go about establishing whether this is true or false? The most basic thing you need to know is which tree is in question. Without that, you cannot really begin. And what provides you with that knowledge of which tree is in question is your perception of the tree.

Consider now your own use of the first person. Suppose, for example, that you say, "I am tired and sleepy." How do you know that this is true? If we employ the model of a perceptual demonstrative, we should say that the first thing you have to establish is which person is being talked about. How do you know which person that use of "I" refers to? On the model of the perceptual demonstrative, perception, or something like it, should provide you with your knowledge of which thing is in question. The trouble is now to understand how to apply that parallel.

The key point here, made most forcibly by Hume and Anscombe, is that there is no way of applying the parallel. The first point is that remarks like, "I am tired and sleepy," self-ascriptions of psychological states, are typically not made on the basis of observation of oneself. It can happen that you catch sight of your exhausted face in a mirror and say, "I am tired and sleepy," but that is a somewhat unusual case. Ordinarily, you do not need to observe yourself at all to know that you are tired and sleepy. So it does not seem that your knowledge of which person you are talking about is provided by, for example, visual observation of yourself. But, you might argue, there is an "inner analogue" of perception of external objects. In ordinary introspection, you do not just establish what psychological properties are around and about, you also have inner perception of the self, the object that has those properties. This is exactly the idea that Hume and Anscombe challenge so persuasively. In introspection, as Hume put it, "I always stumble on some particular perception or other, of heat or cold, light or shade, love or hatred, pain or pleasure. I never can catch myself at any time without a perception, and never can observe any thing but the perception" (*Treatise*, Bk 1, pt 4, §6). Or here is Anscombe:

> At first, it seems as if what "I" stands for ought to be the clearest and certainest thing – what anyone thinking of his own thinking and his own awareness of anything is most evidently aware of. It is most certain because, as Augustine said, it is involved in the knowledge of all mental acts or states by the one who has them. They could not be doubted. But the I, the "mind," the "self," was their subject, not their object, and looking for it as an object resulted, some people thought, in total failure. It was not to be found. It was rather as it were an area of darkness out of which light shone on everything else. So some racked their brains over what this invisible subject and the "thinking of it" could be; others thought there was no such thing, there were just all the objects, and hence that "I," rather, was the name of the whole collection of perceptions. But that hardly fitted its grammar, and anyway – a problem which utterly stumped Hume – by what was I made into a unity? Others in effect treat selves as postulated objects for "I" to be names of in different people's mouths. Yet others denied that the self was invisible, and claimed that there is a unique feeling of oneself which is indescribable but very, very important, especially in psychology, in clinical psychology, and psychiatry. (Anscombe 1975)

The basic point here is that nothing stands to the use we actually make of the first person as perception of the tree stands to the use that we make of the term, "that tree." Our use of the first person does not seem to be grounded in knowledge of the reference of the term. This point needs much more discussion. But if it is correct, there seems no reason to suppose there is any such thing as the reference of the first person. Perhaps there is only the use. If that is the case, then we could still enquire into the use that we make of the first person: how it figures in our ascriptions of psychological states, moral responsibility, our plans and projects, the workings of the law, and so on. That could still be an illuminating enquiry. But there would be no such thing as an enquiry into the nature of the self, for there is no such thing.

References

Allbright, Daniel (1994) "Literary and Psychological Models of the Self," in Ulric Neisser and Robin Fivush (eds), *The Remembering Self*, Cambridge: Cambridge University Press.

Anscombe, G. E. M. (1975) "The First Person," in Samuel Guttenplan (ed.), *Mind and Language: Wolfson College Lectures 1974*, Oxford: Oxford University Press, pp. 45–65.

Dennett, Daniel (1992) "The Self as a Center of Narrative Gravity," in F. Kessel, P. Cole, and D. Johnson (eds) *Self and Consciousness: Multiple Perspectives*, Hillsdale, NJ: Erlbaum, pp. 103–115.

Hume, David (1973) *A Treatise of Human Nature*, 2nd edn, edited by L. A. Selby-Bigge and P. H. Nidditch, Oxford: Oxford University Press.

Locke, John (1975) *An Essay Concerning Human Understanding*, edited by P. H. Nidditch, Oxford: Oxford University Press.

Neisser, Ulric (1988) "Five Kinds of Self-Knowledge," *Philosophical Psychology* 1: 35–59.

Olson, Eric T. (1997) *The Human Animal: Personal Identity Without Psychology*, Oxford: Oxford University Press.

Noonan, Harold (2003) *Personal Identity*, London: Routledge & Kegan Paul.

Parfit, Derek (1971) "Personal Identity," *Philosophical Review* 80 (1971), 3–27; reprinted in Perry, John (ed.) *Personal Identity*, Berkeley: University of California Press, 1975.

—— (1984) *Reasons and Persons*, Oxford: Oxford University Press.

Shoemaker, Sydney (1970) "Persons and Their Pasts," *American Philosophical Quarterly* 7: 269–85.

Snowdon, Paul (1995) "Persons, Animals, and Bodies," in José Bermúdez, A. J. Marcel, and Naomi Eilan (eds) *The Body and the Self*, Cambridge, MA: MIT Press, pp. 71–86.

Williams, Bernard (1956–7) "Personal Identity and Individuation," *Proceedings of the Aristotelian Society* 57: 229–52.

A SHORT GLOSSARY OF METAPHYSICS

Peter Simons
with additional entries by Ross P. Cameron

Note: Many of the words in this glossary have everyday meanings which are different from these. We give only the more specialized philosophical meanings.

Johnsonian health warning: Like all glossaries and dictionaries, not infallible and not complete, but an honest attempt to capture the senses of principal usages and occasionally to recommend some over others.

abstract   Can mean one of several things when said of an object. (1) Existing outside space and time and lacking causal powers: said e.g. of numbers, universals, sets, types, etc. (2) Unable to exist alone (synonym: moment). (Used in this sense by Husserl, Williams, Campbell.) (3) Discernible or recognizable only through a process of abstraction. (The object abstracted is called the *abstractum*, any object abstracted from is called a *concretum*.)

abstraction   A real or logical process revealing or on some accounts creating an abstract object (in one or another sense of "abstract"). (1) In empiricism, a process of discerning something by directing attention on certain features and ignoring others. (2) Introduction of a singular term for an object via an equivalence relation; e.g. the weight of an object is given by considering objects which are or are not as heavy as it: its weight is the abstractum given by the principle of weight abstraction: the weight of A = the weight of B if and only if A is as heavy as B. Here A and B are the *concreta*; *being as heavy as* is the equivalence relation; and the weights are the *abstracta*, or products of abstraction. (3) Any of several logical and mathematical operations introducing a new singular term, such as set abstraction: "$\{x: x$ is a dog$\}$" is a singular term for the set of all dogs using the predicate "is a dog"; also lambda abstraction, e.g. "$\lambda x(x^2 + 5x - 3)$" names a certain numerical function.

accident   (1) Contrast with essence: something incidental to a thing: e.g. it is accidental that a dentist is musical but not accidental that a tree has leaves. A thing may exist with or without its accidents, e.g. a dog may or may not be black-coated, but it is not accidental that it is vertebrate (has a backbone). (2) An attribute instance or trope, usually a property, e.g. the individual redness of an individual snooker ball, by contrast with the exactly similar redness of another such ball.

adicity Said of an attribute: the number of places it has. A property has one place, so is monadic (e.g. being square); a relation has two or more places, so is dyadic (e.g. being larger than); there are also triadic (giving), tetradic, etc. Occasional synonym is "arity."

anti-realism Any view opposed to realism of a certain kind and concerning whether or not certain items (Xs) exist or exist independently of mind and language. Comes in various kinds, according to what it is about, e.g. anti-realism about numbers, values, the future, universals, God, the world, etc. (1) Strong anti-realism about Xs, opposed to weak realism about Xs, states that there are no Xs (at all). (2) Weak anti-realism about Xs, opposed to strong realism about Xs, states that Xs exist but depend on mind or language to do so. (3) In Michael Dummett's philosophy, anti-realism about Xs is the view that certain statements about Xs are verification-transcendent, that is, cannot be established to be true or false by humanly accessible procedure. Dummett claims this for statements about the open future, about unmanifested dispositions, and about certain infinite collections. Dummett claims that verification-transcendence means there is no "fact of the matter" about the Xs in this respect, so it is neither true nor false to make such statements about them.

artefact (also **artifact**) Any object made intentionally by design or plan, e.g. spears, pots, houses, spacecraft. Not all artefacts are human, e.g. beavers build dams; elephants paint; and octopi build gardens. But usually the term is chauvinistically confined to hominid artefacts. According to theists the natural universe is a divine artefact. Often contrasted with "natural" objects. Because e.g. birds' nests are both natural and artificial, not a good contrast.

A-theory A view about time according to which there is real passage of time, so that the difference between past, present and future is ontologically significant. Often the present or present objects are taken as privileged. Often connected with the semantic theory that what is true now is what is true *simpliciter*, while what was or will be true is no longer or is not yet true *simpliciter*. Presentism, growing block, and the moving spotlight are common versions of the A-theory.

atom (1) In Greek metaphysics, a small thing indivisible (*a-tomos*) by physical means, the kinds and relationships which explain the behaviour of larger things. (2) In mereology, an object without any proper parts (like a Euclidean point). In this sense, also called a *simple*. (3) In chemistry, the smallest unit of chemical combination (not atomic in sense [1] or [2]).

attribute In abstraction: a property or a relation. Also attributively, an attribute of a thing is a property that it has or a relation that it stands in to another thing, e.g. Queen Elizabeth has the attributes of being female and of being married to Prince Philip.

being (1) In most metaphysics: the fundamental state of anything distinguishing it from nothing or non-being. Sometimes used more widely than "exist," which is reserved for concrete things. This wider use is deprecated here: "being" is used as synonymous with "existence." (2) Sometimes used in contrast to "becoming," to stress permanence, e.g. Platonic forms are said to be, material things to become.

boundary   A limit or extremity of a concrete object which has fewer dimensions than it does, e.g. bodies have surfaces (two dimensions), surfaces may be bounded by lines (one dimension) and lines bounded by points (zero dimensions). In occurrents, temporal boundaries have three dimensions (zero temporal thickness). Sometimes also used for internal boundaries, e.g. the equatorial plane of the Earth, which is the boundary between the northern and southern hemispheres.

B-theory   As opposed to the A-theory; the view that there is no real passage of time, and that the difference between past, present and future is not ontological.

bundle theory   A theory according to which a concrete individual or substance is constituted by either a collection of universal attributes (universalist bundle theory) or a collection of tropes (particularist bundle theory), without need of a substratum. Universalist bundle theory tends to run afoul of the problem of indiscernibles; particularist bundle theory may run into infinite regresses or have difficulty explaining why only one trope of each kind occurs in a bundle.

Cambridge change   Term of art devised by Peter Geach, name due to the popularity of the idea among Cambridge philosophers in the early twentieth century. An object "undergoes" a Cambridge change whenever some proposition about it changes its truth-value. Some Cambridge changes are real changes, e.g. when a leaf changes colour, but others are not. Some are relational changes, others are not even that. For example, the philosophically artificial proposition "Julius Caesar is such that Arsenal are this season's FA Cup winners" changes its truth-value whenever a season starts in which Arsenal newly loses or newly gains the cup, so Caesar "undergoes" these changes long after his death. Other Cambridge changes of this kind are quite sensible, e.g. a historical figure can "become" more or less popular, admired, etc., after death. Geach stresses that despite its artificiality, Cambridge change is the only exact notion of change we have. That is probably wrong but not obvious.

category   From Greek *kategoria*, predicate. (1) Most general class or kind of being, correlatively, the corresponding concept or word. (2) In Aristotle, one of the most general classes of being, related to ways in which things are predicated of individuals. (3) In Kant, pure concept of the understanding, under which phenomena are brought, and related to the formal properties of judgments. Every object of thought is characterized by four categories, one from each kind of three.

change   A transition of some object from one state to a qualitatively or quantitatively dissimilar state. For example, a leaf changes colour in autumn, a ball changes shape when it hits a solid obstacle. Aristotle, whose analysis has not been surpassed, analyses change into three components: the bearer (subject or substratum of change), the original state (*terminus a quo*) and the final state (*terminus ad quem*). Here they are: leaf, green, red; or ball, spherical, ellipsoidal. On this account a thing does not change when it comes into existence or ceases to exist, because it is not there both before and after. But such so-called substantial changes are often regarded as changes in something else, e.g. the matter of the object, or the system of objects. See also Cambridge change, relational change.

class (1) Vague term used for both collections and sets. Often a complete collection of things having something in common, e.g. (all) dogs, (all) terriers, (all) numbers. (2) In set theory, an abstract entity like a set but which is too "large" to be a set, i.e. to be an element of something else. Sometimes called a "proper class" or (Quine) "ultimate class," when classes are taken to comprise both sets and proper classes.

collection Several things, as distinct from an individual. Collections come in many sorts: some are given merely by the existence of their members (e.g. the kings and queens of England): these are pluralities. Others require a special relationship to bind them into a collection, e.g. an orchestra, which requires its members to play music together. Some collections require all their members to co-exist at a time, others do not. Sets are not collections but abstract individuals. See also multiplicity.

concrete Of an object: not abstract. (1) Opposed to abstract (1): existing in space and time, part of the spatiotemporal order. (2) Opposed to abstract (2): able to exist alone, a substance. (3) Opposed to abstract (3): of the directly given basis of abstraction, the *concreta*.

contingent (1) Of a proposition, possibly true and possibly false. (2) As above, but in fact true. (3) Of a thing or state of affairs: existent but such that it might not have existed (i.e. such that "contingent" in sense [2] applies to the proposition that it exists).

continuant Term invented by W. E. Johnson. A thing existing in time but with no temporal parts, i.e. such that at every time it exists it is present as a whole. A continuant may thus change (the same thing may have different properties and parts at different times). Contrast occurrent.

counterpart In the modal metaphysics of David Lewis, the counterpart in world W_2 of an entity A that exists in world W_1 is that entity B which exists in W_2 and is most like A, where because individuals are world-bound, necessarily $A \neq B$. When we say things like "Abraham Lincoln might not have been assassinated" then according to Lewis this is made true by there being a Lincoln-counterpart in some other world than the actual one who is not assassinated. Lewis's view was anticipated in its essentials by Leibniz. Contrast transworld identity.

dependence The relation between an object and another when the first cannot exist without the second (specific dependence), or on objects of a certain kind (generic dependence). Thus e.g. a boundary is dependent on the thing it bounds, a trope on the concrete individual it is in. A headache is specifically dependent on the sufferer, but the sufferer is generically dependent on oxygen (some portion or other, it doesn't matter which). Other flavours of dependence concern e.g. whether the object depends on its parts or on things which are not its parts. See also functional dependence.

descriptive metaphysics Term invented by Strawson (in 1959). The metaphysics inherent in our standard everyday conceptual scheme. Said by Strawson to "have no history." Contrasted with revisionary metaphysics. Strawson regards Aristotle and Kant as descriptive metaphysicians.

determinable   Term invented by W. E. Johnson for any higher-order property or family of properties (e.g. heights, colours, velocities) that an object may have and in respect to which objects may change. The properties or attributes in the family are called the determinates (q.v.).

determinacy   As opposed to indeterminacy (q.v.).

determinates   Properties or attributes for the most specific or determinate attributes under a determinable (q.v.), e.g. 1 gram, 2.5 kilogram, 12.5 microgram are determinates of the determinable *mass*.

determinism   The view that how the future will be is settled as a result of how the present is together with the laws of nature. Often taken to rule out the claim that the future is open, although this is not uncontroversial.

difference   (1) Numerical difference: non-identity, e.g. even so-called "identical" twins are different. (2) Qualitative dissimilarity. (3) Quantitative difference, e.g. a difference of weight of 2 kilograms between two people, one weighing 51 kilograms, the other 53 kilograms.

dualism   Any view according to which there are two basic kinds of object or substance, e.g. minds and bodies.

duplicate   Two possible objects are duplicates if and only if they are exactly resembling in their intrinsic properties. Various analyses of duplication have been proposed to give an analysis of "intrinsic" (see intrinsic and extrinsic properties).

emergence   The property of a complex object whereby some of its attributes cannot be inferred or predicted from the attributes of its components and their interrelations. For example the role of the base sequences in DNA cannot be inferred or predicted from their chemistry. The properties of the whole so emerging are called "emergent properties." Further differentiable into epistemic emergence, where we are unable to predict or explain (actually or in principle) the novel attribute in terms of what we know about the object's components; and ontic emergence, where the attribute in question fails to be generated or produced by the attributes of the components and their interrelations.

endurantism   The view that common-or-garden objects like tables, animals and planets persist through time by enduring. Contrast perdurantism.

endure   The way a continuant exists from one time to others, i.e. not by accrual of temporal parts but by continuing to exist through time as the self-same thing (hence the name "continuant").

entity   (From Latin *ens*, object). Object of any kind that exists. Often used more widely than "thing" (Latin *res*). Entities comprise any object taken to exist, not just individual things, e.g. universals, sets, states of affairs. In Meinongian philosophy, entities are existing objects, contrasting with non-entities, which are non-existent objects (e.g. Pegasus, the golden mountain, the round square).

equivocity of "being"   In Aristotle, scholastics and neo-Aristotelians, the view that "is" and cognates have several meanings. In Aristotle, these are as follows: accidental being, being in the sense of truth, being in the sense of potentiality, and being in the senses of the different categories. In modern philosophy (Mill, Frege, Russell and others), varying numbers of senses of "be" or "is" are distinguished, most commonly the "is" of existence ("There is a man at the front door"), the "is" of predication ("He is tall"), the "is" of identity ("He is my long-lost cousin, Alf"), the "is" of subsumption ("The blue whale is a mammal") and others. No consensus exists as to how many different meanings there are, how language-dependent they are, or how to classify them, but the question is now widely seen as of merely lexicological, not metaphysical, interest.

essence Aristotelian term of art. Usually the collection of essential properties of an individual. Sometimes taken as given irrespective of whether an object exists or not, e.g. it is essential to a unicorn to have just one horn.

essential Of an attribute or part: such that its bearer cannot exist if it does not have it, e.g. being massive is an essential property of a star, having two protons in the nucleus is essential to a helium atom (these are essential parts). Traditionally, being rational is said to be essential to human beings, but this is overly optimistic.

eternalism The view that past and future objects exist and are as real as present objects. Most commonly combined with the B-theory, but can be combined with the A-theory (giving rise to the moving-spotlight view).

event A change or unified whole consisting of many changes, e.g. a collision, a football match, a battle. Events are occurrents: aside from instantaneous events, they have phases or temporal parts. They also (usually or always) have participants: one or more continuants, the changes in or among which constitute the event. Some philosophers use "event" very broadly for all occurrents.

existence From *ex-sistere, ex-stare*, Latin for "to stand out," a relatively late coinage. The fundamental notion of metaphysics. There are numerous theories as to what existence is, but it is probably best taken to be primitive or indefinable. On some views the existence of a particular is taken as primitive, on others (the majority) it is existence as a second-order property (property of properties) which is basic. The second-order view is found in Kant, Bolzano, Frege, Russell and most modern logic-influenced metaphysics.

existential ontology In Ingarden, the study of the modes of being of objects and the constituent existential moments of these modes of being. Distinguished by him from formal and material ontology.

existential quantifier The logical expression usually written "$\exists$" and to be read as "there exists." Expression combining two features: (1) it binds variables; (2) it expresses existence or non-nothingness. So in predicate logic "there are ghosts" is expressed "$\exists x(x$ is a ghost)" and is read "there exists x such that x is a ghost." Taken by many e.g. Frege, Quine, to be the way in which existence is expressed. See particular quantifier.

external relation A relation accidental to one or both of its terms. For example that Bill and Hillary are married is external to them; either could have existed and not have been married to the other. Contrasted with internal relation. In the logical atomism of Russell, all relations are external. In absolute idealism, none are. The correct position is G. E. Moore's compromise: some relations are internal, some are external.

extrinsic   Of a property or attribute: characterizing an object in part because of that object's relations to its surroundings or things outside itself, e.g. a person is a leader by virtue of leading others, land is an island by virtue of being surrounded by water. Contrast intrinsic.

fact   (1) An existing or obtaining state of affairs, e.g. that Britain is an island, as distinct from a non-obtaining state of affairs, e.g. that France is an island. In many theories of truth, the fundamental truthmaker, what makes a proposition true, e.g. the fact that Britain is an island makes true the proposition that Britain is an island. In Russell and Wittgenstein a distinction is made between atomic and non-atomic facts. Atomic facts make logically simple or atomic propositions true. (2) In Frege and Ramsey, whose theories of truth eschew truthmakers, a true proposition. Suggested by the locution "it's a fact that," e.g. "it's a fact that Cherie dislikes cats," which seems here synonymous with "it's true that Cherie dislikes cats" and hence perhaps with "Cherie dislikes cats."

factor   An element partially determining the nature of something, usually in combination with other elements, as e.g. Ingarden's existential moments or Empedocles's temperature and humidity factors.

factored ontology   An ontology where the basic classes or categories are determined by combinations of factors (e.g. Empedocles, Kant, Ingarden).

fictionalism   Fictionalism about certain entities (such as numbers) is a type of anti-realism about those entities, whereby they are said not to really exist but merely be convenient fictions. Sentences apparently about such things may either be taken to be false but useful, or true not in virtue of the existence of such things but rather as a result of correctly representing the fiction.

form   Term with many meanings. (1) In Plato, an abstract, timeless, ungenerable, immutable and incorruptible idea or model, e.g. Justice, contrasted with individual cases both by its permanence and its perfection. (2) In Aristotle, that which makes a thing what it is, its substance (2). Contrast with matter.

formal   Pertaining to form in one or other of its senses.

formal ontology   (1) Term coined by Husserl for general metaphysics: ontology of the most abstract characteristics or form of things, by contrast with their specific kinds, which is the subject of material or regional ontologies. Also contrasted by Husserl with formal logic, the theory of (logical) forms of proposition. (2) In Ingarden the study of the formal properties of objects, as distinct from their particular kinds (material ontology) and their mode of being (existential ontology). (3) Used by logic-oriented ontologists such as Nino Cocchiarella and Edward Zalta for ontologies based on a formal (logical) language and its associated semantics. The assumption is that the formal language and its semantics together determine an ontology.

four-dimensionalism   Sometimes used as a synonym for eternalism, sometimes as a synonym for perdurantism, sometimes for their conjunction.

function   Mathematical notion invented by Leibniz and exploited by mathematicians such as Dirichlet, extended into logic by Frege. A function f is defined by three constituents: (1) a set of objects D on which the function is defined, called its *domain*, or collectively termed its *arguments*; (2) a set of entities R into which the function maps objects from D, called its *range* and collectively its *values*; (3) a relation, rule or mapping which associates each member of D with a unique member of R. Of these, R is the most important part; the rest is book-keeping. The square function in natural numbers is that function which associates each natural number n with its square n^2, or which maps n to n^2, or which takes n^2 as value for n as argument. Functions may be one-placed (unary, monadic), as in this example, or multi-placed (binary, ternary, etc., or dyadic, triadic, etc., in general: polyadic). For example the sum function on real numbers takes a pair of real numbers r and s to a third number $r + s$, their (unique) sum. Opinions vary as to whether functions are a fundamental category (Frege, Church) or are abbreviatory conveniences exploiting the idea of a many–one relation (Russell, Tarski). Frege defines relations via functions and truth-values, whereas Russell and Tarski define functions via relations. For more on functions see any textbook of basic modern mathematics.

functional dependence Situation whereby the value of a determinate attribute of some object or objects is determined by the values of other attributes of this thing or of other things. For example the pressure of a confined body of gas at a fixed temperature is determined by the volume the gas occupies (Boyle's law). By varying the volume (e.g. by moving a piston) we may vary the pressure (this is how bicycle pumps work). There are in fact a number of different species of functional dependence and their interrelations are not well understood. In statistics for example correlations may be evidence for functional dependence. In natural science, functional dependences are typically expressed using equations connecting the different quantities, and allowing mathematical functions to represent the quantitative features of the dependence.

fundament The converse to a moment: that on which a moment depends, its existential ground.

genidentity The relationship obtaining between successive phases of a perduring object or occurrent. The phases are not identical (existing at different times) but collectively constitute the occurrent as a whole over time (genetically). The term was originally used in 1922 by the German psychologist Kurt Lewin.

Gestalt German for "form" or "shape." Any entity which is not simple (i.e. has proper parts) and which is what it is in virtue of some attribute not derived from the attributes of the parts. Contrast with "totality" or "multiplicity." The term *Gestalt-qualität*, "Gestalt quality," was used by Christian von Ehrenfels in 1891 to describe a quality of something which it has as a whole and which may be perceived in it relatively independently of variations among the parts. For example the melody of "Three Blind Mice" is perceived as the same, despite being transposed into different keys. The perception of *Gestalten* and the physiological conditions for this form the primary subject matter of Gestalt psychology.

God In philosophy, supreme or perfect being, often defined as a being possessing all perfections. Traditionally God is the only being to exist unconditionally or necessarily, all other things being contingent. God's necessity and perfection are usually considered grounds for reverence and worship. Philosophical treatment of God is usually confined to natural theology, that is, those propositions about God which are supposed to be shown true on the basis of reason alone and unaided by divine revelation. Despite the best efforts of both theists and atheists, the existence of God has been neither conclusively proven nor conclusively disproven.

growing block   The view that the past and present exist but that the future does not, and hence that what there is increases as time progresses. Often thought to be motivated by the intuition that the past is "fixed" while the future is "open." Contrast shrinking tree.

haecceity   From the Medieval Latin *haecceitas*, "thisness." A property which uniquely *individuates* a single thing, peculiar to it alone. Associated especially with the theory of John Duns Scotus. Some take haecceities to be qualitative concepts, others take them to be formal properties such as *being identical with Winston Churchill*.

holism   Any of a number of views according to which roughly speaking what is important is a complex whole rather than its parts. More specifically, that the properties of a whole system cannot be explained in terms of those of its parts. Contrast with reductionism. The term comes from Greek *holos*, "whole," and was coined in 1926 by Jan Smuts.

idealism   In metaphysics, any theory according to which all that exists is mental or spiritual. There are three major forms: (1) Subjective idealism: the things are ideas in or qualifications of individuals' minds. (2) Absolute idealism: the things are ideas in or qualifications of the mind of a supreme and unique spiritual being, the Absolute (apart from the Absolute itself, presumably). (3) Transcendental idealism. A form of idealism invented by Kant, in some ways close to (1), because the things we know are largely as we make them (with the exception of the unknown contribution of the "thing in itself"). However because the things of the world are not dependent on individual minds, a form of intersubjective idealism.

identity   That "relation" which everything has to itself alone and to no other thing (Joseph Butler: "Everything is what it is and not another thing"). Because of the necessity of self-identity, often taken to be not a "real" relation. Along with truth and existence, one of the metaphysical cornerstones of logic.

identity of indiscernibles   The principle that if x and y are exactly alike then they are numerically identical. Comes in stronger and weaker versions depending on how we interpret "are exactly alike." If we mean "share all properties" and include properties like "being identical to x" then the principle is trivially true. If we limit the properties in question to intrinsic properties, or to purely qualitative properties, then it becomes very controversial.

impossible   (1) Of a proposition: not possibly true, necessarily false. (2) Of a thing or state of affairs: such that it cannot exist.

indeterminacy   A claim is indeterminate if it is unsettled between truth and falsity. Often this is taken to be a result of our using vague language: e.g. "that man is bald" might have no settled truth-value because he has a thinning head of hair and our use of "bald" is just not precise enough to place him decidedly in either the bald camp of the not bald camp. But some think that sometimes the world itself is indeterminate; for example, the claim that the future is open (as was held by Aristotle) is the claim that at least some statements about how things will be, such as "there will be a sea battle tomorrow," are indeterminate.

indiscernibility Property of two or more things whereby they cannot be discerned, distinguished or told apart. A necessary, and in Leibniz also a sufficient condition of identity. The strength of the indiscernibility depends on what resources are available to "tell things apart."

indiscernibility of identicals The principle that if *x* and *y* are numerically identical then they are exactly alike. This is almost always taken to be uncontroversial even in its strongest form: that if *x* = *y* then every property *x* has, *y* has. However, the principle nonetheless leads to puzzles when applied to entities that persist throughout time: I am identical to a certain child, yet he is a child and I am not.

individual Single thing, numerically one and distinct from others, having its own identity, and distinct from a multiplicity or collection or set of things; also usually distinguished from universals (but see particular).

individuation That whereby something becomes determined as an individual or one single, unrepeatable thing. Some philosophers think that since the primary form of being is general, an individual must require some special item or agency to bring it about that it is an individual. For example according to Thomas Aquinas it is the matter of a body that individuates it, while according to Duns Scotus it is an individual's haecceity (q.v.). Other philosophers such as Ockham consider that since all things are individuals, no individuation is necessary.

internal relation A relation essential to its terms, i.e. such that if its terms exist, it must hold between them. For example the relation of *being darker than* holding between the universals Royal Blue and Sky Blue is internal to these. Also, a relation such that if it ceases to hold, one or more of its terms must cease to exist. Contrasted with external relation. In the philosophy of Absolute idealism (Bradley, Bosanquet et al.) all relations were said to be internal, and all things were related to all others, so the interconnectedness of everything was essential.

intrinsic (1) A property is intrinsic to its bearer if the bearer has it independently of its relations to things outside itself. Mass is intrinsic, because what mass a thing has depends solely on how it is in and of itself, whereas weight is not intrinsic (i.e. is extrinsic) because an object has the weight it has because there are others outside it exerting a gravitational pull on it. Contrast extrinsic. (2) Formerly a synonym for "essential."

location The place or places where an object is, sometimes the spatiotemporal region an object occupies. Sometimes also the relation between the place and its occupant. Some theories (e.g. Quine's) take there to be only one way in which objects occupy their locations, in other theories there are various modes of occupation, e.g. events differ from continuants, particulars from universals.

mass   In metaphysics a word for a particular which is not an individual or collection of individuals, e.g. a certain mass of coffee in a cup. Synonyms: amount, quantity. Some metaphysicians think masses are items in the world along with individuals and collections; others think there are no masses but simply various mass terms (e.g. "water") true of individuals and/or collections. In some cases (e.g. Locke's "mass of matter") the parts of a mass must all be connected, but in many uses this is not necessary (e.g. the mass of all the water in the world). This use is only loosely connected with the use of "mass" in physics.

material   Contrasted with formal in any of its senses.

materialism   The view that all that exists is material or made of matter. Now made obsolete by science, its general scientistic spirit lingers on in physicalism and naturalism.

material ontology   In Ingarden, the study of objects according to their particular (material) kind. Similar to Husserl's regional ontology.

matter   In Aristotle, that which is qualified by form. Divides into proximate and remote matter, the ultimate underlying matter is called "prime matter" and is said by Aristotle to exist only potentially.

Meinongian object   After Alexius Meinong (1853–1920), an object which does not exist, subsist or have any kind of being, for example the golden mountain, the round square. Meinong's objects categorically have the properties that they are said to have – e.g. the golden mountain is golden and mountainous, the round square is round and square – in just the same way as ordinary objects. Further, many Meinongian objects are impossible, they could not possibly exist, either because like the golden mountain they have incompatible properties, or like fictional characters they are incomplete. Russell tried to show that assuming there are Meinongian objects leads to contradictions, but with some care such contradictions can be avoided.

mereological essentialism   The view that a thing has its parts essentially, so that no thing could exist and fail to be made up of the parts it actually has: for example, I could not have been born without my left leg. Some theories accept mereological essentialism for a restricted class of entities, e.g. spatiotemporal regions, events.

mereology   The theory of part, whole and cognate concepts. In nominalism sometimes taken as a partial substitute for set theory, the parts of a concrete thing being concrete, whereas sets are abstract. From Greek *meros*, "part."

metaphysics   The philosophical discipline which comprises the most fundamental concepts and principles. Sometimes divided into a general part and several special parts. Cf. ontology, systematics. Etymology: From the Greek, *ta meta ta physika*, "the (books) after the physics (books on nature)," originally used by Aristotle's editors to denote a miscellaneous collection of fourteen treatises by him on basic principles, the divine, and the "science of being *qua* being." Aristotle did not use the word, calling this area "first philosophy." The connotation of metaphysics as dealing with things above, beyond or prior to nature, based on an ambiguity in *meta*, is not ungrounded in Aristotle's ideas, but is no necessary part of the meaning.

moment   From the German, *das Moment*, a dependent part or aspect, by contrast with *der Moment*, an instant or moment of time. Any object dependent for its existence on one or more others. Tropes are one kind of moment, boundaries another.

monism Any view according to which reality is in some sense "one." Comes in several flavours: (1) Substance- or kind-monism: any view according to which there is only one basic kind of object or substance, e.g. materialism. (2) More specifically, any view denying mind/matter duality (so materialism or immaterialism). (3) Existence monism: any view according to which there is only one "real" or proper object in the universe e.g. only one substance; found in different forms in e.g. Parmenides, Spinoza, Hegel, Bradley. (4) Priority monism: the doctrine that there are many things but only one fundamental thing, on which all else depends (common among theists). Contrast pluralism, dualism.

multiplicity Any collection of more than one thing, especially one where the relations among the members are of no consequence for its existence. A multiplicity of four string players may exist whether they play together or not, but if they are to comprise a string quartet the players need to meet and play together from time to time, so the meeting and playing together relations are constitutive of the quartet, but not the multiplicity. Contrast a Gestalt.

natural An expression or distinction is natural insofar as it "carves the world at its joints." For example, a predicate is natural if it marks out a natural kind (e.g. "is an electron" as opposed to "is an electron near the moon or is a basketball player"). An operator is natural if it picks out a fundamental feature of reality (e.g. a tense operator like "It was the case that ...," will be taken to be natural by the A-theorist but not the B-theorist).

naturalism One of several related views in which the world is equated with nature or with what natural science tells us exists. (1) In Quine, the view that metaphysics is not an *a priori* discipline (first philosophy) but is simply the continuation of natural science into more general considerations. Allows in particular that metaphysical theses may be refuted by discoveries in natural science. (2) The view that all entities are to be found in nature (usually entails anti-Platonism).

natural kind A kind of thing whose distinctness from other kinds is independent of human or other intelligent activity or convention. Typical examples are kinds of fundamental particle, elements and compounds, minerals, heavenly bodies. The physical sciences thus deal in natural kinds. In some but not all theories, biological species and higher *taxa* are natural kinds. A natural kind may be artificially produced: e.g. polythene: what matters is not whether it occurs naturally but whether its distinctness from other kinds is intrinsic or internal.

nature (1) Synonym for "essence." (2) The collection of all properties (essential and accidental) of a thing. (3) The collection of all attributes (including relations) of a thing. (4) (Often capitalized) the totality or system of all things existing in space and time, especially with regard to those things and attributes not made by human beings (non-artefacts).

necessary (1) Of a proposition: such that it must be true, cannot be false. (2) Of a thing or state of affairs: such that it exists necessarily.

nominalism (1) Generally (and most strongly), a metaphysical theory denying the existence of abstract objects. (2) More specifically, a theory denying the existence of real (independent) universals. (3) More specifically still, a theory like (2) but taking universals to be linguistic entities. (4) Special sense due to Nelson Goodman: theory denying the existence of sets (Goodman accepts universals).

non-existent objects In Meinong's and similar metaphysics, not all objects exist or have being: there are objects which have no being (*Sein*), which nevertheless have a nature (*Sosein*). Most philosophers do not believe there are non-existent objects, a stance which Meinong considers a prejudice caused by our preoccupation with everyday practical things.

nuclear vs. extra-nuclear properties In Meinongian ontologies, a distinction between properties characterizing an object's nature (nuclear) and those which apply to it but not as part of its nature (extra-nuclear). Normal properties like being square, green and sat on by Tony Blair are nuclear, whereas extra-nuclear properties include the more arcane or philosophical ones of existing, having only nuclear properties, being incomplete, being simple, being worshipped by the Greeks.

object (1) The most general term, used for everything, not just individuals or substances. Often synonymous with "entity" or Airlinespeak "item." Anything that is something rather than nothing. (2) In the derelativized sense of "object of thought," anything whatever that can be thought about or conceived, contrasted with "subject." Often taken in this sense to be not confined to that which exists (cf. non-existent object). (3) In Frege's ontology, an individual, the referent of a singular term or proper name, as distinct from a function. In Wittgenstein's logical atomism an individual as in Frege, but in addition for Wittgenstein all objects are atomic (have no proper parts) and exist of necessity.

occurrent (Term invented by W. E. Johnson.) Any object existing in time and having temporal parts or phases: includes events, processes and states. Term derives from preferential use of "occur" instead of "exist" for events etc. An occurrent, unlike a continuant, is extended or spread out in the temporal dimension: when one part of it is occurring, others are not, e.g. the final five minutes of a football match have no common part with its first five minutes (though they share many participants, i.e. continuants participating in both parts of the game).

ontological commitment Following Quine, the entities which a given view or theory takes to exist. For example, theism is committed to the existence of a deity, Darwinian evolutionary theory is committed to the occurrence of new species, number theory is committed to numbers. In general, a theory is committed ontologically to a certain entity or a certain kind of entities if in its own terms it cannot be true unless that entity or those entities exist. Quine further holds that the test of ontological commitment is what a theory quantifies over: "To be is to be the value of a variable." So because number theory quantifies over numbers (as in, "there are prime numbers greater than a million") it is committed to numbers. Others consider that ontological commitment is shown not by quantification but by what entities a theory states to exist, so e.g. theism states outright "God exists."

ontology From *onto–logos*, the science of being. A surprisingly late coinage. The Latin term *ontologia* was felicitously invented in 1613, independently, by two German philosophers, Rudolf Göckel (Goclenius) in his *Lexicon Philosophicum* and Jacob Lorhard (Lorhardus), in his *Theatrum Philosophicum*, but first entered general circulation when popularized by Christian Wolff in his Latin writings, especially his *Philosophia Prima sive Ontologia* of 1730. The first known English use of the term "ontology" is 1720. (1) General as distinct from special metaphysics. (2) More limitedly, the list or table of basic kinds of entities. (3) Attributively, as in "Quine's ontology," the basic kinds of entities assumed by a given philosopher. (4) In Ingarden's philosophy, the study of all possible general arrangements of the world, by comparison with metaphysics which concerns only what actually exists. (5) Recently and loosely, in computer science, a set of categories for programming and data representation which is independent of particular hardware, software or implementations.

part Fundamental relationship between an object and others, its parts, as e.g. the blade and handle are parts of a knife. Some parts like these are functional components, others (e.g. the top half of an orange) are arbitrary chunks or fragments. A part is proper if it is less than the whole, otherwise it is improper.

particular Contrasted with universal: an object which is not a universal, which does not occur repeatedly. Particulars include especially individuals, but may also include masses and collections.

particular quantifier From the use in traditional logic, meaning "pertaining to a part": propositions of the form "some As are Bs" or "some As are not Bs," concerning part but not necessarily the whole of (all of) the As. Hence the quantifier "for some *x*." Usually identified with the existential quantifier, but in those theories where quantifiers do not carry existential import, the particular quantifier may fail to entail existence, e.g. in "some unicorns are male," which in Meinongian theory is true despite no unicorns' existing.

perdurantism The view that objects persisting in time do so by perduring. Contrast endurantism.

perdure How occurrents continue to exist from time to time, namely by accumulating new temporal parts or phases which succeed and displace preceding ones.

perfection In natural theology especially, a positive property possessing a (theoretical) maximum. It is much easier to give examples of non-perfections than perfections. Thus blindness is not a perfection, since it is negative, consisting in the absence of sight in a being which might be expected to have it, while size, age and mass are not perfections, since they have no theoretical *maxima*. Power, goodness and love are regarded as perfections in much natural theology, but whether they are is highly disputable. It is said that every perfection is compatible with every other because contradictions arise through negation and limitation, but again this is not clear, so the basis for ontological arguments is shaky to say the least.

physicalism The view that all things are ultimately and properly describable with the vocabulary of physical science alone.

Platonic realism (1) A realist theory of universals according to which universals exist even if they have no instances (e.g. unicornhood, perfect justice, perfectly honest politicianhood). (2) See Platonism, realism.

Platonism (sometimes uncapitalized)   (1) The view, originating with Plato, that there is a separate realm of abstract objects, forms or ideas. (2) More generally, any theory upholding the independent existence of abstract objects such as universals, numbers, sets.

pluralism   (1) Opposite of monism (1): there is more than one basic kind of object. (2) Opposite of monism (2): there is more than one proper object, e.g. substance.

possibility   A possible state of affairs.

possible   (1) Of a proposition: such that it can be true; not necessarily false. (2) Of a thing or state of affairs: such that it can or could exist.

possible world   A way the totality of things might have been. Device used to explicate the truth-values of modal propositions. There are several views among those who believe there are such about what possible worlds are: (1) Realism: that they are items existing independently of mind and language. (2) Conceptualism: that they are products or constructs of thought. (3) Nominalism: that they are linguistic constructs.

presentism   The view that the only time is the present and only things that are present exist, so there are no past or future entities.

process   (1) An occurrent which consists in the usually steady and continuous changing or development of something, e.g. growth, a chemical reaction. (2) In the philosophy of Whitehead the "becoming" of new actual entities, which are themselves of very short duration. Whitehead's philosophy and the theology it inspired are therefore called "process philosophy" and "process theology," but the idea of process philosophy has much older roots, e.g. in the Presocratic philosopher Heraclitus.

property   A way something is in itself, as distinct from how it is related to other things. Originally, an essential, special, distinctive or peculiar quality of a thing. Properties are usually conceived as universal or general, sometimes as particular.

proposition   (1) In semantics, the abstract timeless meaning or sense of a complete declarative sentence, the object of propositional attitudes. Frege's "thought." Truth-value pertains to it timelessly. (2) In medieval philosophy, a statement type. Differs from (1) in that its truth-value may change over time, e.g. "Socrates is sitting" is true while he is sitting but becomes false when he stands up. This notion of proposition is preferred by proponents of tense logic, such as Arthur Prior; it is employed in defining Cambridge change.

realism   (1) In general, realism about Xs is the view that Xs exist (weak realism with respect to Xs). (2) The view that Xs exist independently of mind and language (strong realism about Xs). (3) Strong realism about universals. (4) In epistemology especially, strong realism about the so-called "external world." See also anti-realism.

reduction   There are various conceptions of reduction. (1) Paraphrase reduction: Items A are said to be reduced (or reducible) to items B if all propositions ostensibly about A can be translated or paraphrased into talk about items B only. (2) Explanatory or epistemic reduction: Items A are reduced to items B if we can explain or predict items A through our knowledge of items B. For example chemical properties of matter are thought to be explanatorily reducible to their physical properties (whether or not it can be paraphrased into the language of physics). (3) Ontic reduction: Items A are reduced to items B if items B through their properties and interrelations naturally produce or generate items A. For example molecules are ontically reducible to fundamental particles.

reductionism   Any one of a family of views according to which talk about one somehow suspect kind of entity can be reduced to talk about another supposedly less suspect kind. For example phenomenalism holds that physical objects may be reduced to phenomena; materialism holds that mind may be reduced to matter. Very few reductionist programmes have been carried through with success; metaphysicians tend to confine themselves to asseverating that this or that reduction can in principle be carried through. There are various shades of reductionism depending on the concept of reduction employed.

referential interpretation   The standard semantic account of quantifiers, according to which the variables range over a domain of suitable entities, and it is these and what pertains to them that determine the truth-value of sentences containing the quantifiers. On this view "for some x, x is a prime number and x is greater than a million" is true because among the things (numbers) ranged over by the bound variable "x" there are some prime numbers greater than a million. This view gives rise to Quine's criterion of ontological commitment. The name comes from the idea that the objects in the domain are referrable to by suitable expressions, not that they actually are referred to individually (in some cases there are too many of them for that). Quine favours the more restrictive objectual interpretation, according to which all objects quantified over are individuals, no matter what shape the quantified variables have.

regional ontology   Term of art invented by Husserl and contrasting with formal ontology. Similar to Wolff's *metaphysica specialis*. A regional ontology is one which deals not with all things but with those of a certain very general kind or coming from a very general sub-domain or "region of being." For example natural things, mathematical objects, cultural products, persons, the divine, might be seen as defining five distinct regions. Such divisions are almost always contentious, whence the term "systematics" (q.v.) is to be preferred.

relation   An attribute having more than one place, which links or binds two or more things, and expressible by a predicate needing supplementation by two or more names. Relations may be (in realism) universals or (in trope theory) particulars. In any particular case or relationship, the things related by a relation are called its terms. E.g. Bill and Hillary are terms of the relation of being married to.

relational change   "Change" in something due to a change in its relationship to something else. Need not be a real change. For example, Xanthippe becomes a widow when Socrates dies, but this need not be accompanied by any actual change in her (e.g. if she does not know about his demise). If Cassius is taller than Brutus but Brutus outgrows him while he remains the same height, Cassius has undergone a merely relational change, "becoming" shorter than Brutus, but not by shrinking, while Brutus has undergone a real change.

relational property   A property of something consisting in a relation's holding between the thing and something else, e.g. Socrates's property of being older than Plato, or Sam's being a brother. In Aristotelian and medieval philosophy, relational properties were simply called "relations." Most modern metaphysical theories treat the relations as primitive and the relational properties, if they exist at all, as derivative.

resemblance   Likeness or similarity of one thing to another. With difference (2), the datum for predication.

resemblance nominalism   Version of nominalism in which the crucial relation is one of resemblance of greater and lesser degrees among concrete particulars.

revisionary metaphysics   Strawson's term for any metaphysics contrasting with descriptive metaphysics and concerned to reform or replace the conceptual scheme inherent in everyday thought. Most metaphysical schemes start out as revisionary, most stay that way. Strawson cites Leibniz as a revisionary metaphysician: others in the twentieth century include McTaggart and Whitehead.

set   Term of art introduced to translate Bolzano's term *Menge* ("multitude"), as used by Georg Cantor. Object investigated by set theory. Sets are abstract entities distinct from their members or elements. Sets have extensional identity conditions, that is, sets A and B are identical just if they have the same elements. In standard set theories there is a unique empty or null set (having no members; there cannot be more than one by extensionality), each object has a set having it alone as element (its singleton set), for any finite collection of objects there is a set having just these as elements, and many general conditions define or delineate a set of things, the things satisfying the condition. On pain of contradiction (Russell's paradox), not all expressible conditions define sets. Some set theories (e.g. Quine's) allow a universal set.

set theory   Type of mathematical theory invented by Georg Cantor in the nineteenth century to provide a basis for his theory of transfinite numbers. Set theory was axiomatized by Ernst Zermelo in 1908, and his theory is the basis of most modern theories, which, however, differ in details and in the strength of their existential assumptions. Like Cantor, Zermelo was not obsessed about avoiding paradoxes, but developed set theory for mathematical purposes. Set theory typically has strong ontological commitments to infinities of sets, because it is designed to provide a foundation for mathematical theories such as number theory, analysis, topology, etc., but the extent of the commitment may vary from one theory to another.

shrinking tree   An indeterministic view of time developed by Storrs McCall, according to which reality consists of a single train of events from the past to the present but a branching tree of possibilities in the future. As time goes by, new events come to pass which exclude many of the branching possibilities, so the tree is continually being "pruned." Since there is an ontological distinction between the future and the non-future, and the present (as the boundary of the linear part of the tree) is distinguished, it is a form of A-theory; however, the possible future events are as real as the present and past ones, until they are excluded, so it has features of eternalism. Contrast growing-block theory.

situation   Synonym for "state of affairs," sometimes used by semantic theorists.

sparse   Said of metaphysical theories of attributes (properties and relations) which recognize only certain ("natural") attributes and reject the idea that every well-formed predicate, simple or complex, denotes its own attribute. For example while being an electron, being spherical, or being more massive than are natural attributes, being a non-electron, being red-or-green.

state   (1) Unchanging condition of something, which persists for a certain time. Thus a state is an occurrent, marked, unlike an event or a process, by absence of change. This absence can be either (a) absolute: nothing at all changes about the thing, or (b) relative: the thing does not change in a certain respect. For example a train travelling across a desert is changing its location with respect to the ground, but if its speed and direction are constant its "state of motion" is constant. If it speeds up, slows down or changes direction its state of motion changes. (2) Also used for an instantaneous "snapshot" of the attributes of a thing, as in "the state of the nation," "the train's state of motion at time *t*." Not a state in sense (1) because it does not persist, it nevertheless excludes change for the simple reason that, being instantaneous, there is no time for change. Sense (2) is much used in applications of differential calculus.

state of affairs   In many theories, the truthmaker for propositions. Often used as synonym for fact (1). If a state of affairs exists (obtains, subsists), then its corresponding proposition is true, whereas if it does not, the proposition is false. Some theories distinguish between atomic, molecular and general states of affairs, corresponding to atomic, molecular and general propositions. An atomic state of affairs is the possession of a property by something or the holding of a relation among several things. In Wittgenstein's logical atomism, only atomic states of affairs exist: Russell has conjunctive, negative and general ones too, but no disjunctive ones.

structuralism   A kind of view according to which the entities in a particular domain have only structural attributes and no nature, or that their nature consists solely in the formal relations they have to one another. Structuralism is particularly popular as a view of the nature of mathematical objects, but the term is also used for the view that mathematics has no objects of its own but is about all objects having certain given structures, e.g. numerical structuralism says that number theory is about all simply infinite sequences. Some philosophers hold that structuralism applies to entities in the physical world, that they are "structures all the way down" or "structures and nothing more." It is not clear what this means.

subsistence   In some metaphysical theories, the being or mode of being of objects that are not concrete, e.g. facts, or abstract objects. In such theories "exist" is reserved for concrete things. The term is often used to translate Meinong's term *bestehen*.

substance   From Latin *sub-stare*, to stand under, very inexact equivalent of Aristotle's term *ousia*. In much of metaphysics, the primary category of being. A substance is a continuant capable of existing by itself and of undergoing change without ceasing to exist. Typical examples in Aristotle are individual bodies and organisms. The term comes from the substance's being that which underlies change and which bears attributes (cf. substratum). In Aristotle's later metaphysics (as distinct from the view of the *Categories*) substance is taken as that which gives form to matter and makes something what it is, the scholastics called this substantial form. In rationalist philosophy the moment of independence is stressed, so that e.g. Spinoza takes there to be only one substance, while Leibniz takes there to be infinitely many indivisible substances or monads. Scientific advance since the nineteenth century has largely undermined the technical uses of "substance," and it is now used loosely for any individual falling under a sortal term.

substitutional interpretation   A semantic account of the meaning of the quantifiers according to which they carry no existential import because their meaning is given by the range of expressions which can be substituted for the variables in their scope. So e.g. "for some x: x is a prime number and x is greater than a million" is not to be understood as "there exists a prime number greater than a million" but rather as "there is an expression x which when put in the places so marked in the following clause turns it into a truth: x is a prime number and x is greater than a million." While the substitutional interpretation avoids (direct) ontological commitment to numbers it appears to incur other commitments, namely to expressions. To interpret "there are uncountably many irrational numbers" one would appear to be committed to the existence of uncountably many names for irrational numbers, which many regard as implausible or absurd. See referential interpretation.

substratum   Close cognate of "substance" but generally meaning more specifically that which underlies or bears attributes. Often the substratum is considered invisible and undetectable, by contrast with its attributes. Locke, while endorsing its existence, calls it "something we know not what." Sometimes called a "bare particular."

supervenience   Somewhat unclear term of recent philosophy, related to dependence. Items S are said to supervene on other items B if there can be no difference in S without difference in B. S are the supervenient items, B the *subvenient basis*. Supervenience is often used to get the benefits of reduction (q.v.) without incurring the supposed negative connotations of reductionism. It remains unclear whether the supervenient items (a) exist but depend existentially on their basis; (b) exist independently of their basis but have attributes that are necessarily functionally dependent on those of their basis; or (c) don't exist at all but are useful fictions.

systematics   In metaphysics, the theory of the various kinds of entity and the relationships among them. Contrasted with formal ontology. Analogous to Husserl's regional ontology (q.v.) but making no contentious assumptions about what kinds or regions of things there are. The term generalizes its use in biology.

taxon (pl. **taxa**)   (1) In biological systematics, a group of organisms all descended from a common ancestor which are sufficiently distinct to be regarded as worthy of an official name and given a taxonomic rank. (2) In metaphysical systematics, any proper or genuine class of entities.

taxonomy   The science and practice of classification.

thing in itself   Translation of Kant's term of art *Ding an sich*: thing as it is independently of our knowledge or conceptualization of it. According to Kant, existent but unknown. According to more extreme idealists, there are no things in themselves. According to realist philosophy, many things in themselves are partially known and their being so does not make them any less *an sich*.

three-dimensionalism   As opposed to four-dimensionalism in its various forms, the view that common-or-garden objects are extended in three spatial dimensions but not in the fourth, temporal dimension.

totality   A multiplicity of *all* the things of a certain kind. For example in Wittgenstein's *Tractatus* the world is defined as the totality (complete multiplicity) of facts.

transworld identity   Concept used in modal metaphysics for the notion of one and the same thing's being in more than one world, e.g. since we consider that Abraham Lincoln, who was in fact assassinated, might not have been assassinated, then those who believe in transworld identity will say that the same person exists in another possible world and is not there assassinated. Contrast with counterpart theory, according to which all individuals are confined to a single world.

trope   Term of art introduced in 1953 by Donald C. Williams for an individual property or relation instance. Tropes are particulars, dependent on their concrete particulars. Williams's views have been developed by Keith Campbell (who calls tropes "abstract particulars"), John Bacon and others in Australia, but have their forerunners in Aristotelian and scholastic individual accidents, G. F. Stout's particularized properties, and many more. In view of the plethora of terms, "trope" is a good short word. Campbell does not believe there are relational tropes, others do.

trope theory (trope nominalism)   A moderate version of nominalism in which properties and sometimes also relations are taken to exist but to be tropes. This allows spatiotemporally situated individuals to provide truthmakers for predications about concrete things, without ontological commitment to universals.

truthmaker (sometimes hyphenated, as **truth-maker**)   Term of art invented for English by Charles B. Martin and independently by Kevin Mulligan, Barry Smith and Peter Simons, but corresponding to earlier uses of *wahrmachen* by Husserl and ideas drawn from Russell and earlier philosophers. Role-term for any entity fulfilling the semantic role of making some proposition true simply by existing. In some theories, e.g. of facts or states of affairs, the role is fulfilled by such special items, in other theories there are different categories of truthmaker, not just one category.

type   (1) Generally and loosely: a kind. (2) Special usage due to Charles S. Peirce: the repeatable abstract pattern of e.g. a letter, word or other linguistic object, contrasted with *token*, an individual occurrence or instance thereof. In the sentence "The cat sat on the mat" there are two tokens of "the" but only one type "the," which occurs twice. The terminology comes from typesetting practice. (3) In logic, a grand class of objects which can be regarded as logico-grammatically equivalent in that they have expressions of a particular grammatical category standing for them, and cannot be designated by expressions of any other category. For example individuals, properties of individuals, properties of properties of individuals and so on form different types. See type theory. (4) In computer science, a class of expressions kept for a special purpose, e.g. integer, floating point number, logical, string. Like logical types, they are not freely interchangeable, but their use is mainly for clarity and efficiency, not to avoid paradox. (5) In biological systematics, an individual specimen biological object (preserved after death or fossilized) which serves as the point of reference for the name given to a *taxon* of organisms.

typed   Said of any theory or representation (e.g. in logic, mathematics or computer science) that uses types. Contrasts with "type-free."

type theory   (1) Logico-ontological theory anticipated by Ernst Schröder and first formulated by Bertrand Russell and others to block set-theoretical and other paradoxes. These are essentially eliminated by constraints on grammaticality, so e.g. an expression for an individual (a proper name) is not grammatically replaceable by an expression for a property (a monadic predicate). Types form an infinite hierarchy with individuals at the bottom. Whether the types are of classes (Schröder), functions (Frege), propositional functions (Russell) or attributes varies. There are two flavours of type theory: (1.1) simple type theory has a single hierarchy of types corresponding to different levels of entity. Found in Schröder, Frege and early Russell, it was regained after the complications of ramified type theory by simplifications due to Chwistek, Ramsey and Church. (1.2) Ramified type theory intersperses between each type an infinite hierarchy of orders, designed to avoid "circular" or impredicative definitions, which Russell, following Henri Poincaré, took to be the basis of the paradoxes. Nowadays rarely considered on account of its complication and the expressive weakness of the associated logic. (2) In the constructive type theory of the Swedish logician Per Martin-Löf, types are classes of entities constructed logically according to various constructive principles. As with standard type theory, objects from different types are not interchangeable, but Martin-Löf takes types to be created rather than discovered.

uniqueness   The formal property of being the only one of its kind. Every individual is by definition unique. The term "unique" is more meaningfully used of individuals which are the only ones of their kind although there might have been more than one. For example, to date, Margaret Thatcher is the unique (only) female British Prime Minister.

universal   Contrasted with particular: (1) For a realist, a universal is an object which may occur repeatedly in more than one place and/or time, for example having an electric charge of $e-$ occurs again and again in each electron. In so doing it does not multiply itself, but remains one over and against its occurrences or instances. (2) Conceptualists and nominalists who believe there are universals but that they are dependent on minds, hold them to be general concepts or general words, applicable to more than one thing.

universal quantifier   From the use in traditional logic, meaning "pertaining to the whole": propositions of the form "All As are Bs" or "No As are Bs," the whole of (all of) the As. Hence in predicate logic the quantifier "for all x."

universe   The totality of all that exists. Often synonymous with "world." Sometimes "universe" is confined to the natural world, if that is a restriction. There are several ways in which the term "universe" may be taken: as the name of a mereologically maximal individual, or as the plural name encompassing every object. The former makes best sense in a materialistic universe. If the latter is to have reference, it must be possible to refer to everything all in one phrase. Opponents of this idea include Frege and Russell (because of type theory). Proponents include Husserl.

world Frequent synonym of "universe," sometimes used more broadly to include non-natural objects. According to Wittgenstein, the totality of facts, not things (*Die Welt ist die Gesamtheit der Tatsachen, nicht der Dinge*). According to many others, the totality of things (which may or may not include facts) – *die Gesamtheit der Dinge*.

INDEX